2012
Children's
Writer's & Illustrator's
MARKET®

DISCARD

W9-BLH-538

Includes a 1-year online subscription to **Children's Writer's & Illustrator's Market** on

WritersMarket.com

Where & How to Sell What You Write

THE ULTIMATE MARKET RESEARCH TOOL FOR WRITERS

To register your *2012 Children's Writer's & Illustrator's Market* and **start your 1-year online children's subscription**, scratch off the block below to reveal your activation code, then go to WritersMarket.com. Click on "Sign Up Now" and enter your contact information and activation code. It's that easy!

UPDATED MARKET LISTINGS FOR YOUR INTEREST AREA
EASY-TO-USE SEARCHABLE DATABASE • RECORD-KEEPING TOOLS
PROFESSIONAL TIPS & ADVICE • INDUSTRY NEWS

Your purchase of *Children's Writer's & Illustrator's Market* gives you access to updated listings related to this genre of writing (valid through 12/31/12). For just $9.99, you can upgrade your subscription and get access to listings from all of our best-selling Market books. Visit **WritersMarket.com** for more information.

WritersMarket.com
Where & How to Sell What You Write

Activate your WritersMarket.com subscription to get instant access to:

- **UPDATED LISTINGS IN YOUR WRITING GENRE:** Find additional listings that didn't make it into the book, updated contact information and more. WritersMarket.com provides the most comprehensive database of verified markets available anywhere.

- **EASY-TO-USE SEARCHABLE DATABASE:** Looking for a specific magazine or book publisher? Just type in its name. Or widen your prospects with the Advanced Search. You can also search for listings that have been recently updated!

- **PERSONALIZED TOOLS:** Store your best-bet markets, and use our popular record-keeping tools to track your submissions. Plus, get new and updated market listings, query reminders, and more—every time you log in!

- **PROFESSIONAL TIPS & ADVICE:** From pay rate charts and sample query letters to Q&A's with literary agents and how-to articles, we have the resources freelance writers need.

- **INDUSTRY UPDATES:** Debbie Ridpath Ohi's Market Watch column keeps you up-to-date on the latest publishing industry news, so you'll always be in-the-know.

YOU'LL GET ALL OF THIS WITH YOUR SUBSCRIPTION TO

To put the full power of WritersMarket.com to work for you, upgrade your subscription and get access to listings from all of our best-selling Market books. Find out more at **WritersMarket.com**

12CMI0M

24TH ANNUAL EDITION

2012
Children's
Writer's & Illustrator's
MARKET

Chuck Sambuchino, Editor

DISCARD

WD

WRITER'S DIGEST
BOOKS

WritersDigest.com
Cincinnati, Ohio

Publisher & Editorial Director, Writing Community: Phil Sexton
Managing Editor, Writer's Digest Market Books: Adria Haley

Writer's Market website: www.writersmarket.com
Writer's Digest website: www.writersdigest.com
Writer's Digest Bookstore: www.writersdigestshop.com

Distributed in Canada by Fraser Direct
100 Armstrong Avenue
Georgetown, Ontario, Canada L7G 5S4
Tel: (905) 877-4411

Distributed in the U.K. and Europe by F&W Media International
Brunel House, Newton Abbot, Devon, TQ12 4PU, England
Tel: (+44) 1626-323200, Fax: (+44) 1626-323319
E-mail: postmaster@davidandcharles.co.uk

Distributed in Australia by Capricorn Link
P.O. Box 704, Windsor, NSW 2756 Australia
Tel: (02) 4577-3555

ISSN: 0897-9790
ISBN-13: 978-1-59963-231-5
ISBN-10: 1-59963-231-4

Attention Booksellers: This is an annual directory of F+W Media, Inc. Return deadline for this edition is December 31, 2012.

Edited by: Chuck Sambuchino
Cover designed by: Jessica Boonstra
Interior designed by: Claudean Wheeler
Page layout by: Terri Woesner
Production coordinated by: Greg Nock
Cover illustration by: Emily Keafer

CONTENTS

RESOURCES

INDEXES

PHOTO: Al Parrish

FROM THE EDITOR

The very fact that I'm actually writing this letter is extremely surreal to me. I've worked with Writer's Digest Books for five years now editing the *Guide to Literary Agents,* and I've always read and admired the *Children's Writer's & Illustrator's Market.* When the *CWIM* editor position recently became available, it was a dream come true that they asked me to helm the 2012 edition. It's an honor and a privilege to continue this book's rich history (500,000 copies sold) of helping writers see their work reach others through print and ebooks.

If you flip through this book's pages, the first thing you may notice is a whole ton of upfront instructional articles. We've beefed up the article count in *CWIM* to give you even more info and interviews than ever before. You'll find interviews with best-selling authors like Meg Cabot, M.T. Anderson and Maggie Stiefvater. You'll also find instruction on popular topics such as synopsis writing, working with co-writers, the evolution of publishing, and how to compose a query that hooks an agent.

And in addition to all the upfront articles, *CWIM* is still your trusted source for market listings of all kinds: publishing houses, agents, magazines, illustration opportunities and more. All the good stuff you'd expect from an edition of *CWIM* is still here.

When you're done looking through the book, please stay in touch with me at guideto literaryagents.com/blog. Also, please continue to pass along success stories, improvement ideas and news from the ever-changing world of kids' publishing. In the meantime, good luck—and maybe we'll meet at a writers conference or online this year.

Chuck Sambuchino
literaryagent@fwmedia.com
@chucksambuchino
Editor, *Children's Writer's & Illustrator's Market / Guide to Literary Agents*
Author, *How to Survive a Garden Gnome Attack*

HOW TO USE *CWIM*

As a writer, illustrator or photographer first picking up *Children's Writer's & Illustrator's Market*, you may not know quite how to start using the book. Your impulse may be to flip through the book and quickly make a mailing list, then submit to everyone in hopes that someone will take interest in your work. Well, there's more to it. Finding the right market takes time and research. The more you know about a market that interests you, the better chance you have of getting work accepted. We've made your job a little easier by putting a wealth of information at your fingertips. Besides providing listings, this directory includes a number of tools to help you determine which markets are the best ones for your work. By using these tools, as well as researching on your own, you raise your odds of being published.

USING THE INDEXES

This book lists hundreds of potential buyers of freelance material. To learn which companies want the type of material you're interested in submitting, start with the indexes.

Names Index

This index lists book and magazine editors and art directors as well as agents and art reps, indicating the companies they work for. Use this index to find company and contact information for individual publishing professionals.

Age-Level Index

Age groups are broken down into these categories in the Age-Level Index:

- **PICTURE BOOKS OR PICTURE-ORIENTED MATERIAL** are written and illustrated for preschoolers to 8-year-olds.

- **YOUNG READERS** are for 5- to 8-year-olds.
- **MIDDLE READERS** are for 9- to 11-year-olds.
- **YOUNG ADULT** is for ages 12 and up.

Age breakdowns may vary slightly from publisher to publisher, but using them as general guidelines will help you target appropriate markets. For example, if you've written an article about trends in teen fashion, check the Magazines Age-Level Index under the Young Adult subheading. Using this list, you'll quickly find the listings for young adult magazines.

Subject Index

But let's narrow the search further. Take your list of young adult magazines, turn to the Subject Index, and find the Fashion subheading. Then highlight the names that appear on both lists (Young Adult and Fashion). Now you have a smaller list of all the magazines that would be interested in your teen fashion article. Read through those listings and decide which ones sound best for your work.

Illustrators and photographers can use the Subject Index as well. If you specialize in painting animals, for instance, consider sending samples to book and magazine publishers listed under Animals and, perhaps, Nature/Environment. Since illustrators can simply send general examples of their style to art directors to keep on file, the indexes may be more helpful to artists sending manuscript/illustration packages who need to search for a specific subject. Always read the listings for the potential markets to see the type of work art directors prefer and what type of samples they'll keep on file, and obtain art or photo guidelines if they're available through the mail or online.

Photography Index

In this index, you'll find lists of book and magazine publishers that buy photos from freelancers. Refer to the list and read the listings for companies' specific photography needs. Obtain photo guidelines if they're offered through the mail or online.

USING THE LISTINGS

Many listings begin with symbols. Refer to the inside covers of the book for quick reference and find a handy pull-out bookmark (shown in this article) right inside the front cover.

Many listings indicate whether submission guidelines are available. If a publisher you're interested in offers guidelines, get them and read them. The same is true with catalogs. Sending for and reading catalogs or browsing them online gives you a better idea of whether your work would fit in with the books a publisher produces. (You should also look at a few of the books in the catalog at a library or bookstore to get a feel for the publisher's material.)

⊕ market new to this edition

Ⓐ market accepts agented submissions only

◔ award-winning market

◑ Canadian market

◓ market located outside of the U.S. and Canada

◐ online opportunity

◒ comment from the editor of *Children's Writer's & Illustrator's Market*

○ publisher producing educational material

◯ book packager/producer

ms, mss manuscript(s)

SCBWI Society of Children's Book Writers and Illustrators

SASE self-addressed, stamped envelope

IRC International Reply Coupon, for use in countries other than your own

b&w black & white (photo)

(For definitions of unfamiliar words and expressions relating to writing, illustration and publishing, see the Glossary.)

Especially for artists & photographers

Along with information for writers, listings provide information for illustrators and photographers. Illustrators will find numerous markets that maintain files of samples for possible future assignments. If you're both a writer and an illustrator, look for markets that accept manuscript/illustration packages and read the information offered under the **Illustration** subhead within the listings.

If you're a photographer, after consulting the Photography Index, read the information under the **Photography** subhead within listings to see what format buyers prefer. For example, some want 35mm color transparencies, others want black-and-white prints. Note the type of photos a buyer wants to purchase and the procedures for submitting. It's not uncommon for a market to want a résumé and promotional literature, as well as tearsheets from previous work. Listings also note whether model releases and/or captions are required.

Especially for young writers

If you're a parent, teacher or student, you may be interested in Young Writer's & Illustrator's Markets. The listings in this section encourage submissions from young writers and artists. Some may require a written statement from a teacher or parent noting the work is original. Also watch for age limits.

Young people should also check Contests & Awards for contests that accept work by young writers and artists. Some of the contests listed are especially for students; others accept both student and adult work. These listings contain the phrase **open to students** in bold. Some listings in Clubs & Organizations as well as Conferences & Workshops may also be of interest to students. Organizations and conferences that are open to or are especially for students also include **open to students**.

GRAPHIA

Harcourt Houghton Mifflin, 222 Berkeley St., Boston, MA 02116. (617)351-5000. Website: www.graphiabooks.com. **Manuscript Acquisitions:** Julia Richardson. "Graphia publishes quality paperbacks for today's teen readers, ages 14 and up. From fiction to nonfiction, poetry to graphic novels, Graphia runs the gamut, all unified by the quality of writing that is the hallmark of this imprint."

FICTION Young adult: adventure, contemporary, fantasy, history, humor, multicultural, poetry. Recently published: *The Off Season,* by Catherine Murdock; *Come in from the Cold,* by Marsha Qualey; *Breaking Up is Hard to Do,* with stories by Niki Burnham, Terri Clark, Ellen Hopkins and Lynda Sandoval; *Zahrah the Windseeker,* by Nnedi Okorafot-Mbachu.

NONFICTION Young adult: biography, history, multicultural, nature/environment, science, social issues.

HOW TO CONTACT Query. Responds to queries/mss in 3 months. Will consider simultaneous submissions and previously published work.

ILLUSTRATION Do not send original artwork or slides. Send color photocopies, tearsheets or photos to Art Dept. Include SASE if you would like your samples mailed back to you.

TERMS Pays author royalties. Offers advances. Sends galleys to authors. Catalog available on website (www.houghtonmifflin.com).

E-MAIL ADDRESSES AND WEBSITES

SPECIFIC CONTACT NAMES

INFO ON WHAT A PUBLISHER HANDLES

DETAILED SUBMISSION GUIDELINES

Don't forget your webinar!

To access the webinar that is included with your book, go to www.writersmarket.com/2012CWIM and learn more about getting your work published.

QUICK TIPS FOR WRITERS & ILLUSTRATORS

If you're new to the world of children's publishing, buying *Children's Writer's & Illustrator's Market* may have been one of the first steps in your journey to publication. What follows is a list of suggestions and resources that can help make that journey a smooth and swift one:

1. MAKE THE MOST OF *CHILDREN'S WRITER'S & ILLUSTRATOR'S MARKET*. Be sure to read "How to Use This Book" for tips on reading the listings and using the indexes. Also be sure to take advantage of the articles and interviews in the book. The insights of the authors, illustrators, editors and agents we've interviewed will inform and inspire you.

2. JOIN THE SOCIETY OF CHILDREN'S BOOK WRITERS AND ILLUSTRATORS. SCBWI, more than 19,000 members strong, is an organization for both beginners and professionals interested in writing and illustrating for children. It offers members a slew of information and support through publications, a website, and a host of Regional Advisors overseeing chapters in almost every state in the U.S. and a growing number of locations around the globe (including France, Canada, Japan and Australia). SCBWI puts on a number of conferences, workshops, and events on the regional and national levels (many listed in the Conferences & Workshops section of this book). For more information, contact SCBWI, 8271 Beverly Blvd., Los Angeles CA 90048, (323)782-1010, or visit their website: scbwi.org.

3. READ NEWSLETTERS. Newsletters, such as *Children's Book Insider, Children's Writer* and the *SCBWI Bulletin*, offer updates and new information about publishers on a timely basis and are relatively inexpensive. Many local chapters of SCBWI offer regional newsletters as well. (See Helpful Books & Publications later in this book for contact information on the newsletters listed above and others.) For information on regional SCBWI newsletters, visit scbwi.org and click on "Publications."

4. READ TRADE AND REVIEW PUBLICATIONS. Magazines like *Publishers Weekly* (which offers two special issues each year devoted to children's publishing and is available on newsstands), *The Horn Book* and *Booklinks* offer news, articles, reviews of newly published titles and ads featuring upcoming and current releases. Referring to them will help you get a feel for what's happening in children's publishing.

5. READ GUIDELINES. Most publishers and magazines offer writer's and artist's guidelines that provide detailed information on needs and submission requirements, and some magazines offer theme lists for upcoming issues. Many publishers and magazines state the availability of guidelines within their listings. Send a self-addressed, stamped envelope (SASE) to publishers who offer guidelines. You'll often find submission information on publishers' and magazines' websites.

6. LOOK AT PUBLISHERS' CATALOGS. Perusing publishers' catalogs can give you a feel for their line of books and help you decide where your work might fit in. If catalogs are available (often stated within listings), send for them with a SASE. Visit publishers' websites, which often contain their full catalogs. You can also ask librarians to look at catalogs they have on hand. You can even search Amazon.com by publisher and year. (Click on "book search" then "publisher, date" and plug in, for example, "Lee & Low" under "publisher" and "2010" under year. You'll get a list of Lee & Low titles published in 2010, which you can peruse.)

7. VISIT BOOKSTORES. It's not only informative to spend time in bookstores—it's fun, too! Frequently visit the children's section of your local bookstore (whether a chain or an independent) to see the latest from a variety of publishers and the most current issues of children's magazines. Look for books in the genre you're writing or with illustrations similar in style to yours, and spend some time studying them. It's also wise to get to know your local booksellers; they can tell you what's new in the store and provide insight into what kids and adults are buying.

8. READ, READ, READ! While you're at that bookstore, pick up a few things, or keep a list of the books that interest you and check them out of your library. Read and study the latest releases, the award winners and the classics. You'll learn from other writers, get ideas and get a feel for what's being published. Think about what works and doesn't work in a story. Pay attention to how plots are constructed and how characters are developed or the rhythm and pacing of picture book text. It's certainly enjoyable research!

9. TAKE ADVANTAGE OF INTERNET RESOURCES. There are innumerable sources of information available on the Internet about writing for children (and anything else you could possibly think of). It's also a great resource for getting (and staying) in touch with other writers and illustrators through listservs, blogs, social networking sites and e-mail, and it can serve as a vehicle for self-promotion. (Visit some authors' and illustrators' sites for ideas. See "Useful Online Resources" in this book for a list of websites.)

10. CONSIDER ATTENDING A CONFERENCE. If time and finances allow, attending a conference is a great way to meet peers and network with professionals in the field of children's publishing. As mentioned above, SCBWI offers conferences in various locations year round. (See scbwi.org and click on "Events" for a full conference calendar.) General writers' conferences often offer specialized sessions just for those interested in children's writing. Many conferences offer optional manuscript and portfolio critiques as well, giving you a chance for feedback from seasoned professionals. See the Conferences & Awards section for information on SCBWI and other conferences. The section features a Conferences & Workshops Calendar to help you plan your travel.

11. NETWORK, NETWORK, NETWORK! Don't work in a vacuum. You can meet other writers and illustrators through a number of the things listed above—SCBWI, conferences, online. Attend local meetings for writers and illustrators whenever you can. Befriend other writers in your area (SCBWI offers members a roster broken down by state)—share guidelines, share subscriptions, be conference buddies and roommates, join a critique group or writing group, exchange information and offer support. Get online—sign on to listservs, post on message boards and blogs, visit social networking sites and chatrooms. Exchange addresses, phone numbers and e-mail addresses with writers or illustrators you meet at events. And at conferences, don't be afraid to talk to people, ask strangers to join you for lunch, approach speakers and introduce yourself, or chat in elevators and hallways.

12. PERFECT YOUR CRAFT AND DON'T SUBMIT UNTIL YOUR WORK IS ITS BEST. It's often been said that a writer should try to write every day. Great manuscripts don't happen overnight; there's time, research and revision involved. As you visit bookstores and study what others have written and illustrated, really step back and look at your own work and ask yourself—honestly—*How does my work measure up? Is it ready for editors or art directors to see?* If it's not, keep working. Join a critique group or get a professional manuscript or portfolio critique.

13. BE PATIENT, LEARN FROM REJECTION, AND DON'T GIVE UP! Thousands of manuscripts land on editors' desks; thousands of illustration samples line art directors' file drawers. There are so many factors that come into play when evaluating submissions. Keep in mind that you might not hear back from publishers promptly. Persistence and patience are important qualities in writers and illustrators working toward publication. Keep at it—it will come. It can take a while, but when you get that first book contract or first assignment, you'll know it was worth the wait. (For proof, read the "First Books" article later in this book!)

BEFORE YOUR FIRST SALE

///

If you're just beginning to pursue your career as a children's book writer or illustrator, it's important to learn the proper procedures, formats and protocol for the publishing industry. This article outlines the basics you need to know before you submit your work to a market.

FINDING THE BEST MARKETS FOR YOUR WORK

Researching publishers thoroughly is a basic element of submitting your work successfully. Editors and art directors hate to receive inappropriate submissions; handling them wastes a lot of their time, not to mention your time and money, and they are the main reason some publishers have chosen not to accept material over the transom. By randomly sending out material without knowing a company's needs, you're sure to meet with rejection.

If you're interested in submitting to a particular magazine, write to request a sample copy or see if it's available in your local library or bookstore. For a book publisher, obtain a book catalog and check a library or bookstore for titles produced by that publisher. Most publishers and magazines have websites that include catalogs or sample articles (websites are given within the listings). Studying such materials carefully will better acquaint you with a publisher's or magazine's writing, illustration and photography styles and formats.

Most of the book publishers and magazines listed in this book offer some sort of writer's, artist's or photographer's guidelines for a self-addressed, stamped envelope (SASE). Guidelines are also often found on publishers' websites. It's important to read and study guidelines before submitting work. You'll get a better understanding of what a particular publisher wants. You may even decide, after reading the submission guidelines, that your work isn't right for a company you considered.

SUBMITTING YOUR WORK

Throughout the listings, you'll read requests for particular elements to include when contacting markets. Here are explanations of some of these important submission components.

Queries, cover letters & proposals

A query is a no-more-than-one-page, well-written letter meant to arouse an editor's interest in your work. Query letters briefly outline the work you're proposing and include facts, anecdotes, interviews or other pertinent information that give the editor a feel for the manuscript's premise—enticing her to want to know more. End your letter with a straightforward request to submit the work, and include information on its approximate length, date it could be completed, and whether accompanying photos or artwork are available.

In a query letter, think about presenting your book as a publisher's catalog would present it. Read through a good catalog and examine how the publishers give enticing summaries of their books in a spare amount of words. It's also important that query letters give editors a taste of your writing style. For good advice and samples of queries, cover letters and other correspondence, consult the article "Crafting a Query" in this book, as well as *Formatting & Submitting Your Manuscript, 3rd Ed.* and *How to Write Attention-Grabbing Query & Cover Letters* (both Writer's Digest Books).

- **QUERY LETTERS FOR NONFICTION.** Queries are usually required when submitting nonfiction material to a publisher. The goal of a nonfiction query is to convince the editor your idea is perfect for her readership and that you're qualified to do the job. Note any previous writing experience and include published samples to prove your credentials, especially samples related to the subject matter you're querying about.
- **QUERY LETTERS FOR FICTION.** For a fiction query, explain the story's plot, main characters, conflict, and resolution. Just as in nonfiction queries, make the editor eager to see more.
- **COVER LETTERS FOR WRITERS.** Some editors prefer to review complete manuscripts, especially for picture books or fiction. In such cases, the cover letter (which should be no longer than one page) serves as your introduction, establishes your credentials as a writer, and gives the editor an overview of the manuscript. If the editor asked for the manuscript because of a query, note this in your cover letter.
- **COVER LETTERS FOR ILLUSTRATORS AND PHOTOGRAPHERS.** For an illustrator or photographer, the cover letter serves as an introduction to the art director and establishes professional credentials when submitting samples. Explain what services you can provide as well as what type of follow-up contact you plan to make, if any. Be sure to include the URL of your online portfolio if you have one.

- **RÉSUMÉS.** Often writers, illustrators and photographers are asked to submit résumés with cover letters and samples. They can be created in a variety of formats, from a single page listing information to color brochures featuring your work. Keep your résumé brief, and focus on your achievements, including your clients and the work you've done for them, as well as your educational background and any awards you've received. Do not use the same résumé you'd use for a typical job application.
- **BOOK PROPOSALS.** Throughout the listings in the Book Publishers section, publishers refer to submitting a synopsis, outline and sample chapters. Depending on an editor's preference, some or all of these components, along with a cover letter, make up a book proposal.

A *synopsis* summarizes the book, covering the basic plot (including the ending). It should be easy to read and flow well.

An *outline* covers your book chapter by chapter and provides highlights of each. If you're developing an outline for fiction, include major characters, plots and subplots, and book length. Requesting an outline is uncommon, and the word is somewhat interchangeable with "synopsis."

Sample chapters give a more comprehensive idea of your writing skill. Some editors may request the first two or three chapters to determine if they're interested in seeing the whole book. Some may request a set number of pages.

Manuscript formats

When submitting a complete manuscript, follow some basic guidelines. In the upper-left corner of your title page, type your legal name (not pseudonym), address and phone number. In the upper-right corner, type the approximate word count. All material in the upper corners should be single-spaced. Then type the title (centered) almost halfway down that page, the word "by" two spaces under that, and your name or pseudonym two spaces under "by."

The first page should also include the title (centered) one-third of the way down. Two spaces under that, type "by" and your name or pseudonym. To begin the body of your manuscript, drop down two double spaces and indent five spaces for each new paragraph. There should be one-inch margins around all sides of a full typewritten page. (Manuscripts with wide margins are more readable and easier to edit.)

Set your computer to double-space the manuscript body. From page two to the end of the manuscript, include your last name followed by a comma and the title (or key words of the title) in the upper-left corner. The page number should go in the top right corner. Drop down two double spaces to begin the body of each page. If you're submitting a novel, type each chapter title one-third of the way down the page. For more information on manuscript formats, read *Formatting & Submitting Your Manuscript, 3rd Ed.* (Writer's Digest Books).

Picture book formats

The majority of editors prefer to see complete manuscripts for picture books. When typing the text of a picture book, don't indicate page breaks and don't type each page of text on a new sheet of paper. And unless you are an illustrator, don't worry about supplying art. Editors will find their own illustrators for picture books. Most of the time, a writer and an illustrator who work on the same book never meet or interact. The editor acts as a go-between and works with the writer and illustrator throughout the publishing process. *How to Write and Sell Children's Picture Books*, by Jean E. Karl (Writer's Digest Books), offers advice on preparing text and marketing your work.

If you're an illustrator who has written your own book, consider creating a dummy or storyboard containing both art and text, and then submit it along with your complete manuscript and sample pieces of final art (color photocopies or computer printouts—never originals). Publishers interested in picture books specify in their listings what should be submitted. For tips on creating a dummy, refer to *How to Write and Illustrate Children's Books and Get Them Published*, edited by Treld Pelkey Bicknell and Felicity Trotman (North Light Books), or Frieda Gates' book, *How to Write, Illustrate, and Design Children's Books* (Lloyd-Simone Publishing Company).

Writers may also want to learn the art of dummy-making to help them through their writing process with things like pacing, rhythm and length. For a great explanation and helpful hints, see *You Can Write Children's Books*, by Tracey E. Dils (Writer's Digest Books).

Mailing submissions

Your main concern when packaging material is to be sure it arrives undamaged. If your manuscript is fewer than six pages, simply fold it in thirds and send it in a #10 (business-size) envelope. For a SASE, either fold another #10 envelope in thirds or insert a #9 (reply) envelope, which fits in a #10 neatly without folding.

Another option is folding your manuscript in half in a 6x9 envelope, with a #9 or #10 SASE enclosed. For larger manuscripts, use a 9x12 envelope both for mailing the submission and as a SASE (which can be folded in half). Book manuscripts require sturdy packaging for mailing. Include a self-addressed mailing label and return postage. If asked to send artwork and photographs, remember they require a bit more care in packaging to guarantee they arrive in good condition. Sandwich illustrations and photos between heavy cardboard that is slightly larger than the work. The cardboard can be secured by rubber bands or with tape. If you tape the cardboard together, check that the artwork doesn't stick to the tape. Be sure your name and address appear on the back of each piece of art or each photo in case the material becomes separated. For the packaging, use either a manila envelope, a foam-padded envelope, brown paper or a mailer lined with plastic air bubbles. Bind nonjoined edges with reinforced mailing tape and affix a typed mailing label or clearly write your address.

Mailing material first class ensures quick delivery. Also, first-class mail is forwarded for one year if the addressee has moved, and it can be returned if undeliverable. If you're concerned about your original material safely reaching its destination, consider other mailing options such as UPS. No matter which way you send material, never send it where it requires a signature. Agents and editors are too busy to sign for packages.

Remember, companies outside your own country can't use your country's postage when returning a manuscript to you. When mailing a submission to another country, include a self-addressed envelope and International Reply Coupons, or IRCs. (You'll see this term in many listings in the Canadian & International Book Publishers section.) Your postmaster can tell you, based on a package's weight, the correct number of IRCs to include to ensure its return. If it's not necessary for an editor to return your work (such as with photocopies), don't include return postage.

Unless requested, it's never a good idea to use a company's fax number to send manuscript submissions. This can disrupt a company's internal business. Study the listings for specifics and visit publishers' and market websites for more information.

Keeping submission records

It's important to keep track of the material you submit. When recording each submission, include the date it was sent, the business and contact name, and any enclosures (such as samples of writing, artwork or photography). You can create a record-keeping system of your own or look for record-keeping software in your area computer store.

Keep copies of articles or manuscripts you send together with related correspondence to make follow-up easier. When you sell rights to a manuscript, artwork or photos, you can "close" your file on a particular submission by noting the date the material was accepted, what rights were purchased, the publication date and payment.

Often writers, illustrators and photographers fail to follow up on overdue responses. If you don't hear from a publisher within their stated response time, wait another month or so and follow up with a note asking about the status of your submission. Include the title or description, date sent and a SASE for response. Ask the contact person when she anticipates making a decision. You may refresh the memory of a buyer who temporarily forgot about your submission. At the very least, you'll receive a definite "no" and free yourself to send the material to another publisher.

Simultaneous submissions

If you opt for simultaneous submissions—sending the same material to several publishers at the same time—only submit to publishers who state in their submission guidelines that they accept simultaneous submissions. In such cases, always specify in your cover letter that you've submitted to more than one editor/agent.

It's especially important to keep track of simultaneous submissions, so if you get an offer on a manuscript sent to more than one publisher, you can instruct other publishers to withdraw your work from consideration.

AGENTS & ART REPS

Most children's writers, illustrators and photographers, especially those just beginning, are confused about whether to enlist the services of an agent or representative. The decision is strictly one that each writer, illustrator or photographer must make for herself. Some are confident with their own negotiation skills and believe acquiring an agent or rep is not in their best interest. Others feel uncomfortable in the business arena or are not willing to sacrifice valuable creative time for marketing.

About half of children's publishers accept unagented work, so it's possible to break into children's publishing without an agent. Writers targeting magazine markets don't need the services of an agent. In fact, it's practically impossible to find an agent interested in marketing articles and short stories—there simply isn't enough financial incentive.

One benefit of having an agent, though, is it may speed up the process of getting your work reviewed, especially by publishers who don't accept unagented submissions. If an agent has a good reputation and submits your manuscript to an editor, that manuscript will likely bypass the first-read stage (which is generally done by editorial assistants and junior editors) and end up on the editor's desk sooner.

When agreeing to have a reputable agent represent you, remember that she should be familiar with the needs of the current market and evaluate your manuscript/artwork/photos accordingly. She should also determine the quality of your piece and whether it is saleable. When your manuscript sells, your agent should negotiate a favorable contract and clear up any questions you have about payments.

Keep in mind that however reputable the agent or rep is, she has limitations.

Representation does not guarantee sale of your work. It just means an agent or rep sees potential in your writing, art or photos. Though an agent or rep may offer criticism or advice on how to improve your work, she cannot make you a better writer, artist or photographer.

Literary agents typically charge a 15 percent commission from the sale of writing; art and photo representatives usually charge a 25–30 percent commission. Such fees are taken from advances and royalty earnings. If your agent sells foreign rights or film rights to your work, she will deduct a higher percentage because she will most likely be dealing with an overseas agent with whom she must split the fee.

Be advised that not every agent is open to representing a writer, artist or photographer who lacks an established track record. Just as when approaching a publisher, the manuscript, artwork, or photos and query or cover letter you submit to a potential agent must be attractive and professional looking. Your first impression must be as an organized, articulate person. For listings of agents and reps, turn to the Agents & Art Reps section.

For additional listings of art reps, consult *Artist's & Graphic Designer's Market*; for photo reps, see *Photographer's Market*; for more information and additional listings of literary agents, see *Guide to Literary Agents* (all Writer's Digest Books).

RUNNING YOUR BUSINESS

The basics for writers & illustrators.

A career in children's publishing involves more than just writing skills or artistic talent. Successful authors and illustrators must be able to hold their own in negotiations, keep records, understand contract language, grasp copyright law, pay taxes and take care of a number of other business concerns. Although agents and reps, accountants and lawyers, and writers' organizations offer help in sorting out such business issues, it's wise to have a basic understanding of them going in. This article offers just that—basic information. For a more in-depth look at the subjects covered here, check your library or bookstore for books and magazines to help you. We also tell you how to get information on issues like taxes and copyright from the federal government.

CONTRACTS & NEGOTIATION

Before you see your work in print or begin working with an editor or art director on a project, there is negotiation. And whether negotiating a book contract, a magazine article assignment, or an illustration or photo assignment, there are a few things to keep in mind. First, if you find any clauses vague or confusing in a contract, get legal advice. The time and money invested in counseling up front could protect you from problems later. If you have an agent or rep, she will review any contract.

A contract is an agreement between two or more parties that specifies the fees to be paid, services rendered, deadlines, rights purchased and, for artists and photographers, whether original work is returned. Most companies have standard contracts for writers, illustrators and photographers. The specifics (such as royalty rates, advances, delivery dates, etc.) are typed in after negotiations.

Though it's okay to conduct negotiations over the phone, get a written contract once both parties have agreed on terms. Never depend on oral stipulations; written contracts protect both parties from misunderstandings. Watch for clauses that may not be in your best interest, such as "work-for-hire." When you do work-for-hire, you give up all rights to your creations.

When negotiating a book deal, find out whether your contract contains an option clause. This clause requires the author to give the publisher a first look at her next work before offering it to other publishers. Though it's editorial etiquette to give the publisher the first chance at publishing your next work, be wary of statements in the contract that could trap you. Don't allow the publisher to consider the next project for more than 30 days and be specific about what type of work should actually be considered "next work." (For example, if the book under contract is a young adult novel, specify that the publisher will receive an exclusive look at *only* your next young adult novel.)

Book publishers' payment methods

Book publishers pay authors and artists in royalties, a percentage of either the wholesale or retail price of each book sold. From large publishing houses, the author usually receives an advance issued against future royalties before the book is published.

After your book has sold enough copies to earn back your advance, you'll start to get royalty checks. Some publishers hold a reserve against returns, which means a percentage of royalties is held back in case books are returned from bookstores. If you have a reserve clause in your contract, find out the exact percentage of total sales that will be withheld and the time period the publisher will hold this money. You should be reimbursed this amount after a reasonable time period, such as a year. Royalty percentages vary with each publisher, but there are standard ranges.

Book publishers' rates

First-time picture book authors can expect advances of $500–10,000; first-time picture book illustrators' advances range from $2,000–10,000. Rates go up for subsequent books. Experienced authors can expect higher advances. Royalties for picture books are generally about five percent (split between the author and illustrator) but can go as high as 10 percent. Those who both write and illustrate a book, of course, receive the full royalty. Advances for novels can fetch advances of $1,000–100,000 and 10 percent royalties.

As you might expect, advance and royalty figures vary from house to house and are affected by the time of year, the state of the economy and other factors. Some smaller houses may not even pay royalties, just flat fees. Educational houses may not offer advances or may offer smaller amounts. Religious publishers tend to offer smaller advances than trade publishers. First-time writers and illustrators generally start on the low end of the scale, while established and high-profile writers are paid more. For more information, SCBWI members can request or download SCBWI publication "Answer to Some Questions About Contracts." (Visit scbwi.org.)

Pay rates for magazines

For writers, fee structures for magazines are based on a per-word rate or range for a specific article length. Artists and photographers have a few more variables to contend with before contracting their services.

Payment for illustrations and photos can be set by such factors as whether the piece(s) will be black and white or four-color, how many are to be purchased, where the work appears (cover or inside), circulation, and the artist's or photographer's prior experience.

Remaindering

When a book goes out of print, a publisher will sell any existing copies to a wholesaler who, in turn, sells the copies to stores at a discount. When the books are "remaindered" to a wholesaler, they are usually sold at a price just above the cost of printing. When negotiating a contract with a publisher, you may want to discuss the possibility of purchasing the remaindered copies before they are sold to a wholesaler, then you can market the copies you purchased and still make a profit.

KNOW YOUR RIGHTS

A copyright is a form of protection provided to creators of original works, published or unpublished. In general, copyright protection ensures the writer, illustrator or photographer the power to decide how her work is used and allows her to receive payment for each use.

Essentially, copyright also encourages the creation of new works by guaranteeing the creator power to sell rights to the work in the marketplace. The copyright holder can print, reprint or copy her work; sell or distribute copies of her work; or prepare derivative works such as plays, collages or recordings. The Copyright Law is designed to protect work (created on or after January 1, 1978) for her lifetime plus 70 years. If you collaborate with someone else on a written or artistic project, the copyright will last for the lifetime of the last survivor plus 70 years. The creators' heirs may hold a copyright for an additional 70 years. After that, the work becomes public domain. Works created anonymously or under a pseudonym are protected for 120 years, or 95 years after publication. Under work-for-hire agreements, you relinquish your copyright to your "employer."

Copyright notice & registration

Although it's not necessary to include a copyright notice on unregistered work, if you don't feel your work is safe without the notice (especially if posting work online), it is your right to include one. Including a copyright notice—(©) (year of work, your name)—should help safeguard against plagiarism.

Registration is a legal formality intended to make copyright public record, and it can help you win more money in a court case. By registering work within three months of publication or before an infringement occurs, you are eligible to collect statutory damages and attorney's fees. If you register later than three months after publication, you will qualify only for actual damages and profits.

Ideas and concepts are not copyrightable, only expressions of those ideas and concepts can be protected. A character type or basic plot outline, for example, is not subject to a copyright infringement lawsuit. Also, titles, names, short phrases or slogans, and lists of contents are not subject to copyright protection, though titles and names may be protected through the Trademark Office.

You can register a group of articles, illustrations, or photos if it meets these criteria:
- the group is assembled in order, such as in a notebook
- the works bear a single title, such as "Works by (your name)"
- it is the work of one writer, artist or photographer
- the material is the subject of a single claim to copyright

It's a publisher's responsibility to register your book for copyright. If you've previously registered the same material, you must inform your editor and supply the previous copyright information; otherwise, the publisher can't register the book in its published form.

For more information about the proper way to register works and to order the correct forms, contact the U.S. Copyright Office, (202)707-3000. For information about how to use the copyright forms, request a copy of Circular I on Copyright Basics. All of the forms and circulars are free. Send the completed registration form along with the stated fee and a copy of the work to the Copyright Office.

For specific answers to questions about copyright (but not legal advice), call the Copyright Public Information Office at (202)707-3000 weekdays between 8:30 a.m. and 5 p.m. EST. Forms can also be downloaded from the Library of Congress website: copyright. gov. The site also includes a list of frequently asked questions, tips on filling out forms, general copyright information, and links to other sites related to copyright issues.

The rights publishers buy

The copyright law specifies that a writer, illustrator or photographer generally sells one-time rights to her work unless she and the buyer agree otherwise in writing. Many publications will want more exclusive rights to your work than just one-time usage; some will even require you to sell all rights. Be sure you are monetarily compensated for the additional rights you relinquish. If you must give up all rights to a work, carefully consider the price you're being offered to determine whether you'll be compensated for the loss of other potential sales.

Writers who only give up limited rights to their work can then sell reprint rights to other publications, foreign rights to international publications, or even movie rights, should the opportunity arise. Artists and photographers can sell their work to other markets such as paper product companies who may use an image on a calendar, greeting card or mug. Illustrators and photographers may even sell original work after it has been published. And there are a number of galleries throughout the U.S. that display and sell the original work of children's illustrators.

Rights acquired through the sale of a book manuscript are explained in each publisher's contract. Take time to read relevant clauses to be sure you understand what rights each contract is specifying before signing. Be sure your contract contains a clause allowing all rights to revert back to you in the event the publisher goes out of business. (You may even want to have the contract reviewed by an agent or an attorney specializing in publishing law.)

The following are the rights you'll most often sell to publishers, periodicals and producers in the marketplace:

FIRST RIGHTS. The buyer purchases the rights to use the work for the first time in any medium. All other rights remain with the creator. When material is excerpted in this way (from a soon-to-be-published book in this manner) for use in a newspaper or periodical, first serial rights are also purchased.

ONE-TIME RIGHTS. The buyer has no guarantee that she is the first to use a piece. One-time permission to run written work, illustrations or photos is acquired, and then the rights revert back to the creator.

FIRST NORTH AMERICAN SERIAL RIGHTS. This is similar to first rights, except that companies who distribute both in the U.S. and Canada will stipulate these rights to ensure that another North American company won't come out with simultaneous usage of the same work.

SECOND SERIAL (REPRINT) RIGHTS. In this case, newspapers and magazines are granted the right to reproduce a work that has already appeared in another publication. These rights are also purchased by a newspaper or magazine editor who wants to publish part of a book after the book has been published. The proceeds from reprint rights for a book are often split evenly between the author and his publishing company.

SIMULTANEOUS RIGHTS. More than one publication buys one-time rights to the same work at the same time. Use of such rights occurs among magazines with circulations that don't overlap, such as many religious publications.

ALL RIGHTS. Just as it sounds, the writer, illustrator or photographer relinquishes all rights to a piece—she no longer has any say in who acquires rights to use it. All rights are purchased by publishers who pay premium usage fees, have an exclusive format, or have other book or magazine interests from which the purchased work can generate more mileage. If a company insists on acquiring all rights to your work, see if you can negotiate for the rights to revert back to you after a reasonable period of time. If they agree to such a proposal, get it in writing. Note: Writers, illustrators and photographers should be wary of "work-for-hire" arrangements. If you sign an agreement stipulating that your work will be done as work-for-hire, you will not control the copyrights of the completed work—the company that hired you will be the copyright owner.

FOREIGN SERIAL RIGHTS. Be sure before you market to foreign publications that you have sold only North American—not worldwide—serial rights to previous markets. If so, you are free to market to publications that may be interested in material that's appeared in a North American-based periodical.

SYNDICATION RIGHTS. This is a division of serial rights. For example, if a syndicate prints portions of a book in installments in its newspapers, it would be syndicating second serial rights. The syndicate would receive a commission and leave the remainder to be split between the author and publisher.

SUBSIDIARY RIGHTS. These include serial rights, dramatic rights, book club rights or translation rights. The contract should specify what percentage of profits from sales of these rights go to the author and publisher.

DRAMATIC, TELEVISION AND MOTION PICTURE RIGHTS. During a specified time, the interested party tries to sell a story to a producer or director. Many times options are renewed because the selling process can be lengthy.

DISPLAY RIGHTS OR ELECTRONIC PUBLISHING RIGHTS. They're also known as "Data, Storage and Retrieval." Usually listed under subsidiary rights, the marketing of electronic rights in this era of rapidly expanding capabilities and markets for electronic material can be tricky. Display rights can cover text or images to be used in a CD or online, or they may cover use of material in formats not even fully developed yet. If a display rights clause is listed in your contract, try to negotiate its elimination. Otherwise, be sure to pin down which electronic rights are being purchased. Demand the clause be restricted to things designed to be read only. By doing this, you maintain your rights to use your work for things such as games and interactive software.

SOURCES FOR CONTRACT HELP

Writers organizations offer a wealth of information to members, including contract advice:

SOCIETY OF CHILDREN'S BOOK WRITERS AND ILLUSTRATORS members can find information in the SCBWI publication "Answers to Some Questions About Contracts." Contact SCBWI at 8271 Beverly Blvd., Los Angeles CA 90048, (323)782-1010, or visit their website: scbwi.org.

THE AUTHORS GUILD also offers contract tips. Visit their website: authorsguild.org. (Members of the guild can receive a 75-point contract review from the guild's legal staff.) See the website for membership information and application form, or contact The Authors Guild at 31 E. 28th St., 10th Floor, New York NY 10016, (212)563-5904. Fax: (212)564-5363. E-mail: staff@authorsguild.org.

STRICTLY BUSINESS

An essential part of being a freelance writer, illustrator or photographer is running your freelance business. It's imperative to maintain accurate business records to determine if you're making a profit as a freelancer. Keeping correct, organized records will also make your life easier as you approach tax time.

When setting up your system, begin by keeping a bank account and ledger for your business finances apart from your personal finances. Also, if writing, illustration or photography is secondary to another freelance career, keep separate business records for each.

You will likely accumulate some business expenses before showing any profit when you start out as a freelancer. To substantiate your income and expenses to the IRS, keep all invoices, cash receipts, sales slips, bank statements, canceled checks and receipts related to travel expenses and entertaining clients. For entertainment expenditures, record the date, place and purpose of the business meeting, as well as gas mileage. Keep records for all purchases, big and small. Don't take the small purchases for granted; they can add up to a substantial amount. File all receipts in chronological order. Maintaining a separate file for each month simplifies retrieving records at the end of the year.

Record keeping

When setting up a single-entry bookkeeping system, record income and expenses separately. Use some of the subheads that appear on Schedule C (the form used for recording income from a business) of the 1040 tax form so you can easily transfer information onto the tax form when filing your return. In your ledger, include a description of each transaction—the date, source of income (or debts from business purchases), description of what was purchased or sold, the amount of the transaction, and whether payment was by cash, check or credit card.

Don't wait until January 1 to start keeping records. The moment you first make a business-related purchase or sell an article, book manuscript, illustration or photo, begin tracking your profits and losses. If you keep records from January 1 to December 31, you're using a calendar-year accounting period. Any other accounting period is called a fiscal year.

There are two types of accounting methods you can choose from—the cash method and the accrual method. The cash method is used more often: You record income when it is received and expenses when they're disbursed.

Using the accrual method, you report income at the time you earn it rather than when it's actually received. Similarly, expenses are recorded at the time they're incurred rather than when you actually pay them. If you choose this method, keep separate records for "accounts receivable" and "accounts payable."

Satisfying the IRS

To successfully—and legally—work as a freelancer, you must know what income you should report and what deductions you can claim. But before you can do that, you must prove to the IRS you're in business to make a profit, that your writing, illustration or photography is not merely a hobby. The Tax Reform Act of 1986 says you should show a profit for three years out of a five-year period to attain professional status. The IRS considers these factors as proof of your professionalism:

- accurate financial records
- a business bank account separate from your personal account
- proven time devoted to your profession
- whether it's your main or secondary source of income
- your history of profits and losses
- the amount of training you have invested in your field
- your expertise

If your business is unincorporated, you'll fill out tax information on Schedule C of Form 1040. If you're unsure of what deductions you can take, request the IRS publication containing this information. Under the Tax Reform Act, only 30 percent of business meals, entertainment and related tips, and parking charges are deductible. Other deductible expenses allowed on Schedule C include: car expenses for business-related trips; professional courses and seminars; depreciation of office equipment, such as a computer; dues and publication subscriptions; and miscellaneous expenses, such as postage used for business needs.

If you're working out of a home office, a portion of your mortgage interest (or rent), related utilities, property taxes, repair costs and depreciation may be deducted as business expenses—under special circumstances. To learn more about the possibility of home office deductions, consult IRS Publication 587, Business Use of Your Home.

The method of paying taxes on income not subject to withholding is called "estimated tax" for individuals. If you expect to owe more than $500 at year's end and if the total amount of income tax that will be withheld during the year will be less than 90 percent of the tax shown on the current year's return, you'll generally make estimated tax payments. Estimated tax payments are made in four equal installments due on April 15, June 15, September 15, and January 15 (assuming you're a calendar-year taxpayer). For more information, request Publication 533, Self-Employment Tax.

The Internal Revenue Service's website (irs.gov) offers tips and instant access to IRS forms and publications.

Social Security tax

Depending on your net income as a freelancer, you may be liable for a Social Security tax. This is a tax designed for those who don't have Social Security withheld from their paychecks. You're liable if your net income is $400 or more per year. Net income is the difference between your income and allowable business deductions. Request Schedule SE, Computation of Social Security Self-Employment Tax, if you qualify.

If completing your income tax return proves to be too complex, consider hiring an accountant (the fee is a deductible business expense) or contact the IRS for assistance. (Look in the White Pages under U.S. Government—Internal Revenue Service or check their website, irs.gov.) In addition to offering numerous publications to instruct you in various facets of preparing a tax return, the IRS also has walk-in centers in some cities.

Insurance

As a self-employed professional, be aware of what health and business insurance coverage is available to you. Unless you're a Canadian who is covered by national health insurance or a full-time freelancer covered by your spouse's policy, health insurance will no doubt be one of your biggest expenses. Under the terms of a 1985 government act (COBRA), if you leave a job with health benefits, you're entitled to continue that coverage for up to 18 months; you pay 100 percent of the premium and sometimes a small administration fee. Eventually, you must search for your own health plan. You may also choose to purchase disability and life insurance. Disability insurance is offered through many private insurance companies and state governments. This insurance pays a monthly fee that covers living and business expenses during periods of long-term recuperation from a health problem. The amount of money paid is based on the recipient's annual earnings.

Before contacting any insurance representative, talk to other writers, illustrators or photographers to learn which insurance companies they recommend. If you belong to a writers' or artists' organization, ask the organization if it offers insurance coverage for professionals. (SCBWI has a plan available to members in certain states. Look through the Clubs & Organizations section for other groups that may offer coverage.) Group coverage may be more affordable and provide more comprehensive coverage than an individual policy.

AGENTS TELL ALL

Literary agents answer some common (and not-so-common) questions.

by Chuck Sambuchino, Ricki Schultz and Donna Gambale

Whether during their travels to conferences or on their personal blogs, literary agents get a lot of questions from writers—some over and over. Below is a roundup of such questions answered by some of the top children's agents in the business.

ON STARTING STRONG

When you're reviewing a partial fiction manuscript, what do you hate to see in Chapter 1?

I hate to see a whiny character who's in the middle of a fight with one of their parents, slamming doors, rolling eyes and displaying all sorts of other stereotypical behavior. I hate seeing character "stats" ("Hi, I'm Brian. I'm 10 years and 35 days old with brown hair and green eyes."). I also tend to have a hard time bonding with characters who talk to the reader ("Let me tell you about the summer when I ...").

—**KELLY SONNACK** *is a literary agent with the Andrea Brown Literary Agency*

In YA and teen, what are some page 1 clichés you come across?

The most common problem I see is a story that's been told a million times before, without any new twists to make it unique enough to stand out. Same plot, same situations, same set up = the same ol' story. For example: abusive parents/kid's a rebel; family member(s) killed tragically/kid's a loner; divorced parents/kid acts out. Another problem I often see is when the protagonist/main characters don't have an age-appropriate voice. For example: If your main character is 14, let him talk like a 14-year-old. And lastly, being unable to "connect" with the main character(s). For example: Characters are too whiny or bratty, or a character shows no emotion/angst.

—**CHRISTINE WITTHOHN** *is the founder of Book Cents Literary*

What are some Chapter 1 clichés you often come across when reading a partial manuscript?

One of my biggest pet peeves is when writers try to stuff too much exposition into dialogue rather than trusting their abilities as storytellers to get information across. I'm talking stuff like the mom saying, "Listen, Jimmy, I know you've missed your father ever since he died in that mysterious boating accident last year, but I'm telling you, you'll love this summer camp!" So often writers feel like they have to hook the reader right away. In some ways that's true, but in others you can hook a reader with things other than explosions and big secrets being revealed. Good, strong writing and voice can do it, too.

—**CHRIS RICHMAN** *is a literary agent with Upstart Crow Literary*

Tell me about some Chapter 1 clichés that you come across from time to time that immediately make you stop reading.

The "information dump" is one—paragraphs of information about the protagonist, the protagonist's parents, background information about the protagonist's situation. Often, this information is unnecessary, and if it is necessary, a blend of telling and showing, along with a measured unfolding of information, is a stronger approach. Another is starting the first chapter with the wrong action. Writers are often instructed to start a story in the middle of the action, but it's important that it be the right action. For example, I recently read a manuscript in which the protagonists embark on a dangerous outing in the first chapter. But since I didn't have a clear sense yet for the significance of this outing, the action was undermined and I wasn't invested in the outcome. It was a crucial scene, but the author needed to back up and start with completely different action that placed me more firmly in the world of the story. Finally, I stop reading when the first chapter starts with the protagonist saying something like, "Hi, my name is (fill in the blank)."

—**JEN ROFE** *is an agent with Andrea Brown Literary Agency*

What are some reasons you stop reading a YA manuscript?

Once I've determined that the writing is strong enough, it's usually a question of plot (we receive many works that are derivative or otherwise unoriginal) or voice. As we know from the young adults in our lives, anything that sounds even vaguely parental will not be well received. And there's nothing worse than narration that reads like a text message from a grandmother. In the past month, I've received 29 YA partials. Looking back on my notes, I see that I rejected eight for writing, seven for voice, six for derivative or unoriginal plots, four because they were inappropriate for the age group, and two that simply weren't a good fit for the agency but may find a home elsewhere. Then there were two I liked and passed them on to others in my office. Also, I think a lot of writers, seeing the success of *Twilight*, have tried to force their manuscripts into this genre. I know you've heard it before, but it's so true: Write what you are meant to write—don't write what you think will sell.

—JESSICA SINSHEIMER *is a literary agent with the Sarah Jane Freymann Literary Agency*

ON VOICE, CONCEPT AND SUBJECT MATTER

I've heard that nothing is taboo anymore in young adult books and you can write about topics such as sex and drugs. Is this true?

I would say this: Nothing is taboo if it's done well. Each scene needs to matter in a novel. I've read a number of "edgy" young adult books where writers seem to add in scenes just for shock value and it doesn't work with the flow of the rest of the novel. "Taboo" subjects need to have a purpose in the progression of the novel—and of course, need to be well written! If it does, then yes, I would say nothing is taboo. Taboo topics do, however, affect whether the school and library market will pick up the book—and this can have an effect on whether a publisher feels they can sell enough copies.

—JESSICA REGEL *is a literary agent with the Jean V. Naggar Literary Agency*

What are three of the biggest mistakes you see writers make when writing for kids/teens?

I find being very preachy is a big turnoff for me. Nine and a half times out of ten, when a query letter for a YA or MG starts talking about all the lessons the novel will teach kids, I reject it. Literature can be very powerful and it can teach lessons, but I think it is most important to focus on writing something that kids will want to read first. I've also seen a lot of things lately set in the '80s or '90s that don't need to be; I think it is because this is when the writers remember being teenagers. However, it is important to remember that a 15-year-old now was born in 1997. The '90s are historical fiction to them, and if the story can work at all set in 2011, it probably should be. Finally—and this isn't a mistake, per se—but writing an authentic teenage voice is very difficult, and I see a lot of writers struggling with it. If there is one thing YA and MG writers should practice and work to perfect, it is writing a teenage voice.

—LAUREN MACLEOD *is an agent with The Strothman Agency*

What are some subjects or styles of writing that you rarely receive in a submission and wonder why more writers don't tackle such a subject/style?

In terms of style and execution, I'd love to see more MG and YA submissions use innovative narrative strategies deliberately and well. For example: alternating voices/points of view, or a structure that plays with narrative time. Kids are sophisticated readers.

Books that engage them on the level of storytelling, as well as story, could break out. In terms of subject matter, I don't see as many stories as you'd think about multicultural families and friendships. I'd also love to see more YA submissions depict awkward, funny and real—rather than flat and glossy—teen romance.

—**MICHELLE ANDELMAN** *is a literary agent with Regal Literary*

Regarding submissions, what do you see too much of? What do you see too little of?

I'm definitely looking for projects with something timeless at their core, whether it's the emotional connection a reader feels to the characters, or the universal humor, or issues that are relevant now and will still be relevant years from now. Can readers truly understand what it's like to be the prince of Denmark? Probably not, but they can identify with feeling disconnected from a dead loved one and the anger at watching him be replaced by a conniving uncle. I want stories that, no matter what the setting, feel true in some way to the reader. I definitely see too many people trying to be something else. I used to make the mistake of listing Roald Dahl as one of my favorite writers from my childhood, but I've found that just inspires a bunch of Dahl knockoffs. And trust me, it's tough to imitate the greats. I get far too much emulation of Dahl, Snicket, Rowling, and whatever else has worked in the past. It's one thing to aspire to greatness; it's another to imitate it. I want people who can appeal to me in the same way as successful writers of yore, with a style that's their own. I see too few writers willing to take chances. I just finished Markus Zusak's wonderful novel, *The Book Thief.* It breaks so many so-called rules for kids' books—there are tons of adult characters and points of view, it's a historical at heart, and it's narrated by Death for crying out loud. It's one of the best young adult novels I've read recently.

—**CHRIS RICHMAN** *is a literary agent at Upstart Crow Literary*

Are there any subjects you feel are untapped and would, therefore, be a refreshing change from the typical multicultural story?

When I was a [bookstore buyer], I was tired of certain subject matters only because those subjects have been explored so well, so often, that you really needed to bring something special to the page to make anyone take notice. Send me a story about some modern immigrant stories, some multi-generational stuff, like the YA novels of Carlos Ruiz Zafon. There are deeply rich stories about being an outsider, and yet how assimilation means a compromise and loss. I'd also love to see more issues of race discussed in modern terms, where there is the melting pot happening across the U.S., yet the tensions are still there, like the fear of the other. I think these stories, when done well, are universal stories, as we all feel that way at some point. Look at Junot Diaz's *The Brief Wondrous Life of Oscar Wao* as exhibit A.

—**JOE MONTI** *is a literary agent with Barry Goldblatt Literary*

ON PICTURE BOOKS & ILLUSTRATIONS

Do you often get queries from authors who have also illustrated their children's book? Are the illustrations usually of enough quality to include them with the submission to publishers?

I do receive many queries from author/illustrators, or from authors who aren't necessarily illustrators but fail to understand that they don't have to worry about submitting illustrations. But most often I find that most illustrators are not the best at coming up with compelling storylines or can't execute the words like a well-seasoned writer (or vice versa: The better writers usually are not the best illustrators).

—**Regina Brooks** *is the founder of Serendipity Literary*

With picture books, I suspect you get a lot of submissions and most of them get rejected. Where are writers going wrong?

Rhyming! So many writers think picture books need to rhyme. There are some editors who won't even look at books in rhyme, and a lot more who are extremely wary of them, so it limits an agent on where it can go and the likelihood of it selling. It's also particularly hard to execute perfectly. Aside from rhyming, I see way too many picture books about a family pet or bedtime.

—**Kelly Sonnack** *is a literary agent with the Andrea Brown Literary Agency*

Many people tend to try their hand at children's writing and picture books, but it's often said that writing such books is much more difficult than writers first consider. Why is this so?

I suspect the common thinking goes that if a writer "knows" children, she can write for them. But a successful children's author doesn't simply "know" children—what makes them tick, what their internal and emotional lives are like—she also knows children's literature. She's an avid reader, so she's familiar with what's age-appropriate and authentic to her category of the market. If she's writing a picture book, she's a skilled visual storyteller and can offer up a plot, character, relationship or emotional arc in miniature—but still, and this is the difficult part, in full.

—**Michelle Andelman** *is a literary agent with Regal Literary*

What can writers do to increase their chances of getting a picture book published?

I know it sounds simplistic, but write the very best picture books you can. I think the market contraction has been a good thing, for the most part. I'm only selling the very best picture books my clients write—but I'm definitely selling them. Picture books are generally skewing young, and have been for some time, so focus on strong read-alouds and truly kid-friendly styles. I'm having a lot of luck with projects that have the feel of being created by an author-illustrator even if the author is not an artist, in that they're fairly simple, have all kinds of room for fun and interpretation in the illustrations, and have a lot of personality. I see a lot of picture book manuscripts that depend too heavily on dialogue, which tends to give them the feel of a chapter book or middle grade novel. The style isn't a picture book style.

—**ERIN MURPHY** *is the founder of the Erin Murphy Literary Agency*

ON CHILDREN'S NONFICTION

Can you give us some 101 tips on writing nonfiction for kids?

You can write about almost anything when it comes to children's nonfiction, even if it's been done before. But you need to come at the subject from a different angle. If there is already a book on tomatoes and how they grow, then try writing about tomatoes from a cultural angle. There are a ton of books on slavery, but not many on slaves in Haiti during the Haitian Revolution. (Is there even one? There's an idea—someone take it and query me!) Another thing to always consider is your audience. Kids already have textbooks at school, so you shouldn't write your book like one. Come at the subject in a way that kids can relate to and find interesting. Humor is always a useful tool in nonfiction for kids. Adding to a series is a great way to get started as a writer of nonfiction. But it can't hurt to research the market and try to come up with an idea of your own.

—**JOANNA STAMPFEL-VOLPE** *is an agent with Nancy Coffey Literary*

You're looking for nonfiction for young adults, such as picture book biographies. Can you give a few good examples of this for people to read and learn from?

The most important thing to me is that the nonfiction reads like fiction—that there is a "story behind the story." For example, Pamela S. Turner's *George Schaller: Life in the Wild*, from FSG/Kroupa (2008), is a biography of the great field biologist George Schaller. The book explores Dr. Schaller's career both as a scientist and as an advocate for vanishing wildlife. Appealing to children who are interested in animals, science, adventure and the outdoors, each chapter of the book will also be a "mini-biography" of the species being studied. Several of Pamela's other books study certain environments or animals and make science fun and interesting for kids.

—**CARYN WISEMAN** *is a literary agent with the Andrea Brown Literary Agency*

ON CHILDREN'S WRITING CATEGORIES

You seek books with dystopian themes. That seems to be a healthy area of market—particularly in YA. Why do you think this is so? As well, what do you see for the future? Will it always be so hot?

YA topics and trends are cyclical, but I think dystopian is always relevant and in-demand. It's funny that the term "science fiction" is still not "cool" or commercial, still relegated to genre fiction—but *dystopian*—suddenly that word is very cool. Do people not realize that most of it is science fiction? Or magical realism? In that sense, the theme has been hot forever.

It's fascinating to ponder the question "what if?" These books make us think about the world and humanity—how people act toward each other when pushed to the brink, when fighting for survival. It's so interesting to think how quickly these societies we've built could break down and we'd be left with the most basic human instincts.

—**MELISSA SARVER** *is an agent with Elizabeth Kaplan Literary*

If someone asked about the line between middle grade and young adult, how would you explain the difference?

Is there a line? It seems to me there is scale more than a line. An editor said to me recently that if the main character is 14, it automatically gets shelved in YA in the chain stores. There's a line. But I work with authors whose light and wholesome novels, with teen main characters, are read mostly by tweens; and others whose novels are populated by middle graders going through such intense experiences that the readership skews to the high end of MG/low end of YA. I try to focus on helping my clients make their stories the best stories they can be rather than fitting them into boxes. The line sometimes feels like a moving target, and the writer has little control over it; better to focus on what you can control, which is how good it is. That said, characters should feel as though they are truly the age they are supposed to be—and that age *today*. Kids are savvier than they used to be even five or 10 years ago. They are exposed to more and more at a younger age. Writers should respect their readership accordingly.

—**ERIN MURPHY** *is the founder of the Erin Murphy Literary Agency*

Can you explain exactly how chapter books differ from middle grade?

There is a lot of overlap between categories, so the difference between older chapter books and younger middle grade is often just a matter of marketing. Younger chapter books are for kids who have graduated from easy readers and are starting to read more fluently. They usually have 8–10 short chapters, each with a cliffhanger ending. They are often a series, like Captain Underpants or Magic Tree House, and can be lightly or heavily illustrated. Middle grade is for readers in the 8–12 age group. They can have a complex plot and subplot, and while often humorous, they can certainly be more serious. The vocabulary is more sophisticated than chapter books, and the emphasis is on character. *The Qwikpick Adventure Society* by Sam Riddleburger (Dial) is an example of a middle grade book in which the targeted reader is at the younger end of the spectrum. At the older end of the middle grade spectrum is "tween." It's realistic, often contemporary, often edgier than traditional middle-grade, and deals with identity issues, school-based situations, family vs. friends, and just how hard it is to be 12.

—**CARYN WISEMAN** *is a literary agent with the Andrea Brown Literary Agency*

Does "tween" exist as a category?

Tween *does* exist, and various publishers even have specific tween imprints in place. As for queries, the same standard holds true for me in terms of tween as it does with YA or MG: If the voice is authentic, then I'm probably interested. However, I do look more at plot with tween novels. Right now, it's not enough just to have a great tween voice—the storyline also needs to be unique enough to stand out in the marketplace.

—**MEREDITH KAFFEL** *is a literary agent at The Charlotte Sheedy Literary Agency*

ON EVERYTHING ELSE

What's your best piece of advice for new writers who wish to submit their work to agents?

My best one word of advice: professionalize. A new writer who has done her homework on the children's market ahead of time, and submits to agents in a way that suggests a professional approach to a writing career, is going to stand out. Professionalizing may mean doing a few different things that make all the difference: joining a critique group that can help you polish your manuscript before you query, researching and approaching agents according to submission guidelines, crafting a query that aims to pique interest in—rather than fully explain—your project, and joining the Society of Children's Book Writers & Illustrators (SCBWI).

—**MICHELLE ANDELMAN** *is a literary agent with Regal Literary*

One of the areas you seek is young adult. That is a healthy market—and has been for quite some time. However, what do you see for the future? Will it always be so hot?

It's hot; it's just that the competition is huge. Especially in the paranormal romance genre. I think that the YA market will continue to grow in the future, and we will see more variety and dimension in the work that is offered to this market. Authors who are targeting this market really need to bring the groundbreaking stories in order to be competitive due to the saturation factor in the paranormal genre. The window is still open; it's just not open as wide.

—**JENNIFER SCHOBER** *is a literary agent with Spencerhill Associates*

What do you see for the future of young adult literature?

A shift to enhanced e-book domination. My older kids are 9 and 13, and while they love stories and enjoy reading, they also like the computer and the iPad and the television more—in spite of having parents and stepparents that are all voracious readers. Young adult authors are going to have to abandon the urge to be old-school about their writing, in most cases, if they want to find a healthy audience among tomorrow's kids. I've personally got little use for links to music and video and other material I consider extraneous, but the minds of kids today work completely differently than they did even just 10 years ago, for better or for worse. It's just a different, more fragmented requirement for all entertainment.

—DAVID DUNTON *is a literary agent at Harvey Klinger, Inc.*

Best piece of advice we haven't talked about yet?

Don't hold back from your passion. Too many folks get caught up in what the marketplace is supposedly looking for, and they lose sight of what they're trying to write. That, and read your drafts (Note the plural usage!) aloud for imperfections of language and cadence. It's an old horse, but not done enough because it may take you days to finish—but the results are astounding.

—JOE MONTI *is a literary agent with Barry Goldblatt Literary*

CHUCK SAMBUCHINO is an editor and a writer. He works for Writer's Digest Books and edits *Guide to Literary Agents* (guidetoliteraryagents.com/blog) as well as *Children's Writer's & Illustrator's Market*. His humor book, *How to Survive a Garden Gnome Attack* (gnomeattack.com), was released in Sept. 2010 and has been featured by *Reader's Digest, USA Today*, the *New York Times* and AOL News. His first book was writing-related: the third edition of *Formatting & Submitting Your Manuscript* (2009). Besides that, he is a produced playwright, magazine freelancer, husband, cover band guitarist, chocolate chip cookie fiend, and owner of a flabby-yet-lovable dog named Graham.

RICKI SCHULTZ (rickischultz.com) is a Virginia-based freelance writer and recovering high school English teacher. In addition to interviewing literary agents for the Guide to Literary Agents Blog, she speaks at writers' conferences. Her work has been featured in several publications, including past editions of *Guide to Literary Agents* and *Children's Writer's & Illustrator's Market* as well as *Northern Virginia Magazine, St. Ignatius Magazine* and *The John Carroll Review*. She also writes young adult fiction. Originally from Ohio, Schultz taught English and journalism for five years, and she holds a BA in English and an M.Ed. in secondary education, both from John Carroll University in Cleveland. As coordinator of the Write-Brained Network (writebrainednetwork.com), she is planning the group's inaugural writing workshop to be held in September 2011 in Harrisonburg, Virginia—where she lives with her husband and beagle.

DONNA GAMBALE works an office job by day, writes young adult novels by night, and travels when possible. She is a contributing editor for the Guide to Literary Agents Blog and freelances as a copyeditor and proofreader of both fiction and nonfiction. She is the author of a mini kit, *Magnetic Kama Sutra* (Running Press, 2009). You can find her online at firstnovelsclub.com, where she and her critique group blog about writing, reading, networking and the rest of life.

VOICE IN TEEN FICTION

Write with style and sell your work.

....

by Mary Kole

///

Crafting exceptional middle grade and young adult fiction for tweens and teens takes unforgettable character, one-of-a-kind voice and supreme writing confidence. The first two are necessary to make the third happen. After you have all three pieces in place, you are ready to tackle this vibrant market.

Too often in my work as a literary agent, I see weak characterization, sterile voice and unsteady writing craft. These flaws will prevent *any* project from getting published, for *any* audience, but they're particularly fatal when a writer aspires to speak to the tween (called "middle grade," for readers 8+) and teen (called "young adult," for readers 12+) audiences. These age groups experience life in a very specific way: It's life processed in Photoshop to add brightness, saturation, color and light. Young adults live a lot of emotional firsts in a very short amount of time. Their life is electric.

The best books written for tweens and teens possess that same brilliant, exciting, innovative quality. Bland writing, weak character, flat dialogue and a slow plot are cardinal sins in teen fiction. So how do you do it right? Let's tackle character first.

CHARACTERS WITH CHARACTER

In my experience—this is true for me as an agent, as a reader and as a human being—character is the portal to a story. Without a great character, we don't care about the plot, we're not breathless about the stakes, and we lack the motivation to keep turning those pages.

There is a lot of advice out there on making your characters likable and realistic, on making them relatable or universal or putting them on a hero's journey. And a lot of writers read a lot of books on writing character and still turn out forgettable people who lie flat on the page.

What's the secret?

The first thing miring writers is character backstory. How do you give a character's fascinating history without slowing down pacing with a dreaded "info-dump"? In Louis Sachar's Newbury Award-winning middle grade novel *Holes* (Farrar, Straus, and Giroux, 2008), we learn about Stanley Yelnats' unlucky lineage in a way that also keeps the story's forward momentum going:

> *Everyone in [Stanley's] family had always liked the fact that "Stanley Yelnats" was spelled the same frontward and backward. So they kept naming their sons Stanley. Stanley was an only child, as was every other Stanley Yelnats before him.*
>
> *All of them had something else in common. Despite their awful luck, they always remained hopeful. As Stanley's father liked to say, "I learn from failure."*
>
> *But perhaps that was part of the curse as well. If Stanley and his father weren't always hopeful, then it wouldn't hurt so much every time their hopes were crushed.*
>
> *"Not every Stanley Yelnats has been a failure," Stanley's mother often pointed out, whenever Stanley or his father became so discouraged that they actually started to believe in the curse. The first Stanley Yelnats, Stanley's great-grandfather, had made a fortune in the stock market. "He couldn't have been too unlucky."*
>
> *At such times she neglected to mention the bad luck that befell the first Stanley Yelnats. He lost his entire fortune when he was coming from New York to California. His stagecoach was robbed by the outlaw Kissin' Kate Barlow.*
>
> *If it weren't for that, Stanley's family would now be living in a mansion on a beach in California. Instead, they were crammed in a tiny apartment that smelled of burning rubber and foot odor.*
>
> *If only, if only…(p. 9)*

This snippet provides us with enough backstory to put this latest Stanley in context, but we also get a lot of tension, which is the basic engine that keeps fiction driving forward. We know right away there's a curse, and you better believe it will be part of the plot. We also know that the Yelnats men were never happy with their lot, always wishing, "*If only, if only.*" That longing, and the possibility of failure, is a great shade to give to Stanley's character right off the bat.

Secondly, successful characters need a worldview. It's what suffuses the story with their particular outlook and makes them pop off the page. In Lauren Oliver's debut, *Before I Fall* (HarperCollins, 2010), we may not immediately like bitchy Sam Kingston, the popular girl who is killed in a car accident in the first chapter, but we find ourselves strangely riveted by her paranormal opportunity to go back and fix her past, *Groundhog Day*-style. It's her immediate and unabashed attitude that draws us to her, as expressed in scenes like this:

> *"Last year I got twenty-two roses." Lindsay flicks her cigarette butt out of the window and leans over for a slurp of coffee. "I'm going for twenty-five this year."*

> *Each year before Cupid Day, the student council sets up a booth outside the gym. For two*
> *dollars each, you can buy your friends Valograms—roses with little notes attached to them—*
> *and then they get delivered by Cupids (usually freshman or sophomore girls trying to get in*
> *good with the upperclassmen) throughout the day.*
>
> *"I'd be happy with fifteen," I say. It's a big deal how many roses you get. You can tell who's*
> *popular and who isn't by the number of roses they're holding. It's bad if you get under ten and*
> *humiliating if you don't get more than five—it basically means that you're either ugly or un-*
> *known. Probably both. Sometimes people scavenge for dropped roses to add to their bouquets,*
> *but you can always tell. (p. 13)*

You start to know Sam's insecurities, her value judgments, her neediness, her fears, in the
way she talks about popular people—her and her friends—and the "ugly or unknown." If this
wasn't clear enough, she also gives readers a monologue that reinforces her philosophy:

> *If you draw a circle, there will always be an inside and an outside, and unless you're a total nut*
> *job, it's pretty easy to see which is which. It's just what happens.*
>
> *I'm not going to lie, though. It's nice that everything's easy for us. It's a good feeling know-*
> *ing you can basically do whatever you want and there won't be any consequences. When we*
> *get out of high school we'll look back and know we did everything right, that we kissed the cut-*
> *est boys and went to the best parties, got in just enough trouble, listened to our music too loud,*
> *smoked too many cigarettes, and drank too much and laughed too much and listened too little,*
> *or not at all. If high school were a game of poker, Lindsay, Ally, Elody, and I would be holding*
> *80 percent of the cards.*
>
> *And believe me: I know what it's like to be on the other side. I was there for the first half of*
> *my life. The bottom of the bottom, lowest of the low. I know what it's like to have to squabble*
> *and pick and fight over the leftovers.*
>
> *So now I have first pick of everything. So what. That's the way it is.*
>
> *Nobody ever said life was fair. (p. 18)*

There's also a lot of tension in these sentences. Shot through every line is Sam's fear that she
may lose everything—that the hand of cards she's holding may be a wash. Call Sam cruel; call her callous, a monster. Others think she's brash and honest. Why are we having all
these strong reactions to Sam Kingston? Because she's a character, loud and clear, with an
unmistakable set of opinions. You're in a great place if your readers either love or hate your
character. It's the boring middle ground that you should be afraid of.

Finally, and most importantly, we always have to know what your characters want.
Take this example from *The Disreputable History of Frankie Landau-Banks*, a National
Book Award Finalist and Printz Honor by E. Lockhart (Disney-Hyperion, 2008). The book's
namesake, Frankie, is a favorite in the recent canon. A lot of readers can sympathize with
her angst as she clashes with her family:

> *"If I were a boy, then would you let me [walk into town]?"*

"You want to spoil the last day of our vacation with a fight?" snapped Ruth. "Is that what you want?"

"No."

"So stop talking back. Leave it alone and enjoy the beach."

"Fine. I'll go down to the boardwalk." Frankie stood and shoved her feet into her flip-flops, grabbed the bag where her wallet was, and stalked across the sand.

"Be back in an hour!" called Ruth. "Call me on my cell if you're going to be late."

Frankie didn't answer.

It wasn't that she wanted postcards—or even that she wanted to go into town so much. It wasn't that Ruth had too many rules, either; or that Paulie Junior got to go on his own last year.

The problem was that to them—to Uncle Ben and her mother, and maybe even to Uncle Paul—Frankie was Bunny Rabbit.

Not a person with intelligence, a sense of direction, and the ability to use a cell phone. Not a person who could solve a problem.

Not even a person who could walk fifteen blocks all by herself without getting run over by a car.

To them, she was Bunny Rabbit.

Innocent.

In need of protection.

Inconsequential. (p. 12–13)

Here, Frankie's scene objective (what she wants in the short term) may be small—a walk into town—but it stands for something so much bigger. Her character is revealed very clearly in this scene because we discover her main objective, which will be center stage throughout the book: to be taken seriously as a smart, independent, powerful young woman. Once we know what a character wants, we will sympathize with them and follow their story.

As you establish character, you'll also need something to sustain the reader as you unfurl the plot. That can only be character's right-hand man: voice.

VOICE, LOUD AND CLEAR

Voice is the thing that sings from the page, that magical mix of an author's natural tone, the music of the character and the harmony of the narrator. Good voice is unforgettable, but very hard to explain.

Successful children's writer Laurie Halse Anderson, whose sample is discussed below, once tweeted that voice is all about "Taking out the parts that suck and making the rest sound natural."

I'd say that voice is also about which words you use, your sentence syntax, the observations you choose to bring to your reader's attention and how you keep showcasing character. Our first voice example is middle grade novel and National Book Award Winner *The*

Penderwicks by Jeanne Birdsall (Knopf, 2005), about four sisters and a dog named Hound on summer vacation:

> Now it was time for the sisters to go upstairs and choose their bedrooms.
>
> "Dibs first choice." Skye headed toward the steps with her suitcase.
>
> "Not fair!" said Jane. "I hadn't thought of it yet."
>
> "Right. I thought of it first, which is why I get first choice," said Skye, already halfway up to the second floor.
>
> "Come back, Skye," said Rosalind. "Hound draws for order."
>
> Skye groaned and reluctantly came back downstairs. She hated leaving important things up to Hound, and besides, he usually drew her last.
>
> The Hound Draw for Order was a time-honored ritual with the sisters. Names were written on small pieces of paper, then dropped on the ground along with broken bits of dog biscuit. As Hound snuffled among the biscuit pieces, he couldn't help but knock into the papers. The person whose paper his big nose hit first was given first choice. Second hit, second choice, and so on.
>
> Rosalind and Jane readied the slips of paper, Batty crumbled the dog biscuit, and Skye held Hound, whispering her name over and over in his ear, trying to hypnotize him. Her efforts were useless. Once let go, he touched Jane's paper first, then Rosalind's, and then Batty's. Skye's piece of paper he ate along with the last piece of biscuit.
>
> "Great," said Skye sadly. "I've got fourth choice and Hound's going to throw up again." (p. 15-16)

This perfectly executed mini-scene reveals each character, especially Skye, and also the characters' dynamics with one another. (Note: At no point did the author tell us anything about these sisters. It was all showing, in scene, and yet we know so much about them and their bonds.) We get a slightly affected drawl in the writing ("Skye's piece of paper he ate…"), some choice words ("snuffled"), as well as the author's great sense of humor. We zoom from two sisters writing, to one crumpling biscuits, to the last whispering. Birdsall's grasp of choosing where to guide the reader's attention in a scene is all part of her voice.

If that example of voice is too subtle for you, here's a YA novel that will knock you over the head. M.T. Anderson's *Feed* (Candlewick, 2002), a National Book Award Finalist and *Boston Globe*-Horn Book Book Award Winner, plunges the reader into its own riffing syntax and vocabulary. Here, Titus, the narrator, describes his guy friends:

> Link is tall and butt-ugly and really rich, that kind of old rich that's like radiation, so that it's always going deet deet deet in invisible waves and people are suddenly like, "Unit! Hey! Unit!" and they want to be guys with him. Marty, his thing is that he's good at like anything, any game, and I just stand there silent and act cool, and we're this trio, the three of us guys, being like, total guys, which usually makes people let us in and give us beer. (p. 10)

From the radiating "*deet deet deet*" sound effects to the colloquial, conversational sentence flow, we get the narrator's voice very clearly. It feels like he's standing over our shoulder—or tapped directly into our brains via a feed, which is more fitting with the book's plot—as we read; like he's speaking straight to us.

If you find yourself struggling with your writing voice, read the samples in this article aloud, and then read your own prose. Write your next few pages by dictation. It's called story*telling* for a reason.

WORDPLAY

When I know I'm in the hands of a writer who is ready for publication, I can feel their confidence and agility with words. You don't have to show off to a reader—300 pages of that would be torture—but I like seeing a writer who is comfortable and inspired enough to write joyfully on the sentence level. Here are some of my favorite examples of wordplay. The first is from a book on the cusp of middle grade and young adult, *Plain Kate* by Erin Bow (Arthur A. Levine Books/Scholastic, 2010), in which the author details a disease spreading through a fantasy village:

> *Witch's fever was an ugly thing. The sick tossed in their beds, burning up, sobbing about the devils that were pulling their joints apart. They raved of horrors and pointed into shadows, crying, "Witch, witch." And then they died, all but a few. It seemed to Plain Kate that even those who were not sick were looking into shadows. The cressets in the market square—the iron nests of fire where people gathered to trade news and roast fish—became a place of hisses and silences. More fingers crooked at her than ever before. (p. 4)*

Look at the sentence craft at work here. Bow combines visceral imagery ("devils ... pulling their joints apart") with a whispered, nearly breathless tone echoed in the slithering "s" sounds ("the market square ... became a place of hisses and silences") to create a dangerous atmosphere. This writing is full of artistry *and* tension as it makes us care about Plain Kate, the heroine, and what might befall her in this town.

As you can see, clear imagery makes description come alive. It makes the setting into another character of the story. Look at the subtle artistry in Jennifer Donnelly's Printz Honor *A Northern Light* (Harcourt, 2003):

> *If spring has a taste, it tastes like fiddleheads. Green and crisp and new. Mineralish, like the dirt that made them. Bright, like the sun that called them forth. I was supposed to be picking them, me and Weaver both. We were going to fill two buckets—split one for ourselves and sell one to the chef over at the Eagle Bay Hotel—but I was too busy eating them. I couldn't help it. I craved something fresh after months of old potatoes, and beans from a jar. (p. 27)*

She's given us a visceral look at spring, from its taste to the sensation of sun on our skin. This prose is lovely but tension is never far behind. We can surmise from this passage that Mattie, the protagonist, is suffering financially—a struggle for her throughout the book. Even in the smallest details of spring, Donnelly is busy revealing character and planting hooks to pull the plot forward.

On a darker note, Laurie Halse Anderson adopts a beat poet's invented vocabulary in her exploration of protagonist Lia's descent into eating disorder hell with *Wintergirls* (Viking, 2009):

> *The box opens and the razors slide out, whisper sweet.*
>
> *Used to be that my whole body was my canvas—hot cuts licking my ribs, ladder rungs climbing my arms, thick milkweed stalks shooting up my thighs. When I moved to jennifer-land, my father made one condition. A daughter who forgets how to eat, well that was bad, but it was just a phase and I was over it. But a daughter who opens her own skin bag, wanting to let her shell fall to the ground so she can dance? That was just sick. No cutting, Lia Marrigan Overbrook. Not under Daddy's roof. Bottom line. Deal breaker. (p. 61)*

You can feel Lia's anger and the tremendous weight of her secrets here. From the "whisper sweet" call of the razor blades, to Lia's true self, her "shell" hidden within her "skin bag," to her unease at living in her stepmother's house ("jenniferland"), we see Anderson's language tell this story with an unflinching intensity.

PUTTING IT ALL TOGETHER

Character, voice and writing confidence are three of the most difficult writing elements to master when you're tackling middle grade or young adult fiction. As you work on your writing craft, you should be reading as much, if not much more, than writing. We can't know how to craft a character until we've read some of the best. Our voice won't speak properly until we've heard the voices of others. Writing confidence can only come from knowledge, and that knowledge is best had at the feet of master teachers. Use this collection of works as a starting required reading list, keep learning, keep reading and, finally, keep writing.

When you're done, the agents and publishers listed within these pages, myself included, will be eager to hear what you have to say.

MARY KOLE is an agent at the Andrea Brown Literary Agency (andreabrownlit.com) and, in her quest to learn all sides of publishing, has also worked at Chronicle Books and earned her MFA in creative writing at the University of San Francisco. For the children's market, she seeks young adult stories and middle grade fiction and truly exceptional picture books from authors, illustrators and author/illustrators. She operates the Andrea Brown East office from Brooklyn, NY. She also runs the award-winning Kid Lit Blog (kidlit.com) all about children's writing and publishing.

WRITING NONFICTION

The essentials of writing true-life books for kids.

....

by Audrey Vernick

Today's nonfiction for kids bears little similarity to the nonfiction books I had to read in grade school. I vividly, palpably remember the anguish caused by having to get through a yellow library book about Florence Nightingale. An avid reader of *good* books, I found that biography to be torture. I shouted out updates on my halting progress from the bedroom: "Seventy-four more pages!"

Today's nonfiction pops. It rocks. It makes me want to read everything. Who knew there could be books for kids about the history of the hot dog and spies and Barbie and sugar and Superman and ice cream? Nonfiction is reaching a wider audience, a trade audience, because the books are finally, well, interesting. And well written.

"Children deserve our absolute best work," says Tami Lewis Brown, author of the nonfiction picture book *Soar Elinor*. "They deserve to know the truth as best as we can tell it."

So where's an author to begin? The straight-up answer: with a rock-solid idea. And a lot of thoughtful consideration.

THE IDEA

Some people are idea hunters. Others are like me: good ideas have been kind enough to seek us out. We just had to pay attention (see sidebar).

However the idea finds you, or you it, the next steps usually go like this: research/think/ write, repeat. Mixed in there are the following questions to continuously ask yourself: Is this idea good enough? Can it sustain a book? Has it been done before? Can I develop something new and unique? Does it have an audience?

"Have a killer idea," suggests Erin Murphy of the Erin Murphy Literary Agency. "Easy, right? Something relatable to kids that hasn't been done to death, preferably with some universal curriculum tie-ins. Something fresh!"

It's a heady, think-heavy time when you're all excited about a new idea. Some writers let their idea marinate for a while. Others dive right into research on their subject. Some might do a broad market search to see what, if anything, has been published on the same or similar topics.

Thorough research, with proper citations, is essential. Murphy suggests that writers "prove yourself to be respectful of the nonfiction genre—do your research, cite it, have as many primary sources as possible, and include an author's note fleshing out the information as needed."

"I tend to think about projects a lot before I actually start doing any work on them—or rather, I let them sit, and if I find myself thinking about one a lot, then I know that it's a project that would sustain my interest for a good long while," says Chris Barton, author of *The Day-Glo Brothers* and *Can I See Your I.D.?*

The thinking a writer does at this stage can go a long way toward preventing all kinds of rookie mistakes—from insufficient or undocumented research to incorrectly identifying who your readers will be.

WHO'S THE AUDIENCE?

This usually gets folded into the research/think/write mix, but it's worthy of its own heading because it's so important. For some projects, the intended audience is clear at the outset. Some books, for example, are only suitable for a middle grade or teen audience because the subject matter would be inappropriate for picture book readers. But other times, determining the proper audience—and thus the appropriate format for the book—can be murky business.

"The intended age of my audience evolves as I get to know the story," says Tanya Lee Stone, author of award-winning nonfiction books including *Almost Astronauts* and *The Good, the Bad, and the Barbie*. "I have started several picture books that have turned into long-form nonfiction for older readers. The structure can only really come after I know what the story is I need to tell."

Remaining open to that kind of change is difficult, but it's essential. You don't only need to be a master of the subject matter—you need to know who needs to know that story, and what would be the best way to tell it.

"I knew that *The Day-Glo Brothers* had to be a picture book—the whole point was to show the colors—but that (unfortunately) didn't stop me from initially shopping around a 6,200-word draft," Barton says. "The stories in *Can I See Your I.D.?* contain elements best suited for older readers, but whether that older-than-a-picture-book format would be geared toward middle grades or YA became clearer only as I decided which of those elements truly needed to be included."

KNOW AND RESPECT THE CATEGORY

Readers count on the author to present an authentic representation of the truth. And writers often feel a tremendous responsibility to tell their subject's story in a way that would do the subject proud. Brown says, "As a pilot, a writer and a woman, I felt a big responsibility to get Elinor's story right and tell it well."

Telling a compelling story while providing enough context for young readers without being didactic is an extremely delicate balancing act. "Writing for kids doesn't mean writing down, which is a frequent mistake even experienced writers make," says Jennifer Greene, senior editor at Clarion Books. "At the same time, one can't assume kids have the same knowledge base as educated adults."

Getting all your nonfiction ducks in a row—that's the easy way to show an agent or an editor that you know what you're doing.

PROPOSAL OR FULL MANUSCRIPT?

As with most things in publishing, there's no set-in-stone answer to whether you need to submit a completed manuscript or a thorough proposal when seeking publication. Generally, though not always, first-time authors will need to complete the work before submitting. Greene says, "From first-time nonfiction writers, I have only acquired projects that were complete. Nonfiction writing, especially for kids, is just as much of a craft as fiction writing, and even with a great topic and hook and previous writing experience, there's no guarantee a writer will be able to do it well, or have an understanding of the level of research and work that is entailed."

There are occasional exceptions. Cynthia Levinson, author of the 2012 release *We Have A Job: The 1963 Birmingham Children's March*, was a first-timer when Peachtree acquired her project based upon a proposal. According to Levinson, it was "a very detailed and solid proposal, which consisted of five sample chapters; a narrative outline with several paragraphs on each of the remaining chapters; an extensive bibliography that included background reading, personal interviews and other primary-source research, and a trip to Birmingham; and a list of ancillary materials and back matter."

It's more common for seasoned authors than first-timers to sell their books based on a proposal. According to Stone, "I have been able to sell a new book based on an idea, an outline and a sample. But I'm not sure I prefer it. There are upsides and downsides to selling something before having figured it out completely."

MY OWN STORY

I never imagined I'd be an author of nonfiction picture books. Even after I wrote one.

The first picture book I published, *Bark and Tim: A True Story of Friendship,* co-written with my sister Ellen Glassman Gidaro, was supposed to be a one-shot deal. I didn't seek out a nonfiction book project; it was more like Bark sat on my lap.

I saw a painting by outsider artist Tim Brown and fell in love. I showed the picture to my sister who said, "That would be such a good illustration in a children's book." One thing led to another. We were given permission to interview Tim (through an intermediary—Tim lives alone in a home without electricity) and to use his paintings to illustrate our book.

It wasn't easy to find a publisher for that project, but that's when I learned the tremendous role small regional publishers can play in publishing quirky children's nonfiction. Overmountain Press is a family-owned publisher, with a primary focus on Southern history and nonfiction. Working with them was a fabulous introduction to the world of children's nonfiction.

I returned to writing fiction after the publication of *Bark and Tim* until another nonfiction subject started calling.

A short piece about Effa Manley in a children's news magazine caught my attention. As an avid baseball fan, I could not believe that a woman—a woman I had never heard of—was about to be inducted into the National Baseball Hall of Fame.

I researched her story (which included an awesome road trip to the Hall of Fame in Cooperstown, NY), and my agent sent out my picture book manuscript. Two editors requested a revision, both looking for the same kind of changes. (I offer this as a reminder of what a subjective business publishing is.) Upon reading the revision, one editor said, "Wow, this is kind of all over the place, huh?" And the other said, "Wow, you really hit it out of the park."

Thankfully, it only takes one.

She Loved Baseball: The Effa Manley Story was published by HarperCollins in 2010, a Junior Library Guild selection.

Even before Effa's official publication date, one more story started calling me. This one had local roots. I knew a man, a friend of my husband, whose father was one of twelve baseball-playing brothers. The family team had been honored by the Hall of Fame as the longest-playing all-brother baseball team.

Hello? Audrey Vernick? this story said. *I'm your next book.*

I invited myself to the home of one of the three surviving brothers. I was told to come on Tuesday, as that was spaghetti night. It was a remarkable, memorable experience—

listening to the stories, food forced upon me for hours, laughing, friends new and old joining us at the table.

The resulting book, *Brothers at Bat: The True Story of an Amazing All-Brother Team*, will be published in March 2012.

Jennifer Greene, senior editor at Clarion, who will be publishing the book, says, "With *Brothers at Bat*, at first glance this might seem like a project not well suited for me. I like the energy and atmosphere of a good baseball game as well as anyone else, but I don't consider myself a real fan. But I loved this manuscript for the *story*—a family with twelve boys who loved baseball and had their own team! It's a slice of Americana, and it has so many moving moments throughout as we watch this family grow."

As for what's ahead … there's one story—yet another baseball story. Right now, it's calling quietly. We shall see.

You can visit Audrey Vernick online at audreyvernick.com and read her blog posts at shelovedbaseball.wordpress.com.

MAKING THAT FIRST SALE

It's the perpetual frustration of the not-yet-published writer: Having something published gets you noticed by agents and editors. Ahem. *How do you get something published without having that first credit?*

"Develop your writing chops and your contacts," advises Murphy. "Get paid to do interesting research that could lead to viable book projects by writing for kids' magazines and websites. Much more so with nonfiction than fiction, when an author queries me, I find a list of published magazine credits to be persuasive."

"Present your project in the most professional way possible," Greene suggests. "Try to offer the publisher the best possible picture of your vision for the book. Comparing it to successful books on the market in terms of feel, length, and audience doesn't hurt, either, if your comparison is fair."

Of course, all the typical publishing advice also applies. Write well. Revise vigorously. Attend conferences. Network. Listen. Brown heard her future editor, Melanie Kroupa, speak at Vermont College. "She spoke about books she'd edited and I knew right away she was 'the one' for me and for *Elinor*."

PLATFORMS

Writers of adult nonfiction are advised that it's all about the *platform*; no publisher will take a chance on a writer who's not an expert in her field or who doesn't have an army of book-buying supporters already lined up. While a platform can only help you, it doesn't seem to be a deal-breaker when looking for that first children's nonfiction sale.

"The author's credentials, experience in the field and track record as a nonfiction writer all come into consideration when I look at a manuscript or proposal," Scott says. "It's always nice when someone is an expert in the field about which they are writing, but it's not essential. More important is the author's writing ability—that indefinable skill at making words on paper exciting and accessible to children."

STAY THE COURSE

Take your pick of all the publishing clichés—most have to do with persistence. My first nonfiction picture book was rejected 27 times before it was accepted.

It's a good idea to remain mindful that the writing, and what you get out of the writing, counts too. It's not all about publication. Listen to Tanya Lee Stone—she knows of what she speaks: "Embrace change; everything you write, whether you end up using it or not, takes you to the next place in your writing. It is all valuable to the process."

Scott adds, "Keep up the faith! I think there are a lot more opportunities in nonfiction, for newcomers and established authors alike, than in traditional picture book fiction."

It's a long road from idea to published book, and it's usually riddled with detours and potholes and accidental side trips. But it's a great time to be writing nonfiction for kids. Children have a plethora of fantastic, exciting nonfiction books at their disposal. Instead of counting down the pages until finally, finally reaching the end, today's nonfiction reader is working to make it last, turning the last few pages slowly and calling out a different refrain: "I don't want it to end!"

AUDREY VERNICK (audreyvernick.com) is the author of three nonfiction books: *Bark and Tim: A True Story of Friendship*; *She Loved Baseball: The Effa Manley Story*; and *Brothers at Bat: The True Story of an Amazing All-Brother Team*. Audrey also wrote *Is Your Buffalo Ready for Kindergarten?*; *Teach Your Buffalo to Play Drums*; and *Edgar's Second Word*. Her debut upper middle grade novel, *Water Balloon*, was published last year. Audrey lives near the ocean with one of each of the following: husband, son, daughter, dog.

You can visit Audrey's website at audreyvernick.com and her blog at shelovedbaseball.wordpress.com.

HOW TO GIVE A GOOD SPEECH

How to present without fainting, vomiting or dropping dead.

by Donna Gephart

Many people rank fear of public speaking higher than fear of dying. In other words, they'd be happier dropping dead than giving a half-hour speech. I am not among them.

I'm going to share the secrets to creating drop-dead fantastic speeches and delivering them with joy and verve. Ready? Here we go.

There you are, minding your own business, when Joe King from Gottaloveit School/Conference/Club/Association/Library invites you to give a speech. You are shocked at the words that fly from your mouth: "I'd love to."

What were you thinking?!

There are exactly two months, one week, four days, six hours and nine minutes before you will deliver this speech. During this time, you can do any of the following:

1. Enter the Witness Protection Program so Joe King will never find you.
2. Spend each of those minutes in sheer and utter panic that will cause your blood pressure to soar dangerously high.
3. Join the circus.
4. Pay attention to the tips below.

TIP #1: IT'S NOT ABOUT YOU

Your initial reaction is probably to imagine a gigantic group of people staring at you as you flub your speech, stare blankly in horror, then trip and fall off the stage into a weeping heap of humiliation and shame. Change your thinking!

You have a limited time before your speech. Do you really want to fill your brain space with negative thoughts that will serve only to undermine your performance? The first step is to think not about yourself, but about your audience.

Who are they? What do they care about? What are they hoping to gain from your talk?

See? It's not about you. It's all about them! And the sooner you take the spotlight off yourself, the sooner you can direct it to where it belongs: on your audience's needs.

My husband helps organize conferences where the luncheon speaker earns about $20,000 for a talk that takes less time than I usually spend checking my e-mail.

What is the first thing these speakers do when my husband contacts them on behalf of his company? They find out everything they can about the organization, the attendees and the expected outcomes. And that's what you must do, too. (Even if you're not earning $20,000, what you will be earning is an excellent reputation as a speaker.)

TIP #2: BEGIN AT THE BEGINNING

Let your audience know why you're there and why they should listen to you. Are you an expert on the topic about which you've written your book? Have you had a long association with the organization at which you're speaking? Do you have information that will be useful to them?

I give a talk to fifth and sixth grade students titled, "6-1/2 Ways to Survive and Thrive in Middle School." My first sentence is: "I'm a dork." I let the kids know I've walked in their shoes, I've slathered on their acne cream, and I've suffered their heartbreaks. After letting them know about my middle school (junior high, back then) humiliations, I launch into my 6½ tips. Begin by giving your audience a good reason to listen to you . . . and they will.

6½ TIPS FOR CREATING SUCCESSFUL SCHOOL VISITS

1. BE VERY CLEAR WITH THE PERSON COORDINATING THE VISIT AS TO WHAT YOUR NEEDS AND REQUIREMENTS ARE. I use a contract and then I also connect with the school about two weeks ahead of time to confirm everything (equipment, number of presentations, schedule, travel issues). It also lets me check in to see how much preparation the school has done for my visit. For a novel, I tweak my presentation based on whether or not the kids have all read the book, so it helps to know that ahead of time.

2. AFTER THE KIDS ARE SEATED, BE INTRODUCED BY SOMEONE AT THE SCHOOL. That person has authority with the students, and that will be passed on to you through that introduction. That person will also know the school's way of getting kids' attention (two fingers up, clapping, etc).

The first few minutes set the tone for the whole presentation, so you want to engage the kids quickly. The most challenging student behaviors will come in the "down" times and the "dull" times, so the best thing you can do for classroom management is to keep the down time to a minimum and have an interactive and engaging presentation. Think of your presentation like a novel: a strong beginning, followed by rising emotion, logical

---

sequencing with exciting scenes, and a strong and satisfying ending. And leave some time for questions at the end.

3. IF YOU USE POWERPOINT, KEEP YOUR SLIDES SIMPLE. Use only keywords and high-quality images. It will keep you from being tempted to read off your slides, and the kids will be paying attention to you and not reading the slides.

A remote to advance your slides is a very worthwhile investment. You can get a good one for around $40, and it will allow you to move around the stage—which keeps the kids' attention more than if you are stuck behind a podium. Also, in a big group, some kids will have a better view of you than others. By moving around, you give more kids a chance to see you.

4. THE SCHOOL WANTS A PERSONAL CONNECTION FOR THEIR STUDENTS. Be sure that *you* are the star of your presentation, not your slides. Have at least a few things to show the kids or stories to tell them that they cannot find on your website or read in interviews with you. If the school has prepared the students well, students will have already been to your website and read available interviews with you. They should get something new from seeing you and hearing you speak.

5. GIVE STUDENTS PRACTICAL WRITING ADVICE THAT SUPPORTS SCHOOL WRITING CUR-RICULUM—teachers will love you for it. Some examples would be: thoughts about first drafts, adding sensory details, revision tips, etc.

6. IF THE STUDENTS HAVE BEEN A GOOD AUDIENCE, COMPLIMENT THEM AND TELL THE TEACHERS THEY CAN BE VERY PROUD OF THEM. It builds a lot of good will. Also tell the principal how wonderful the media specialist (or whoever organized the visit with you) has been to work with. It's a nice way to affirm the hard work that went into bringing you to the school.

6½. AFTER A SUCCESSFUL VISIT, ASK THAT MEDIA SPECIALIST TO WRITE A RECOMMENDA-TION OR TO RECOMMEND YOU ON HER STATE LIBRARIANS' LISTSERVE. Word of mouth is always a powerful tool in marketing for your school visits.

School visits can be a wonderful, fun way to get up close and personal with your #1 audience: kids!

Newbery Honor Medal winner **CYNTHIA LORD** does about 50 speaking events a year. Her books include *Rules; Touch Blue;* and *Hot Rod Hamster.* To learn more, visit cynthialord.com.

TIP #3: EVERYONE LOVES A GOOD STORY

One of the best, most memorable ways to get your point across when giving a talk is to tell stories. We are storytellers, after all.

When I talk with school children and want to let them know how important the library is, I tell the story of Ben Carson. In fifth grade, in a poor, single-parent household, Ben Carson decided he was the stupidest kid in school.

And his classmates readily agreed.

His mother decided he and his brother wouldn't spend their free time watching TV or playing outside. She would take them to the public library, and they would be required to take out two books every week and write a book report on each.

HOW TO GET GIGS

Meeting your readers at school visits makes fans, helps sell books and can augment your income significantly. Appearances help you build a larger audience "platform" for your future books and can keep older books in print longer.

So how do you get invited to do school visits? Simple answer: *Become famous locally first.* Name recognition—of you and of your book titles—is paramount. Here are a few of the ways to establish name recognition and help potential hosts find you.

1. BE ACTIVE IN YOUR COMMUNITY. The activities you're involved with where you live (city and county), the listservs you participate in and the associations you belong to (professional and social) all count. SCBWI Regional Advisors field many requests from hosts to find authors, so make sure your RA knows you and your books. To find your RA, go to scbwi.org. Shake hands with local librarians, booksellers, community newspaper reporters. Let everyone know that you *love* doing school visits.

2. DISTRIBUTE PRINTED MATERIALS. Have your professional brochures, postcards, bookmarks or business cards ready to hand out at all times. You might also consider doing direct mailings of your brochures to targeted lists of public and private schools.

3. MAINTAIN AN AUTHOR WEBSITE. If you don't have one, you might as well be invisible.

4. PRESENT AT MEETINGS AND CONFERENCES. Most authors are hired as a result of word-of-mouth recommendations rather than solely from a print source such as a brochure. Submit proposals to regional or state conferences for teachers, librarians, administrators, parents, booksellers and writers/illustrators. Circulate at city, county and state conferences and events. Walk the trade show floor. Offer to do five-minute presentations at meetings of librarians or teachers in your city. Work with your regional reading council and investigate opportunities at the state level. Example: Reading.org/General/Local Associations/NorthAmerica.aspx

5. JOIN SPEAKERS' LISTS. Literary organizations often post lists of their author members on their websites (i.e., SCBWI, Authors Guild, The Children's Book Council, etc.). Typically, this service is free with your membership in the parent organization. You might also consider joining a speakers' bureau. Speakers' bureaus are agencies that represent and promote a select group of authors and illustrators for school visits. Some have performance requirements for inclusion. They charge a fee for you to be included or take a percentage of your speaking honorarium after you're hired.

6. JOIN PUBLISHERS' LISTS. Let your publisher know that you are eager to do presentations. Publishers will send the school's request to you or to your booking agency.

7. DO SHOWCASES. Local performing arts organizations, county education offices, libraries or bookstores sometimes host "Program Preview Days" or "Local Author Days" where presenters do a short showcase presentation. This will highlight your books and your presentation personality. Consider creating a team of authors and illustrators and offer a showcase to your local bookstore or library, or as part of an existing conference.

8. PARTICIPATE IN BOOK FAIRS AND LITERARY EVENTS. The Center for the Book: Library of Congress publishes a list of book fairs and festivals held throughout the country. See which ones have events that include children's book authors and illustrators. Contact the event organizer and ask if you might be included to do a presentation or sign books. Visit read.gov/resources/statefairs.php

It takes time—and multiple methods—to establish name recognition and have word-of-mouth do its magic. The more active you are *locally*, the more people you'll meet and the more likely someone will ask, "Do you ever do school visits?" And *voilá!* You're hired!

....

ALEXIS O'NEILL, Ph.D., is the author of *The Recess Queen* and other award-winning books for children. She has been an elementary school teacher, a teacher of teachers and a museum educator. She is a popular school visit presenter and helps other authors create and deliver quality programs. Visit her at schoolvisitexperts.com.

....

This did not go over well with the boys, but they did it. And Ben discovered that he liked the nonfiction section, especially books about rocks. Each week, he would borrow more books about rocks. Eventually, he knew everything about rocks.

So, when his fifth grade teacher began a unit on rocks, Ben was able to answer every question and teach the class a few things the teacher didn't know. The students looked at

Ben differently after that day. He looked at himself differently. He soon realized he could learn about anything as he had learned about rocks.

And he did, ultimately graduating at the top of his class and eventually becoming a famous pediatric neurosurgeon, author and speaker. It was many years after writing these book reports and showing them to his mother for a quick glance and checkmark that Ben learned his mother was actually illiterate.

Stories.

What great ways to engage your listener and make your points more memorable.

TIP #4: PROPS

You do not need to use props, but in some cases they can be a whole lot of fun for you and your audience. For example, if you're speaking to students, having hands-on items to show what your book is about can be a great asset. Do you have a fossil, a unicycle, an ant farm to show kids? My book, *How to Survive Middle School*, stars a talented hamster named Hammy, so I bring a stuffed toy hamster to book signings and school visits. Was I ever surprised when one young reader brought his *live* hamster to meet Hammy.

Can you don a cape during your talk, wave a magic wand or dress up with big glasses and a wild hat? Do what's appropriate for your talk and what you feel comfortable with.

I've been known to wear outrageously huge sunglasses and don a rubber chicken necklace, but then again, I often speak about writing humor.

TIP #5: PRACTICE KEEPS YOU FROM FAINTING

Once your speech is written and rewritten, and filled with a few memorable stories and perhaps a prop or two, it's time to practice. Read it. Out loud. In front of a mirror. And time yourself. When you practice in front of a mirror, you will notice any odd tics or gestures you use. And you can correct them immediately.

When I was in tenth grade, we were required to give a speech in front of the class. Afterward, my teacher gave me a critique. "Wonderful job, but you used 'um' a lot." I don't use "um" anymore. And neither will you if you practice in front of a mirror.

Make sure your language is appropriate for the age group to which you're speaking. Plain and simple language, without ever talking down or being condescending, is preferable. Be sure that with their limited experiences, your young audience will understand your references. If you bring up your Monkees album collection and your favorite manual typewriter, expect confused stares.

Be yourself. Be enthusiastic. Be passionate about your subject matter. And even if they don't show it ("not cool"), your audience will love you. After practicing, you will find ways to make your speech even better. Note the changes and improvements. Practice the new

version. And practice again a couple days before you're scheduled to speak and then the day before the big event. Then forget about it. You'll do a great job!

TIP #6: THE BIG SECRET

Here's a secret no one tells you. While you're thinking about your speech, writing it and practicing it, there is one other thing you must do: Imagine.

Imagine yourself doing a fantastic job. Imagine your audience spellbound by your words. Imagine them smiling, nodding and laughing in all the right places. Imagine them so moved by what you've said that they give you a standing ovation when you're done.

Imagining a positive experience will help you walk onto the stage happy and relaxed and prepared to succeed. Remember, the most important factor in a successful talk is to *have fun*! Then maybe when you finish, someone will come up to you, as happened to me (after a recent conference speech) and say six words that will make your day: "You totally kicked butt up there!"

DONNA GEPHART's first novel, *As If Being 12¾ Isn't Bad Enough, My Mother Is Running for President!* won the Sid Fleischman Humor Award. Her new novel, *How to Survive Middle School*, received starred reviews from *Kirkus* and *School Library Journal*. She's spoken at elementary and middle schools, book festivals, libraries and conferences, including the SCBWI National Conference. Learn more about her at donnagephart.com.

THE STATE OF YOUNG ADULT BOOKS

Agents and editors dish on the category.

....

by Jessica Strawser

Harry Potter cast a spell: The wizardry of J.K. Rowling descended on the literary landscape like magic. Kids couldn't get enough. Teens decided reading was cool again. Adults were lining up to buy YA—one copy for the kids, and one for themselves. And what's more, they weren't embarrassed to say so.

At the end of the day, if there was any lingering doubt that YA was hot, it vanished at *Twilight*.

It's official: Today's YA has the power to transcend the boundaries of genre, perhaps more than any other. Today's YA has the potential to set trends—not just for books, but for movies, TV, even fashion—for all ages. And today's YA doesn't seem to be going away anytime soon.

If you aspire to write books for young readers, your timing couldn't be better. But with so many writers flocking to the genre, how can you rise above the rest? As with all trends, even expert opinions vary—so we decided to present a range of perspectives so you can make the best decisions for you and your work.

Here, influential agents and editors weigh in on what you can do to break in, how to keep pace with a genre that's still evolving, and much, much more about YA today.

How can a writer assessing the market determine what topics might be reaching a saturation point (how many vampires is too many?), and which ones will stay hot?

STEPHEN FRASER: Vampires have already reached a saturation point. … I don't think a single additional book needs to be added to the vampire/werewolf canon.

Books about disenfranchised teens will always be around, though. Books about a struggle with the world will always be around. A book with a fresh voice will always sell.

THE ROUND TABLE

STEPHEN FRASER (jdlit.com) has been an agent with the Jennifer DeChiara Literary Agency since 2005. He previously worked as an editor with HarperCollins, Scholastic, Simon & Schuster and *Highlights for Children*, and has edited the work of such talents as Gregory Maguire and Brent Hartinger. He represents children's, YA and adult books in a wide range of genres.

AIMEE FRIEDMAN (aimeefriedmanbooks.com) is a senior editor at Scholastic. She is also a *New York Times* best-selling author of several YA books.

WENDY LOGGIA is an executive editor at Delacorte Press. Recent novels she's edited include *Fallen* by Lauren Kate and *The Ever Breath* by Julianna Baggott. She responds to strong voices, as well as exciting premises and writers interested in the collaborative process. Romance, girl thriller, paranormal and humor are all genres she'd like to see more of in her YA submissions.

GEORGE NICHOLSON (sll.com) has been an agent with Sterling Lord Literistic since 1995. Prior to joining SLL, he founded Delacorte Press Books for Young Readers and Yearling Books. He also served as publisher of Books for Children and Young People at The Viking Press, as well as publisher of Bantam Doubleday Dell Books for Children. He is particularly interested in developing new writers in fiction and nonfiction for both YA and children.

ANICA MROSE RISSI is a senior editor at Simon Pulse. Rissi acquires commercial, high-concept and literary fiction for teen readers. She looks for quirky humor, smart writing, compelling storytelling and characters that she can't get out of her head. Rissi especially enjoys nurturing and building the careers of debut novelists.

AIMEE FRIEDMAN: This is a question—or, perhaps, as of late, *the* question—that very often preoccupies publishers. But I generally encourage aspiring authors to avoid getting too deep into these types of guessing games. This is not to say an author needs to remain wholly removed from the ups and downs of the marketplace (and, increasingly, that's becoming less and less realistic). But I do encourage writers to stay focused on what excites them—what ignites their passion and keeps them inspired—rather than on the needs of the market.

ANICA MROSE RISSI: It's smart to know your market, but please don't write for current trends—those trends will probably be over by the time your book is ready for submission or publication. Editors aren't looking to acquire current trends; we're looking for the next hot thing. Sometimes the next hot thing builds off the success of what's currently hot, but remember: By the time your book is written, revised, acquired, edited and published, at least a year will have passed, and the trend you're trying to tap into is likely to be tapering, morphing or long gone. Write the story that only you can tell, and let the agents and publishers worry about how to pitch and package your manuscript to fit the market.

That said, an aspiring writer should do her research (i.e., read, read, read) and take note of the basic characteristics that most YA novels share. YA plots are teen-focused. Adults tend to play only minor roles, and friends and love interests are central. The majority of YA is written in first person (this helps it feel relatable and immediate), and that voice/viewpoint is strictly teen. Even literary, voice-driven YA novels are also driven by plot.

What sorts of submissions are you seeing too many of?

WENDY LOGGIA: Poorly written paranormal fiction.

GEORGE NICHOLSON: Because fantasy and paranormal are the currency of today's successes, there are far too many poorly thought-out proposals for series, particularly trilogies. It's not that the ideas for the books are not powerful, just inexperience and inadequate knowledge on the part of the writer.

FRIEDMAN: I'm definitely seeing a whole slew of paranormal submissions right now, particularly of the angel variety. Because of the success of titles like *Hush, Hush* and *Fallen*, I always pay these titles a little extra attention, but on the whole, fallen angels haven't grabbed me in the way other paranormal topics—such as vampires/werewolves and ghosts—have. I'm also seeing a wave of Percy Jackson–esque novels about young boys with latent powers and magical ancestors, which I think have a perennial appeal but right now run the risk of feeling a bit too derivative.

FRASER: I'm a bit tired of the dystopian view. ... If human beings experience just what they hold in thought, why are we perpetuating those images? Let's be more creative and see something more positive. How about humor? How about surprising kindness? And let's give human beings more credit than to think everyone is basically greedy and hateful.

What would you like to see more of in your inbox—and which YA subgenres do you see as up-and-coming?

LOGGIA: Well-written paranormal fiction! Gripping stories—something different that's exciting. When I read the galley of [Suzanne Collins'] *The Hunger Games*, I couldn't stop thinking about it, wishing it had come my way. Manuscripts I've bought lately are a combination of great voice and compelling plot. Stories that are compulsively readable, stories that teens will gobble up.

FRASER: I've seen a couple of books about the music industry, which is interesting, given the huge success of TV shows like "American Idol" and "America's Got Talent," YouTube videos, etc.—but they have to be good.

I'd like to see a good gay novel, but one in which sexuality isn't an "issue" but part of the fabric of the story.

Religion or faith is rarely dealt with in YA novels, and again, if it isn't the "issue" but an integral part of the story, that would be good to see.

RISSI: I'm always looking for dark, edgy fiction. I like books about characters who make bad choices, then have to work through the consequences of those decisions. Whether dark novels are verse, realistic fiction or paranormal, they tackle tough, emotional issues and feature relatable characters who find themselves in challenging—or even life-threatening—situations. Teen readers perennially connect with these types of stories, and what better place for them to explore darkness and push boundaries than on the page and in the imagination?

FRIEDMAN: I love historical fiction, in particular historical romance (with or without paranormal elements), and it's pretty rare to find that done well for the YA audience. I'm a big fan of Libba Bray's Gemma Doyle trilogy, as well as The Luxe books, which I think both very successfully remain authentic to their time period while still feeling fresh and contemporary and fun. I'd love to see more such submissions coming down the pike.

For now, I think paranormal romance in all its forms has some staying power, but I do wonder if there will eventually be a backlash, and then more of a return to the straightforward coming-of-age, chick-lit-y romances that were all the rage about five years back. Then again, it's so hard to be able to prognosticate these sort of trends.

NICHOLSON: This sounds hopelessly old-fashioned, but what I look for in new work is pacing and emotional resonance in characterization and plot. The best praise I can give a client is that "tears came to my eyes." I'd like to see fiction in which moral and ethical concerns are at the core of the novel's complexities. I do think that most young people are honestly and honorably trying to think about who they are and who they wish to become.

How would you describe the styles and voices that YA readers seem to be responding to today?

LOGGIA: Fresh and frank writing—the hallmark of what teen fiction has been and continues to be. Honesty and realness. And there's a real variety in what readers can find; there really is a book for everyone.

NICHOLSON: I do think that young people respond to integrity of voice and style and that emotional resonance I mentioned. Whatever the changes in diction and current slang, I still think it should be used sparingly. When I first came to the business, slang of any sort was strictly forbidden, yet there was still richness in language. I may be wrong, but I think slang dates good fiction more easily than any other single thing.

FRIEDMAN: I think teen readers are—and have always been—a lot smarter and savvier than many give them credit for. Today's teens in particular tend to be remarkably mature, articulate and pop-culturally aware. And I find that teens have an amazing radar for inauthenticity—for "phonies," as our dear Holden Caulfield would put it. So with all that in mind, I think YA readers really respond to an authentic voice—one that doesn't feel pandering or dumbed down in any way. And if that voice is authentic—if it rings true and doesn't try too hard—I think YA readers are really open to wherever those voices can range: from ones that are earnest and heartbroken, to wry, witty, hilarious takes on life and love.

How is today's YA market different from that of 10 years ago? How is good YA writing the same?

RISSI: We've seen changes in format and trim size (more hardcovers, more trade paperbacks, fewer mass-market paperbacks), and a shift away from open-ended series toward closed series arcs and single-title fiction. Cover trends have changed (currently, photographic and iconic covers are more popular than illustrated covers), and we've cycled through different trends in topic and voice. Publishing is a cyclical business, and Simon Pulse has had incredible success with backlist gems such as L.J. Smith's best-selling Night World series and Christopher Pike's best-selling Thirst series, both of which we've introduced to a new generation of readers through new packaging.

Good YA writing is still immediate and relatable, with an unwavering teen perspective and emotional truth.

FRASER: It's harder to shock these days. Judy Blume really knocked people's socks off in the '70s, [as have] books like Laurie Halse Anderson's *Speak* in more recent times. To me, one of the most important YA writers of the 20th century (maybe beyond) is Francesca Lia Block. I think her fresh-voice, quirky writing really changed the landscape. I'm looking for a new voice like that. An Adam Lambert of words!

LOGGIA: It's more of a hot commodity: In general, everyone has shifted focus to the tween/teen market as a profitable area. It seems that there are more and more wonderful writers turning their talents toward YA, with writers like Meg Cabot, Ann Brashares, Scott Westerfeld, Rick Riordan and Sarah Dessen, to name a few, paving the way and showing how it should and can be done.

NICHOLSON: Today's … publishing machine is commodity driven. The most careless writing fills that maw only. The best writing remains the product of a thoughtful mind.

FRIEDMAN: The YA of the last 10 years is varied and sophisticated, and it sometimes takes bigger risks than adult fiction. I don't think it's an accident that one of the biggest book phenoms of the past decade, *Twilight*, was a YA novel.

Of course, the classics will always endure—with J.D. Salinger's recent death, *The Catcher in the Rye* has been on everyone's mind now as this example of a novel that was "YA before YA." Judy Blume will endure. And I think what these classics have in common with the best YA of today is that same authenticity and richness of voice—the characters who come alive and speak to the reader in a meaningful way. That's timeless.

BEFORE YOU SUBMIT

Here's YA editor Anica Mrose Rissi's list of what you can do to increase your book's chances of making it out of the slush pile and into the spotlight.

1. Revise, revise, revise! I don't want to read your first draft, ever. (Tip: Your novel isn't ready to send to me until you can describe it in one sentence.)
2. Start with conflict and tension to raise questions, arouse curiosity and (like musical dissonance) create the need for resolution.
3. Start with the story you're telling, not with the backstory. Throw the reader directly into a conflict and let her get to know your characters through their actions. (Yes, this is another way of saying, "Show, don't tell.")
4. Give the reader something to wonder about and a sense of where the story is going—of what's at stake.
5. Avoid explaining too much too soon. And, don't be obvious. Trust your readers. Trust your characters. Trust your writing. If you find that chunks of your story need to include long explanations, go back in and write those chunks better, until the story explains itself.
6. Make sure your story has both a plot arc and an emotional arc. Cross internal conflict with external conflict. Give your characters moral dilemmas, and force them to deal with the consequences of their choices.
7. Read your dialogue out loud. When revising, ask yourself, "What is the point of this dialogue?" (Just as you should be asking, "What is the point of this sentence? What is the point of this scene?")
8. Use adjectives, adverbs and dialogue tags only sparingly. (See "trust your readers," above.)
9. Make sure your details matter.

In the wake of series like Harry Potter and the Twilight saga, more adults are reading YA. How (if at all) should YA authors take that into account?

RISSI: It's true: Thanks in part to Twilight and The CW, adults are reading teen books and watching teen shows—the stigma is gone. I think YA authors should be glad to have an ever-increasing audience but shouldn't change a thing about the way they craft their stories. Adults, like teens, go the YA section of the bookstore looking for great writing and storytelling. They're finding it in plot-driven and voice-driven novels with unforgettable characters, intense emotions and strong hooks.

BUILD YOUR BOOKSHELF

If you want to go to the head of the class, you'll need to do your homework. Read up on works by these contemporary YA authors mentioned in our round table.

1. Laurie Halse Anderson
2. Francesca Lia Block
3. Ann Brashares
4. Libba Bray
5. Meg Cabot
6. Suzanne Collins
7. Sarah Dessen
8. Anna Godbersen
9. Rick Riordan
10. Scott Westerfeld

LOGGIA: I'm not sure it works to try to make your book all things for all people. Write the story you want to write, and at the end of the day it might be that it's not teen. It's middle grade. Or adult. Sometimes writers are the most surprised of all to find out that the story they've written is for teens.

FRASER: The line between YA and adult is very slight. While YA authors still need to be conscious that teens don't have the life experience that adults do, the word choices, choice of topic, narrative skill, should be similar. I have always felt literature for children and teens should be evaluated on the same terms as adult literature. Good writing is good writing. There should be no cheapening or dumbing down for children, and certainly not for teens. And I suppose it's like those great Disney movies; there can be a layer for the adult, a layer of meaning, humor, depth, that the younger readers won't catch. Though the smarter ones always do.

FRIEDMAN: I would say not at all. If a book crosses over, that's fantastic. I do think more and more adults are dipping into YA, because it's such a rich and intriguing field right now. As an author myself, I get e-mails from women in their 20s and 30s and beyond about my books, which is always a lovely surprise. But I think a YA author by definition is writing for a teen audience.

What are some of the biggest mistakes aspiring YA authors make?

FRASER: Probably the same mistake all aspiring writers make: They assume readers care about their characters the way they do. You need to make your readers care about your characters. Some writers do capture the way teens speak and think, but they are simply recording and not writing. Writing creates the illusion of reality, the illusion which is great art. Banality comes into bad writing. Writers need to learn to excise all banality, anything that doesn't further the story.

NICHOLSON: The biggest mistake new YA authors make is not trusting their own voice. There's too much derivative, even copycat, writing and publishing.

FRIEDMAN: Feeling as if they should be jumping on a certain bandwagon or following a trend. Write what excites you, not what you think you should be writing. If fantasy is not your forte, if it doesn't make your heart pound, but you think that fantasy novels get all the success, I think it's a mistake to try and force yourself to write in the genre. In the end, the writing process will be all the more difficult, and not as rewarding. While I am all for book concepts with big, catchy hooks, I don't think an author should feel as if their manuscript needs to have that kind of commercial *gotcha!* from the get-go.

What is the best thing an aspiring YA author can do to learn what it takes to appeal to today's young readers?

RISSI: YA writers must have an authentic teen voice, which comes from tapping into the intense emotional experience of being a teen. The technology, trends and slang may change dramatically over the years, but the emotions are universal.

FRASER: Teens can spot a fake miles away. I think this is because they're so close to their authentic, developing selves, emotionally, sexually, physically, personally. Wouldn't you want to offer some kind of loving gesture to a group of teens listening to you?

LOGGIA: Old advice that still rings true: Read as much as you can, stay abreast of what's appealing to teens and where they live, and be a sponge of the culture we live in.

JESSICA STRAWSER is the chief editor of *Writer's Digest* magazine. In more than 10 years working in the publishing industry, she has served as an editor for commercial nonfiction imprint Emmis Books, as the managing editor for both North Light Books and Memory Makers Books, as a marketing and public relations editor, and as a freelance writer, editor and writing instructor.

SUPPLEMENT YOUR WRITING INCOME

Know your options.

....

by Jean Daigneau

British romance author Michelle Paver rewrote a 22-year-old manuscript and received the equivalent of almost five million dollars U.S. for her YA novel, *Wolf Brother*, published in 2004. Not a bad way to make a living. Now that your manuscript is out, it's time to think about how to spend all *your* millions once *they* start rolling in. And they will roll in, right? Well, maybe in an alternate universe. Or if you're Michelle Paver. But in reality? Probably not.

One thing that can be said about life as a children's writer is that it's not getting any easier to make a living at it. Even if you already have a book published—or two or three—there are no guarantees that editors will give your next project much more than a passing glance what with increasingly smaller publishing slots to fill.

So, what's a writer to do? While it may seem daunting even in a *good* economy, there are ways to supplement your income as a writer, whether you're waiting for the book deal you've dreamed of or your next contract. Here are a few ideas to consider.

YOU CAN TEACH AN OLD DOG NEW TRICKS

Magazines have always been touted as a way to break into children's publishing. Besides the income, it's a chance to add credits to your résumé as well. When it comes to magazines, it's all about filling those pages, month after month, with material that will entertain and engage. But with today's kids cutting their teeth on iPads and Wii's, keeping their interest is absolutely essential. And whether it's full-blown articles or fillers—like puzzles and crafts—creativity can make the difference between acceptance or rejection.

Award-winning author Kelly Milner Halls has written more than 1,000 magazine articles. She suggests, "If you're out to break into magazine nonfiction for kids, holiday themes are rich with potential. If you come up with a fresh angle on a seasonal favorite—I wrote about reindeer ranching, for example—your odds of acceptance increase significantly. Find a new twist and you'll see a crack in the magazine doors open." This goes for short stories and other fictional pieces, too. While themes are universal—friendship, family, self-esteem, acceptance, school—presenting it in a new way might get an editor's attention.

Another plus to magazine writing is reprints. With more than a hundred magazine credits, children's author Joan Marie Arbogast has had checks show up in her mailbox more than a decade after selling a craft idea or puzzle. According to Arbogast, "Reprints are a treat! Not only for the monetary value, but for the fact that someone else saw merit in your work. Plus, complimentary copies are helpful when studying another magazine's focus and style." Keep in mind that once your rights are returned to you, your article can be submitted elsewhere—depending, of course, on the terms of your contract. Just be sure to mention that it's been published before.

There's another bonus to working with magazine editors most writers might not realize. Arbogast says, "All three of my books were a result of having first worked with editors on the 'magazine side' of publishing—a *Highlights* article published as a nonfiction book with Boyds Mills Press and two books (and one forthcoming) with Pauline Books and Media as a result of work with *My Friend* magazine. You never know how one project will lead to another."

When considering magazine markets, don't overlook the number of well-established newsletters specifically geared towards children's authors and illustrators such as *Children's Writer*, *Children's Book Insider* and the SCBWI Bulletin. Magazines such as *The Writer* and *Writer's Digest* are also open to submissions. Some of these publications don't require previous publishing credits.

FREELANCING RESOURCES

There are an unlimited number of websites available to help you expand your writing credentials and income. A simple search on writing subjects, freelancing, markets or submissions and you'll have more information than you'll have time to wade through.

Here are some leads to pursue both in the children's and adult fields of publishing. As always, check publishers' websites for the latest submission guidelines.

AMERICAN BOOK PRODUCERS ASSOCIATION: You do not need to be a member to get information on book packagers and links to their websites. Look under Membership Directory and do a search for "juvenile" or "children's." To filter your search, use the "narrow search" option and choose a category. Visit abpaonline.org/mc/page.do?sitePageI d=83298&orgId=abpa

ANDREWS MCMEEL PUBLISHING: Publishes children's and adult books on a range of subjects—including activity and hobby, gift books, cookbooks, puzzles and games, biography, poetry and many more. andrewsmcmeel.com/submissions.html

THE ASSOCIATION OF EDUCATIONAL PUBLISHERS: A list of publishers who produce supplemental instructional material. aepweb.org/

CHICKEN SOUP FOR THE SOUL: Includes current call for submission information and guidelines. chickensoup.com/cs.asp?cid=guidelines

CHILDREN'S BOOK INSIDER/LAURA BACKES: Information is available on joining the CBI Clubhouse, signing up for subscriptions to Children's Book Insider and Author's Bootcamps, along with details on critiquing services. cbiclubhouse.com

CHILDREN'S MAGAZINE MARKETS: A list of magazines with links to their websites and submission information. freelancewriting.com/guidelines/pages/Children

CHILDREN'S WRITER: A 12-page newsletter featuring articles on all aspects of the field of children's publishing. childrenswriter.com

CHILDREN'S WRITER'S AND ILLUSTRATOR'S MARKET: A wealth of information—including articles on writing for children as well as a current list of children's publishers, guidelines, etc. Available in most bookstores and online. cwim.com

DAN CASE WRITING FOR DOLLARS: Articles and opportunities for freelance writing, mostly in the magazine market, along with an extensive magazine database with a sign-up option to receive regular e-mail alerts. writingfordollars.com

DOVER PUBLISHING: A publishing company that specializes in books ranging from clip art and math and science books to craft and coloring books. http://store.doverpublications.com/condov.html

EDUCATIONAL MARKETS: Author Evelyn B. Christensen provides information on educational publishers along with some submission guidelines and links to websites. evelynchristensen.com/mktnotes.html#bp

GRYPHON HOUSE: A publisher of books that supplement teaching and curriculum, including those that extend beyond the educational market. gryphonhouse.com/authors/authorGuidelines.asp

HIGHLIGHTS MAGAZINE: A general interest magazine published for more than 65 years, its mission is to help children develop positive self-worth. The magazine features fiction and nonfiction stories, puzzles, poems, crafts, and finger play and action rhymes. highlights.com/contributor-guidelines

THE INSTITUTE FOR CHILDREN'S LITERATURE: The Institute is known for its online children's writing classes, but there are plenty of articles, links and other information on their website that have to do writing for children. institutechildrenslit.com

INTERNATIONAL ASSOCIATION OF GHOSTWRITERS: Information on all aspects of ghostwriting, with a sign-up option to receive a free e-mail newsletter. iapgw.org

JUNE COTNER: A list of current calls for submissions. junecotner.com/jccallsub.html

KID MAGAZINE WRITERS: Information on all aspects of magazine writing for children with links to magazine publishers' websites. kidmagwriters.com/others/aboutus.htm

SCBWI BULLETIN: For members only. Submissions of interest to writers and illustrators are welcome. scbwi.org/Pages.aspx/Submission-Guidelines

SKYPE AN AUTHOR NETWORK: A free service for authors and illustrators seeking opportunities for Skype visits. skypeanauthor.wetpaint.com

STERLING PUBLISHERS: Children's books focus mostly on crafts, experiments, puzzles and hands-on activities. sterlingpublishing.com/sterling/author-guidelines

WORLD-NEWSPAPERS.COM: A listing of adult and children's magazines with the option to search by subject. Links to websites included. world-newspapers.com/environment.html

THE WRITER: A national magazine for writers of all genres that includes regular features, articles, market listings, interviews and up-to-date information on all aspects of writing. Includes a free e-mail newsletter (subscription not required). writermag.com

WRITER'S DIGEST: A national magazine to keep writers of all genres up to date on the most current information available about the world of publishing, trends, real-life experiences and life as a writer today, etc. Includes a free e-mail newsletter (subscription not required). writersdigest.com/SubmissionGuidelines

WRITER'S MARKET: A wealth of information—including articles on writing as well as a current list of magazine and book publishers, guidelines, etc. Available in most bookstores and online. writersmarket.com

WRITING FOR THE EDUCATION MARKET: A website dedicated to educational writing, including a list of educational publishers. Includes a sign-up option to receive regular e-mail alerts. educationwriting.blogspot.com

NONFICTION IS NOT JUST FOR GEEKS

Many authors make a living writing nonfiction for both the educational and trade markets. If you haven't considered it, perhaps you should, especially if you love research and you're a stickler for accuracy. Nonfiction is not just about putting facts on the page; it's about making them exciting and engaging your readers. An author looking to break in needs to write a book that gets kids excited, whether it's about the endangered snow leopard or the Pythagorean Theorem.

Kelly Milner Halls has more than 25 nonfiction books to her name. But for Halls, the cornerstone of her success has a lot to do with subject matter—and for Halls, the weirder the better. "For a lot of years I felt as if I was chasing a bus that had already left the stop," she says. "I kept thinking 'I wish I'd written *this* book, or I wish I'd written *that* book' instead of searching for a place that was uniquely my own. All that ended—and my career took a giant step forward—when I trusted my instincts and set out to write the books I would have loved to read as a kid. I loved weird then and I love it now, and I suspected I was not alone." Her advice for breaking into the nonfiction book market is the same as that for magazines: "Find a new angle on an old favorite and you've won half the battle."

Besides children's titles, there are a number of companies that publish books, games, posters and activities targeted for teachers and educators. While your readers aren't children, ultimately they benefit when you bring a subject to life through a teacher. Colleen Kessler has written in this market professionally and full time since 2007. She says it's a good market for writers because an educational background is helpful, but it is not a requirement. "Publishers are looking for people who can put words in a teacher's mouth so that kids can understand." Essentially, "it's a way of writing nonfiction that teachers can use."

The industry standard for submission is an "introductory packet," which usually includes a cover letter, résumé and credit list (if any). But some publishers are very specific about what they want, so follow guidelines to the letter.

Kessler includes a check-off postcard with choices such as: 1) Not interested; 2) Will hold for future projects; and 3) I would like to discuss a project with you. Please call me at _____. Of course, she immediately calls any publishers that are interested, but she sends a follow-up letter and résumé every three months to those who will hold her information and every six months to others. Setting up a submissions' database is one way she keeps track.

When she started, she recalls she might get one "hit" for every 30 submission packets sent. But that didn't stop her. Kessler says, "Publishers are always looking for writers and you never know when you'll fit a future project. It's about being in the right place at the right time." For Kessler, perseverance paid off.

Another side to the educational writing is test writing—or *assessment*, as it's often called. Some companies prefer someone with teaching experience, but many do not, according to Rita Milios, who has written for the test and educational markets for 20 years.

Milios says that while the market is tougher to break into than when she started, "it is still far from closed. If a writer is new to this genre and has no track record or teaching experience, they could still have a shot. If they focus on small educational testing companies and prepare a good sample writing passage along with good sample test questions, they could catch a break, especially if they have subject-matter expertise."

DON'T BE AFRAID OF GHOSTS

Don't worry, this has nothing to do with Casper, but did you know that many children's series—including some of the Goosebumps, Nancy Drew, and Boxcar Children books—were ghostwritten? Ghostwriting is a great place for authors to break into the market because it's less about artistry and more about being a good technical writer. YA author Emma Carlson Berne ghostwrites at least one teen novel per year, in addition to publishing under her own name. Why would someone ghostwrite when they can't take credit for their work? For Berne, it gives her a chance to explore other genres and to support herself financially as a working writer.

A good ghostwriter must be someone who understands the craft of writing, is able to write from an outline (not all authors can) and is adaptable. Packagers and publishers who work with ghostwriters—most often for series—have very specific ideas of what they want in the finished product, so while credentials help and might eventually lead to more contracts, this is a legitimate starting place for beginning writers, according to Berne. However, be aware that ghostwriters usually have a short turnaround time—about 12 to 16 weeks for a first draft of perhaps 60,000 words—and another four weeks for revisions.

Berne adds that "if you're interested in writing for packagers, I have found them to be easy to approach through cold calls or e-mail." But you often won't make royalties when ghostwriting and don't be surprised if you're required to "audition." This means a packager will ask you to write a chapter or two from an outline to see if your voice and style fit the project.

On the plus side, Berne suggests authors—especially unpublished authors—might want to consider this additional benefit: "I don't think I could have written my own first novel without the techniques I learned from ghostwriting. It really gives you a chance to learn the ins and outs of novel writing in a number of different genres as well as to work closely with an editor, since ghostwriting is very much a collaborative effort."

FIND YOUR NICHE

Other freelance opportunities for children's authors to consider are specialty books such as the Chicken Soup books. A number of their successful titles involve stories about kids, including *Preteens Talk*, *Christian Kids*, and *Teens Talk Tough Times*. A quick search can find what current topics are being considered, along with submission information and any relevant deadlines.

June Cotner's poetry anthologies include children's poetry books such as *Teen Sunshine Reflections* and *Amazing Graces*. Many are filled with poems that were purchased as a result of a call for submissions.

Publishers such as Gryphon House and Sterling Publishing are always on the lookout for great craft and teacher-resource material. Consider also publishers like Andrews McMeel or Dover Publishing, whose children's books include "animotion" and specialties such as activity books, science kits, hidden puzzles and cookbooks, among others. A little sleuthing can help you find some of these niche publishers.

TALKING MONEY

So how much can you *really* make? Here are some *general* guidelines for what markets pay. Of course, information presented is always subject to change, given the current state of the publishing industry in general.

CHICKEN SOUP FOR THE SOUL: $200 and 10 contributor copies of the anthology in which the story appears.

CHILDREN'S BOOK INSIDER: One-page articles (750 words) pay $25 and a 6-month subscription to CBI newsletter; two-page Special Reports (1,500 words) pay $50 and a one-year subscription to the newsletter.

CHILDREN'S WRITER: Lead and feature articles (1,700–2,000 words) pay $300; columns of 750 words with a sidebar (125 words) pay $200.

EDUCATIONAL MARKETS: As with trade publishers, payment varies depending on the assignment, writer's experience, length of the project, etc.

GHOSTWRITING: Payment varies with publishers and is usually higher for experienced writers or with a proven track record with a packager.

GREETING CARDS: Payment (for text only) varies with publishers, but can range from $25 up to $200 per card.

JUNE COTNER: $25 per poem and one contributor copy of the anthology in which a poem appears.

MAGAZINES (CHILDREN): Children's magazine payments, on average, range from $25 and up for a poem, puzzle or activity, to $100 and more for an in-depth article. Publishers that pay per word average around $.20 to $.25 per printed word. Professional quality photographs can also add to an article, and, as a general rule, payment varies from $15 (b/w) to $25 (color) for a quarter-page photo to $100 for a full page. Magazines with a smaller circulation can pay as little as $.05 to $.15 per word.

MAGAZINES (GENERAL TRADE): Less than $125 per article on the low-paying side to $500 or more on the high-paying side; payment and submission guidelines vary per publication.

NONFICTION BOOKS: As for trade publications, advances and payments vary greatly. Authors with more publications can often negotiate higher rates. Authors are typically paid an advance against sales.

REPRINTS: In the general magazine market (including magazines for adults), the standard rule is 25–50 percent of the original payment, but it can vary among publishers; reprint income can come when the same publisher reprints an article or feature within their publishing house or when an author resells an article to another magazine, *depending on the terms of your contract.*

SCBWI BULLETIN: Payment for articles is typically $50, plus a year's membership in the organization.

SCHOOL VISITS: Payment varies, but can start at $500–$1,500 or more, often contingent on the author's publishing credits and success; costs for travel and accommodations are usually extra.

SKYPE VISITS: Payment varies, but a general range is $75–$250 for a 40–50 minute program.

WOW: Women on Writing: Varies from $75 to $150 for articles and features from 1,500 to 3,000 words.

GO BACK TO SCHOOL

No, this doesn't involve college courses. This is about visits to elementary, middle and high schools. Authors and illustrators often can't survive on book advances alone, and school visits are a great way to supplement income. Because of the kids' enthusiasm, they also present opportunities to sell books to an excited audience. According to author Stephanie Greene, whose books range from early chapter books to middle grade, getting your foot in the door can be tough if you don't have more than one book in print.

But for those who don't or who are unpublished, a program that excites children is what will help open doors. Then market yourself like crazy. According to Greene, the first step is "to get your name out there and let your reputation build. I try to donate one school visit to a North Carolina school every year." She also suggests, "Authors who hope to do school visits have to have a website with a page on it devoted to school visits. Their schedule, what they talk about, suggestions for schools that will help them plan the best possible visit, should all be on there." But Greene also warns that "time away from my desk is time I'm not writing."

One way to get around that issue is to Skype. Skyping takes minimal equipment—usually just a computer with a microphone and a web camera—and can virtually bring the world into your home. Children's author Mona Kerby and Sarah Chauncey, Director of Information Resources and Learning Technologies – Rockland BOCES, have created a website that makes the names of authors and illustrators who want to Skype available to schools and other organizations. Their site, Skype an Author Network, is a free service that grew out of a desire to connect children with books and the authors and illustrators who create them. Chauncey says that because of tight dollars, Skyping is one way schools can afford to bring authors and illustrators directly into the classroom. "When children can put a face to someone and ask a question—even little kids know this is special and get excited about reading again." For authors and illustrators, it's a way to open their lives to eager readers and to supplement income without a major time commitment. But, don't kid yourself. Less time for travel doesn't mean taking shortcuts when putting together a presentation. Unique and exciting will translate into future requests for virtual visits.

WHERE TO FIND OPPORTUNITY

I'm a big believer in walking through any door that's open to see what's on the other side. And thanks to that adage, I've made some gains in the publishing field that I don't believe I might have found otherwise.

Although I sold two picture books within a few short months of pursuing children's publishing, neither book was ever published. (It's a long story with boring details, so I'll spare you.) Suffice it to say that while there was a lot of teeth gnashing and disappointment—not to mention money spent on a lawyer to get my manuscripts back. The acceptance gave me the confidence to believe in myself and pursue my dream.

Fast forward 10 years and I'm still waiting for that big book deal. In the meantime, I've sold educational testing material; greeting card text; crafts, poetry and puzzles; nonfiction newspaper and magazine articles; and articles for *Writer's Digest*. I am currently a freelance writer for a healthy lifestyle newsletter.

Many of these successes came about because of opportunities brought to my attention by fellow writers (Thanks, Joan, Kate and LaVora) or through calls for submissions that I read about on the Internet. The difference for me was that I was too dumb to think that I couldn't do it, so I stepped through the door when the opportunities presented themselves. After speaking to *Guide to Literary Agents* editor Chuck Sambuchino and getting a verbal acceptance for a freelance article, I clearly remember thinking to myself,

"Oh my gosh. What have I done?" Then I put on my big girl pants, hit the keyboard, and a few weeks later turned in my first article on spec.

While I'm still not quitting my day job, I am building up a nice writing résumé that I hope will lead to bigger and better things. I've also made my accountant happy with some much needed income, including two surprise checks that appeared in my mailbox as a result of reprints.

So if you want to add to your writing credits *and* supplement your income, you can do it, too. You must be willing to do your homework first and walk through any doors that open, or go out and find them for yourself. After all, no one is going to do it for you.

SHARE WHAT YOU KNOW

If you know your way around a manuscript, teaching writing classes and holding workshops are great ways to supplement your income. They also offer a lot of flexibility: where you hold classes (in a physical location or online), the number of students you teach and if you instruct at a beginner or advanced writing level are all up to you.

Laura Backes has been involved in the children's book field in many capacities since 1988 and is currently the publisher of *Children's Book Insider, The Newsletter for Children's Writers*. She and Christopher Award-winning author Linda Arms White hold Children's Author Bootcamps around the country—usually three or four a year. Backes also teaches one-day and half-day workshops for local organizations and adult continuing ed centers. The most challenging part is getting the publicity out and finding a reasonably priced location. "It helps if you can do it for an established organization or you have some way of marketing to a large group of people," Backes says.

For authors interested in teaching, Backes says, "I think experienced writers have the potential to be good workshop teachers. But there's quite a difference between being able to write your book and being able to teach others how to write theirs. You need to take that very personal writing experience and translate it into universal techniques."

Then, too, conferences and other writer venues are other options to explore. Regional SCBWI organizations often pay program speakers in order to provide the best and most current information to help their members become successful authors and illustrators. As a former SCBWI regional advisor, I can tell you that the conference presenters who got the best ratings were the ones that hit it out of the ballpark when it came to what they offered attendees—being prepared and organized, offering current and relevant material, and being knowledgeable about subject matter. Positive evaluations can be a great way to market yourself for future presentations. Then, too, community colleges and local adult education courses are viable opportunities to check into. Children's programs are another way to share your passion with an excited audience and increase your writer income. So consider libraries and other organizations like Scout groups or YMCA organizations that would love to have a writer speak to their kids.

SHARPEN YOUR RED PENCIL

A number of authors critique to successfully fill income gaps. Keep in mind it takes a certain personality to critique, especially when working with new writers, since so many put their hearts and souls into their projects and may or may not be prepared to hear the truth. Laura Backes also offers a personal critique service through her website. She suggests that "one special skill is being able to look at each book individually." Backes believes that empathy is extremely important, too. "I try to tap into the passion that an author feels for the story and give the author ways to convey that passion to the reader in a book that will compete in today's market." Remember, too, that if you can help bring a manuscript to life and get it submission ready, a grateful author will be your best marketing tool for new business.

THE BOTTOM LINE

If you're determined to make a living as a children's writer, you *do* have options. With access to the Internet and books like the one you're holding, there's a world of information waiting for you to tap into to find potential markets and information on ways to get started. You'll have to invest some time and follow a lot of leads, but it can definitely be worthwhile.

And this advice from Kelly Milner Halls will serve you no matter what approach you take to supplementing your income. "Talk to everyone ... pay attention to everything ... be aware at all times. That sounds so overwhelming and unreasonable, but I've made it as a freelancer for 10 years by taking the opportunities that present themselves. I carry my business cards, a notebook and a copy of my latest book just about everywhere. I talk to strangers and ask lots of questions. I make notes if someone says or does something I think might be useful in a book or article. My card and book verify my legitimacy, so people tend to respond well."

On the other hand, if none of these ideas work for you, perhaps you might want to consider a career as a television or movie celebrity. Everyone knows they *all* can write children's books! Yeah, right. Perhaps in an alternate universe.

JEAN DAIGNEAU has been published in the adult and children's newspaper and magazine markets, including *Highlights*, and has sold educational testing material, craft ideas and greeting card text. Her picture book manuscript, *Tice Davids' Underground Road*, won an honorable mention in the 2008 Barbara Karlin competition and is being adapted as a short play by the Kentucky Historical Society for their 2012 season. Jean is a former regional and assistant regional advisor for the SCBWI Northern Ohio and serves on the executive board.

WRITING FOR MAGAZINES

The toughest job you'll ever love.

by Diana Jenkins

After writing hundreds of stories, articles and comic strips for kids' and teens' magazines, I can honestly say I love magazine work. Except when I hate it.

I love it when a story really comes together. Or when a publication forwards me a letter from a young fan. At other times, magazine work makes me crazy. Like when I've spent hours duking it out with a story that's still a mess—and way too long. Whether I'm elated or frustrated, one thing is always true: Writing for kids' magazines is tough work.

So why do I do it? Should you try writing for magazines, too? How can you be successful in this challenging market?

FIRST THINGS FIRST

Having realistic expectations will keep you going—and help you succeed in this field. So before you get started, take a moment to consider the downside of writing for kids' and teens' magazines.

Since kids' magazines don't usually run advertisements, their budgets aren't huge. This means they can't pay you a lot. Most kids' magazines pay between $100 and $300 for a story or article, but some pay much less. A short story in a small magazine might earn you only $25. Or you might be "paid" in copies of the issue in which your work appears. You won't get rich doing magazine work (though it makes a nice supplement to other family income).

Writing for kids' magazines is hard work—harder than many people think. Fiction presents the challenge of setting up a story, creating characters, fitting in enough description, developing a complete storyline, and teaching a good lesson in just 1,400 words. (Or even fewer, depending on the magazine.) In nonfiction, you face the daunting task of getting across abstract and complex concepts with age-appropriate vocabulary and syntax.

Meeting the demands of this market takes exhaustive (and exhausting!) revisions: tightening, rephrasing, cutting and rewriting, rewriting, rewriting.

Some writers find magazine work stressful. You can't usually write about whatever you want since most magazines for kids and teens have themes planned for each issue or otherwise limit the material they accept. If you're lucky enough to have an editor ask you to write a story or article, you'll have to stick to a particular subject or style. Such restrictions can be helpful because they narrow the list of possible topics and focus your writing. However, some people don't respond well to creating on demand.

Deadlines add to the pressure of writing for magazines. You can't work at a leisurely pace, setting aside a story when you reach a snag and picking it up whenever your muse finally strikes again. It's due when it's due—probably very soon—and your editor is counting on you. Even if you're writing on spec, you may have to meet submission deadlines just to have your story considered.

ON THE POSITIVE SIDE

Fortunately, the positives about writing for magazines far outweigh the negatives. (That's why I do it!) Let's take a look at them.

Things move faster in the magazine world than they do in the book world. Writing a novel takes months and months, even years and years. You can write a whole magazine story or article in hours. The consideration process for a book is long and complicated; magazine editors can accept—or reject!—your story in just minutes. And you're likely to be paid more quickly for magazine work. Many publications even pay writers upon acceptance. Best of all, you'll soon see your magazine work in print—usually in less than a year.

Writing for magazines helps you improve as a writer—even when your work is rejected. Since you're allowed so few words in magazine stories and articles, you learn to carefully choose each one. You can't afford to clutter things up with excessive description, unnecessary adjectives and adverbs, passive voice or rambling dialogue. Magazine work also forces you to tighten up your plots, breathe life into your characters and make your stories emotionally powerful. Every time you write for a magazine, you're developing skills you can use whenever and whatever you write.

Publication in kids' magazines lays the groundwork for other writing successes. Your published stories or articles might be purchased for inclusion in a book or as testing material. Writing about a particular topic or theme for a magazine can help you develop an idea more thoroughly and maybe even lead to a book on that subject. And magazine credits show a potential agent or book publisher that you can write well, you're dependable and you know how to work with editors.

The best thing about writing for kids' and teens' magazines is that it's rewarding. You reach tons of kids with your work—sometimes even more than you would as a book author.

Magazine circulations can be larger than the print runs of some books. And since magazines continue to be available in waiting rooms, libraries and classrooms after their initial publication, your work might pick up new readers for years. As a magazine writer, you can have a powerful influence—entertaining young readers, moving them, making them think and teaching important lessons. That's why I love writing for magazines despite all the challenges. Maybe you will, too!

HOW TO DO IT

Like other writing markets, the world of kids' and teens' magazines is competitive. Magazine editors receive many more submissions than they have room to include in their publications. And in recent years, a number of kids' magazines have gone under, leaving fewer opportunities for aspiring writers. So how can you beat out the competition and become successful in this field?

First of all, hone your skills; getting published in kids' magazines takes excellent writing. Your work must be able to quickly capture the attention of young readers and hold onto it until the last word. That requires flawless pacing, potent word choice, snappy dialogue, superior plotting and plenty of other talents that don't come easy. You can develop the skills you need with classes, articles, books, writers' groups, conferences, and websites, but there's no substitute for spending lots of time actually writing.

You also need to learn all you can about kids' and teens' magazines. You're on the right track already with this book. The "Magazines" section includes essential information about how to contact magazine editors, what they're looking for, what they don't want, etc. You can also check out magazines' websites for writers' guidelines, theme lists and other useful information. Read sample issues online or in the library to see what topics have already been covered and to get a feel for tone and style. Of course, it's easier to send out your work without doing this research, but why waste everybody's valuable time? Editors only publish material that meets their needs. Target your submissions to fit their requirements, and your chances of acceptance increase.

Successful magazine writers don't give editors *only* what they want—they give them something more. The same-old, same-old themes come up again and again in kids' magazines: honesty, responsibility, family, friendship, caring for the environment, doing the right thing. If you can give a new twist to a classic theme, your work will stand out. When considering a theme, toss out the first few ideas that come to your mind—everybody else is probably thinking along the same lines—and find an original approach. Using humor is one of the most effective ways to freshen up an old theme, and editors are always looking for funny stories and articles. However, anything unexpected—a non-stereotypical character, a situation viewed from an unusual perspective, a surprising development—can make your work shine.

Even if you've never had anything published, you can—and should—act like a professional. Busy magazine editors need writers who format their manuscripts correctly, stick to required word counts and meet deadlines. If you're asked to make changes in a manuscript, do so in a pleasant and timely manner. When you start selling your work, be sure to keep good records about where you've submitted, what rights you've sold, and when you expect publication. You don't want to cause problems for editors by selling two different magazines first rights to the same story or having a story appear in competing magazines at the same time.

To be a successful magazine writer, you'll have to deal with the downside of the business. Maximize the not-so-high income by writing more than one story or article based on the same research, selling reprints to other magazines after the first-rights publication, or transforming a work (for which you hold the rights) into a new genre. (Rewrite a story as a play, for example.) Join a critique group or find a critique partner to help with the demanding process of writing for kids. Decrease your stress by starting to work well ahead of deadlines whenever possible. (You can almost always do this for magazines with theme lists.) That gives you time to wrestle with a story, get it down on paper and let it ferment awhile before tackling final revisions.

IN THE BEGINNING

Because writing for magazines is challenging, you can expect to face rejection. Understand that it's just part of the process. (My work has been rejected hundreds and hundreds of times over the years. And I still get rejected today!) Don't let the possibility of rejection discourage you from trying this market. Begin with just one project, make it the best you can and send it out. Then write something new and submit it, too. Carry on like that and eventually you'll have a number of projects out there, increasing your odds of acceptance. When something is rejected, analyze it and revise it as needed, and then send it out again. Keep working at it, and maybe you'll come to love this tough job as much as I do!

DIANA JENKINS has had hundreds of stories, articles, comic strips and plays published in magazines for kids and teens. She's also written several play collections, including *All Year Long! Funny Readers Theatre for Life's Special Times* (teacherideaspress.com). Her other books include *Saints of Note—The Comic Collection, The Stepping Stones Journals,* and *Goodness Graces! Ten Short Stories about the Sacraments* (pauline.org). She lives in Ohio with her husband, a medical physicist. Visit dianarjenkins.bravehost.com and read her blog at djsthoughts-dj.blogspot.com.

WORKING WITH CO-WRITERS

Enrich your story by working with others.

....

by Ferida Wolff

When I first started writing books for children, I never considered writing with another person. After all, how could someone else express my ideas, write with my voice, know what I wanted to say?

But then a car-pooling partner introduced me to Dolores Kozielski, a woman who lived on the street I was moving to and who happened to write also. Only we didn't write the same things; she was a poet and I wrote kids' books. We did lots of things together as our friendship grew; we even shared our writing through a support group we both attended. Sometime after my first two books were published, I said, "Why don't we write a book together? I can write the prose and you can write the poetry." I just thought it would be fun to work together. She had never written poems for children before but was willing to try. We sent out queries and got rejections, but one editor suggested that instead of just stories and poems we should add games, crafts and activities. That was new for both of us, though it sounded like something we could do. So we started meeting at each other's houses, scavenging household items for easy-to-do crafts, and expanded our writing repertoire. We put together a Halloween activity book. It sold and led to another. We discovered that our friendship worked on a professional level for us as well. We wrote everything as one, sharing our ideas and words equally. We went on to co-author seven books for children.

Co-authoring is a different kind of writing discipline, as we learned. Each writer needs to put aside the idea of absolute control over the work and to be open to another's perspective. But it can be an expanding experience, one that leads to professional growth. If you are thinking about co-writing, here are some things to consider.

WORKING WITH LOTS OF CO-AUTHORS

I belong to a writer's support group. It is small in one sense (only six members) but huge in another: We are co-writing a YA book. That's right—all six of us are writing one book! We didn't come together for that purpose though we all are writing for children. It sort of happened when one of us, Dina DiRenzo, brought the beginning of a YA story to read. Her main character was quirky and charming and we encouraged her to continue. But after a while, she said that the story wasn't going anywhere and would we all like to write the book with her? "All of us?" we asked. "Why not?" she said. She felt we could bring in characters with a variety of personalities and plot out the story together. It would be a challenge but it intrigued all of us so we agreed to try it. We decided to write under the pseudonym B.F. JADE, which is composed of the initials of each of our first names.

We bring our own perspectives to the project and that is reflected in our characters. But when you are writing with a group, you have to be carefully responsive to the other characters as they develop. We take turns in writing our individual chapters so that we can reflect on and further what the prior member had written. It is an ongoing project that tends to take longer than if one of us was writing alone but it is also deeply satisfying working with people you like and trust.

Here are some of our thoughts on group co-writing:

Barbara Stavetski: "Co-authoring a story with five other authors is a whole lot of fun. We seem to feed off each other's energy and creativity, which makes it easier to advance the plot."

Ferida Wolff: "I don't take anything personally. With so many personalities, skills and preferences feeding into the project, there is always something that will need changing to make the pieces of the story work for all of us. The constant critiquing moves the book along and deepens it."

Jody Bilbo Staton: "I hear about TV writers sitting around a table working on an episode script for a series and wonder how much our experience is like theirs. It's challenging but fun to work on our JADE project, and it's different to be in charge of just one character. It will be interesting to see what happens when we finish it and take it to agents."

April Woolley: "One of the best things (and challenges) about working with a group of writers is the immediate feedback, whether good or bad. Working solo, you may have the luxury of waiting for the second draft to rethink an idea, but the instant feedback of a group dynamic breeds an openness and level of trust that's hard to match elsewhere and, when embraced, fosters creativity."

> **Dina DiRenzo**: "Although there are challenges to writing with so many co-authors, one great benefit is the variety of viewpoints and ways to problem-solve that we have at our disposal. Co-authoring isn't for everyone. Pick your co-authors carefully!"
>
> **Ellen Dunkel:** "Each person's strengths help carry us through the book. As a journalist, I am very good at writing short, tight and snappy. But I appreciate the help in plotting out a longer project. We mostly write separately and then come together to fit each piece into the puzzle. It's challenging getting everyone in the same room at the same time, though. We're six busy adults with vastly different lives and schedules."

FINDING A CO-WRITER

There are many ways to connect with a possible co-writer. I met Dolores right on my own block, but that is not the way most people find a writing partner. I connected with another co-author, Harriet May Savitz, at a local writers conference. She was facilitating the workshop on Writing for Juveniles; I was a beginning writer in her workshop. She became my mentor, guiding my writing with her penetrating sense of story, but it wasn't until years later that we decided to write together.

Corey Rosen Schwartz found her first co-author, Tali Klein, for the picture book *HOP! PLOP!* at the company where they both worked. She met another co-author, Rebecca Gomez, at an online critique group.

When Natalie Zaman attended a mentor session at an NJSCBWI program, she asked for a group recommendation from the critique group coordinator, who suggested Charlotte Bennardo's group. Zaman said, "We found out that we (she and Charlotte) had a lot in common—and only lived a few blocks from each other!"

A writer's support group may be just the place to find a compatible writing partner. Don't overlook groups at the local library or programs at bookstores; the speaker may know of someone interested in collaborating, possibly even herself.

SPLITTING UP THE WORK

There are various ways to divide the writing; what works well for one partnership may not at all for another. I worked differently with Harriet Savitz than with Dolores Kozielski. Harriet's strength was in YA novels while mine was in picture books. Somewhere along our 30-year relationship, she came up with an idea for a picture book but said she couldn't write it on her own—that she didn't have the same kind of visual images for that age level that I did. She asked if I would write with her. We developed a working pattern; Harriet often came up with the initial idea, we'd talk it out, then I'd put it into story form. We'd tweak it, usually over the phone or by e-mail, until we both were happy with the final draft.

Schwartz said that she and Gomez have a 50/50 collaboration, "We go line by line. We discuss what we like and where it needs to be improved."

Becky Gomez agreed. "We will start with a brainstorming session. Sometimes we'll have a concept or a clever title and we'll see where that takes us. We bounce ideas back and forth until something sticks. Once we agree on an idea worth pursuing, our writing process is very similar to brainstorming. Lots of back and forth until we finally get the plot nailed down, settle on a structure (prose, rhyme or a mix), etc. We work strictly online, through instant messaging, e-mails, and Google docs."

Cyn Balog and her co-author Mandy Hubbard wrote alternating chapters for their YA book, *Getting Caught*. "Each alternating chapter was written from the view of one of the two main characters," Balog said. "Since we live on opposite coasts, we did the entire thing by e-mail."

Lisa and Laura Roecker are sisters and co-authors. They write YA books and have their own way of working. They describe it this way: "Lisa always writes the first chapter and Laura edits, writes the next chapter and sends it back to Lisa. Lisa does the same and we continue until we have a complete first draft. Then we edit like mad. We mainly work at night (or into the morning depending upon how you look at it) because our days are full of carpooling, ballet classes and toddler meal prep."

WORKING TOGETHER/ALONE

For those who have trouble wrapping themselves around the idea of co-writing, you have a compatriot in Mel Glenn, New York poet and author of YA books. He says his Alter Ego is always angling to be his co-author but he's not having any of it.

MG: You're kidding me, right? You want to write with me?

AE: Why not? We'd make a great team. You never heard that two heads are better than one?

MG: But we're in the same head.

AE: I can bring new ideas to the table.

MG: I need my own table. That's the way I roll.

AE: You're being quite obstinate.

MG: That's just another word for "genius." My own vision, that's what's important. Besides, I don't want to fight with anyone, particularly myself.

AE: You never heard that great art comes out of conflict?

MG: I hate conflict; it's so counterproductive. What am I going to do? Battle with you over every word?

AE: We wouldn't battle; we'd share.

> **MG:** I don't share. I want all the credit.
>
> **AE:** So it's a matter of ego?
>
> **MG:** Of course it is. That's what all writers are—all ego, thinking that their words have extraordinary meaning. We write, therefore we are.
>
> **AE:** I see there's no talking to you.
>
> **MG:** Guess not, and if you'll excuse me now, I have some writing to do.
>
> **AE:** Alone?
>
> **MG:** Yes, alone.

HANDLING THE CHALLENGES

Writing with another person can be wonderful yet challenging at the same time. Inevitably, there will be times when a story stops in its tracks. That's the time to brainstorm with your co-writer.

Schwartz finds that particularly helpful. She says she is an extrovert and needs to talk things out. "Oh my. If only I had counted how many times one of us typed a big 'UGH' in the chat box!" said Gomez. "There have been times when we have debated for an hour over one word."

Dolores and I would occasionally sit side by side, each at our own computer, thinking aloud, when we weren't agreeing on some wording. We would not be satisfied until we could both feel good about it. Eventually one of us would blurt out just the right words and we'd continue on.

Zaman sees the need for honesty as an issue in co-writing. "This sticky point is something that I think all co-authors will face, and it's also the one that breaks up a lot of partnerships. It all has to do with communication. Co-authors *cannot* be afraid to voice their opinions and concerns to one another. You have to put aside the notion that you will offend (you might) or upset (you probably will) your partner, and that will kill the relationship and project all together (it won't). *Not* saying anything is far more deadly and will definitely lead to resentment and ill feelings."

Another challenge comes with revision. "The biggest challenge for me," said Bennardo, "is that we have two different writing styles. When we edit, we have to resist the temptation to make the other person sound like ourself. Using two styles without blending them into one is hard, especially when it's in one book. It helped that in *Sirenz* we have two different characters with two distinct voices and points of view. As long as we keep our paws off the other person's chapter, there's no problem."

And sometimes the challenge comes from the publisher. After the contract for our picture book, *The Story Blanket,* was signed, the editor told me that we had to cut the manuscript in half, from 950 words to 500 words! Harriet and I argued over what stayed, what went, what was important, what didn't need to be in the story. When we were finished, we agreed that the resulting story was stronger; reading it aloud, we couldn't even tell what had been cut.

Balog and Hubbard had an enviable challenge; as they both had agents, who would be the one to handle the book? They left it to their agents to decide.

APPRECIATING THE PARTNERSHIP

Co-writing is a partnering experience. If you have the right partner, the work is a joy—but it is still work. I find the exchange of ideas energizing. Each new thought sparks another possibility, which either furthers the book along or can be tucked away for later—and maybe another book.

The most satisfying thing about the process for the sisters Roecker is "typing and editing and deleting and reworking the last sentence of the first draft until we think it's perfect. It comes complete with all the hope in the world that your little baby could go far and do great things. It's an amazing feeling."

For Schwartz, it's the interaction. She said, "I need a sounding board so I want to and need to work with someone else. It helps keep me focused."

Zaman is enthusiastic about co-authoring. "You only have to do half the work!" she said. "You catch *way* more mistakes and inconsistencies when you have two sets of eyes looking for them, and it's like a built in crit-group as well; you automatically get another perspective."

Bennardo added her own reasons for liking co-writing. "What I like about the process of co-authoring is that you never get stuck for long. There's twice the amount of ideas, suggestions and unfortunately criticisms too—but it's all good! We each bring different experiences to the process; it makes the book richer." And should the manuscript be turned down? It's a "guaranteed shoulder to cry on when the rejections come slithering in."

TAKING CARE OF BUSINESS

Working with a co-author gets the creative juices flowing and can be great fun. So in the delight of the process, we often forget to consider what might come in the future. Anita Fore, director of legal service for The Author's Guild, advocates a co-author agreement, separate from the publisher's agreement, to take care of contingencies such as incapacitation or death of one of the authors. "We want to preserve respectful relationships," she said. "All decisions made in mutual agreement." She said that, "Most often the copyright and income become part of the literary estate." However, an agreement would designate who would be primary decision-maker about the book and if the copyright would belong to the surviving author.

This also applies to books should they go out of print. "We wish books would stay in print forever," Fore said. But as that is often not the case, "a pre-agreement would spell out who had the right to make the decision to pursue bringing the book back into print." She said that sometimes an author prefers that an earlier work remain out of print; that is something that might well be addressed in a co-author agreement. Questions that can be addressed beforehand will not be a problem later.

Is co-authoring for you? Schwartz feels there isn't a downside to co-authoring. She said she hates working alone. Besides the books she wrote with Gomez that are being shopped around, and her book with Klein, she has another co-written book, *Goldi Rocks and the Three Bears* (due out in 2013) with Beth Coulton. She has invited others to co-author but they often say, "I don't know if I can be a team player." For Schwartz, "It's worth a shot. If it doesn't work you don't have to continue. Find someone whose strength complements yours, who provides a good counterbalance."

FERIDA WOLFF is the author of 17 books for children, including the picture books *Is a Worry Worrying You?* and *The Story Blanket*, both co-authored with Harriet May Savitz. She is a former teacher and presents programs at elementary schools about the process of writing. Her essays have been in *The New York Times*, *The Philadelphia Inquirer*, *The Christian Science Monitor* and *Woman's World*, and she is a frequent contributor to the Chicken Soup for the Soul books and the HCI Ultimate series. Wolff writes a nature-based blog (feridasbackyard.blogspot.com) and is a columnist for senior women.com. Besides the six-author book she is currently co-writing with her writing group, she is co-authoring early readers with Stephanie Mirmina. Her website is feridawolff.com.

A LOOK AT THE FUTURE OF BOOKS

E-books, e-readers and more.

....

by Laura Backes

///

With the publishing industry in a state of upheaval and companies large and small scrambling to adjust to new realities, it may seem odd to hear a seasoned veteran like Michael Hyatt, CEO of Thomas Nelson, declare, "This is the best possible time to be in the publishing business." It turns out, though, that there's good reason for such optimism, thanks to the growing market for e-books, apps and web-based content.

To gauge the opportunities and challenges that await children's book authors seeking to enter the digital domain, I spoke with three entrepreneurs who are blazing a trail through the e-wilderness. They're each proving that, with some ingenuity, vision and smart marketing, it's possible to not only survive the new landscape but to thrive. And in doing so, they're helping to shape history.

First, though, a quick look at where things stand right now.

E-publishing is still in its infancy, and the full impact of electronic sales has yet to be felt. Even so, the numbers are impressive. The Association of American Publishers' 2010 domestic sales report showed that e-book sales overall (adult and children's titles) rose 164.4 percent over the previous year. Verso Advertising's 2010 Survey of Book-Buying Behavior found that 7.9 percent of book consumers own dedicated e-readers—a huge jump over 2009. And if Kindle owners are any indication, those consumers purchase multiple e-books: as of January 1, 2011, Amazon reported that U.S. customers bought 115 Kindle e-books for every 100 paperbacks sold, and Kindle titles are outselling hardcovers by three to one.

These remarkable statistics focus only on e-books and e-readers such as Amazon's Kindle, Barnes & Noble's Nook, and the Sony Reader. What the numbers don't show are sales for the thousands of apps available for smartphones, iPods and tablet computers, many of which feature children's books. On January 22, 2011, Apple announced its *one billionth* app store download, and one telling statistic from the iPad launch day on April 3, 2010—that the Apple store had more than one million downloads with children's picture book apps occupying six of the top 10 slots—hints at the willingness of book lovers of all ages to embrace the electronic era.

And there's still lots of room to grow. In September 2010, when the ABC Children's Group of the American Booksellers Association asked 509 parents of American children ages 7–12 how often their children read e-books, 83 percent responded "Not at all." It's quite possible, then, that the sales of children's e-books and apps to date are just the tip of the iceberg. Plus, schools are getting in on the action: *The New York Times* reported last January that schools are testing iPad use in the classroom for teaching everything from history to math to reading. Prices on electronic devices are coming down, and we still don't have a dedicated e-reader designed for young children. When one does hit the market, the potential for children's e-book sales is enormous.

While many children's publishers are moving into the digital age by offering both print and digital formats of their titles, some of the most exciting innovations are coming from entrepreneurs creating their own platforms and apps for children's books. Let's take a look at three of the most prominent game changers.

THE LEARN-TO-READ APP

In early 2009, Michael Kripalani founded the app development company Oceanhouse Media (oceanhousemedia.com) with the motto, "Creativity with Purpose." Fifty of the publisher's 160 apps are for picture books, including Dr. Seuss, Berenstain Bears and Little Critter titles, with plans to release another 80–100 in 2011. In January 2011, Oceanhouse celebrated its one millionth paid download from Apple's App store.

Oceanhouse's apps for children are designed to work well on smartphones and small screens, and their primary purpose is to teach basic reading skills. "We made a conscious decision from the beginning that every effort we put into the app had to support learning and literacy," said Kripalani. "We have a lot of interactivity on each page, where a child can tap the illustration of a hat and see the word 'hat' float up on the screen. This is also reinforced by the narrator speaking the word. We call this 'picture/word association.' Tap a picture, see the word and hear the word. This will teach a child to read. By contrast, we could have the hat fly up in the air, spin around, do a dance and drop back, but this raises costs quite a bit without adding any educational qualities. Leaving out the complex animations does allow us to keep our apps affordable ($0.99–$3.99). Again, it's equally important to us that first and foremost, our apps teach kids how to read, so we choose to emphasize those features instead."

Oceanhouse Media works with publishers and directly with authors and illustrators to create the picture book apps. "Specifically, we want to speak with people who own the electronic or digital rights to books that have already been successful in print. The brand awareness that accompanies these books is key in making the apps stand out in this increasingly crowded market," said Kripalani. Authors and publishers can contact Oceanhouse through the company website or by sending an e-mail to info@oceanhousemedia.com.

Oceanhouse Media's success can be attributed to timing, hard work and technology. "We're using our technological expertise and a unique business model to create a new type of product that is extremely relevant to today's consumers," Kripalani added. "Children's publishing has been a very static industry for many years now. It took the combination of things like new touch screen technologies, the commoditization of smartphones and other mobile devices, and highly efficient distribution channels such as iTunes to create the platform for the revolution we're seeing in children's publishing today." At the same time, Kripalani strives to keep the integrity of the original work intact. "We consider it an honor to work with companies like Dr. Seuss Enterprises in transitioning their cherished stories from print form to digital. We're happy to be a major player in bringing this technology to children's publishing."

THE READ-TO-ME E-BOOK

A Story Before Bed (astorybeforebed.com) was launched in November 2009 by Jackson Fish Market, a small software start-up in Seattle. It was the first—and remains the only—enhanced e-book platform that allows consumers to record a video of themselves reading a children's book, which then plays in the corner of the screen as the child views the e-book. Children can play back the story as often as they like, either on a computer or on the iPad and iPhone with the A Story Before Bed app. In January 2011, A Story Before Bed was awarded the first-ever Publishing Innovation Award for Children at the Digital Book World conference.

Though co-founder Hillel Cooperman emphasizes that the company is still in the start-up stage, their offerings grew from 25 titles in 2010 to over 250 in early 2011. The average price of a picture book is $6.99, with choices ranging from a few free titles to $39.95 for unlimited recordings of 50 select books. "Our mailing list is growing every day. I think the main issue is letting people know that it is even possible to do this. Right now this is the only place on the Internet where you can actually record a video of yourself reading a children's book to your kid whether they are on your lap or across the country, and that is pretty compelling for lot of people." As of March 2011, A Story Before Bed was close to its goal of giving away 100,000 e-books to parents serving in the U.S. military.

A Story Before Bed currently carries books from publishers such as Charlesbridge, Chronicle and Sourcebooks, as well as publishing original versions of classic stories for their Jackson Fish Market imprint. They also work directly with authors and illustrators who hold the digital rights to their books. A royalty is paid on every e-book sold. "We sign an agreement with each rights holder, and every time we sell one of their books they get a cut. In our subscription offering, we set aside a chunk of revenue for the [rights holders] so that they get revenue with each of our subscription sales. I think what is key for us is that we have designed our business so that when we succeed, the folks who own the rights to the content succeed as well. We are not building our business around giving away something for free. We are building our business around creating a fantastic environment where people want to pay for great children's books, and we are designed to share that with the publishers, authors and illustrators."

A Story Before Bed provides the details of what needs to be submitted by authors and publishers, but Cooperman says even technical neophytes can handle it. "It is really simple—just the PDF. It needs to be of appropriate quality and prepared properly but there is nothing fancy about it. If their book has been published with any sort of semi-modern desktop publishing tools ... then they are in pretty good shape. If the book is older than that they may need to look into getting it converted digitally and scanned at a high resolution." For more details, e-mail publishers@astorybeforebed.com.

Cooperman offers this advice to authors, illustrators and small publishers: "The day has arrived. You need to get your content in digital form now. You do not need to be a computer programmer or software developer to be able to put your books out electronically, but you do need to start understanding digital publishing, and once you do the research, you'll realize it's not scary. It is pretty straightforward stuff. After you have your content in a flexible, high-resolution digital form and you have some basic understanding of how to get it out there, then your job is to sign as many nonexclusive deals as possible with companies that are doing a good job representing children's book content in a professional and thoughtful way."

GOING BEYOND THE BOOK

Back in 2008, practically the e-book dark ages, Internet entrepreneur Bradley Inman had the vision of uniting books, audio, video and Internet into one complete, blended story. The Vook (vook.com) allows users to read the text, watch videos that enhance the story, and connect with authors and friends through social media all on one screen—without switching between platforms. Starting as a web-based product, Vook now has apps that work on smartphones, tablet readers and e-readers. The company expects to have 1,000 children's and adult titles available in 2011. MotherVook, the digital conversion platform Vook uses to create its own titles, was made available in February 2011 for license by publishers to turn their backlists into the Vook format. The company's newest innovation, TextVook, is an e-book series of nonfiction, college-level topics such as history, economics, law, politics and science that blends traditional book content with animation.

The initial offering of children's titles are public domain works, but a look at Vook's *Alice's Adventures in Wonderland* shows the potential for virtually any book. It combines the original story and illustrations with videos filmed in Oxford where Lewis Carroll lived, narration about his inspiration for Alice and other characters, and web links for additional resources. Nonfiction can also be brought to life with multimedia. A perfect example is *JFK: 50 Days*. Designed as a companion to the book, *JFK: Day by Day* (Running Press/Perseus), this app takes an intimate look at 50 select moments of the Kennedy presidency. The video includes rare footage retrieved by NBC researchers, some of which has not been seen since it first aired 50 years ago. While *JFK: 50 Days* would be at home in a high school history class, the format can easily be adapted to younger nonfiction as well. The layered information delivered visually, aurally and through the written word casts a wide net to capture kids' different learning styles. Plus, Vook e-books are just plain fun to read.

Vook has worked with large and small publishers, and directly with authors. "The publishing community relies a lot on authors to do their own marketing," said Mike Arnot, Vook's marketing director. "We'll take a book and make it available as a web-based e-book, launch it as an app, sell it in the iBook store, and at the same time launch it for the Kindle. We're also now on the Android platform. A lot of authors have humongous followings on Twitter and Facebook and the like and yet they still don't necessarily know how to get their content in front of the audience, and so that's one of our strong points."

If you imagine your middle grade mystery as an e-book that lets readers visit the protagonist's neighborhood via live streetcam; read the newest, real-time entries on the villain's blog; check web links that lead to clues and e-mail their friends about your book all without switching platforms, then the Vook might be for you. Authors and publishers can find more information at publish.vook.com.

WHERE DO YOU GO FROM HERE?

"Everybody is just getting started and there is still plenty of room here," said Hillel Cooperman. "There are a lot of parents, a lot of grandparents and a lot of kids out there, and they all need children's books." And, as Michael Kripalani explained, "In today's world, people expect everything to be available at their fingertips, immediately and affordably."

But how does an author or illustrator keep track of the newest developments? The Internet is full of information, but you don't have to absorb everything. Just get comfortable with the basic terminology. Sign up for Digital Book World's free e-newsletter (digitalbook world.com) and stay up to date on e-publishing's latest news and events. Do the same for *PW Daily Newsletter* and *Children's Bookshelf* from *Publishers Weekly* at publishersweek ly.com. Read a multimedia interview on the app-building process with Michael Kripalani at gotstorycountdown.wordpress.com/2011/02/09/from-games-to-childrens-story-apps/. Then get out there.

"There is nothing stopping the smart and aggressive and thoughtful publisher from putting their books on as many e-book sites as they want to," said Cooperman. "The incremental cost of doing this after the first time is negligible. It's basically as if you have an unlimited number of chips and you can put them on every square on the roulette table. It doesn't matter if Red 14 or Black 26 loses because it's cost you essentially nothing to bet them all." With odds like that, at least a few squares are bound to pay off in a big way.

LAURA BACKES is publisher of *Children's Book Insider, The Newsletter for Children's Writers* and co-founder of The CBI Clubhouse, an online membership community for aspiring and published children's authors (CBIClubhouse.com). She also blogs at Write4Kids.com/blog and eWriting4Kids.com, where she focuses on the exciting new world of children's e-books.

CRAFTING A QUERY

How to write a great letter.

by Kara Gebhart Uhl

So you've written a book. And now you want an agent. If you're new to publishing, you probably assume that the next step is to send your finished, fabulous book out to agents, right? Wrong. Agents don't want your finished, fabulous book. In fact, they probably don't even want *part* of your finished, fabulous book—at least, not yet. First, they want your query.

A query is a short, professional way of introducing yourself to an agent. If you're frustrated by the idea of this step, imagine yourself at a cocktail party. Upon meeting someone new, you don't greet them with a boisterous hug and kiss and, in three minutes, reveal your entire life story including the fact that you were late to the party because of some gastrointestinal problems. Rather, you extend your hand. You state your name. You comment on the hors d'oeuvres, the weather, the lovely shade of someone's dress. Perhaps, after this introduction, the person you're talking to politely excuses himself. Or, perhaps, you become best of friends. It's basic etiquette, formality, professionalism—it's simply how it's done.

Agents receive hundreds of submissions every month. Often they read these submissions on their own time—evenings, weekends, on their lunch break. Given the number of writers submitting, and the number of agents reading, it would simply be impossible for agents to ask for and read entire book manuscripts off the bat. Instead, a query is a quick way for you to, first and foremost, pitch your book. But it's also a way to pitch yourself. If an agent is intrigued by your query, she may ask for a partial (say, the first three chapters of your book). Or she may ask for your entire manuscript. And only then may you be signed.

As troublesome as it may first seem, try not to be frustrated by this process. Because, honestly, a query is a really great way to help speed up what is already a monumentally slow-paced industry. Have you ever seen pictures of slush piles—those piles of unread queries on many well-known agents' desk? Imagine the size of those slush piles if they held full manuscripts instead of one-page query letters. Thinking of it this way, query letters begin to make more sense.

Here we share with you the basics of a query, including its three parts and a detailed list of dos and don'ts.

PART I: THE INTRODUCTION

Whether you're submitting a 100-word picture book or a 90,000-word novel, you must be able to sum up the most basic aspects of it in one sentence. Agents are busy. And they constantly receive submissions for types of work they don't represent. So upfront they need to know that, after reading your first paragraph, the rest of your query is going to be worth their time.

An opening sentence designed to "hook" an agent is fine—if it's good and if it works. But this is the time to tune your right brain down and your left brain up—agents desire professionalism and queries that are short and to the point. Remember the cocktail party. Always err on the side of formality. Tell the agent, in as few words as possible, what you've written, including the title, genre and length.

Within the intro you also must try to connect with the agent. Simply sending 100 identical query letters out to "Dear Agent" won't get you published. Instead, your letter should be addressed not only to a specific agency but a specific agent within that agency. (And double, triple, quadruple check that the agent's name is spelled correctly.) In addition, you need to let the agent know why you chose her specifically. A good author-agent relationship is like a good marriage. It's important that both sides invest the time to find a good fit that meets their needs. So how do you connect with an agent you don't know personally? Research.

1. Make a connection based on an author or book the agent already represents.
Most agencies have websites that list who and what they represent. Research those sites. Find a book similar to yours and explain that, because such-and-such book has a similar theme or tone or whatever, you think your book would be a great fit. In addition, many agents will list specific topics they're looking for, either on their websites or in interviews. If your book is a match, state that.

2. Make a connection based on an interview you read.
Search by agents' names online and read any and all interviews they've participated in. Perhaps they mentioned a love for X and your book is all about X. Or, perhaps they mentioned that they're looking for Y and your book is all about Y. Mention the specific

interview. Prove that you've invested as much time researching them as they're about to spend researching you.

3. Make a connection based on a conference you both attended.

Was the agent you're querying the keynote speaker at a writing conference you were recently at? Mention it, specifically commenting on an aspect of his speech you liked. Even better, did you meet the agent in person? Mention it, and if there's something you can say to jog her memory about the meeting, say it. And better yet, did the agent specifically ask you to send your manuscript? Mention it.

Finally, if you're being referred to a particular agent by an author who that agent already represents—that's your opening sentence. That referral is guaranteed to get your query placed on the top of the stack.

PART II: THE PITCH

Here's where you really get to sell your book—but in only three to 10 sentences. Consider the jacket flap and its role in convincing readers to plunk down $24.95 to buy what's in between those flaps. Like a jacket flap, you need to hook an agent in the confines of very limited space. What makes your story interesting and unique? Is your story about a woman going through a midlife crisis? Fine, but there are hundreds of stories about women going through midlife crises. Is your story about a woman who, because of a midlife crisis, leaves her life and family behind to spend three months in India? Again, fine, but this story, too, already exists—in many forms. Is your story about a woman who, because of a midlife crisis, leaves her life and family behind to spend three months in India, falls in love with someone new while there and starts a new life—and family?—and then has to deal with everything she left behind upon her return? *Now* you have a hook.

Practice your pitch. Read it out loud, not only to family and friends, but to people willing to give you honest, intelligent criticism. If you belong to a writing group, workshop your pitch. Share it with members of an online writing forum. Know anyone in the publishing industry? Share it with them. Many writers spend years writing their books. We're not talking about querying magazines here, we're talking about querying an agent who could become a lifelong partner. Spend time on your pitch. Perfect it. Turn it into jacket-flap material so detailed, exciting and clear that it would be near impossible to read your pitch and not want to read more. Use active verbs. Write your pitch, put it aside for a week, then look at it again. Don't send a query simply because you finished a book. Send a query because you finished your pitch and are ready to take the next steps.

DOS AND DON'TS FOR QUERYING AGENTS

DO:

- Keep the tone professional.
- Query a specific agent at a specific agency.
- Proofread. Double-check the spelling of the agency and the agent's name.
- Keep the query concise, limiting the overall length to one page (single space, 12-point type in a commonly used font).
- Focus on the plot, not your bio, when pitching fiction.
- Pitch agents who represent the type of material you write.
- Check an agency's submission guidelines to see how it would like to be queried—for example, via e-mail or mail—and whether or not to include a SASE.
- Keep pitching, despite rejections.

DON'T:

- Include personal info not directly related to the book. For example, stating that you're a parent to three children doesn't make you more qualified than someone else to write a children's book.
- Say how long it took you to write your manuscript. Some best-selling books took 10 years to write—others, six weeks. An agent doesn't care how long it took—an agent only cares if it's good. Same thing goes with drafts—an agent doesn't care how many drafts it took you to reach the final product.
- Mention that this is your first novel or, worse, the first thing you've ever written aside from grocery lists. If you have no other publishing credits, don't advertise that fact. Don't mention it at all.
- State that your book has been edited by peers or professionals. Agents expect manuscripts to be edited, no matter how the editing was done.
- Bring up screenplays or film adaptations; you're querying an agent about publishing a book, not making a movie.
- Mention any previous rejections.
- State that the story is copyrighted with the U.S. Copyright Office or that you own all rights. Of course you own all rights. You wrote it.
- Rave about how much your family and friends loved it. What matters is that the agent loves it.
- Send flowers, baked goods or anything else except a self-addressed stamped envelope (and only if the SASE is required).
- Follow up with a phone call. After the appropriate time has passed (many agencies say how long it will take to receive a response) follow up in the manner you queried—via e-mail or mail.

PART III: THE BIO

If you write fiction, unless you're a household name or you've recently been a guest on "Oprah," an agent is much more interested in your pitch than in who you are. If you write nonfiction, who you are—more specifically, your platform and publicity—is much more important. Regardless, these are key elements that must be present in every bio:

1. Publishing credits

If you're submitting fiction, focus on your fiction credits—previously published works and short stories. That said, if you're submitting fiction and all your previously published work is nonfiction—magazine articles, essays, etc.—that's still fine and good to mention. Don't be overly long about it. Mention your publications in bigger magazines or well-known literary journals. If you've never had anything published, don't say you lack official credits. Simply skip this altogether and thank the agent for his time.

2. Contests and awards

If you've won many, focus on the most impressive ones and the ones that most directly relate to your work. Don't mention contests you entered and weren't named in. Also, feel free to leave titles and years out of it. If you took first place at the Delaware Writers Conference for your fiction manuscript, that's good enough. Mentioning details isn't necessary.

3. MFAs

If you've earned or are working toward a Master of Fine Arts in writing, say so and state the program. Don't mention English degrees or online writing courses.

4. Large, recognized writing organizations

Agents don't want to hear about your book club and the fact that there's always great food, or the small critique group you meet with once a week. And they really don't want to hear about the online writing forum you belong to. But if you're a member of something like the Romance Writers of America (RWA), the Mystery Writers of America (MWA), the Society of Children's Book Writers and Illustrators (SCBWI), the Society of Professional Journalists (SPJ), etc., say so. This shows you're serious about what you do and you're involved in groups that can aid with publicity and networking.

5. Platform and publicity

If you write nonfiction, who you are and how you're going to help sell the book once it's published becomes very important. Why are you the best person to write it and what do you have now—public speaking engagements, an active website or blog, substantial cred in your industry—that will help you sell this book?

Finally, be cordial. Thank the agent for taking the time to read your query and consider your manuscript. Ask if you may send more, in the format she desires (partial, full, etc.).

Think of the time you spent writing your book. Unfortunately, you can't send your book to an agent for a first impression. Your query *is* that first impression. Give it the time it deserves. Keep it professional. Keep it formal. Let it be a firm handshake—not a sloppy kiss. Let it be a first meeting that evolves into a lifetime relationship—not a rejection slip. But expect those slips. Just like you don't become lifelong friends with everyone you meet at a cocktail party, you can't expect every agent you pitch to sign you. Be patient. Keep pitching. And in the meantime, start writing that next book.

KARA GEBHART UHL (karagebhartuhl.com) was formerly a managing editor at *Popular Woodworking Magazine* and, later, *Writer's Digest* magazine. Kara now freelance writes and edits for trade and consumer publications from her 100-year-old foursquare in Fort Thomas, KY. She also actively writes about the joys and challenges of raising a 3-year-old daughter and twin 1-year-old boys at pleiadesbee.com, which is part of Cincinnati.com's Locals on Living blog network. An essay she wrote, which she originally read for WVXU's "This I Believe" program, will be published in the forthcoming *This I Believe: Life Lessons* (Wiley; fall 2011). You can read more of her work at karagebhartuhl.com.

Dear Mr. Malawer:

I would like you to represent my 65,000-word contemporary teen novel *My Big Nose & Other Natural Disasters*.

(1) Seventeen-year-old Jory Michaels wakes up on the first day of summer vacation with her same old big nose, no passion in her life (in the creative sense of the word), and all signs still pointing to her dying a virgin. Plus, her mother is busy roasting a chicken for Day #6 of the Dinner For Breakfast Diet.

(2) In spite of her driving record (it was an accident!), Jory gets a job delivering flowers and cakes to Reno's casinos and wedding chapels. She also comes up with a new summer goal: saving for a life-altering nose job. She and her new nose will attract a fabulous boyfriend. Nothing like the shameless flirt Tyler Briggs, or Tom who's always nice but never calls. Maybe she'll find someone kind of like Gideon at the Jewel Café, except better looking and not quite so different. Jory survives various summer disasters like doing yoga after sampling Mom's Cabbage Soup Diet, Enforced Mother Bonding With Crazy Nose Obsessed Daughter Night, and discovering Tyler's big secret. But will she learn to accept herself and maybe even find her passion, in the creative (AND romantic!) sense of the word?

(3) I have written for *APPLESEEDS*, *Children's Playmate*, *Confetti*, *FACES*, *Hopscotch*, *Story Friends*, *Wee Ones Magazine*, the *Deseret News* and Blooming Tree Press' *Summer Shorts* anthology. I won the Utah Arts Council prize for *Not-A-Dr. Logan's Divorce Book*. My novels *Jungle Crossing* and *Going Native!* each won first prize in the League of Utah Writers contest. I am currently serving as a Regional Advisor for SCBWI.

(4) I submitted *My Big Nose & Other Natural Disasters* to Krista Marino at Delacorte because she requested it during our critique at the summer SCBWI conference (no response yet).

Thank you for your time and attention. I look forward to hearing from you.

Sincerely,
Sydney Salter Husseman

(1) With hundreds and hundreds of queries each month, it's tough to stand out. Sydney, however, did just that. First, she has a great title that totally made me laugh. Second, she sets up her main character's dilemma in a succinct and interesting way. In one simple paragraph, I have a great idea of who Jory is and what her life is about—the interesting tidbits about her mother help show the novel's sense of humor, too. **(2)** Sydney's largest paragraph sets up the plot and the conflict, and introduces some exciting potential love interests and misadventures that I was excited to read about. Again, Sydney really shows off her fantastic sense of humor, and she leaves me hanging with a question that I needed an answer to. **(3)** She has writing experience and has completed other manuscripts that were prize-worthy. Her SCBWI involvement—while not a necessity—shows me that she has an understanding of and an interest in the children's publishing world. **(4)** The fact that an editor requested the manuscript is always a good sign. That I knew Krista personally and highly valued her opinion was, as Sydney's main character Jory would say, "The icing on the cake."

SAMPLE QUERY NO. 2: YOUNG ADULT
AGENT'S COMMENTS: LAUREN MACLEOD (STROTHMAN AGENCY)

Dear Ms. MacLeod,

I am seeking literary representation and hope you will consider my tween novel, REAL MERMAIDS DON'T WEAR TOE RINGS.

First zit. First crush. First … mermaid's tail?

❶ Jade feels like enough of a freak-of-nature when she gets her first period at almost fifteen. She doesn't need to have it happen at the mall while trying on that XL tankini she never wanted to buy in the first place. And she really doesn't need to run into Luke Martin in the Feminine Hygiene Products **❷** aisle while her dad Googles "menstruation" on his Blackberry **❹** .

❸ But "freak-of-nature" takes on a whole new meaning when raging hormones and bath salts bring on another metamorphosis—complete with scales and a tail. And when Jade learns she's inherited her mermaid tendencies from her late mother's side of the family, it raises the question: if Mom was once a mermaid, did she really drown that day last summer?

Jade is determined to find out. Though, how does a plus-sized, aquaphobic mer-girl go about doing that, exactly … especially when Luke from aisle six seems to be the only person who might be able to help?

❺ REAL MERMAIDS DON'T WEAR TOE RINGS is a light-hearted fantasy novel for tweens (10-14). It is complete at 44,500 words and available at your request. The first ten pages and a synopsis are included below my signature. I also have a completed chapter book for boys (MASON AND THE MEGANAUTS), should that be of interest to you.

My middle grade novel, ACADIAN STAR, was released last fall by Nimbus Publishing and has been nominated for the 2009/2010 Hackmatack Children's Choice Book Award. I have three nonfiction children's books with Crabtree Publishing to my credit (one forthcoming) as well as an upcoming early chapter book series. Thank you for taking the time to consider this project.

Kind regards,
Hélène Boudreau
www.heleneboudreau.com

❶ One of the things that can really make a query letter stand out is a strong voice, and it seems that is one of the things writers struggle with the most. Hélène, however, knocked it out of the park with her query letter. I find young readers are very sensitive to inauthentic voices, but you can tell by just the first few paragraphs that she is going to absolutely nail the tween voice in the manuscript—you can see this even by the way she capitalized Feminine Hygiene Products **❷**.

❸ The first time I read this query, I actually did laugh out loud. Instead of merely promising me RMDWTR was funny (which it absolutely is), Hélène showed me how funny she can be, which made me want to request the manuscript even before I got to her sample pages.

I also loved how clearly and with just a few words she could invoke an entire scene. Hélène doesn't tell us Jade gets embarrassed in front of a local hunk, she plops us right down in the middle of the pink aisle with the well-intentioned but hopelessly nerdy Dad **❹**. I felt this really spoke to her talents—if she could bring bits of a query to life, I couldn't wait to see what she could do with a whole manuscript. **❺** And on top of all of this, she had a phenomenal title, a bio that made it very clear she was ready to break out, and a hook so strong it even made it onto the cover!

Dear Ms. Humphrey,

I'm contacting you because I've read on various writing websites that you are expanding your young adult client list.

In LOSING FAITH, fifteen-year-old Brie Jenkins discovers her sister's death may not have been an accident **1**. At the funeral, an uncorroborated story surfaces about Faith's whereabouts the night of her tragic fall from a cliff. When Brie encounters a strange, evasive boy **3** at Faith's gravesite, she tries to confront him, but he disappears into a nearby forest.

Brie searches out and questions the mysterious boy, finding more information than she bargained for: Faith belonged to a secret ritualistic group, which regularly held meetings at the cliff where she died. Brie suspects foul play, but the only way to find out for sure is to risk her own life and join the secret cult. **2**

LOSING FAITH (76k/YA) will appeal to readers of **4** John Green's LOOKING FOR ALASKA and Laurie Halse Anderson's CATALYST. My published stories have won an editor's choice award in *The Greensilk Journal* and appeared in *Mississippi Crow* magazine. I'm a member of Romance Writers of America, where my manuscript is a finalist in the Florida chapter's Launching a Star Contest. For your convenience, I've pasted the first chapter at the bottom of this e-mail. Thank you for your time and consideration.

Sincerely,
Denise Jaden
www.denisejaden.com **5**

Everything about Denise's query appealed to me. She gave me a quick sentence about why she chose to query me, and then went right into the gist of her novel. **1** Her "gist" is very much a teaser, or like the back blurb of a book. She gives plot clues without revealing too much of the plot. She keeps the plot points brief and keeps the teaser moving; most important is where she ends—on a note that makes the agent curious to know more. **2** Denise also gives us vivid characters **3** in this teaser: the smart, investigative protagonist, Brie; the mysterious boy at the gravesite; the sister, Faith, who's not what she seems. By creating hints of vivid characters and quick engaging plot points in a paragraph, Denise demonstrates her storytelling ability in the query—and I suspected it would carry through to her novel. **4** Denise includes some other elements that I like to see in queries: comparisons to other well-known books (two or three is enough) and credentials that show her ability to write fiction. **5** I like, too, that she included her website—I often visit websites when considering queries.

SAMPLE QUERY NO. 4: MIDDLE GRADE
AGENT'S COMMENTS: ELANA ROTH (CAREN JOHNSON LITERARY)

Dear Ms. Roth,

A boy with a hidden power and the girl who was sent to stop him have 24 hours to win a pickle contest.

1 12-year-old Pierre La Bouche is a *cornichon*. That's French for "pickle," but it also means "good-for-nothing." A middle child who gets straight C's, he's never been No. 1 at anything. When the family farm goes broke, grandfather Henri gives Pierre a mission: to save the farm by winning an international pickle contest.

2 En route to the contest, Pierre meets Aurore, the charming but less-than-truthful granddaughter of a rival farmer. She's been sent to ensnare Pierre, but after a wake up call from her conscience, she rescues him. Together, they navigate the ghostly Paris catacombs, figure out how to crash-land a plane, and duel with a black-hearted villain who will stop at nothing to capture their pickles. In their most desperate hour, it is Pierre's incredible simplicity that saves the day. Always bickering but becoming friends, Pierre and Aurore discover that anything is possible, no matter how hard it may seem.

3 *Pickle Impossible* is complete at 32,500 words. I'm a technical writer by day, optimistic novelist by night. Recently, I've interviewed a host of pickle makers and French natives. My own pickles are fermenting in the kitchen. I grew up in Toronto and live with my wife and children in Israel.

Thank you for your consideration. I hope to hear from you.

Kind Regards,

Eli Stutz

1 The first paragraph introduces the main character and the set-up. He uses concrete things to describe Pierre. He throws in the French flair of the book right away. And he doesn't beat around the bush to tell me what Pierre has to accomplish. **2** The second delves a little deeper into the plot. It gives me the complication that will drive the story forward—someone is out to stop Pierre. And then Eli accomplishes the most important trick here: He gives me some fun examples of what will happen in the book without summarizing the entire plot. That is key because I don't want to read the whole book in the query letter. But he gives me flavor. **3** The bio paragraph is straight to the point, not overcrowded with his whole life history, and also ties light-heartedly right back to the subject of the book. I loved that he tried fermenting his own pickles. (He later told me they weren't very good.) Here's the kicker. The total word count on this letter is 242 words. 242! Look how much he fits into 242 words. There's plot, character, personality and quirk. From this tightly written letter I know I'm going to get a fun, zany story. Those of you who wanted 250 words just to pitch your book, take heed! Shorter is better.

Dear Ms. Wiseman:

(1) Everyone assumes Camp David must be one of the safest places on earth, but what would happen if a natural disaster caused the security systems to turn the retreat into a prison? *Escape From Camp David* is a young adult manuscript approximately **(3)** 40,000 words in length. I read on your bio you were interested in stories that would appeal to boys, so I thought you might be interested in this **(2)**.

Just once Luke Brockett would like to do something slightly dangerous, but when your father is the President of the United States, that is not an option. Always surrounded by Secret Service agents and kept in a bubble of safety, Luke sees Camp David, the presidential retreat in the woods of Maryland, as the only place where he can be almost normal. For one week in August, Luke's mother has arranged for Luke to have a "summer camp" experience, if summer camp had only three kids and the counselors carried automatic weapons **(4)**. The experience comes to a quick end when a forest fire surrounds Camp David. Luke and his friends are trapped inside, left on their own, the Secret Service agents incapacitated, forcing the three to outwit security systems designed to be unbeatable before the fire gets to them.

While it isn't possible for the average person to know exactly how Camp David is protected, some educated guesses can be made to make this story plausible. I have a degree in International Relations from Tufts University, and have been careful to research both the lives of presidential children and the details of any government references in the story. This is the first of a planned series; a president's son as a main character can have many adventures other children could not.

Thank you,

Dee Garretson

This query interested me for several reasons. **(1)** It's a great high-concept premise, and the author gives me the hook right in the first line. **(2)** She also shows in the first paragraph that she really has looked at our website and identified me as the right agent for her, due to my interest in "boy" books. Too often, this is not the case. Although our website clearly states that I don't handle adult work, you'd be amazed at how many adult queries I receive! Although the query letter is on the short side, the author definitely did her job in piquing my interest with it. **(3)** She gives me the word count right up front, so I know that her manuscript is not way too short or way too long for the genre.

(4) In the second and third paragraphs, the author gives a succinct synopsis of the plot, that demonstrates, even in this brief paragraph, that she is a talented writer with a humorous side. I was also pleased to note that, although this is fiction, she had done her research, making for a more believable story.

SYNOPSIS WORKSHOP

Compose an effective novel summary.

....

by Chuck Sambuchino

Before you submit your novel to an agent or publisher, there are things you need to do. First and foremost, you must finish the work. If you contact an agent and she likes your idea, she will ask to see some or all of the manuscript. You don't want to have to tell her it won't be finished for another six months. If your novel is complete and polished, it's time to write your query and synopsis. After that, you're ready to test the agent and editor waters.

How you submit your novel package will depend on each agent or publisher's specified submission guidelines. You'll find that some want only a query letter; others request a query letter and the complete manuscript; some prefer a query letter plus three sample chapters and a synopsis; and still others request a query letter, a few sample chapters, an outline *and* a synopsis. All want a SASE (self-addressed, stamped envelope) with adequate postage, unless they request an electronic submission. To determine what you need to submit, visit the agent or publisher's website for guidelines, or consult a current edition of a market resource such as *Novel & Short Story Writer's Market*, *Writer's Market* or *Guide to Literary Agents*. These sources have submission specifications that come straight from the editors and agents telling you just what to send, how to send it and when to anticipate a response.

Be prepared to send at least a query letter, a synopsis and three consecutive sample chapters. These are the most important—and most requested—parts of your novel package. You may not need to send them all in the same submission package, but you probably will need to use each of them at one time or another, so prepare everything before you start submitting. Here we'll focus on what writers often find the most difficult component of their novel submission package: the synopsis.

DEFINING SYNOPSIS

The synopsis supplies key information about your novel (plot, theme, characterization, setting), while also showing how these coalesce to form the big picture. You want to quickly tell what your novel is about without making an editor or agent read the novel in its entirety.

There are no hard and fast rules about the synopsis. In fact, there's conflicting advice about the typical length of a synopsis. Most editors and agents agree, though: The shorter, the better.

When writing your synopsis, focus on the essential parts of your story, and try not to include sections of dialogue unless you think they're absolutely necessary. (It's OK to inject a few strong quotes from your characters, but keep them brief.) Finally, even though the synopsis is only a condensed version of your novel, it must seem complete.

Keep events in the same order as they happen in the novel (but don't break them down into individual chapters). Remember that your synopsis should have a beginning, a middle and an ending (yes, you must tell how the novel ends to round out your story).

That's what's required of a synopsis: You need to be concise, compelling and complete, all at the same time.

CRAFTING TWO SYNOPSES

Because there is no definitive length to a synopsis, it's recommended you have two versions: a long synopsis and a short synopsis.

In past years, there used to be a fairly universal system regarding synopses. For every 35 or so pages of your manuscript, you would have one page of synopsis explanation, up to a maximum of eight pages.

So, if your book was 245 pages, double-spaced, your synopsis would be approximately seven pages. This was fairly standard, and allowed writers a decent amount of space to explain their story. You should write a synopsis following these guidelines first. This will be your long synopsis.

The problem is that during the past few years, agents started to get busier and busier, and now they want to hear your story now-now-now. Many agents today request synopses of no more than two pages. Some even say one page, but two pages is generally acceptable. To be ready to submit to these agents, you'll also need to draft a new, more concise summary—the short synopsis.

So, once you've written both, which do you submit? If you think your short synopsis is tight and effective, always use that. However, if you think the long synopsis is actually more effective, then you will sometimes submit one and sometimes submit the other. If an agent requests two pages max, send only the short one.

If she says simply, "Send a synopsis," and you feel your longer synopsis is superior, submit the long one. If you're writing plot-heavy fiction, such as thrillers and mysteries, you might really benefit from submitting a longer, more thorough synopsis.

Your best bet on knowing what to submit is to follow the guidelines of the agency or publisher in question.

FORMATTING ELECTRONIC SUBMISSIONS

Some editors or agents might ask you to submit your synopsis via e-mail or on a CD. The editor or agent can provide you with specific formatting guidelines indicating how she wants it sent and the type of files she prefers.

If an agent or editor does request an electronic submission, keep the following four points in mind:

1. Follow the same formatting specs as for a paper (hard copy) synopsis submission.
2. When sending your synopsis via e-mail, put the name of your novel in the subject line (but don't use all capital letters—it's just obnoxious).
3. Send the synopsis as an attachment to your e-mail unless the agent requests you cut and paste it in the e-mail body.
4. Include a cover letter in the body of your e-mail, and your cover page and table of contents in the file along with the synopsis.

PUTTING IT ALL TOGETHER

Now you know the basics of synopsis writing. Read on for explanations of mistakes to avoid in your synopsis, as well as an example of what a well-crafted, properly formatted synopsis should look like.

Excerpted from *Formatting & Submitting Your Manuscript*, 3rd edition © 2009 by Chuck Sambuchino and the Editors of Writer's Digest Books, with permission from Writer's Digest Books.

MISTAKES TO AVOID IN YOUR SYNOPSIS

John Q. Writer ❶
123 Author Lane
Writerville, USA 95355 ❷

Officer on the Run ❸

Investigative officer ❹ David Black doesn't know where to begin when he gets word Police Chief John Murphy is found dead on his bed—with a silver bullet between his eyes and half-inch nail marks running down his back. Black has to answer two questions: Who would kill the Chief, and why?

It turns out quite a few people aren't too pleased with the Chief. He's been on the force for 23 years and no doubt made some enemies. On the home front, the Chief was completely out of control. He'd lost all affection for his wife, Mary, who was once the apple of his eye.

Black interviews all of the women that the Chief had affairs with, whom he called his "Seven Deadly Sins," and finds no leads until Marlene Preston, the Chief's seventh "sin." ❺ She reveals how the Chief repeatedly would handcuff her arms and legs to four metal poles under the bleachers at the school football stadium. Black drinks himself into a stupor and pours out his problems to a young barmaid, who tells him that the Chief deserved to die.

Black continues investigating the Chief and uncovers all kinds of sordid details. ❻ The killer is revealed at the end, and it is a total shock and surprise ❼ to all, especially Black. ❽

❶ The genre of the novel is not mentioned, nor is the word length. ❷ Phone number and e-mail address are missing; make sure the agent or editor will be able to contact you. ❸ The title of the book should be in all caps, or at the very least bold and italicized. ❹ The first time a character is introduced, the name should be in all caps. ❺ Pivotal plot points are glossed over—they should be highlighted. ❻ Be sure to reveal your novel's ending. ❼ A short synopsis is preferable, but this is actually too short; it doesn't give enough information about the characters or the plot to make it compelling. ❽ The characters' motivations and emotions aren't conveyed at all in this synopsis, leaving the editor or agent to think, "Why should I care about these characters?"

THE MAKING OF A SUCCESSFUL SYNOPSIS

John Q. Writer   **2** Mystery
123 Author Lane   70,000 words
Writerville, CA 95355
(323) 555-0000
johnqwriter@e-mail.com **1**

> **1** List contact information on the top left corner of first page. **2** Include novel's genre and word length here. **3** Avoid numbering the first page. **4** Center title in all caps. **5** Use all caps the first time a character is introduced. **6** Double-space all text. **7** Establish a good hook, introduce important characters and set up a key conflict.

4 OFFICER ON THE RUN
Synopsis

Investigative officer **5** DAVID BLACK doesn't know where to begin when he gets word Police Chief JOHN MURPHY is found dead on his bed—with a silver bullet between his eyes and half-inch nail marks running down his back. Black has to answer two questions: **6** Who would kill the Chief, and why? **7**

It turns out quite a few people aren't too pleased with the Chief. He'd been on the force for 23 years and no doubt made some enemies. All the townspeople called him Bulldog because he looked like a pit bull, and certainly acted like one.

Countless stories passed through City Hall about how the Chief wouldn't hesitate to roll up his cuffs and beat suspects into submission until they would confess to a crime. That was his method and it worked. He could take control of any person and any situation.

Except his wife and his marriage. On that front, the Chief was completely out of control. He'd lost all affection for his wife, MARY, who was once the apple of his eye but now weighs in at 260 lbs. That was fine with the Chief—the less he had to see Mary, the more time for his own pursuits. But he really had only one pursuit: younger women. That fact he didn't hide. He'd often brag to guys on the force about being the only Chief in the history of law enforcement to "burn through seven dispatchers in just as many years." He even called them his "Seven Deadly Sins." Little did he know that one day they'd all be suspects for his murder.

❷ Black interviews all seven women and finds no leads until MAR-LENE PRESTON, the Chief's "Seventh Deadly Sin," reveals how the Chief repeatedly would handcuff her arms and legs to four metal poles under the bleachers at the school football stadium. Marlene says she's never told anyone about any of it. Black then interrogates ❸ the six other "sins" to see if they had also been physically mistreated. They all say the Chief never tried anything like that with them.

Black drinks himself into a stupor and pours out his problems to a young barmaid, SARAH, who just happens to be the best friend of the Police Lieutenant's daughter, KELLY LIEBERMAN. Sarah tells Black the Chief deserved to die and that he was a jerk, especially to Kelly when she'd baby-sit for the Chief and his wife. According to Sarah, the Chief used to talk dirty to Kelly and then warn her not to tell her father because LIEUTENANT LIEBERMAN was in line for a promotion.

Black interviews Kelly. She denies the Chief did anything but make a few lewd comments on occasion. When Black approaches Kelly's father, Lieutenant Lieberman says Kelly never mentioned a word about the Chief. Black returns to talk with Kelly and asks why she's never mentioned anything to her father. She says she's afraid he'd get upset at her for bringing it up. Black presses further, asking Kelly if the Chief ever did anything other than verbally harass her. Kelly says no.

❹ Black decides to walk back under the bleachers to the spot where Marlene says the Chief repeatedly handcuffed her. There, he notices two sneaker shoestrings on the ground by the four poles Marlene pointed out. The strings had been tied in knots and then cut. Black shows the strings to Marlene and asks if the Chief ever tied her to the poles with them. "Not once," she says. "Handcuffs every time."

❶ Format headers with your name, the title, the word "Synopsis" and the page number. ❷ Begin text three lines below the header. ❸ Write your synopsis in third person, present tense. ❹ In a long synopsis, begin a new scene or twist with the start of a new paragraph (there is not enough room to do this in a short synopsis).

CONFERENCES

Get the most out of a writing event.

....

by Mary Kole

You've finally taken the plunge and decided to invest in a writers conference. Or perhaps you're planning this year's conference schedule and hitting all your favorite events. Great! There's no better way to network with publishing professionals, meet fellow writers, learn about the current marketplace, and get a jolt of inspiration for your craft.

When you're choosing your next conference, keep in mind that there are two major types: big group and small group. The big group conferences feature breakout speaker sessions, panels and other information-packed classes for large audiences of writers. Small group conferences, like workshops or retreats, often break attendees into smaller classes and focus directly on participants' writing samples.

I go to dozens of events every year as a faculty member and can share a few tips to help you get the most from your experience at both types of events. Read below for hints on big conferences, small workshops, pitching and aligning your expectations.

BIG CONFERENCES

At a big group conference, you'll be going to sessions with dozens or hundreds of your writing peers. This was the case at the DFW Writers' Conference (dfwwritersconference.org), the Society of Children's Book Writers and Illustrators (scbwi.org) New York and Los Angeles National conferences, the Florida Writers Association (floridawriters.net), the San Diego Writers' Conference (writersconferences.com), the Writer's Digest Writers Conference (writersdigest.com/conferences-events), and many more. Independent regional conferences and big writing groups like the Romance Writers of America (rwa.org) often host these types of events, too.

Sessions at big conferences range from the general—perhaps "Trends in the Children's Marketplace"—to the specific—"Humor for Picture Book Illustrators," for example. You'll also get informational sessions from agents and editors about their agencies, tastes and houses. Big conferences can be overwhelming, and the issue is often too many great sessions to choose from!

Here's how you make the most of a big conference:

- **MIX UP YOUR SCHEDULE:** Check the schedule with an eye toward variety. Mix craft seminars with talks by publishing bigwigs. If a session isn't satisfying you, it's perfectly okay to get up and visit a concurrent one. Make sure you go to all of the panels, too.

- **MINGLE:** Even if you're naturally shy, you'll get more out of a big event by meeting other writers, talking to the publishing professionals, asking questions during sessions (we love getting smart questions!) and otherwise putting yourself out there. Writing is a solitary pursuit, but this isn't the time to hold back on the socializing!

- **PRINT BUSINESS CARDS.** Whether you get a set designed or use free services like VistaPrint (vistaprint.com) you'll want something with your name and e-mail to give out. This is Networking 101, and if you don't have them, you'll end up regretting it.

- **MEET YOUR NEW CRITIQUE GROUP.** Connect with other writers at the event so you can exchange pages after you go home and the conference buzz wears off.

I urge every writer to go to a big conference at least once. You'll get relevant information, meet other writers and rub elbows with agents and editors. Such a massive event is also a jolt of creative inspiration, which is worth the price of admission every time.

SMALL CONFERENCES, WORKSHOPS AND RETREATS

Smaller conferences and workshops focus on an attendee's work in a hands-on environment. Here, you'll be in small groups with a writing teacher or publishing professional and you'll work on your writing sample in a critique setting.

Workshops and retreats are great because you're getting personalized advice on your writing. You're also working in small groups. These events are intense—lots of information to soak up, lots of critique to give, lots of interactions with writers and faculty—but totally worth it. The Andrea Brown Literary Agency hosts the Big Sur Writing Workshop twice a year (December and March, henrymiller.org/workshops.html) on the beautiful Northern California Coast, and I am always amazed by how much writers evolve from Friday to Sunday. There's nothing quite like a focused workshop to really take craft to the next level.

I've seen the same happen at other workshops I've attended, like the SCBWI LA Retreat, the SCBWI New York Writers Intensive, and the workshops put on by the Highlights Foundation (highlightsfoundation.org) on their secluded property in Pennsylvania. That's the other benefit of small conferences: They're often held in scenic locations that are perfect for courting your muse.

Here are my tips for taking advantage of a small group workshop or retreat:

- **COME READY TO WORK.** A retreat should be relaxing, right? Wrong! While you'll benefit from a gorgeous setting or a lot of personal attention, you should also come with a notepad, a laptop and your regular writing tools. Attendees are often inspired to make changes to their writing sample mid-workshop, so make sure you're equipped to do so.

- **ADJUST YOUR CRITIQUE ATTITUDE.** Writers learn to revise—the biggest skill in a working author's toolbox—by first looking constructively at the work of others. Don't just sit in workshop waiting for them to talk about your work. Actively critique, participate, examine and analyze the work of your fellow writers. They'll return the favor, and your editorial eye will be that much sharper as a result, which you'll need to finesse your own work.

- **USE THE FACULTY.** We show up to a retreat weekend knowing that our time belongs to the attendees. You'll have unprecedented access to authors, agents and editors. Ask questions, really drill into craft topics and take full advantage of the faculty's knowledge base.

Whether it's your first retreat or your tenth, you'll leave the weekend with new connections and a deeper understanding of your work and the bigger writing craft.

PITCHING

You'll most likely have the opportunity to pitch the faculty at both kinds of conferences. My biggest piece of advice on this fraught writing topic is: relax. Seriously. I've had people burst out crying during a pitch. I've had people mumble their memorized monologue into their laps. People read off of cue cards. People shake. People forget their words.

Don't do any of the above. Just talk to me. Tell me about your book. Pique my curiosity. Have a conversation and make a personal connection ... *that's* what I'll remember as I head off to the airport. I have experienced thousands of pitches. Don't put undue pressure on yourself to knock my socks off or get an offer of representation right off the bat. Just being casual and interesting is enough. And for goodness sake, don't worry about memorizing your lines or fret if you misremember them. Only you know how it's supposed to go, so don't put so much emphasis on getting every word right.

Once you loosen up and talk to me, you'll be ahead of the pack.

KNOW BEFORE YOU GO

As an agent, I wish more writers went into conferences with the right attitude. You should be prepared to have fun, make new friends, network with the pros, pitch casually, leave with new ideas to take your work to the next level. You shouldn't go in expecting a contract or a big break. You shouldn't pack your suitcase with 20 copies of your full manuscript and spend all weekend trying to slip them to faculty. That's unrealistic. If you ever leave a conference feeling *crushed* and unable to go on, you need to revise your expectations. You don't have to be a "conference success story" in order to have a successful conference.

The benefits of a conference are inspiration and knowledge. You may see the positive effects immediately, or you may wake up with a brainstorm months after the event. Either way, a conference is something every writer should invest in at least once in their career.

See you on the conference circuit!

RISING STARS

Editors of small and midsize publishing houses talk books and writing.

....

by Madeline Smoot

Editor. That one simple word on a fellow attendee's name badge can inspire so many different emotions in the average conference-goer. After all, the editor is the dragon at the gate of the publishing world, the one individual who must love your manuscript, the person that sends out the dreaded rejection letter. And even when we're interested in the work, we'll still find flaws in your previously flawless manuscript and force you to consider tedious and monumental rewrites in an effort to conform your literary masterpiece to the current marketplace. Right?

These perceptions can make editors like me seem unapproachable, even terrifying, to the unpublished author. It can explain the uneasy smiles, the shaky palms and jittery legs that have sat across from me at conference critique sessions. However, most editors are not these paragons of evil that many unpublished authors' fears turn us into. In fact, the editor is your greatest friend and guide in the publishing process. The editor is the one who wants to help craft your vision into something extraordinary. The editor is your champion at the publishing house who battles the combined foes of other editorial projects, marketing and sales to see that your book gets a chance. And along the way, he or she might become a writing confidante and friend and somehow transition from "the" editor to "your" editor.

So, to help demystify editors, I've decided to get to know (really get to know) a few of them for you. I've taken up their time, pried into their lives, and have asked them personal questions about their reading preferences all in an effort to unveil the people hidden behind those editorial desks. Like me, all of the editors are from small, independent presses with focused publishing preferences. Also each of these editors came highly recommended to me from authors, mentors and former classmates. And, most importantly, all of them take unsolicited manuscripts at some point during the year.

PEGGY TIERNNEY, TANGLEWOOD PRESS

I first met Peggy several years ago at my very first BookExpo America—that huge yearly trade show that brings authors, editors publishers, and booksellers together in a giant, crazy melting pot. Back then, I was editorial director for Blooming Tree Press, trying to find distributors to present to my publisher. As part of that, I was trying to talk to publishers to see what they thought of their distributor. I was referred to Peggy and found her to be a wonderful, engaging, easily approachable editor.

Originally an Americanization editor for the British publisher Usborne, Peggy founded Tanglewood Press when the author Audrey Penn, best known for her picture book *The Kissing Hand*, offered her a novel for publication. As Peggy puts it, "Of course I accepted! This was also at a time when way too many books for children had heavy messages or were moralistic or seeking to indoctrinate children in some way. I just wanted kids to love books and reading as much as I did, and I wanted to give them funny, smart, interesting stories."

And that is exactly what Tanglewood publishes. Although Peggy loves all the books Tanglewood has produced, when pushed to name a favorite, she could only narrow it down to three. She mentioned *The Kissing Hand*, which besides being the most successful, has a fond place in Peggy's heart because the book "has touched so many lives and is such a gift to children and their parents." Her favorite book to work on was *The Mice of Bistrot des Sept Frères*, because she was "so deeply involved in that book, even coming up with a cheese soup recipe" and because Peggy is secretly (or not so secretly) "a total Francophile." Finally, the most meaningful book for Peggy has been *Surviving the Angel of Death*, the memoir of Eva Kor, a 10-year-old Mengele twin in Auschwitz.

Although Peggy publishes everything from picture book through YA, she has been focusing more on widening her middle reader and YA lists. Peggy acknowledges that "the picture book market is smaller than it used to be, and picture books are more expensive to produce." Nowadays she is looking for "humor in all books, but particularly for the youngest kids." For teens, Peggy says, "It doesn't have to be funny if it has great drama. Overall, I want intelligence, writing skill, professionalism, originality, respect (for readers) and authenticity."

In the past, Peggy has found these things in manuscripts in her slush pile. For instance, one manuscript, *The Tiptoe Guide to Tracking Fairies*, went on to win great reviews and was selected by the Association of Booksellers for Children as one of the "Best Children's Books of 2009." Another book, *68 Knots*, has also been successful for Tanglewood. As Peggy puts it when discussing the slush pile, "I haven't had the breakout mega-seller yet, but I know it will happen!"

BEN BARNHART, MILKWEED EDITIONS

Ben Barnhart, editor for Milkweed Editions, has also had positive experiences with unsolicited manuscripts. One of these stories happens to involve a former classmate of mine, Jessica Lee Anderson. Her debut novel, *Trudy*, originally sat in Ben's slush pile awaiting another rejection until Ben picked it up and discovered the "first novel I'd found in the slush pile that had held my interest from beginning to end." After working a bit with Jessica, Ben acquired *Trudy* and later her second and third books as well. "I'm immensely proud to have Jessica on our list," says Ben, "and I think of her publishing career as an example of the kind of work we hope to do with each of our authors."

Ben has worked with many authors in his traditional editorial career that started as an intern and has allowed him to climb to the ranks of editor. Since Milkweed Editions is "a literary, nonprofit, independent publisher of compelling, meaningful stories for young readers and teens," Ben looks for books for "readers as young as 8 or as old as 18." When asked about his publishing preferences, Ben says, "Personally, I'm drawn to contemporary, character-driven stories, and I'm a fan of ambitious novels that do their best to break out of standard storylines (like Marcus Zusak's *The Book Thief*) as well as genuine, heartwarming novels (like Madeleine L'Engle's *Meet the Austins*)."

So, it's no surprise that when it comes to submissions, Ben is "most aware of voice and whether or not the author establishes that narrative voice in the first few pages. 'Voice' is one of those catch-all categories for me that includes tone, dialogue and some description of setting. The right voice is an immediate tip-off as to whether the author has fully realized a character and the right trajectory for the plot."

Ben has acquired some great books with strong voices. One of his favorites, and in his opinion the most unique, powerful novel he has worked with, is *The Keening* by A. LaFaye. Set in Maine during the Spanish Flu epidemic just after World War I, the protagonist as Ben put it, "sets out on a journey to safeguard her eccentric father and help her best friend realize his dream of seeing the big city. There's a fantasy element to the story, as well as a compelling, brave lead character, and I think the novel nicely explores the way family members rely on one another in times of tragedy."

Like *The Keening* and *Trudy*, Ben is looking for more solid character-driven stories and good writing. What he would love to find is something that combines those elements with the kinds of otherworldly stories that science fiction and fantasy traffic in, but so far the right story hasn't been presented to him.

BRIAN FARREY, FLUX

Brian Farrey's experience with his slush pile as acquisitions editor at Flux has been similar to Ben's. Although most of the work in the slush pile gets rejected, he does occasionally come across some real gems. One of those, now published as *A Blue So Dark,* concerns a young girl who inadvertently becomes the sole caretaker for her schizophrenic mother. Written by Holly Schindler, the manuscript "immediately captivated" Brian. It was just the kind of thing Brian is looking for: "the next great writer who can tell a terrific story." Uninterested in fads or trends, Brian wants things that are new and exciting, and recommends reading *A Blue So Dark, Gigged* or *Popular* to get a feel for his tastes.

These books would also help you get a feel for Flux where Brian works. The young adult imprint for Llewellyn Worldwide, Flux publishes edgy and provocative fiction for teens that cross all sorts of subgenres. You'll find Flux books that fall in the realistic drama, comedy, urban fantasy, science fiction, romance and literary realms. What you won't find is high fantasy. "Our fantasy needs to be grounded in the real world," says Brian, and high fantasy is one of the few categories that will earn your manuscript an "automatic reject." He is also not a fan of what he calls the "snarky teen girl voice" or books "where the emphasis is on snappy one liners and putdowns as opposed to character development and an intriguing plot. They certainly have an audience, but it's not something that gets me excited as an editor." Otherwise he likes it when a wide variety of teen voices, styles and genres cross his desk.

In fact, originality is exactly what Brian is looking for. "I want to see something I haven't seen before. I think the mistake many beginning writers make is looking at something like Harry Potter and saying, 'I can do that!' My immediate reaction is: 'Well, why? It's been done. Do something new.' ... I'm looking for the next great writer who can tell a terrific story."

Besides originality, Brian also wants a clear, strong voice. In fact, he's "a sucker for a strong voice. It's the first thing I notice and it often makes or breaks a submission for me." Although plot, character development and all key writing skills are important, Brian adds, "An intriguing plot won't cut it for me if the voice isn't there. Skillful use of language, impeccable pacing, strong plot ... they all play roles as well. But first and foremost, I need a strong voice." If you manage to nail a superb voice, then he looks at the characters. "I need to connect with them in some way, even if it's someone who is so unlike me in every way imaginable (*especially* if they're not like me)."

And strong voices and great characters can be found in all of the books Brian has worked on. He won't play favorites with his books, saying, "You're not allowed to ask editors about their favorite book they've acquired. We love all our children." However, he would tell me about one of the most successful books he's acquired, Karen Kincy's *Other*. A breakout book for Flux in 2010, Brian has now contracted two more books from her and is hard at work editing her second book in the series, *Bloodborn*.

Success stories like Karen Kincy remind us that when the right manuscript finds the right editor, magic (and sometimes multi-book deals) can happen. The only way to increase the chance that the right editor will see your work is to submit to an editor with the tastes and inclinations that are most likely to appreciate it. In order to do that, you have to get to know potential editors. And the best way to do that is by asking them questions at conferences, on their blogs, or when they are on official chats online.

Now, don't ask editors intrusive personal questions about their messy divorce or refer to their constant drug relapses by inquiring whether rehab is prettier in the fall or the spring. Besides being quite creepy, questions like that are unprofessional and won't get you what you want. Asking questions about an editor's publishing and reading preferences and finding out if they are looking for the kind of book you've written will take you a long way towards finding "your" editor.

MADELINE SMOOT is the publisher of Children's Brains are Yummy Books (CBAY Books), an independent press that focuses primarily on fantasy and science fiction books for children and teens (cbaybooks.com). Madeline also publishes the blog Buried in the Slush Pile, where she posts as the semi-anonymous Buried Editor. The blog was named one of the 101 Best Websites for Writers by *Writer's Digest* in 2008. To visit Buried in the Slush Pile, go to buriededitor.com.

M.T. ANDERSON

On experimentation in fiction.

....

by Lee Wind

M.T. Anderson is one heck of a writer. Whether it's science fiction (like the amazing *Feed*, a finalist for the National Book Award) or historical young adult fiction (like *The Astonishing Life of Octavian Nothing, Traitor To The Nation, Volume One: The Pox Party*, a Michael L. Printz Honor book and winner of the National Book Award) or even wacky middle grade fantasy adventure (like *Jasper Dash and the Flame-Pits of Delaware*) his voice and books are unique, compelling, hard to put down … and they stay with you long after you've read them.

He's written about vampires (*Thirsty*), romance and revenge in a fast food restaurant (*Burger Wuss*) and has even published three picture books! (Including a biography of the surrealist French composer Erik Satie of which the *Washington Post* said, "Anderson makes a music of his own with words.")

His website (mt-anderson.com) is remarkable, full of ancient documents, clippings, telegrams, photographs and eldeitch texts regarding the mysteries under Mount Noeumbega (backstory for his novel *The Suburb Beyond the Stars*) and the "guaranteed to be erroneous" Tourist's Guide To Deepest, Darkest Delaware—complete with computer error messages directly from His Terrible Majesty, the Awful and Adorable Autarch of Dagsboro! It even talks about his books.

He was also the fiction editor for *3rd bed*, a literary journal devoted to surreal and absurdist prose, and in that guise published experimental work in other similar literary journals (*Conjunctions, The Northwest Review*, etc.).

At the 2010 Society of Children's Book Writers and Illustrators Conference in Los Angeles, M.T. did a session on "Literary Experiment in Books for Children" that was beyond capacity—attendees were sitting on the floor, in the aisles, standing by the walls—packed into the room to hear what would be the most talked-about session of the conference. I was fortunate to be there, and am delighted to continue the conversation here.

In your presentation, you said, "To read is to learn to read." Can you explain what you meant by that?

Every story teaches you how to read it. Sometimes those lessons are easy ones. For example, in the first few pages, some book sends out all the typical signals and devices of a mystery novel: a body on the carpet, say, and a dining room full of astonished guests. So already, the novel is whispering to you about what to expect: a detective figure of some kind, a solution. But the other things it's slipping you, while you're concentrating on the story, are more subtle: first or third person? Is the language eccentric or banal, ornate or clichéd? If it's clichéd, are they the clichés of mystery writing from a particular period? And if it's eccentric, does that destabilize your sense of this being a straightforward tale with a clean solution at the end of it? After all, there's a body on the carpet and there are shocked guests in, say, Ann Patchett's *Bel Canto,* but it's not a mystery novel. And is the story told from the earliest events to the latest events, or does it shift back and forth in time? And if it shifts back and forth—as in Carolyn Coman's *Tell Me Everything* or Robert Cormier's *I Am the Cheese* or an Alison McGhee novel—what is the logic of those shifts in time? The book teaches you its rules.

Or think about one of my favorite experimental texts for kids, Jon Stone's *The Monster at the End of This Book.* Like many picture books, it has a definite structure. And like many picture books, it teaches you, the reader, how that structure works. In each spread, loveable, furry old Grover tells you *not* to turn the page, because otherwise, you nincompoop, you'll get to *the monster at the end of the book.* And each page, you do turn the page. And Grover gets more incensed. Part of the fun of the book for the child reader (and the adult!) is knowing just enough about that structure to take pleasure in the page turn—and in the shock of how things work out. In each of these examples, some obvious, some subtle, you as a reader are being asked to pick up on decisions the author makes and to make certain assumptions about where the story is going. And sometimes, with a slap, you're surprised!

Why is it easier to be experimental in literature for children?

Kids don't have preconceived notions of story shape yet. At age seven, eight and nine, they're starting to really learn a lot of the common options for telling stories—and corporate storytelling tends to teach them a very simple, straightforward structure. But they're still open to play. They love it. If they're used to being told bedtime stories, for example, they're used to bending the narrative, and becoming part of it, and incorporating things in the room, say, all of which are typical elements of literary experimentation.

In picture books especially, there can be experimentation of all kinds and it just seems joyful, playful, part of the fun of learning how stories can work. Somehow, when you're older and more set in your ways, it's harder for people to play around like that without it seeming pretentious to readers. Which is too bad … because there are so many wonderful books out there that exuberantly break all the rules we know.

EXPERIMENT IN YOUR WRITING

M.T. Anderson shares some typical terms for "experimental" elements that often appear in books for young people (and also books for older people!).

1. **Metafiction.** Any element that is about the story being a story. Like Jon Stone's *The Monster at the End of This Book*, David Weisner's *The Three Pigs*, and Aidan Chambers's *Breaktime*.

2. **Fabulism/Magic Realism.** Parts of a narrative that use the logic of myth, fable and dream. Like George MacDonald's *The Princess and the Goblins*, and his bizarre Symbolist novel for adults, *Phantastes*; Mordecai Gerstein's *The Old Country*; David Almond's *Skellig*; Kelly Link's *Pretty Monsters*, etc.

3. **Typographical Play and Intrusion.** Instead of taking the form of the book for granted, some books actually play with the typeface they're written in, using that to change the meaning of the words. For example, Lauren Child's *Clarice Bean* (and sequels), Lane Smith and Jon Scieszka's *True Story of the Three Little Pigs* (and others), Emily Gravett's *Wolves*, etc.

4. **Formalism.** Linguistic play that revolves around various kinds of repetitions, grammatical parallels, transformations of words, strange sentence structure, etc. Anything that clearly plays with the form of language. In fact, picture books routinely do this!

5. **Words as Sound Instead of Meaning.** Not just the bams, klonks, swishes and bings, but also other ways of making us hear words intensely as sound, regardless of what they mean. This often happens in Dr. Seuss's books, for example, as he repeats real words and made up ones together until it's hard to remember which are which. For those who love this kind of thing, check out Alastair Reid's *Ounce, Dice, Trice*, which was recently reissued.

6. **Nonsense/Whimsy.** The defiance of sense. Lewis Carroll and Edward Lear most famously, but also, for example, Daniel Pinkwater's young adult novel, *Young Adult Novel.* ("It is a Dada story.")

7. **Hypertext.** Any text that does not demand that you read it in a particular order, or that provides links or avenues for you to read it in an alternative order.

8. **Self-Contradiction.** As in Robert Cormier's chilling *I Am the Cheese*, for example—in which parallel narratives don't quite add up.

9. **Organic, Non-Plotted Structures.** Like William S. Burroughs's *Naked Lunch*. Or Dr. Seuss's *One Fish, Two Fish*, which turns from a counting book into a random, crazy menagerie.

You've spoken of how an artist's task is to show us the familiar in an unfamiliar (or fresh) way. How can we, as writers, best do that?

In a thousand different ways! That's one of the great things about being a writer. Some people use very weird, high-octane language that jolts us out of what we know. Some writers use very stripped-down, unexceptional language in each sentence, but they know just when to break our hearts, or make us gasp. Some writers take us to worlds that are completely unrecognizable, and force us to find a home there. Others stick with us at home, and focus on a few banal details so closely that we're forced to really open our eyes and see something we hadn't recognized about (for instance) how linoleum choices can break up a marriage. The great thing about literature is that there are a thousand ways to surprise us.

But I do think that the key to books that survive their own time is that element of defamiliarization. Books that play by all the rules of their genre and their time can be delicious at the moment, but tend to taste pretty stale a few years later. (For example, take a bite out of Oliver Optic's middle-grade novels from the turn of the last century. Hugely popular in their own time! And now, dry as dust, I'm afraid to say. Though I'll eat anything if it's deep-fried.)

Is the secret to having the world of your book be believable (whether it's sci-fi or fantasy or historical) the reverse of that—making the unfamiliar (be it the moon, your Delaware, or Revolutionary America) feel familiar to your readers?

Very well put. I think it does indeed go both ways.

What I've tried to do in many of my books is stick the reader someplace they think they know and estrange them from that place. So, yes, the Delaware in my Pals in Peril novels is a world of exotic fantasy adventure, rich in wizards, pterodactyls, ancient cities and spies. And yet, as you say, it's my hope that after a while, the place in my books becomes so real that kids driving along Delaware Route 1 will feel kind of disappointed they aren't attacked by ogres.

In a slightly more serious vein, in my Revolutionary War-era *Octavian Nothing* books, I try to bring forward details—real facts, real events—that might shed new and unexpected light on the era … but which also, after a time, produce their own strong sense of place. As I'm writing, I want to try to smell and hear Boston in the 18th century, the seagulls overhead and the haze of woodsmoke in the air. I want to walk those streets, and I'm hoping the reader will walk along with me.

Either way, I'm hoping we'll end the tour by seeing the familiar world anew.

(Incidentally, I have not yet heard back from Delaware regarding the state song I wrote them.)

Is being experimental and telling your stories in non-traditional ways something that you only get to do once you've already established yourself as an author? Or do you think writers working towards getting published can also successfully experiment?

Good question. Who knows? Many agents and some editors are clearly going to be frightened off by something that's not familiar. Especially in a world where profits are precarious and publishers seem thirsty primarily for bestsellers.

But someone, somewhere, is going to take a chance on something unusual. And that something—which none of us know about yet—will in fact be the thing that sticks out because it's different, and it will attract attention, and it will *become* the next big seller. And then all the rest of us will think, *Isn't that obvious? Why didn't I think of that?*

Given that you were the department chair of the M.F.A. in Writing for Children and Young Adults program at Vermont College, I wanted to ask you about your take on that old maxim, "You can't break the rules until you know the rules." True or false?

Generally true. Except for geniuses and idiot savants. Most of us, when we try to just write "what comes straight from the heart," without self-examination and knowledge of what's been done before, surprisingly arrive at something formulaic. I know that sounds counterintuitive, but I think it's true. We don't even realize how the thick, mulched layer of everything we've read and watched and know actually determines the way we think and dream. The novel liberated from self-examination is often not groundbreakingly original, but (sadly) extremely bland and conventional.

In my view, it's the job of the writing teacher to help each student find that part of themselves that is truly, urgently, desperately *them* … and that lies outside of the realm of convention.

With iPads and Kindles and Nooks and all the technological changes in how stories can now be delivered and enjoyed by readers, is this perhaps the best time ever to be an innovator in how we tell stories to children and teens?

Absolutely true! We have the blessing or the curse to be alive at the very moment of a media revolution as profound as Gutenberg's development of moveable type. Five hundred years of one format are coming to an end, and we're moving into a new world. You can either find this depressing, demoralizing and even irritating, or you can embrace these new possibilities and see that they will yield new forms of narrative, the like of which have hardly yet been known.

I choose the former path. It all makes me want to stay in bed with the covers over my head, eating Cap'n Crunch and reading Herodotus.

How funny! I cope by reading the Cap'n Crunch cereal box and eating heroes (or what we called "subs" back East.) From the Choose Your Own Adventure books of yesterday to the computer games of tomorrow, the experimental technique of hypertext seems to be ascendant in our multi-tasking-a-million-distractions-every-minute culture. What does all this interactivity and scattered attention mean for the future of long-form narratives that suck us in and tell us an amazing story?

Well, I'm not sure that the longer-form narrative will ever go away—though who knows what we'll be reading it on in a hundred years, or even in the next decade.

I do worry that consciousness and attention span will change. That can have a problematic effect culturally and politically. It's a complex world, and narratives need to be sustained sufficiently to represent that complexity.

But there are tremendous opportunities for new kinds of stories that involve us in new ways. Choose Your Own Adventure books are a great example of this. Video games will, I'm sure, develop their own "literary" models—the game as an art form. And you already have series like the 39 Clues, which tell a story over many books—but also draw in all kinds of online elements, too. For my Norumbegan Quartet (*The Game of Sunken*

Places, et al), I created a website that can be read as a kind of exploded book of short stories: little newspaper clippings about mysterious events in the Vermont mountains; ancient manuscripts describing a weird, elfin court; telegrams; old photographs; video clips; and so on. All these snippets revolve around the books but explore the place further and extend the mythology of the setting. They are interconnected, but they can be read in any order, and no set path through them is predetermined. I imagine we'll see much more of that kind of thing in the future—and that can be exciting! As a kid, who doesn't love charts of imaginary places and additional stuff that gives the reader special insight into something else they've read? All of that is a fun sideline for people right now, but it will undoubtedly evolve into its own serious literary form in the next few years.

I've listened to some great audio books of your novels, including the wonderful bonus track on the audio book version of *Jasper Dash and the Flame-Pits of Delaware*, where you sing the "State Song of Delaware." (Hysterical! And really, how rude that they haven't gotten back to you on that.) And yet listening to someone read a book to you is a very different experience than reading the text off a page—or, even, reading the text on an e-reader. Is a story somehow "purer" in the way it's first made real? Does it matter to you how your readers experience your stories?

Well, part of my revision process is to read a book out loud. (It's a useful exercise because it makes me very self-conscious about the parts that don't work.) So I don't have any problem with people encountering the books that way. In a way, I write them to be heard, even if just with the inner ear. And as for other formats … I recently had a kid write to me to tell me he'd just read an early vampire novel of mine on a black screen with blood-red letters.

Hey, whatever floats your gory boat.

LEE WIND's award-winning blog "I'm Here. I'm Queer. What the Hell Do I Read?" covers GLBTQ teen books, culture and politics, and has had over half a million visits from teen readers and their allies. He is the advisor for the Trevor Project's book club and visits middle and high schools to create Safe Space and lead Smashing Stereotypes workshops. His interviews and articles have been published online and in print, and he is a member of SCBWI Team Blog. A co-regional advisor for SCBWI Los Angeles, he is currently writing both a YA and MG novel. You can find out more at leewind.org.

MEG CABOT

On how to balance writing projects.

....

by Ricki Schultz

With more than 25 series under her belt—and counting!—Meg Cabot knows the secrets to publishing success. She claims she's not actually the first successfully cloned human, but her body of work suggests she's, at the very least, a cyborg: Cabot has written nearly 70 novels, ranging from middle grade to teen to adult fiction—including around 50 *New York Times* bestsellers.

With a *curriculum vitae* like that, it's hard to believe she had to climb the literary ladder just like the rest of us and overcome a fair amount of rejection with her first and perhaps most popular series, The Princess Diaries.

So, how does this incredi-writer get all that writing done? And how does she craft a bestseller? Although there is no surefire way to success, Cabot was gracious enough to share what works for her.

With so many series out there, your schedule has to be crazy. Do you work on multiple projects at once? And how do you compartmentalize?

I'm perhaps the best compartmentalizer on the planet, but none of what I do would be possible without the wonderful team of people with whom I work daily—and who do the really hard stuff—including my fantastic agent, my amazing assistants, my publicist and web team, everyone at HarperCollins and Scholastic, my husband, friends and family, all of whom support me all the way.

And I think the perception is a bit different than the reality. I really do work on only one book at a time.

Two series books came out in 2011—Abandon, a new young adult paranormal series that debuted from Scholastic in April; and Overbite, the next book in the Insatiable series (for adults), was released by HarperCollins in July. How long does it typically take you to write a novel?

I wish I were a two-page-a-day-every-day type of person, which is how I hear Ernest Hemingway used to work. But I can go for weeks at a time writing nothing at all but blog entries and Tweets. Then I'll go into a room and power through 300 pages in a few weeks. During that time, I will not go out or speak to anyone or wash my hair or do anything else at all but write. It is very dysfunctional and unpleasant.

Walk us through your writing process. Do your story ideas come first? Your characters? And where do you go from there?

I guess you could say I'm still discovering my writing process. In general it seems to be that I get an idea for a book (Who knows where ideas come from? Mine usually seem to come from out of nowhere), my agent will pitch it to my publisher, hopefully the publisher will say yes (I have learned not to write until they say they want it), and then usually things will happen that will prevent me from being able to work on that particular book, such as edits for other books that are due, or book tours for another book, or various other crises.

And then the date the book is due will come, and I will have no book (although I will still have the idea for the book, and probably some rough notes and maybe a few chapters).

Then I will inform my husband that I am going into what Eddie Murphy called in the movie *Beverly Hills Cop II* "deep, deep, *deep* undercover," and that he will not be seeing me for a while. In reality, he will be seeing me every day, and also doing all the cooking, cleaning and laundry for the next three weeks while I sit in a room of our house, ignoring the phone and freaking out while writing.

At the end of this period, I will emerge from deep undercover with very dirty hair and a book.

With so many books, how do you go about making each cast of characters fresh and unique? How do you keep them all straight?

My lovely assistant has created something called a "story bible" for each series (unless it's a standalone book), which contains all the pertinent data for each character—such as eye and hair color—in case I forget between books (this has been known to happen).

But usually once I get back into the book, it's pretty easy to remember, since the characters are like old friends, and we don't forget what our friends look like, or their backstories (while we might forget what color their eyes are).

You cover such a wide range of topics, from your characters' interests to your overall plots: Mia Thermopolis struggles with algebra; Emerson and Christopher

are really into computer games; Ellie Harrison has extensive knowledge of Arthurian legends, etc. You obviously need to know a great deal about each subject in order to include these details believably. That said, how do you go about your research?

Online research is great for stuff like locations, dates, etc., but I find it very limiting as far as the kind of data I usually need to go in depth on a subject (whether or not any actual physical evidence of King Arthur exists, for instance).

For that kind of thing, I find it much more helpful to read people's published dissertations, or to go straight to the source and interview the authors themselves (they are usually very happy to answer questions).

The best piece of writing advice I ever got was, "Shut up and listen." This was from the writer Joyce Hackett, who taught a writing workshop I took at NYU. Her advice was to go to a bar and just listen to other people talk, if we wanted to write believable dialogue. I did as she said, and my dialogue improved dramatically.

When I decided I wanted to write books for a younger audience, I started hanging out with the children of friends of mine—just listening to them to talk. I still follow Joyce's advice and listen to everything people are saying around me wherever I am.

As writers, our job is to find what's next and what's new, and I can guarantee that's something people are talking about somewhere face to face, not something that's being posted somewhere on the Internet. So it's important to put down our laptops and get out there and listen.

Do you ever have writer's block? (It doesn't seem like that is even in your vocabulary!) How do you push through it?

Ha, that is a funny question. I hope most writers have experienced writer's block at some time in their lives. I certainly have. Like everyone else, I try talking through whatever problem I am having with my project with my spouse, who gets very irritated and walks away. Then I watch TV. If that doesn't work, I talk about it with anyone else who will listen, generally my friends and neighbors and family members. So far that has worked. The day it doesn't will be the day you stop hearing about any new upcoming releases from me.

What would you say is a writing weakness of yours? How do you go about overcoming it?

I do not like writing descriptions of things or people. I don't like reading them either. I was very happy in the '80s, when the style was not to describe anything, except for maybe a key word or two (Robert B. Parker was the master of this. He could describe a perp with just a name and a piece of clothing and you knew exactly who this person was).

I think readers are intelligent enough to imagine how things or people look for themselves without the writer having to go on and on about it.

Now it seems like with everything you read, there are pages and pages of description, sometimes of a character's complete childhood and his entire backstory. I don't care. I always try to skip describing as much as possible in my stories, and I always get nailed about this by readers (and editors) who complain they want more description.

So now I overdescribe to compensate. It is an endless uphill road.

Anyone who has read any of your series knows you are a backstory dynamo—and you'd have to be! With The Princess Diaries in particular, there is a ton to weave in, and although most people picking up those books probably have read the previous installments, there is always the pressure to make each book a standalone, for any new readers. Any tips on how to make sure you're incorporating everything you need in order to make each book a standalone success?

Oh my goodness, thank you. I think when you're telling a story, you just need to concentrate on the few things the reader (and you) needs to know in order to understand the current narrative, in case he or she hasn't read any of the past books.

You definitely don't want to "info dump." If you watch romantic comedies, you'll see that there's often a character who gives an "info dump" somewhere in the first four minutes: "But Amanda, you haven't been on a date since you walked in on your ex doing it with that flight attendant! And since then, you've been living alone with your cat, trying to get along with your really mean boss who won't promote you!" That is an info dump. I try to avoid those by showing, not telling, this information, but it's sometimes impossible to avoid.

You have said you're more of a "pantser" than a "plotter." However, when writing a series, there has to be a fair amount of plotting involved—particularly, in a more succinct series (Airhead comes to mind because it's only three books). In another interview, you said that, when writing a series, you must "hold things

back." Can you talk a little more about this—how do you know what info to hold back, etc., and how do you find the right places to sprinkle it in?

Honestly, I don't know. I call it "driving with the low beams on." You are driving in the dark, and all you can see is what's right in front of you. You know you are going to get there. You have a map. You know the key places you need to get to.

The rest is just a mystery.

I start with a brief outline, which I give to the publisher, telling them what's going to happen over the entire three-book arc. By "brief," I mean one page.

How are the characters going to get to what happens by the third book? I have no idea. I have several vivid scenes pictured in my head. However, if I tell anyone what those scenes look like before I write them, or outline them in any way, even "collage" them as some authors suggest I do, it will put what I call "the curse" on the entire project, and I will lose my low beams on my car and never be able to write those scenes.

So I just keep driving in the dark. I know that's of no help, but it's the best way I can describe it. I have tried outlining, I have tried collaging, all that stuff. None of it works for me.

Being that you have written everything from middle grade to adult novels, what would you say are the biggest differences? What sets a middle grade novel apart from a young adult novel? A YA from an adult book? Are there specific things you incorporate—or keep out of—each? And how does your approach change?

Obviously books for middle graders (considered ages 8–12) are not going to contain sexual themes or even kissing, beyond a possible peck on the cheek. This would not be suitable in an elementary school library.

My YAs have been removed from middle school libraries just for mentioning the word "condom," and sometimes just the words "French kiss." There are some parents who believe that any mention at all of teens engaging in sexual behavior in a book, even safely, is wrong.

Obviously, explicit sex scenes are not going to go over well with either middle school or high school libraries. So, I save these for the adult books.

There are some battles that are worth fighting, and some that are not. Over the years, I have learned to pick my battles.

I try to write my books exactly the way I would tell them to a friend—keeping in mind that if she's a nine-year-old friend of mine, her parents might kill me later . . . but that she needs to know this stuff.

Even in your middle grade *Allie Finkle* series, you don't write "down" to the young readers. How do you balance using sophisticated words/concepts without losing your authentically YA voice?

If you think back to yourself at nine, you were not stupid. You understood a lot more than anyone gave you credit for. I remember being extremely bored by the books people kept giving me to read at the age of nine, preferring adult books because they were not as boring, plus they had violence and smut in them.

So, I just assume all nine-year-olds are the same way that I was, and I write accordingly (minus the violence and smut). Today's nine-year-olds probably understand even more than I did, and the same is true of today's 13-year-olds, etc.

Which has been your most challenging book (or series) to write? What made it challenging? On the flip side, which was your easiest? Why do you think that is?

The easiest book I ever wrote was a YA regency romance called *Nicola and the Viscount*. It also happens to be one of my favorite books I ever wrote. I wrote it in 10 days, with a horrible head cold, in bed, right after 9/11, about 10 blocks from Ground Zero. I think it was so easy and enjoyable to write because it was such a wonderful escape from everything that was happening right outside my window (my husband worked across the street from the World Trade Center, and all the windows of his office building were blown out that day. I was so happy he was alive).

I should also mention that's the only book I ever turned in that required no revising whatsoever.

The most challenging book I ever had to write was probably *Abandon*, the first book in my new paranormal series for teens. I think it was so challenging to write because it's such a departure from my past YAs, in that the heroine is so young but has experienced some extremely emotionally difficult issues—not just being swept down to the Underworld against her will—and will continue to experience many more during the course of the series. The first draft was very upbeat and funny, but I realized this wasn't appropriate, because it's a modern retelling of the myth of Persephone, a story about death with very dark sexual undertones, basically.

So I had to completely rewrite it, and now it's very, very dark and completely serious, which fits the story, but truthfully, I had a lot of nightmares writing it.

Now I'm stuck writing the sequel, which is going to be even darker, because it's called *Underworld*, and it's mostly set in the Underworld, a place no one wants to be. I don't know why I get myself into these situations.

What is one thing you wish you'd known when you were starting out writing?

That it was going to become such an obsession. With any other hobby, when it becomes such an obsession, they take it away from you. But because it's considered socially acceptable to be a writer, no one ever takes writers' pens away. But sometimes I think they should. I would probably start writing with a piece of bark or something, though, if they did.

ALLY CARTER

On creating likeable characters and hooking your readers early.

....

by Lee Wind

Ally Carter has a knack for giving us mere mortals inside access to elite worlds: world-class spies and covert operations, art thieves and billionaires, and teenage girls trying to save the day—while still getting the super-cute guy.

In her Gallagher Girls series (*I'd Tell You I Love You But Then I'd Have To Kill You, Cross My Heart and Hope to Spy, Don't Judge a Girl By Her Cover* and *Only the Good Spy Young*), we're along for the adventures with Cammie and her friends at the Gallagher Academy for Exceptional Young Women—a boarding school for teenage spies. In *Heist Society,* we're accomplices with Kat as she's forced to pull off the biggest heist ever to save her "family"—whose business is stealing priceless works of art. And with *Heist Society*'s follow-up, *Uncommon Criminals,* Ally's second YA series is well underway!

From the Gallagher Girls' repeatedly blowing their covers ... onto the *New York Times* Bestseller lists to *Heist Society* stealing the honor of being a 2010 YALSA Teens Top Ten Book, readers are clamoring for more.

In addition to action and romance, *I'd Tell You I Love You But Then I'd Have To Kill You* has some really funny moments. I laughed out loud a number of times, like on page 43, when Cammie is arguing with her mother: "But then I looked at the woman who had raised me and who, rumor had it, once sweet-talked a Russian dignitary into dressing in drag and carrying a beach ball full of liquid nitrogen under his shirt like a pregnant lady, and I knew I was sufficiently outgunned…" Do you see humor as springing from character or from the events of the story?

Well, I think making someone laugh out loud is one of the highest compliments in this business, so thank you very much for that. As to where humor comes from, I think that's the great mystery and one of the reasons "funny" is so hard to write. The one thing I do know for certain is that characters and plot are always interconnected. Always. If you take two different characters and present them with the same conflict, you will certainly get two different stories. For me, personally, I think humor comes largely from the intersection of character and conflict. You can have a funny character, but you don't really get the full benefit from that unless they're also facing a situation that challenges them in the most interesting way possible.

While your books are fun and very funny, there are also real emotions of grief and vulnerability for Cammie (in the Gallagher Girls books) and Kat (in *Heist Society*). There's a poignant moment in the latter (page 112) when you write, "Kat had often wondered what was more cruel: to so closely resemble a mother who had left too soon, making you equal parts daughter and ghost, or to have nothing of your parent in your features—to be, aesthetically speaking, more than one generation removed." How do you go about finding (and keeping) that "right" tone?

Again, it comes from character. I don't think anyone is ever funny or confident or adventurous 100 percent of the time. We all have down moments, or quiet times. We all get introspective. And to rob a character of those moments in a story feels like cheating somehow. So I think about the character and the challenges he or she is trying to overcome, and I give them opportunities to experience the full range of emotion.

Cammie and Kat are immensely likable. When creating a character, how do you balance between fantasy (making a character perfect: smart, gorgeous, brave) and relatability (allowing a character to feel insecure, or have acne or make mistakes...) to come up with someone readers will believe in, root for and love?

I think it is, first and foremost, about authenticity. I like to say that I don't make these things up—I just write them down. And that's as true as it can be when dealing with fictional people, events and worlds. It's part of my job to get to the core of the character—who she is, what she likes, what she fears and how she copes. If you don't show all of those things, you might drift into "Mary Sue" territory. However, if you make your characters as well-rounded and real as possible, I think you'll have someone that the reader will be far more likely to see as real and relatable.

[Editor's note: The Urban Dictionary defines "Mary Sue" as a female fanfiction character who is so perfect as to be annoying.]

Voice is that element that editors and agents are always looking for, and yet it seems to be elusive when those same people try to explain it. I've heard many

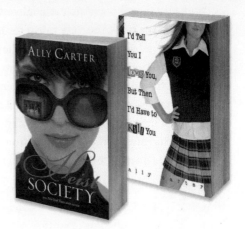

times at conferences, "I know it when I read it." Or, "I can fix plot, I can fix character, but I can't fix voice." You've really nailed voice in your novels—like this moment from your first YA novel (page 22):

"You okay?" she asked, because that's a best friend's job.

"Yes," I lied, because that's what spies do.

Do you have a working definition or equation to achieve *voice* that you can share with us?

> Voice is probably the most mysterious thing about this business, and I have never had any luck in decoding it. The only thing I've learned that might be useful is that point of view is crucial. It is perhaps the only voice-based decision that we, as writers, make. And it's a big one. Choose the wrong point of view and the story will always suffer from it. It's also one of the few ways I think we can force ourselves to change voices, even if just slightly. For example, my Gallagher Girls series is written in first person, but when I decided to start a second series I chose to write that in a loose third that's really more semi-omniscient because that was one way I could help myself to write Kat's story in a way that she wouldn't sound too much like Cammie.

Beginnings of novels are always crucial. You need a strong opening to hook your reader (and before that, an agent and editor). And while it can be tempting to start a story right in the middle of the action, if we don't know or care about any of the characters, we won't be nervous for them or care that they're in peril. You started off book four in your Gallagher Girls series, *Only the Good Spy Young*, with a sense of danger and a really strong voice—but when I went back and looked again, the "action" really starts at the end of chapter two. Can you share with us your advice for how to figure out where a story should start?

Someone (I'm afraid I can't remember who) once said of filmmaking that you should start a scene right after it gets interesting and end right before it gets boring. I think that's a good rule for everything. It's important to note that interesting doesn't necessarily mean "dodging bullets." The key, I believe, is to start when the character begins facing change and conflict is on the horizon. As a reader, I need to get a sense of who this person is and what makes them tick, but I'd rather learn that as we go. I'd rather *see* that than be told, in other words. And it's up to us, as writers, to imagine a scenario where that can be shown in the most interesting way possible.

REVISION ON THE PATH TO A BESTSELLER

Stories rarely leap fully formed onto the pages of that first draft. In fact, to quote Anne Lamott (from her brilliant book on writing, *Bird by Bird: Some Instructions on Writing and Life*), you've got to get out that "shitty first draft." Once you do, the writing mantra shifts to: "revise, revise, revise!" With two adult and six young adult novels published (and more on the way), *New York Times* best-selling author Ally Carter shares with us her top five revision tips:

1. Don't be afraid to make mistakes—even in revision. It's not like you just get two drafts to get it right.

2. If you can't pinpoint where the problem is, make a storyboard out of Post-its or a spreadsheet or scraps of paper spread across the living room floor—whatever you need to do to "see" the story all spread out in one place.

3. Some revisions are best done with a scalpel. Some you do with a chainsaw. Chances are your book will need both before it's through.

4. Change the margins and font of your manuscript to mimic those of a finished book. That will give yourself a different experience and help you see the novel with fresh eyes.

5. "Murdering your darlings" is easier when you don't delete them altogether. Open a "scraps" file that you can cut and paste those things into. That way, you have them if you decide you want to use them later. (Hint: You probably never will, but it still makes cutting them far easier.)

There's a bunch of sayings about endings and beginnings of books, and how they are interrelated. "The beginning is your ending, in disguise." "The beginning and ending should shake hands." "If you don't know how your book ends, you don't know what it's about." *Heist Society* ends with an emotional punch I didn't expect, that resonated long after I finished reading it. What's your take on the relationship between beginnings and endings?

My mother was a speech, English and creative writing teacher, and she always used to talk about the need to wrap up a story or a speech into a "nice little package." That's something I come back to time and time again. People frequently ask me if I outline my entire story before I begin. I don't. But I do usually know where the book is headed—I do know the end and I do think about that when I'm writing the beginning, because it's always a goal to pick up all the loose ends and tie them into a pretty bow. My mother wouldn't have it any other way.

Series books have a challenge that standalone titles don't—in every book, you need your main character to change, to grow, to learn something, to have some kind of internal arc in addition to the external arc of action that they go through. Keeping a character constantly changing and growing over multiple books would seem to create an enormous challenge. And yet, often writers who have a series idea in mind are told to write the first book so it can stand on its own. And then, if it's successful, the sequels may happen. You've written and are writing more books in two different YA series. Can you explain how you approach character arc in a macro (series) and micro (individual book) way?

I never think about the macro character arc. When I started *I'd Tell You I Love You But Then I'd Have to Kill You*, I didn't sit down and ponder where Cammie would be six books later. I knew she would be older and wiser and would probably have more scars—both literally and figuratively—but I didn't think about quirks or likes or dislikes or any number of things that people do for writing exercises and the like. Basically, I'm a firm believer that every book changes my characters. Even though I've been writing the same characters now for several years, they are different characters at the beginning and ending of each book. Maybe it's my process, but I don't know who those characters will be until the book has ended. I won't know exactly how those characters will react to the new challenges they will face until the next book begins. I can say that I have never thought that writing a series is easier because I "already know my characters." My characters are very different people book to book because the events of each book *do* change them. And that's the way I like it.

Can you tell us a bit about your writing process? I loved the rhythm you established in *I'd Tell You I Love You But Then I'd Have To Kill You*, where Cammie learns something in her Covert Operations class that she then puts to immediate use in tracking down Josh, the boy she has a crush on. Is that kind of structure something you saw by stepping back and looking at the outline of your story, or did it grow more organically as you wrote?

I absolutely hate my writing process. I really do. I usually do one very rough draft that isn't even a real draft. It's more like a book-length collection of thoughts and snippets of dialogue and questions to myself. Then I painstakingly go through that and do a real first draft. Then a second. Then probably a third and a fourth. It's very cumbersome and time-consuming and ugly, and with every book, I swear I'm going to change it, but I've never managed to break the pattern. Along the way, I utilize a very large whiteboard and some big Post-it notes, and I'll make a storyboard where every scene gets written on a Post-it and put on the board. Then, as I write, I can move the Post-its around like a puzzle until I figure the plot out. In television writing, they call that "breaking the story," and, for me, that's the hardest part of the process by far.

As for the parallels that Cammie faces in her academic and personal life, those definitely weren't by accident. It took several drafts, I'm sure, to get all the appropriate plot developments in all the right places, but I certainly had in mind from the beginning that it would be a story about a girl who was learning to be a girl and learning to be a spy at the same time. I knew it was important for those two endeavors to meet at the most interesting cross-sections possible.

Your world-building feels authentic and, at the same time, original. And yet, there's the real world of spies and the movies/books/television world of spies. The real world of thieves and the movies/books/television world of thieves. Often fiction on these themes can seem derivative of other fiction—resulting in a lot of stereotypes and clichés. I'm guessing you're too busy being an author to actually be a *real* world-class spy or art thief, so how do you go about doing your research and spinning it to make your novels convincing and still uniquely yours?

You're exactly right in that being a real spy or thief has very little correlation to what it's like to do those things in the movies. There is the real world and there is also the world of the genre. And, truth be told, I try very hard to walk the line between each. As for research, the International Spy Museum has been incredibly helpful. They have a great gift/book shop and a very knowledgeable staff that loads me up with reading material whenever I'm in D.C. There are also a number of great how-to guides for things like vehicular surveillance and losing a tail. There are also some great books and documentaries that cover famous art crimes and the detectives who work in that field. And, of course, there are movies and TV shows and novels. I think it's important to know the truth and to know the rules, so to speak, of the genre. And, most importantly, it's important for me to build my "world" in a way that allows me to be as true as possible to both.

How do you balance the expectations of others (readers, editors, agents) with doing your own creative thing? After your first published YA novel hit the *New York Times* Bestseller list, did writing change for you? Did it make it harder to write the next book?

I don't know that writing ever gets easier, in the way that many people hope. The challenges of story and plot and character never really go away—or haven't gone away for me yet. Experiencing a degree of success does lighten the load in some ways, though. I now get to write full time and have a little more leeway with deadlines and slightly more time and help overall. But I also have to tour more and attend more conferences, so I have more to do with that time. And, as you mentioned, there are more stakes overall—just more riding on me and on the books—and on the days when the writing isn't going well (which is most days, to tell you the truth), I long for the time when I was an unpublished writer—when it was just me and a story and a pen and I could work at my own pace and for my own satisfaction. Really, that is a blessing, and I hate to see so many people wishing those days away like I did.

In *Heist Society*, you play with point of view, starting a number of chapters off with a new minor character's background and inner thoughts that then leads us to their interaction with Kat on her journey to pull of her heist and save the lives of those she loves. Each time it's like a red herring, making us as readers think we're going one way when in fact you're taking us somewhere else! How do you figure out the best way to tell a scene?

I think part of why I hate my process is I never really know what will work until I try it. If that doesn't work, I try something else. And over and over and over again. It's ugly and messy and makes my life miserable much of the time, but at the end of the day, the reader doesn't see that. He or she only sees the finished product, so try things if you have to. Don't assume there's a formula or method. Or, if there is, please tell me what it is!

What's the most useful advice you've ever received as an author?

The best advice I've received is probably the simplest: Read as much as you can and write as much as you can. You learn to do this by doing.

BECCA FITZPATRICK

On her writing journey.

....

by Frankie Mallis

Becca Fitzpatrick's debut young adult novel, *Hush, Hush,* (Simon and Schuster) was an instant *New York Times* bestseller when it released in 2009. The highly anticipated sequel, *Crescendo,* was also a huge success upon its release a year later. The care and creativity Fitzpatrick put into her romantic leads Patch and Nora have inspired tons of fan websites and a very devoted following. Now fans all across the globe are counting down the days until the trilogy is complete with the release of *Silence.*

But despite the overnight success *Hush, Hush* seemed to gain, the first novel in this trilogy took Fitzpatrick five years to write. The story of *Hush, Hush* actually began when Fitzpatrick's husband surprised her on her birthday with a creative writing class. From there, Fitzpatrick felt the encouragement she needed to finally pursue her lifelong dream of becoming a writer and to seek out an agent.

Fitzpatrick always had a deep love for mysteries, particularly Nancy Drew. And before becoming a writer, she knew she wanted to live a dangerous and sexy life. For a while, that meant becoming a spy. Now she gets to write dangerous and sexy stories. Here, Fitzpatrick talks about her road to publication, the evolution of her characters, herself and her writing style, and the best advice she ever received. For more information on Becca Fitzpatrick, visit beccafitzpatrick.com.

Hush, Hush was definitely a breakout novel, with lots of buzz leading up to its publication and debut on the *New York Times* Bestseller list. Did you have any idea when you were writing what a success it would become?

No, not at all. The first scene I wrote for *Hush, Hush* was for a writing class: a simple craft assignment to show humiliation. I still remember the first time my teacher said, "You've got something special here. Don't give up." With his encouragement, I joined a critique group and continued to write *Hush, Hush* after the class ended. It was about that time that I decided to take the next step. I sent my first query letter to an agent in 2003 and, over the next five years, accumulated just shy of 100 rejection letters. I believed it would take a miracle to get the book published. Ironically, the night before *Hush, Hush* sold, I ran into a friend while taking my son to soccer practice. I told her if I could *just* find a publisher, I'd give them the book for free.

With two successful novels in the series, *Hush, Hush* and *Crescendo*, and the third book *Silence* on the way, how has your life changed?

I'm a lot busier! That's probably the most pronounced change. I'm now a stay-at-home mom *and* a full-time writer. I've mastered the art of folding laundry while drafting scenes in my head. There are intangible changes, too, including the belief that I'm capable of more than maybe I give myself credit for. I'm more confident in my ability to tell better and more honest stories. I'm starting to understand why setting goals and achieving them is such a crucial part of learning.

What part about becoming not only a published author, but a best-selling author most surprised you?

I've always tried to make myself accessible to readers, especially online, but I don't think I was prepared for the flood (in a good way!) of e-mails and letters. As a teen, I'm quite positive I never e-mailed any of my favorite authors. Granted, most of them were dead, but the point is, it never would have occurred to me to search out the authors of my favorite novels, except in the card catalog. I think the Internet has played a huge role in the interaction between authors and readers, which is why it's vital that authors have a website. Social networking also gives readers a way to reach out to me, and for authors who are comfortable with the idea of creating an online presence, sites like Facebook and Twitter can be both useful and fun.

Can you describe your writing process and how it's evolved from when you began writing to what it looks like now?

I began writing *Hush, Hush* in 2003 after my husband surprised me by enrolling me in a writing class for my birthday. I'll be the first to admit I had no idea what I was doing. My strategy looked something like this: Take experiences from my own high school years, change a few names and details, and slap them down on paper. I didn't worry about plot and I was fond of melodrama. Over the years, I realized the only way I was ever going to make *Hush, Hush* come together (and hopefully publishable) was by outlining first. Now before I even think about writing a novel, I pull out a stack of index cards and scribble down key plot points.

You spent more than five years writing Patch and Nora before *Hush, Hush* sold. Can you describe how their characters and relationship evolved as you continued to write and revise?

When I go back and read some of the earliest drafts of *Hush, Hush,* it's very clear to me that Patch has changed very little. Yes, he's a bit softer now, but that was a change my editor and I worked on together after the book sold. Patch's character was inspired by a guy I once knew, so I didn't experience that getting-to-know you stage that I did with some of the other characters. Case in point: Nora Grey. Originally, Nora's character was named Ellie Fairchild and she was every bit as arrogant and cunning as Patch. The two constantly fought and undermined each other, and I came to accept that in order to make the story work, Patch needed an opposite. Someone a little less worldly and little more sensitive. It took years to get to know Nora Grey, and feel comfortable sharing her side of the story.

Talk about the research that went into the creation of your angel mythology.

I always feel a little like I'm cheating when I give this answer, but I grew up attending Sunday School every week and hearing stories from the Bible. When I started writing *Hush, Hush*, it never occurred to me to do serious research into angel mythology. I felt like I had a pretty good grasp of the angels that would be in my stories. Rather than making them like angels from the Bible, however, I wanted to make them more human. I wanted them capable of making the same mistakes we make. I wanted them to face the same challenges we face.

What do you think is your greatest strength as a writer? And how have you cultivated that strength?

I think it's hard for me to see my writing objectively, but if my biggest strength is also my first love, then writing dialogue wins, hands down. I've always been an introvert and a people-watcher, standing quietly on the outside, sponging up facial cues, gestures and dialogue. I find eavesdropping invaluable research and much of it goes directly into my stories. Before I send the finished draft of a book to my editor, I stand in front of the mirror and read aloud the exchanges between my characters. I want their voices to snap off the pages.

Which part of the writing process do you find the most challenging? And how do you go about conquering it?

Oddly enough, it changes from book to book. *Hush, Hush* was, in essence, "crashed" into my publisher's schedule, which means editing had to be done in a fraction of the

normal time. I also had to face the challenge of learning how to handle criticism, a big hurdle for all debut authors, I think. With *Crescendo*, the biggest challenge was tackling a massive rewrite. The story that's published today, and the story I originally turned in to my editor, bear no resemblance. With *Silence*, the third book in the series, the biggest challenge has been making sure that I exceed readers' expectations. Not the easiest of feats, but I'm determined to do it!

On a day-to-day basis, discouragement is a constant challenge. Is my story not coming together? Did I just read an e-mail from an unhappy reader? Has it been a busy week and I haven't had time to write? I attack all of these problems differently, but I think one of the key ingredients to every solution is surrounding myself with encouraging friends. I feel so very fortunate to have such a wonderful support system in my friends and family. They remind me that in the big scheme of things, one bad day won't ruin everything.

When you began writing *Hush, Hush*, did you only plan to write one book? Or did you envision a series from the start?

I always dreamed of seeing *Hush, Hush* published, but for a long time it was just that— a dream. After years of rejection, I accepted the fact that publication probably wasn't going to happen. Still, I was determined not to put the book aside until I'd made it the best I could. My vision was narrowed to those three hundred and some odd pages, and I never looked beyond. Imagine my surprise when my agent called with the news that not only had several publishers made offers on *Hush, Hush*, but they all wanted a sequel as well!

You always create playlists to accompany your stories. Can you talk about what role music plays in your creative process?

With two small boys at home, you would think I'd find it relatively easy to write surrounded by noise, but the truth is the exact opposite. I need near silence when I write. It's probably a product of circumstance—I write mostly at night, after everyone has gone to sleep. But I do plot to music. Most of the plotting for *Hush, Hush* came early in the morning, when I was out running, iPod blaring, and I began crafting specific scenes to songs.

You've been very protective of your movie option rights. How important is it for you to see *Hush, Hush* as a movie? What concerns do have you about the translation from book to screen?

Before I sold *Hush, Hush*, I loved reading the Kinsey Millhone mysteries by Sue Grafton, and I remember hearing Ms. Grafton say she refused to sell the film rights because she didn't want a movie to destroy readers' image of Kinsey. I don't think I could say it any better than that. I'm in the business of writing books, not making movies. Of course, I can see the allure in watching your favorite fictional characters onscreen. I've often wished someone would make a movie based on Diana Gabaldon's Outlander series.

Can you describe the moment you knew in your gut you wanted to be a writer?

When I was eight years old, I watched *Romancing the Stone* for the first time and promptly announced to my mom that I would grow up to be a romance writer. Granted, I thought all romance writers hunted for treasure in Colombia and fell in love with a sexy, mysterious stranger who wore crocodile boots.

What was the best piece of writing advice you ever got?

It's easy to tear something down; it's much more difficult to create. Likewise, the most difficult things in life are always the most rewarding.

What can we expect to see after Patch and Nora's story wraps up? Do you have plans for other series? Or switching to other genres?

I've started writing a contemporary young adult novel, which I would consider a big genre switch. So far there are no supernatural elements, but the temptation to go in that direction is definitely there ...

Keep a journal and write in it daily—you never know when your own life experiences will inspire a story.

FRANKIE MALLIS is a young adult writer who blogs frequently at Frankie Writes (frankiediane.blogspot.com) and with The First Novels Club (firstnovelsclub. com), where she mostly enjoys writing parodies of *The Vampire Diaries*. When not blogging or tweeting (@frankiediane) she teaches college-level writing, belly dances and eats lots of vegan food. She is represented by Laura Rennert of the Andrea Brown Literary Agency.

MAGGIE STIEFVATER

On the importance of creativity.

....

by Frankie Mallis

Maggie Stiefvater's first young adult novel, *Lament,* was published by Flux in October 2008. But in August 2009, with the release of *Shiver* (Scholastic), Stiefvater became one of the leading ladies in young adult literature. *Shiver* spent months on the *New York Times* bestseller list, and its sequel, *Linger,* debuted at #1. Now everyone is anticipating the release of *Forever,* the final book in her *Wolves of Mercy Falls* trilogy, as well as another standalone fantasy novel from Scholastic.

Stiefvater made a living as a musician and artist before becoming a full time novelist and has been able to incorporate those talents into her current works. Stiefvater not only writes beautiful, lyrical novels, but she also composes music to accompany them, often creating her own animated book trailers that feature her original art and music. Stiefvater plays the Celtic harp, piano and bagpipes, and these musical elements often find their way into her tales.

With four novels published and four more on the way—plus an anthology with her critique group, the Merry Sisters of Fate—Stiefvater keeps busy. Here, she talks about her writing evolution, the crazy ways her life has changed since publication, including the time she was a clue on *Jeopardy,* as well as her advice to aspiring writers. For more information on Stiefvater, check out her website at maggiestiefvater.com.

Shiver was your breakout novel, though it was your second release. Did you have any idea when you were writing *Shiver* what a success it would become? What were your expectations for publication?

I was, in fact, not even expecting to be published. Even back when I first finished writing *Shiver*, I thought the marketplace looked a bit saturated with werewolves and vampires, and my gut feeling was that *Shiver* didn't even sit comfortably among what was already out there. It was this strange sort of literary, sort of fantasy novel with broken German poetry and many, many incomplete sentences. My worst fear was that it wouldn't sell. My best hope was that I would sell it for more than my first novel, which sold for enough to buy a mattress.

Since *Shiver* became a *New York Times* bestseller and *Linger* debuted at #1, how has your life changed?

I used to tell people that my life hadn't really changed at all, because for a long time, it was true. Novels didn't care if you were a bestseller—they still took just as much work to write. Kids didn't care if you were a bestseller—they still want to sell girl scout cookies to unsuspecting strangers. Most people still didn't know my name. Life continued apace. But somewhere along the way, things began to snowball, and now, things are quite different. Some things are positive: Out of the 4,000 e-mails I receive every month, some are absolutely amazing and touching reader mail. Some are negative: Everything I type online on my blog seems to carry a strange significance. (At one point I commented on Twitter about a movie still of *Breaking Dawn*. It got transmitted to major Twilight sites: "Maggie Stiefvater weighs in on *Breaking Dawn*!") Some are just unpredictable: The series just appeared as a clue on "Jeopardy," and I've discovered very quickly just how many people I know who watch "Jeopardy." The nicest part, creatively, is the freedom to write just about anything I'd like to and being fairly certain my publisher will print it.

What part about becoming not only a published author, but a best-selling author, most surprised you?

How you cease to be a person and start to be a commodity in the eyes of the readers. Like you might introduce yourself as a Lady Gaga fan to someone to tell them something about yourself. My books and I somehow move from creative project and actual human to an abstract object that defines someone else on their Facebook "likes."

Can you describe your writing process and how it's evolved from when you began writing to what it looks like now?

It's changed very little. I know what I need more than I used to, so I've abandoned some of the steps I used to toy with—like the two-page synopsis I used to write and then completely ignore. Now I know that I need an idea, a setting, a mood, and character arcs. Then I brainstorm until I have an ending and then a beginning, and finally, a half dozen "core scenes" that get me from A to B. It's a messy sort of process that requires

taking some wrong turns and being absolutely ruthless with rewriting. I edit as I go. I generally end up with a pretty complete draft.

How have Grace and Sam and their relationship evolved as you continued to write and revise?

It was a challenge to go from writing about falling in love, which is quite simple, to writing about being in love, which is complicated. It's the difference between snogging and dirty socks in the middle of the floor—I wanted to try to show how there's still romance after that first blush. I also very much wanted to show this couple getting stronger both individually and as a couple, and how their strength changed when they were apart or together. There's more to this, but since *Forever*'s not out yet, I can't tell you.

Can you describe the research that went into the creation of your werewolf science and mythology?

I did a lot of reading on brains. Also, of course, on meningitis and leptospirosis and other fevers that go bump in the night. Epi-pens and malaria and drug abuse, too. The agonizing thing about this research is that so little of it makes it into the novel; you just see the tip of the iceberg. But of course you don't want the reader to feel educated, you want them to feel persuaded and entertained. Also all of the science is seen through the eyes of teens with little training and even less scientific instrumentation, so you can only get so involved.

What do you think is your greatest strength as a writer? And how have you cultivated that strength?

Hmmm . . . maybe characterization. For me, every scene is about making at least one character change at least a little by the end; I'm much more interested in how events have changed someone rather than changing the world. For instance, *Shiver* could've been about how the world reacted to werewolves in their midst. But I was much more interested at an intimate person-by-person level. As far as cultivating it, I take lots of mental notes when I read a book that does character really well. I also do the same when I watch movies—a great movie establishes a character in two seconds flat, and that's something to be aware is possible.

Which part of the writing process do you find the most challenging? And how do you go about conquering it?

Pacing is always my bogey man, I guess, if I have to choose one. Like all writing challenges, I think the best defense is merely to be aware of it, especially while revising. I have complicated lever and pulley and chart systems I use during complicated revisions.

When you began writing *Shiver,* did you only plan to write one book? Or did you envision a series from the start?

When I first began *Shiver*, yes, it was just one book. It stayed that way for quite a long time until I realized I was just as interested in what happened after "happily ever after."

What inspired you to include Isabel and Cole as narrators in *Linger*?

One of the things I love as a reader is seeing my beloved characters from another character's point of view. You know the scenes in movies where the two side characters comment on the hero's antics or quiz the heroine about the hero's personal life and you shudder with happiness because you get to see the hero from outside himself? Well, maybe it's only me who shudders with happiness. I love looking at a box from all angles. I also love opposites, and Isabel and Cole were originally intended to showcase traits of Sam and Grace's relationship by being polar opposites. Of course, that evolved a little ...

You always create playlists to accompany your stories and you're talented enough to create original songs for them as well. Can you talk about what role music plays in your creative process?

I must have it. I find it impossible to focus without music playing (it's playing right now), and while I'm writing, I concoct dedicated playlists for the mood I want the novel to be in. I play them while writing and while brainstorming and no other time so that when I have to take a break—to go on tour, for example—when I come back, I can put that music on and I'm right back in the moment. As to the compositional aspect, it's just another side of the creative box. Just another way to describe the story.

One of your goals was to create a screenplay, which is pretty different from a novel. What other artistic aspirations do you have and hope to achieve?

The biggest one I have right now is to write a graphic/illustrated novel for teens.

Growing up, which writers did you most admire and want to be like? And which writers do you most admire now?

I very much admired Susan Cooper, Lloyd Alexander and Diana Wynne Jones. I loved the long running British fantasy series. When I was in college, my favorite history professor told me my prose was like a dead Englishman's, and those books are probably why. Nowadays, I still admire them hugely, but I'm also a tremendous fan of Leif Enger and Audrey Niffeneggar.

Can you describe the moment when you knew you wanted to be a writer?

I can't. Because I can't remember ever not writing. I can describe the moment I knew in my gut that I was not going to be a history professor, however. Do you want that one? Ah. I thought not.

What was the best piece of writing advice you ever got?

Write what you wish was already on the shelf.

Your readers have really come to love your mix of fantasy and romance. Have you ever considered writing in another genre outside of fantasy?

Not really. Sometimes I think of writing something dystopic, which is not really fantasy, but what can I say. I like me a little magic.

What advice would you give to an aspiring author?

That same advice I was given: Write what you wish was on the shelf. And I'd add: Write it the way only you could.

CHERYL KLEIN

Giving writers the gift of a second sight.

....

by Donna Gambale

Cheryl Klein, senior editor at Arthur A. Levine Books, is best known for being the continuity editor of the last three Harry Potter books and Scholastic's resident "Potterologist." During her decade-plus in publishing, though, she's worked on numerous acclaimed children's books, such as *Marcelo in the Real World* by Francisco X. Stork (2009), *The Snow Day* by Komako Sakai (2009), and *Millicent Min, Girl Genius* by Lisa Yee (2003).

Her keen editorial eye has made her a popular conference speaker, and in 2005, she began posting those talks on her website. Around that time, she also began regularly updating her blog, Brooklyn Arden, with commentary on writing, publishing, her books and the editorial process.

In response to reader requests, Klein compiled the talks—as well as various blog posts and practical-application worksheets—into a book called *Second Sight*, which she self-published in March 2011. In *Second Sight*, she shares her insights on a number of writerly topics, offering writers tools to develop their craft and bring their work to the next level through analysis and revision.

Here, Klein discusses key elements from *Second Sight*, her lifelong passion for children's literature and more. For more on Cheryl Klein, visit her website at cherylklein.com and her blog at chavelaque.blogspot.com.

In *Second Sight*, you state that your goal is to teach writers "to help evaluate and revise their manuscripts and develop their craft as a whole" via the methods and principles you use as an editor. How did your "second sight" develop through-out your years as an editor?

> Whatever insight I have into the writing process, I developed through a combination of theoretical learning, practical experience and lots of thinking about both of those things. That is: I like reading books on writing and what other editors and writers have to say about writing (not to mention reading real books myself); I've worked on more than 50 books, each one of which presented its own challenges and joys; and I've spent a lot of time considering "How did that book *do* that?" or "Why didn't that work for me?" or "I know I want to make this edit, but why? What is it exactly that feels wrong here? And what's the best way to communicate that?"

You encourage writers to reread their manuscript not only on screen, but also on paper. Why are both techniques important?

> This is something I've found in my own writing, that words feel very different on a screen, where they're ephemeral and disappear in a keystroke, versus paper, where they're tangible and have actual weight. It's easier to see copyediting mistakes on pa-per; it's easier to feel the pacing—to realize, "Good grief, I've turned over 135 pages here and I still haven't reached that first turning point! Maybe I need to cut." And it's easier to find redundancies, as the previous bit of conversation hasn't slipped completely out of physical view as it does on a screen.

> Also, most writers and editors working now grew up reading books on paper, so paper = a book for us, and that solidity lends added weight to the revision process. It will be interesting to see how this aspect of readers' and writers' experiences changes with e-books.

What's one skill you'd like to improve upon as an editor?

> Brevity.

In your book, you say a character can be broken down into two parts: "essence qualities" and "action qualities." What does that mean, and how do the two work together to create a memorable character?

> A character can be defined the same way a spoon can: by what he is (essence) and by what he does (action). A spoon is, according to *Webster's*, "an eating or cooking im-plement consisting of a small shallow bowl with a relatively long handle." But it is just a small, shallow bowl with a handle until it is used. The thing that makes it more than a small shallow bowl with a handle—its very spoonness—consists of its utility in stirring, measuring and eating.

> And it's the same way with a character in fiction. She can have all these charming quirks, all the personality and kindness in the world—a truly wonderful essence—but they don't matter until she begins to do something within the novel—her actions. Yet

at the same time, if she didn't have that personality and those quirks, there would be nothing to distinguish her from a robot or an animal, or any other creature capable of carrying out the function she serves in the story. What makes a character come alive on the page is the unity of essence and action.

You acknowledge that multiple revisions may be necessary, but you discourage writers from aiming for "perfect" because, ultimately, it's a waste of time in light of future revision suggestions from a critique partner, agent or editor. How does a writer know when it's time to move forward?

When you have done the best you can in (1) articulating your themes, (2) making your plot work, and (3) developing your characters, let it go. I know some people might be saying now, "But my best would be *perfect*"—I know, because I have that thought all the time myself! But until other people read the manuscript, you're stuck in the echo chamber of your head; and it's *really* necessary to get out of there eventually when you're working on a piece of writing, because writing is meant to communicate, and if you're not letting it do so, it doesn't work as writing.

Failing that, I'd say you should move forward within one year after you've completed a first draft. If you're not getting feedback on it (from other writers, at least) within that year, you're letting your fear of other people's opinions get in the way of your actually making a book, and you need to move past that if you truly want to be published.

After more than a decade of working at Scholastic, what keeps you passionate about the process of editing children's books?

I work with fascinating authors who ask and answer important questions in their fiction, about how we form our identities, how we relate to other people both one on one and in community, what are the most important things in life—and yes, they do this even in picture books! These authors (and my coworkers) are also kind, smart and interesting people, which makes collaborating with them lots of fun. And I like the actual work of editorial work, which (if I can say this without sounding too pretentious) feels something like *tikkun olam* to me: helping the world become more whole by helping one little piece of it to function better—in this case, a story.

Second Sight offers varied and practical examination techniques for revision, including charts, questionnaires, tables and maps. What would you say to a writer who is intending to revise solely via instinct?

I think that is perfectly fair. Some writers have a really good sense of what their book needs and just require a little time away from it or feedback from another reader to refocus their vision and what they need to do to achieve it. Others need help figuring out those larger-picture questions of who is the protagonist, how does she change, and

what events bring about that change in her—and that's what the charts and so forth are designed to help writers articulate.

It's no secret that the industry is publishing fewer picture books than in previous years, but *Second Sight* includes a section on creating a satisfying picture book manuscript. What makes a picture book stand out from the crowd in today's market?

The perfect marriage of a smart, fresh concept (ideally rooted in a child's emotions) and beautiful execution.

You say that "voice is the foundation on which your whole novel is built," and in your book, you go into great depth on how to build this foundation. What are your top three keys for an excellent narrative voice?

While I was working on the voice essay in the book, I came across a terrific quote from Evelyn Waugh, who said the three elements necessary to a writer's style were "lucidity, elegance and individuality." And I agree with him absolutely: the ability to say something clearly, with efficiency and beauty, and in a way that nobody else would say it.

In *Second Sight*, you provide a brief exercise for authors to write out their vision/aims for a book to help focus their editing. Why do authors commonly lose sight of their original goals in the drafting process?

Authors build realities from the ground up, and there are a lot of details to take care of in making a reality: what a room looks like, how characters move through it, whether what those characters say or do in the scene set in the room is consistent with what they said or did in the previous scene (or, if it's inconsistent, is that inconsistency deliberate and what effect are you going for there), how what they say or do advances the plot ... And all of that is very hard to keep track of, never mind how it all serves the grand vision and aims of the book! So once you have a first draft completed, it's good to reconnect with those goals and aims before diving into a revision.

In the section on the author-editor relationship, you mention that part of the editor's job is to tailor his or her advice to what each specific author and manuscript needs. What can authors do to help facilitate the editorial process?

Be honest about your needs, while also respecting the editor's time, style and workload. If you know that you receive feedback and develop new ideas best in conversation, ask if your editor would be willing to have a long phone chat with you rather than sending you an editorial letter. If you're working on a draft and you feel like you need a sounding board for a number of points, collect all these points in an e-mail and ask if you might set up a time to discuss them with the editor. In my experience, if you give us a little time to respond, we're often pleased to be consulted and useful! Finally, always turn in the very best draft you can, having solved all the problems and made all creative decisions to the very best of your ability. This will vary from situation to situation, of course, but if you talk to your editor beforehand, I think it's usually safe to say we'd rather have a *late* draft you feel good about, than an on-time draft that isn't your best work.

In order for an author to answer the basic question, "What is your book about?" you emphasize that they need to know the book's thematic and emotional points. Can you describe the difference between the two?

An emotional point is what you want your reader to feel as a result of the book, what kind of emotional experience you want him to have by the end. Terrified? Exhausted? Exhilarated? Do you want him to have learned something? Thought about something? Or just to have had a good time? A thematic point is what you want your reader to think about as a result of the book, what subject is at the heart of your work, what kind of questions you want your story to inspire or answer. The writer David Lodge said, "A novel is a long answer to the question, 'What is it about?' "—so, *what is your novel about?* That's the thematic point.

As examples, I would say the emotional point of *Pride and Prejudice* is to make readers laugh at human folly and sigh over the romance and the characters' self-improvement, while the thematic point is about how our own vanities—our prides and prejudices—can keep us from seeing or acting rightly. Meanwhile, the emotional point of Captain Underpants, I would conjecture, is to make readers roll on the floor laughing at the hilarity and cleverness of the antics, while the thematic point is that kids can be smarter than grown-ups! (Which is always a popular thematic point in children's literature.)

It is perhaps a bit dangerous to define these too completely or certainly, especially in the early stages of the writing: An overly articulated thematic point can become a hit-you-over-the-head moral message, and the emotions in a book should encompass the full range of human feeling, not just those of the emotional point. (We readers sigh more over Elizabeth and Darcy's ultimate happiness at the end because we felt so afraid it wouldn't happen earlier.) But setting out general goals or directions for each of these points is enormously helpful in revision, because they give you a benchmark by which to judge the success of the novel and what elements are or aren't contributing to it.

One of the most enlightening parts of *Second Sight* is the inclusion of editorial notes from you and Arthur Levine on multiple drafts of the first chapter of Lisa Yee's *So Totally Emily Ebers*. Why did you choose that opening scene to show the progression of revision?

At the time I wrote that talk (the fall of 2006), we had just finished editing *Emily Ebers*, so its editorial process was fresh in my mind. Moreover, that scene is a nice example of an opening evolving as the book did: As Lisa developed the characters and their relationships in more depth, she also developed new ways of showing those relationships in the way Emily wrote to her father—what she'd include, what she'd leave out—so it was fascinating to see how each of those drafts changed. And it raised interesting reader-relationship points as well, in that some of the details in early drafts felt as if they came too early in the reader's relationship with Emily for them to be productively included ... The same way you might be really confused if a perfect stranger came up to you at a party and started talking about a bunch of people you didn't know, we readers didn't know Emily well enough during these first pages to care about her crazy first-grade teacher, though Emily talked about him with such comfort in the early drafts, she obviously expected us readers to do so! So the edits on that chapter provided a great example of both authorial and editorial minds at work.

It's easy for subplots to overrun a book. How does a writer know which to keep and which can be cut?

Think through all the plots and relationships in the novel and what each one is doing for your main character—what each one teaches her, how they force her to change and grow. Do any of the functions those plots/relationships serve duplicate each other—e.g., the subplot with the main character's best friend teaches her to look beyond surfaces, and so does the subplot with her social studies teacher? Maybe you don't need both of those subplots if so. And does each subplot contribute to the central plots in some way, either by bringing an additional complication or element to the action plot, or by giving the character something she needs for the emotional plot? If it doesn't, can you make that subplot contribute in that way? And if you can't—again, maybe that's one that should go, if it can't be woven smoothly into the rest of the novel.

How long should an author wait before tackling revision?

An author should take as much time off from the project as she can while still maintaining her interest in and momentum for it. That way, when she does go back to revise the manuscript, the author will be looking at it with fresh eyes, which is just how a beta reader, agent or editor will read it for the first time.

What are your top five revision resources (books or websites) that you recommend to writers?

Besides *Second Sight*, I recommend: Orson Scott Card's *Character and Viewpoint*—probably the most useful book on writing fiction that I've ever read. For picture book writers, Uri Shulevitz's *Writing with Pictures*, which is just genius. Anita Nolan's article "The End Is Only the Beginning" (available at anitanolan.com/theend.html) for people who think structurally, or need help thinking structurally. Darcy Pattinson's website, which has a lot of interesting advice and revision techniques (darcypattinson.com). *The Artful Edit* by Susan Bell, a beautifully written book that uses examples from the editing process for *The Great Gatsby*.

DONNA GAMBALE works an office job by day, writes young adult novels by night, and travels when possible. She is a contributing editor for the Guide to Literary Agents Blog and freelances as a copyeditor and proofreader of both fiction and nonfiction. She is the author of a mini-kit, *Magnetic Kama Sutra* (Running Press, 2009). You can find her online at firstnovelsclub.com, where she and her critique group blog about writing, reading, networking and the rest of life.

WENDY TOLIVER

On creating authentic teen character and voice.

....

by Ricki Schultz

Although Utah native Wendy Toliver wrote chick lit when she started writing novels, her editors suggested her "fun, young voice" might better fit the young adult genre. Three teen novels later, it's hard to imagine Toliver writing anything else.

Her latest book, *Lifted*, a contemporary young adult tale about one teen's struggle with a shoplifting addiction, came out in June 2010 (Simon Pulse).

Toliver is currently hard at work on book number four, but that doesn't stop her from helping aspiring YA novelists in their pursuit of publication. She speaks at writers conferences, teaches workshops, blogs at Boys, Books, Buzz (yawriters.blogspot.com)—and she was kind enough to let us steal some of her methods for creating authentic teen characters and memorable stories.

How do you write with an authentically teen voice? What advice would you have for someone trying to recreate a voice appropriate for a young adult book?

To be honest, I don't do anything scientific or fancy; I just write like I believe my character "sounds." For example, in *The Secret Life of a Teenage Siren*, I wanted to convey that the main character, Roxy Zimmerman, thinks her sixteenth birthday dinner with her family is going to be boring. Instead of "My birthday dinner is going to be boring," which is, well, *boring*, or comparing it to watching paint dry, which is a cliché, her internal dialogue reads: "Having a birthday dinner with my family, like I'm doing tonight, is as exciting as watching nail polish dry. Clear nail polish." These two sentences allow

Roxy's unique personality to shine through. To test it, I might read it out loud, and if I can say to myself, "Yep, that sounds like Roxy all right," I know I've pegged it.

So how does someone who hasn't been in high school for eons write in a way that will sound authentically teen? Just like any kind of writing, it pays to be observant. Listen to teens around you and ask yourself: What's cool? What's lame? What matters to them? How do they structure their sentences? What are popular words or phrases? It also helps to watch TV shows and movies that appeal to a teen audience (and usually star teen actors), subscribe to teen magazines and blogs, and read novels that are getting young adults excited about reading (booksellers and your local librarians can recommend some if you're unsure). The more you observe the world of teens, the more comfortable you'll feel creating and nurturing your authentic teen voice(s).

Once during a school visit, a 14-year-old girl walked up to me and said, "Man, you're *old*. When I read your book, I just assumed you were my age." It's one of the biggest compliments I've ever received.

Along the same lines, how easy or difficult do you find writing male characters? How do you approach this?

For the most part, I approach writing a male character the same way as writing a female one. Whether he's a love interest or a villain, I want him to have both flaws and redeeming qualities. Like my female characters, what he wears reveals something about his personality, as does his vocabulary, mood, what he notices, what riles him up, what makes him happy and so on.

To be sure my writing doesn't scream "female writer trying to sound like a dude," I might read my male character's dialogue out loud, and I've been known to run passages by high school boys I know. I really enjoy writing my male characters, and my favorite so far is David Hillcrest from *Lifted*, about whom *Booklist*'s review noted: "Especially well drawn is Poppy [Browne's] crush, a quirky, sincere minister's son."

Do your characters or your story ideas tend to come first? And where do you go from there?

1. Inspiration. I definitely come up with the idea first. For example, with *Lifted*, I saw a documentary on shoplifting and how teens in particular are drawn to it. I knew I wanted to write a book about a character (or characters) that shoplift.
2. Brainstorm sessions. Next, I brainstorm. Not only do I think about plot, I brainstorm factors to cause and deepen the conflicts and make my story stand out. I remind myself to steer clear of clichés and stereotypes and not be afraid to take risks.
3. Research. By this time, I usually realize I have some behind-the-scenes work to do. With *Lifted*, I had to research why and how people shoplift, what are the legal consequences of shoplifting, why and how people can become addicted to shoplifting,

what it's like to live in a Bible-belt town and go to a private Baptist high school, and so forth. I wanted all of these aspects of the story to ring true.

4. Character development. I like to make a "cast of characters," where I list all the main characters' names followed by some basic info (physical traits, their goals, their fears, family situation, etc.). I also like to find an image of someone who looks like I imagine my character looking, which serves as a reference as well as inspiration.

5. Write! Now I'm ready to start writing. I might write about three chapters to "get into it" and then go back and write a synopsis or outline. I'm not a very good synopsis writer, but I have found that it's a great organizational tool and it keeps the plot moving along if writer's block strikes.

6. Edit, revise, critique, repeat. I'm a self-editor so I typically try to work out the kinks as I go, but I have to admit that once the entire story is written, I love going back to add more feeling, more detail, stronger verbs, and so forth. Sometimes I don't have time for a critique partner's turnaround, but those times I do, I'm always glad I have someone I trust give my manuscript a thorough read and critique. And then it's time to do some more editing and revising before I send it off to my editor. While waiting for his or her editorial letter, I start at Step 1 with a whole new book idea.

All three of your books are written in first person. What draws you to this point of view? How do you think it enhances your stories?

I started using first person because I enjoy reading YA novels written in it and it seemed to work well for each of the books I wanted to write. I believe it enhances my stories because it allows me to get right into the character's head, which is especially beneficial for expressing how the character feels at any given moment. A well-written first person POV novel brings the reader right into the story, giving the reader the feeling that she *is* that character, or that she is having a conversation with a best friend.

Your first two books, *The Secret Life of a Teenage Siren* and *Miss Match*, are both written in present tense, while your latest, *Lifted*, is in past tense. Why the switch? Was this a conscious decision? And what do you find are the advantages or disadvantages of writing each?

Present tense is fun because it's more immediate. It allows the reader to be right in the story as it's unfolding. I chose this for the first two books because they are romantic comedies and it seemed like a good fit. It's like Roxy and Sasha (the main characters for each) are saying, "Come along and see what I do." I think present tense makes the whole book seem like you're watching a movie. You don't know what will happen next, which causes suspense.

As for *Lifted*, which deals with much edgier subject matters, I chose past tense because it allows Poppy (the main character) to retell her story for the reader. It's like she's saying, "Come here and I'll tell you what I did." It's the most popular storytelling tense and tends to allow for more flexibility in your writing style.

You use a lot of fabulous verbs in all your books. So active, so clear! How do you come up with them? Do you "collect" them in some kind of verb journal, or do they simply come naturally to you?

Wow, what a great compliment! Thank you. I do have a file on my computer to keep track of interesting words (not just verbs) I've come across, and sometimes I pull it up to see if there's one I can use. When I read my sentences, I ask myself if they're interesting and clear and if not, I doctor them up, and sometimes all it takes is a new verb. Like many writers, coming up with the perfect word choice makes me happy.

That said, I'm not going to write an awkward sentence just to use a cool verb. I'm not afraid of using passive verbs if that's the best way to get my idea across. Also, most people don't use fancy verbs when they're chatting with their friends, so I keep this in mind as I'm writing dialogue.

Particularly in *Lifted*, you give characters certain characteristics or tics that helped identify them. For instance, whenever Mary Jane Portman says something derogatory about someone else, she follows it up with a "Bless her heart." Was this on purpose? Talk to us about why you used little details like these. Also, what are some other characteristics you've used that function in the same way?

When I was in college, I got into a wreck. My friend, who happened to be 11 stories up in a tower, saw me on the street below. He knew it was me because of the way I stood: one arm bent across my chest, the other arm straight down at my side. I remember thinking that was really amazing, and ever since, I've paid attention to the little things that make people who they are. (I also have a degree in speech communication and a little bit of an acting background, which also helps.)

So, yes, my characters have signature sayings, gestures and tics, like twirling their hair when in the presence of a cute guy, smacking their gum or chewing their thumb nails when nervous, picking at their food when sad and so forth. I also like to use what they're wearing, what music they're listening to, etc., as extensions of their personalities and moods. These sorts of details give characters dimension and help the readers connect with them.

In *Lifted*, Poppy is a character with a snarky attitude who gets herself in over her head in a shoplifting ring. What was it like for you to round out her character? What kinds of things did you do/insert to make sure she'd be redeemable from the get-go, even with her flaws?

I think it's important for the reader to find out at some point where the character, especially one with flaws as major as Poppy's, is coming from. With Poppy, I hoped to earn her a little sympathy from the beginning, as she was forced to move from liberal Boulder, Colorado, to ultra-religious Pleasant Acres, Texas. I also expose that she doesn't really have any close friends and her relationship with her single mother is a continuous struggle.

Then, as her story unfolds, I try to show her honesty, her insecurities (despite her tough-girl façade), her hunger to be accepted and loved, and the reasons she makes the decisions she makes (character motivation), illustrating through Poppy that good people sometimes make bad choices.

Tell us a bit about your research for *Lifted*. The shoplifting scenes seemed so real. Did you *gasp* ever have first-hand experience in this area?

I'm glad they felt real. I found some shoplifting tips online (it's true, you can find almost anything on the Internet these days), read testimonials of people who were trying to stop shoplifting, watched documentaries, interviewed a police officer and a store owner, and even witnessed a shoplifter being arrested. Whenever I told people what I was writing about, they almost always had shoplifted themselves, or knew someone who had, and they were more than happy to share these stories. I also did research on addiction in general and addiction to shoplifting. That's how I gleaned most of my information.

As for first-hand experience, I stole a wallet (a new one at a store, not out of someone's pocket) for my dad for Father's Day when I was four or five, but I don't really remember it. My mom says I felt very guilty and confessed before getting into the car.

The supernatural element of Roxy turning into a siren in *The Secret Life of a Teenage Siren* makes the novel an urban fantasy. What are some ways your writing/

preparation differed in writing that novel as opposed to your two straight-up contemporary novels?

In order to write about a modern-day siren, I became very familiar with the sirens of Greek mythology. Some of the details found in *The Secret Life of a Teenage Siren* are based on this information, and some I made up.

I thought it would be beneficial for Roxy to have a guide as she learns about her new life as a siren (think Yoda for Luke Skywalker), and who better than her spunky, beautiful and mysterious Grandma Perkins, who also turned into a siren on her sixteenth birthday?

Next, with the help of a friend, I created the *The Enchiridion of the Seirenes*, which is basically a magical handbook for sirens, holding in it the history and rules Roxy needs to know. I wove excerpts from this ancient tome throughout the story.

Finally, I just had to make sure everything Roxy did after turning into a siren stayed true to the myth-inspired elements and rules I'd created. It was really fun to write a main character with magical powers.

One hot topic in YA is swearing. While your books aren't littered with swear words, they do appear. What are your thoughts on this? How you determine whether or not to use swear words, and how do you know when you've used enough?

I only use swear words when I feel they're a part of a particular character's personality or a character who wouldn't normally swear has reached his or her breaking point. In other words, I allow my characters to swear if it's *authentic*, not just for the general shock factor. I realize that swear words disqualify my books from certain awards and are a deterrent for some readers, a cost definitely worth mentioning. However, it was my conscious decision to "keep it real," and in the three YA books I've written so far, I'm glad I took the risk.

Of all of my YA novels, *Miss Match* has the least swear words, and that's because I've observed that teens living in the vicinity of Salt Lake City, Utah, don't cuss as often (or as extremely) as teens living in other places. For example, Utahns use the phrase "Oh my heck," so I have my characters say it in order to make them sound authentic. In *Lifted*, Poppy swears in the beginning, but as she becomes more integrated into her new religious setting, where her peers very rarely swear and taking the Lord's name in vain is frowned upon, she begins to notice her language and attempts to cut down on her cussing. This felt natural for Poppy's character and her growth.

You use Texas, Colorado, and Utah (all places you have lived) as your settings—or you feature transplant characters *from* those places. Can you speak a bit to how your settings enhance your characters and plots?

To be honest, it started out as a "write what you know" thing with *Siren*. I felt comfortable with the lay of the land, the weather, the smells, the foliage, the way teens in Denver dress and talk, and the things teens like to do there. As for using Utah for *Miss Match*, I thought it would be interesting because at the time there weren't many commercial novels with Utah settings. Plus, it's a comedy and there's plenty of funny stuff that happens in the Utah culture. When you use a setting that you've lived in or visit often, details such as the types of homes, grocery stores, gas stations, roads, schools, music, art, activities, etc., come without too much effort. As long as it works for your particular story, I believe it's natural to consider the place where you live or have lived as a setting.

As for *Lifted*, I decided to situate it in the Bible belt in order to up the conflict for a group of girls who break the law. I had fresh memories of East Texas as I was just there for my grandfather's funeral, but I've never lived in that part of the state. In creating the fictitious Pleasant Acres, I borrowed characteristics from several Southern towns and spoke with friends and relatives who live in those towns or attend private Baptist schools. Painting an authentic picture of Pleasant Acres took more effort than the previous books' settings, but I truly believe *Lifted* wouldn't have turned out to be the same book if I'd chosen somewhere different.

What's one thing you wish you'd known when you were starting out writing?

Luckily, when I decided to write my first book, a professor at the local university recommended I join writing organizations. I can honestly say groups such as RWA and SCBWI have helped me meet the right people and make educated and effective decisions from the get-go.

Sure, there are things I wish I would have done so I could've learned to be a more organized writer, like writing short stories and reading books and taking courses about writing books (which I've gone back and done now). But honestly, my journey to becoming a published author has been a series of ups and downs, all equally important in getting me to where I am today. Not knowing what's up around the bend is one of the many things that makes being an author so exciting.

JAMES DASHNER

On revision, world-building and why being a movie buff helps your writing.

....

by Donna Gambale

James Dashner's first young adult novel, *The Maze Runner* (Delacorte), was released in October 2009 amid much buzz, and it certainly lived up to readers' expectations. Kirkus selected *The Maze Runner* as one of the best young adult books of 2009, and both it and its sequel, *The Scorch Trials*, made the *New York Times* bestseller list. Fans now wait impatiently for *The Death Cure*, the third and final book in the dystopian trilogy, which releases in October 2012.

Dashner's success didn't come overnight, though. When *The Maze Runner* hit bookstores, he'd been writing for 10 years and had already published four middle grade books regionally with a small press. He broke onto the national scene in 2008 with his second middle grade fantasy series, The 13th Reality, which began with *The Journal of Curious Letters* (Shadow Mountain). The first three books have been published thus far, with two more to come.

Before becoming a full-time writer, Dashner worked as an accountant, a job he was ecstatic to quit. Here, he talks about the perils of revision, his advice for aspiring writers, how being a movie buff improves his writing, and what he's learned about thriving in the business. For more on Dashner, visit jamesdashner.com.

Why do you choose to write for children and teens?

That was the age when I personally fell in love with reading, and there's a magic about it that I love to experience over and over again. I also like how you can get away with almost anything in books for younger readers—mixing genres, throwing in humor and crazy creatures and horror and romance, all in the same book. It's just fun. There's the easy answer.

What challenges did you come across when plotting the three-book arc of the Maze Runner trilogy? How much did you know from the beginning, and what was a surprise?

It's a complex story, and it's been a challenge to make sure every little thing ties together. My editor (Krista Marino) has been brilliant in helping with that. I did know the overall story arc from the beginning, though many, many things were changed along the way. Now that we're almost done with revisions on the third book, I feel very relieved. I think readers will be very satisfied with how it all ends.

How has being a movie buff helped your writing?

More than I can possibly express. Movies are an important part of my life, and I see almost every single one that comes out. They really help the idea factory in my brain churn and stay fresh. Often I'll go see a movie in the middle of the day, and some of my best writing comes right after doing so. There's just something about seeing an entire story arc in two hours, with all the scenes and dialogue and characters and visuals. I love it.

You've done national book tours for The Maze Runner and The Scorch Trials. Any advice for an author embarking on his or her first tour?

Enjoy every minute of it. It's a high honor for a publisher to choose to spend money on you, and they treat you really well while you're out and about. Enjoy the hotels, the food, the people, the bookstores, everything. Expect to be tired—lots of early mornings and airports. I think my biggest advice is to never complain or act like a prima donna. For one, you'll anger aspiring writers who would do anything to be in your shoes, and two, it makes you look like a sourpuss and turns people off. Smile even if you don't feel like it!

How do you balance your writing schedule when you're writing two series and promoting your newest release?

It's not easy, that's for sure. Ideally I like to separate them as much as possible—two or three months on one at a time. But that doesn't always work out, so then I try to split it between morning and afternoon, things like that. The hardest is when I have to write or edit while on tour.

You mentioned on your blog that you worked hard in your revisions for The Maze Runner to differentiate your large cast of characters—and it worked! How did you make them so distinct?

Developing the characters for that story was difficult because they've had their memories erased, and it really hit me how much you pull from a character's prior experiences to flush out their personality and traits. But I worked on doing it through their dialogue and interactions with each other, as well as their reactions to situations. I always start with a defining trait for each person, then let my mind expand and fill in the blanks.

There's heavy world-building in both your 13th Reality series and in the Maze Runner books. How do you develop the world of your story?

It's somewhat similar to my characters. Very much so, actually. When I envision a certain aspect of my world, I begin with one or two obvious descriptions or features then let my mind naturally expand upon it. A lot of it comes as I'm actually writing.

You're a huge fan of writers conferences. What helpful tips can you pass along to conference-goers?

You can't overstate the importance of conferences. Almost every published author I know can trace some bit of their success back to a conference or someone they met at a conference. Be prepared; attend every class you possibly can; and most importantly, network like crazy. Meet the agents and editors and other writers. It will all come back to help you at some point.

Who are your favorite YA authors?

That's a hard one because I know so many and I'd hate to hurt anyone's feelings by leaving them out. Better to say who I loved to read when I was that age: Judy Blume, Madeleine L'Engle, Tolkien, Stephen King. How's that for variety?

What's your favorite part of promoting your books? What do you find most effective?

I love interacting with my readers, hearing from them, meeting them, etc. I'm so glad we live in this age of blogs and e-mail and Twitter and all that. That makes it a lot of fun. I would say the most effective method of marketing is to get people talking about them—word of mouth. And the Internet is probably the most valuable way to make that happen. Other than the obvious, of course, which is make sure your book doesn't stink!

Tell us about when you found out you hit the *New York Times* bestseller list for *The Maze Runner*. Where were you, what were you doing, who were you with, and what was your exact reaction?

Great question! Fittingly, I was in the middle of a movie at the theater. Embarrassingly, I was all by myself, which is very typical on a weekday afternoon. But I knew we had a chance to hit the list, so when I saw my agent was calling, I ran out of the theater and ended up having to call him back because I wasn't fast enough. He told me the great news, and it really overwhelmed me. The *NY Times* isn't really the greatest indicator of sales, per se, but there's just something so symbolic about it, and I felt like I'd reached a major milestone. Something I'd dreamed about my whole life. After sharing the joy

with my agent, I then called my wife, and then my mom. And, I'll admit it, a few tears were shed. It's a day I'll never forget. I'm proud to say we've spent several months on the list now!

What have you learned about maintaining positive relationships with agents, editors and others in the business?

It's extremely important. Never burn a bridge. Never. It's a small world in this industry, and you never know what might come back to help you or haunt you. Most of the successful authors I know are genuinely good people and aren't jerks. That had to have helped their publishing journey in some regard. Who wants to work with a jerk? So, don't be a jerk.

What does your workspace look like? Do you have any rituals or superstitions you follow when you write?

We moved about a year ago and I finally have my own office. It's my favorite place in the world besides a bookstore or library (where I often go to work for a change of scenery). I have a comfy couch, a comfy chair and ottoman, a desk, lots of bookshelves. It's heaven. I don't really have any rituals or anything. I just sit down and go at it. But one thing that helps me: movie soundtrack music. Things like *Lord of the Rings, Aliens, The Matrix, Braveheart*. Those really bring out my creative juices and help me visualize what I'm writing.

What's your favorite murdered darling from your books—the one character, scene, plot or even line that you really wanted to keep but ultimately had to cut?

One of my 13th Reality books had a really dark, horrifying scene that I loved. I'd channeled my evil Stephen King side to write it. But, in the end, my editor thought it was *too* dark and I reluctantly agreed to change it significantly. What's so wrong with scarring someone for life?

What do you do when you get stuck on a scene or chapter, or have general writer's block?

It's certainly a sinking feeling when that happens, but honestly, I don't suffer from writer's block very often. I think the problem that hits me is before I even sit down with my laptop, I just feel a general lack of desire to write. What snaps me out of that is to read for a bit or watch a movie. Or exercise. That time is better spent than staring at a computer screen or writing dreck.

You've admitted to not being a fan of revision, but of course there's no avoiding it. How do you tackle the evil beast?

Guilty! It's certainly not my favorite part. I'm all about the original creative process—the first draft. But I'm also smart enough to know that revisions are equally important. I don't want a bad product landing in the hands of my readers, so it's actually not that hard to get motivated to do what needs to be done. But I do find myself having to be a little more disciplined in terms of setting daily goals to get the task completed. I always give myself a day or two off after reading the initial editorial letter, however. It needs to sink in and I have to get over my depression, psyche myself up. For some reason our brain convinces us that *this* time, your editor thought it was *perfect*.

What's the best advice you have for aspiring writers?

Attend conferences, write every day and be persistent. Please don't listen to all the negative stuff. Yes, be realistic. But shoot for the stars. If I'd listened to every naysayer who tried to tell me that I could never make a living doing this, I would've given up. But those things always went in one ear and out the other with me. You can do it.

Your novels contain all kinds of unpleasant situations and events—to say the least—but what element from any of your books do you wish were a part of your real life?

Definitely the telepathic ability. That'd be so cool to be able to talk to my wife and kids that way. That certainly would make texting obsolete, now wouldn't it? There are some really cool things in the second and third books of The Maze Runner that I'd also love to have, but I don't want to spoil anything. I'll just say four words: Flat Trans and Bergs.

You're a very goal-oriented writer. In 2003, you announced you wanted to be a full-time writer in five years, and in 2008 you were able to quit your finance job. What's your current writing-related goal?

Now that I'm a *New York Times* bestseller, I guess my next goal is to hit #1. Never quit reaching for the stars!

FIRST BOOKS

Hear from debut authors of picture books, middle grade and young adult.

....

by Chuck Sambuchino

There's something fresh and amazing about debut novels that's inspiring to other writers. It's with that in mind that we collected eight successful debuts from the past year and sat down to ask the authors questions about how they broke in, what they did right and what advice they have for scribes who are trying to follow in their footsteps. These are writers of picture books, middle grade stories and young adult novels—same as you—who saw their work come to life through hard work and determination. Read on to learn more about their individual journeys.

PICTURE BOOKS

① BETHANIE MURGUIA AQUAPUP.COM

Buglette, The Messy Sleeper (**TRICYCLE PRESS**)

QUICK TAKE: "Buglette is a tidy little bug by day, but at night, her messy sleeping annoys the family and threatens to wake the crow."

WRITES FROM: Sausalito, Calif.

PRE-*BUGLETTE*: A few years ago, I began to focus on writing and illustrating for children. Before receiving the offer for *Buglette*, I did illustrations for a variety of children's magazines.

TIMEFRAME: The idea of "messy sleeping" was in my mind for a year or two before writing the story. I had done a few sketches in my sketchbook. Then, the little bug character came to me. Once I had the character fleshed out, I wrote the first draft in a few days. I was especially motivated because I had just joined a new writing group and knew that I needed a story to share.

ENTER THE AGENT: My agent is Mary Kole with the Andrea Brown Literary Agency. I submitted my book dummy to a handful of publishers and agents. I received an offer of publication and a few agents expressed interest. It was an exciting time! I spoke with Mary and everything fell into place.

WHAT YOU LEARNED: As a debut author and illustrator, I have realized how important it is for me to think about marketing myself. I don't have the benefit of being paired with a well-known illustrator as a debut author might be (or vice versa in the case of an illustrator). At times it is daunting, but I'm embracing it as another part of the creative process. I've really enjoyed creating interactive marketing pieces and child-focused props for my readings.

WHAT YOU DID RIGHT: I simplified my art and my writing. Previously, I had been trying to do too much with both. I was forcing my illustrations to be complex. My writing was message heavy. Once I began to focus on the characters themselves, the stories and images came together much more easily.

DO DIFFERENT NEXT TIME: I would have joined a critique group sooner. I've gained such valuable insight and camaraderie from meeting with other writers and illustrators.

PLATFORM: I had a website showcasing my illustration when *Buglette* was sold. Recently, I began a blog with (almost) weekly illustrations. I have also been blogging about "lessons learned" while working on this first book. I am currently expanding my website and blog to include more information for fellow children's literature enthusiasts as well as activities for children and teachers. In the real world, I enjoy sharing my book and my process with both kids and adults. I love those face-to-face opportunities!

NEXT UP: My next book will be published by Arthur A. Levine Books/Scholastic in 2012. I am also working on a companion book to *Buglette* for Knopf.

② TAMEKA FRYER BROWN TAMEKAFRYERBROWN.COM
Around Our Way on Neighbors' Day (**ABRAMS BOOKS**)

QUICK TAKE: "A rhythmic love story between a young girl and her close-knit, multicultural community."

WRITES FROM: Charlotte, N.C.

PRE-BOOK: Ever since I joined the Society of Children's Book Writers and Illustrators in November of 2005, my focus has been on studying and writing picture books. Prior to signing the contract for *Around Our Way on Neighbors' Day*, I was awarded a first prize in the 2008 Cheerios Spoonfuls of Stories Contest for a story.

TIMEFRAME: The first version of this book was called *ABCs Around Our Way* and it came to me one morning in that twilight phase between sleep and wakefulness. Before I ever opened my eyes, I had the first verse written and the rhyme scheme worked out. Within 24 hours, the first draft was complete. The whole serendipitous thing was extremely cool. I keep waiting for it to happen again. The current version of the book was written based on a revision request from an editor. Between pondering and actual writing, it took about a month to complete.

ENTER THE AGENT: My agent is Jennifer Rofe of Andrea Brown Literary Agency. While visiting the ABLA website, I read her agent bio and thought my manuscripts might appeal to her.

WHAT YOU LEARNED: Getting published is not the end goal; selling books is. Promotion takes a tremendous amount of time and effort—far more than writing the story does. It becomes important to find ways to work smarter.

WHAT YOU DID RIGHT: The best thing I did was joining SCBWI. I don't think I'd be published yet had I not.

DO DIFFERENT NEXT TIME: Maybe I could have done more networking and pursued a lot more professional mentors. But I am more comfortable with small social circles, and the writing friends and mentors I do have are the best.

PLATFORM: I have a website; I've participated in a variety of online interviews on some popular blogs like Bowllan's Blog, Cynsations, and Multiculturalism Rocks!; I am a contributing member of The Brown Bookshelf; and I have a very accessible Facebook Author Page. Awareness + interest = readership. At this point, my primary goal is to inform as many people as possible that my book exists.

NEXT UP: My next picture book, *In a Mood,* is scheduled for 2012 with Viking Children's. It will be illustrated by the award-winning Shane Evans.

MIDDLE GRADE

③ CRYSTAL ALLEN CRYSTALALLENBOOKS.COM
How Lamar's Bad Prank Won a Bubba-Sized Trophy (**BALZAR + BRAY**)

QUICK TAKE: "Lamar Washington is the maddest, baddest most spectacular bowler ever, but he doesn't have game with the ladies, so he vows to spend the summer changing his image from dud to stud."

WRITES FROM: Sugar Land, Texas

PRE-LAMAR: *Lamar* was in the makings for several years. I attended numerous conferences, workshops and writers' meetings to prepare it for submission.

TIMEFRAME: *Lamar* began as a ghostwriting possibility for a famous comedian who wanted a story focused on a group of multicultural kids in a school setting. I didn't get the job, but I loved the characters and tried to keep the story alive. But after a few weeks, the story, written in third person, lost its luster and I stopped working on it. About two weeks later, while I was deep in an episode of "CSI: Las Vegas," a boy appeared in my mind, strutting around my brain like he owned the place. He took me places that I recognized from my ghostwriting venture. We ended up at a bowling alley. I immediately realized this boy was Lamar, knew he had a story to tell, and I wanted to tell it.

WHAT YOU LEARNED: Patience. The publishing world moves slower than snails in molasses.

WHAT YOU DID RIGHT: Besides going to workshops and conferences, I stayed in contact with people in the publishing business and they kept me focused, encouraged and determined.

DO DIFFERENT NEXT TIME: I definitely would have followed this dream a lot earlier.

PLATFORM: By managing a tween-friendly website, doing blog interviews, and attending school visits, book fairs, festivals and signings, I have the opportunity to strengthen my presence as an author and gain readership in the process.

YOUNG ADULT

④ KARSTEN KNIGHT KARSTENKNIGHT.COM
Wildefire (SIMON & SCHUSTER)

QUICK TAKE: "16-year-old Ashline Wilde, a dormant Polynesian volcano goddess, enters into a dark sibling rivalry with her manipulative older sister as a war between the gods looms over her Northern California boarding school."

WRITES FROM: Boston, Mass.

PRE-NOVEL: When I entered the workforce, my writing time evaporated faster than a puddle in Death Valley. After I lost my job in 2009, I enrolled in the MFA program at Simmons College and started writing a volcano goddess biography. That first chapter eventually became *Wildefire*. So I landed my dream job because I got laid off.

TIMEFRAME: It was about 10 months from writing the first sentence ("Ashline Wilde was a human mood ring.") to the book deal.

WHAT YOU LEARNED: Mostly how fast your career can change. At 9 a.m. one day, I was an unpublished author who had just stumbled out of the shower. At 9:15, I got a call from my future editor saying she was about to make me an offer.

WHAT YOU DID RIGHT: I wrapped my mind around what it meant to write a character-driven fantasy novel. I kept reminding myself, "This needs to be the story of a girl first, and a volcano goddess second."

DO DIFFERENT NEXT TIME: Not a thing. Not even the two years when I didn't write a word. I needed that hiatus for writing to feel fresh for me again.

PLATFORM: I have a blog. I also film a weekly video blog as a member of the YA Rebels, a merry band of young adult authors. You can tune in at youtube.com/yarebels.

NEXT UP: The next two books in the *Wildefire* trilogy.

⑤ JOSEPHINE ANGELINI JOSEPHINEANGELINI.COM
Starcrossed (HARPERTEEN)

QUICK TAKE: "A modern day re-imagining of the *Iliad* set in the world of teenaged demigods."

WRITES FROM: Los Angeles

PRE-NOVEL: I started trying to write screenplays, but I'm too long-winded for such a strict format! I never got anything produced, but I did learn a lot about pace, structure and the importance of a solid outline. It's helped me enormously.

TIMEFRAME: My husband encouraged me to quit my job bartending and devote myself to writing full time, so I only had until the money from his most recent screenplay sale ran out. I outlined and wrote *Starcrossed* in only eight months.

ENTER THE AGENT: I got my agent, Mollie Glick at Foundry Literary + Media, through Rachel Miller at Tom Sawyer Entertainment. My husband was a Facebook friend of Rachel's, although neither of them knows how that "friending" happened to begin with. He reached out to her online. Rachel had a rare slow day and decided to read my manuscript, and then she immediately passed it on to Mollie. I got a call the next morning—it actually happened *that* fast.

WHAT YOU LEARNED: It takes longer to edit a novel than it does to write it. My high school English teacher was absolutely right; writing really is rewriting.

WHAT YOU DID RIGHT: I married the most supportive, understanding and amazing man in the universe who believed in me so much he was willing to go completely broke so I could write.

PLATFORM: My goal is to set up a forum where I can really interact with my readers. I want to give them an experience that they can't get from just reading the books.

NEXT UP: Edit book two while I write book three. At least I already know which of those two things will take longer!

⑥ LISA AND LAURA ROECKER THELIARSOCIETY.COM
The Liar Society (**SOURCEBOOKS FIRE**)

QUICK TAKE: "Kate Lowry didn't think dead best friends could send e-mails, but when she gets an e-mail from Grace, she finally has the chance to prove that her friend's death was more than just a tragic accident."

WRITES FROM: Cleveland, Ohio

PRE-SOCIETY: We both enjoyed writing but could never imagine writing a book. During a late-night phone conversation, we came up with the "next *Gossip Girl*" and began writing the next day. The bad news was the book sucked. But the good news was that we fell in love with writing, and, after querying every agent known to man, we started in on a new idea. *The Liar Society* was born five million drafts later.

ENTER THE AGENT: Our agent is Catherine Drayton of Inkwell Management. We queried her with the first doomed manuscript and were over the moon when she requested pages.

And not quite as happy when we were rejected a week later. The second time around, we managed to learn from our mistakes. We applied feedback from beta readers, edited our first 250 words based on comments we received during Miss Snark's First Victim Contest and sent our query through the ringer. All the prep work paid off when we received three offers of representation.

WHAT YOU LEARNED: To laugh at ourselves and try really hard not to take ourselves too seriously. There are no guarantees in this business, and the more fun you can have, the better.

WHAT YOU DID RIGHT: The night after we decided to start writing together, we began our blog. We now have 1,000 readers who support our work and have followed our journey. Our critique partners and beta readers are all people who we've met through the blog.

DO DIFFERENT NEXT TIME: We wish we would have gone out on submission under the title *The Liar Society*. When our editor saw our manuscript titled *The Haunting of Pemberly Brown*, he said it reminded him of a historical piece, which … um … is not our book.

PLATFORM: An online platform of blog readers and Twitter followers. We're also involved in WriteOnCon, an online writers conference.

NEXT UP: A YA thriller called *Bloodlines*. And then, of course, the second book in *The Liar Society* series!

⑦ MINDI SCOTT MINDISCOTT.COM

Freefall **(SIMON PULSE)**

QUICK TAKE: "The story of what comes next for a teen who was the last person to see his best friend alive and the first one to find him dead."

WRITES FROM: Near Seattle, Wash.

PRE-NOVEL: Before *Freefall*, I completed and queried another contemporary YA, but I did not end up getting representation for it.

TIMEFRAME: From the first spark of the idea (July 2006) to hitting bookstores shelves, it was a four-year process. For only about 21 months was I actively writing and revising it, though. The rest of the time I was waiting.

ENTER THE AGENT: My agent is Jim McCarthy with Dystel & Goderich, and we found each other after one of his clients read my manuscript and recommended it to him.

BIGGEST SURPRISE: When I first started, I was very naive and thought that I could get an agent, a deal and see the book on sale within a year. It took about a year just for me to get the agent!

WHAT YOU DID RIGHT: I did a lot of networking (mostly online). I found that being willing to talk about my writing and help others with theirs opened many doors for me.

DO DIFFERENT NEXT TIME: If I'd known about it, I would have started researching book blogs and interacting within that community of readers long before my book sold.

PLATFORM: I've been active on Twitter and with The Tenners, a group for 2010 debut YA and MG authors. Also, I'm a member of The Contemps, organized by authors who are spotlighting contemporary YA fiction for the 2010/2011 school year.

NEXT UP: I'm working on more contemporary young adult novels!

⑧ KODY KEPLINGER KODYKEPLINGER.COM
The DUFF: Designated Ugly Fat Friend (POPPY)

WRITES FROM: Upstate New York

QUICK TAKE: "A high school girl realizes with absolute horror that she's falling for the guy she thought she hated more than anyone."

PRE-NOVEL: I started writing when I was 11, and that's when my first "novels" appeared. Most of them were blatant rip-offs of Judy Blume books or Harry Potter, but gradually they became more and more original. In high school, I wrote a lot of fan fiction before focusing my attention on my own characters and stories. It was at the end of my senior year when my agent offered on *The DUFF*, which I had written earlier that winter.

ENTER THE AGENT: I found Joanna Volpe [of the Nancy Coffey Literary Agency] on one of my beta reader's lists of agents she'd queried. I found out much, much later that any e-query I'd sent with more than five sample pages in the body of the e-mail hadn't sent! So it turned out, Joanna being a rare agent who specified that she didn't want sample pages was a blessing.

BIGGEST SURPRISE: How open and friendly the publishing industry is. I've made some of the best friends in writing groups.

WHAT YOU DID RIGHT: I was patient. I watched so many of my friends jump the gun on querying. I saw people query books before they were finished or query a million agents at the same time. I also queried in rounds so that, if I had any notes in rejections, I could revise my manuscript with them.

PLATFORM: I've started becoming more and more involved in social networking. I've reached out to others and started working for a few different blog and vlog groups.

NEXT UP: I'm working on my next Poppy novel for a fall 2011 release.

AMY KROUSE ROSENTHAL

On how to create—every day.

....

by Meg Leder

At the end of Thornton Wilder's *Our Town*, an incredulous Emily, having been given one more day to be with the people she loves, asks the stage manager, "Do any human beings ever realize life while they live it?—every, every minute?" He replies, "No. Saints and poets, maybe—they do some."

The passage is one Amy Krouse Rosenthal thinks every aspiring writer should read. It gives her goosebumps. It also explains what drives the extremely prolific writer, filmmaker and all-around "maker" of stuff.

"Since I was a child, I have always had an acute awareness of time," she says. "I think that's what it's about for me—it's the thing that I'm obsessed with, just making the most of my time. For everyone who's alive, as long as you're answering the question *Are you making the most of your time here?*, you're going to be doing the right things."

And how does Rosenthal make the most of her time? Quite simply, by making things.

MAKING BOOKS

Whether it's for adults or children, when you pick up a book by Rosenthal, you're entering a unique world, one in which the everyday is explored, questioned and seen with new eyes—all with wondrous results. A small pig wants to be clean, not muddy; a charming spoon wishes its life were as exciting as those of knife, fork and chopsticks; a life is chronicled in encyclopedic form. The ordinary is turned on its head, and the new perspective is nothing short of joyous.

While each book is different, there's an underlying positivity to all of Rosenthal's work: a call to pay attention to the small moments of ordinary life, to look at what you have in a new light and to celebrate the joy and loveliness that comes from that act of reexamining. And there's a devout audience of readers responding to the message: her memoir, *Encyclopedia of Ordinary Life,* was named by Amazon as one of the top 10 memoirs of the decade, while *Duck! Rabbit!,* based on a famous optical illusion, was named by *Time* as the top children's book of 2009.

Rosenthal practices what she preaches, finding inspiration for her works within the material of her everyday life. Take, for instance, the trio *Little Pea, Little Hoot,* and *Little Oink,* with illustrations by Jen Corace—dubbed a "Bizarro World trilogy for kids" by the *New York Times.* The first, which features a pea who doesn't want to eat candy for dinner, grew out of a bedtime story Rosenthal told her daughter.

"When my kids were small, there were countless stories told. Often for the boys, I'd tell them stories about dinosaurs, monsters or something in a cape—all these nonsense stories they loved. Ninety-nine percent of the stories I made up for my kids were nonsensical things. But once in a while there was some kind of cool stuff. You have to tell one thousand bad ones to get to the one good one."

Rosenthal says finding that one good one amidst all the others is a little bit like dating. "When a relationship isn't right, even if you think *I know this is going to work out, he's really cute,* it always has some convoluted glitch—this nonfluid, nonseamless barrage of obstacles. But true love is this flawless, shiny, perfectly smooth thing, at least in the beginning. When I'm writing something, I'm coming at it from a number of different angles. With the ones that end up working, everything falls into place more fluidly."

That feeling of fluidity can also come from working well with an illustrator. For one of her most recent books, *Plant a Kiss* (which explores what might grow if you, quite literally, planted a kiss), Rosenthal worked closely with illustrator Peter Reynolds to develop the vision and feel of the book—a process she says has "been a dream." Not only was it a chance for her to work with one of her favorite artists, but she was thrilled with the vision he brought to the book.

"When I started, I had mocked up the book with stick-figure illustrations. It was tidy, executed visually 100 percent. There was a moment of talk when we thought maybe the book should look like this. It was kind of cute. But thank goodness we reached out to Peter and he said yes. During the first conference call he said he'd send us some sketches. Later, I opened the document, and he had illustrated the entire book. And it was just this moment of 'Oh my god, he nailed it.' The characters are beautiful."

With all of her picture books, Rosenthal has strived for this type of creative partnership. "I really value the collaboration. Oftentimes the writers are kept apart from the illustrator, but that paradigm never made sense to me. From the first 'yes' [for *Little Pea* and *Cookies*]

I made the plea to be involved. I couldn't imagine not doing it. The books gain so much by the writer and illustrator interacting."

Along with the books for children and adults, Rosenthal has also created a line of journals including ones for new parents, grandparents, and big siblings—as well as a charming set of Karma Checks, sixty literal checks on which to write acts of good karma or admonish bad ones.

For Rosenthal, transitioning between writing picture books, memoirs, and journals hasn't been difficult. "When I sit down to write books for children or grownups, there isn't a schism for me. It's not as different as you'd think. But at the same time, I'm doing my damndest to write the thing I want to write. I'm trying to be true to myself and what I want to say."

MAKING FILMS

In May of 2008, Rosenthal discovered a new way of saying what she wants to say. "I had never been drawn to video before; I was never the one filming my kids. I've chronicled my kids in scrapbooks and written things, but I was never drawn to filming back then. But I saw a headline in the *New York Times* about the Flip camera that said 'When good enough is good enough.' The camera was described as having one button and it fit in your hand. When I got it, it actually felt like the pencil version of a camera."

The first short film she made came a month later. It was inspired by a live performance from Glen Hansard and Marketa Irglova from the movie *Once*. The result—"17 Things I Made"—is a quirky, two-plus minute look at 17 things Rosenthal has created—from a mess in the sink to her three children to an impromptu song to her books. At the end, Rosenthal makes a promise, inviting viewers to meet her on 08/08/08, at the "Bean" sculpture in Millennium Park, to make a "cool 18th thing together." She didn't know what would happen, but the results were, in a word, lovely.

Several hundred strangers showed up that evening to participate with Rosenthal in making another film, *The Beckoning of Lovely,* in less than an hour. Described on her website as "a beautiful testament to the power of community, cooperation and hope amongst strangers in the name of all things lovely," the wondrous seven-minute piece features Rosenthal asking people to "make" a variety of things—make something pretty, make do with what you have, kiss and make up, make someone's day and so on. And they do—couples kiss, a stranger gives flowers to people who pass him by, groups of people hold up tiny umbrellas to "make do," friends do cartwheels. The film was such a success, Rosenthal is working on making a feature-length *Beckoning of Lovely* film, created entirely by viewers and funded "by the universe."

"I've been working on it nonstop in my own head and in my own house. There's a lot of work and a lot of thinking going on. My goal is to have the movie released 11/11/11. I have the material; the question is how this all comes together, how do we weave it, is it a story, what kind of movie is this thing?"

As to how film impacts her writing and vice versa, it's opened a new method of sharing her ideas with the world. "I've had this one book idea forever, and it existed as a manuscript, and it just didn't happen. There's stuff in there that I'm excited about. But then I got the idea to pull three examples and make 30-second films of them. They're called 'Drawing Conclusions.' They work for me right now as short films. Now, when I have an idea, I ask *Is this a book, a journal, a film?*"

> "When I sit down to write books for children or grownups, there isn't a schism for me. It's not as different as you'd think. But at the same time, I'm doing my damndest to write the thing I want to write. I'm trying to be true to myself and what I want to say."

Along with her own films, Rosenthal also creates a series of short films associated with Mission Amy KR, a blog she has started with Chicago public radio station WBEZ. Every week, Rosenthal gives readers and listeners "missions"—short creative endeavors her website describes as "always interactive, always easily doable and always excruciatingly earnest."

"I do a mission a week. There's a range of them. I do a short film inviting people to do something, and then over the week, things happen." These things have included calls for doing cartwheels in public places and leaving positive messages for strangers on ATM machines, changing the acronym from "automated teller machine" to "Always trust magic." Rosenthal is also using the blog to write a children's book with her blog readers—*Imagine Nation*—described as "an amazing place to live because when you imagine something good/cool/wonderful/revolutionary—poof—it comes to be!"

MAKING TIME

So how does Rosenthal fit in writing amidst her other creative pursuits? "I take my laptop and I go to a coffeehouse and sit and write—getting out and getting away from distractions. I can't get online; I go somewhere where there's no free wireless."

For Rosenthal, writing is a practice and discipline, and she makes the most of her writing time. "There's this sort of illusion that you wait for this big burst of inspiration and then you're receiving it, and it's this fluid easy thing. For me at least, the little moments of inspiration are sprinkled throughout the day. The hard work is sitting down for two hours to work. It's the calisthenics of literature: you have to sit down and do the thing. It would be impossible to do it floating through the inspiration avenue. It's about sitting down and whatever happens, happens."

And through the work of sitting down to allow things to happen, the good stuff can come. "The process of making the thing feels like what a potter experiences. I'm throwing stuff and letting my hands build it. It's that push and pull of bringing ideas and intention and specific hopes for something, and then letting that organic, hopefully magical thing happen that you hadn't anticipated develop. It's trying to merge those."

MAKING CONNECTIONS

Rosenthal started her professional career as a copywriter. It was a career she loved, and she "never saw it as a stepping stone." On the side, however, she was doing her own writing—exploring words and wordplay—and she began seeking a home for the work.

"For a long time, I'd be making all these same things, and I couldn't find the person to listen to me. Half of it was finding the right person." For Rosenthal, that right person was literary agent Amy Rennert.

"I was talking to a few different agents, and at first, I was sort of confused; they were all accomplished, nice people and doing good things. I found [Rennert] through a colleague, a fellow writer. She highly recommended her, and I had this moment of clarity and went with her—thank God I did. Amy is smart, she's good, she's loyal, she's honest, she's efficient, she's a pal."

> "There's this sort of illusion that you wait for this big burst of inspiration and then you're receiving it, and it's this fluid easy thing. For me at least, the little moments of inspiration are sprinkled throughout the day. The hard work is sitting down for two hours to work."

Now, more than 10 years later, Rosenthal's group of "right people" not only includes Rennert but a number of editors at different houses with whom she's cultivated working relationships. "I'm elated because I get to make this stuff and there are folks who will want to look at the things I'm making."

While she values having these first readers to bounce ideas off of, she uses her time carefully, eschewing other forms of critique in favor of writing time. "The writing group hasn't been my path. I'm really sort of insular, and my time is a double-edged sword. I've had to be hyper-cognizant of how I use every moment."

MAKING THE MOST OF HER LIFE

Being cognizant of how she uses her time is a recurring them in Rosenthal's life and work. (The end message of *The Beckoning of Lovely?* "Make the most of your time here.")

"Everybody has their own version of what they want to fill their hours with; for me it's making things. *This* is what I want to fill my time with, I love it. I don't know how to not make things. For me it's not a conscious decision to make or not make; it's my natural leaning, I don't know what it feels like to not want to. But you can't impose that on someone else.

"Someone might feel the need to do the luge—that's their thing. Mine is a need to create—to translate what I love to words and films. You have to find the thing that makes *you* want to do it so bad you don't know how not to do it.

"It's one big happy mess to me, I love writing, I love children's books, I love doing grown-up books, I love the journal line, I love doing film.

"I love thinking and I love ideas, and whatever form that's going to take, that's a satisfying life to me."

MEG LEDER is a nonfiction editor at Perigee Books, an imprint of Penguin Group, where she acquires and edits creativity, popular reference, humor and craft books. She is the co-author of *The Happy Book* and *Boys of a Feather*, and an upcoming title with Sourcebooks. Her writing has appeared in *Cincinnati Magazine*, *The Bellingham Review* and *Writer's Digest*, and she's worked at Writer's Digest Books, McGraw-Hill, and Joseph-Beth Booksellers. She lives in Brooklyn where she enjoys reading young adult books on the subway, singing the praises of "Friday Night Lights," and looking for cool vintage finds at the Brooklyn Flea.

BOOK PUBLISHERS

There's no magic formula for getting published. It's a matter of getting the right manuscript on the right editor's desk at the right time. Before you submit, it's important to learn publishers' needs, see what kind of books they're producing and decide which publishers your work is best suited for. *Children's Writer's & Illustrator's Market* is but one tool in this process. (Those just starting out, turn to "Quick Tips for Writers & Illustrators" in this book.)

To help you narrow down the list of possible publishers for your work, we've included several indexes at the back of this book. The **Subject Index** lists book and magazine publishers according to their fiction and nonfiction needs or interests. The **Age-Level Index** indicates which age groups publishers cater to. The **Photography Index** indicates which markets buy photography for children's publications. The **Poetry Index** lists publishers accepting poetry.

If you write contemporary fiction for young adults, for example, and you're trying to place a book manuscript, go first to the Subject Index. Locate the fiction categories under Book Publishers and copy the list under Contemporary. Then go to the Age-Level Index and highlight the publishers on the Contemporary list that are included under the Young Adults heading. Read the listings for the highlighted publishers to see if your work matches their needs.

Remember, *Children's Writer's & Illustrator's Market* should not be your only source for researching publishers. Here are a few other sources of information:

- The Society of Children's Book Writers and Illustrators (SCBWI) offers members an annual market survey of children's book publishers for the cost of postage or free online at scbwi.org. (SCBWI membership information can also be found at www.scbwi.org.)

- The Children's Book Council website (www.cbcbooks.org) gives information on member publishers.
- If a publisher interests you, send a SASE for submission guidelines or check publishers' websites for guidelines *before* submitting. To quickly find guidelines online, visit The Colossal Directory of Children's Publishers at www.signaleader.com.
- Check publishers' websites. Many include their complete catalogs that you can browse. Web addresses are included in many publishers' listings.
- Spend time at your local bookstore to see who's publishing what. While you're there, browse through *Publishers Weekly* and *The Horn Book*.

SUBSIDY & SELF-PUBLISHING

Some determined writers who receive rejections from royalty publishers may look to subsidy and co-op publishers as an option for getting their work into print. These publishers ask writers to pay all or part of the costs of producing a book. We strongly advise writers and illustrators to work only with publishers who pay them. For this reason, we've adopted a policy not to include any subsidy or co-op publishers in *Children's Writer's & Illustrator's Market* (or any other Writer's Digest Books market books).

If you're interested in publishing your book just to share it with friends and relatives, self-publishing is a viable option, but it involves time, energy and money. You oversee all book production details. Check with a local printer for advice and information on cost or check online for print-on-demand and e-book publishing options (which are often more affordable).

Whatever path you choose, keep in mind that the market is flooded with submissions, so it's important for you to hone your craft and submit the best work possible. Competition from thousands of other writers and illustrators makes it more important than ever to research publishers before submitting—read their guidelines, look at their catalogs, check out a few of their titles and visit their websites.

ABBEVILLE FAMILY

Abbeville Press 137 Varick St. New York NY 10013. Estab. 1977. (212)366-5585. Fax: (212)366-6966. E-mail: abbeville@abbeville.com; cvance@abbeville.com. Website: www.abbeville.com. Specializes in trade books. **Manuscript/Art Acquisitions:** Cynthia Vance, director of Abbeville Family. Publishes 8 picture books/year. 10% of books by first-time authors and 20% for subsidy published.

FICTION Picture books: animal, anthology, concept, contemporary, fantasy, folktales, health, hi-lo, history, humor, multicultural, nature/environment, poetry, science fiction, special needs, sports, suspense. Average word length 300–1,000 words. Recently published *Everett, the Incredibly Helpful Helper* by Sue Anne Morrow with illustrations by CG Williams (ages 1-4, picture/nonfiction book); *Red, Yellow, Blue, and You* by Cynthia Vance with illustrations by Candace Whitman (ages 2-5 picture/board book) with padded cover and rhyming text; *The Journey: Plateosarus (Dinosaurs illustrated comics series)* by Matteo Bacchin and Marco Signore, with foreword by Mark Norell (ages 9 and up). Educational comic series, 64 pages with hardcover.

HOW TO CONTACT Fiction: Please refer to website for submission policy. Not accepting unsolicited manuscripts. If you wish to have your manuscript or materials returned, a SASE with proper postage must be included.

ILLUSTRATION Works with approx 2-4 illustrators/year. Uses color artwork only.

PHOTOGRAPHY Buys stock and assigns work.

ABRAMS BOOKS FOR YOUNG READERS

115 W. 18th St., New York NY 10011. Website: www.abramsyoungreaders.com.

○ Abrams no longer accepts unsolicted manuscripts or queries. Abrams title *365 Penguins,* by Jean-Luc Fromental, illustrated by Joelle Jolivel, won a Boston Globe-Horn Book Picture Book Honor Award in 2007. *Abrams also publishes Laurent De Brunhoff, Graeme Base and Laura Numeroff, among others.*

FICTION Picture books ages 0–12, fiction and non-fiction.

HOW TO CONTACT Does not accept unsolicited manuscripts or queries.

ILLUSTRATION Illustrations only: Do not submit original material; copies only. Contact: Chad Beckerman, art director.

Ⓐ○ ACTION PUBLISHING

P.O. Box 391, Glendale CA 91209. (323)478-1667. Fax: (323)478-1767. Website: www.actionpublishing.com. **Contact:** Art Director. Publishes 2 middle readers/year.

FICTION Picture book: fantasy. Middle readers: adventure. Recently published *The Family of Ree* series, by Scott E. Sutton.

HOW TO CONTACT Only interested in agented material.

ILLUSTRATION Works with 2-4 illustrators/year. Reviews illustration packages from artists. Query. Send promotional literature. Contact: art director. Responds only if interested. Samples returned with SASE or kept on file if interested and OK with illustrator.

PHOTOGRAPHY Buys stock and assigns work. Contact: art director. "We use photos on an as-needed basis. Mainly publicity, advertising and copy work." Uses 35mm or 4×5 transparencies. Submit cover letter and promo piece.

TERMS Pays authors royalty based on wholesale price. Offers advances against royalties. Pays illustrators by the project or royalty. Pays photographers by the project or per photo. Sends galleys to authors. Original art returned as negotiated depending on project.

TIPS "We use a small number of photos. Promo is kept on file for reference if potential interest. If you are sending a book proposal, send query letter first with web link to sample photos if available."

ALADDIN/PULSE

1230 Avenue of the Americas, 4th Floor, New York, NY 10020. (212)698-2707. Fax: (212)698-7337. Website: www.simonsays.com. Hardcover/paperback imprints of Simon & Schuster Children's Publishing Children's Division. Publishes 175 titles/year. **Vice President/Publisher, Aladdin/Pulse:** Bethany Buck **Vice President/Associate Publisher, Aladdin:** Ellen Krieger; Liesa Abrams, executive editor (Aladdin); Emily Lawrence, associate editor (Aladdin); Kate Angelella, assistant editor (Aladdin) Jennifer Klonsky, Editorial Director (Pulse); Anica Rissi, editor (Pulse); Michael del Rosario, associate editor (Pulse). **Manuscript Acquisitions:** Attn: Submissions Editor. **Art**

Acquisitions: Karin Paprocki, Aladdin; Russell Gordon, Simon Pulse.

FICTION Aladdin publishes picture books, beginning readers, chapter books, middle grade and tween fiction and nonfiction, and graphic novels and nonfiction in hardcover and paperback, with an emphasis on commercial, kid-friendly titles. Simon Pulse publishes original teen series, single-title fiction, and select nonfiction, in hardcover and paperback. Recently published Nancy Drew and the Clue Crew chapter book series (Emily Lawrence, editor); Pendragon middle grade series (Liesa Abrams, editor); Edgar & Ellen middle grade series (Ellen Krieger, editor); Uglies series (Bethany Buck, editor); *Wake, Bloom, Uninvited, Disenchanted Princess, The Straight Road to Kylie* (Jennifer Klonsky, editor); *Chill*; *Model* (Anica Rissi, editor); *I Heart You, You Haunt Me*; *Unleashed*; *My Summer on Earth*; Drama series (Michael del Rosario, editor).

HOW TO CONTACT Fiction: Accepts query letters with proposals (Aladdin); accepts query letters (Simon Pulse).

🌑 AMBASSADOR BOOKS, INC.

(201)825-7300; (800)218-1903. Fax: (800)836-3161. E-mail: info@paulistpress.com; ggoggins@paulistpress.com; jconlan@paulistpress.com. Website: www.ambassadorbooks.com. Publishes hardcover and trade paperback originals. Published 50% debut authors within the last year. Averages 7 total titles/year. Juvenile, literary, picture books, religious, spiritual, sports, young adult, women's. **Contact:** Acquisitions Editor. "We are a Christian publishing company seeking spirituality-focused books for children and adults." Publishes hardcover and trade paperback originals. 500 queries received/year. 100 mss received/year.

○ Preference is given to non-simultaneous submissions (responds in 1-2 months). Accepts simultaneous submissions.

FICTION Not accepted except in adult or juvenile fables. Query with SASE. Submit complete ms.

NONFICTION Adult books must have spiritual theme. Query with a sample chapter and SASE or complete ms. Children's books published as Ambassador Children's Books, and must have spiritual or self-help topic and 32-page format for ages 3-7, and under 100 pages for juvenile biography and religious topics for ages 8-13. Books with a spiritual theme. Query with proposal and SASE or submit complete ms.

HOW TO CONTACT Query with SASE or submit complete ms. Responds in 3-4 months to queries. Accepts simultaneous submissions.

TERMS Pays 8-10% royalty on retail price. Publishes ms 1 year after acceptance. Book catalog free or online.

AMERICAN PRESS

60 State St., Suite 700, Boston MA 02109. (617)247-0022. E-mail: americanpress@flash.net. Website: www.americanpresspublishers.com. *Integrating Technology Into Physical Education and Health*, by Ken Felker and D.J. Bradley. **Contact:** Jana Kirk, editor. Publishes college textbooks. 350 queries received/year. 100 mss received/year.

○ "Mss proposals are welcome in all subjects & disciplines."

NONFICTION "We prefer that our authors actually teach courses for which the manuscripts are designed." Query, or submit outline with tentative TOC. *No complete mss.*

⊕ AMULET BOOKS

Abrams Books for Young Readers, 115 W. 18th St., New York NY 10001. Website: www.amuletbooks.com. **Manuscript Acquisitions:** Susan Van Metre, vice president and publisher. Tamar Brazis, editorial director. Cecily Kaiser, publishing director. Produces 15 middle readers/year, 15 young adult titles/year. 10% of books by first-time authors.

FICTION Middle readers: adventure, contemporary, fantasy, history, science fiction, sports. Young adults/teens: adventure, contemporary, fantasy, history, science fiction, sports, suspense. Recently published *Diary of a Wimpy Kid*, by Jeff Kinney; *The Sisters Grimm*, by Michael Buckley (mid-grade series); *ttyl*, by Lauren Miracle (YA novel); *Heart of a Samurai*, by Margi Preus (Newberry Honor Award winner).

HOW TO CONTACT Fiction: Does not accept unsolicited manuscripts or queries.

ILLUSTRATION Works with 10-12 illustrators/year. Uses both color and b&w. Query with samples. Contact: Chad Beckerman, art director. Samples filed.

PHOTOGRAPHY Buys stock images and assigns work.

TERMS Offers advance against royalties. Illustrators paid by the project. Author sees galleys for review. Illustrators see dummies for review. Originals returned to artist at job's completion.

Ⓐ AVALON BOOKS

Thomas Bouregy & Sons, Inc., 160 Madison Ave., 5th Floor, New York NY 10016. (212)598-0222. Fax: (212)979-1862. E-mail: editorial@avalonbooks.com; avalon@avalonbooks.com; lbrown@avalonbooks.com. E-mail: editorial@avalonbooks.com. Website: www.avalonbooks.com. Publishes hardcover originals. **Publishes 60 titles/year**. Publishes manuscript 12-18 months after acceptance. Responds in 6 months to queries. No answer to manuscripts. **Pays 15% royalty. Offers advance**. "We publish contemporary romances (4 every 2 months), historical romances (2 every 2 months), mysteries (2 every 2 months) and traditional westerns (2 every 2 months). Submit first 3 sample chapters, a 2-3 page synopsis and SASE. Books range in length from a minimum of 50,000 words to a maximum of 70,000 words. However, if the ms is exceptional, we will accept somewhat longer books. Manuscripts that are too long will not be considered. The books shall be wholesome fiction, without graphic sex, violence or strong language. We are actively looking for romantic comedy, chick lit." **Contact:** Lia Brown, editor. Format publishes in hardcover originals

FICTION "We publish wholesome contemporary romances, mysteries, historical romances and westerns. Our books are read by adults as well as teenagers, and the main characters are all adults. All mysteries are contemporary. Submit first 3 sample chapters, a 2-3 page synopsis and SASE. The manuscripts should be between 50,000–70,000 words. However, if the ms is exceptional, we will accept somewhat longer books. Time period and setting are the author's preference. The historical romances will maintain the high level of reading expected by our readers. The books shall be wholesome fiction, without graphic sex, violence or strong language." Published *Death in the French Quarter*, by Kent Conwell (mystery); *Judgment at Gold Butte*, by Terrell L. Bowers (western); *Adieu, My Love*, by Lynn Turner (historical romance); *Everything But a Groom*, by Holly Jacobs (romantic comedy). "We do accept unagented material. We no longer accept e-mail queries. When submitting, include a query letter, a 2-3 page (and no longer) synopsis of the entire ms, and the first three chapters. All submissions must be typed and double spaced. If we think that your novel might be suitable for our list, we will contact you and request that you submit the entire manuscript. **Please note that any unsolicited full manuscripts will not be returned.** There is no need to send your partial to any specific editor at Avalon. The editors read all the genres that are listed above. Address your letter to: The Editors.

HOW TO CONTACT Query with SASE.

TIPS "Avalon Books are geared and marketed for librarians to purchase and distribute."

Ⓐ AVON BOOKS/BOOKS FOR YOUNG READERS

10 E. 53rd St., New York, NY 10022. (212)207-7000. Website: www.harperchildrens.com.

🚫Avon is not accepting unagented submissions.

➕ AZRO PRESS

PMB 342, 1704 Llano St. B, Santa Fe NM 87505. Tel: (505)989-3272. Fax: (505)989-3832. E-mail: books@azropress.com. Website: www.azropress.com. Estab. 1997. Specializes in illustrated children's books. **Writers contact:** Gae Eisenhardt. Produces 3-4 picture books/year; 1 young reader/year. 75% of books by first-time authors. "We like to publish illustrated children's books by Southwestern authors and illustrators. We are always looking for books with a Southwestern look or theme."

FICTION Picture books: animal, history, humor, nature/environment. Young readers: adventure, animal, hi-lo, history, humor. Average word length: picture books—1,200; young readers—2,000-2,500. Recently published *Paloma and The Dust Devil at The Balloon Festival*, by Marcy Heller, illustrated, by Nancy Poes; *Emus and Owlhoots*, by Sid Hausman.

NONFICTION Picture books: animal, geography, history. Young readers: geography, history.

HOW TO CONTACT Accepts international submissions. Fiction/nonfiction: Query or submit complete ms. Responds to queries/mss in 3-4 months. Publishes book 1-2 years after acceptance. Considers simultaneous submissions.

ILLUSTRATION Accepts material from international illustrators. Works with 3 illustrators/year. Uses color and b&w artwork. Reviews ms/illustration packages. Reviews work for future assignments. Query with samples. Submit samples to illustrations editor. Responds in 3-4 months. Samples not returned. Samples are filed.

TERMS Pays authors royalty of 5–10% based on wholesale price. Pays illustrators by the project ($2,000) or royalty of 5%. Author sees galleys for review. Illustrators see dummies for review. Originals returned to artist at job's completion. Catalog available for #10 SASE and 3 first-class stamps. Catalog online. See website for artist's, photographer's guidelines.

TIPS "We are not currently accepting new manuscripts. Please see our website for acceptance date."

⊕ BAILIWICK PRESS

309 East Mulberry St., Fort Collins CO 80524. (970) 672-4878. Fax: (970) 672-4731. E-mail: info@baili wickpress.com. Website: www.bailiwickpress.com. "We're a micro-press that produces books and other products that inspire and tell great stories. Our motto is: "Books with something to say."

○ "We are now considering submissions, agented and unagented, for children's and young adult fiction. We're looking for smart, funny, and layered writing that kids will clamor for. Illustrated fiction is desired but not required. (Illustrators are also invited to send samples.) Make us laugh out loud, ooh and aah, and cry, "Eureka!" Please read the Aldo Zelnick series to determine if we might be on the same page, then fill out our submission form. Please do not send submissions via snail mail. You must complete the online submission form to be considered. If, after completing and submitting the form, you also need to send us an e-mail attachment (such as sample illustrations or excerpts of graphics), you may e-mail them to info@bailiwickpress.com."

HOW TO CONTACT Query by e-mail at infor@bai liwickpress.com. Or mail to: 309 East Mulberry St., Fort Collins CO 80524.

ILLUSTRATION Illustrated fiction desired but not required. Send samples.

BALZER & BRAY

HarperCollins Children's Books, 10 E. 53rd St., New York, NY 10022. (212)207-7000. Website: www.harpercol linschildrens.com. Estab. 2008. Specializes in fiction. Publishes 10 picture books/year; 8 middle readers/year; 7 young adult/year.

FICTION Picture books, young readers: adventure, animal, anthology, concept, contemporary, fantasy, history, humor, multicultural, nature/environment, poetry, science fiction, special needs, sports, suspense. middle readers, young adults/teens: adventure, animal, anthology, contemporary, fantasy, history, hu-

mor, multicultural, nature/environment, poetry, science fiction, special needs, sports, suspense.

NONFICTION All levels: animal, biography, concept, cooking, history, multicultural, music/dance, nature/environment, science, self-help, social issues, special needs, sports. "We will publish very few nonfiction titles, maybe 1-2 per year."

HOW TO CONTACT Interested in agented material. Publishes a book 18 months after acceptance.

ILLUSTRATION Works with 10 illustrators/year. Uses both color and b&w. Illustrations only: send tearsheets to be kept on file. **Contact:** Editor. Responds only if interested. Samples are not returned.

PHOTOGRAPHY Works on assignment only.

TERMS Offers advances. Pays illustrators by the project. Sends galleys to authors. Originals returned to artist at job's completion. Catalog is available on our website.

○ BARRONS EDUCATIONAL SERIES

250 Wireless Blvd. Hauppauge NY 11788. Fax: (631)434-3723. E-mail: waynebarr@barronseduc. com. Website: www.barronseduc.com. **Manuscript Acquisitions:** Wayne R. Barr, acquisitions manager. **Art Acquisitions:** Bill Kuchler. Publishes 20 picture books/year; 20 young readers/year; 20 middle readers/year; 10 young adult titles/year. Most are from packagers.

FICTION Picture books: animal, concept, multicultural, nature/environment. Young readers: adventure, multicultural, nature/environment, fantasy, suspense/mystery. Middle readers: adventure, fantasy, multicultural, nature/environment, problem novels, suspense/mystery. Young adults: problem novels. Examples: *Night of the Dragon*, by Michael Steele; *Renoir and the Boy in the Long Hair*, by Wendy Wax. Stories with an educational element are appealing.

NONFICTION Picture books: concept, reference. Young readers: biography, how-to, reference, self-help, social issues. Middle readers: hi-lo, how-to, reference, self-help, social issues. Young adults: reference, self-help, social issues, sports.

HOW TO CONTACT Fiction: Query via e-mail with no attached files. Snail mail query letters for children's books discouraged. Nonfiction: Submit outline/synopsis and sample chapters. "Nonfiction submissions must be accompanied by SASE for response." Responds to queries in 2 months; mss in 4 months. Publishes a book 9–12 months after acceptance. Will consider simultaneous submissions.

ILLUSTRATION Works with 20 illustrators/year. Reviews ms/illustration packages from artists. Query first; 3 chapters of ms with 1 piece of final art, remainder roughs. Illustrations only: Submit tearsheets or slides plus résumé. Responds in 2 months.

TERMS Pays authors royalty of 10-12% based on net price or buys ms outright for $2,000 minimum. Pays illustrators by the project based on retail price. Sends galleys to authors; dummies to illustrators. Book catalog, ms/artist's guidelines for 9×12 SAE.

TIPS Writers: "We publish pre-school storybooks, concept books and middle grade and YA chapter books. No romance novels. Those with an educational element." Illustrators: "We are happy to receive a sample illustration to keep on file for future consideration. Periodic notes reminding us of your work are acceptable." Children's book themes "are becoming much more contemporary and relevant to a child's day-to-day activities, fewer talking animals. We are interested in fiction (ages 7-11 and ages 12-16) dealing with modern problems."

BEHRMAN HOUSE INC.

11 Edison Place, Springfield, NJ 07081. (973)379-7200. Fax: (973)379-7280. Website: www.behrmanhouse. com. **Managing Editor:** Editorial Department. Publishes 3 young readers/year; 3 middle readers/year; 3 young adult titles/year. 12% of books by first-time authors; 2% of books from agented writers. Publishes books on all aspects of Judaism: history, cultural, textbooks, holidays. "Behrman House publishes quality books of Jewish content—history, Bible, philosophy, holidays, ethics—for children and adults."

FICTION All levels: Judaism.

NONFICTION All levels: Judaism, Jewish educational textbooks. Average word length: young reader—1,200; middle reader—2,000; young adult—4,000. Recently published *I Kid's Mensch Handbook*, by Scott E. Blumenthal; *Shalom Ivrit 3*, by Nili Ziv.

HOW TO CONTACT Fiction/nonfiction: Submit outline/synopsis and sample chapters. Responds to queries in 1 month; mss in 2 months. Publishes a book 2.5 years after acceptance. Will consider simultaneous submissions.

ILLUSTRATION Works with 6 children's illustrators/year. Reviews ms/illustration packages from artists. "Query first." Illustrations only: Query with samples;

send unsolicited art samples by mail. Responds to queries in 1 month; mss in 2 months.

PHOTOGRAPHY Purchases photos from freelancers. Buys stock and assigns work. Uses photos of families involved in Jewish activities. Uses color and b&w prints. Photographers should query with samples. Send unsolicited photos by mail. Submit portfolio for review.

TERMS Pays authors royalty of 3-10% based on retail price or buys ms outright for $1,000-5,000. Offers advance. Pays illustrators by the project (range: $500-5,000). Sends galleys to authors; dummies to illustrators. Book catalog free on request.

TIPS Looking for "religious school texts" with Judaic themes or general trade Judaica.

○ Ⓐ BENCHMARK BOOKS

99 White Plains Rd., Tarrytown NY 10591. (914)332-8888. Fax: (914)332-1082. E-mail: mbisson@marshall cavendish.com. Website: www.marshallcavendish. us. **Benchmark Books is not accepting any unsolicited manuscripts at this time; they are still, however, considering agented mss.** Publishes approx. 300 young reader, middle reader and young adult books/year. "We look for interesting treatments of only nonfiction subjects related to elementary, middle school and high school curriculum." **Contact:** Michelle Bisson, manuscript acquisitions.

NONFICTION Most nonfiction topics should be curriculum related. Average word length: 4,000-20,000. All books published as part of a series. Recently published *Barbarians, Amazing Machines, Perspectives On.*

HOW TO CONTACT Nonfiction: "Please read our catalog or view our website before submitting proposals. We only publish series. We do not publish individual titles." Submit outline/synopsis and 1 or more sample chapters. Responds to queries/mss in 3 months. Publishes a book 2 years after acceptance. Will consider simultaneous submissions.

PHOTOGRAPHY Buys stock and assigns work.

TERMS Buys work outright. Sends galleys to authors. Book catalog available online. All imprints included in a single catalog.

Ⓐ THE BERKLEY PUBLISHING GROUP

375 Hudson St., New York NY 10014. (212)366-2000. E-mail: online@us.penguingroup.com. Website: http://us.penguingroup.com/. **Contact:** Leslie Gelbman, president and publisher. The Berkley Publishing Group publishes a variety of general nonfiction

and fiction including the traditional categories of romance, mystery and science fiction. Publishes paperback and mass market originals and reprints.

○ "Due to the high volume of manuscripts received, most Penguin Group (USA) Inc. imprints do not normally accept unsolicited manuscripts."

FICTION No occult fiction. *Prefers agented submissions.*

NONFICTION No memoirs or personal stories. *Prefers agented submissions.*

HOW TO CONTACT "The preferred and standard method for having manuscripts considered for publication by a major publisher is to submit them through an established literary agent."

BETHANY HOUSE PUBLISHERS

(616)676-9185. Fax: (616)676-9573. Website: www. bethanyhouse.com. 6030 E. Fulton Rd., Ada MI 49301. "Bethany House Publishers specializes in books that communicate Biblical truth and assist people in both spiritual and practical areas of life. While we do not accept unsolicited queries or proposals via telephone or e-mail, we will consider 1-page queries sent by fax and directed to Adult Nonfiction, Adult Fiction, or Young Adult/Children." Publishes hardcover and trade paperback originals, mass market paperback reprints.

○ *All unsolicited mss returned unopened.*

HOW TO CONTACT Bethany House does not accept unsolicited mss.

TIPS "Bethany House Publishers' publishing program relates Biblical truth to all areas of life—whether in the framework of a well-told story, of a challenging book for spiritual growth, or of a Bible reference work. We are seeking high-quality fiction and nonfiction that will inspire and challenge our audience."

○ BIRDSONG BOOKS

1322 Bayview Rd. Middletown DE 19709. (302)378-7274. E-mail: Birdsong@BirdsongBooks.com. Website: www.BirdsongBooks.com. **Manuscript and Art Acquisitions:** Nancy Carol Willis, president. Publishes 1 picture book/year. "Birdsong Books seeks to spark the delight of discovering our wild neighbors and natural habitats. We believe knowledge and understanding of nature fosters caring and a desire to protect the Earth and all living things. Our emphasis

is on North American animals and habitats, rather than people."

NONFICTION Picture books, young readers: activity books, animal, nature/environment. Average word length: picture books—800-1,000 plus content for 2-4 pages of back matter. Recently published *The Animals' Winter Sleep*, by Lynda-Graham Barber (age 3-6, nonfiction picture book); *Red Knot: A Shorebird's Incredible Journey*, by Nancy Carol Willis (age 6-9, nonfiction picture book); *Raccoon Moon*, by Nancy Carol Willis (ages 5-8, natural science picture book); *The Robins In Your Backyard*, by Nancy Carol Willis (ages 4-7, nonfiction picture book).

HOW TO CONTACT Nonfiction: Submit complete manuscript package with SASE. Responds to mss in 3 months. Publishes book 2-3 years after acceptance. Will consider simultaneous submissions (if stated).

ILLUSTRATION Accepts material from residents of U.S. Works with 1 illustrator/year. Reviews ms/illustration packages from artists. Send ms with dummy (plus samples/tearsheets for style). Illustrations only: Query with brochure, résumé, samples, SASE, or tearsheets. Responds only if interested. Samples returned with SASE.

PHOTOGRAPHY Uses North American animals and habitats (currently wading birds—herons, egrets, and the like). Submit cover letter, résumé, promo piece, stock photo list.

TIPS "We are a small independent press actively seeking manuscripts that fit our narrowly defined niche. We are only interested in nonfiction, natural science picture books or educational activity books about North American animals and habitats. We are not interested in fiction stories based on actual events. Our books include several pages of back matter suitable for early elementary classrooms. Mailed submissions with SASE only. No e-mail submissions or phone calls, please. Cover letters should sell author/illustrator and book idea."

BLACK ROSE WRITING

E-mail: creator@blackrosewriting.com. Website: www. blackrosewriting.com. "Black Rose Writing is an independent publishing house that believes in developing a personal relationship with our authors. We publish only one genre—our genre. Publishes nonfiction books, novels, short story collections, novellas, juvenile. Actively seeking fiction, novels and short story collections. We are seeking growth in an array of different genres and searching for new publicity venues for our authors everyday. Black Rose Writing doesn't promise our authors the world, leading them to become overwhelmed by the competitive and difficult venture. We are honest with our authors, and we give them the insight to generate solid leads without wasting their time. Black Rose Writing is able to promote, showcase, and produce your dedicated stories through the company itself and with our publishing/printing connections. We want to make your writing successes possible and eliminate the fear of a toilsome and lengthy experience." **Contact:** Reagan Rothe.

FICTION Young adult, juvenile, picture books, short story collections.

NONFICTION Query with SASE. Submit synopsis, author bio.

ILLUSTRATION Accepts picture books.

TIPS "Please query first with synopsis and author information. Allow 3-4 weeks for response. Always check spelling and do not forward your initial contact e-mails."

Ⓐ BLOOMSBURY CHILDREN'S BOOKS

E-mail: bloomsbury.kids@bloomsburyusa.com. Imprint of Bloomsbury PLC, 175 Fifth Ave., 8th Floor, New York, NY 10010. Website:www.bloomsburykids. com. Specializes in fiction, picture books. Publishes 15 picture books/year; 10 young readers/year; 20 middle readers/year; 25 young adult titles/year. 25% of books by first-time authors.

◯ No phone calls or e-mails.

FICTION Picture books: adventure,animal, contemporary, fantasy, folktales, history, humor, multicultural, poetry, suspense/mystery. Young readers: adventure, animal, anthology, concept,contemporary, fantasy, folktales, history, humor, multicultural, suspense/mystery. Middle readers: adventure, animal, contemporary, fantasy,folktales, history, humor, multicultural, poetry, problem novels. Young adults:adventure, animal, anthology, contemporary, fantasy, folktales, history, humor, multicultural, problem novels, science fiction, sports, suspense/mystery. Recently published *Too Purpley*, by Jean Reidy (picture book); *A Whole Nother Story*, by Dr. Cuthbert Soup (middle reader); *The Captivate*, by Carrie Jones (young adult). "We publish picture books, chapter books, middle grade, and YA novels, and some nonfiction." Query with SASE. Submit clips, first 3 chapters with SASE.

HOW TO CONTACT *Agented submissions only.* Guidelines available online.

TERMS Pays authors royalty or work purchased outright for jackets. Offers advances. Pays illustrators by the project or royalty. Pays photographers by the project or per photo. Sends galleys to authors; dummies to illustrators. Originals returned to artist at job's completion. Writer's and art guidelines available on their website: www.bloomsburykids. com/FAQ .

TIPS "All Bloomsbury Children's Books submissions are considered on an individual basis. Bloomsbury-Children's Books will no longer respond to unsolicited manuscripts or art submissions. Please include a telephone AND e-mail address where we may contact you if we are interested in your work. Do NOT send a self-addressed stamped envelope. We regret the inconvenience, but unfortunately, we are too understaffed to maintain a correspondence with authors. There is no need to send art with a picture book manuscript. Artists should submit art with a picture book manuscript. We do not return art samples. Please do not send us original art! Please note that we do accept simultaneous submissions but please be courteous and inform us if another house has made an offer on your work. Do not send originals or your only copy of anything. We are not liable for artwork or manuscript submissions. Please address all submissions to the attention of 'Manuscript Submissions'. Please make sure that everything is stapled, paper-clipped, or rubber-banded together. We do not accept e-mail or CD/DVD submissions. Be sure your work is appropriate for us. Familiarize yourself with our list by going to bookstores or libraries."

BRIGHT RING PUBLISHING, INC.

P.O. Box 31338, Bellingham WA 98228. (360)592-9201. Fax: (360)592-4503. E-mail: maryann@brightring. com. Website: www.brightring.com. **Editor:** Mary-Ann Kohl. Bright Ring is no longer accepting manuscript submissions.

◯ Bright Ring is no longer accepting manuscript submissions.

CALKINS CREEK

Boyds Mills Press, 815 Church St., Honesdale, PA 18431. Website: www.calkinscreekbooks.com. Estab. 2004. "We aim to publish books that are a well-written blend of creative writing and extensive research, which emphasize important events, people, and places in U.S. history."

FICTION All levels: history. Recently published *Healing Water*, by Joyce Moyer Hostetter (ages 10 and up, historical fiction); *The Shakeress*, by Kimberly Heuston (ages 12 and up, historical fiction).

NONFICTION All levels: history. Recently published *Farmer George Plants a Nation* by Peggy Thomas (ages 8 and up, nonfiction picture book); *Robert H. Jackson*, by Gail Jarrow (ages 10 and up, historical fiction);

HOW TO CONTACT Accepts international submissions. Fiction: Submit outline/synopsis and 3 sample chapters. Nonfiction: Submit outline/synopsis and 3 sample chapters. Considers simultaneous submissions. Label package "Manuscript Submissions" and inlcude SASE.

ILLUSTRATION Accepts material from international illustrators. Works with 25 (for all Boyds Mills Press imprints) illustrators/year. Uses both color and b&w. Reviews ms/illustration packages. For ms/illustration packages: Submit ms with 2 pieces of final art. Submit ms/illustration packages to address above, label package " Manuscript Submission." Reviews work for future assignments. If interested in illustrating future titles, query with samples. Submit samples to address above. Label package "Art Sample Submission."

PHOTOGRAPHY Buys stock images and assigns work. Submit photos to: address above, label package "Art Sample Submission". Uses color or b&w 8×10 prints. For first contact, send promo piece (color or b&w).

TERMS Authors paid royalty or work purchased outright. Offers advances. Illustrators paid by the project or royalties; varies. Photographers paid by the project, per photo, or royalties; varies. Manuscripts/artist's guidelines available on Website.

TIPS "Read through our recently-published titles and review our catalog. When selecting titles to publish, our emphasis will be on important events, people, and places in U.S. history. Writers are encouraged to submit a detailed bibliography, including secondary and primary sources, and expert reviews with their submissions."

CANDLEWICK PRESS

99 Dover St., Somerville MA 02144. (617)661-3330. Fax: (617)661-0565. E-mail: bigbear@candlewick. com. Website: www.candlewick.com. Publishes 160 picture books/year; 15 middle readers/year; 15 young adult titles/year. 5% of books by first-time authors. "Our books are truly for children, and we strive for the very highest standards in the writing, illustrating, designing and production of all of our books. And we are not averse to risk." Recently published *The Astonishing Life of Octavian Nothing, Traitor to the Nation: Volume One: The Pox Party* by M.T. Anderson (young adult fiction); *Surrender*, by Sonya Hartnett (young adult fiction); *Good Masters! Sweet Ladies! by* Laura Amy Schlitz, illustrated by Robert Byrd (middle grade poetry collection), *Dragonology*, by Ernest Drake; Encyclopedia Prehistorica: *Dinosaurs*, by Robert Sabuda and Matthew Reinhart. Recently published *Twelve Rounds to Glory: The Story of Muhammad Ali*, by Charles R. Smith Jr., illustrated by Bryan Collier. *Does not accept unsolicited illustration packages/dummies.* **Contact:** Deb Wayshak, executive editor (fiction); Joan Powers, editor-at-large (picture books); Liz Bicknell, editorial director/associate publisher (poetry, picture books, fiction); Mary Lee Donovan, executive editor (picture books, nonfiction/fiction); Hilary Van Dusen, senior editor (nonfiction/fiction); Sarah Ketchersid, senior editor (board, toddler). "Candlewick Press publishes high-quality, illustrated children's books for ages infant through young adult. We are a truly child-centered publisher." Publishes hardcover and trade paperback originals and reprints.

○ *Candlewick Press is not accepting queries and unsolicited mss at this time.* Candlewick title *Good Masters! Sweet Ladies! Voices from a Medieval Village*, by Amy Schlitz won the John Newbery Medal in 2008. Their title *Twelve Rounds to Glory: The Story of Muhammad Ali*, by Charles R. Smith Jr.illustrated by Bryan Collier, won a Coretta Scott King Author Honor Award in 2008. Their title *The Astonishing Life of Octavian Nothing*, by M.T. Anderson won the Boston Globe-Hornbook Award for Fiction and Poetry in 2007.

FICTION Picture books: animal, concept, contemporary, fantasy, history, humor, multicultural, nature/environment, poetry. Middle readers, young adults: contemporary, fantasy, history, humor, multicultural, poetry, science fiction, sports, suspense/mystery. *No unsolicited mss.* "We do not accept editorial queries or submissions online. If you are an author or illustrator and would like us to consider your work, please read our submissions policy (online) to learn more."

NONFICTION Picture books: concept, biography, geography, nature/environment. Young readers: biography, geography, nature/environment. Good writing is essential; specific topics are less important than strong, clear writing. *No unsolicited mss.*

ILLUSTRATION Works with approx. 40 illustrators/year. "We prefer to see a range of styles from artists along with samples showing strong characters (human or animals) in various settings with various emotions."

TERMS Pays authors royalty of 2½-10% based on retail price. Offers advances. Pays illustrators 2½-10% royalty based on retail price. Sends galleys to authors; dummies to illustrators. Pays photographers 2½-10% royalty. Original artwork returned at job's completion.

TIPS *"We no longer accept unsolicited mss. See our website for further information about us."*

CAROLRHODA BOOKS, INC.

A division of Lerner Publishing Group, 1251 Washington Ave. N.,Minneapolis, MN 55401. Website: www.lernerbooks.com. Estab. 1969. Publishes hardcover originals. Averages 8-10 picture books each year for ages 3-8, six fiction titles for ages 7-18, and 2-3 nonfiction titles for various ages. Starting in 2007, Lerner Publishing Group no longer accepts submissions to any of their imprints except for Kar-Ben Publishing.

◯ Starting in 2007, Lerner Publishing Group no longer accepts submissions to any of their imprints except for Kar-Ben Publishing.

HOW TO CONTACT "We will continue to seek targeted solicitations at specific reading levels and in specific subject areas. The company will list these targeted solicitations on our website and in national newsletters, such as the SCBWI Bulletin."

CARTWHEEL BOOKS

Imprint of Scholastic Inc. 557 Broadway, New York, NY 10012. Website: www.scholastic.com. Estab. 1991. Book publisher. **Manuscript Acquisitions:** Rotem Moscovich, editor; Jeffrey Salane, editor. **Art Acquisitions:** Daniel Moreton, executive art director. Publishes 15-25 picture books/year; 10-15 easy readers/year; 40-50 novelty/concept/board books/year.

FICTION Picture books, young readers: seasonal/holiday, humor, family/love. Average word length: picture books—100-500; easy readers 100-1,500.

NONFICTION Picture books, young readers: seasonal/curricular topics involving animals (polar animals, ocean animals, hibernation), nature (fall leaves, life cycles, weather, solar system), history (first Thanksgiving, MLK Jr., George Washington, Columbus). "Most of our nonfiction is either written on assignment or is within a series. We do not want to see any arts/crafts or cooking." Average word length: picture books 100-1,500; young readers 100-2,000.

HOW TO CONTACT Cartwheel Books is no longer accepting unsolicited mss. All unsolicited materials will be returned unread. Fiction/nonfiction: For previously published or agented authors, submit complete ms. Responds to mss in 6 months. Publishes a book within 2 years after acceptance. SASE required with all submissions.

ILLUSTRATION Works with 30 illustrators/year. Reviews illustration packages from artists. Illustrations only: Query with samples; arrange personal portfolio review; send promo sheet, tearsheets to be kept on file. Contact: Creative Director. Responds in 6 months. Samples returned with SASE; samples filed. Please do not send original artwork.

PHOTOGRAPHY Buys stock and assigns work. Uses photos of kids, families, vehicles, toys, animals. Submit published samples, color promo piece.

TERMS Pays advance against royalty or flat fee. Sends galley to authors; dummy to illustrators. Originals returned to artist at job's completion.

TIPS "With each Cartwheel list, we seek a pleasing balance of board books and novelty books, hardcover picture books and gift books, nonfiction, paperback storybooks and easy readers. Cartwheel seeks to acquire projects that speak to young children and their world: new and exciting novelty formats, fresh seasonal and holiday stories, curriculum/concept-based titles, and books for beginning readers. Our books are inviting and appealing, clearly marketable, and have inherent educational and social value. We strive to provide the earliest readers with relevant and exciting books that will ultimately lead to a lifetime of reading, learning and wondering. Know what types of books we do. Check out bookstores or catalogs first to see where your work would fit best, and why."

◯ CHARLESBRIDGE

85 Main St., Watertown, MA 02472. (617)926-0329. Fax: (617)926-5720. E-mail: tradeeditorial@charlesbridge.com. Website: www.charlesbridge.com. Estab. 1980. Book publisher. **Contact:** Trade Editorial

Department. Publishes 60% nonfiction, 40% fiction picture books and early chapter books. Publishes nature, science, multicultural, social studies, and fiction picture books and transitional "bridge books" (books ranging from early readers to middle grade chapter books).

FICTION Picture books and chapter books: "Strong, realistic stories with enduring themes." Considers the following categories: adventure, concept, contemporary, health, history, humor, multicultural, nature/environment, special needs, sports, suspense/mystery. Recently published *The Searcher and Old Tree*, by David McPhail; *Good Dog, Aggie* by Lori Ries; *The Perfect Sword* by Scott Goto; *Not So Tall for Six*, by Dianna Hutts Aston; *Wiggle and Waggle* by Caroline Arnold; *Rickshaw Girl* by Mitali Perkins.

NONFICTION Picture books and chapter books: animal, biography, careers, concept, geography, health, history, multicultural, music/dance, nature/environment, religion, science, social issues, special needs, hobbies, sports. Average word length: picture books, 1,000.

HOW TO CONTACT Send mss as exclusive submission for three months. Responds only to mss of interest. Full mss only; no queries. Please do not include a self-addressed stamped envelope.

ILLUSTRATION Works with 5-10 illustrators/year. Uses color artwork only. Illustrations only: Query with samples; provide resume, tearsheets to be kept on file. "Send no original artwork, please." Responds only if interested. Samples returned with SASE; samples filed. Originals returned at job's completion. Pays authors and illustrators in royalties or work purchased outright. Manuscript/art guidelines available for SASE. Exclusive submissions only.

TIPS "Charlesbridge publishes picture books and transitional 'bridge books'. We look for fresh and engaging voices and directions in both fiction and nonfiction."

⊕ CHELSEA HOUSE, AN INFOBASE LEARNING COMPANY

Facts on File, 132 West 31st Street, 17th Floor, New York, New York 10001. (800)322-8755. Fax: (917)339-0326. E-mail: jciovacco@factsonfile.com. Website: www.chelseahouse.com. Specializes in nonfiction chapter books. **Manuscript Acquisitions:** Laurie Likoff, editorial director; Justine Ciovacco, managing editor. Imprints: Chelsea Clubhouse; Chelsea House.

Produces 150 middle readers/year, 150 young adult books/year. 10% of books by first-time authors.

HOW TO CONTACT "All books are parts of series. We do not publish stand-alone books. Most series topics are developed by in-house editors, but suggestions are welcome. We prefer authors with a degree or solid experience in science or a history niche. Authors may query with résumé and list of publications."

○ CHICAGO REVIEW PRESS

814 N. Franklin St., Chicago, IL 60610. (312)337-0747. Fax: (312)337-5110. E-mail: frontdesk@chicagoreviewpress.com. Website: www.chicagoreviewpress.com. **Manuscript Acquisitions:** Cynthia Sherry, publisher. **Art Acquisitions:** Allison Felus, managing editor. Publishes 4-5 middle readers/year; 2-3 young adult titles/year. 33% of books by first-time authors; 30% of books from agented authors. "Chicago Review Press publishes high-quality, nonfiction, educational activity books that extend the learning process through hands-on projects and accurate and interesting text. We look for activity books that are as much fun as they are constructive and informative."

○ Chicago Review Press only publishes nonfiction.

NONFICTION Young readers, middle readers and young adults: activity books, arts/crafts, multicultural, history, nature/environment, science. "We're interested in hands-on, educational books; anything else probably will be rejected." Average length: young readers and young adults—144-160 pages. Recently published *Amazing Rubber Band Cars*, by Michael Rigsby (ages 9 and up); *Don't Touch That!*, by Jeff Day M.D. (ages 7 to 9); and *Abraham Lincoln for Kids*, by Janis Herbert (ages 9 and up).

HOW TO CONTACT Enclose cover letter and no more than a table of contents and 1-2 sample chapters; prefers not to receive e-mail queries. Send for guidelines. Responds to queries/mss in 2 months. Publishes a book 1-2 years after acceptance. Will consider simultaneous submissions and previously published work.

ILLUSTRATION Works with 6 illustrators/year. Uses primarily b&w artwork. Reviews ms/illustration packages from artists. Submit 1-2 chapters of ms with corresponding pieces of final art. Illustrations only: Query with samples, résumé. Responds only if interested. Samples returned with SASE.

PHOTOGRAPHY Buys photos from freelancers

("but not often"). Buys stock and assigns work. Wants "instructive photos. We consult our files when we know what we're looking for on a book-by-book basis." Uses b&w prints.

TERMS Pays authors royalty of $7^1\!/_2$-$12^1\!/_2$% based on retail price. Offers advances of $3,000-6,000. Pays illustrators by the project (range varies considerably). Pays photographers by the project (range varies considerably). Original artwork "usually" returned at job's completion. Book catalog/ms guidelines available for $3.

TIPS "We're looking for original activity books for small children and the adults caring for them—new themes and enticing projects to occupy kids' imaginations and promote their sense of personal creativity. We like activity books that are as much fun as they are constructive. Please write for guidelines so you'll know what we're looking for."

CHILDREN'S BRAINS ARE YUMMY (CBAY) BOOKS

P.O. Box 92411, Austin TX 78709. (512)789-1004. Fax: (512)473-7710. E-mail: submissions@cbaybooks.com. Website: www.cbaybooks.com. Publishes 1 picture book/year, 2-4 middle readers/year and 1-2 young readers/year. 30% of books by first-time authors. Recent titles: *Dry Souls*, by Denise Getson (teen science fantasy); *The Forgotten Worlds Trilogy* (*The Emerald Tablet, The Navel of the World*, et al.), by PJ Hoover, (middle grade science fiction); *The Sacred Books Series* (*The Book of Nonsense, The Book of Knowledge*, et al.), by David Michael Slater (middle grade fantasy). **Contact:** Madeline Smoot, Publisher.

FICTION "CBAY Books currently focuses on quality fantasy and science fiction books for the middle grade and teen markets. Although we are exploring the possibility of publishing fantasy and science fiction books in the future, we are not seeking submissions for them at this time. We do welcome books that mix genres—a fantasy mystery for example—but since our press currently has a narrow focus, all submissions need to have fantasy or science fiction elements to fit in with our list."

HOW TO CONTACT Accepts international material. Submit outline/synopsis and 3 sample chapters. Responds in 3 months to mss. Average length of acceptance of a book-length manuscript and publication of the work is 2 years. Considers simultaneous submissions.

ILLUSTRATION Accepts international material. Works with 0-1 illustrators/year. Uses color artwork only. Reviews artwork. Send manuscripts with dummy. Send résumé and tearsheets. Send samples to Madeline Smoot. Responds to queries only if interested.

PHOTOGRAPHY Buy stock images.

TERMS Pays authors royalty 10%-15% based on wholesale price. Offers advances against royalties. Average amount $500. Send galleys to authors. Brochure available on website. Guidelines available for writers online.

TIPS "CBAY Books only accepts unsolicited submissions from authors at specific times for specific genres. Please check the website to see if we are accepting books at this time. Manuscripts received when submissions are closed are not read."

○ CHRISTIAN ED. PUBLISHERS

P.O. Box 26639, San Diego CA 92196. E-mail: crogers@cehouse.com. Website: www.ChristianEdWarehouse.com. Book publisher. Acquisitions: Janet Ackelson, assistant editor; Carol Rogers, managing editor; Nicole Tom, production coordinator. Publishes 110 Bible curriculum titles/year. "We publish curriculum for children and youth, including program and student books and take-home papers—all handled by our assigned freelance writers only." **Contact:** Janet Ackelson, assistant editor. "Christian Ed. Publishers is an independent, nondenominational, evangelical company founded over 50 years ago to produce Christ-centered curriculum materials based on the Word of God for thousands of churches of different denominations throughout the world. Our mission is to introduce children, teens, and adults to a personal faith in Jesus Christ, and to help them grow in their faith and service to the Lord. We publish materials that teach moral and spiritual values while training individuals for a lifetime of Christian service. Currently emphasizing Bible curriculum for preschool-preteen ages, including program and student books and take-home papers—all handled by our assigned freelance writers only. Do not send unsolicited manuscripts. Ask for a writer's application."

○ Publishes 110 Bible curriculum titles/year.

FICTION Young readers: contemporary. Middle readers: adventure, contemporary, suspense/mystery. "We publish fiction for Bible club take-home papers. All fiction is on assignment only."

NONFICTION Publishes Bible curriculum and take-home papers for all ages. Recently published *All-Stars for Jesus*, by Lucinda Rollings and Laura Gray, illustrated by Aline Heiser (Bible club curriculum for grades 4-6); *Honeybees Classroom Activity Sheets*, by Janet Miller and Wanda Pelfrey, illustrated by Ron Widman (Bible club curriculum for ages 2-3).

HOW TO CONTACT Fiction/nonfiction: Query. Responds to queries in 5 weeks. Publishes assignments 1 year after acceptance. Send SASE for guidelines or contact Christian Editor at crogers@cehouse.com. Ask for a writer's application. Do not send manuscripts.

ILLUSTRATION Works with 2-3 illustrators/year. Query by e-mail. Contact: Nicole Tom, production coordinator (ntom@cehouse.com). Responds in 1 month. Samples returned with SASE.

TERMS Work purchased outright from authors for 3¢/word. Pays illustrators $18-20/page. Book catalog available for 9×12 SAE and 4 first-class stamps; ms and art guidelines available for SASE or via e-mail.

TIPS "Read our guidelines carefully before sending us a manuscript or illustrations. Do not send unsolicited manuscripts. All writing and illustrating is done on assignment only and must be age-appropriate (preschool-6th grade). Ask for a writer's application. Do not send manuscripts."

CHRONICLE BOOKS

680 Second St., San Francisco CA 94107. Website: www.chroniclekids.com. Publishes 90 (both fiction and nonfiction) books/year; 5-10% middle readers/year; young adult nonfiction titles/year. 10-25% of books by first-time authors; 20-40% of books from agented writers. **Contact:** Acquisitions: Victoria Rock, founding publisher and editor-at-large; Andrea Menotti, senior editor; Julie Romeis, editor; Melissa Manlove, editor, Naomi Kirsten, assistant editor; Mary Colgan, assistant editor.

FICTION Picture books, young readers, middle readers, young adults: "We are open to a very wide range of topics." Recently published *Wave* by Suzy Lee (all ages, picture book); *Ivy and Bean* (series), by Annie Barrows, illustrated by Sophie Blackall (ages 6-10, chapter book).

NONFICTION Picture books, young readers, middle readers, young adults: "We are open to a very wide range of topics." Recently published *Delicious: The Life & Art of Wayne Thiebaud* by Susan Rubin (ages 9-14, middle grade)

HOW TO CONTACT Fiction/nonfiction: Submit complete ms (picture books); submit outline/synopsis and 3 sample chapters (for older readers). Responds to queries in 1 month; will not respond to submissions unless interested. Publishes a book 1-3 years after acceptance. Will consider simultaneous submissions, as long as they are marked "multiple submissions." Will not consider submissions by fax, e-mail or disk. Do not include SASE; do not send original materials. No submissions will be returned; to confirm receipt, include a SASP.

ILLUSTRATION Works with 40-50 illustrators/year. Wants "unusual art, graphically strong, something that will stand out on the shelves. Fine art, not mass market." Reviews ms/illustration packages from artists. "Indicate if project *must* be considered jointly, or if editor may consider text and art separately." Illustrations only: Submit samples of artist's work (not necessarily from book, but in the envisioned style). Slides, tearsheets and color photocopies OK. (No original art.) Dummies helpful. Résumé helpful. Samples suited to our needs are filed for future reference. Samples not suited to our needs will be recycled. Queries and project proposals responded to in same time frame as author query/proposals."

PHOTOGRAPHY Purchases photos from freelancers. Works on assignment only.

TERMS Generally pays authors in royalties based on retail price, "though we do occasionally work on a flat fee basis." Advance varies. Illustrators paid royalty based on retail price or flat fee. Sends proofs to authors and illustrators. Book catalog for 9 x 12 SAE and 8 first-class stamps; ms guidelines for #10 SASE.

TIPS "Chronicle Books publishes an eclectic mixture of traditional and innovative children's books. We are interested in taking on projects that have a unique bent to them—be it subject matter, writing style, or illustrative technique. As a small list, we are looking for books that will lend us a distinctive flavor. We are also interested in growing our fiction program for older readers, including chapter books, middle grade, and young adult projects."

CHRONICLE BOOKS FOR CHILDREN

(415)537-4200. Fax: (415)537-4460. E-mail: frontdesk@chroniclebooks.com. Website: www.chroniclekids.com. **Contact:** Children's Division. "Chronicle

Books for Children publishes an eclectic mixture of traditional and innovative children's books. Our aim is to publish books that inspire young readers to learn and grow creatively while helping them discover the joy of reading. We're looking for quirky, bold artwork and subject matter. Currently emphasizing picture books. De-emphasizing young adult." Publishes hardcover and trade paperback originals. 30,000 queries received/year.

FICTION "We do not accept proposals by fax, via e-mail, or on disk. When submitting artwork, either as a part of a project or as samples for review, do not send original art."

NONFICTION Query with synopsis.

TIPS "We are interested in projects that have a unique bent to them—be it in subject matter, writing style, or illustrative technique. As a small list, we are looking for books that will lend our list a distinctive flavor. Primarily we are interested in fiction and nonfiction picture books for children ages up to eight years, and nonfiction books for children ages up to twelve years. We publish board, pop-up, and other novelty formats as well as picture books. We are also interested in early chapter books, middle grade fiction, and young adult projects."

CLARION BOOKS

Website: www.houghtonmifflinbooks.com; www. hmco.com. Guidelines available on website. **Contact:** Dinah Stevenson, vice president and publisher; Jennifer B. Greene, senior editor (contemporary fiction, picture books for all ages, nonfiction); Jennifer Wingertzahn, editor (fiction, picture books); Lynne Polvino, editor (fiction, nonfiction, picture books). "Clarion Books publishes picture books, nonfiction, and fiction for infants through grade 12. Avoid telling your stories in verse unless you are a professional poet." Publishes hardcover originals for children. *Identify multiple submissions.*

"We are no longer responding to your unsolicited submission unless we are interested in publishing it. Please do not include a SASE. Submissions will be recycled, and you will not hear from us regarding the status of your submission unless we are interested. We regret that we cannot respond personally to each submission, but we do consider each and every submission we receive."

FICTION "Clarion is highly selective in the areas of historical fiction, fantasy, and science fiction. A novel must be superlatively written in order to find a place on the list. Mss that arrive without an SASE of adequate size will *not* be responded to or returned. Accepts fiction translations." Submit complete ms. No queries, please. Send to only *one* Clarion editor.

NONFICTION Recently published *Who Was First? Discovering the Americas*, by Russell Freedman (ages 9-12, history) No unsolicited mss. Query with SASE. Submit proposal package, sample chapters, SASE.

ILLUSTRATION Pays illustrators royalty; flat fee for jacket illustration.

TERMS Pays royalties and advance to writers; both vary.

TIPS "Looks for freshness, enthusiasm—in short, *life*."

CLEAR LIGHT PUBLISHERS

(505)989-9590. Fax: (505)989-9519. E-mail: market@ clearlightbooks.com. Website: http://clearlightbooks. com/. Publishes 4 middle readers/year; 4 young adult titles/year. "We're looking for authentic American Indian art and folklore." **Contact:** Harmon Houghton, publisher. "Clear Light publishes books that accurately depict the positive side of human experience and inspire the spirit." Publishes hardcover and trade paperback originals. 100 queries received/year.

NONFICTION Middle readers and young adults: multicultural, American Indian and Hispanic only. Query with SASE.

HOW TO CONTACT Fiction/nonfiction: Submit complete ms with SASE. "No e-mail submissions. Authors supply art. Manuscripts not considered without art or artist's renderings." Will consider simultaneous submissions. Responds in 3 months. Only send *copies.*

ILLUSTRATION Reviews ms/illustration packages from artists. "No originals please." Submit ms with dummy and SASE.

TERMS Pays authors royalty of 10% based on wholesale price. Offers advances (average amount: up to 50% of expected net sales within the first year). Sends galleys to authors.

CONCORDIA PUBLISHING HOUSE

3558 S. Jefferson Ave., St. Louis MO 63118. E-mail: publicity@cph.org;rosemary.parkinson@cph.org. Website: www.cph.org. (314)268-1187. Fax: (314)268-1329. "Concordia Publishing House produces quality resources that communicate and nurture the Christian faith and ministry of people of all ages, lay and professional. These resources include curriculum, worship aids, books, and religious supplies. We publish approximately 30 quality children's books each year. We boldly provide Gospel resources that are Christ-centered, Bible-based and faithful to our Lutheran heritage." **Contact:** Peggy Kuethe, senior editor (children's product, adult devotional, women's resources); Dawn Weinstock, managing production editor (adult nonfiction on Christian spirituality and culture, academic works of interest in Lutheran markets). "Concordia publishes Protestant, inspirational, theological, family, and juvenile material. All mss must conform to the doctrinal tenets of The Lutheran Church—Missouri Synod. No longer publishes fiction." Publishes hardcover and trade paperback originals.

NONFICTION Picture books, young readers, young adults: Bible stories, activity books, arts/crafts, concept, contemporary, religion. "All books must contain explicit Christian content." Recently published *Three Wise Women of Christmas*, by Dandi Daley Mackall (picture book for ages 6-10); *The Town That Forgot About Christmas*, by Susan K. Leigh (ages 5-9, picture book); *Little Ones Talk With God* (prayer book compilation, aged 5 and up).

HOW TO CONTACT Submit complete ms (picture books); submit outline/synopsis and samples for longer mss. May also query. Responds to queries in 1 month; mss in 3 months. Publishes a book 2 years after acceptance. Will consider simultaneous submissions. "Absolutely no phone queries."

ILLUSTRATION Works with 20 illustrators/year. Illustrations only: Query with samples. Contact: Norm Simon, art director. Responds only if interested. Samples filed.

TERMS Pays authors royalties based on retail price or work purchased outright ($750-2,000). Manuscript guidelines for 1 first-class stamp and a #10 envelope. Pays illustrators by the project.

TIPS "Do not send finished artwork with the manuscript. If sketches will help in the presentation of the manuscript, they may be sent. If stories are taken from the Bible, they should follow the Biblical account closely. Liberties should not be taken in fantasizing Biblical stories."

CREATIVE COMPANY

P.O. Box 227, Mankato MN 56002. (800)445-6209. Fax: (507)388-2746. E-mail: info@thecreativecompany.us. Website: www.thecreativecompany.us. **Manu**-script **Acquisitions:** Aaron Frisch. Publishes 5 picture books/year; 40 young readers/year; 70 young adult titles/year. 5% of books by first-time authors.

NONFICTION Picture books, young readers, young adults: animal, arts/crafts, biography, careers, geography, health, history, hobbies, multicultural, music/dance, nature/environment, religion, science, social issues, special needs, sports. Average word length: young readers—500; young adults—6,000. Recently published *Empire State Building*, by Kate Riggs (age 7, young reader); *The Assassination of Archduke Ferdinand*, by Valerie Bodden (age 14, young adult/teen).

HOW TO CONTACT "We are not accepting fiction submissions." **Nonfiction:** Submit outline/synopsis and 2 sample chapters, along with division of titles within the series. Responds to queries in 3 months; mss in 3 months. Publishes book 2 years after acceptance. Does not accept illustration packages.

PHOTOGRAPHY Buys stock. Contact: Tricia Kleist, photo editor. Model/property releases not required; captions required. Uses b&w prints. Submit cover letter, promo piece. Ms and photographer guidelines available for SAE.

TIPS "We are accepting nonfiction, series submissions only. Fiction submissions will not be reviewed or returned. Nonfiction submissions should be presented in series (4, 6, or 8) rather than single."

CRICKET BOOKS

(603)924-7209. Fax: (603)924-7380. Carus Publishing Company, 70 East Lake St., Suite 300, Chicago IL 60601. Website: www.cricketmag.com. Art Acquisitions: John Sandford. **Contact:** Submissions Editor. Cricket Books publishes picture books, chapter books, and middle grade novels. Publishes hardcover originals.

○ *Currently not accepting queries or mss.* Check website for submissions details and updates.

ILLUSTRATION Works with 4 illustrators/year. Use color and b&w. Illustration only: Please send artwork submissions via e-mail to: mail@cicadamag.com. Make sure "portfolio samples—cricket books" is the subject line of the e-mail. The file should be 72 dpi RGB jpg format. Contact: John Sandford. Responds only if interested.

TIPS "Take a look at the recent titles to see what sort of materials we're interested in, especially for nonfiction. Please note that we aren't doing the sort of strictly educational nonfiction that other publishers specialize in."

CROSSWAY BOOKS

E-mail: submissions@crossway.org. Division of Good News Publishers, 1300 Crescent St., Wheaton IL 60187-5800. (630)682-4300. Fax: (630)682-4785. Website: www.crossway.org. **Contact:** Jill Carter. Estab. 1938. " 'Making a difference in people's lives for Christ' as its maxim, Crossway Books lists titles written from an evangelical Christian perspective." Midsize evangelical Christian publisher. Publishes hardcover and trade paperback originals. Averages 85 total titles, 1 fiction title/year. Member ECPA. Distributes titles through Christian bookstores and catalogs. Promotes titles through magazine ads, catalogs.

HOW TO CONTACT Does not accept unsolicited mss. Agented fiction 5%.

TERMS Pays negotiable royalty. Average advance: negotiable. Publishes ms 18 months after acceptance. Ms guidelines online.

DARBY CREEK PUBLISHING

Lerner Publishing Group, 241 First Ave. N., Minneapolis, MN 55401-1607. (612)332-3344. Fax: (612)332-7615. Website:www.darbycreekpublishing.com. **Manuscript/Art Acquisitions:** Andrew Karre, editorial director. Publishes 18-25 children's books/year, mostly series. Does not publish picture books. "Darby Creek publishes series fiction titles for emerging, striving and reluctant readers ages 7 to 18 (grades 2-12). From beginning chapter books to intermediate fiction and page-turning YA titles, Darby Creek books engage readers with strong characters and formats they'll want to pursue."

○ Darby Creek does not publish picture books. Publishes children's chapter books, middle readers, young adult. Mostly series.

FICTION Middle readers, young adult. Recently published: *The Surviving Southside* series by various authors; *The Agent Amelia* series by Michael Broad; *The Mallory McDonald* series by Laurie B. Friedman; and *The Alien Agent* series by Pam Service.

NONFICTION Middle readers: biography, history, science, sports. Recently published *Albino Animals*, by Kelly Milner Halls, illustrated by Rick Spears; *Miracle: The True Story of the Wreck of the Sea Venture*, by Gail Karwoski.

HOW TO CONTACT Fiction: Darby Creek does not consider unsolicited submissions of any kind.

ILLUSTRATION Illustrations only: Send photocopies and résumé with publishing history. "Indicate which samples we may keep on file and include SASE and appropriate packing materials for any samples you wish to have returned."

TERMS Offers advance-against-royalty contracts.

TIPS "We are currently not accepting any submissions. If that changes, we will provide all children's writing publications with our new info."

Ⓐ DELACORTE PRESS

1745 Broadway, Mail Drop 9-2, New York NY 10019. (212)782-9000. Website: www.randomhouse.com/kids.

○ Publishes middle grade and young adult fiction in hardcover, trade paperback, mass market and digest formats.

HOW TO CONTACT Unsolicited manuscripts are only accepted as submissions to the Delacorte Press Contest for a First Young Adult Novel. See www.randomhouse.com/kids/writingcontests for rules and guidelines or send a written request addressed to Delacorte Press Contest, Random House, Inc. 1745 Broadway, New York, NY 10019 and include a SASE. All other query letters or manuscript submissions must be submitted through an agent or at the request of an editor. No e-mail queries.

Ⓐ DIAL BOOKS FOR YOUNG READERS

(212)366-2000. Website: www.penguin.com/youngreaders. Penguin Young Readers Group, 345 Hudson St.New York NY 10014. President and Publisher: Lauri Hornik. **Acquisitions:** Kathy Dawson, Associate Publisher; Kate Harrison, senior editor; Liz Waniewski, editor; Alisha Niehaus, editor; Jessica Garrison, editor. **Art Director:** Lily Malcom. Publishes 20 picture books/year; 3 young readers/year; 12 middle readers/year; 15 young adult titles/year. **Fiction** Recently published *Savvy*, by Ingrid Law (ages10-14); *Incarceron* by Catherine Fisher (ages 12 and up); *The Sky Is Everywhere* by Jandy Nelson (ages 14 and up); *Dragonbreath*, by Ursula Vernon (ages 9-11); *Ladybug Girl*, by Jacky Davis and David Soman (ages 3-7). **Contact:** Submissions Editor. "Dial Books for Young Readers publishes quality picture books for ages 18 months-6 years; lively, believable novels for middle readers and young adults; and occasional nonfiction for middle readers and young adults." Publishes hardcover originals. 5,000 queries received/year.

FICTION Especially looking for lively and well-written novels for middle grade and young adult children involving a convincing plot and believable characters. The subject matter or theme should not already be overworked in previously published books. The approach must not be demeaning to any minority group, nor should the roles of female characters (or others) be stereotyped, though we don't think books should be didactic, or in any way message-y. No topics inappropriate for the juvenile, young adult, and middle grade audiences. No plays. Accepts unsolicited queries & up to 10 pages for longer works and unsolicited mss for picture books.

NONFICTION Will consider query letters for submissions of outstanding literary merit. Recently published *Listen to the Wind* by Greg Mortenson and Susan L. Roth (ages 5-8) and *Omnivore's Dilemma* by Michael Pollan (ages 10-14). **How to Contact/Writers** "Due to the overwhelming number of unsolicited manuscripts we receive, we at Dial Books for Young Readers have had to change our submissions policy: As of August 1, 2005, Dial will no longer respond to your unsolicited submission unless interested in publishing it. Please do not include SASE with your submission. You will not hear from Dial regarding the status of your submission unless we are interested, in which case you can expect a reply from us within four months. We accept entire picture book manuscripts and a maximum of 10 pages for longer works (novels, easy-to-reads). When submitting a portion of a longer work, please provide an accompanying cover letter that briefly describes your manuscript's plot, genre (i.e. easy-to-read, middle grade or YA novel), the intended age group, and your publishing credits, if any." Accepts unsolicited queries.

TIPS "Our readers are anywhere from preschool age to teenage. Picture books must have strong plots, lots of action, unusual premises, or universal themes treated with freshness and originality. Humor works well in these books. A very well-thought-out and intelligently presented book has the best chance of being taken on. Genre isn't as much of a factor as presentation."

DISKUS PUBLISHING

E-mail: editor@diskuspublishing.com. Website: www.diskuspublishing.com. **Contact:** Joyce McLaughlin, inspirational and children's editor; Holly Janey, submissions editor. Publishes e-books.

At this time DiskUs Publishing is closed for submissions. We will reopen for submissions in the near future. We get thousands of submissions each month and our editors need time to get through the current ones. Keep checking our website for updates on the status of our submissions reopen date.

FICTION Submit publishing history, bio, estimated word count and genre. Submit complete ms.

DISNEY HYPERION BOOKS FOR CHILDREN

114 Fifth Ave., New York, NY 10011-5690. (914)288-4100. Fax: (212)633-4833. Website: www.hyperionbooksforchildren.com. **Manuscript Acquisitions:** Editorial Director. 10% of books by first-time authors. Publishes various categories. **All submissions must come via an agent.** Hyperion title *Are You Ready to Play Outside*, by Mo Willems, won the Theodor Seuss Geisel Award in 2009. The title *We Are the Ship* by Kadir Nelson won a Coretta Scott King Author Award. Their title *The Disreputable History of Frankie Landou-Banks*, by E. Lockhart was a National Book Award Finalist and won a Michael L. Printz Honor.

FICTION Picture books, early readers, middle readers, young adults: adventure, animal, anthology (short stories), contemporary, fantasy, history, humor, multicultural, poetry, science fiction, sports, suspense/mystery. Middle readers, young adults: commercial fiction.

NONFICTION Narrative nonfiction for elementary schoolers.

HOW TO CONTACT Only interested in agented material.

ILLUSTRATION Works with 100 illustrators/year. "Picture books are fully illustrated throughout. All others depend on individual project." Illustrations only: Submit résumé, business card, promotional literature or tearsheets to be kept on file. Responds only if interested. Original artwork returned at job's completion.

PHOTOGRAPHY Works on assignment only. Provide résumé, business card, promotional literature or tearsheets to be kept on file.

TERMS Pays authors royalty based on retail price. Offers advances. Pays illustrators and photographers royalty based on retail price or a flat fee. Sends galleys to authors; dummies to illustrators.

DIVERSION PRESS

E-mail: diversionpress@yahoo.com. Website: www.diversionpress.com. **Contact:** Attn: Acquisition Editor. Publishes hardcover, trade and mass market paperback originals.

FICTION "We will happily consider any children's or young adult books if they are illustrated. If your story has potential to become a series, please address that in your proposal. Fiction short stories and poetry will be considered for our anthology series. See website for details on how to submit your ms."

NONFICTION "The editors have doctoral degrees and are interested in a broad range of academic works. We are also interested in how-to, slice of life, and other nonfiction areas." Does not review works that are sexually explicit, religious, or put children in a bad light. Send query/proposal first. Mss accepted by request only.

TIPS "Read our website and blog prior to submitting. We like short, concise queries. Tell us why your book is different, not like other books. Give us a realistic idea of what you will do to market your book—that you will actually do. We will ask for more information if we are interested."

Ⓐ DK PUBLISHING

375 Hudson St., New York, NY 10014. (646)674-4000. Website: www.dk.com. **Acquisitions:** Submissions editor. "DK publishes photographically illustrated nonfiction for children of all ages."

HOW TO CONTACT DK Publishing does not accept unagented manuscripts or proposals.

DNA PRESS & NARTEA PUBLISHING

DNA Press, P.O. Box 9311, Glendale CA 91226-0311. E-mail: editors@dnapress.com. Website: www.dnapress.com. Estab. 1998. Book publisher for young adults, children, and adults. Publishes hardcover and trade paperback originals. 500 queries received/year. 400 mss received/year.

FICTION All books should be oriented to explaining science even if they do not fall 100% under the category of science fiction. Submit complete ms.

NONFICTION "We publish business, real estate and investment books."

HOW TO CONTACT See website.

TIPS Quick response, great relationships, high commission/royalty.

Ⓐ DOG-EARED PUBLICATIONS

P.O. Box 620863, Middletown WI 53562-0863. (608)831-1410. Fax: (608)831-1410. E-mail: field@dog-eared.com. Website: www.dog-eared.com. **Art Acquisitions:** Nancy Field, publisher. Publishes 2-3 middle readers/year. 1% of books by first-time authors. "Dog-Eared Publications creates action-packed nature books for children. We aim to turn young readers into environmentally aware citizens and to foster a love for science and nature in the new generation."

NONFICTION Middle readers: activity books, animal, nature/environment, science. Average word length: varies. Recently published *Discovering Black Bear*, by Margaret Anderson, Nancy Field and Karen Stephenson, illustrated by Michael Maydak (middle readers, activity book); *Leapfrogging Through Wetlands*, by Margaret Anderson, Nancy Field and Karen Stephenson, illustrated by Michael Maydak (middle readers, activity book); *Ancient Forests*, by Margaret Anderson, Nancy Field and Karen Stephenson, illustrated by Sharon Torvik (middle readers, activity book).

HOW TO CONTACT Nonfiction: **Currently not accepting unsolicited mss.**

ILLUSTRATION Works with 2-3 illustrators/year. Reviews ms/illustration packages from artists. Submit query and a few art samples. Illustrations only: Query with samples. Responds only if interested. Samples not returned; samples filed. "Interested in realistic, nature art!"

TERMS Pays authors royalty based on wholesale price. Offers advances (amount varies). Pays illustrators royalty based on wholesale price. Sends galleys to authors. Originals returned to artist at job's completion. Brochure available for SASE and 1 first-class stamp or on website.

PAUL DRY BOOKS

(215)231-9939. Fax: (215)231-9942. E-mail: pdry@pauldrybooks.com. Website: http://pauldrybooks.com. "We publish fiction, both novels and short stories, and nonfiction, biography, memoirs, history, and essays, covering subjects from Homer to Chekhov, bird watching to jazz music, New York City to shogunate Japan." Hardcover and trade paperback originals, trade paperback reprints.

> "Take a few minutes to familiarize yourself with the books we publish. Then if you think your book would be a good fit in our line, we invite you to submit the following: A one- or

two-page summary of the work. Be sure to tell us how long--pages or words--in the full book will be; a sample of 20 to 30 pages; your bio. A brief description of how you think the book (and you, the author) could be marketed."

FICTION Submit sample chapters, clips, bio. Sample 2-3 pages are also acceptable.

NONFICTION Submit proposal package.

TIPS "Our aim is to publish lively books 'to awaken, delight, and educate'—to spark conversation. We publish fiction and nonfiction, and essays covering subjects from Homer to Chekhov, bird watching to jazz music, New York City to shogunate Japan."

DUTTON CHILDREN'S BOOKS

Imprint of Penguin Group (USA), Inc. 345 Hudson St., New York NY 10014. (212)4143700. Fax: (212)414-3397. Website: www.penquin.com/youngreaders. **Contact**: Lauri Hornik, president and publisher; Julie Strauss-Gabel, associate publisher (literary contemporary young adult fiction); Lucia Monfried, senior editor (picture books and middle grade fiction); Sara Reynolds, art director. Estab. 1852. Dutton Children's Books publishes fiction and nonfiction for readers ranging from preschoolers to young adults on a variety of subjects. Publishes hardcover originals as well as novelty formats. Averages 50 titles/year. **Needs:** Dutton Children's Books has a diverse, general-interest list that includes picture books, and fiction for all ages and occasional retail-appropriate nonfiction. Recently published *Skippyjon Jones Lost in Space*, by Judy Schachner (picture book); *Thirteen*, by Lauren Myracle (middle grade novel); *Paper Towns*, by John Green (young adult novel); and *If I Stay*, by Gayle Forman (young adult novel). **Contact:** Acquisitions Editor. Currently emphasizing middle grade and young adult novels that offer a fresh perspective. De-emphasizing photographic nonfiction and picture books that teach a lesson. Approximately 80 new hardcover titles are published every year, fiction and nonfiction for babies through young adults.

"Cultivating the creative talents of authors and illustrators and publishing books with purpose and heart continue to be the mission and joy at Dutton."

FICTION Dutton Children's Books has a diverse, general interest list that includes picture books; easy-to-read books; and fiction for all ages, from first chapter books to young adult readers. Query with SASE.

NONFICTION Query with SASE.

HOW TO CONTACT Query letter only; include SASE.

TERMS Pays royalty on retail price. Offers advance.

EDCON PUBLISHING GROUP

30 Montauk Blvd., Oakdale, NY 11769. (631)567-7227. Fax: (631)567-8745. Website: www.edconpublishing. com. **Manuscript Acquisitions:** Editor. Publishes 6 young readers/year, 6 middle readers/year, 6 young adult titles/year. 30% of books by first-time authors. Looking for educational games and nonfiction work in the areas of math, science, reading and social studies.

FICTION Recently adapted/published *A Christmas Carol*; *Frankenstein*; *Around the World in 80 Days*; *The Picture of Dorian Grey*.

NONFICTION Grades 1-12, though primarily 6-12 remedial.

HOW TO CONTACT Submit outline/synopsis and 1 sample chapter. Publishes book 6 months after acceptance. Will consider simultaneous submissions. Submission kept on file unless return is requested. Include SASE for return.

ILLUSTRATION Buys b&w and color illustrations and currently seeking computerized graphic art. Send postcards, samples, links to edcon@EDCON Publishing.com. Mailed submissions kept on file, not returned.

TERMS Work purchased outright from authors for up to $1,000. Pays illustrators by the project (range: $100-$500). Catalog available at www.edconpublishing.com/Edcon-Catalog.pdf.

EDUPRESS, INC.

P.O. Box 8610, Madison, WI 53708-8610. (800)694-5827. Fax: (800)835-2329. E-mail: edupress@high smith.com; lbowie@highsmith.com. Website: www.edupressinc.com. **Manuscript Acquisitions:** Liz Bowie, product development manager. "Our mission is to create products that make kids want to go to school!"

HOW TO CONTACT Nonfiction: Submit complete ms via mail or e-mail at lbowie@highsmith.com with "Manuscript Submission" as the subject line. Responds to queries/mss in 2-4 months. Publishes book 1-2 years after acceptance.

ILLUSTRATION Query with samples. Contact: Cathy Baker, product development manager. Responds only if interested. Samples returned with SASE.

PHOTOGRAPHY Buys stock.

TERMS Work purchased outright from authors. Pays illustrators by the project. Book catalog available at no cost. Catalog available on website.

TIPS "We are looking for unique, research-based, quality supplemental materials for Pre-K through eighth grade. We publish all subject areas in many different formats, including games. Our materials are intended for classroom and home schooling use."

🎧 EERDMANS BOOKS FOR YOUNG READERS

An imprint of Wm. B. Eerdmans Publishing Co., 2140 Oak Industrial Dr. NE, Grand Rapids, MI 49505 (616) 459-4591. Fax: (616) 776-7683. E-mail: youngreaders@eerdmans.com. Website: www.eerdmans.com/youngreaders. Produces 10-12 picture books/year; 2 middle readers/year; 2 young adult books/year. 10% of books by first-time authors. "We seek to engage young minds with words and pictures that inform and delight, inspire and entertain. From board books for babies to picture books, nonfiction, and novels for children and young adults, our goal is to produce quality literature for a new generation of readers. We believe in books!"

Contact: Shannon White, acquisitions editor. "We are seeking books that encourage independent thinking, problem-solving, creativity, acceptance, kindness. Books that encourage moral values without being didactic or preachy." Board books, picture books, middle reader fiction, young adult fiction, nonfiction, illustrated storybooks. 6,000 mss received/year. Pays 5-7% royalty on retail price. Publishes middle reader and YA books in 1 year; publishes picture books in 2-3 years. "We do not accept or reply to queries or submissions via e-mail or fax. Responds in 3-4 months for exclusive submissions sent to Eerdmans Books for Young Readers." Do not call or e-mail to inquire about the status of your manuscript. "Right now we are not acquiring books that revolve around a holiday. (No Christmas, Thanksgiving, Easter, Halloween, Fourth of July, Hanukkah books.)" Reviews artwork/photos. Send color photocopies rather than original art. "We do not publish retold or original fairy tales, nor do we publish books about witches or ghosts or vampires." Send exclusive ms submissions (marked so on outside of envelope) to acquisitions editor. *A River of Words*, by Jen Bryant, illustrated by Melissa Sweet (2009 Caldecott Honor Book); *Garmann's Summer*, by Stian Hole (2009 Batchelder Honor Book); *Ethan, Suspended*, by Pamela Ehrenberg (novel); *Attack of the Turtle*, by Drew Carlson (novel). "A submission stands out when it's obvious that someone put time into it—the publisher's name and address are spelled correctly, the package is neat, and all of our submission requirements have been followed precisely. We look for short, concise cover letters that explain why the ms fits with our list, and/or how the ms fills an important need in the world of children's literature. Send EXCLUSIVE ms submissions to acquisitions editor. We regret that due to the volume of material we receive, we cannot comment on ms we are unable to accept."

🎧 "We accept unsolicited submissions. We respond within 4 months only to submissions we are interested in publishing."

FICTION Picture books: animal, contemporary, folktales, history, humor, multicultural, nature/environment, poetry, religion, special needs, social issues, sports, suspense. Young readers: animal, contemporary, fantasy, folktales, history, humor, multicultural, poetry, religion, special needs, social issues, sports, suspense. Middle readers: adventure, contemporary, fantasy, history, humor, multicultural, nature/environment, problem novels, religion, social issues, sports, suspense. Young adults/teens: adventure, contemporary, fantasy, folktales, history, humor, multicultural, nature/environment, problem novels, religion, sports, suspense. Average word length: picture books—1,000; middle readers—15,000; young adult—45,000. Recently published *My Name is Sangoel* by Karen Lynn Williams and Khadra Mohammed, illustrated by Catharine Stock (picture book, ages 7-10); *A River of Words* written by Jen Bryant, illustrated by Melissa Sweet (picture book, ages 7 & up); *Garmann's Summer*, written and illustrated by Stian Hole (picture book, ages 5-8); *Tillmon County Fire*, by Pamela Ehrenberg (YA fiction ages 14 & up); *Joe Rat*, by Mark Barratt (YA fiction ages 11 & up). Send exclusive ms submissions (marked so on outside of envelope) to acquisitions editor.

NONFICTION Middle readers: biography, history, multicultural, nature/environment, religion, social issues. Young adults/teens: biography, history, multicultural, nature/environment, religion, social issues. Average word length: middle readers—35,000; young adult books—35,000. Recently published *Eva's Story*, by Eva Schloss.

HOW TO CONTACT We only consider submissions sent EXCLUSIVELY to Eerdmans. YA and Middle Reader fiction: Please send query, synopsis, and 3 sample chapters. Children's picture books: Please send full manuscript. "We accept unsolicited submissions. We respond within 4 months only to submissions we are interested in publishing."

ILLUSTRATION Accepts material from international illustrators. Works with 10-12 illustrators/year. Uses color artwork primarily. Reviews work for future assignments. If interested in illustrating future titles, send promo sheet. Submit samples to Gayle Brown, Art Director. Samples not returned. Samples filed.

TERMS Offers advance against royalties. Author sees galleys for review. Illustrators see proofs for review. Originals returned to artist at job's completion. Catalog available upon request. Offers writer's guidelines for SASE. See website for writer's guidelines. (www. eerdmans.com/youngreaders/submit.htm)

TIPS "Find out who Eerdmans is before submitting a manuscript. Look at our website, request a catalog, and check out our books."

EGMONT USA

Website: www.egmontusa.com. 443 Park Ave. S., Suite 806, New York, NY 10016. (212)685-0102. E-mail: egmontusa@egmont.com. **Acquisitions:** Elizabeth Law (VP and publisher), Regina Griffin (executive editor). Estab. 2008. Specializes in trade books. Publishes 5 picture books/year; 5 young readers/year; 20 middle readers/year; 20 young adult/year. 25% of books by first-time authors. "Egmont USA publishes quality commercial fiction. We are committed to editorial excellence and to providing first-rate care for our authors. Our motto is that we turn writers into authors and children into passionate readers."

FICTION Picture books: animal, concept, contemporary, humor, multicultural. Young readers: adventure, animal, contemporary, humor, multicultural. Middle readers: adventure, animal, contemporary, fantasy, humor, multicultural, problem novels, science fiction, special needs. Young adults/teens: adventure, animal, contemporary, humor, multicultural, problem novels, science fiction, special needs. *Leaving the Belleweathers*, by Kristen Venuti (fall 2009); *Back*, by Julia Keller (fall 2009); *The Cinderella Society* (spring 2010).

HOW TO CONTACT Only interested in agented material. Fiction: Submit complete query. Responds to queries in 4 weeks; mss in 6 weeks. Publishes a book 18 months after acceptance. Will consider e-mail submissions.

ILLUSTRATION Only interested in agented in material. Works with 5 illustrators/year. Uses both color and b&w. Illustrations only: Query with samples. Responds only if interested. Samples are not returned.

TERMS Pays authors royalties based on retail price. Pays illustrators royalties.

ENSLOW PUBLISHERS INC.

Box 398, 40 Industrial Rd., Berkeley Heights, NJ 07922-0398. (908)771-9400. Fax: (908)771-0925. E-mail: info@enslow.com; CustomerService@enslow.com. Website: www.enslow.com or www.myreportlinks.com. **Acquisitions:** Brian D. Enslow, vice president. Imprint: MyReportLinks.com Books. Publishes 30 young readers/year; 70 middle readers/year; 100 young adult titles/year. 30% of books by first-time authors.

○ Enslow Imprint MyReportLinks.com Books produces books on animals, states, presidents, continents, countries, and a variety of other topics for middle readers and young adults, and offers links to online sources of information on topics covered in books.

NONFICTION Young readers, middle readers, young adults: animal, arts/crafts, biography, careers, geography, health, history, multicultural, nature/environment, science, social issues, sports. Middle readers, young adults: hi-lo. "Enslow is moving into the elementary (grades 3-4) level and is looking for authors who can write biography and suggest other nonfiction themes at this level." Average word length: young readers—2,000; middle readers—5,000; young adult—18,000. Published *It's About Time! Science Projects*, by Robert Gardner (grades 3-6, science); *Georgia O'Keeffe: Legendary American Painter*, by Jodie A. Shull (grades 6-12, biography); *California: A MyReportLinks.com Book*, by Jeff Savaga (grades 5-8, social studies/history).

HOW TO CONTACT Nonfiction: Send for guidelines. Query. Responds to queries/mss in 2 weeks. Publishes a book 18 months after acceptance. Will not consider simultaneous submissions.

ILLUSTRATION Submit résumé, business card, or tearsheets to be kept on file. Responds only if interested. Samples returned with SASE only.

TERMS Pays authors royalties or work purchased outright. Pays illustrators by the project. Pays photographers by the project or per photo. Sends galleys to authors. Book catalog/ms guidelines available for $3, along with an 8½×11 SASE and $2 postage.

FACTS ON FILE

Website: www.factsonfile.com. 132 W. 31st St., New York, NY 10001. (212)967-8800. Fax: (212)967-9196. E-mail: editorial@factsonfile.com. Website: www.factsonfile.com. Estab. 1941. Book publisher. Editorial Director: Laurie Likoff. **Acquisitions:** Frank Darmstadt, science and technology/nature; Andrew Gyory, American history and cultural studies; Jeff Soloway, language and literature; Owen Lancer, world studies; Jim Chambers, arts, health and entertainment. "We produce high-quality reference materials for the school library market and the general nonfiction trade." Publishes 25-30 young adult titles/year. 5% of books by first-time authors; 25% of books from agented writers; additional titles through book packagers, co-publishers and unagented writers.

NONFICTION Middle readers, young adults: animal, biography, careers, geography, health, history, multicultural, nature/environment, reference, religion, science, social issues and sports.

HOW TO CONTACT Nonfiction: Submit outline/synopsis and sample chapters. Responds to queries in 10 weeks. Publishes a book 10-12 months after acceptance. Will consider simultaneous submissions. Sends galleys to authors. Book catalog free on request. Send SASE for submission guidelines.

TERMS Submission guidelines available via website or with SASE.

TIPS "Most projects have high reference value and fit into a series format."

♥ FARRAR, STRAUS & GIROUX INC.

175 Fifth Ave., New York, NY 10010. (212)741-6900. E-mail: childrens.editorial@fsgbooks.com. Website: www.fsgkidsbooks.com. Estab. 1946. Book publisher. Imprints: Frances Foster Books. Children's Books Editorial Director: Margaret Ferguson. **Manuscript Acquisitions:** Margaret Ferguson, editorial director; Frances Foster, Frances Foster Books; Wesley Adams, executive editor; Janine O'Malley, Senior editor. **Art Director:** Robbin Gourley, art director, Books for Young Readers. Publishes 40 picture books/year; 30 middle grade books/year; 10 young adult titles/year. 5% of books by first-time authors; 20% of books from agented writers.

FICTION All levels: all categories. "Original and well-written material for all ages." Recently published *The*

Cabinet of Wonders, by Marie Rutkoski; *Last Night*, by Hyewon Yum.

NONFICTION All levels: all categories. "We publish only literary nonfiction."

HOW TO CONTACT As of January 2010, Farrar Straus & Giroux does not accept unsolicited manuscripts. "We recommend finding a literary agent to represent you and your work."

ILLUSTRATION Works with 30-60 illustrators/year. Reviews ms/illustration packages from artists. Submit ms with 1 example of final art, remainder roughs. Do not send originals. Illustrations only: Query with tearsheets. Responds if interested in 3 months. Samples returned with SASE; samples sometimes filed.

TERMS "We offer an advance against royalties for both authors and illustrators." Sends galleys to authors; dummies to illustrators. Original artwork returned at job's completion. Book catalog available for 9×12 SASE with $1.95 postage; ms guidelines for SASE with 1 first-class stamp, or can be viewed at www.fsgkidsbooks.com.

TIPS "Study our catalog before submitting. We will see illustrators' portfolios by appointment. Don't ask for criticism and/or advice. Due to the volume of submissions we receive, it's just not possible. Never send originals. Always enclose SASE."

○○ FIVE STAR PUBLICATIONS, INC.

P.O. Box 6698, Chandler AZ 85246-6698. (480)940-8182. Fax: (480)940-8787. E-mail: info@fivestarpublications.com. Website: www.fivestarpublications.com. Publishes seven middle readers/year. **Contact:** Linda Radke, president. "Helps produce and market award-winning books."

○ "Five Star Publications publishes and promotes award-winning fiction, nonfiction, cookbooks, children's literature and professional guides. More information about Five Star Publications, Inc., a 25-year leader in the book publishing/book marketing industry, is available online at our website."

NONFICTION Recently published *Tic Talk Book: Living with Tourette Syndrome*, by Dylan Peters, illustrated by Zachary Wendland (www.TicTalkBook.com); *Alfie's Bark Mitzvah* by Shari Cohen, songs by Cantor Marcello Gindlin, illustrated by Nadia Komorova (www.AlfiesBarkMitvah.com). Other websites: www.LittleFivestar.com, www.FiveStarLegends.com; www.FiveStarSleuths.com; www.SixPointsPress.com.

HOW TO CONTACT Nonfiction: Query.

ILLUSTRATION Works with 3 illustrators/year. Reviews ms/illustration packages from artists. Query. Illustrations only: Query with samples. Responds only if interested. Samples filed.

PHOTOGRAPHY Buys stock and assigns work. Works on assignment only. Submit letter.

TERMS Pays illustrators by the project. Pays photographers by the project. Sends galleys to authors; dummies to illustrators.

TIPS Features the Purple Dragonfly Book Awards and Royal Dragonfly Book Awards, which were conceived and designed with children in mind. "Not only do we want to recognize and honor accomplished authors in the field of children's literature, but we also want to highlight and reward up-and-coming newly published authors, as well as younger published writers. In our efforts to include everyone, the awards are divided into distinct subject categories, ranging from books on the environment and cooking to books on sports and family issues. (Please see the complete categories list on the entry form on our website.)

FLUX

Llewellyn Worldwide, Ltd., 2143 Wooddale Dr., Woodbury, MN 55125. (651)312-8613. Fax: (651)291-1908. Website: www.fluxnow.com; fluxnow.blogspot.com. Imprint estab. 2005; Lllewellyn estab. 1901. Publishes 21 young adult titles/year. 50% of books by first-time authors. "Flux seeks to publish authors who see YA as a point of view, not a reading level. We look for books that try to capture a slice of teenage experience, whether in real or imagined worlds." **Contact:** Brian Farrey, acquisitions editor.

FICTION Young Adults: adventure, contemporary, fantasy, history, humor, problem novels, religion, science fiction, sports, suspense. Average word length: 50,000. Recently published *Ballad* by Maggie Stiefvater; *The Dust of 100 Dogs*, by A.S. King; *Return to Paradise*, by Simone Elkeles; *Gigged*, by Heath Gibson.

HOW TO CONTACT Per website: "As of March 1, 2011, FLUX will no longer be accepting unsolicited submissions. Any unsolicited submission sent after February 28, 2011 will be deleted unread."

TERMS Pays royalties of 10-15% based on wholesale price. Offers advance. Authors see galleys for review. Book catalog available on website. Writer's guidelines available for SASE or in website at www.fluxnow.com/submission_guidelines.php.

TIPS "Read contemporary teen books. Be aware of what else is out there. If you don't read teen books, you probably shouldn't write them. Know your audience. Write incredibly well. Do not condescend."

FORT ROSS INC. INTERNATIONAL RIGHTS

26 Arthur Place, Yonkers NY 10701. (914)375-6448. E-mail: fortross@optonline.net. Website: www.fortrossinc.com. Buys and sells rights for more than 500 titles per year, mostly in Russian and in Russia. Genres include children adapted classics, adventure, fantasy, horror, romance, science fiction, biography, history and self-help. **Contact:** Dr. Kartsev, executive director. "Generally, we publish Russia-related books in English or Russian. Sometimes we publish various fiction and nonfiction books in collaboration with the east European publishers in translation. We are looking mainly for well-established authors." Publishes paperback originals. 100 queries received/year; 100 mss received/year. Pays 6-8% royalty on wholesale price or makes outright purchase of $500-1,500; negotiable advance. Publishes in hardcover and paperback originals.

FREE SPIRIT PUBLISHING, INC.

217 Fifth Ave. N., Suite 200, Minneapolis MN 55401-1299. (612)338-2068. Fax: (612)337-5050. E-mail: acquisitions@freespirit.com. Website: www.freespirit.com. Publishes 25-30 titles/year for pre-K through 12, educators and parents. "Free Spirit is the leading publisher of learning tools that support young people's social and emotional health, helping children and teens to think for themselves, succeed in life, and make a difference in the world." Accepts nonfiction submissions from prospective authors or through agents. **Contact:** Acquisitions Editor. "We believe passionately in empowering kids to learn to think for themselves and make their own good choices." Publishes trade paperback originals and reprints.

○ Free Spirit does not accept fiction, poetry or storybook submissions.

NONFICTION "Many of our authors are educators, mental health professionals, and youth workers involved in helping kids and teens." No fiction or picture storybooks, poetry, single biographies or autobiographies, books with mythical or animal characters, or books with religious or New Age content. "We are not looking for academic or religious materials, or books that analyze problems with the nation's school systems." Query with cover letter stating qualifications, intent, and intended audience and market analysis (how your book stands out from the field), along with outline, 2 sample chapters, résumé, SASE. Do not send original copies of work.

HOW TO CONTACT "Please review catalog and author guidelines (both available online) before submitting proposal." Reponds to queries in 4-6 months. "If you'd like material returned, enclose a SASE with sufficient postage." Accepts queries only—not submissions—by e-mail.

ILLUSTRATION Works with 5 illustrators/year. Submit samples to creative director for consideration. If appropriate, samples will be kept on file and artist will be contacted if a suitable project comes up. Enclose SASE if you'd like materials returned.

PHOTOGRAPHY Uses stock photos. Does not accept photography submissions.

TERMS Pays authors royalty based on net receipts. Offers advance. Pays illustrators by the project.

TIPS "Our books are issue-oriented, jargon-free and solution-focused. Our audience is children, teens, teachers, parents and youth counselors. We are especially concerned with kids' social and emotional well-being and look for books with ready-to-use strategies for coping with today's issues at home or in school—written in everyday language. We are not looking for academic or religious materials, or books that analyze problems with the nation's school systems. Instead, we want books that offer practical, positive advice so kids can help themselves, and parents and teachers can help kids succeed."

FREESTONE/PEACHTREE, JR.

Peachtree Publishers, 1700 Chattahoochee Ave., Atlanta, GA 30318-2112. (404)876-8761. Fax: (404)875-2578. E-mail: hello@peachtree-online.com. Website: www.peachtree-online.com. **Acquisitions:** Helen Harriss. Publishes 4-8 young adult titles/year.

○ Freestone and Peachtree, Jr. are imprints of Peachtree Publishers. See the listing for Peachtree for submission information. No e-mail or fax queries or submissions, please.

FICTION Picture books: animals, folktales, health, history, humor, multicultural, nature/environment, special needs, sports. Young readers: history, humor, health, multicultural, sports. Middle readers: adventure, contemporary, history, humor, multicultural, problem novels, sports, suspense/mystery. Young adults/teens: adventure, contemporary, history, humor, multicultural, problem novels, sports, suspense/mystery. Recently published *Martina the Beautiful Cockroach* byCarmen Agra Deedy, illustrated by Michael Austin (ages 4-8, picture book); *Young Charles Darwin and the Voyage of the Beagle*, written by Ruth Ashby (ages 7-10; early reader); *The Sorta Sisters*, by Adrian Fogelin (ages 8-12, middle reader); *Giving Up the Ghost*, by Sheri Sinykin (ages 12-16, young adult).

NONFICTION Picture books, young readers, middle readers, young adults: history, sports. Picture books: animal, health, multicultural, nature/environment, science, social issues, special needs.

HOW TO CONTACT Responds to queries/mss in 6 months.

ILLUSTRATION Works with 10-20 illustrators/year. Responds only if interested. Samples not returned; samples filed. Originals returned at job's completion.

TERMS Pays authors royalty. Pays illustrators by the project or royalty. Pays photographers by the project or per photo.

FRONT STREET

Imprint of Boyds Mills Press, 815 Church Street, Honesdale, PA 18431. Website: www.frontstreetbooks. com. Publishes 20-25 titles/year. "We look for fresh voices for children and young adults. Titles on our list entertain, challenge or enlighten, always employing novel characters whose considered voices resonate." High-end picture books. **Contact:** Acquisitions Editor. "We are an independent publisher of books for children and young adults." Publishes hardcover originals and trade paperback reprints. 2,000 queries received/year. 5,000 mss received/year.

FICTION Recently published *I'm Being Stalked by a Moonshadow*, by Doug MacLeod; *Runaround*, by Helen Hemphill; *Baby*, by Joseph Monninger. Query with SASE. Submit complete ms, if under 100 pages, with SASE. Keeps illustration samples on file. Reviews artwork/photos w/ms. Send photocopies. "High-quality fiction for children and young adults." Publishes hardcover originals and trade paperback reprints. Books: coated paper; offset printing; case binding; 4-color illustrations. Averages 15 fiction titles/year. Distributes titles through independent sales reps, wholesalers, and via order line directly from Front Street. Promotes titles through sales and professional conferences, sales reps, reviews, catalogs, website and direct marketing.

HOW TO CONTACT Fiction: Submit cover letter and complete ms if under 30 pages; submit cover letter, 1 or 2 sample chapters and plot summary if over 30 pages. Label package "Manuscript Submission." Include SASE with submissions if you want them returned. "We try to respond within three months. "

ILLUSTRATION "Send sample illustrations. Label package 'Art Smaple Submission.'"

TIPS "Read through our recently published titles and review our website. Check to see what's on the market and in our catalog before submitting your story. Feel free to query us if you're not sure."

FULCRUM PUBLISHING

4690 Table Mountain Drive, Suite 100 Golden CO 80403. (303)277-1623. Fax: (303)279-7111. Website: www.fulcrum-books.com. **Manuscript Acquisitions:** T. Baker, acquisitions editor.

NONFICTION Middle and early readers: Western history, nature/environment, Native American.

HOW TO CONTACT Submit complete ms or submit outline/synopsis and 2 sample chapters. "Publisher does not send response letters unless we are interested in publishing." Do not send SASE.

PHOTOGRAPHY Works on assignment only.

TERMS Pays authors royalty based on wholesale price. Offers advances. Book catalog available for 9×12 SAE and 77¢ postage; Ms submission guidelines available on website under "Authors" tab.

TIPS "Research our line first. We look for books that appeal to the school market and trade. "

GAUTHIER PUBLICATIONS, INC.

Frog Legs Ink, P.O. Box 806241, Saint Clair Shores MI 48080. Fax: (586)279-1515. E-mail: info@gauthier publications.com. E-mail: submissions@gauthierpub lications.com. Website: www.eatabook.com. **Contact:** Elizabeth Gauthier, Creative Director (Children's/ Fiction). Hardcover originals and trade paperback originals

  Frog Legs Ink (imprint) is always looking for new writers and illustrators. We are currently looking for horror/thriller short stories for an upcoming collection.

FICTION "We are particularly interested in mystery, thriller, graphic novels, horror and young adult areas for the upcoming year. We do, however, consider most subjects if they are intriguing and well written."

NONFICTION Query with SASE.

HOW TO CONTACT Query with SASE. "Please do not send full ms unless we ask for it If we are interested we will request a few sample chapters and outline. Since we do take the time to read and consider each piece, response can take up to 8 weeks. Mailed submissions without SASE included are destroyed if we are not interested."

ILLUSTRATION "Please send a résumé with professional experience and credentials along with copies or tear-sheets of work. Do not send originals. We will contact you if we will be keeping your work on file or if it seems appropriate for a current project. If you do not send a SASE, your materials will be destroyed if we do not have a place for them. Response time can take up to 4 weeks."

GIBBS SMITH, PUBLISHER

P.O. Box 667, Layton, UT 84041. (801)544-9800. Fax: (801)544-5582. E-mail: duribe@gibbs-smith. com. Website: www.gibbs-smith.com. **Manuscript Acquisitions:** Suzanne Taylor, associate publisher and creative director (children's activity books). **Art Acquisitions:** Jennifer Grillone. Book publisher; copublisher of Sierra Club Books for Children. Imprint: Gibbs Smith. Publishes 2-3 books/year. 50% of books by first-time authors. 50% of books from agented authors. "We accept submissions for picture books with particular interest in those with a Western (cowboy or ranch lifestyle) theme or backdrop."

  Gibbs Smith is not accepting fiction at this time.

NONFICTION Middle readers: activity, arts/crafts, cooking, how-to, nature/environment, science. Average word length: picture books—under 1,000 words; activity books—under 15,000 words. Recently published *Hiding in a Fort*, by G. Lawson Drinkard, illustrated by Fran Lee (ages 7-12); *Sleeping in a Sack: Camping Activities for Kids*, by Linda White, illustrated by Fran Lee (ages 7-12).

HOW TO CONTACT Nonfiction: Submit an outline and writing samples for activity books; query for other types of books. Responds to queries/mss in 2 months. Publishes a book 1-2 years after acceptance. Will consider simultaneous submissions. Manuscript returned with SASE.

ILLUSTRATION Works with 2 illustrators/year. Reviews ms/illustration packages from artists. Query.

Submit ms with 3-5 pieces of final art. Illustrations only: Query with samples; provide résumé, promo sheet, slides (duplicate slides, not originals). Responds only if interested. Samples returned with SASE; samples filed.

TERMS Pays authors royalty of 2% based on retail price or work purchased outright ($500 minimum). Offers advances (average amount: $2,000). Pays illustrators by the project or royalty of 2% based on retail price. Sends galleys to authors; color proofs to illustrators. Original artwork returned at job's completion. Book catalog available for 9×12 SAE and $2.30 postage. Manuscript guidelines available; e-mail duribe@gibbs-smith.com.

TIPS "We target ages 5-11. We do not publish young adult novels or chapter books."

DAVID R. GODINE, PUBLISHER

9 Hamilton Place, Boston, MA 02108. (617)451-9600. Fax: (617)350-0250. E-mail:info@godine.com. Website: www.godine.com. Estab. 1970. Book publisher. Publishes 1 picture book/year; 1 young reader/year; 1 middle reader/year. 10% of books by first-time authors; 90% of books from agented writers. "We publish books that matter for people who care."

This publisher is no longer considering unsolicited manuscripts of any type.

FICTION Picture books: adventure, animal, contemporary, folktales, nature/environment. Young readers: adventure, animal, contemporary, folk or fairy tales, history, nature/environment, poetry. Middle readers: adventure, animal, contemporary, folk or fairy tales, history, mystery, nature/environment, poetry. Young adults/teens: adventure, animal, contemporary, history, mystery, nature/environment, poetry. Recently published *Little Red Riding Hood*, by Andrea Wisnewski (picture book); *The Merchant of Noises*, by Anna Rozen, illustrated by François Avril.

NONFICTION Picture books: alphabet, animal, nature/environment. Young readers: activity books, animal, history, music/dance, nature/environment. Middle readers: activity books, animal, biography, history, music/dance, nature/environment. Young adults: biography, history, music/dance, nature/environment.

HOW TO CONTACT Only interested in agented material. Query. Include SASE for return of material.

ILLUSTRATION Only interested in agented material. Works with 1-3 illustrators/year. "Please do not send original artwork unless solicited. Almost all of the

children's books we accept for publication come to us with the author and illustrator already paired up. Therefore, we rarely use freelance illustrators." Samples returned with SASE.

TIPS "E-mail submissions are not accepted. Always enclose a SASE. Keep in mind that we do not accept unsolicited manuscripts and that we rarely use freelance illustrators."

GOLDEN BOOKS

1745 Broadway, New York, NY 10019. (212)782-9000. **Editorial Directors:** Courtney Silk, color and activity; Chris Angelilli, storybooks; Dennis Shealy, novelty. **Art Acquisitions:** Tracey Tyler, executive art director.

See listing for Random House-Golden Books for Young Readers Group.

FICTION Publishes board books, novelty books, picture books, workbooks, series (mass market and trade).

HOW TO CONTACT Does not accept unsolicited submissions.

GRAPHIA

Harcourt Houghton Mifflin, 222 Berkeley St., Boston, MA 02116. (617)351-5000. Website: www.graphiabooks.com. **Manuscript Acquisitions:** Julia Richardson. "Graphia publishes quality paperbacks for today's teen readers, ages 14 and up. From fiction to nonfiction, poetry to graphic novels, Graphia runs the gamut, all unified by the quality of writing that is the hallmark of this imprint."

FICTION Young adult: adventure, contemporary, fantasy, history, humor, multicultural, poetry. Recently published: *The Off Season* by Catherine Murdock; *Come in from the Cold* by Marsha Qualey; *Breaking Up is Hard to Do* with stories by Niki Burnham, Terri Clark, Ellen Hopkins, and Lynda Sandoval; *Zahrah the Windseeker* by Nnedi Okorafot-Mbachu.

NONFICTION Young adult: biography, history, multicultural, nature/environment, science, social issues.

HOW TO CONTACT Query. Responds to queries/mss in 3 months. Will consider simultaneous submissions and previously published work.

ILLUSTRATION Do not send original artwork or slides. Send color photocopies, tearsheets or photos to Art Dept. Include SASE if you would like your samples mailed back to you.

TERMS Pays author royalties. Offers advances. Sends galleys to authors. Catalog available on website (www. houghtonmifflin.com).

GREENHAVEN PRESS

Imprint of the Cengage Gale, 27500 Drake Road, Farmington, Hills MI 48331. E-mail: Kristine.burns@ cengage.com. Website: www.gale.com/greenhaven. **Acquisitions:** Kristine Burns. Publishes 220 young adult academic reference titles/year. 50% of books by first-time authors. Greenhaven continues to print quality nonfiction anthologies for libraries and classrooms. Our well known Opposing Viewpoints series is highly respected by students and librarians in need of material on controversial social issues. Greenhaven accepts no unsolicited manuscripts. All writing is done on a work-for-hire basis.

NONFICTION Young adults (high school): controversial issues, social issues, history, literature, science, environment, health. Recently published (series): Issues That Concern You; Writing the Critical Essay: An Opening Viewpoint Guide; Introducing Issue with Opposing Viewpoints; Social Issues in Literature; and Perspectives on Diseases and Disorders.

HOW TO CONTACT Send query, résumé, and list of published works by e-mail.

TERMS Work purchased outright from authors; write-for-hire, flat fee.

GREENWILLOW BOOKS

1350 Avenue of the Americas, New York NY 10019. (212)261-6500. Website: www.harpercollinschild rens.com. Book publisher. Imprint of HarperCollins. Vice President/Publisher: Virginia Duncan. **Art Acquisitions:** Paul Zakris, Art Director. Publishes 30 picture books/year; 5 middle readers/year; 5 young adult books/year. "Greenwillow Books publishes picture books, fiction for young readers of all ages, and nonfiction primarily for children under seven years of age.We hope that at the heart of each book there is honesty, emotion and depth—conveyed by an author or an artist who has something that is worth saying to children and who says it in a way that is worth reading." Publishes hardcover originals and reprints.

FICTION Juvenile.

ILLUSTRATION Art samples (postcards only) should be sent in duplicate to Paul Zakris and Virginia Duncan.

TERMS Pays authors royalty. Offers advances. Pays illustrators royalty or by the project. Sends galleys to authors.

TIPS Currently not accepting unsolicited mail, mss or queries.

GROSSET & DUNLAP PUBLISHERS

Penguin Group (USA), Inc 345 Hudson St.New York NY 10014. Website: http://us.penguingroup.com/ youngreaders. Estab. 1898. **Acquisitions:** Francesco Sedita, Vice-President/Publisher. Publishes approximately 140 titles/year. "Grosset & Dunlap publishes high interest, affordable books for children ages 0-10 years. We focus on original series, licensed properties, readers and novelty books." Grosset & Dunlap publishes children's books that show children that reading is fun, with books that speak to their interests, and that are affordable so that children can build a home library of their own. Focus on licensed properties, series and readers. Publishes hardcover (few) and mass market paperback originals.

○ *Not currently accepting submissions.*

FICTION Recently published series: Frankly Frannie; George Brown, Class Clown; Bedeviled; Hank Zipzer; Camp Confidential; Katie Kazoo; Magic Kitten; Magic Puppy; The Hardy Boys; Nancy Drew; The Little Engine That Could. *Upcoming series:* Splurch Academy for Disruptive Boys; Gladiator Boy; Dinkin Dings; Hello, Gorgeous!; **Licensed series:** Angelina Ballerina; Disney Club Penguin; Charlie & Lola; Star Wars: The Clone Wars; WWE; Disney's Classic Pooh; Max & Ruby; The Penguins of Madagascar; Batman: The Brave and the Bold; Strawberry Shortcake. All book formats except for picture books. Submit a summary and the first chapter or two for longer works. Agented submissions only.

NONFICTION *Young readers:* nature/environment, science. Recently published series: *All Aboard Reading*; *Who Was..?* series. Agented submissions only.

HOW TO CONTACT "We do not accept e-mail submissions. Unsolicited manuscripts usually receive a response in 6-8 weeks."

TIPS Nonfiction that is particularly topical or of wide interest in the mass market; new concepts for novelty format for preschoolers; and very well-written easy readers on topics that appeal to primary graders have the best chance of selling to our firm.

GRYPHON HOUSE, INC.

(800)638-0928. Fax: (301)595-0051. E-mail: kathy@gh books.com. Website: www.gryphonhouse.com. Parent and teacher resource books, textbooks. Recently published *Reading Games*, by Jackie Silberg; *Primary*

Art, by MaryAnn F. Kohl; *Teaching Young Children with Autism Spectrum Disorder*, by Clarissa Willis; *The Complete Resource Book for Infants*, by Pam Schiller. "At Gryphon House, our goal is to publish books that help teachers and parents enrich the lives of children from birth through age 8. We strive to make our books useful for teachers at all levels of experience, as well as for parents, caregivers, and anyone interested in working with children." Query. Submit outline/synopsis and 2 sample chapters. Responds to queries/mss in 6 months. Publishes a book 18 months after acceptance. Will consider simultaneous submissions, e-mail submissions. Book catalog and ms guidelines available via website or with SASE. "We are looking for books of creative, participatory learning experiences that have a common conceptual theme to tie them together. The books should be on subjects that parents or teachers want to do on a daily basis." **Contact:** Kathy Charner, editor-in-chief. "Gryphon House publishes books that teachers and parents of young children (birth-age 8) consider essential to their daily lives." Publishes trade paperback originals.

NONFICTION Currently emphasizing social-emotional intelligence and classroom management; de-emphasizing literacy after-school activities. "We prefer to receive a letter of inquiry and/or a proposal, rather than the entire manuscript. Please include: The proposed title The purpose of the book, Table of contents, Introductory material, 20-40 sample pages of the actual book. In addition, please describe the book, including the intended audience, why teachers will want to buy it, how it is different from other similar books already published, and what qualifications you possess that make you the appropriate person to write the book. If you have a writing sample that demonstrates that you write clear, compelling prose, please include it with your letter."

HOW TO CONTACT "Send a SASE for our catalog and manuscript guidelines. Look at our books, then submit proposals that complement the books we already publish or supplement our existing books." P.O. Box 207, Beltsville MD 20704-0207. (301)595-9500. Fax: (301)595-0051. E-mail: kathy@ghbooks.com. Website: www.gryphonhouse.com.

ILLUSTRATION Works with 4-5 illustrators/year. Uses b&w realistic artwork only. Query with samples, promo sheet. Responds in 2 months. Samples returned with SASE; samples filed. Pays illustrators by the project.

PHOTOGRAPHY Pays photographers by the project or per photo. Sends edited ms copy to authors. Original artwork returned at job's completion.

H & W PUBLISHING INC

P.O. Box 53515, Cincinnati, OH 45253. (513)687-3968. E-mail: info@handwpublishing.com. Website: www.handwpublishing.com. Estab. 2007. Specializes in African American children's literature. Publishes 2 books/year. 90% of books by first-time authors. "Our company empowers, inspires, and uplifts."

FICTION Picture Books: concept, contemporary, humor, poetry, religion. Young Readers: adventure, contemporary, nature/environment, poetry. Middle Readers: contemporary, problem novels. Average word length: picture books-1,200; young readers-850; middle readers-2,500. Recently published *Coralee's Best Run Yet*, by Karen N. Harkness, Alpha Frierson, (ages 6-8 picture book).

NONFICTION Young Readers: biography, social issues. Average word length: picture books-700; young readers-1,200. Recently published *Obama, Our Hero*, by Karen N. Harkness, Elbert Lewis Jr. (ages 5-12, biography).

HOW TO CONTACT Submit complete manuscript or submit outline/synopsis. Responds to queries in 1 month. Responds to mss in 2 months. Publishes a book 18 months after acceptance.

ILLUSTRATION Works with 3 illustrators/year. Uses both color and b&w. Submit work history and 3 samples or URL that displays a minimum of 3 original illustrations. Contact: Karen Harkness, submissions department.

TERMS Pays authors royalty 5% and work purchased outright for $2,500-4,000. Pays illustrators by the project (range $1,800-3,500) and royalty of 3-5% based on retail price. Originals returned to artist at job's completion. Writers and artists guidelines available at www.handwpublishing.com.

TIPS "We specialize in literature for African American children. Illustrations should be detailed and reflect positive images. Story lines should either be humorist, contemporary or teach without being preachy. No books on slavery, please."

HARPERTEEN

10 East 53rd Street, New York, NY 10022. Phone: (212)207-7000. Fax: (212)702-2583. Web sites: www.harpercollins.com, www.harperteen.com. Book publisher. HarperTeen is an imprint of HarperCol-

lins Children's Books. Publishes about 100 teen titles/year.

○ HarperTeen is a teen imprint that publishes hardcovers, paperback reprints and papberback originals.

HOW TO CONTACT HarperCollins Children's Books is not accepting unsolicited and/or un-agented manuscripts or queries. Unfortunately the volume of these submissions is so large that they cannot receive the attention they deserve. Such submissions will not be reviewed or returned. Manuscripts and queries: Agent submissions may be sent to Elise Howard.Responses only if interested. Materials returned with SASE.

○ HAYES SCHOOL PUBLISHING CO. INC.

321 Pennwood Ave.Wilkinsburg PA 15221-3398. (412)371-2373. Fax: (800)543-8771. E-mail: chayes@ hayespub.com. Website: www.hayespub.com. Estab. 1940. **Acquisitions:** Mr. Clair N. Hayes. Produces folders, workbooks, stickers, certificates. Wants to see supplementary teaching aids for grades K-12. Interested in all subject areas. Will consider simultaneous and electronic submissions.

HOW TO CONTACT Query with description or complete ms. Responds in 6 weeks. SASE for return of submissions.

ILLUSTRATION Works with 3-4 illustrators/year. Responds in 6 weeks. Samples returned with SASE; samples filed. Originals not returned at job's completion.

TERMS Work purchased outright. Purchases all rights.

HOLIDAY HOUSE INC.

425 Madison Ave., New York NY 10017. (212)688-0085. Fax: (212)421-6134. E-mail: info@holidayhouse.com. Website: www.holidayhouse.com. Publishes 35 picture books/year; 3 young readers/year; 15 middle readers/year; 8 young adult titles/year. 20% of books by first-time authors; 10% from agented writers. Mission statement: "To publish high-quality books for children."

FICTION Recently published: *Here We Go Round the Mulberry Bush*, by Jane Cabrera; *Time Zones*, by David A. Adler; *The Day of the Dead/El Dia de los Muertos*, by Bob Barner; *Thank You, Miss Doover*, by Robin Pulver; *Nightshade City*, by Hilary Wagner; *Storm Mountain* by Tom Birdseye; *Lafayette and the American Revolution*, by Russell Freedman.

NONFICTION All levels, but more picture books and fewer middle grade nonfiction titles: animal, biography, concept, contemporary, geography, historical, math, multicultural, music/dance, nature/environment, religion, science, social issues.

HOW TO CONTACT Send complete manuscripts to the acquisitions editor. "We respond only to manuscripts that meet our current needs."

ILLUSTRATION Works with 35 illustrators/year. Reviews ms illustration packages from artists. Send ms with dummy. Do not submit original artwork or slides. Color photocopies or printed samples are preferred. Responds only if interested. Samples filed.

TERMS Pays authors and illustrators an advance against royalties. Originals returned at job's completion. Book catalog, ms/artist's guidelines available for a SASE.

TIPS "We need books with strong stories, writing and art. We do not publish board books or novelties. No easy readers."

◯ HOUGHTON MIFFLIN HARCOURT

Children's Trade Books, 222 Berkeley St. Boston MA 02116-3764. (617)351-5000. Fax: (617)351-1111. E-mail: Children'sBooks@hmhpub.com. Website: www.houghtonmifflinbooks.com. Manuscript Acquisitions: Submissions Coordinator; Betsy Groban, publisher; Margaret Raymo, senior executive; Ann Rider, executive editor; Mary Wilcox, editorial director; Julia Richardson, paperback director; Kate O'Sullivan, executive editor; Monica Perez, franchise senior editor; Erica Zappy, associate editor. Art Acquisitions: Sheila Smallwood, creative director. Imprints include Houghton Mifflin, Harcourt, Clarion, Sandpiper and Graphia. Averages 60 titles/year. Publishes hardcover originals and trade paperback reprints and originals. "Houghton Mifflin gives shape to ideas that educate, inform, and above all, delight."

○ Houghton title *Kakapo Rescue* won the 2011 Sibert Medal, while *Dark Emperor and Other Poems of the Night* by Joyce Sidman, illustrated by Rick Allen, was a 2011 Newbery Honor Medalist Children's.

FICTION All levels: all categories except religion. "We do not rule out any theme, though we do not publish specifically religious material." Recently published *Red Sings from Treetops: a year in colors*, by Joyce Sidman, illustrated by Pamela Zagarenski (ages 5-8, picture book/poetry); *The Entomological Tales of Augustus T. Percival: Petronella Saves Nearly*

Everyone (ages 5 and up, middle grade); *Cashay* (ages 12 and up, YA novel).

NONFICTION All categories except religion. Recently published *Down, Down, Down; A Journey to the Bottom of the Sea*, by Steven Jenkins (ages 5-8, picture); *The Frog Scientist*, by Pamela S. Turner, photographs by Andy Comins (ages 10 and up).

HOW TO CONTACT Submit entire ms typed (letter quality), double-spaced manuscript on unfolded plain white paper in a 9×12 envelope. "We do not accept manuscripts that are handwritten or submitted on computer disk. You do not have to furnish illustrations, but if you wish, copies of a few comprehensive sketches or duplicate copies of original art will suffice. "Nonfiction: Submit outline/synopsis and sample chapters. Responds within 4 months ONLY if interested. DO NOT SEND SELF-ADDRESSED STAMPED ENVELOPE. All declined material will be recycled.

ILLUSTRATION Works with 60 illustrators/year. Reviews ms/illustration packages or illustrations only from artists: Query with samples (colored photocopies are fine); provide tearsheets. Responds in 4 months if interested. Samples returned with SASE; samples filed if interested. Address art submissions to: Art Department, Children's Trade Books.

HOUGHTON MIFFLIN HARCOURT BOOKS FOR CHILDREN

Imprint of Houghton Mifflin Trade & Reference Division, 222 Berkeley St., Boston MA 02116. (617)351-5000. Fax: (617)351-1111. E-mail: children's_books@hmco.com. Website: www.houghtonmifflinbooks.com. Houghton Mifflin Harcourt gives shape to ideas that educate, inform, and above all, delight. Does not respond to or return mss unless interested. Publishes hardcover originals and trade paperback originals and reprints. **Contact:** Erica Zappy, associate editor; Kate O'Sullivan, senior editor; Anne Rider, executive editor; Margaret Raymo, editorial director. 5,000 queries received/year. 14,000 mss received/year.

○ Does not respond to or return mss unless interested.

FICTION Submit complete ms.

NONFICTION Interested in innovative books and subjects about which the author is passionate. Query with SASE. Submit sample chapters, synopsis.

HOW TO CONTACT Query with SASE. Submit sample chapters, synopsis.

TIPS Faxed or e-mailed manuscripts and proposals are not considered. Complete submission guidelines available on website.

HOUGHTON MIFFLIN HARCOURT CHILDREN'S BOOKS

Imprint of Houghton Mifflin Harcourt Children's Book Group, 215 Park Ave South, New York, NY 10003. Website: www.harcourtbooks.com. **Senior Vice President and Publisher:** Betsy Groban. **Vice President and Editorial Director:** Jeannette Larson. 20% of books by first-time authors; 50% of books from agented writers. "Harcourt Children's Books publishes hardcover picture books and fiction only." Harcourt Children's Books no longer accepts unsolicited manuscripts, queries or illustrations. Recent Harcourt titles *Ten Little Fingers and Ten Little Toes*, by Mem Fox, illustrated by Helen Oxenbury; *Help Me, Mr. Mut!* by Janet Stevens and Susan Stevens Crummel; *How I Became a Pirate and Pirates Don't Change Diapers*, by Melinda Long, illustrated by David Shannon; and *Frankenstein Makes a Sandwich*, by Adam Rex, are all New York Times bestsellers. *My Abuelita* by Tony Johnston, illustrated by Yuyi Morales was named an ALA Notable Children's book for 2010. Publishes hardcover originals and trade paperback reprints.

FICTION *No unsolicited mss or queries.* No phone calls.

NONFICTION *No unsolicited mss or queries.* No phone calls.

HOW TO CONTACT Only interested in agented material.

ILLUSTRATION Only interested in agented material at this time.

PHOTOGRAPHY Works on assignment only.

TERMS Pays authors and illustrators royalty based on retail price. Pays photographers by the project. Sends galleys to authors; dummies to illustrators. Original artwork returned at job's completion.

HUNTER HOUSE PUBLISHERS

P.O. Box 2914, Alameda, CA 94501-0914. (510)865-5282. Fax: (510)865-4295. E-mail: acquisitions@hunterhouse.com. Website: www.hunterhouse.com. **Manuscript Acquisitions:** Acquisitions editor. Publishes 1-3 nonfiction titles for children/teens per year. 50% of books by first-time authors.

NONFICTION Books are fitness/diet/exercise and activity games/social skills/classroom management-oriented. Does *not* want to see books for young children, fiction, illustrated picture books, memoir or autobiography. Published SmartFun activity book series (currently about 20 books): each has 101 games that encourage imagination, social interaction, and self-expression in children (generally between ages 3-15). Widely used in homes, schools, day-care centers, clubs, and camps. Each activity includes set-up, age range, difficulty level, materials list and a time suggestion. **HOW TO CONTACT** Query: Visit website for submission guidelines. Submit overview and chapter-by-chapter synopsis, sample chapters, and statistics on subject area, support organizations or networks, personal bio, and marketing ideas. "Testimonials from professionals or well-known authors are helpful, especially for health books." Responds to queries in 1-3 months; mss in 3-6 months. Publishes a book 12-18 months after acceptance. Will consider simultaneous submissions. **TERMS** Payment varies. Sends galleys to authors. Book catalog available. But most updated information is on website; ms guidelines for standard SAE and 1 first-class stamp. **TIPS** "Looking for children's activity books focused on education, teamwork, skill-building, ETC. The Children's Books we publish are for a select, therapeutic audience. No fiction! Please, no fiction."

IDEALS CHILDREN'S BOOKS AND CANDYCANE PRESS

Imprints of Ideals Publications, 2630 Elm Hill Pike, Suite 100, Nashville, TN 37214. Website: www.idealsbooks.com. **Manuscript Acquisitions:** Submissions. **Art Acquisitions:** Art Director. Publishes 4-6 new picture books/year; 4-6 new board books/year. 50% of books by first-time authors. **FICTION** Picture books: animal, concept, history, religion. Board books: animal, history, nature/environment, religion. Average word length: picture books—1,500; board books—200.

ILLUMINATION ARTS

P.O. Box 1865, Bellevue WA 98009. (425)644-7185. Fax: (425)644-9274. E-mail: liteinfo@illumin.com. Website: www.illumin.com. **Acquisitions:** Ruth Thompson, editorial director. **FICTION** Word length: Prefers under 1,000, but will consider up to 1,500 words. Recently published *God's Promise*, by Maureen Moss, illustrated by Ger-

ald Purnell; *Roonie B. Moonie: Lost and Alone*, by Janan Cain. **HOW TO CONTACT** Note that our submission review process is on hold until notice on website so submissions are not currently being reviewed. Normal requirements include no electronic or CD submissions for text or art. Considers simultaneous submissions. **ILLUSTRATION** Uses color artwork only. Reviews both ms submissions from authors and illustration packages from artists. Artists may query with color samples, résumé and promotional material to be kept on file or returned with SASE only. Responds within 3 months with SASE only. Samples returned with SASE or filed. **TERMS** Pays authors and illustrators royalty based on wholesale price. Book fliers available for SASE. **TIPS** "Read our books or visit website to see what our books are like. Follow submission guidelines found on website. Be patient. We are unable to track unsolicited submissions."

IMPACT PUBLISHERS, INC.

P.O. Box 6016, Atascadero CA 93423-6016. (805)466-5917. E-mail: submissions@impactpublishers.com. Website: www.impactpublishers.com. **Manuscript Acquisitions:** Freeman Porter, submissions editor. **Art Acquisitions:** J. Trumbull, production. Imprints: Little Imp Books, Rebuilding Books, The Practical Therapist Series. Publishes 1 young reader/year; 1 middle reader/year; 1 young adult title/year. 20% of books by first-time authors. "Our purpose is to make the best human services expertise available to the widest possible audience. We publish only popular psychology and self-help materials written in everyday language by professionals with advanced degrees and significant experience in the human services." **NONFICTION** Young readers, middle readers, young adults: self-help. Recently published *Jigsaw Puzzle Family: The Stepkids' Guide to Fitting It Together*, by Cynthia MacGregor (ages 8-12, children's/divorce/emotions). **HOW TO CONTACT** Nonfiction: Query or submit complete ms, cover letter, résumé. Responds to queries in 12 weeks; mss in 3 months. Will consider simultaneous submissions or previously published work. **ILLUSTRATION** Works with 1 illustrator/year. Uses b&w artwork only. Reviews ms/illustration packages from artists. Query. Contact: Children's Editor. Illustrations only: Query with samples. Contact: Jean Trumbull, production manager. Responds only if interested. Samples returned with SASE; samples filed. Originals returned to artist at job's completion.

TERMS Pays authors royalty of 10-12%. Offers advances. Pays illustrators by the project. Book catalog available for #10 SAE with 2 first-class stamps; ms guidelines available for SASE. All imprints included in a single catalog.

TIPS "Please do not submit fiction, poetry or narratives."

JEWISH LIGHTS PUBLISHING

LongHill Partners, Inc., Sunset Farm Offices, Rt. 4, P.O. Box 237, Woodstock VT 05091. (802)457-4000. Fax: (802)457-4004. E-mail: editorial@jewishlights. com; sales@jewishlights.com. Website: www.jewish lights.com. **Art Acquisitions:** Tim Holtz. Publishes 2 picture books/year; 1 young reader/year. 50% of books by first-time authors; 25% of books from agented authors. All books have spiritual/religious themes. "Jewish Lights publishes books for people of all faiths and all backgrounds who yearn for books that attract, engage, educate and spiritually inspire. Our authors are at the forefront of spiritual thought and deal with the quest for the self and for meaning in life by drawing on the Jewish wisdom tradition. Our books cover topics including history, spirituality, life cycle, children, self-help, recovery, theology and philosophy. We do not publish autobiography, biography, fiction, haggadot, poetry or cookbooks. At this point we plan to do only two books for children annually, and one will be for younger children (ages 4-10)." **Contact:** Acquisitions Editor. "People of all faiths and backgrounds yearn for books that attract, engage, educate and spiritually inspire. Our principal goal is to stimulate thought and help all people learn about who the Jewish people are, where they come from, and what the future can be made to hold." Publishes hardcover and trade paperback originals, trade paperback reprints.

FICTION Picture books, young readers, middle readers: spirituality. "We are not interested in anything other than spirituality." Recently published *God's Paintbrush*, by Sandy Eisenberg Sasso, illustrated by Annette Compton (ages 4-9).

NONFICTION Picture book, young readers, middle readers: activity books, spirituality. Recently published *When a Grandparent Dies: A Kid's Own*

Remembering Workbook for Dealing with Shiva and the Year Beyond, by Nechama Liss-Levinson, Ph.D. (ages 7-11); *Tough Questions Jews Ask: A Young Adult's Guide to Building a Jewish Life*, by Rabbi Edward Feinstein (ages 12 and up). "We do *not* publish haggadot, biography, poetry, or cookbooks." Submit proposal package, including cover letter, TOC, 2 sample chapters and SASE (postage must cover weight of ms).

HOW TO CONTACT Fiction/nonfiction: Query with outline/synopsis and 2 sample chapters; submit complete ms for picture books. Include SASE. Responds to queries/mss in 4 months. Publishes a book 1 year after acceptance. Will consider simultaneous submissions and previously published work.

ILLUSTRATION Works with 2 illustrators/year. Reviews ms/illustration packages from artists. Query. Illustrations only: Query with samples; provide résumé. Samples returned with SASE; samples filed.

TERMS Pays authors royalty of 10% of revenue received; 15% royalty for subsequent printings. Offers advances. Pays illustrators by the project or royalty. Pays photographers by the project or royalty. Sends galleys to authors; dummies to illustrators. Book catalog available for $6^{1}_{2} \times 9^{1}_{2}$ SAE and 59¢ postage; ms guidelines available on website.

TIPS "We publish books for all faiths and backgrounds that also reflect the Jewish wisdom tradition. Explain in your cover letter why you're submitting your project to us in particular. Make sure you know what we publish."

JOURNEYFORTH

Imprint of BJU Press, 1700 Wade Hampton Blvd., Greenville SC 29614. (864)242-5100, ext. 4350. Fax: (864)298-0268. E-mail: jb@bju.edu. Website: www. journeyforth.com. Specializes in trade books. Publishes 1 picture book/year; 2 young readers/year; 4 middle readers/year; 4 young adult titles/year. 10% of books by first-time authors. "We aim to produce well-written books for readers of varying abilities and interests and fully consistent with biblical worldview." Book catalog and writers guidelines are at www.bju press.com/books/freelance.html. "Review our backlist to be sure your work is a good fit." **Contact:** Nancy Lohr. "Small independent publisher of trustworthy novels and biographies for readers pre-school through high school from a conservative Christian perspective, Christian living books, and Bible studies for adults." Publishes paperback originals.

FICTION Young readers, middle readers, young adults: adventure, animal, contemporary, fantasy, folktales, history, humor, multicultural, nature/environment, problem novels, suspense/mystery. Average word length: young readers—10,000-12,000; middle readers—10,000-40,000; young adult/teens—40,000-60,000. Our fiction is all based on a moral and Christian worldview. Does not want short stories. Submit 5 sample chapters, synopsis, SASE.

NONFICTION Young readers, middle readers, young adult: biography. Average word length: young readers—10,000-12,000; middle readers—10,000-40,000; young adult/teens—40,000-60,000. Nonfiction Christian living, Bible studies, church and ministry, church history. We produce books for the adult Christian market that are from a conservative Christian worldview.

HOW TO CONTACT Fiction: Query or submit outline/synopsis and 5 sample chapters. "Do not send stories with magical elements. We are not currently accepting picture books. We do not publish: romance, science fiction, poetry and drama." Nonfiction: Query or submit outline/synopsis and 5 sample chapters. Responds to queries in 4 weeks; mss in 3 months. Publishes book 12-15 months after acceptance. Will consider previously published work.

ILLUSTRATION Works with 2–4 illustrators/year. Query with samples. Send promo sheet; will review website portfolio if applicable. Responds only if interested. Samples returned with SASE; samples filed.

TERMS Pays authors royalty based on wholesale price. Pays illustrators by the project. Originals returned to artist at job's completion.

TIPS "Study the publisher's guidelines. No picture books and no submissions by e-mail."

⦿ KAMEHAMEHA PUBLISHING

567 S. King St., Suite 118, Honolulu, HI 96813. (808)534-8205. E-mail: publishing@ksbe.edu. Website: www.KamehamehaPublishing.org. **Manuscript Acquisitions:** Acquisitions Editor. "Kamehameha Schools Press publishes in the areas of Hawaiian history, Hawaiian culture, Hawaiian language and Hawaiian studies."

FICTION Young reader, middle readers, young adults: biography, history, multicultural, Hawaiian folklore.

NONFICTION Young reader, middle readers, young adults: biography, history, multicultural, Hawaiian folklore.

ILLUSTRATION Uses color and b&w artwork. Illustrations only: Query with samples. Responds only if interested. Samples not returned.

TERMS Work purchased outright from authors or by royalty agreement. Pays illustrators by the project. Sends galleys to authors. Book catalog available (call or write for copy). All imprints included in a single catalog. Catalog available on website.

TIPS "Writers and illustrators must be knowledgeable in Hawaiian history/culture and be able to show credentials to validate their proficiency. Greatly prefer to work with writers/illustrators available in the Honolulu area."

ⓐⓖⓞ KANE/MILLER BOOK PUBLISHERS

Kane/Miller: A Division of EDC Publishing, 4901 Morena Blvd., Suite 213, San Diego CA 92117. (858)456-0540. Fax: (858)456-9641. E-mail: info@kanemiller.com. E-mail: submissions@kanemiller.com. Website: www.kanemiller.com. Estab. 1985. Specializes in trade books, fiction, multicultural material. Publishes 20 picture books/year; 10 young readers/year; 20 middle grade readers/year. 50% of books by first-time authors. **Contact:** Kira Lynn, Editorial Department. "Kane/Miller Book Publishers is a division of EDC Publishing, specializing in award-winning children's books from around the world. Our books bring the children of the world closer to each other, sharing stories and ideas, while exploring cultural differences and similarities. Although we continue to look for books from other countries, we are now actively seeking works that convey cultures and communities within the US. We are looking for picture book fiction and nonfiction on those subjects which may be defined as particularly American: sports such as baseball, historical events, American biographies, American folk tales, etc. We are committed to expanding our early and middle grade fiction list. We're interested in great stories with engaging characters in all genres (mystery, fantasy, adventure, historical, etc.) and, as with picture books, especially those with particularly American subjects. All submissions sent via USPS should be sent to: Editorial Department. Please do not send anything requiring a signature. Work submitted for consideration may also be sent via e-mail. Please send either the complete picture book ms, the published book (with a summary and outline in English, if that is not the language of origin) or a synopsis of the work and two sample chapters. DO NOT SEND ORIGINALS. Illustrators may send color copies, tear sheets, or other non-returnable illustration samples. If you have a website with additional samples of your work, please include the web address. Please do not send original artwork, or samples on CD. A SASE must be included if you send your submission via USPS; otherwise you will not receive a reply. If we wish to follow up, we will notify you."

○ "We like to think that a child reading a Kane Miller book will see parallels between his own life and what might be the unfamiliar setting and characters of the story. And that by seeing how a character who is somehow or in some way dissimilar—an outsider—finds a way to fit comfortably into a culture or community or situation while maintaining a healthy sense of self and self-dignity, she might be empowered to do the same."

FICTION Picture Books: concept, contemporary, health, humor, multicultural. Young Readers: contemporary, multicultural, suspense. Middle Readers: contemporary, humor, multicultural, suspense.

HOW TO CONTACT Only interested in agented material. Fiction/nonfiction: Submit outline/synopsis and 2 sample chapters. Responds to queries in 6 weeks; mss in 12 weeks. Publishes a book 1 year after acceptance. Will consider simultaneous submissions.

ILLUSTRATION Only interested in agented material. Uses both color and b&w. Reviews ms/illustration packages from artists. Query. Responds in 3 weeks. Samples returned with SASE.

TERMS Book catalog available online. All imprints included in a single catalog. Writer's and artist's guidelines are available online.

KAR-BEN PUBLISHING, INC.

A division of Lerner Publishing Group, Inc. 241 First Ave. N. Minneapolis, MN 55401. (612)332-3344. Fax: (612)-332-7615. E-mail: editorial@karben.com. Website: www.karben.com. **Manuscript Acquisitions:** Joni Sussman, publisher. Publishes 10-15 books/year (mostly picture books); 20% of books by first-time authors. All of Kar-Ben's books are on Jewish themes for young children and families.

FICTION Picture books: Adventure, concept, folktales, history, humor, multicultural, religion, special needs; must be on a Jewish theme. Average word length: picture books—1,000. Recently published *Engineer Ari and the Rosh Hashanah Ride*, by Deborah Bodin Cohen, illustrated by Shahar Kober; and *The Wedding That Saved a Town*, by Yale Strom, illustrated by Jenya Prosmitsky.

NONFICTION Picture books, young readers: activity books, arts/crafts, biography, careers, concept, cooking, history, how-to, multicultural, religion, social issues, special needs; must be of Jewish interest.

HOW TO CONTACT Submit complete ms. Responds to queries/mss in 6 weeks. Publishes a book 24-36 months after acceptance. Will consider simultaneous submissions.

ILLUSTRATION Works with 10-12 illustrators/year. Prefers four-color art in any medium that is scannable. Reviews illustration packages from artists. Submit sample of art or online portfolio (no originals).

TERMS Pays authors royalties of 3-5% of net against advance of $500-1,000; or purchased outright. Original artwork returned at job's completion. Book catalog free on request. Manuscript guidelines on website.

TIPS Looks for books for young children with Jewish interest and content, modern, nonsexist, not didactic. Fiction or nonfiction with a Jewish theme can be serious or humorous, life cycle, Bible story, or holiday-related. Looking in particular for stories that reflect the ethnic and cultural diversity of today's Jewish family.

Ⓐ KNOPF, DELACORTE, DELL BOOKS FOR YOUNG READERS

Imprint of Random House Children's Books, Division of Random House, Inc., 1745 Broadway, New York NY 10019. (212)782-9000. Website: www.randomhouse.com/kids. Book publisher.

○ See listings for Random House/Golden Books for Young Readers Group, Delacorte and Doubleday Books for Young Readers, Alfred A. Knopf and Crown Books for Young Readers, and Wendy Lamb Books.

HOW TO CONTACT Not seeking manuscripts at this time. **No e-mail samples are accepted. No calls accepted. Only mailings to the address listed above.**

ILLUSTRATION Contact: Isabel Warren-Lynch, executive director, art & design. Responds only if interested. Samples returned with SASE; samples filed.

TERMS Pays illustrators and photographers by the project or royalties. Original artwork returned at job's completion.

KOENISHA PUBLICATIONS

3196 53rd St., Hamilton MI 49419-9626. Phone/Fax: (269)751-4100. E-mail: koenisha@macatawa.org. Website: www.koenisha.com. Acquisitions: Sharolett Koenig, publisher; Earl Leon, acquisition editor. Publishes trade paperback originals. 10-12/year. 500 queries received/year. 500 mss received/year. Allow 6 months for response. Accepts simultaneous submissions. Guidelines available online. Not accepting submissions from new authors at this time. **Contact:** Sharolett Koenig, publisher; Earl Leon, acquisition editor. Publishes trade paperback originals. 500 queries received/year. 500 mss received/year.

FICTION "We do not accept manuscripts that contain unnecessary foul language, explicit sex or gratuitous violence." Query with SASE. Submit proposal package, clips, 3 sample chapters.

NONFICTION *Not accepting submissions from new authors at this time.*

TIPS "We're not interested in books written to suit a particular line or house or because it's trendy. Instead write a book from your heart—the inspiration or idea that kept you going through the writing process."

KRBY CREATIONS, LLC

Website: www.KRBYCreations.com. PO Box 327, Bay Head, NJ 08742. (732)691-3010. Fax: (815)846-0636. E-mail: info@KRBYCreations.com. Website: www. KRBYCreations.com. Estab. 2003.

FICTION Recently published *The Snowman in the Moon*, by Stephen Heigh (picture book); *Mulch the Lawnmower*, by Scott Nelson (picture book); *My Imagination*, by Katrina Estes-Hill (picture book).

HOW TO CONTACT Fiction/nonfiction: Writers *must* request guidelines by e-mail prior to submitting mss. See website. Submissions without annotation found in guidelines will not be considered. Responds to e-mail queries in 1 week; mss in 1-3 months. Publishes book 1 year after acceptance. Considers simultaneous submissions.

ILLUSTRATION Detailed contact guidelines available on website. Illustrator terms negotiable. Pays advance plus royalties for experienced illustrators. Avoids work-for-hire contracts. 40-60% of illustrators are first-time children's picture book published.

TERMS Pays authors royalty of 6-15% based on wholesale price. Catalog on website. Offers writer's guidelines by e-mail.

TIPS "Submit as professionally as possible; make your vision clear to us about what you are trying to capture. Know your market/audience and identify it in your proposal. Tell us what is new/unique with your idea. All writers submitting must first request guidelines by e-mail."

KREGEL PUBLICATIONS

(616)451-4775. Fax: (616)451-9330. E-mail: kregel books@kregel.com. Website: www.kregelpublications. com. P.O. Box 2607, Grand Rapids MI 49501. **Contact:** Dennis R. Hillman, publisher. "Our mission as an evangelical Christian publisher is to provide—with integrity and excellence—trusted, Biblically-based resources that challenge and encourage individuals in their Christian lives. Works in theology and Biblical studies should reflect the historic, orthodox Protestant tradition." Publishes hardcover and trade paperback originals and reprints.

FICTION Fiction should be geared toward the evangelical Christian market. Wants books with fast-paced, contemporary storylines presenting a strong Christian message in an engaging, entertaining style.

NONFICTION "We serve evangelical Christian readers and those in career Christian service."

TIPS "Our audience consists of conservative, evangelical Christians, including pastors and ministry students."

WENDY LAMB BOOKS

Imprint of Random House, 1745 Broadway, New York, NY 10019. Website: www.randomhouse.com. **Manuscript Acquisitions:** Wendy Lamb. Receives 1,500-2,000 submissions/year. Publishes 12-15 novels/year for middle grade and young adult readers. WLB does not publish picture books at present. 15% of books by first-time authors and 10% unagented writers. Publishes hardcover originals.

○ Literary fiction and nonfiction for readers 8-15. Query with SASE.

FICTION Recently published *When You Reach Me*, by Rebecca Stead; *Love, Aubrey*, by Suzanne LaFleur; *Eyes of the Emperor*, by Graham Salisbury; *A Brief Chapter in My Impossible Life*, by Dana Reinhardt; *What They Found: Love on 145th Street*, by Walter Dean Myers; *Eleven*, by Patricia Reilly Giff. Other WLB authors include Christopher Paul Curtis, Gary Paulsen, Donna Jo Napoli, Peter Dickinson, Marthe-Jocelyn, Graham McNamee.

HOW TO CONTACT "Query letter with SASE for reply. A query letter should briefly describe the book you have written, the intended age group and your brief biography and publishing credits, if any. Please send the first 10 pages (or to the end of the chapter) of your manuscript. Our turnaround time is approximately 4–8 weeks."

TIPS "Please note that we do not publish picture books. Please send the first 10 pages of your ms (or until the end of the first chapter) along with a cover letter, synopsis, and SASE. Before you submit, please take a look at some of our recent titles to get an idea of what we publish."

Ⓐ LAUREL-LEAF

(212)782-9000. Website: www.randomhouse.com/teens.

Ⓠ Quality reprint paperback imprint for young adult paperback books. *Does not accept unsolicited mss.*

LEE & LOW BOOKS

95 Madison Ave., #1205, New York NY 10016. (212)779-4400. E-mail: general@leeandlow.com. Website: www.leeandlow.com. Publishes 12-14 children's books/year. 25% of books by first-time authors. Lee & Low Books publishes books with diverse themes. "One of our goals is to discover new talent and produce books that reflect the diverse society in which we live." **Contact:** Louise May, editor-in-chief (multicultural children's fiction/nonfiction). "Our goals are to meet a growing need for books that address children of color, and to present literature that all children can identify with. We only consider multicultural children's books. Currently emphasizing material for 5-12 year olds. Sponsors a yearly New Voices Award for first-time picture book authors of color. Contest rules online at website or for SASE." Publishes hardcover originals and trade paperback reprints of our own titles. Receives 100 queries/year; 1,200 mss/year.

FICTION Picture books, young readers: anthology, contemporary, history, multicultural, poetry. " We are not considering folktales or animal stories." Picture book, middle reader: contemporary, history, multicultural, nature/environment, poetry, sports. Average word length: picture books--1,000-1,500 words. Recently published *Gracias~Thanks*, by Pat Mora; *Balarama*, by Ted and Betsy Lewin; *Yasmin's Hammer*, by Ann Malaspina; *Only One Year*, by Andrea Cheng (chapter book). "We do not publish folklore or animal stories." Send complete ms.

NONFICTION Picture books: concept. Picture books, middle readers: biography, history, multicultural, science and sports. Average word length: picture books-1,500-3,000. Recently published *Seeds of Change*, by Jen Cullerton Johnson; *Sharing Our Homeland*, by Trish Marx. "We publish only books featuring people of color for children ages 5-10 (illustrated picture books) plus a limited number of middle grade and YA stories." Submit completed ms.

HOW TO CONTACT Fiction/nonfiction: Submit complete ms. No e-mail submissions. Responds within 6 months, only if interested. Publishes a book 2-3 years after acceptance. Will consider simultaneous submissions. Guidelines on website.

ILLUSTRATION Works with 12-14 illustrators/year. Uses color artwork only. Reviews ms/illustration packages from artists. Contact: Louise May. Illustrations only: Query with samples, résumé, promo sheet and tearsheets. Responds only if interested. Samples returned with SASE; samples filed. Original artwork returned at job's completion.

PHOTOGRAPHY Buys photos from freelancers. Works on assignment only. Model/property releases required. Submit cover letter, résumé, promo piece and book dummy.

TERMS Pays authors advances against royalty. Pays illustrators advance against royalty. Photographers paid advance against royalty. Book catalog available for 9×12 SAE and $1.68 postage; catalog and ms and art guidelines available via website or with SASE.

TIPS "Check our website to see the kinds of books we publish. Do not send mss that don't fit our mission."

LEGACY PRESS

P.O. Box 261129, San Diego CA 92196. (858)277-1167. E-mail: editor@rainbowpublishers.com. Website: www.rainbowpublishers.com; www.legacypresskids.com. Publishes 4 young readers/year; 4 middle readers/year; 4 young adult titles/year. 50% of books by first-time authors. "Our mission is to publish Bible-based, teacher resource materials that contribute to and inspire spiritual growth and development in kids ages 2-12." **Contact:** Editorial Department.

NONFICTION Young readers, middle readers, young adult/teens: activity books, arts/crafts, how-to, reference, religion.

HOW TO CONTACT Responds to queries in 6 weeks; mss in 3 months. Publishes a book 60 months after acceptance. Will consider simultaneous submissions, submissions via disk and previously published work.

ILLUSTRATION Works with 25 illustrators/year. Reviews ms/illustration packages from artists. Submit ms with 2-5 pieces of final art. Illustrations only: Query with samples. Responds in 6 weeks. Samples returned with SASE; samples filed.

TERMS For authors work purchased outright (range: $500 and up). Pays illustrators by the project (range: $300 and up). Sends galleys to authors.

TIPS "Our Rainbow imprint publishes reproducible books for teachers of children in Christian ministries, including crafts, activities, games and puzzles. Our Legacy imprint publishes titles for children such as devotionals, fiction and Christian living. Please write for guidelines and study the market before submitting material."

LERNER PUBLISHING GROUP

Editorial Office, 11430 Strand Dr., #2, Rockville MD 20852-4371. (301)984-8733. Fax: (301)881-9195. E-mail: editorial@karben.com. Website: www.karben.com. Primarily publishes books for children ages 7-18. List includes titles in geography, natural and physical science, current events, ancient and modern history, high interest, sports, world cultures, and numerous biography series.

○ Starting in 2007, Lerner Publishing Group no longer accepts submission in any of their imprints except for Kar-Ben Publishing.

HOW TO CONTACT "We will continue to seek targeted solicitations at specific reading levels and in specific subject areas. The company will list these targeted solicitations on our website and in national newsletters, such as the SCBWI *Bulletin*."

○● ARTHUR A. LEVINE BOOKS

Imprint of Scholastic, Inc. 557 Broadway, New York NY 10012. (212)343-4436. Fax: (212)343-4890. Website: www.arthuralevinebooks.com. **Acquisitions:** Arthur A. Levine, editorial director; Cheryl Klein, senior editor. Publishes approximately 8 picture books/year; 8 full-length works for middle grade and young adult readers/year. Approximately 25% of books by first-time authors. Publishes hardback and soft cover prints and reprints.

FICTION Recently published *Bobby vs. Girls (accidentally)*, by Lisa Yee (chapter book); *The Perfect Gift* by Mary Newell Depalma, (picture book); *Moribito: Guardian of the Darkness*, by Nahoko Uehashi, trans.

by Cathy Hirano (novel); *The Memory Bank* by Carolyn Coman (chapter book); and *Plain Kate* by Erin Bow (novel).

NONFICTION Recently published *Peaceful Heroes*, by Jonah Winter, illustrated by Sean Addy (picture book); *The Fabulous Feud of Gilbert and Sullivan* by Jonah Winter, illustrated by Richard Egielski (picture book).

HOW TO CONTACT Fiction/nonfiction: Accepts queries only. Responds to queries in 1 month; mss in 5 months. Publishes a book $1\frac{1}{2}$ years after acceptance.

ILLUSTRATION Works with 8 illustrators/year. Will review ms/illustration packages from artists. Query first. Illustrations only: Send postcard sample with tearsheets. Samples not returned.

Ⓐ LITTLE, BROWN AND CO. BOOKS FOR YOUNG READERS

Hachette Book Group USA, 237 Park Ave., New York NY 10017. (212)364-1100. Fax: (212)364-0925. Website: www.lb-kids.com; www.lb-teens.com. "Little, Brown and Co. Children's Publishing publishes all formats including board books, picture books, middle grade fiction, and nonfiction YA titles. We are looking for strong writing and presentation, but no predetermined topics." Publishes picture books, board books, chapter books, novelty books, and general nonfiction and novels for middle and young adult readers.

FICTION Picture books: humor, adventure, animal, contemporary, history, multicultural, folktales. Young adults: contemporary, humor, multicultural, suspense/mystery, chick lit. Multicultural needs include "any material by, for and about minorities." Average word length: picture books—1,000; young readers—6,000; middle readers—15,000-50,000; young adults—50,000 and up. Picture books, middle grade and young adult. "We are looking for strong fiction for children of all ages in any area. We always prefer full manuscripts for fiction." Agented submissions only.

NONFICTION Middle readers, young adults: arts/crafts, history, multicultural, nature, self-help, social issues, sports, science. Average word length: middle readers—15,000-25,000; young adults—20,000-40,000. Recently published *American Dreaming*, by Laban Carrick Hill; *Exploratopia*, by the Exploratorium; *Yeah! Yeah! Yeah!: The Beatles, Beatlemania, and the Music that Changed the World*, by Bob Spitz. Writers should avoid looking for the 'issue' they think publishers want to see, choosing instead topics they know best and are most enthusiastic about/inspired by. *Agented submissions only.*

HOW TO CONTACT Only interested in solicited agented material. Fiction: Submit complete ms. Nonfiction: Submit cover letter, previous publications, a proposal, outline and 3 sample chapters. Do not send originals. Responds to queries in 2 weeks. Responds to mss in 2 months.

ILLUSTRATION Works with 40 illustrators/year. Illustrations only: Query art director with b&w and color samples; provide résumé, promo sheet or tearsheets to be kept on file. Does not respond to art samples. Do not send originals; copies only.

PHOTOGRAPHY Works on assignment only. Model/property releases required; captions required. Publishes photo essays and photo concept books. Uses 35mm transparencies. Photographers should provide résumé, promo sheets or tearsheets to be kept on file.

TERMS Pays authors royalties based on retail price. Pays illustrators and photographers by the project or royalty based on retail price. Sends galleys to authors; dummies to illustrators.

TIPS "In order to break into the field, authors and illustrators should research their competition and try to come up with something outstandingly different."

○ LOLLIPOP POWER BOOKS

Imprint of Carolina Wren Press, 120 Morris St., Durham, NC 27701. (919)560-2738. Fax: (919)560-2759. E-mail: carolinawrenpress@earthlink.net. Website: www.carolinawrenpress.org. **Manuscript Acquisitions:** Children's Book Editor. **Art Acquisitions:** Art Director. "In the past, Carolina Wren Press and Lollipop Power specialized in children's books that counter stereotypes or debunk myths about race, gender, sexual orientation, etc. We are also interested in books that deal with health or mental health issues—our two biggest sellers are *Puzzles* (about a young girl coping with Sickle Cell Disease) and *I Like It When You Joke With Me, I Don't Like It When You Touch Me* (about inappropriate touching) and we are currently promoting *Peace Comes to Ajani*, about anger management. Many of our children's titles are bilingual (English/Spanish). Please note, however, that as of 2009, we are no longer holding open submission periods for children's literature."

FICTION Average word length: picture books—500.

HOW TO CONTACT No open submissions at this time. "Please check our website to see if we have reopened submissions."

ILLUSTRATION "Send one example and link to website with further examples. We will respond only if interested. Samples not returned."

TERMS Pays authors royalty of 10% minimum based on retail price or work purchased outright from authors (range: $500-$2,000). Pays illustrators by the project (range: $500-$2,000). Sends galleys to authors; dummies to illustrators. Originals returned to artist at job's completion. Catalog available on website.

⊕ MAGICAL CHILD

Shades of White, 301 Tenth Ave., Crystal City MO 63019. E-mail: Acquisitions@Magicalchildbooks. com. Website: www.magicalchildbooks.com. Estab. 2007. Specializes in trade books, fiction. **Art Acquisitions:** art director. Publishes 1-3 picture books/year; 1-3 young readers/year; 1-3 middle readers/year. 80% of books by first-time authors. "The Neo-Pagan Earth Religions Community is the fastest growing demographic in the spiritual landscape, and Pagan parents are crying out for books appropriate for their Pagan kids. It is our plan to fill this small but growing need."

FICTION Picture Books: adventure, contemporary, nature/environment, submit only stories appropriate for Earth Religions *not* Native American. Young Readers: adventure, contemporary, nature/environment. Middle Readers: adventure, contemporary, nature/environment, submit only stories appropriate for Earth Religions *not* Native American. Average word length; picture books- 500-800; young readers- 500-4,500; middle readers-11,200-28,000. Recently published *Aiden's First Full Moon Circle*, by W. Lyon Martin (ages 5-8, picture book); *An Ordinary Girl, A Magical Child*, by W. Lyon Martin (ages 5-8, chapter book); *Smoky and the Feast of Mabon*, by Catherynne M. Valente (ages 4-8, picture book).

NONFICTION Middle Readers: biography, history (Earth religions only for both). Average word length: middle readers-11,200-28,000.

HOW TO CONTACT Fiction: Query or submit outline/synopsis for picture books only or submit outline/synopsis and 3 sample chapters. Nonfiction: Query or submit outline/synopsis and 3 sample chapters. Responds to queries in 3 weeks; mss in 3-6 months. Publishes a book 18+ months after acceptance. Will consider simultaneous submissions.

ILLUSTRATION Works with 1-2 illustrators/year. Uses color artwork only. Reviews ms/illustration packages from artists. Send manuscript with dummy. Contact: Art Director. Illustrations only: Send résumé, client list, tearsheets. Contact: Art Director. Samples returned with SASE; samples filed if interested.

TERMS Pays authors royalty based on retail price. Offers advances. Pays illustrators royalty based on wholesale price. Sends galleys to authors; dummies to illustrators. Originals returned to artist at job's completion. Book catalog available for SASE (#10 envelope with 1 first-class stamps). All imprints included in single catalog.

TIPS "Visit our submissions guidelines on the website. Follow the information provided there. We expect our authors to take an active role in promoting their books. If you can't do that, please don't submit your manuscript. *No calls, please.* Our list is *very* specific. Please do not send us manuscripts outside of our requested needs."

MAGINATION PRESS

750 First Street, NE, Washington, DC 20002-4242. (202)336-5618. Fax: (202)336-5624. E-mail: magination@apa.org. Website: www.maginationpress.com. **Acquisitions:** Kristine Enderle, managing editor. Publishes 12 books/year (picture books/year, middle readers/year, teen nonfiction). 75% of books by first-time authors. "We publish books dealing with the psycho/therapeutic resolution of children's problems and psychological issues with a strong self-help component."

⊕Magination Press is an imprint of the American Psychological Association.

FICTION All levels: psychological and social issues, self-help, health, parenting concerns and, special needs. Picture books, middle school readers. Recently published *Nobody's Perfect: A Story for Children about Perfection* by Ellen Flanagan Burns, illustrated by, Erica Peltron Villnave (ages 8-12); *Murphey's Three Homes: A Story for Children in Foster Care* by Jan Levinson Gilman, illustrated by Kathy O'Malley (ages 4-8).

NONFICTION All levels: psychological and social issues, self-help, health, multicultural, special needs. Recently published *Putting on the Brakes: Under-* *standing and Controlling Your ADD or ADHD* (ages 8-13), by Patricia Quinn and Judith M. Stern, illustrated by Joe Lee.

HOW TO CONTACT Fiction/nonfiction: Submit complete ms. Responds to queries in 1-2 months; mss in 2-6 months. Will consider simultaneous submissions. Materials returned only with a SASE. Publishes a book 18-24 months after acceptance.

ILLUSTRATION Works with 10-15 illustrators/year. Reviews ms/illustration packages. Will review artwork for future assignments. Responds only if interested, or immediately if SASE or response card is included. "We keep samples on file."

◐○⊕● MARSHALL CAVENDISH CHILDREN'S BOOKS

Imprint of Marshall Cavendish, 99 White Plains Rd., Tarrytown NY, 10591-9001. (914)332-8888. Website: www.marshallcavendish.us. Publishes 60-70 books/year. "Marshall Cavendish is an international publisher that publishes books, directories, magazines and digital platforms. Our philosophy of enriching life through knowledge transcends boundaries of geography and culture. In line with this vision, our products reach across the globe in 13 languages, and our publishing network spans Asia and the USA. Our brands have garnered international awards for educational excellence, and they include Marshall Cavendish Reference, Marshall Cavendish Benchmark, Marshall Cavendish Children, Marshall Cavendish Education and Marshall Cavendish Editions. Several have also achieved household name status in the international market. We ceaselessly explore new avenues to convey our products to the world, with our extensive variety of genres, languages and formats. In addition, our strategy of business expansion has ensured that the reach and benefits of Marshall Cavendish's products extend across the globe, especially into previously uncharted markets in China and Eastern Europe. Our aspiration to further the desire for lifelong learning and self-development continues to guide our efforts."

FICTION Publishes fiction for all ages/picture books.

HOW TO CONTACT Marshall Cavendish is no longer accepting unsolicited mss. However, the company will continue to consider agented mss.

ILLUSTRATION Contact: Anahid Hamparian, art director.

TERMS Pays authors/illustrators advance and royalties.

○ MASTER BOOKS

Website: www.masterbooks.net. Imprint of New Leaf Publishing Group, Inc, P.O. Box 726, Green Forest, AR 72638. (870)438-5288. Fax: (870)438-5120. E-mail: nlp@newleafpress.net. Website: www.nlpg.com. **Manuscript Acquisitions:** Craig Froman, acquisitions editor. 3 middle readers/year; 2 young adult nonfiction titles/year; 15 adult trade books/year. 10% of books by first-time authors.

NONFICTION Picture books: activity books, animal, nature/environment, creation. Young readers, middle readers, young adults: activity books, animal, biography Christian, nature/environment, science, creation. Recently published *Passport to the World* (middle readers); *The Earth* (science book); *Demolishing Supposed Bible Contradictions*, compiled by Ken Ham (adult series).

HOW TO CONTACT Nonfiction: Submission guidelines at our website. Responds to queries/mss in 4 months. Publishes book 1 year after acceptance. Will consider simultaneous submissions. Must download submissions form from website.

ILLUSTRATION We are not looking for illustrations.

TERMS Pays authors royalty of 3-15% based on wholesale price. Sends galleys to authors. Book catalog available per request; ms guidelines available on website. Catalog available on website.

TIPS "All of our children's books are creation-based, including topics from the Book of Genesis. We look also for home school educational material that would be supplementary to a home school curriculum."

◉ MARGARET K. MCELDERRY BOOKS

Imprint of Simon & Schuster Children's Publishing Division, 1230 Avenue of the Americas, New York, NY 10020. (212)698-7000. Website: www.simonsayskids. com. **Publisher:** Justin Chanda, vice president. Acquisitions: Karen Wojtyla, editorial director; Gretchen Hirsch, associate editor; Emily Fabre, assistant editor. Art Acquisitions: Ann Bobco, executive art director. Publishes 12 picture books/year; 5-8 middle readers/year; 8-10 young adult titles/year. "Margaret K. McElderry Books publishes hardcover and paperback trade books for children from pre-school age through young adult. This list includes picture books, middle grade and teen fiction, poetry, and fantasy. The style and subject matter of the books we publish is almost unlimited. We do not publish textbooks, coloring and activity books, greeting cards, magazines, pamphlets, or religious publications."

FICTION All levels. "Always interested in publishing young read-aloud picture books, humorous middle grade fiction, and original teen fiction or fantasy." Average word length: picture books-500; young readers-2,000; middle readers-10,000-20,000; young adults-45,000-50,000. Recently Published: *Monster Mess* by Margery Cuyler, illustrated by S. D. Schindler (picture book); *The Joy of Spooking: Fiendish Deeds* by P. J. Bracegirdle (MGF); *Identical* by Ellen Hopkins (teen); *Where is Home, Little Pip?* by Karma Wilson, illustrated by Jane Chapman (picture book); *Dr. Ted* by Andrea Beaty; illustrated by Pascal LeMaitre (picture book); *To Be Mona* by Kelly Easton (teen).

HOW TO CONTACT **Simon & Schuster children's publishing division does not accept unsolicited queries, manuscripts, or art samples unless submitted by an agent.**

TERMS Pays authors royalty based on retail price. Pays illustrator royalty or by the project. Pays photographers by the project. Original artwork returned at job's completion.

TIPS "We're looking for strong, original fiction, especially mysteries and middle grade humor. We are always interested in picture books for the youngest age reader. Study our titles."

MEADOWBROOK PRESS

5451 Smetana Dr., Minnetonka MN 55343. Fax: (952)930-1940. E-mail: info@meadowbrookpress. com. Website: www.meadowbrookpress.com. 20% of books by first-time authors; 10% of books from agented writers. Publishes children's poetry books, activity books, arts-and-crafts books and how-to books. **Contact:** Art Director. Publishes trade paperback originals and reprints. 1,500 queries received/year.

○ "We are not currently accepting unsolicited manuscripts or queries for the following genres: adult fiction, adult poetry, humor, and children's fiction. Also note that we do not currently publish picture books for children, travel titles, scholarly, or literary works. For children's poetry guidelines, please go to our website."

NONFICTION Publishes activity books, arts/crafts, how-to, poetry. Average word length: varies. Recently published *The Siblings' Busy Book*, by Heather Kempskie & Lisa Hanson (activity book); *I Hope I Don't Strike Out*, by Bruce Lansky (poetry). "We prefer a query first; then we will request an outline and/or sample material. Send for guidelines." No children's fiction, academic, or biography. Query or submit outline with sample chapters.

HOW TO CONTACT Nonfiction: See guidelines on website before submitting. Responds only if interested. Publishes a book 1-2 years after acceptance. Will consider simultaneous submissions.

ILLUSTRATION Works with 4 illustrators/year. Submit ms with 2-3 pieces of nonreturnable samples. Responds only if interested. Samples filed.

PHOTOGRAPHY Buys photos from freelancers. Buys stock. Model/property releases required.

TERMS Pays authors royalty of 5-7% based on retail price. Offers average advance payment of $1,000-3,000. Pays illustrators per project. Pays photographers by the project. Book catalog available for 5×11 SASE and 2 first-class stamps; ms guidelines and artists guidelines available for SASE.

TIPS "Always send for guidelines before submitting material. Always submit nonreturnable copies; we do not respond to queries or submissions unless interested."

MERIWETHER PUBLISHING LTD.

885 Elkton Dr., Colorado Springs, CO 80907. (719)594-9916. Fax: (719)594-9916. E-mail: editor@meriwether.com. Website: www.meriwetherpublishing.com. **Manuscript Acquisitions:** Ted Zapel, comedy plays and educational drama; Rhonda Wray, religious drama. "We do most of our artwork in-house; we do not publish for the children's elementary market." 75% of books by first-time authors; 5% of books from agented writers. "Our niche is drama. Our books cover a wide variety of theatre subjects from play anthologies to theatrecraft. We publish books of monologs, duologs, short one-act plays, scenes for students, acting textbooks, how-to speech and theatre textbooks, improvisation and theatre games. Our Christian books cover worship on such topics as clown ministry, storytelling, banner-making, drama ministry, children's worship and more. We also publish anthologies of Christian sketches. We do not publish works of fiction or devotionals."

FICTION Middle readers, young adults: anthology, contemporary, humor, religion. "We publish plays, not prose-fiction." Our emphasis is comedy plays instead of educational themes.

NONFICTION Middle readers: activity books, how-to, religion, textbooks. Young adults: activity books, drama/theater arts, how-to church activities, religion. Average length: 250 pages. Recently published *Acting for Life*, by Jack Frakes; *Scenes Keep Happening*, by Mary Krell-Oishi; *Service with a Smile*, by Daniel Wray.

HOW TO CONTACT Nonfiction: Query or submit outline/synopsis and sample chapters. Responds to queries in 3 weeks; mss in 2 months or less. Publishes a book 6-12 months after acceptance. Will consider simultaneous submissions.

ILLUSTRATION "We do our illustration in house."

TERMS Pays authors royalty of 10% based on retail or wholesale price. Book catalog for SAE and $2 postage; ms guidelines for SAE and 1 first-class stamp.

TIPS "We are currently interested in finding unique treatments for theater arts subjects: scene books, how-to books, musical comedy scripts, monologs and short comedy plays for teens."

MILKWEED EDITIONS

(612)332-3192. E-mail: submissions@milkweed.org. Website: www.milkweed.org. Publishes 3-4 middle readers/year. 25% of books by first-time authors. "Milkweed Editions publishes with the intention of making a humane impact on society, in the belief that literature is a transformative art uniquely able to convey the essential experiences of the human heart and spirit. To that end, Milkweed Editions publishes distinctive voices of literary merit in handsomely designed, visually dynamic books, exploring the ethical, cultural, and esthetic issues that free societies need continually to address." Publishes hardcover, trade paperback, and electronic originals; trade paperback and electronic reprints.

○ Please consider our previous publications when considering submissions.

FICTION Middle readers: adventure, contemporary, fantasy, multicultural, nature/environment, suspense/mystery. Does not want to see folktales, health, hi-lo, picture books, poetry, religion, romance, sports. Average length: middle readers-90-200 pages. Recently published *Perfect* by Natasha Friend (contemporary); *The Linden Tree*, by Ellie Mathews (contemporary); *The Cat*, by Jutta Richter (contemporary/translation). Novels for adults and for readers 8-13. High literary quality. For adult readers: literary fiction, nonfiction, poetry, essays. For children (ages 8-13): literary novels. Translations welcome for both audiences. No romance, mysteries, science fiction. Query with SASE, submit completed ms.

NONFICTION Please consider our previous publications when considering submissions to Milkweed Editions. Submit complete ms with SASE. Milkweed strongly encourages digital submissions through our website.

HOW TO CONTACT Fiction: Use submissions manager online at www.milkweed.org. Publishes a book 1 year after acceptance. Will consider simultaneous submissions.

TERMS Pays authors variable royalty based on retail price. Offers advance against royalties. Sends galleys to authors. Book catalog available for $1.50 to cover postage; ms guidelines available for SASE or at website. Must include SASE with ms submission for its return.

TIPS "We are looking for excellent writing with the intent of making a humane impact on society. Please read submission guidelines before submitting and acquaint yourself with our books in terms of style and quality before submitting. Many factors influence our selection process, so don't get discouraged. Nonfiction is focused on literary writing about the natural world, including living well in urban environments."

THE MILLBROOK PRESS

Website: www.lernerbooks.com.

Lerner Publishing Group no longer accepts submission in any of their imprints except for Kar-Ben Publishing.

HOW TO CONTACT "We will continue to seek targeted solicitations at specific reading levels and in specific subject areas. The company will list these targeted solicitations on our website and in national newsletters, such as the SCBWI Bulletin."

MITCHELL LANE PUBLISHERS, INC.

Editorial Department, Mitchell Lane Publishers, P.O. Box 196, Hockessin DE 19707. (302)234-9426. Fax: (866)834-4164. E-mail: barbaramitchell@mitchelllane.com. Website: www.mitchelllane.com. Publishes 80 young adult titles/year. "We publish nonfiction for children and young adults." **Contact:** Barbara Mitchell, publisher. Publishes hardcover and library bound originals. 100 queries received/year. 5 mss received/year.

NONFICTION Young readers, middle readers, young adults: biography, multicultural. Average word length: 4,000-50,000 words. Recently published Stephenie Meyer and Drew Brees (both Blue Banner Biographies); Justin Bieber (A Robbie Reader); Earth Science Projects for Kids series; Your Land and My Land: Latin America series; and World Crafts and Recipes series. Query with SASE. *All unsolicited mss discarded.*

HOW TO CONTACT Most assignments are work-for-hire.

ILLUSTRATION Works with 2-3 illustrators/year. Reviews ms/illustration packages from artists. Query. Illustration only: Query with samples; send résumé, portfolio, slides, tearsheets. Responds only if interested. Samples not returned; samples filed.

PHOTOGRAPHY Buys stock images. Needs photos of famous and prominent minority figures. Captions required. Uses color prints or digital images. Submit cover letter, résumé, published samples, stock photo list.

TERMS Work purchased outright from authors (range: $350-2,000). Pays illustrators by the project (range: $40-400). Sends galleys to authors.

TIPS "We hire writers on a 'work-for-hire' basis to complete book projects we assign. Send résumé and writing samples that do not need to be returned."

MOODY PUBLISHERS

(800)678-8812. Fax: (312)329-4157. E-mail: authors@moody.edu. 820 N. LaSalle Blvd., Chicago IL 60610. Website: www.moodypublishers.com. **Contact:** Acquisitions Coordinator. "The mission of Moody Publishers is to educate and edify the Christian and to evangelize the non-Christian by ethically publishing conservative, evangelical Christian literature and other media for all ages around the world, and to help provide resources for Moody Bible Institute in its training of future Christian leaders." Publishes hardcover, trade, and mass market paperback originals. 1,500 queries received/year. 2,000 mss received/year.

FICTION Submit query letter, bio, one-page description of book, word count, table of contents, two chapters fully written, marketing information and SASE.

NONFICTION We are no longer reviewing queries or unsolicited manuscripts unless they come to us through an agent. Unsolicited proposals will be returned only if proper postage is included. We are not able to acknowledge the receipt of your unsolicited proposal. Does not accept unsolicited nonfiction submissions.

HOW TO CONTACT "Mss should be neatly typed, double-spaced, on white letter-size typing paper. Grammar, style and punctuation should follow normal English usage. We use *The Chicago Manual of Style* (University of Chicago Press) for fine points."

TIPS "In our fiction list, we're looking for Christian storytellers rather than teachers trying to present a message. Your motivation should be to delight the reader. Using your skills to create beautiful works is glorifying to God."

○ MOUNTAINLAND PUBLISHING, INC.

P.O. Box 150891, Ogden UT 84415. E-mail: editor@ mountainlandpublishing.com. Website: www.mountainlandpublishing.com. "Mountainland Publishing Inc. is a complete, main-line publishing house that offers complete book publishing and promotion for authors with exceptional abilities. We publish both fiction and nonfiction as long as it is a captivating, well-written story." *Not currently accepting submissions until further notice.* **Contact:** Michael Combe, managing editor (fiction, nonfiction). Hardcover, mass market paperback, and electronic originals

○ *We are no longer accepting unsolicited submissions either via mail or e-mail.*

FICTION "True fiction should be able to grab readers and hold their attention with dynamic writing, interesting characters, and compelling plot." Submit synopsis, 1 sample chapter via e-mail.

NONFICTION "Nonfiction should read like fiction. It should be captivating to the audience and on an intriguing subject." Query via e-mail. Submit proposal package, including outline, 3 sample chapters.

TIPS "Our audience is a new generation of readers who enjoy well-told stories and who want to be entertained. They want characters they can feel close to and/or love to hate. Make sure your ms is ready for print. Publishing companies will not wait for you to finish editing your story. Be confident that the work you are submitting is your best work. Please submit all ms electronically. Submissions received by mail will be returned unopened."

NEW CANAAN PUBLISHING COMPANY LLC.

2384 N. Hwy 341, Rossville, GA 30741. (423)285-8672. Fax: (678)306-1471. E-mail: djm@newcanaanpublishing.com. Website: www.newcanaanpublishing.com. Book publisher. Publishes 1 picture book/year; 1 young reader/year; 1 middle reader/year; 1 young adult title/year. 50% of books by first-time authors. "We seek books with strong educational or traditional moral content and books with Christian themes."

○ To curb the number of unsolicited submissions, New Canaan Publishing only accepts: 1—books for children of military families; and 2—middle readers and young adult books addressing Christian themes (e.g., devotionals, books addressing teen or pre-teen issues with a Christian focus, whether in a fictional context or otherwise).

FICTION All levels: adventure, history, religion (Christianity), suspense/mystery. Picture books: Christian themes. Average word length: picture books—1,000-3,000; young readers—8,000-30,000; middle readers—8,000-40,000; young adults—15,000-50,000.

NONFICTION All levels: religion (Christian only), textbooks. Average word length: picture books—1,000-3,000; young readers—8,000-30,000; middle readers—8,000-40,000; young adults—15,000-50,000.

HOW TO CONTACT New Canaan no longer reviews unsolicited manuscripts.

ILLUSTRATION Works with 1-2 illustrators/year. Reviews ms/illustration packages from artists. Query or send ms with dummy. Illustrations only: Query with samples. Responds in 1-2 months if need exists.

TERMS *New Canaan no longer reviews unsolicited manuscripts.* Pays authors royalty of 7-12% based on wholesale price. Royalty may be shared with illustrator where relevant. Pays illustrators royalty of 4-6% as share of total royalties. Submission guidelines available on website.

TIPS "We are small, so please be patient."

NOMAD PRESS

2456 Christain St., White River Junction, VT 05001. (802)649-1995. Fax: (802)649-2667. E-mail: info@ nomadpress.net. Website: www.nomadpress.net. Estab. 2001. Specializes in nonfiction, educational material. **Contact:** Alex Kahan, publisher. Produces 8-12 young readers/year. 10% of books by first-time authors. "We produce nonfiction children's activity books that bring a particular science or cultural topic into sharp focus."

○ Nomad Press does not accept picture books or fiction.

NONFICTION Middle readers: activity books, history, science. Average word length: middle readers—30,000. Recently published *Explore Transportation* by Marylou Moran Kjelle (ages 6-9); *Discover the Oceans* by Lauri Berkenkamp (ages 8-12); *Amazing Biomes* by Donna Latham (ages 9-12); *Explore Colonial America* by Verna Fisher (ages 6-9); *Discover the Desert* by Kathy Ceceri (ages 8-12).

HOW TO CONTACT Accepts international submissions. Nonfiction: "Nomad Press does not accept unsolicited manuscripts. If authors are interested in contributing to our children's series, please send a writing resume that includes relevant experience/expertise and publishing credits." Responds to queries in 3-4 weeks. Publishes book 1 year after acceptance.

TERMS Pays authors royalty based on retail price or work purchased outright. Offers advance against royalties. Catalog on website. All imprints included in single catalog. See website for writer's guidelines.

TIPS "We publish a very specific kind of nonfiction children's activity book. Please keep this in mind when querying or submitting."

○ ONSTAGE PUBLISHING

190 Lime Quarry Rd., Suite 106-J, Madison AL 35758-8962. (256)308-2300, (888)420-8879. E-mail: onstage123@knology.net. Website: www.onstagepublishing.com. Publishes 1-2 middle readers/year; 1-2 young adult titles/year. 80% of books by first-time authors. **Contact:** Dianne Hamilton, senior editor. OnStage Publishing is a small, independent publishing house specializing in children's literature. We currently publish chapter books, middle grade fiction and YA. At this time, we only produce fiction books for ages 8-18. We will not do anthologies of any kind. Query first for nonfiction projects as nonfiction projects must spark our interest. See our submission guidelines for more information.

○ To everyone who has submitted a ms, we are currently about 18 months behind. We should get back on track eventually. Please feel free to submit your ms to other houses. OnStage Publishing understands that authors work very hard to produce the finished ms and we do not have to have exclusive submission rights. Please let us know if you sell your ms. Meanwhile, keep writing and we'll keep reading for our next acquisitions.

FICTION Middle readers: adventure, contemporary, fantasy, history, nature/environment, science fiction, suspense/mystery. Young adults: adventure, contemporary, fantasy, history, humor, science fiction, suspense/mystery. Average word length: chapter books—4,000-6,000 words; middle readers—5,000 words and up; young adults—25,000 and up. Recently published *China Clipper* by Jamie Dodson (an adventure for boys ages 12+); *Merlin's Curse* by Darren J. Butler (a chapter book for grades 3 to 5). "We do not produce picture books."

NONFICTION Query first; currently not producing nonfiction.

HOW TO CONTACT Fiction: Now accepting e-mail queries and submissions. For submissions: Put the first 3 chapters in the body of the e-mail. Do not use attachments! We will no longer return any mss. Only an SASE envelope is needed. Send complete ms if under 20,000 words, otherwise send synopsis and first 3 chapters. Responds to queries/mss in 6-8 months. Publishes a book 1-2 years after acceptance. Will consider simultaneous submissions.

ILLUSTRATION Reviews ms/illustration packages from artists. Submit with 3 pieces of final art. Contact: Dianne Hamilton, senior editor. Illustrations only. Samples not returned.

TERMS Pays authors/illustrators/photographers advance plus royalties. Sends galleys to authors; dummies to illustrators. Catalog available on website.

TIPS "Study our titles and get a sense of the kind of books we publish, so that you know whether your project is likely to be right for us."

ORCHARD BOOKS

E-mail: mcroland@scholastic.com. Website: www.scholastic.com. **Editorial Director:** Ken Geist. **Manuscript Acquisitions:** Ken Geist, V.P. and editorial director. Art Acquisitions: David Saylor, V.P. and creative director. "Orchard publishes 20 books yearly, including picture books and early readers." 10% of books by first-time authors.

○ Orchard is not accepting unsolicited manuscripts;

FICTION All levels: animal, contemporary, history, humor, multicultural, poetry. Recently published *Bulldog's Big Day*, by Kate McMullan and Pascal Lemaitre; *Story County: Here We Come!*, by Derek Anderson; *Robin Hood and the Golden Arrow*, by Robert San Souci and E.B. Lewis; *Eight Days*, by Edwidge

Danticat and Alix Delinois; *If You're a Monster and You Know It*, by Rebecca Emberley and Ed Emberley; *One Drowsy Dragon*, by Ethan Long; *Max Spaniel: Funny Lunch*, by David Catrow; *Firehouse!*, by Mark Teague; *Farm*, by Elisha Cooper, *Princess Pigtoria and the Pea*, by Pamela Duncan Edwards and Henry Cole; *While the World Is Sleeping*, by Pamela Duncan Edwards and Daniel Kirk; *One More Hug for Madison*, by Caroline Jayne Church.

HOW TO CONTACT Art director reviews ms/illustration portfolios. Submit "tearsheets or photocopies of the work." Responds to art samples in 1 month. Samples returned with SASE.

ILLUSTRATION No disks or slides, please. Most commonly offers an advance against list royalties. Original artwork returned at job's completion.

TERMS Most commonly offers an advance against list royalties. Sends galleys to authors; dummies to illustrators. Original artwork returned at job's completion.

TIPS "Read some of our books to determine first whether your manuscript is suited to our list."

OUR CHILD PRESS

P.O. Box 4379, Philadelphia, PA 19118. Phone/fax: (610)308-8088. E-mail: info@ourchildpress.com. Website: www.ourchildpress.com. **Acquisitions:** Carol Perrott, president. 90% of books by first-time authors.

FICTION All levels: adoption, multicultural, special needs. Published *Like Me*, written by Dawn Martelli, illustrated by Jennifer Hedy Wharton; *Is That Your Sister?*, by Catherine and Sherry Burin; *Oliver: A Story About Adoption*, by Lois Wichstrom.

HOW TO CONTACT Query or submit complete ms. Responds to queries/mss in 6 months. Publishes a book 6-12 months after acceptance.

ILLUSTRATION Works with 1-5 illustrators/year. Reviews ms/illustration packages from artists. Manuscript/illustration packages and illustration only: Query first. Submit résumé, tearsheets and photocopies. Responds to art samples in 2 months. Samples returned with SASE; samples kept on file.

TERMS Pays authors royalty of 5-10% based on wholesale price. Pays illustrators royalty of 5-10% based on wholesale price. Original artwork returned at job's completion. Book catalog for business-size SAE and 67¢ postage.

OUR SUNDAY VISITOR, INC.

200 Noll Plaza, Huntington IN 46750. E-mail: jlindsey@osv.com. Website: www.osv.com. Publishes religious, educational, parenting, reference and biographies. OSV is dedicated to providing books that are specifically Catholic, periodicals and other products that serve the Catholic Church. "We are a Catholic publishing company seeking to educate and deepen our readers in their faith. Currently emphasizing devotional, inspirational, Catholic identity, apologetics, and catechetics." Publishes paperback and hardbound originals.

Our Sunday Visitor, Inc. is publishing only those children's books that are specifically Catholic. See website for submission guidelines."

NONFICTION Picture books, middle readers, young readers, young adults. Recently published *Little Acts of Grace*, by Rosemarie Gortler and Donna Piscitelli, illustrated by Mimi Sternhagen. Prefers to see well-developed proposals as first submission with annotated outline and definition of intended market; Catholic viewpoints on family, prayer, and devotional books, and Catholic heritage books.

HOW TO CONTACT Query, submit complete ms, or submit outline/synopsis and 2-3 sample chapters. Responds to queries/mss in 2 months. Publishes a book 18-24 months after acceptance. Will consider simultaneous submissions, electronic submissions via disk or modem, previously published work.

ILLUSTRATION Reviews ms/illustration packages from artists. Illustration only: Query with samples. Contact: Art Director. Responds only if interested. Samples returned with SASE; samples filed.

PHOTOGRAPHY Buys photos from freelancers. Contact: Art Director.

TERMS Pays authors royalty of 10-12% net. Pays illustrators by the project (range: $25-1,500). Sends page proofs to authors. Book catalog available for SASE; ms submission guidelines available online at www.osv.com.

TIPS "Stay in accordance with our guidelines."

RICHARD C. OWEN PUBLISHERS, INC.

P.O. Box 585, Katonah NY 10536. (914)232-3903; (800)262-0787. E-mail: richardowen@rcowen.com. Website: www.rcowen.com. "We publish child-focused books, with inherent instructional value, about characters and situations with which five-, six-, and seven-year-old children can identify—books that can be read for meaning, entertainment, enjoyment and information. We include multicultural stories that present minorities in a positive and natural way. Our stories show the diversity in America." Not interested in lesson plans, or books of activities for literature studies or other content areas. **Contact:** Richard Owen, publisher. "Due to high volume and long production time, we are currently limiting to nonfiction submissions only."

NONFICTION Picture books, young readers: animals, careers, history, how-to, music/dance, geography, multicultural, nature/environment, science, sports. Multicultural needs include: "Good stories respectful of all heritages, races, cultural--African-American, Hispanic, American Indian." Wants lively stories. No "encyclopedic" type of information stories. Average word length: under 500 words. Recently published *The Coral Reef*. Our books are for kindergarten, first- and second-grade children to read on their own. The stories are very brief—under 1,000 words—yet well structured and crafted with memorable characters, language and plots.

HOW TO CONTACT Fiction/nonfiction: Submit complete ms and cover letter. Responds to mss in 1 year. Publishes a book 2-3 years after acceptance. See website for guidelines.

ILLUSTRATION Works with 20 illustrators/year. Uses color artwork only. Illustration only: Send color copies/reproductions or photos of art or provide tearsheets; do not send slides or originals. Include SASE and cover letter. Responds only if interested; samples filed.

TERMS Pays authors royalty of 5% based on net price or outright purchase (range: $25-500). Offers no advances. Pays illustrators by the project (range: $100-2,500). Pays photographers by the project (range: $100-2,000) or per photo ($100-150). Original artwork returned 12-18 months after job's completion. Book brochure, ms/artists guidelines available with SASE.

TIPS "We don't respond to queries or e-mails. Please do not fax or e-mail us. Because our books are so brief, it is better to send an entire manuscript. We publish story books with inherent educational value for young readers—books they can read with enjoyment and success. We believe students become enthusiastic, independent, life-long learners when supported and guided by skillful teachers using good books. The professional development work we do and the books we publish support these beliefs."

PACIFIC PRESS

P.O. Box 5353., Nampa ID 83653-5353. (208)465-2500. Fax: (208)465-2531. E-mail: booksubmissions@pacificpress.com. Website: www.pacificpress.com/writers/books.htm. **Manuscript Acquisitions:** Scott Cady. **Art Acquisitions:** Gerald Monks, creative director. Publishes 1 picture book/year; 2 young readers/year; 2 middle readers/year. 5% of books by first-time authors. Pacific Press brings the Bible and Christian lifestyle to children.

FICTION Picture books, young readers, middle readers, young adults: religious subjects only. No fantasy. Average word length: picture books-100; young readers—1,000; middle readers—15,000; young adults-40,000. Recently published *A Child's Steps to Jesus* (3 vols), by Linda Carlyle; *Octopus Encounter*, by Sally Streib; *Sheperd Warrior*, by Bradley Booth.

NONFICTION Picture books, young readers, middle readers, young adults: religion. Average word length: picture books-100; young readers—1,000; middle readers—15,000; young adults-40,000. Recently published *Escape*, by Sandy Zaugg; *What We Believe*, by Seth Pierce.

HOW TO CONTACT Fiction/nonfiction: Query or submit outline/synopsis and 3 sample chapters. Responds to queries in 3 months; mss in 1 year. Publishes a book 6-12 months after acceptance. Will consider e-mail submissions.

ILLUSTRATION Works with 2-6 illustrators/year. Uses color artwork only. Query. Responds only if interested. Samples returned with SASE.

PHOTOGRAPHY Buys stock and assigns work. Model/property releases required.

TERMS Pays author royalty of 6-15% based on wholesale price. Offers advances (average amount: $1,500). Pays illustrators royalty of 6-15% based on wholesale price. Pays photographers royalty of 6-15% based on wholesale price. Sends galleys to authors. Originals returned to artist at job's completion. Manuscript guidelines for SASE. Catalog available on website (www.adventistbookcenter.com).

TIPS Pacific Press is owned by the Seventh-day Adventist Church. The Press rejects all material that is not Bible-based.

PACIFIC VIEW PRESS

P.O. Box 2897, Berkeley, CA 94702. (415)285-8538. Fax: (510)843-5835. E-mail: pvpress@sprynet.com; Nancy@pacificviewpress.com. Website: www.paci ficviewpress.com. Publishes 1-2 picture books/year. 50% of books by first-time authors. "We publish unique, high-quality introductions to Asian cultures and history for children 8-12, for schools, libraries and families. Our children's books focus on hardcover illustrated nonfiction. We look for titles on aspects of the history and culture of the countries and peoples of the Pacific Rim, especially China, presented in an engaging, informative and respectful manner. We are interested in books that all children will enjoy reading and using, and that parents and teachers will want to buy."

NONFICTION Young readers, middle readers: Asia-related multicultural only. Recently published *Cloud Weavers: Ancient Chinese Legends*, by Rena Krasno and Yeng-Fong Chiang (all ages); *Exploring Chinatown: A Children's Guide to Chinese Culture*, by Carol Stepanchuk (ages 8-12).

HOW TO CONTACT Query with outline and sample chapter. Responds in 3 months.

ILLUSTRATION Works with 2 illustrators/year. Responds only if interested. Samples returned with SASE.

TERMS Pays authors royalty of 8-12% based on wholesale price. Pays illustrators by the project (range: $2,000-5,000).

TIPS "We welcome proposals from persons with expertise, either academic or personal, in their area of interest. While we do accept proposals from previously unpublished authors, we would expect submitters to have considerable experience presenting their interests to children in classroom or other public settings and to have skill in writing for children."

PAULINE BOOKS & MEDIA

50 St. Paula's Ave., Boston MA 02130. (617)522-8911. Fax: (617)541-9805. E-mail: design@paulinemedia. com; editorial@paulinemedia.com. Website: www. pauline.org. Publishes 8 picture books/year; 2 board books/year; 5 young readers/year; 5 middle readers/ year. "One to two books per year by first-time authors. Through our children's literature we aim to provide wholesome and entertaining reading that can help children develop strong Christian values." "Submissions are evaluated on adherence to Gospel values, harmony with the Catholic tradition, relevance of topic, and quality of writing." Publishes trade paperback originals and reprints.

FICTION Children's fiction only. We are now accepting submissions for easy-to-read and middle-reader chapter fiction. Please see our Writer's Guidelines. "Submit proposal package, including synopsis, 2 sample chapters, and cover letter; complete ms."

NONFICTION Picture books, young readers, middle readers: religion. Average word length: picture books-500-1,000; young readers-8,000-10,000; middle readers-15,000-25,000. Recently published *God Made Wonderful Me!* by Genny Monchamp; *O Holy Night* by Maite Roche; *Starring Francie O'Leary*, by Maryann; *Adventures of Saint Paul* by Oldrich Selucky; *Anna Mei, Cartoon Girl* by Carol A. Grund; *Goodness Graces! Ten Short Stories about the Sacraments* by Diana R. Jenkins. No biography/autobiography, poetry or strictly nonreligious works considered. Submit proposal package, including outline, 1- 2 sample chapters, cover letter, synopsis, intended audience and proposed length.

HOW TO CONTACT For board books and picture books, the entire manuscript should be submitted. For easy-to-read, young readers, and middle reader books, please send a cover letter accompanied by a synopsis and two sample chapters. "Electronic submissions are encouraged. We make every effort to respond to unsolicited submissions within two months."

ILLUSTRATION Works with 10-15 illustrators/year. Uses color and black-and-white artwork. Illustrations only: Send résumé and 4-5 color samples. Samples and résumé will be kept on file unless return is requested and SASE provided.

TERMS Varies by project, but generally are royalties with advance. Flat fees sometimes considered for smaller works. Manuscript and art guidelines available by SASE or on website. Catalog available on website.

TIPS "Manuscripts may or may not be explicitly catechetical, but we seek those that reflect a positive worldview, good moral values, awareness and appreciation of diversity, and respect for all people. All material must be relevant to the lives of young readers and must conform to Catholic teaching and practice."

PAULIST PRESS

997 Macarthur Blvd., Mahwah NJ 07430-9990. (201)825-7300. Fax: (201)825-8345. E-mail: info@

paulistpress.com; dcrilly@paulistpress.com. Website: www.paulistpress.com. **Contact:** Donna Crilly, editorial. "Paulist Press publishes ecumenical theology, Roman Catholic studies, and books on scripture, liturgy, spirituality, church history, and philosophy, as well as works on faith and culture. Our publishing is oriented toward adult-level nonfiction. We do not publish poetry." Publishes hardcover and electronic originals and electronic reprints.

FICTION Submit résumé, ms, SASE. Accepts unsolicited mss, but most of our titles have been commissioned.

TERMS Advance payment is $500, payable on publication. Illustrators sometimes receive a flat fee when all we need are spot illustrations.

TIPS "Our typical reader is probably Roman Catholic and wants the content to be educational about Catholic thought and practice, or else the reader is a spiritual seeker who looks for discovery of God and the spiritual values that churches offer but without the church connection."

PEACE HILL PRESS

Affiliate of W.W. Norton, 18021, The Glebe Lane, Charles City, VA, 23030. (804)829-5043. E-mail: info@peacehillpress.com. Website: www.peacehill press.com. Estab. 2001. Publishes hardcover and trade paperback originals. **Contact:** Peter Buffington, acquisitions editor. Publishes hardcover and trade paperback originals.

NONFICTION Submit proposal package, outline, 1 sample chapter.

HOW TO CONTACT Submit proposal package, outline, 1 sample chapter.

PEACHTREE PUBLISHERS, LTD.

1700 Chattahoochee Ave., Atlanta, GA 30318-2112. (404)876-8761. Fax: (404)875-2578. E-mail: hello@ peachtree-online.com. Website: www.peachtree-on line.com. **Acquisitions:** Helen Harriss. **Art Director:** Loraine Joyner. Production Manager: Melanie Mc-Mahon Ives. Publishes 30-35 titles/year.

FICTION Picture books, young readers: adventure, animal, concept, history, nature/environment. Middle readers: adventure, animal, history, nature/environment, sports. Young adults: fiction, mystery, adventure. Does not want to see science fiction, romance.

NONFICTION Picture books: animal, history, nature/environment. Young readers, middle readers,

young adults: animal, biography, nature/environment. Does not want to see religion.

HOW TO CONTACT Fiction/nonfiction: Submit complete ms (picture books) or 3 sample chapters (chapter books) by postal mail only. Responds to queries/mss in 6-7 months. Publishes a book 1-2 years after acceptance. Will consider simultaneous submissions.

ILLUSTRATION Works with 8-10 illustrators/year. Illustrations only: Query production manager or art director with samples, résumé, slides, color copies to keep on file. Responds only if interested. Samples returned with SASE; samples filed.

TERMS "Manuscript guidelines for SASE, visit website or call for a recorded message. No fax or e-mail submissions or queries please."

PELICAN PUBLISHING COMPANY

1000 Burmaster St., Gretna LA 70053. (504)368-1175. Fax: (504)368-1195. E-mail: editorial@pelicanpub. com. Website: www.pelicanpub.com. Publishes 20 young readers/year; 3 middle readers/year. 4% of books from agented writers. "Pelican publishes hardcover and trade paperback originals and reprints. Our children's books (illustrated and otherwise) include history, biography, holiday, and regional. Pelican's mission is "to publish books of quality and permanence that enrich the lives of those who read them." **Contact:** Nina Kooij, editor-in-chief. "We believe ideas have consequences. One of the consequences is that they lead to a best-selling book. We publish books to improve and uplift the reader. Currently emphasizing business and history titles." Publishes hardcover, trade paperback and mass market paperback originals and reprints.

FICTION Young readers: history, holiday, science, multicultural and regional. Middle readers: Louisiana History. Multicultural needs include stories about African-Americans, Irish-Americans, Jews, Asian-Americans, and Hispanics. Does not want animal stories, general Christmas stories, "day at school" or "accept yourself" stories. Maximum word length: young readers-1,100; middle readers-40,000. Recently published *The Oklahoma Land Run* by Una Belle Townsend (ages 5-8, historical/regional). We publish maybe 1 novel a year, usually by an author we already have. Almost all proposals are returned. No young adult, romance, science fiction, fantasy, gothic, mystery, erotica, confession, horror, sex, or violence. Also no psychological novels. Query with SASE. Submit outline, clips, 2 sample chapters, SASE.

NONFICTION Young readers: biography, history, holiday, multicultural. Middle readers: Louisiana history, holiday, regional. Recently published *Batty about Texas*, by J. Jaye Smith (ages 5-8, science/regional). "We look for authors who can promote successfully. We require that a query be made first. This greatly expedites the review process and can save the writer additional postage expenses." No multiple queries or submissions. Query with SASE.

HOW TO CONTACT Fiction/nonfiction: Query. Responds to queries in 1 month; mss in 3 months. Publishes a book 9-18 months after acceptance.

ILLUSTRATION Works with 20 illustrators/year. Reviews ms/illustration packages from artists. Query first. Illustrations only: Query with samples (no originals). Responds only if interested. Samples returned with SASE; samples kept on file.

TERMS Pays authors in royalties; buys ms outright "rarely." Sends galleys to authors. Illustrators paid by "various arrangements." Book catalog and ms guidelines available on website.

TIPS "We do extremely well with cookbooks, popular histories, and business. We will continue to build in these areas. The writer must have a clear sense of the market and knowledge of the competition. A query letter should describe the project briefly, give the author's writing and professional credentials, and promotional ideas."

PHILOMEL BOOKS

Penguin Young Readers Group (USA), 345 Hudson St., New York, NY 10014. Website: www.penguin.com. **Manuscript Acquisitions:** Submissions Editor. **Art Acquisitions:** Annie Ericsson, junior designer. Publishes 8-10 picture books/year; 15-18 middle grades/year; 5 young readers/year. 5% of books by first-time authors; 80% of books from agented writers. "We look for beautifully written, engaging manuscripts for children and young adults."

FICTION All levels: adventure, animal, boys, contemporary, fantasy, folktales, historical fiction, humor, sports, multicultural. Middle readers, young adults: problem novels, science fiction, suspense/mystery. No concept picture books, mass-market "character" books, or series. Average word length: picture books—1,000; young readers—1,500; middle readers—14,000; young adult—20,000.

NONFICTION Picture books.

HOW TO CONTACT "As of January 1, 2007, Philomel will no longer respond to your unsolicited submission unless interested in publishing it. Rejected submissions postmarked January 1, 2007, or later will be recycled. Please *do not* include a self-addressed stamped envelope with your submission. You will not hear from Philomel regarding the status of your submission unless we are interested in publishing it, in which case you can expect a reply from us within approximately four months. We regret that we cannot respond personally to each submission, but rest assured that we do make every effort to consider each and every one we receive."

ILLUSTRATION Works with 8-10 illustrators/year. Reviews ms/illustration packages from artists. Query with art sample first. Illustrations only: Query with samples. Send résumé and tearsheets. Responds to art samples in 1 month. Original artwork returned at job's completion. Samples returned with SASE or kept on file.

TERMS Pays authors in royalties. Average advance payment "varies." Illustrators paid by advance and in royalties. Sends galleys to authors; dummies to illustrators. Book catalog, ms guidelines free on request with SASE (9×12 envelope for catalog).

TIPS Wants "unique fiction or nonfiction with a strong voice and lasting quality. Discover your own voice and own story and persevere." Looks for "something unusual, original, well-written. Fine art or illustrative art that feels unique. The genre (fantasy, contemporary, or historical fiction) is not so important as the story itself and the spirited life the story allows its main character."

○ PIANO PRESS

P.O. Box 85, Del Mar CA 92014-0085. (619)884-1401. Fax: (858)755-1104. E-mail: pianopress@pianopress.com. Website: www.pianopress.com. **Manuscript Acquisitions:** Elizabeth C. Axford, M.A, editor. "We publish music-related books, either fiction or nonfiction, coloring books, songbooks and poetry."

FICTION Picture books, young readers, middle readers, young adults: folktales, multicultural, poetry, music. Average word length: picture books-1,500-2,000. Recently published *Strum a Song of Angels*, by Linda Oatman High and Elizabeth C. Axford; *Music and Me*, by Kimberly White and Elizabeth C. Axford.

NONFICTION Picture books, young readers, middle readers, young adults: multicultural, music/dance. Average word length: picture books-1,500-2,000. Recently published *The Musical ABC*, by Dr. Phyllis J. Perry and Elizabeth C. Axford; *Merry Christmas Happy Hanukkah—A Multilingual Songbook & CD*, by Elizabeth C. Axford.

HOW TO CONTACT Fiction/nonfiction: Query. Responds to queries in 3 months; mss in 6 months. Publishes a book 1 year after acceptance. Will consider simultaneous submissions, electronic submissions via disk or modem.

ILLUSTRATION Works with 1 or 2 illustrators/year. Reviews ms/illustration packages from artists. Query. Illustrations only: Query with samples. Responds in 3 months. Samples returned with SASE; samples filed.

PHOTOGRAPHY Buys stock and assigns work. Looking for music-related, multicultural. Model/property releases required. Uses glossy or flat, color or b&w prints. Submit cover letter, résumé, client list, published samples, stock photo list.

TERMS Pays authors, illustrators, and photographers royalty of 5-10% based on retail price. Sends galleys to authors; dummies to illustrators. Originals returned to artist at job's completion. Book catalog available for #10 SASE and 2 first-class stamps. All imprints included in a single catalog. Catalog available on website.

TIPS "We are looking for music-related material only for any juvenile market. Please do not send non-music-related materials. Query first before submitting anything."

PINEAPPLE PRESS, INC.

P.O. Box 3889, Sarasota FL 34230. (941)739-2219. E-mail: info@pineapplepress.com. Website: www. pineapplepress.com. Publishes 1 picture book/year; 1 young reader/year; 1 middle reader/year; 1 young adult title/year. 50% of books by first-time authors. "Our mission is to publish good books about Florida." **Contact:** June Cussen, exec. editor. "We are seeking quality nonfiction on diverse topics for the library and book trade markets." Publishes hardcover and trade paperback originals. 1,000 queries received/year. 500 mss received/year.

FICTION Picture books, young readers, middle readers, young adults: animal, folktales, history, nature/environment. Recently published *The Treasure of Amelia Island*, by M.C. Finotti (ages 8-12).

NONFICTION Picture books: animal, history, nature/environmental, science. Young readers, middle readers, young adults: animal, biography, geography, history, nature/environment, science. Recently published *Those Magical Manatees*, by Jan Lee Wicker and *Those Beautiful Butterflies* by Sarah Cussen. We will consider most nonfiction topics when related to Florida. Submit proposal package, outline, 3 sample chapters, and introduction.

HOW TO CONTACT Query or submit outline/synopsis and 3 sample chapters. Nonfiction: Query or submit outline/synopsis and intro and 3 sample chapters. Responds to queries/samples/mss in 2 months. Will consider simultaneous submissions. Submit proposal package, 3 sample chapters, clips.

ILLUSTRATION Works with 2 illustrators/year. Reviews ms/illustration packages from artists. Query with nonreturnable samples. Contact: June Cussen, executive editor. Illustrations only: Query with brochure, nonreturnable samples, photocopies, résumé. Responds only if interested. Samples returned with SASE, but prefers nonreturnable; samples filed.

TERMS Pays authors royalty of 10-15%. Pays illustrators royalties. Sends galleys to authors; dummies to illustrators. Originals returned to artist at job's completion. Book catalog available for 9×12 SAE with $1.06 postage; all imprints included in a single catalog. Catalog available on website at www.pine applepress.com.

TIPS "Quality first novels will be published, though we usually only do one or two novels per year and they must be set in Florida. We regard the author/editor relationship as a trusting relationship with communication open both ways. Learn all you can about the publishing process and about how to promote your book once it is published. A query on a novel without a brief sample seems useless."

PIÑATA BOOKS

Imprint of Arte Publico Press, University of Houston, 452 Cullen Performance Hall, Houston TX 77204-2004. (713)743-2845. Fax: (713)743-3080. E-mail: sub mapp@mail.uh.edu. Website: www.artepublicopress. com. Publishes 6 picture books/year; 2 young readers/year; 5 middle readers/year; 5 young adult titles/year. 80% of books are by first-time authors. "Arte Publico's mission is the publication, promotion and dissemination of Latino literature for a variety of national and regional audiences, from early childhood to adult, through the complete gamut of delivery systems, including personal performance as well as print and electronic media." **Contact:** Nicolas Kanellos, director. "Piñata Books is dedicated to the publication of children's and young adult literature focusing on U.S. Hispanic culture by U.S. Hispanic authors." Publishes hardcover and trade paperback originals.

FICTION Recently published *We Are Cousins/Somos primos* by Diane Gonzales Betrand*; Butterflies on Carmen Street/Mariposas en la calle Carmen* by Monica Brown*; Windows into My World: Latino Youth Write Their Lives.* Query with SASE. Submit clips, 2 sample chapters, SASE.

NONFICTION Recently published *Cesar Chavez: The Struggle for Justice/Cesar Chavez: La Lucha Por La Justicia,* by Richard Griswold del Castillo, illustrated by Anthony Accardo (ages 3-7). Piñata Books specializes in publication of children's and young adult literature that authentically portrays themes, characters and customs unique to U.S. Hispanic culture. Query with SASE. Submit outline, 2 sample chapters, synopsis.

HOW TO CONTACT Accepts material from U.S./Hispanic authors only (living abroad OK). Manuscripts, queries, synopses, etc. are accepted in either English or Spanish. Fiction: Submit complete ms. Nonfiction: Query. Responds to queries in 2-4 months; mss in 3-6 months. Publishes a book 2 years after acceptance. Will sometimes consider previously published work.

ILLUSTRATION Works with 6 illustrators/year. Uses color artwork only. Reviews ms/illustration packages from artists. Query or send portfolio (slides, color copies). Illustrations only: Query with samples or send résumé, promo sheet, portfolio, slides, client list and tearsheets. Responds only if interested. Samples not returned; samples filed.

TERMS Pays authors royalty of 10% minimum based on wholesale price. Offers advances (average amount $2,000). Pays illustrators advance and royalties of 10% based on wholesale price. Sends galleys to authors. Catalog available on website; ms guidelines available for SASE.

TIPS "Include cover letter with submission explaining why your manuscript is unique and important, why we should publish it, who will buy it, etc.

PITSPOPANY PRESS

Simcha Media, P.O. Box 5329, Englewood, NJ 07631. (212)444-1657. Fax: (866)205-3966. E-mail: pitspop@ netvision.net.il. Website: www.pitspopany.com. Estab. 1992. Specializes in trade books, Judaica, nonfiction, fiction, multicultural material. **Manuscript Acquisitions:** Yaacov Peterseil, publisher. **Art Acquisitions:** Yaacov Peterseil, publisher. Produces 6 picture books/year; 4 young readers/year; 4 middle readers/year; 4 young adult books/year. 10% of books by first-time authors. "Pitspopany Press is dedicated to bringing quality children's books of Jewish interest into the marketplace. Our goal is to create titles that will appeal to the esthetic senses of our readers and, at the same time, offer quality Jewish content to the discerning parent, teacher, and librarian. While the people working for Pitspopany Press embody a wide spectrum of Jewish belief and opinion, we insist that our titles be respectful of the mainstream Jewish viewpoints and beliefs. We are especially interested in chapter books for kids. Most of all, we are committed to creating books that all Jewish children can read, learn from, and enjoy."

FICTION Picture books: animal, anthology, fantasy, folktales, history, humor, multicultural, nature/environment, poetry. Young readers: adventure, animal, anthology, concept, contemporary, fantasy, folktales, health, history, humor, multicultural, nature/environment, poetry, religion, science fiction, special needs, sports, suspense. Middle readers: animal, anthology, fantasy, folktales, health, hi-lo, history, humor, multicultural, nature/environment, poetry, religion, science fiction, special needs, sports, suspense. Young adults/teens: animal, anthology, contemporary, fantasy, folktales, health, hi-lo, history, humor, multicultural, nature/environment, poetry, religion, science fiction, special needs, sports, suspense. Recently published *Hayyim's Ghost*, by Eric Kimmel, illustrated by Ari Binus (ages 6-9); *The Littlest Pair*, by Syliva Rouss, illustrated by Hally Hannan (ages 3-6); *The Converso Legacy*, by Sheldon Gardner (ages 10-14, historial fiction).

NONFICTION All levels: activity books, animal, arts/crafts, biography, careers, concept, cooking, geography, health, history, hobbies, how-to, multicultural, music/dance, nature/environment, reference, religion, science, self-help, social issues, special needs, sports.

HOW TO CONTACT Accepts international submissions. Fiction/nonfiction: Submit outline/synopsis. Responds to queries/mss in 6 weeks. Publishes book

9 months after acceptance. Considers simultaneous submissions, electronic submissions.

ILLUSTRATION Accepts material from international illustrators. Works with 6 illustrators/year. Uses color artwork only. Reviews ms/illustration packages. For ms/illustration packages: Submit ms with 4 pieces of final art. Submit ms/illustration packages to Yaacov Peterseil, publisher. Reviews work for future assignments. If interested in illustrating future titles, send promo sheet. Submit samples to Yaacov Peterseil, publisher. Samples returned with SASE. Samples not filed.

PHOTOGRAPHY Works on assignment only. Submit photos to Yaacov Peterseil, publisher.

TERMS Pays authors royalty or work purchased outright. Offers advance against royalties. Author sees galleys for review. Originals returned to artist at job's completion. Catalog on website. All imprints included in single catalog. Offers writer's guidelines for SASE.

PLUM BLOSSOM BOOKS

Parallax Press, P.O. Box 7355, Berkeley, CA 94707. (510)525-0101. Fax: (510)525-7129. E-mail: rachel@parallax.org. Website: www.parallax.org. Estab. 1985. Specializes in nonfiction, fiction. **Writers contact:** Rachel Neuman, senior editor. Produces 2 picture books/year. 30% of books by first-time authors. "Plum Blossom Books publishes stories for children of all ages that focus on mindfulness in daily life, Buddhism, and social justice."

FICTION Picture books: adventure, contemporary, folktales, multicultural, nature/environment, religion. Young readers: adventure, contemporary, folktales, multicultural, nature/environment, religion. Middle readers: multicultural, nature/environment, religion. Young adults/teens: nature/environment, religion. Recently published *The Hermit and the Well*, by Thich Nhat Hanh, illustrated by Dinh Mai (ages 4-8, hardcover); *Each Breath a Smile*, by Sister Thuc Nghiem and Thich Nhat Hanh, illustrated by T. Hop (ages 2-5, paperback picture book); *Meow Said the Mouse*, by Beatrice Barbey, illustrated by Philippe Ames (ages 5-8, picture and activity book).

NONFICTION All levels: nature/environment, religion (Buddhist), Buddhist counting books.

HOW TO CONTACT Accepts international submissions. Fiction/nonfiction: Query or submit complete ms. Responds to queries in 1-2 weeks. Responds to mss in 4 weeks. Publishes book 9-12 months after acceptance. Considers electronic submissions.

ILLUSTRATION Accepts material from international illustrators. Works with 3 illustrators/year. Uses both color and b&w. Reviews ms/illustration packages. For ms/illustration packages: Query. Send manuscript with dummy. Reviews work for future assignments. If interested in illustrating future titles, query with samples. Responds in 4 weeks. Samples returned with SASE. Samples filed.

PHOTOGRAPHY Buys stock images and assigns work. Submit photos to Rachel Neuman, senior editor. Uses b&w prints. For first contact, send cover letter, published samples.

TERMS Pays authors royalty of 20% based on wholesale price. Pays illustrators by the project. Author sees galleys for review. Illustrators see dummies for review. Originals returned to artist at job's completion. Catalog available for SASE. Offers writer's, artist's guidelines for SASE. See website for writer's, artist's, photographer's guidelines.

TIPS "Read our books before approaching us. We are very specifically looking for mindfulness and Buddhist messages in high-quality stories where the Buddhist message is implied rather than stated outright."

PRICE STERN SLOAN, INC.

Website: http://us.penguingroup.com/youngreaders. Penguin Group (USA), 345 Hudson St., New York, NY 10014. (212)414-3590. Fax: (212)414-3396. Estab. 1963. Website: http://us.penguingroup.com/youngreaders. **Acquisitions:** Debra Dorfman, president/publisher. "Price Stern Sloan publishes quirky mass market novelty series for children as well as licensed movie tie-in books."

○ Price Stern Sloan does not accept e-mail submissions.

FICTION Publishes picture books and novelty/board books including Mad Libs Movie and Television Tie-ins, and unauthorized biographies. "We publish unique novelty formats and fun, colorful paperbacks and activity books. We also publish the Book with Audio Series *Wee Sing* and *Baby Loves Jazz*." Recently published: *Baby Loves Jazz* board book with CD Series; new formats in the classic *Mr. Men/Little Miss* series; Movie/TV tie-in titles: *Speed Racers, Journey 3D*. Unauthorized biographies: *Mad for Miley* and *Jammin' with The Jonas Brothers*.

HOW TO CONTACT Query. Responds to queries in 6-8 weeks.

TERMS Work purchased outright. Offers advance. Book catalog available for 9×12 SASE and 5 first-class stamps; address to Book Catalog. Manuscript guidelines available for SASE; address to Manuscript Guidelines.

TIPS "Price Stern Sloan publishes unique, fun titles."

🎧 PUFFIN BOOKS

Imprint of Penguin Group (USA), Inc., 345 Hudson St., New York NY 10014. (212)366-2000. Website: www.penguinputnam.com. Imprints: Speak, Firebird, Sleuth. Publishes trade paperback originals and reprints. Publishes 175-200 titles/year. Receives 600 queries and mss/year. 1% of books by first-time authors; 5% from unagented writers. "Puffin Books publishes high-end trade paperbacks and paperback originals and reprints for preschool children, beginning and middle readers, and young adults." **Contact:** Kristin Gilson, editorial director. Publishes trade paperback originals and reprints.

FICTION Picture books, young adult novels, middle grade and easy-to-read grades 1-3: fantasy and science fiction, graphic novels, classics. Recently Published *Three Cups of Tea* young readers edition, by Greg Mortenson and David Oliver Relin, adapted for young readers by Sarah Thomson; *The Big Field*, by Mike Lupica; *Geek Charming*, by Robin Palmer. We do not publish original picture books. *No unsolicited mss.*

NONFICTION Biography, illustrated books, young children's concept books (counting, shapes, colors). Subjects include education (for teaching concepts and colors, not academic), women in history. "Women in history books interest us." *No unsolicited mss.*

HOW TO CONTACT Fiction: Submit 3 sample chapters with SASE. Nonfiction: Submit 5 pages of ms with SASE. "It could take up to 5 months to get response." Publishes book 1 year after acceptance. Will consider simultaneous submissions, if so noted. Does not accept unsolicited picture book mss.

ILLUSTRATION Reviews artwork. Send color copies.

PHOTOGRAPHY Reviews photos. Send color copies.

TERMS Pays royalty. Offers advance (varies). Book catalog for 9×12 SASE with 7 first-class stamps; send request to Marketing Department.

TIPS "Our audience ranges from little children 'first books' to young adult (ages 14-16). An original idea

has the best luck."

🅐 PUSH

Scholastic, 557 Broadway, New York, NY 10012-3999. Website: www.thisispush.com. Estab. 2002. Specializes in fiction. Produces 6-9 young adult books/year. 50% of books by first-time authors. PUSH publishes new voices in teen literature.

⊖ PUSH does not accept unsolicited manuscripts or queries, only agented or referred fiction/memoir.

FICTION Young adults: contemporary, multicultural, poetry. Recently published *Splintering*, by Eireann Corrigan; *Never Mind the Goldbergs*, by Matthue Roth; *Perfect World*, by Brian James.

NONFICTION Young adults: memoir. Recently published *Talking in the Dark*, by Billy Merrell; *You Remind Me of You*, by Eireann Corrigan.

HOW TO CONTACT Only interested in agented material. Accepts international submissions. Fiction/nonfiction: Submit complete ms. Responds to queries in 2 months; mss in 4 months. No simultaneous, electronic, or previously published submissions.

TIPS "We only publish first-time writers (and then their subsequent books), so authors who have published previously should not consider PUSH. Also, for young writers in grades 7-12, we run the PUSH Novel Contest with the Scholastic Art & Writing Awards. Every year it begins in October and ends in March. Rules can be found on our website."

RAINBOW PUBLISHERS

P.O. Box 261129, San Diego CA 92196. (858)277-1167. E-mail: editor@rainbowpublishers.com. Website: www.rainbowpublishers.com; www.legacypresskids.com. Publishes 4 young readers/year; 4 middle readers/year; 4 young adult titles/year. 50% of books by first-time authors. "Our mission is to publish Bible-based, teacher resource materials that contribute to and inspire spiritual growth and development in kids ages 2-12." **Contact:** Editorial Department.

NONFICTION Young readers, middle readers, young adult/teens: activity books, arts/crafts, how-to, reference, religion.

HOW TO CONTACT Responds to queries in 6 weeks; mss in 3 months. Publishes a book 60 months after acceptance. Will consider simultaneous submissions, submissions via disk and previously published work.

ILLUSTRATION Works with 25 illustrators/year. Reviews ms/illustration packages from artists. Submit ms with 2-5 pieces of final art. Illustrations only: Query with samples. Responds in 6 weeks. Samples returned with SASE; samples filed.

TERMS For authors work purchased outright (range: $500 and up). Pays illustrators by the project (range: $300 and up). Sends galleys to authors.

TIPS "Our Rainbow imprint publishes reproducible books for teachers of children in Christian ministries, including crafts, activities, games and puzzles. Our Legacy imprint publishes titles for children such as devotionals, fiction and Christian living. Please write for guidelines and study the market before submitting material."

RAIN TOWN PRESS

Website: www.raintownpress.com. "We are Portland, Oregon's first independent press dedicated to publishing literature for middle grade and young adult readers. We hope to give rise to their voice, speaking directly to the spirit they embody through our books and other endeavors. The gray days we endure in the Pacific Northwest are custom-made for reading a good book—or in our case, making one. The rain inspires, challenges, and motivates us. To that end, we say: "Let it drizzle." Imprint: (In The Future): Raintown Kids; Mary Darcy, Misty V'Marie, William Softich, Leah Brown. Imprints are included in a single catalog. **Contact:** Misty V'Marie, acquisitions editor.

○ "We are Portland, Oregon's first independent press dedicated to publishing literature for middle grade and young adult readers. We hope to give rise to their voice, speaking directly to the spirit they embody through our books and other endeavors. The gray days we endure in the Pacific Northwest are custom-made for reading a good book—or in our case, making one. The rain inspires, challenges, and motivates us. To that end, we say: Let it drizzle. We will soon publish picture books."

FICTION Middle Readers/YA/Teens: Wants adventure, animal, contemporary, fantasy, folktales, graphic novels, health, hi-lo, history, humor, multicultural, nature/environment, problem novels, sci-fi, special needs, sports. Catalog available on website. Query. Submit complete ms. See online submission guide for detailed instructions.

NONFICTION Middle Readers/YA/Teens: biography, concept, graphic novels, hi-lo, how-to. "We are a new press and haven't decided yet how we are going to handle/pursue our nonfiction line when the time comes. I think it would almost take a proposal for us to decide." Query. Submit outline/synopsis and 2 sample chapters. See online submission guide for detailed instructions.

HOW TO CONTACT Submit query by link to online portfolio (preferred).

ILLUSTRATION Reviews ms/illustration packages from artists (will review packages for future titles); uses both color and b&w. Submit query, link to online portfolio. Submit to Ellery Harvey, art director. Originals not returned. Does not show dummies to Illustrators.

PHOTOGRAPHY Buys stock images and assigned work. Model/property releases required with submissions. Photo captions required. Uses high-res digital materials. Send cover letter, client list, portolio (online preferred).

TERMS Pays authors 8-15% royalty on net sales. (No advance offered against royalties.) Illustrators/photographers are paid by the project/scope of the job. Considers simultaneous submissions, previously published work. Prefers electronic submissions.

TIPS "The middle grade and YA markets have sometimes very stringent conventions for subject matter, theme, etc. It's most helpful if an author knows his/her genre inside and out. Read, read, read books that have successfully been published for your genre. This will ultimately make your writing more marketable. Also, follow a publisher's submission guidelines to a tee. We try to set writers up for success. Send us what we're looking for."

ⓐ RANDOM HOUSE CHILDREN'S BOOKS

Imprint of Random House, Inc., 1745 Broadway, New York NY 10019. (212)782-9000. Website: www.random house.com. "Producing books for preschool children through young adult readers, in all formats from board to activity books to picture books and novels, Random House Children's Books brings together world-famous franchise characters, multimillion-copy series and top-flight, award-winning authors and illustrators."

○ Submit mss through a literary agent.

FICTION "Random House publishes a select list of first chapter books and novels, with an emphasis on fantasy and historical fiction." Chapter books, middle grade readers, young adult.

HOW TO CONTACT Does not accept unsolicited mss. *Agented submissions only.* Accepts simultaneous submissions.

ILLUSTRATION The Random House publishing divisions hire their freelancers directly. To contact the appropriate person, send a cover letter and résumé to the department head at the publisher as follows: "Department Head" (e.g., Art Director, Production Director), "Publisher/Imprint" (e.g., Knopf, Doubleday, etc.), 1745 Broadway New York, NY 10019. Works with 100-150 freelancers/year. Works on assignment only. Send query letter with résumé, tearsheets and printed samples; no originals. Samples are filed. Negotiates rights purchased. Assigns 5 freelance design jobs/year. Pays by the project.

TIPS "We look for original, unique stories. Do something that hasn't been done before."

Ⓐ◯ RANDOM HOUSE-GOLDEN BOOKS FOR YOUNG READERS GROUP

Random House, Inc., 1745 Broadway, New York. NY 10019. (212)782-9000. Website: www.randomhouse.com/golden. Estab. 1925. Book publisher. "Random House Books aims to create books that nurture the hearts and minds of children, providing and promoting quality books and a rich variety of media that entertain and educate readers from 6 months to 12 years." Publisher/Vice President: Kate Klimo. VP & Associate Publisher/Art Director: Cathy Goldsmith. **Acquisitions:** Easy-to-read books (step-into-reading and picture books), board and novelty books, fiction and nonfiction for young and mid-grade readers: Heidi Kilgras, editorial director; Stepping Stones: Jennifer Arena, executive editor; middle grade and young adult fiction: Jim Thomas, editorial director. 100% of books published through agents; 2% of books by first-time authors.

> ◯ Random House-Golden Books does not accept unsolicited manuscripts, only agented material. They reserve the right not to return unsolicited material.

HOW TO CONTACT Only interested in agented material. Reviews ms/illustration packages from artists through agent only. Does not open or respond to unsolicited submissions.

TERMS Pays authors in royalties; sometimes buys mss outright. Sends galleys to authors. Book catalog free on request.

RAVEN TREE PRESS

A Division of Delta Publishing Company, 1400 Miller Pkwy., McHenry IL 60050. (800)323-8270. Fax: (800)909-9901. E-mail: raven@deltapublishing.com; raven@raventreepress.com. acquisitions@deltapublishing.com. Website: www.raventreepress.com. Publishes 8-10 picture books/year. 50% of books by first-time authors. "We publish entertaining and educational picture books in a variety of formats. Bilingual (English/Spanish), English-only, Spanish-only and wordless editions." **Contact:** Check website for most current submission guidelines (children's picture books). Publishes hardcover and trade paperback originals. 1,500 mss received/year.

NONFICTION "Submission guidelines available online. Do not query or send mss without first checking submission guidelines on our website for most current information."

HOW TO CONTACT Check website for current needs, submission guidelines and deadlines.

TERMS Pays authors and illustrators royalty. Offers advances against royalties. Pays illustrators by the project or royalty. Originals returned to artist at job's completion. Catalog available on website.

TIPS "Submit only based on guidelines. No e-mail OR snail mail queries please. Word count is a definite issue, since we are bilingual." Staff attended or plans to attend the following conferences: BEA, NABE, IRA, ALA and SCBWI.

RAZORBILL

Penguin Group, 345 Hudson St., New York, NY 10014. Imprint estab. 2003. (212)414-3448. Fax: (212)414-3343. E-mail: razorbill@us.penguingroup.com. Web site: www.razorbillbooks.com. Specializes in fiction. **Acquisitions:** Gillian Levinson, assistant edtor; Jessica Rothenberg, Brianne Mulligan, editors. Publishes about 30 middle grade and YA titles/year. "This division of Penguin Young Readers is looking for the best and the most original of commercial contemporary fiction titles for middle grade and YA readers. A select quantity of nonfiction titles will also be considered."

FICTION Middle Readers: adventure, contemporary, graphic novels, fantasy, humor, problem novels. Young adults/teens: adventure, contemporary, fantasy, graphic novels, humor, multicultural, suspense, paranormal, science fiction, dystopian, literary, romance. Average word length: middle readers—40,000; young adult—60,000. Recently published *Thirteen Reasons Why*, by Jay Asher (ages 14 and up, a NY Times Bestseller); *Vampire Academy* series by Richelle Mead (ages 12 and up; NY Times Bestselling series); *The Teen Vogue Handbook* (ages 12 and up; a NY Times Bestseller); and *I Am a Genius of Unspeakable Evil and I Want to Be Your Class President*, by Josh Lieb (ages 12 and up; a *NY Times* Bestseller).

NONFICTION Middle readers and young adults/teens: concept.

HOW TO CONTACT Submit outline/synopsis and 3 sample chapters along with query and SASE. Responds to queries/mss in 1-3 months. Publishes a book 1-2 years after acceptance. Will consider e-mail submissions and simultaneous submissions.

TERMS Offers advance against royalties. Authors see galleys for review. Catalog available online at www.razorbillbooks.com.

TIPS "New writers will have the best chance of acceptance and publication with original, contemporary material that boasts a distinctive voice and well-articulated world. Check out www.razorbillbooks.com to get a better idea of what we're looking for."

Ⓐ ROARING BROOK PRESS

175 Fifth Ave., New York NY 10010. (646)307-5151. E-mail: david.langva@roaringbrookpress.com; press. inquiries@macmillanusa.com. Website: http://us.macmillan.com/RoaringBrook.aspx. **Contact:** David Langva.

- Roaring Brook Press is an imprint of MacMillan, a group of companies that includes Henry Holt and Farrar, Straus & Giroux. Roaring Brook is not accepting unsolicited manuscripts. Roaring Brook title *First the Egg*, by Laura Vaacaro Seeger, won a Caldecott Honor Medal and a Theodor Seuss Geisel Honor in 2008. Their title *Dog and Bear: Two Friends, Three Stories*, also by Laura Vaccaro Seeger, won the Boston Globe-Horn Book Picture Book Award in 2007.

FICTION Picture books, young readers, middle readers, young adults: adventure, animal, contemporary, fantasy, history, humor, multicultural, nature/environment, poetry, religion, science fiction, sports, suspense/mystery. Recently published *Happy Birthday Bad Kitty*, by Nick Bruel; *Cookie*, by Jacqueline Wilson.

NONFICTION Picture books, young readers, middle readers, young adults: adventure, animal, contemporary, fantasy, history, humor, multicultural, nature/environment, poetry, religion, science fiction, sports, suspense/mystery.

HOW TO CONTACT Primarily interested in agented material. Not accepting unsolicited mss or queries. Will consider simultaneous agented submissions.

ILLUSTRATION Primarily interested in agented material. Works with 25 illustrators/year. Illustrations only: Query with samples. Do not send original art; copies only through the mail. Samples returned with SASE.

PHOTOGRAPHY Works on assignment only.

TERMS Pays authors royalty based on retail price. Pays illustrators royalty or flat fee depending on project. Sends galleys to authors; dummies to illustrators, if requested.

TIPS "You should find a reputable agent and have him/her submit your work."

SASQUATCH BOOKS

E-mail: ttabor@sasquatchbooks.com. 119 South Main St. Seattle WA 98104. (800)775-0817. Fax: (206)467-4301. Website: www.sasquatchbooks.com. Estab. 1986. Specializes in trade books, nonfiction, children's fiction. **Writers contact:** The Editors. **Illustrators contact:** Lisa-Brire Dahmen, production manager. Produces 5 picture books/year. 20% of books by first-time authors. **Contact:** Gary Luke, editorial director; Terence Maikels, acquisitions editor; Heidi Lenze, acquisitions editor. "Sasquatch Books publishes books for and from the Pacific Northwest, Alaska, and California is the nation's premier regional press. Sasquatch Books' publishing program is a veritable celebration of regionally written words. Undeterred by political or geographical borders, Sasquatch defines its region as the magnificent area that stretches from the Brooks Range to the Gulf of California and from the Rocky Mountains to the Pacific Ocean. Our top-selling Best Places® travel guides serve the most popular destinations and locations of the West. We also publish widely in the areas of food and wine, gardening, nature, photography, children's books, and regional history, all facets of the literature of place. With more than 200 books brimming with insider information on the West, we offer an energetic eye on the lifestyle, landscape, and worldview of our region. Publishes regional hardcover and trade paperback originals.

FICTION Young readers: adventure, animal, concept, contemporary, humor, nature/environment. Recently published *Amazing Alaska*, by Deb Vanasse, illustrated by Karen Lewis; *Sourdough Man*, by Cherie Stihler, illustrated by Barbara Lavallee.

NONFICTION Picture books: activity books, animal, concept, nature/environment. Recently published *Larry Gets Lost in New York*, written and illustrated by John Skewes (picture book); *Searching for Sasqatch* by Nathaniel Lachenmeyer, illustrated by Vicki Bradley (picture book). "Considers queries and proposals from authors and agents for new projects that fit into our West Coast regional publishing program. We can evaluate query letters, proposals, and complete mss. When you submit to Sasquatch Books, please remember that the editors want to know about you *and* your project, along with a sense of who will want to read your book. We are seeking quality nonfiction works about the Pacific Northwest and West Coast regions (including Alaska to California). The literature of place includes how-to and where-to as well as history and narrative nonfiction." Query first, then submit outline and sample chapters with SASE. Send submissions to The Editors. E-mailed submissions and queries are not recommended. Please include return postage if you want your materials back.

HOW TO CONTACT Accepts international submissions. Fiction: Query, submit complete ms, or submit outline/synopsis. Nonfiction: Query. Responds to queries in 3 months. Publishes book 6-9 months after acceptance. Considers simultaneous submissions.

ILLUSTRATION Accepts material from international illustrators. Works with 5 illustrators/year. Uses both color and b&w. Reviews ms/illustration packages. For ms/illustration packages: Query. Submit ms/illustration packages to The Editors. Reviews work for future assignments. If interested in illustrating future titles, query with samples. Samples returned with SASE. Samples filed.

PHOTOGRAPHY Buys stock images and assigns work. Submit photos to: Lisa-Brire Dahmen, production manager.

TERMS Pays authors royalty based on retail price. Offers advance against royalties. Offers a wide range of advances. Author sees galleys for review. Originals not returned. Catalog on website. See website for writer's guidelines.

TIPS "We sell books through a range of channels in addition to the book trade. Our primary audience consists of active, literate residents of the West Coast."

SCHOLASTIC INC.

557 Broadway, New York NY 10012. (212)343-6100. Website: www.scholastic.com. Arthur A. Levine Books, Cartwheel Books®, Chicken House®, Graphix™, Little Scholastic™, Little Shepherd™, Michael di Capua Books, Orchard Books®, Point™, PUSH, Scholastic en Español, Scholastic Licensed Publishing, Scholastic Nonfiction, Scholastic Paperbacks, Scholastic Press, Scholastic Reference™, and The Blue Sky Press® are imprints of the Scholastic Trade Books Division. In addition, Scholastic Trade Books included Klutz®, a highly innovative publisher and creator of "books plus" for children.

Scholastic Trade Books is a publisher of original children's books. Scholastic publishes more than 600 new hardcover, paperback and novelty books each year. The list includes the phenomenally successful publishing properties Harry Potter®, Goosebumps®, The 39 Clues™, I Spy™ and The Hunger Games; bestselling and award-winning authors and illustrators, including Blue Balliett, Jim Benton, Meg Cabot, Suzanne Collins, Christopher Paul Curtis, Ann M. Martin, Dav Pilkey, J.K. Rowling, Pam Muñoz Ryan, Brian Selznick, David Shannon, Mark Teague, and Walter Wick, among others; as well as licensed properties such as Star Wars® and Rainbow Magic®.

SCHOLASTIC LIBRARY PUBLISHING

A division of Scholastic, Inc., 90 Old Sherman Turnpike, Danbury CT 06816. (203)797-3500. Fax: (203)797-3197. Website: www.scholastic.com/librarypublishing. Vice President/Publisher: Phil Friedman. **Manuscript Acquisitions:** Kate Nunn, editor-in-chief. **Art Acquisitions:** Marie O'Neil, art director. Imprints: Grolier, Children's Press, Franklin Watts. Publishes more than 400 titles/year. 5% of books by first-time authors; very few titles from agented authors. Publishes informational (nonfiction) for K-12; picture books for young readers, grades 1-3. "Scholastic Library is a leading publisher of reference, educational, and children's books. We provide parents, teachers, and librarians with the tools they need to enlighten children to the pleasure of learning and prepare them for the road ahead." Publishes hardcover and trade paperback originals.

○ *This publisher accepts agented submissions only.*

FICTION Publishes 1 picture book series, Rookie Readers, for grades 1-2. Does not accept unsolicited mss.

NONFICTION Photo-illustrated books for all levels: animal, arts/crafts, biography, careers, concept, geography, health, history, hobbies, how-to, multicultural, nature/environment, science, social issues, special needs, sports. Average word length: young readers—2,000; middle readers—8,000; young adult—15,000.

HOW TO CONTACT Fiction: Does not accept fiction proposals. Nonfiction: Query; submit outline/synopsis, résumé and/or list of publications, and writing sample. SASE required for response. Responds in 3 months. Will consider simultaneous submissions. No phone or e-mail queries; will not respond to phone inquiries about submitted material.

ILLUSTRATION Works with 15-20 illustrators/year. Uses color artwork and line drawings. Illustrations only: Query with samples or arrange personal portfolio review. Responds only if interested. Samples returned with SASE. Samples filed. Do not send originals. No phone or e-mail inquiries; contact only by mail.

PHOTOGRAPHY Contact: Caroline Anderson, photo manager. Buys stock and assigns work. Model/property releases and captions required. Uses color and b&w prints; $2^1_4 \times 2^1_4$, 35mm transparencies, images on CD-ROM.

TERMS Pays authors royalty based on net or work purchased outright. Pays illustrators at competitive rates. Photographers paid per photo. Sends galleys to authors; dummies to illustrators.

Ⓐ SCHOLASTIC PRESS

557 Broadway, New York NY 10012. (212)343-6100. Website: www.scholastic.com. **Manuscript Acquisitions:** David Saylor, editorial director, Scholastic Press, creative director and associate publisher for all Scholastic hardcover imprints. David Levithan, executive editorial director, Scholastic Press fiction, multimedia publishing, and PUSH Lisa Sandell, acquiring editor; Dianne Hess, executive editor (picture book fiction/nonfiction, 2nd-3rd grade chapter books, some middle grade fantasy that is based on reality); Tracy Mack, executive editor (picture book,

middle grade, YA); Rachel Griffiths, Editor; Jennifer Rees, associate editor (picture book fiction/nonfiction, middle grade, YA). **Art Acquisitions:** Elizabeth Parisi, art director, Scholastic Press; Marijka Kostiw, art director; David Saylor, creative director and associate publisher for all Scholastic hardcover imprints. Publishes 60 titles/year. 1% of books by first-time authors. Scholastic Press publishes fresh, literary picture book fiction and nonfiction; fresh, literary non-series or nongenre-oriented middle grade and young adult fiction. Currently emphasizing subtly handled treatments of key relationships in children's lives; unusual approaches to commonly dry subjects, such as biography, math, history, or science. De-emphasizing fairy tales (or retellings), board books, genre, or series fiction (mystery, fantasy, etc.). Publishes hardcover originals. 2,500 queries received/year.

FICTION Looking for strong picture books, young chapter books, appealing middle grade novels (ages 8-11) and interesting and well written young adult novels. Wants fresh, exciting picture books and novels--inspiring, new talent. *Agented submissions and previously published authors only.*

NONFICTION Interested in "unusual, interesting, and very appealing approaches to biography, math, history and science." *Agented submissions and previously published authors only.*

HOW TO CONTACT Fiction/nonfiction: "Send query with 1 sample chapter and synopsis. Don't call! Don't e-mail!" Picture books: submission accepted from agents or previously published authors only.

ILLUSTRATION Works with 30 illustrators/year. Uses both b&w and color artwork. Illustrations only: Query with samples; send tearsheets. Responds only if interested. Samples returned with SASE. Original artwork returned at job's completion.

TERMS Pays advance against royalty.

TIPS "Read *currently* published children's books. Revise, rewrite, rework and find your own voice, style and subject. We are looking for authors with a strong and unique voice who can tell a great story and have the ability to evoke genuine emotion. Children's publishers are becoming more selective, looking for irresistible talent and fairly broad appeal, yet still very willing to take risks, just to keep the game interesting."

TIPS "Be a big reader of juvenile literature before you write and submit!"

SCIENCE & HUMANITIES PRESS

(636)394-4950. E-mail: banis@sciencehumanities press.com. Website: www.sciencehumanitiespress. com. **Contact:** Dr. Bud Banis, publisher. Publishes trade paperback originals and reprints, and electronic originals and reprints. 1,000 queries received/year. 50 mss received/year.

FICTION *Does not accept unsolicited mss* without a SASE. "We prefer books with a theme that gives a market focus." Brief description by e-mail. "We prefer that you send proposals by e-mail to banis@sciencehu manitiespress.com with a brief description, marketing concept, and possibly a sample of the writing."

NONFICTION "Submissions are best as brief descriptions by e-mail, including some description of the author's background/credentials, and thoughts on approach to nontraditional or specialized markets. Why is the book important and who would buy it? Prefer description by e-mail. Need not be a large format proposal. We prefer that you send proposals by e-mail to banis@sciencehumanitiespress.com with a brief description, marketing concept, and possibly a sample of the writing."

TIPS "Our expertise is electronic publishing for continuous short-run-in-house production."

SEEDLING CONTINENTAL PRESS

520 E. Bainbridge St., Elizabethtown, PA 17022. Website: www.continentalpress.com. **Acquisitions:** Megan Bergonzi. 20% of books by first-time authors. Publishes books for classroom use only for the beginning reader in English. "Natural language and predictable text are requisite. Patterned text is acceptable, but must have a unique story line. Poetry, books in rhyme and full-length picture books are not being accepted. Illustrations are not necessary."

FICTION Young readers: adventure, animal, folktales, humor, multicultural, nature/environment. Does not accept texts longer than 12 pages or over 300 words. Average word length: young readers-100.

NONFICTION Young readers: animal, arts/crafts, biography, careers, concept, multicultural, nature/environment, science. Does not accept texts longer than 12 pages or over 300 words. Average word length: young readers-100.

HOW TO CONTACT Fiction/nonfiction: Submit complete ms with SASE. Responds in 6 months. Publishes a book 1-2 years after acceptance. Will consider simultaneous submissions. Prefers e-mail submissions from authors or illustrators outside the U.S.

ILLUSTRATION Works with 8-10 illustrators/year. Uses color artwork only. Reviews ms/illustration packages from artists. Submit ms with dummy. Illustrations only: Color copies or line art. Responds only if interested. Samples returned with SASE only; samples filed if interested.

PHOTOGRAPHY Buys photos from freelancers. Works on assignment only. Model/property releases required. Uses color prints and 35mm transparencies. Submit cover letter and color promo piece.

TERMS Work purchased outright from authors. Pays illustrators and photographers by the project. Original artwork is not returned at job's completion. Catalog available on website.

TIPS "See our website. Follow writers' guidelines carefully and test your story with children and educators."

SHEN'S BOOKS

1547 Palos Verdes Mall, #291, Walnut Creek CA 94597. (925)262-8108. Fax: (888)269-9092. E-mail: info@ shens.com. Website: www.shens.com. Estab. 1986. Specializes in multicultural material. **Acquisitions:** Renee Ting, president. Produces 2 picture books/year. 50% of books by first-time authors.

FICTION Picture books, young readers: folktales, multicultural with Asian Focus. Middle readers: multicultural. Recently published *Cora Cooks Pacit*, by Dorina Lazo Gilmore, illustrated by Kristi Valiant; *Grandfather's Story Cloth*, by Linda Gerdner, illustrated by Stuart Loughridge (ages 4-8); *The Wakame Gatherers*, by Holly Thompson, illustrated by Kazumi (ages 4-8); *Romina's Rangoli*, by Malathi Michelle Iyengar, illustrated by Jennifer Wanardi (ages 4-8); *The Day the Dragon Danced*, by Kay Haugaard, illustrated by Carolyn Reed Barritt (ages 4-8).

NONFICTION Picture books, young readers: multicultural. Recently published *Chinese History Stories,* edited by Renee Ting; *Selvakumar Knew Better,* by Virginia Kroll, illustrated by Xiaojun Li (ages 4-8).

HOW TO CONTACT Accepts international submissions. Fiction/nonfiction: Submit complete ms. Responds to queries in 1-2 weeks; mss in 6-12 months. Publishes book 1-2 years after acceptance. Considers simultaneous submissions.

ILLUSTRATION Accepts material from international illustrators. Works with 2 illustrators/year. Uses color artwork only. Reviews ms/illustration packages. For ms/illustration packages: Send ms with dummy. Submit ms/illustration packages to Renee Ting, president. Reviews work for future assignments. If interested in illustrating future titles, query with samples. Submit samples to Renee Ting, president. Samples not returned. Samples filed.

PHOTOGRAPHY Works on assignment only. Submit photos to Renee Ting, president.

TERMS Authors pay negotiated by the project. Pays illustrators by the project. Pays photographers by the project. Illustrators see dummies for review. Catalog on website.

TIPS "Be familiar with our catalog before submitting."

SIMON & SCHUSTER BOOKS FOR YOUNG READERS

(212)698-7000. Fax: (212)698-2796. Website: www.simonsayskids.com. 1230 Avenue of the Americas, New York NY 10020. Website: www.kids.simonandschuster.com. "Simon and Schuster Books For Young Readers is the flagship imprint of the S&S Children's Division. We are committed to publishing a wide range of contemporary, commercial, award-winning fiction and non-fiction that spans every age of children's publishing. BFYR is constantly looking to the future, supporting our foundation authors and franchises, but always with an eye for breaking new ground with every publication." "We publish high-quality fiction and nonfiction for a variety of age groups and a variety of markets. Above all, we strive to publish books that we are passionate about." Publishes hardcover originals.

> ◯ *No unsolicited mss.* All unsolicited mss returned unopened. Queries are accepted via mail.

FICTION Query with SASE only.

NONFICTION Picture books: concept. All levels: narrative, current events, biography, history. "We're looking for picture book or middle grade nonfiction that has a retail potential. No photo essays." Recently published Insiders Series (picture book nonfiction, all ages). Paula Deen's cookbook for the lunch-box set 9 cookbook (nonfiction, ages 7 up). Query with SASE only.

HOW TO CONTACT Does not accept unsolicited or unagented manuscripts.

ILLUSTRATION Works with 70 illustrators/year. Do not submit original artwork. Do not accept unsolicited or unagented illustration submissions.

TERMS Pays authors royalty (varies) based on retail price. Pays illustrators or photographers by the project or royalty (varies) based on retail price. Original artwork returned at job's completion. Manuscript/artist's guidelines available via website or free on request. Call (212)698-2707.

TIPS "We're looking for picture books centered on a strong, fully-developed protagonist who grows or changes during the course of the story; YA novels that are challenging and psychologically complex; also imaginative and humorous middle grade fiction. And we want nonfiction that is as engaging as fiction. Our imprint's slogan is 'Reading You'll Remember.' We aim to publish books that are fresh, accessible and family-oriented; we want them to have an impact on the reader."

SKINNER HOUSE BOOKS

Unitarian Universalist Association. 25 Beacon St. Boston MA 02108. (617)742-2100. Fax: (617)742-7025. E-mail: skinnerhouse@uua.org. Website: www.uua.org/publications/skinnerhouse/. Estab. 1976. Specializes in nonfiction, educational material, multicultural material. **Manuscript Acquisitions:** Betsy Martin, editorial assistant. **Art Acquisitions:** Suzanne Morgan, design director. Publishes 1 picture book/ year; 1 young reader/year; 1 middle reader/year. 50% of books by first-time authors. "We publish books for Unitarian Universalists. Most of our children's titles are intended for religious education or worship use. They reflect Unitarian Universalist values." **Contact:** Mary Benard, senior editor. "We publish titles in Unitarian Universalist faith, liberal religion, history, biography, worship, and issues of social justice. We also publish inspirational titles of poetic prose and meditations. Writers should know that Unitarian Universalism is a liberal religious denomination committed to progressive ideals. Currently emphasizing social justice concerns." Publishes trade paperback originals and reprints.

FICTION All levels: anthology, multicultural, nature/environment, religion. Recently published *A Child's Book of Blessings and Prayers*, by Eliza Blanchard (ages 4-8, picture book); *Meet Jesus: The Life and Lessons of a Beloved Teacher*, by Lynn Gunney (age's 5-8, picture book); *Magic Wanda's Travel Emporium*, by Joshua Searle-White (ages 9 and up, stories).

NONFICTION All levels: activity books, multicultural, music/dance, nature/environment, religion.

Unitarian Universalism Is a Really Long Name, by Jennifer Dant (picture book, resource that answers children's questions about Unit. Univ., ages 5-9). Query with SASE.

HOW TO CONTACT Fiction/nonfiction: Query or submit outline/synopsis and 2 sample chapters. Responds to queries in 3 weeks. Publishes a book 1 year after acceptance. Will consider e-mail submissions, simultaneous submissions, and sometimes previously published work.

ILLUSTRATION Works with 2 illustrators/year. Uses both color and b&w. Reviews ms/illustration packages from artists. Query. Contact: Suzanne Morgan, design director. Illustrations only: query with samples. Contact: Suzanne Morgan, Design Director. Responds only if interested. Samples returned with SASE.

PHOTOGRAPHY Buys stock images and assign work. Contact: Suzanne Morgan, design director. Uses inspirational types of photos. Model/property releases required; captions required. Uses color, b&w. Submit cover letter, resume.

TERMS Pays authors royalty 8% based on retail price. Pays illustrators/photographers by the project. Sends galleys to authors; dummies to illustrators. Book catalog available for SASE.

TIPS "From outside our denomination, we are interested in manuscripts that will be of help or interest to liberal churches, Sunday School classes, parents, ministers, and volunteers. Inspirational/spiritual and children's titles must reflect liberal Unitarian Universalist values."

SMALL DOGMA PUBLISHING, INC.

E-mail: submissions@smalldogma.com. Website: www.smalldogma.com. **Contact:** Matt Porricelli, M.B.A., Pres. (fiction, self-help, fantasy, sci-fi, religion, lit, poetry). Hardcover and electronic originals, trade and mass market paperback originals; trade paperback reprints.

FICTION Same as nonfiction. Submit completed ms along with query letter by e-mail.

NONFICTION "We are dedicated to making a difference and are always looking for new manuscripts that entertain, teach, challenge, inform or inspire. Please note: We do not accept material with gratuitous violence or sexual content." Submit completed ms along with query letter by e-mail.

TIPS "Be different. Be passionate about your book. Be willing to do book signings/promotions. How do you plan to reach your target audience? What is your sales/promotion strategy?"

SMALLFELLOW PRESS

Imprint of Tallfellow Press, 9454 Wilshire Blvd., Suite 550, Beverly Hills, CA 90212. E-mail: tallfellow@pac bell.net. Website: www.smallfellow.com. **Manuscript/Art Acquisitions:** Claudia Sloan.

Smallfellow no longer accepts manuscript/art submissions.

SOUNDPRINTS/STUDIO MOUSE

Palm Publishing. LLC, 353 Main St., Norwalk CT 06851. (800)228-7839. Fax: (203)864-1776. E-mail: info@soundprints.com. Website: www.soundprints. com. Publishes mass market books, educational material, multicultural material. **Manuscript Acquisitions:** Anthony Parisi, editorial assistant. **Art Acquisitions:** Katie Sears, senior designer. 10% of books by first-time authors.

FICTION Picture books, young readers: adventure, animal, fantasy, history, multicultural, nature/environment, sports. Recently published *Smithsonian Alphabet of Earth*, by Barbie Heit Schwaeber, and illustrated by Sally Vitsky (ages preschool-2, hardcover and paperback available with audio CD plus bonus audiobook and e-book downloads); *First Look at Insects*, by Laura Gates Galvin, illustrated by Charlotte Oh (ages 18 months-5 years board book plus e-book and activities download).

HOW TO CONTACT Query or submit complete manuscript. Responds to queries/mss in 6 months. Publishes a book 1-2 years after acceptance. Illustration: Works with 3-7 illustrators/year. Uses color artwork only. Send tearsheets with contact information, "especially web address if applicable." Samples not returned; samples filed.

PHOTOGRAPHY Buys stock and assign work. Model/property release and captions required. Send color promo sheet.

TERMS Original artwork returned at job's completion. Catalog available on website. Offers writer's/artist's/photographer's guidelines with SASE.

SPINNER BOOKS

Imprint of University Games, 2030 Harrison St., San Francisco, CA 94110. Estab. 1985. (415)503-1600. Fax: (415)503-0085. E-mail: info@ugames.com. Website: www.ugames.com. Specializes in nonfiction. **Contact: Editorial Department. Publishes 6 young readers/year; 6 middle readers/year. "Spinner Books publishes books of puzzles, games and trivia."

NONFICTION Picture books: games & puzzles. Recently published *20 Questions*, by Bob Moog (adult); *20 Questions for Kids*, by Bob Moog (young adult).

HOW TO CONTACT Only interested in agented material. Nonfiction: Query. Responds to queries in 3 months; mss in 2 months. Publishes a book 6 months after acceptance. Will consider e-mail submissions.

ILLUSTRATION Only interested in agented material. Uses both color and b&w. Illustrations only: Query with samples. Responds in 3 months only if interested. Samples not returned.

TERMS Sends galleys to authors; dummies to illustrators. Originals returned to artist at job's completion. Book catalog available on website: www.ugames.com.

STANDARD PUBLISHING

Standex International Corp., 8805 Governor's Hill Dr., Suite 400, Cincinnati OH 45249. (800)543-1353. E-mail: adultministry@standardpub.com; ministrytochildren@standardpub.com; ministrytoyouth@standardpub.com. Website: www.standardpub.com. Publishes resources that meet church and family needs in the area of children's ministry. Visit www.standardpub.com/writers for writers' guidelines and current publishing objectives. **Contact:** Acquisitions Editor. Publishes resources that meet church and family needs in the area of children's ministry.

STERLING PUBLISHING CO., INC.

387 Park Ave. S.10th Floor, New York NY 10016-8810. (212)532-7160. Fax: (212)981-0508. E-mail: ragis@sterlingpub.com; bduquette@sterlingpublishing.com. E-mail: info@sterlingweb.com. Website: www.sterlingpublishing.com/kids. Publishes 10 picture books/year; 50 young readers/year; 50 middle readers/year; 10 young adult titles/year. 15% of books by first-time authors. **Contact:** Category Editor; Children's Book Editor; Children's Art Director: Merideth Harte. "Sterling publishes highly illustrated, accessible, hands-on, practical books for adults and children." Publishes hardcover and paperback originals and reprints.

> "Our mission is to publish high-quality books that educate, entertain and enrich the lives of our readers."

FICTION Picture books. "At present we do not accept fiction."

NONFICTION Young readers: activity books, arts/crafts, cooking, hobbies, how-to, science. Middle readers, young adults: activity books, arts/crafts, hobbies, how-to, science, mazes, optical illusions, games, magic, math, puzzles. Proposals on subjects such as crafting, decorating, outdoor living, and photography should be sent directly to Lark Books at their Asheville, North Carolina offices. Complete guidelines can be found on the Lark site: www.larkbooks.com/submissions. Publishes nonfiction only. Submit outline, publishing history, 1 sample chapter (typed and double-spaced), SASE. Explain your idea. Send sample illustrations where applicable. For children's books, please submit full mss. We do not accept electronic (e-mail) submissions. Be sure to include information about yourself with particular regard to your skills and qualifications in the subject area of your submission. It is helpful for us to know your publishing history—whether or not you've written other books and, if so, the name of the publisher and whether those books are currently in print.

HOW TO CONTACT Nonfiction: Submit outline/synopsis, 1 sample chapter and SASE. Responds to queries/mss in 6 weeks. Publishes book 1 year after acceptance. Will consider simultaneous submissions, previously published work.

ILLUSTRATION Works with 50 illustrators/year. Reviews ms/illustration packages from artists. Illustrations only: Send promo sheet. Contact: Karen Nelson, creative director. Responds in 6 weeks. Samples returned with SASE; samples filed.

PHOTOGRAPHY Buys stock and assigns work. Contact: Karen Nelson.

TERMS Pays authors royalty or work purchased outright from authors. Offers advances (average amount: $2,000). Pays illustrators by the project. Pays photographers by the project or per photo. Sends galleys to authors; dummies to illustrators. Originals returned to artist at job's completion. Offers writer's guidelines for SASE. Catalog available on website.

TIPS "We are primarily a nonfiction activities-based publisher. We have a picture book list, but we do not publish chapter books or novels. Our list is not trend-driven. We focus on titles that will backlist well."

STONE ARCH BOOKS

151 Good Counsel Dr., P.O. Box 669, Mankato, MN 56002-0669. Website: www.stonearchbooks.com. **Acquisitions Editor:** Michael Dahl. **Art Director:** Heather Kindseth. Specializes in "safe graphic novels and high-interest fiction for striving readers, especially boys."

FICTION Young readers, middle readers, young adults: adventure, contemporary, fantasy, humor, light humor, mystery, science fiction, sports, suspense. Average word length: young readers—1,000-3,000; middle readers and early young adults—5,000-10,000.

HOW TO CONTACT Submit outline/synopsis and 3 sample chapters. Electronic submissions are preferred and should be sent to author.sub@stonearchbooks.com. Accepts simultaneous submissions. Only submissions with e-mail addresses will receive a reply.

ILLUSTRATION Works with 35 illustrators/year. Uses both color and b&w.

TERMS Work purchased outright from authors. Illustrators paid by the project. Title list and catalog available on website.

TIPS "A high-interest topic or activity is one that a young person would spend their free time on without adult direction or suggestion."

SYLVAN DELL PUBLISHING

612 Johnnie Dodds, Suite A2, Mt. Pleasant, SC 29464. (843)971-6722. Fax (843)216-3804. Estab. 2004. E-mail: donnagerman@sylvandellpublishing.com. Website: www.sylvandellpublishing.com. **Contact:** Donna German. "The books that we publish are usually, but not always, fictional stories that relate to animals, nature, the environment, and science. All books should subtly convey an educational theme through a warm story that is fun to read and that will grab a children's attention. Each book has a 3-5 page For Creative Minds section in the back to reinforce the educational component of the book itself. This section will have a craft and/or game as well as fun facts to be shared by the parent, teacher or other adult. Authors do not need to supply this information but may be actively involved in its development if they would like. Please read about our submission guidelines on our website." Mss. should be less than 1,500 words and meet all of the following 4 criteria: fun to read—mostly fiction with nonfiction facts woven into the story; national or regional in scope; must tie into early elementary school curriculum; must be marketable through a niche market such as a zoo, aquarium, or museum gift shop. Publishes hardcover, trade paperback, and electronic originals. 2,000 mss received/year.

FICTION Picture books: animal, folktales, nature/environment, math-related. Word length—picture books: no more than 1500. Recently published *Whistling Wings* by first-time author Laura Goering, illustrated by Laura Jacques; *Sort it Out!* by Barbara Mariconda, illustrated by Sherry Rogers; *River Beds: Sleeping in the World's Rivers* by Gail Langer Karwoski, illustrated by Connie McLennan; *Saturn for My Birthday* by first-time author John McGranaghan, illustrated by Wendy Edelson.

NONFICTION "We are not looking for mss about: pets (dogs or cats in particular); new babies; local or state-specific; magic; biographies; history-related; ABC books; poetry; series; young adult books or novels; holiday-related books. We do not consider mss. that have been previously published in any way, including e-books or self-published. We only accept e-submissions."

HOW TO CONTACT Submit complete ms. Prefers to work with authors from the U.S. and Canada because of marketing. Responds to mss in 3-4 months. Publishes a book about 2 years after acceptance. Accepts simultaneous submissions. Accepts electronic submissions only. Snail mail submissions are discarded without being opened.

ILLUSTRATION Works with 10 illustrators/year. Prefers to work with illustrators from the U.S. and Canada. Uses color artwork only. Submit Web link or 2-3 electronic images. Contact: Donna German. "I generally keep submissions on file until I match the manuscripts to illustration needs."

TERMS Pays authors and illustrators step-up, advance royalty. "Authors and illustrators see PDFs of book as it goes to the printer. Any concerns or changes are dealt with then. We keep cover art and return all other art to illustrators." Catalog available on website. Writer's and artist's guidelines available on website.

TIPS "Please make sure that you have looked at our website to read our complete submission guidelines and to see if we are looking for a particular subject. Manuscripts must meet all four of our stated criteria. We look for fairly realistic, bright and colorful art—no cartoons. We envision the books being used at home and in the classroom."

SYNERGEBOOKS

205 S. Dixie Dr., Haines City FL 33844. (863)956-3015. E-mail: synergebooks@aol.com. Website: www.syn ergebooks.com. SynergEbooks publishes at least 40 new titles a year, and only 1-5 of those are put into print in any given year. "SynergEbooks is first and foremost a digital publisher, so most of our marketing budget goes to those formats. Authors are required to direct-sell a minimum of 100 digital copies of a title before it's accepted for print." **Contact:** Debra Staples, publisher/acquisitions editor. Publishes trade paperback and electronic originals. 250 queries received/ year. 250 mss received/year.

FICTION Submit proposal package, including synopsis, 1-3 sample chapters, and marketing plans.

NONFICTION Submit proposal package, 1-3 sample chapters.

HOW TO CONTACT Submit proposal package, including synopsis, 1-3 sample chapters, and marketing plans.

TIPS "At SynergEbooks, we work with the author to promote their work."

TANGLEWOOD BOOKS

P.O. Box 3009, Terre Haute IN 47803. E-mail: ptier ney@tanglewoodbooks.com. Website: www.tangle woodbooks.com. Produces 2-3 picture books/year, 1-2 middle readers/year, 1-2 young adult titles/year. 20% of books by first-time authors. "Tanglewood Press strives to publish entertaining, kid-centric books." **Contact:** Kairi Hamlin, acquisitions editor.

FICTION Picture books: adventure, animal, concept, contemporary, fantasy, humor. Average word length: picture books—800. Recently published *68 Knots*, by Micheal Robert Evans (young adult); *The Mice of Bistrot des Sept Freres*, written and illustrated by Marie Letourneau; *Chester Raccoon and the Acorn Full of Memories*, by Audrey Penn and Barbara Gibson. Query with 3-5 sample chapters.

NONFICTION Does not generally publish nonfiction.

HOW TO CONTACT Accepts international submissions. Fiction: Query with 3-5 sample chapters. Responds to mss in up to 18 months. Publishes book 2 years after acceptance. Considers simultaneous submissions.

ILLUSTRATION Accepts material from international illustrators. Works with 3-4 illustrators/year. Uses both color and b&w. Reviews ms/illustration packages. For ms/illustration packages: Send ms with sample illustrations. Submit ms/illustration packages to Peggy Tierney, publisher. If interested in illustrating future titles, query with samples. Submit samples to Peggy Tierney, publisher. Samples not returned. Samples filed.

TERMS Illustrators paid by the project for covers and small illustrations; royalty of 3-5% for picture books. Author sees galleys for review. Illustrators see dummies for review. Originals returned to artist at job's completion.

TIPS "Please see lengthy 'Submissions' page on our website."

THIRD WORLD PRESS

P.O. Box 19730, Chicago IL 60619. (773)651-0700. Fax: (773)651-7286. E-mail: twpress3@aol.com; GWEN MTWP@aol.com. Website: www.thirdworldpressinc. com. **Contact:** Bennett J. Johnson. "We look for the maximum effect of creative expression and cultural enlightenment in all of the written genres, including fiction, nonfiction, poetry, drama, young adult, and children's books that may not have an outlet otherwise. Third World Press welcomes the opportunity to review solicited and unsolicited manuscripts that explore African-centered life and thought through the genres listed above." Publishes hardcover and trade paperback originals and reprints. 200-300 queries received/year. 200 mss received/year.

Third World Press is open to submissions in July only.

FICTION "We primarily publish nonfiction, but will consider fiction by and about Blacks." Query with SASE. Submit outline, clips, 5 sample chapters.

NONFICTION Query with SASE. Submit outline, 5 sample chapters.

TILBURY HOUSE, PUBLISHERS

103 Brunswick Ave. Gardiner ME 04345. (207)582-1899. Fax: (207)582-8227. E-mail: karen@tilbury house.com. Website: www.tilburyhouse.com. **Publisher:** Jennifer Bunting. **Children's Book Editor:** Audrey Maynard. **Children's Book Editor:** Karen Fisk. Publishes 2-4 picture book/year.

FICTION Picture books: multicultural, nature/environment. Special needs include books that teach children about tolerance and honoring diversity. Recently published *One of Us*, by Peggy Moss; *Moonwatchers: Shirin'sramadan Miracle*, by Reza Jalali; and *The Lunch Thief*, by Anne Bromely, illustrated by Rober Casilla.

NONFICTION Picture books, young readers, middle readers: multicultural, nature/environment. Recently published *Bear-ly There*, by Rebekah Raye.

HOW TO CONTACT Fiction/nonfiction: Submit complete ms or outline/synopsis. Responds to queries/mss in 1 month. Publishes a book 1-2 years after acceptance. Will consider simultaneous submissions "with notification."

ILLUSTRATION Works with 2-3 illustrators/year. Illustrations only: Query with samples. Responds in 1 month. Samples returned with SASE. Original artwork returned at job's completion.

PHOTOGRAPHY Buys photos from freelancers. Works on assignment only.

TERMS Pays authors royalty based on wholesale price. Pays illustrators/photographers by the project; royalty based on wholesale price. Sends galleys to authors. Book catalog available for SAE and postage.

TIPS "We are always interested in stories that will encourage children to understand the natural world and the environment, as well as stories with social justice themes. We really like stories that engage children to become problem solvers as well as those that promote respect, tolerance and compassion. We do not publish books with personified animal characters, historical fiction, chapter books, fantasy."

TOR BOOKS

175 Fifth Ave., New York NY 10010. Website: www.tor-forge.com. Contact: Juliet Pederson, publishing coordinator. **Contact:** Juliet Pederson, publishing coordinator.

○ Tor Books is the "world's largest publisher of science fiction and fantasy, with strong category publishing in historical fiction, mystery, western/Americana, thriller, YA."

FICTION Average word length: middle readers-30,000; young adults-60,000-100,000. We do not accept queries.

NONFICTION Middle readers and young adult: geography, history, how-to, multicultural, nature/environment, science, social issues. Does not want to see religion, cooking. Average word length: middle readers-25,000-35,000; young adults-70,000. Published *Strange Unsolved Mysteries*, by Phyllis Rabin Emert; *Stargazer's Guide (to the Galaxy)*, by Q.L. Pearce (ages 8-12, guide to constellations, illustrated).

TIPS "Know the house you are submitting to, familiarize yourself with the types of books they are publishing. Get an agent. Allow him/her to direct you to publishers who are most appropriate. It saves time and effort."

Ⓐ TYNDALE HOUSE PUBLISHERS, INC.

(800)323-9400. Fax: (800)684-0247. 351 Executive Dr. P.O. Box 80, Wheaton IL 60189. (630)668-8300. Website: www.tyndale.com. **Manuscript Acquisitions:** Katara Washington Patton. **Art Acquisitions:** Talinda Iverson. Publishes approximately 15 Christian children's titles/year. **Contact:** Manuscript Review Committee. "Tyndale House publishes practical, user-friendly Christian books for the home and family." Publishes hardcover and trade paperback originals and mass paperback reprints.

FICTION Juvenile. "Christian truths must be woven into the story organically. No short story collections. Youth books: character building stories with Christian perspective. Especially interested in ages 10-14. We primarily publish Christian historical romances, with occasional contemporary, suspense, or standalones." Agented submissions only. *No unsolicited mss.*

NONFICTION Bible, devotionals, Bible storybooks. Prefers agented submissions.

ILLUSTRATION Uses full-color for book covers, b&w or color spot illustrations for some nonfiction. Illustrations only: Query with photocopies (color or b&w) of samples, résumé.

PHOTOGRAPHY Buys photos from freelancers. Works on assignment only.

TERMS Pay rates for authors and illustrators vary.

TIPS "All accepted manuscripts will appeal to Evangelical Christian children and parents."

⊕ UNTREED READS PUBLISHING

(415)621-0465. Fax: (415)621-0465. E-mail: general@untreedreads.com. E-mail: submissions@untreedreads.com. Website: www.untreedreads.com. "We welcome short story collections. Also, we look forward to publishing children's books, cookbooks, and other works that have been known for illustrations in print as the technology in the multiple ereaders improves. We hope to be a large platform for diverse content and authors. We seek mainstream content, but if you're an author or have content that doesn't seem to always 'fit' into the traditional market we'd like to hear from you." No erotica, picture books, poetry, poetry in translation, or romance. Submit proposal package with 3 sample chapters. Submit completed ms. **Contact:** Jay A. Hartman, editor-in-chief (fiction-all genres). Publishes in electronic originals and reprints. Receives 50 submissions/year.

FICTION "We look forward to long-term relationships with our authors. We encourage works that are either already a series or could develop into a series. We are one of the few publishers publishing short stories and are happy to be a resource for these good works."

NONFICTION "We are very interested in developing our textbook market. E-readers don't currently support graphs, tables, images, etc. as well as print books; however, we plan to be trendsetters in this as the technology in the ereaders improves. Also we are eager to increase our number of business books. We always look for series or works that could develop into a series." Submit proposal package, including 3 sample chapters. Submit completed mss.

TIPS "For our fiction titles we lean toward a literary audience. For nonfiction titles, we want to be a platform for business people, entrepreneurs and speakers to become well known in their fields of expertise. However, for both fiction and nonfiction we want to appeal to many audiences."

⊕ URJ PRESS

633 Third Ave.New York NY 10017. (212)650-4120. Fax: (212)650-4119. E-mail: press@urj.org. Website: www.urj.press.com. **Manuscript/Art Acquisitions:** Rabbi Hara Person, editor-in-chief. Publishes 4 picture books/year; 2 young readers/year; 2 middle readers/year; 2 young adult titles; 4 textbooks/year. "URJ publishes textbooks for the religious classroom, children's tradebooks and scholarly work of Jewish education import—no adult fiction and no YA fiction." **Contact:** Rabbi Hara Person, editor (subjects related to Judaism). URJ Press publishes books related to Judaism. Publishes hardcover and trade paperback originals. 500 queries received/year. 400 mss received/year.

FICTION Picture books: religion. Average word length: picture books—1,500. Recently published *The Purim Costume*, by Peninnah Schran, illustrated by Tammy L. Keiser (ages 4-8, picture book); *A Year of Jewish Stories: 52 Tales for Children and Their Families*, by Grace Ragues Maisel and Samantha Shubert, illustrated by Tammy L. Keiser (ages 4-12, picture book). Jewish, liberal content. Picture book length only. Submit complete ms with author bio.

NONFICTION Picture books, young readers, middle readers: religion. Average word length: picture books—1,500. Recently published *The Seven Spices: Stories and Recipes Inspired by the Foods of the Bible*, by Matt Biers-Ariel, illustrated by Tama Goodman (story and recipe book). Submit proposal package, outline, bio, 1-2 sample chapters.

HOW TO CONTACT Fiction: Submit outline/synopsis and 2 sample chapters. Nonfiction: Submit complete ms. Responds to queries/mss in 4 months. Publishes a book 18-24 months after acceptance. Will consider simultaneous submissions.

ILLUSTRATION Works with 5 illustrators/year. Reviews ms/illustration packages from artists. Send ms with dummy. Illustrations only: Send portfolio to be kept on file. Responds in 2 months. Samples returned with SASE. Looking specifically for Jewish themes.

PHOTOGRAPHY Buys stock and assigns work. Uses photos with Jewish content. Prefers modern settings. Submit cover letter and promo piece.

TERMS Offers advances. Pays photographers by the project (range: $200-3,000) or per photo (range: $20-100). Book catalog free; ms guidelines for SASE.

TIPS "Look at some of our books. Have an understanding of the Reform Judaism community. In addition to bookstores, we sell to Jewish congregations and Hebrew day schools."

⊕ VIEWPOINT PRESS

Website: www.viewpointpress.com/products.html. PMB 400 785 Tucker Road #G Tehachapi, CA. 93561. Phone: (661)821-5110. Fax: (661)821-7515. E-mail: joie99@aol.com.We are not accepting manuscripts at this time. **Contact:** Dr. B.J. Mitchell. We have been in business for 25 years and have three children's books: *Seeds of Violence: the Autobiography of a Subversive; Fiddler of the Opry: The Howdy Forrester Story; and Footprints of the Soul: a Novel.*

Ⓐ VIKING CHILDREN'S BOOKS

345 Hudson St., New York NY 10014. E-mail: studiopublicity@us.penguingroup.com. Website: www.penguingroup.com. **Acquisitions:** Catherine Frank, executive editor (picture books, middle grade and young adult fiction, and nonfiction); Tracy Gates, associate editorial director (picture books, middle grade, and young adult fiction); Joy Peskin, executive editor (middle grade and young adult fiction); Kendra Levin, associate editor (picture books, middle grade and young adult fiction); Leila Sales, editorial

assistant. **Art Acquisitions:** Denise Cronin, Viking Children's Books. Publishes hardcover originals. Publishes 55 books/year. Receives 7,500 queries/year. 25% of books from first-time authors; 33% from unagented writers. "Viking Children's Books is known for humorous, quirky picture books, in addition to more traditional fiction. We publish the highest quality fiction, nonfiction, and picture books for pre-schoolers through young adults." Publishes book 1-2 years after acceptance of artwork. Hesitantly accepts simultaneous submissions. **Contact:** Catherine Frank, exec. editor. Publishes hardcover originals.

○ *Does not accept unsolicited submissions.* Viking Children's Books publishes high-quality trade books for children including fiction, nonfiction and picture books for pre-schoolers through young adults.

FICTION All levels: adventure, animal, contemporary, fantasy, history, humor, multicultural, nature/environment, poetry, problem novels, romance, science fiction, sports, suspense/mystery. Recently published *Llama Llama Misses Mama*, by Anna Dewdney (ages 2 up, picture book); *Wintergirls*, by Laurie Halse Anderson (ages 12 and up); *Good Luck Bear*, by Greg Foley (ages 2 up); *Along for the Ride*, by Sarah Dessen (ages 12 up). **Nonfiction** All levels: biography, concept, history, multicultural, music/dance, nature/environment, science, sports. Recently published *Harper Lee* by Kerry Madden (ages 11 up, biography); *Knucklehead* by Jon Scieszka (ages 7 & up, autobiography); *Marching for Freedom* by Elizabeth Partridge (ages 11 up, nonfiction).

NONFICTION Query with SASE, or submit outline, 3 sample chapters, SASE.

ILLUSTRATION Works with 30 illustrators/year. Responds to artist's queries/submissions only if interested. Samples returned with SASE only or samples filed. Originals returned at job's completion.

TERMS Pays 2-10% royalty on retail price or flat fee. Advance negotiable.

TIPS No "cartoony" or mass-market submissions for picture books.

◉ WALKER & COMPANY

Books for Young Readers, 175 Fifth Ave., New York NY 10010. Website: www.bloomsburykids.com and www.bloomsburyteens.com. Manuscript Acquisitions: Emily Easton, publisher; Stacy Cantor Abrams, editor; Mary Kate Castellani, associate editor. Publishes 8-10 picture books/year; 3-5 nonfiction books/year; 5-10 middle grade titles/year; 15-20 young adult titles/year. 5% of books by first-time authors; 85% of books from agented writers.

FICTION Picture books: adventure, history, humor. Middle readers: coming-of-age, adventure, contemporary, history, humor, multicultural. Young adults: adventure, contemporary, romance, humor, historical fiction, suspense/mystery, paranormal. Recently published fiction: *Ribbit Rabbit*, by Candace Ryan and Mike Lowery (ages 3-5, picture book); *Grandma's Gift*, by Eric Velasquez (ages 4-8, picture book); *Sugar and Ice*, by Kate Messner (8-12, middle grade novel); *Rules of Attraction*, by Simone Elkeles; and *Haunting Violet*, by Alyx Harvey (ages 14 and up).

NONFICTION Recently published nonfiction: *Poop Happened: A History of the World from the Bottom Up*, by Sarah Albee, illustrated by Robert Leighton, (ages 8-12, middle grade nonfiction); *Saving Audie*, by Dorothy Patent and William Munoz (ages 6-9, picture book nonfiction); *101 Ways to Become a Superhero*, by Richard Horne (ages 12 and up, teen nonfiction). Multicultural needs include "contemporary, literary fiction and historical fiction written in an authentic voice. Also high interest nonfiction with trade appeal."

HOW TO CONTACT Fiction/nonfiction: Submit outline/synopsis and sample chapters; complete ms for picture books. Send SASE for writer's guidelines.

ILLUSTRATION Works with 20-25 illustrators/year. Editorial department reviews ms/illustration packages from artists. Query or submit ms with 4-8 samples. Illustrations only: Tearsheets. "Please do not send original artwork."

TERMS Pays authors royalty of 5-10%; pays illustrators royalty or flat fee. Offers advance payment against royalties. Original artwork returned at job's completion. Sends galleys to authors.

TIPS Writers: "Make sure you study our catalog before submitting. We are a small house with a tightly focused list. Illustrators: Have a well-rounded portfolio with different styles." Does not want to see folktales, ABC books, early readers, paperback series. "Walker and Company is committed to introducing talented new authors and illustrators to the children's book field."

◉ WEIGL PUBLISHERS INC.

350 5th Ave., 59th floor, New York NY 10118-0069. (866)649-3445. Fax: (866)449-3445. E-mail: linda@

weigl.com. Website: www.weigl.com. **Manuscript/Art Acquisitions:** Heather Kissock. Publishes 25 young readers/year; 40 middle readers/year; 20 young adult titles/year. 15% of books by first-time authors. "Our mission is to provide innovative high-quality learning resources for schools and libraries worldwide at a competitive price."

NONFICTION Young readers: animal, biography, geography, history, multicultural, nature/environment, science. Middle readers: animal, biography, geography, history, multicultural, nature/environment, science, social issues, sports. Young adults: biography, careers, geography, history, multicultural, nature/environment, social issues. Average word length: young readers—100 words/page; middle readers—200 words/page; young adults—300 words/page. Recently published *Amazing Animals* (ages 9 and up, science series); *U.S. Sites and Symbols* (ages 8 and up, social studies series); *Science Q&A* (ages 9 and up, social studies series). Query by e-mail only; will consider e-mail submissions.

HOW TO CONTACT Nonfiction: Query, by e-mail only. Publishes book 6-9 months after acceptance. Will consider e-mail submissions, simultaneous submissions.

ILLUSTRATION Pays illustrators by the project. Book catalog available for 9$\frac{1}{2}$×11 SASE. Catalog available on website.

PHOTOGRAPHY Pays per photo.

TERMS Work purchased outright from authors. Originals returned to artist at job's completion.

WHITE MANE KIDS

Imprint of White Mane Publishing Co. Inc., 73 W. Burd St., P.O. Box 708, Shippensburg, PA 17257. (717)532-2237. Fax: (717)532-6110. E-mail: marketing@whitemane.com. Website: www.whitemane.com. Acquisitions: Harold Collier, acquisitions editor. Imprints: White Mane Books, Burd Street Press, White Mane Kids, Ragged Edge Press. Publishes 7 middle readers/year. 50% of books are by first-time authors.

FICTION Middle readers, young adults: history (primarily American Civil War). Average word length: middle readers-30,000. Does not publish picture books. Recently published *The Witness Tree and the Shadow of the Noose: Mystery, Lies, and Spies in Manassas* by K.E.M. Johnston; *Drumbeat: The Story of a Civil War Drummer Boy* by Robert J. Trout (grades 5 and up).

NONFICTION Middle readers, young adults: history. Average word length: middle readers-30,000. Does not publish picture books. Recently published *Hey, History Isn't Boring Anymore! A Creative Approach to Teaching the Civil War* by Kelly Ann Butterbaugh (young adult).

HOW TO CONTACT Fiction: Query. Nonfiction: Submit outline/synopsis and 2-3 sample chapters. Responds to queries in 1 month; mss in 3 months. Publishes a book 18 months after acceptance. Will consider simultaneous submissions.

ILLUSTRATION Works with 4 illustrators/year. Illustrations used for cover art only. Responds only if interested. Samples returned with SASE.

PHOTOGRAPHY Buys stock and assigns work. Submit cover letter and portfolio.

TERMS Pays authors royalty of 7-10%. Pays illustrators and photographers by the project. Sends galleys for review. Originals returned to artist at job's completion. Book catalog and writer's guidelines available for SASE. All imprints included in a single catalog.

ALBERT WHITMAN & COMPANY

250 S. Northwest Highway, Suite 320, Park Ridge IL 60068. (800)255-7675. Fax: (847)581-0039. E-mail: mail@awhitmanco.com. Website: www.albertwhitman.com. Manuscript Acquisitions: Editor-in-chief. Art Acquisitions: Carol Gildar. Publishes 40 books/year. 20% of books by first-time authors; 15% of books from agented authors. **Contact:** Submissions Editor. "Albert Whitman & Company publishes books for the trade, library and school library market. We have an open submissions policy: we read unsolicited work, which means that it is not necessary for writers to submit through a literary agent. We are interested in reviewing the following types of projects: Picture book manuscripts for ages 2-8; Novels and chapter books for ages 8-12; Young adult novels; Nonfiction for ages 3-12 and YA; Art samples showing pictures of children." Best known for the classic series The Boxcar Children® Mysteries, its highly-praised picture books, novels, and nonfiction titles for ages 2-12, delighting children and reaching out to children of all backgrounds and experiences. "Albert Whitman publishes good books for children on a variety of topics: holidays (i.e., Halloween), special needs (such as diabetes) and problems like divorce. The majority of our titles are picture books with less than 1,500 words. De-emphasizing bedtime stories." Albert Whitman's

special interest and issue titles address subjects such as disease, social issues and disabilities. Many books deal in a caring and respectful manner with the challenging situations and learning experiences encountered by children, helping them to grow intellectually and emotionally. Publishes in original hardcover, paperback, boardbooks.

○ "We have a new policy for unsolicited submissions. After November 1, 2010, we will respond only to submissions of interest. We read every submission within 4 months of receipt, but we can no longer respond to every one. If you do not receive a response from us after 4 months, we have declined to publish your submission. After November 1, 2010, please do not enclose a SASE. We will not be returning materials received after that date. Please be sure to include current contact information (mail address, e-mail, and phone number) on cover letter and first page of manuscript."

FICTION Picture books, young readers, middle readers: adventure, concept (to help children deal with problems), fantasy, history, humor, multicultural, suspense. Middle readers: problem novels, suspense/mystery. "We are interested in contemporary multicultural stories—stories with holiday themes and exciting distinctive novels. We publish a wide variety of topics and are interested in stories that help children deal with their problems and concerns. Does not want to see, "religion-oriented, ABCs, pop-up, romance, counting." Recently published fiction: *Three Little Gators*, by Hellen Ketteman, illustrated by Will Terry; *Peace Week in Miss Fox's Class* by Eileen Spinelli, Anne Kennedy (Illustrator); *The Bully-Blockers Club*, by Teresa Bateman, illustrated by Jackie Urbanovic; *The Truth about Truman School*, by Dori Hillestad Butler. "You may send the manuscript in its entirety OR a query letter with synopsis and sample chapters. At this time, we are not seeking manuscripts or writers for the Boxcar Children® Mysteries series."

NONFICTION Picture books, young readers, middle readers: animal, arts/crafts, health, history, hobbies, multicultural, music/dance, nature/environment, science, sports, special needs. Does not want to see, "religion, any books that have to be written in, or fictionalized biographies. "Recently published *Abe Lincoln Loved Animals*, by Ellen Jackson, illustrated by Doris

Ettllinger; *An Apple for Harriet Tubman* by Glennette Tilly Turner.

HOW TO CONTACT Fiction/nonfiction: Submit query, outline, and sample chapter. For picture books send entire ms. Include cover letter. Responds to submissions in 4 months. Publishes a book 18 months after acceptance. Will consider simultaneous submissions "if notified."

ILLUSTRATION *"We are not accepting Illustration samples at this time. Submissions will not be returned."*

PHOTOGRAPHY Publishes books illustrated with photos, but not stock photos—desires photos all taken for project. "Our books are for children and cover many topics; photos must be taken to match text. Books often show a child in a particular situation (e.g. kids being home-schooled, a sister whose brother is born prematurely)." Photographers should query with samples; send unsolicited photos by mail.

TERMS Pays author's, illustrator's, and photographer's royalties. Book catalog for 8×10 SAE and 3 first-class stamps.

TIPS "In both picture books and nonfiction, we are seeking stories showing life in other cultures and the variety of multicultural life in the U.S. We also want fiction and nonfiction about mentally or physically challenged children—some recent topics have been autism, stuttering, and diabetes. Look up some of our books first to be sure your submission is appropriate for Albert Whitman & Co. We publish trade books that are especially interesting to schools and libraries. We recommend you study our website before submitting your work."

WILLIAMSON BOOKS

An imprint of Ideals Publications, 2630 Elm Hill Pike, Ste. 100, Nashville, TN 37214. E-mail: pjay@guideposts.org. Website: www.idealsbooks.com. **Manuscript and Art Acquisitions:** Williamson Books Submission. Publishes 2-4 titles/year. 50% of books by first-time authors; 10% of books from agented authors. Publishes "very successful nonfiction series (Kids Can! Series) on subjects such as history, science, arts/crafts, geography, diversity, multiculturalism. Little Hands series for ages 2-6, Kaleidoscope Kids series (age 7 and up) and Quick Starts for Kids! series (ages 8 and up). "Our goal is to help every child fulfill his/her potential and experience personal growth."

NONFICTION Hands-on active learning books, animals, African-American, arts/crafts, Asian, biography, diversity, careers, geography, health, history, hobbies, how-to, math, multicultural, music/dance, nature/environment, Native American, science, writing and journaling. Does not want to see textbooks, picture books, fiction. "Looking for all things African American, Asian American, Hispanic, Latino, and Native American including crafts and traditions, as well as their history, biographies, and personal retrospectives of growing up in U.S. for grades pre K-8th. We are looking for books in which learning and doing are inseparable." Recently published *Keeping Our Earth Green; Leap Into Space; China! and Big Fun Craft Book.*

HOW TO CONTACT Query with annotated TOC/synopsis and 1 sample chapter. Responds to queries/mss in 4 months. Publishes book "about 1 year" after acceptance. Writers may send a SASE for guidelines or reply to submission.

ILLUSTRATION Works with at least 2 illustrators and 2 designers/year. "We're interested in expanding our illustrator and design freelancers." Uses primarily 2-color and 4-color artwork. Responds only if interested. Samples returned with SASE; samples filed.

PHOTOGRAPHY Buys photos from freelancers; uses archival art and photos.

TERMS Pays authors advance against future royalties based on wholesale price or purchases outright. Pays illustrators by the project. Pays photographers per photo. Sends galleys to authors.

TIPS "Please do not send any fiction or picture books of any kind—those should go to Ideals Children's Books. Look at our books to see what we do. We're interested in interactive learning books with a creative approach packed with interesting information, written for young readers ages 3-7 and 8-14. In nonfiction children's publishing, we are looking for authors with a depth of knowledge shared with children through a warm, embracing style. Our publishing philosophy is based on the idea that all children can succeed and have positive learning experiences. Children's lasting learning experiences involve their participation."

WINDRIVER PUBLISHING, INC.

72 N. WindRiver Rd., Silverton ID 83867-0446. (208)752-1836. Fax: (208)752-1876. E-mail: info@windriverpublishing.com. Website: www.windriverpub

lishing.com. **Contact:** E. Keith Howick, Jr., president; Gail Howick, vice president/editor-in-chief. "Authors who wish to submit book proposals for review must do so according to our submissions guidelines, which can be found on our website, along with an online submission form, which is our preferred submission method. We do not accept submissions of any kind by e-mail." Publishes hardcover originals and reprints, trade paperback originals, and mass market originals. 1,000 queries received/year. 300 mss received/year.

FICTION Follow online instructions.

NONFICTION Follow online instructions for submitting proposal, including synopsis and 3 sample chapters. *Ms submissions by invitation only.*

TIPS "We do not accept manuscripts containing graphic or gratuitous profanity, sex or violence. See online instructions for details."

PAULA WISEMAN BOOKS

Imprint of Simon & Schuster, 1230 Sixth Ave. New York NY 10020. (212)698-7000. Website: http://kids.simonandschuster.com/. Publishes 15 picture books/year; 4 middle readers/year; 2 young adult titles/year. 10% of books by first-time authors.

FICTION Considers all categories. Average word length: picture books--500; others standard length. Recently published *Which Puppy?*, by Kate Feiffer, illustrated by Jules Feiffer.

NONFICTION Picture books: animal, biography, concept, history, nature/environment. Young readers: animal, biography, history, multicultural, nature/environment, sports. Average word length: picture books--500; others standard length.

HOW TO CONTACT Do not submit original artwork. **Does not accept unsolicited or unagented manuscript submissions.**

ILLUSTRATION Works with 15 illustrators/year. Does not accept unsolicited or unagented illustrations or submissions.

WIZARDS OF THE COAST BOOKS FOR YOUNG READERS

P.O. Box 707, Renton WA 98057. (425)254-2287. E-mail: nina.hess@wizards.com. Website: www.wizards.com. Publishes 6 middle readers/year; 4 young adult titles/year. 5% of books by first-time authors. "We publish fantasy novels for young readers based on the lore of the Dungeons & Dragons role-playing game." **Contact:** Nina Hess. Wizards of the Coast publishes only science fiction and fantasy shared-world titles. Currently emphasizing solid fantasy writers. De-emphasizing gothic fiction. Dragonlance; Forgotten Realms; Magic: The Gathering; Eberron. Wizards of the Coast publishes games as well, including Dungeons & Dragons® role-playing game. Publishes hardcover and trade paperback originals and trade paperback reprints.

FICTION Young readers, middle readers, young adults: fantasy only. Average word length: middle readers-30,000-40,000; young adults-60,000-75,000. Recently published *A Practical Guide to Dragon-Riding*, by Lisa Trumbauer (ages 6 and up); *The Stowaway*, by R.A. Salvatore and Geno Salvatore (10 and up); *Red Dragon Codex*, by R. Henham (ages 8-12)

HOW TO CONTACT Fiction: Query with samples, writing credits. "No manuscripts, please." Responds to queries if interested. Publishes book 9-24 months after acceptance.

ILLUSTRATION Works with 4 illustrators/year. Query. Illustrations only: Query with samples, résumé.

TERMS Pays authors royalty of 4-6% based on retail price. Offers advances (average amount: $4,000). Pays illustrators by the project. Ms guidelines available on our website. All imprints included in a single catalog. Catalog available on website.

TIPS Editorial staff attended or plans to attend ALA conference.

WORDSONG

815 Church St., Honesdale PA 18431. E-mail: contact@boydsmillspress.com. Website: www.wordsongpoetry.com. Estab. 1990. An imprint of Boyds Mills Press, Inc. 5% of books from agented writers. "We publish fresh voices in contemporary poetry."

HOW TO CONTACT Fiction/ nonfiction: Submit complete ms or submit through agent. Label package "Manuscript Submission" and include SASE. "Please send a book-length collection of your own poems. Do not send an initial query." Responds in 3 months.

ILLUSTRATION Works with approx. 7-10 illustrators/year. Reviews ms/illustration packages from artists. Submit complete ms with 1 or 2 pieces of art. Illustrations only: Query with samples best suited to the art (postcard, 8½ × 11, etc.). Label package "Art Sample Submission." Responds only if interested. Samples returned with SASE.

PHOTOGRAPHY Assigns work.

TERMS Authors paid royalty or work purchased outright. Offers advances. Illustrators paid by the project or royalties; varies. Photographers paid by the project, per photo, or royalties; varies. Manuscripts/artist's guidelines available on website.

TIPS "Collections of original poetry, not anthologies, are our biggest need at this time. Keep in mind that the strongest collections demonstrate a facility with multiple poetic forms and offer fresh images and insights."

WORLD BOOK, INC.

233 N. Michigan Ave., Suite 2000, Chicago, IL 60601. (312)729-5800. Fax: (312)729-5600. Website: www.worldbook.com. **Manuscript Acquisitions:** Paul A. Kobasa, editor-in-chief. **Art Acquisitions:** Art/design manager. World Book, Inc. (publisher of The World Book Encyclopedia), publishes reference sources and nonfiction series for children and young adults in the areas of science, mathematics, English-language skills, basic academic and social skills, social studies, history, and health and fitness.

NONFICTION Young readers: animal, arts/crafts, careers, concept, geography, health, reference. Middle readers: animal, arts/crafts, careers, geography, health, history, hobbies, how-to, nature/environment, reference, science. Young adult: arts/crafts, careers, geography, health, history, hobbies, how-to, nature/environment, reference, science.

HOW TO CONTACT Nonfiction: Submit outline/synopsis only; no mss. Responds to queries/mss in 2 months. Unsolicited mss will not be returned. Publishes a book 18 months after acceptance. Will consider simultaneous submissions.

ILLUSTRATION Works with 10-30 illustrators/year. Illustrations only: Query with samples. Responds only if interested. Samples returned with SASE; samples filed "if extra copies and if interested."

PHOTOGRAPHY Buys stock and assigns work. Needs broad spectrum; editorial concept, specific natural, physical and social science spectrum. Model/property releases required; captions required. Uses color 8×10 glossy and matte prints, 35mm, 2¼×2¼, 4×5, 8×10 transparencies. Submit cover letter, résumé, promo piece (color and b&w).

TERMS Payment negotiated on project-by-project basis. Sends galleys to authors. Manuscript and art guidelines for SASE.

⊕ ◐ ZUMAYA PUBLICATIONS, LLC

3209 S. Interstate 35, #1086, Austin TX 78741. E-mail: submissions@zumayapublications.com. Website: www.zumayapublications.com. **Contact:** Elizabeth Burton, executive editor. Publishes trade paperback and electronic originals and reprints. 1,000 queries received/year. 100 mss received/year.

◐ "We are currently closed to submissions until further notice while we endeavor to catch up on our publishing queue. We will begin accepting queries for some imprints in July of 2010. Please review the guidelines page near that time for information on which imprints will be opened when."

FICTION "We are currently oversupplied with speculative fiction and are reviewing submissions in SF, fantasy and paranormal suspense by invitation only. We are much in need of GLBT and YA/middle grade, historical and Western, New Age/inspirational (no overtly Christian materials, please), non-category romance, thrillers. As with nonfiction, we encourage people to review what we've already published so as to avoid sending us more of the same, at least, insofar as the plot is concerned. While we're always looking for good specific mysteries, we want original concepts rather than slightly altered versions of what we've already published." Electronic query only.

NONFICTION "The easiest way to figure out what I'm looking for is to look at what we've already done. Our main nonfiction interests are in collections of true ghost stories, ones that have been investigated or thoroughly documented, memoirs that address specific regions and eras and books on the craft of writing. That doesn't mean we won't consider something else." Electronic query only.

TIPS "We're catering to readers who may have loved last year's best seller but not enough to want to read 10 more just like it. Have something different. If it does not fit standard pigeonholes, that's a plus. On the other hand, it has to have an audience. And if you're not prepared to work with us on promotion and marketing, it would be better to look elsewhere."

CANADIAN & INTERNATIONAL BOOK PUBLISHERS

//

While the United States is considered the largest market in children's publishing, the children's publishing world is by no means strictly dominated by the U.S. After all, the most prestigious children's book extravaganza in the world occurs each year in Bologna, Italy, at the Bologna Children's Book Fair, and some of the world's most beloved characters were born in the United Kingdom (i.e., Winnie-the-Pooh and Mr. Potter).

In this section you'll find book publishers from English-speaking countries around the world, including Canada, Australia, New Zealand and the United Kingdom. The listings in this section look just like the U.S. Book Publishers section, and the publishers listed are dedicated to the same goal—publishing great books for children.

Like always, be sure to study each listing and research each publisher carefully before submitting material. Determine whether a publisher is open to U.S. or international submissions, as many publishers accept submissions only from residents of their own country. Some publishers accept illustration samples from foreign artists, but do not accept manuscripts from foreign writers. Illustrators do have a slight edge in this category as many illustrators generate commissions from all around the globe. Visit publishers' websites to be certain they publish the sort of work you do. Visit online bookstores to see if publishers' books are available there. Write or e-mail to request catalogs and submission guidelines.

When mailing requests or submissions out of the United States, remember that U.S. postal stamps are useless on your SASE. Always include International Reply Coupons (IRCs) with your SAE. Each IRC is good for postage for one letter. So if you want the publisher to return your manuscript or send a catalog, be sure to enclose enough IRCs to pay the postage. For more help, visit the United State Postal Service website at www.usps.com. Visit www.timeand date.com/worldclock and American Computer Resources, Inc.'s International Calling Code

Directory at www.the-acr.com/codes/cntrycd.htm before calling or faxing internationally to make sure you're calling at a reasonable time and using the correct numbers.

As in the rest of *Children's Writer's & Illustrator's Market*, the maple leaf ☼ symbol identifies Canadian markets. Look for the International ☽ symbol throughout *Children's Writer's & Illustrator's Market* as well. Several of the Society of Children's Book Writers and Illustrators' (SCBWI) international conferences are listed in the Conferences & Workshops section along with other events in locations around the globe. Look for more information about SCBWI's international chapters on the organization's website, www.scbwi.org. You'll also find international listings in Magazines and Young Writer's & Illustrator's Markets. See "Useful Online Resources" in this book for sites that offer additional international information.

☮ ANNICK PRESS, LTD.

(416)221-4802. Fax: (416)221-8400. E-mail: annick press@annickpress.com. Website: www.annickpress. com. Publishes 5 picture books/year; 6 young readers/ year; 8 middle readers/year; 9 young adult titles/year. 25% of books by first-time authors. "Annick Press maintains a commitment to high-quality books that entertain and challenge. Our publications share fantasy and stimulate judgment and abilities." **Contact:** Rick Wilks, director; Colleen MacMillan, associate publisher. Publishes picture books, juvenile and YA fiction and nonfiction; specializes in trade books. 5,000 queries received/year. 3,000 mss received/year.

○ *Does not accept unsolicited mss.*

FICTION "Recently published *The Apprentice's Masterpiece: A Story of Medieval Spain*, by Melanie Little, ages 12 and up; *Chicken, Pig, Cow series* written and illustrated by Ruth Ohi, ages 2-5; *Single Voices series*, Melanie Little, Editor, ages 14 and up; *Crusades*, by Laura Scandiffio, illustrated by John Mantha, ages 9-11. Publisher of children's books. Publishes hardcover and trade paperback originals. Average print order: 9,000. First novel print order: 7,000. Plans 18 first novels this year. Averages 25 total titles/year. Distributes titles through Firefly Books Ltd. Juvenile, young adult. Not accepting picture books at this time.

NONFICTION Recently published *Pharaohs and Foot Soldiers: One Hundred Ancient Egyptian Jobs You Might Have Desired or Dreaded* by Kristin Butcher, illustrations by Martha Newbigging, ages 9-12; *The Bite of the Mango* by Mariatu Kamara with Susan McClelland, ages 14 and up; *Adventures on the Ancient Silk Road*, by Priscilla Galloway with Dawn Hunter, ages 10 and up; *The Chinese Thought of It: Amazing Inventions and Innovations* by Ting-xing Ye, ages 9-11.

ILLUSTRATION Works with 20 illustrators/year. Illustrations only: Query with samples. Contact: Creative Director.

TERMS Samples cannot be returned. Response sent only if SASE included and submission being kept on file. Pays authors royalty of 5-12% based on retail price. Offers advances (average amount: $3,000). Pays illustrators royalty of 5% minimum. Originals returned to artist at job's completion. Book catalog available on website.

☮ BOREALIS PRESS, LTD.

(613)829-0150. Fax: (613)829-7783. E-mail: drt@bo realispress.com. Website: www.borealispress.com.

8 Mohawk Crescent, Napean ONK 2H 7G6 Canada. Our mission is to publish work that will be of lasting interest in the Canadian book market. Currently emphasizing Canadian fiction, nonfiction, drama, poetry. De-emphasizing children's books. Publishes hardcover and paperback originals and reprints.

FICTION Only material Canadian in content and dealing with significant aspects of the human situation. Query with SASE. Submit clips, 1-2 sample chapters. *No unsolicited mss.*

NONFICTION Only material Canadian in content. Looks for style in tone and language, reader interest, and maturity of outlook. Query with SASE. Submit outline, 2 sample chapters. *No unsolicited mss.*

☮ THE BRUCEDALE PRESS

(519)832-6025. E-mail: brucedale@bmts.com. Website: www.bmts.com/~brucedale. P.O. Box 2259, Port Elgin, ON N0H 2C0 Canada. The Brucedale Press publishes books and other materials of regional interest and merit, as well as literary, historical, and/or pictorial works. Accepts works by Canadian authors only. Submissions accepted in September and March ONLY. Publishes hardcover and trade paperback originals. 50 queries received/year. 30 mss received/year.

HOW TO CONTACT Material should be sent in standard manuscript form: typed, double-spaced, one side only on 8.5×11 white paper. Computer-generated text should use a plain font such as Times New Roman.

TIPS "Our focus is very regional. In reading submissions, I look for quality writing with a strong connection to the Queen's Bush area of Ontario. All authors should visit our website, get a catalog, and read our books before submitting."

☮ BUSTER BOOKS

Imprint of Michael O'Mara Books, 16 Lion Yard, Tremadoc Rd., London SW4 7NQ, United Kingdom. (020)7720-8643. Fax: (022)7720-8953. E-mail: enquiries@mombooks.com. Website: www.mom books.com/busterbooks. "We are dedicated to providing irresistible and fun books for children of all ages. We typically publish black-and-white nonfiction for children aged 8-12 and novelty titles—including doodle books."

NONFICTION Middle readers.

HOW TO CONTACT Prefers synopsis and sample text over complete mss. Responds to queries/mss in 6 weeks. Will consider e-mail submissions.

TIPS "We do not accept fiction submissions. Please do not send original artwork as we cannot guarantee its safety." Visit website before submitting.

CHILD'S PLAY (INTERNATIONAL) LTD.

Children's Play International, Ashworth Rd. Bridgemead, Swindon, Wiltshire SN5 7YD, United Kingdom. E-mail: allday@childs-play.com; neil@childs-play.com; office@childs-play.com. Website: www.childs-play.com. (44)(179)361-6286. Fax: (44)(179)351-2795. E-mail: office@childs-play.co. Estab. 1972. Specializes in nonfiction, fiction, educational material, multicultural material. **Art Acquisitions:** Annie Kubler, art director. "A child's early years are more important than any other. This is when children learn most about the world around them and the language they need to survive and grow. Child's Play aims to create exactly the right material for this all-important time." **Contact:** Sue Baker, Neil Burden, manuscript acquisitions. Specializes in nonfiction, fiction, educational material, multicultural material. Produces 30 picture books/year; 10 young readers/year; 2 middle readers/year. 20% of books by first-time authors.

FICTION Picture books: adventure, animal, concept, contemporary, folktales, multicultural, nature/environment. Young readers: adventure, animal, anthology, concept, contemporary, folktales, humor, multicultural, nature/environment, poetry. Average word length: picture books-0-1,500; young readers-2,000. Recently published *Snug*, by Carol Thompson (ages 0-2, picture book); *The Lost Stars*, by Hannah Cumming (ages 4-8 yrs, picture book); *Uuggh!* by Claudia Boldt (ages 4-8 yrs, picture book); *First Time Doctor/Dentist/Hospital/Vet*, by Jess Stockham (ages 2-5 yrs, picture book); *New Baby Series*, by Rachel Fuller (ages 1-3, board books).

NONFICTION Picture books: activity books, animal, concept, multicultural, music/dance, nature/environment, science. Young readers: activity books, animal, concept, multicultural, music/dance, nature/environment, science. Average word length: picture books—2,000; young readers—3,000. Recently published *Roly Poly Discovery, by Kees Moerbeek (ages 3+ years, novelty).*

HOW TO CONTACT Accepts international submissions. Fiction/nonfiction: Query or submit complete ms. Responds to queries in 10 weeks; mss in 15 weeks.

Publishes book 2 years after acceptance. Considers simultaneous submissions, electronic submissions.

ILLUSTRATION Accepts material from international illustrators. Works with 10 illustrators/year. Uses color artwork only. Reviews ms/illustration packages. For ms/illustration packages: Query or submit ms/illustration packages to Sue Baker, editor. Reviews work for future assignments. If interested in illustrating future titles, query with samples, CD, website address. Submit samples to Annie Kubler, art director. Responds in 10 weeks. Samples not returned. Samples filed.

TERMS Work purchased outright from authors (range: $500-15,000). Pays illustrators by the project (range: $500-15,000). Author sees galleys for review. Originals not returned. Catalog on website. Offers writer's, artist's guidelines for SASE.

TIPS "Look at our website to see the kind of work we do before sending. Do not send cartoons. We do not publish novels. We do publish lots of books with pictures of babies/toddlers."

CHRISTIAN FOCUS PUBLICATIONS

Geanies House, Fearn, Tain Ross-shire, IV20 1TW, Scotland, UK. 44 (0) 1862 871 011. Fax: 44 (0) 1862 871 699. E-mail: info@christianfocus.com. Website: www.christianfocus.com. Estab. 1975. Specializes in Christian material, nonfiction, fiction, educational material. **Manuscript Acquisitions:** Catherine Mackenzie. Publishes 4-6 picture books/year; 4-6 young readers/year; 10-15 middle readers/year; 4-6 young adult books/year. 2% of books by first-time authors.

FICTION Picture books, young readers, adventure, history, religion. Middle readers: adventure, problem novels, religion. Young adult/teens: adventure, history, problem novels, religion. Average word length: young readers—5,000; middle reader—max 10,000; young adult/teen—max 20,000. Recently published *Back Leg of a Goat,* by Penny Reeve, illustrated by Fred Apps (middle reader Christian/world issues); *Trees in the Pavement,* by Jennifer Grosser (teen fiction/Christian/Islamic and multicultural issues); *The Duke's Daughter,* by Lachlan Mackenzie; illustrated by Jeff Anderson (young reader folk tale/Christian).

NONFICTION All levels: activity books, biography, history, religion, science. Average word length: picture books—2-5,000; young readers—5,000; middle readers—5,000-10,000; young adult/teens—10,000-20,000. Recently published *Moses the Child-Kept by God*, by Carine Mackenzie, illustrated by Graham Kennedy (young reader, bible story); *Hearts and Hands-History Lives vol. 4,* by Mindy Withrow, cover illustration by Jonathan Williams (teen, church history); *Little Hands Life of Jesus,* by Carine Mackenzie, illustrated by Rafaella Cosco (picture book, Bible stories about Jesus).

HOW TO CONTACT Fiction/nonfiction: Query or submit outline/synopsis and 3 sample chapters. Responds to queries in 2 weeks/mss in 3 months. Publishes 1 year after acceptance. Will consider electronic submissions and previously published work.

ILLUSTRATION Works on 15-20 potential projects. "Some artists are chosen to do more than one. Some projects just require a cover illustration, some require full color spreads, others black and white line art." **Contact:** Catherine Mackenzie, children's editor. Responds in 2 weeks only if interested. Samples are not returned.

PHOTOGRAPHY "We only purchase royalty free photos from particular photographic associations. However portfolios can be presented to our designer." **Contact:** Daniel van Straaten. Photographers should send cover letter, résumé, published samples client list, portfolio.

TERMS Authors: "We do not discuss financial details of this type in public. Contracts can vary depending on the needs of author/publisher. Illustrators/Photographers: "Each project varies—we determine our budget by determining possible sales—but each illustrator is paid a fee. Originals generally are not returned. We keep them on file so that we can rescan if necessary in the future but they may be sent back to the artist on the proviso that we will be able to obtain them again for the future reprints if necessary. For catalog visit our website at www.christianfocus.com." Writers and artists' guidelines are available for SASE.

TIPS "Be aware of the international market as regards writing style/topics as well as illustration styles. Our company sells rights to European as well as Asian countries. Fiction sales are not as good as they were. Christian fiction for youngsters is not a product that is performing well in comparison to nonfiction such as Christian biography/Bible stories/church history, etc."

☼ COTEAU BOOKS LTD.

2517 Victoria Ave., Regina, SK S4P 0T2, Canada. (306)777-0170. E-mail: coteau@coteaubooks.com. Website: www.coteaubooks.com. **Acquisitions:** Acquistion editor. Publishes 6 juvenile and/or young adult books/year; 14-16 books/year; 25% of books by first-time authors. "Coteau Books publishes the finest Canadian fiction, poetry, drama and children's literature, with an emphasis on western writers."

○ Coteau Books publishes Canadian writers and illustrators only; mss from the U.S. are returned unopened.

FICTION Teen, young readers, middle readers, young adults: adventure, contemporary, fantasy, history, humor, multicultural, nature/environment, science fiction, suspense/mystery. "No didactic, message pieces, nothing religious, no horror. No picture books." Recently published *New: Run Like Jäger,* by Karen Bass (ages 15 and up); *Longhorns & Outlaws,* by Linda Aksomitis (ages 9 and up); *Graveyard of the Sea,* by Penny Draper (ages 9 and up).

NONFICTION Young readers, middle readers, young adult/teen: biography, history, multicultural, nature/environment, social issues.

HOW TO CONTACT Accepts unsolicited mss— fiction accepted from Jan. 1 to April 30; Children's/Teen novels from May 1 to August 31, poetry from September 1 to December 31, Nonfiction accepted any time. Submit complete manuscript, or 3-4 sample chapters, author bio. Responds in 2-3 months to queries; 6 months to mss. No simultaneous submissions. Sometimes comments on rejected mss. No e-mail submissions or queries. Include SASE. Responds to queries/mss in 4 months. Publishes a book 1-2 years after acceptance.

ILLUSTRATION Works with 1-4 illustrators/year. Illustrations only: Submit nonreturnable samples. Responds only if interested. Samples returned with SASE; samples filed.

PHOTOGRAPHY "Very occasionally buys photos from freelancers." Buys stock and assigns work.

TERMS Pays authors royalty based on retail price. Pays illustrators and photographers by the project. Sends galleys to authors; dummies to illustrators. Original artwork returned at job's completion. Book catalog free on request with 9×12 SASE.

☾ DUNDURN PRESS, LTD.

(416)214-5544. E-mail: info@dundurn.com. 3 Church St. Suite 500, Toronto, ON M5E 1M2 Canada. Website: www.dundurn.com. "We DO NOT publish children's books for readers under seven years of age. This includes picture books." **Contact:** Kirk Howard, president and publisher. Dundurn publishes books by Canadian authors. Publishes hardcover and trade paperback originals and reprints. 600 queries received/year.

FICTION No romance, science fiction or experimental. Submit sample chapters, synopsis, author fee, SASE/IRCs or submit complete ms.

NONFICTION Submit cover letter, synopsis, cv, sample chapters, SASE/IRC. Submit complete ms.

HOW TO CONTACT Does not accept e-mail submissions. Submit through postal mail addressed to "Acquistions Editor." Accepts multiple submissions.

☾ FABER AND FABER

Bloomsbury House, 74-77 Great Russell St., London WC2B 3DA, United Kingdom. 020 7927 3800. Fax: 020 7927 3801. E-mail: gachildren@faber.co.uk. Website: www.faber.co.uk.

FICTION Recently published *Grubtown Tales: The Wrong End of the Dog*, by Philip Ardagh (ages 7-10); *Holidays According to Humphrey*, by Betty G. Birney (ages 7-9); *The Chamber of Shadows*, by Justin Richards (ages 10+); *New and Collected Poems for Children*, by Carol Ann Duffy (ages 5-7).

HOW TO CONTACT "Faber and Faber published a wide range of children's fiction and poetry titles. For more information and a full set of our titles, please see www.faber.co.uk/kids. *Faber and Faber does not currently accept any unsolicited submissions to the children's list.*"

☾ FENN PUBLISHING CO.

34 Nixon Rd, .Bolton, ON L7E 1W2, Canada. (905)857-7175. Fax: (905)857-7608. E-mail: fennpubs@hbfenn.com. Website: www.hbfenn.com. Manuscript/Art Acquisitions: C. Jordan Fenn, publisher. Publishes 35 books/year. Publishes children's and young adult fiction.

FICTION Picture books: adventure, animal, sports, adult sports.

HOW TO CONTACT Query or submit complete ms. Responds to queries/mss in 2 months. Illustration: Reviews ms/illustration packages from artists.

Responds only if interested. Samples not returned or filed.

☾ DAVID FICKLING BOOKS

31 Beaumont St., Oxford OX1 2NP, United Kingdom. (018)65-339000. Fax: (018)65-339009. E-mail: tburgess@randomhouse.co.uk. Website: www.davidficklingbooks.co.uk. Publishes 12 fiction titles/year.

FICTION Considers all categories. Recently published *Once Upon a Time in the North*, by Phillip Pullman; *The Curious Incident of the Dog in the Night-time*, by Mark Haddon; *The Boy in the Striped Pyjamas*, by John Boyne.

HOW TO CONTACT Submit 3 sample chapters to David Fickling. Please send submission rather than query letter. Responds to mss in approximatley 3 months.

ILLUSTRATION Reviews ms/illustration packages from artists. Illustrations only: Query with samples.

PHOTOGRAPHY Submit cover letter, résumé, promo pieces.

☾ FITZHENRY & WHITESIDE LTD.

195 Allstate Pkwy. Markham ON L3R 4T8 Canada. (905)477-9700. Fax: (905)477-9179. E-mail: charkin@fitzhenry.ca. Website: www.fitzhenry.ca. Book publisher. **President:** Sharon Fitzhenry; Children's Publisher: Cathy Sandusky. Publishes 3 picture books/year; 4 middle novels/year; 3 young adult titles/year; 3 juvenile nonfiction titles/year. 10% of books by first-time authors. Publishes fiction and nonfiction—social studies, visual arts, biography, environment. Emphasis on Canadian authors and illustrators, subject or perspective.

HOW TO CONTACT Submissions Editor: Christie Harkin. Fiction/nonfiction. Publishes a book 12-24 months after acceptance. See full submission guidelines on website.

ILLUSTRATION Works with approximately 10 illustrators/year. Reviews ms/illustration packages from artists. Submit outline and sample illustration (copy). Illustrations only: Query with samples and promo sheet. Samples not returned unless requested.

PHOTOGRAPHY Buys photos from freelancers. Buys stock and assigns work. Captions required. Uses b&w 8×10 prints; 35mm and 4×5 transparencies, 300+ dpi digital images. Submit stock photo list and promo piece.

TERMS Pays authors 8-10% royalty with escalations. Offers "respectable" advances for picture books,

50/50 split between author and illustrator. Pays illustrators by the project and royalty. Pays photographers per photo. Sends galleys to authors; dummies to illustrators.

TIPS "We respond to quality."

○ GROUNDWOOD BOOKS

E-mail: nfroman@groundwoodbooks.com. 110 Spadina.Suite 801, Toronto ON M5V 2K4 Canada. (416)363-4343. Fax: (416)363-1017. Website: www. groundwoodbooks.com. Publishes 10 picture books/ year; 3 young readers/year; 5 middle readers/year; 5 young adult titles/year, approximately 2 nonfiction titles/year. 10% of books by first-time authors.

FICTION Recently published *Harvey*, by Herva Bouchard and Janice Nadeau; *A Queen of Hearts*, by Martha Brooks (Y/A); *Between Sisters*, by Adwoa Badoe (Y/A); *No Safe Place*, by Deborah Ellis (Y/A).

NONFICTION *Technology (A Groundwork Guide)*, by Wayne Grady; picture books recently published: *No*, by Claudia Rueda; *Hello Baby Board Books*, photographs by Jorge Uzon; *Roslyn Rutabaga and the Biggest Hole on Earth!* by Marie-Louise Gay; *Doggy Slippers*, by Jorge Luján, illustrated by Isol; *Arroz con leche / Rice Pudding* (un poema para cocinar / a cooking poem), by Jorge Argueta, illustrated by Fernando Vilela; *Canadian Railroad Trilogy* by Gordon Lightfoot, illustrated by Ian Wallace; *Book of Big Brothers*, by Cary Fagan, illustrated by Luc Melanson; *Viola Desmond Won't Be Budged*, by Jody Nyasha Warner, illustrated by Richard Rudnicki.

HOW TO CONTACT Fiction: Submit synopsis and sample chapters. Responds to mss in 6-8 months. Will consider simultaneous submissions.

ILLUSTRATION Works with 20 illustrators/year. Reviews ms/illustration packages from artists. Illustrations only: Send résumé, promo sheet, slides, color or b&w copies, and tearsheets. Responds only if interested. Samples not returned.

TERMS Offers advances. Pays illustrators by the project for cover art; otherwise royalty. Sends galleys to authors; dummies to illustrators. Originals returned to artist at job's completion. Backlist available on website.

TIPS "Try to familiarize yourself with our list before submitting to judge whether or not your work is appropriate for Groundwood. Visit our website for guidelines (http://www.groundwoodbooks.com/ gw_guidelines.cgm)."

●○○ HINKLER

45-55 Fairchild St.Heatherton, Victoria Australia 3202. (61)(3)9552-1333. Fax: (61)(3)9552-2566. E-mail: enquiries@hinkler.com.au. Website: www.hinkler books.com. **Acquisitions:** Stephen Ungar, CEO/publisher. "Packaged entertainment affordable to every family."

○ KIDS CAN PRESS

25 Dockside Dr., Toronto, ON M5A 0B5, Canada. U.S. address: 2250 Military Rd., Tonawanda, NY 14150. (416)479-7000. Fax: (416)960-5437.

○ Kids Can Press is currently accepting unsolicited manuscripts from Canadian adult authors only.

FICTION Picture books, young readers: concepts. We do not accept young adult fiction or fantasy novels for any age. Adventure, animal, contemporary, folktales, history, humor, multicultural, nature/environment, special needs, sports, suspense/mystery. Average word length: picture books 1,000-2,000; young readers 750-1,500; middle readers 10,000-15,000; young adults over 15,000. Recently published *Rosie & Buttercup* by Chieri Ugaki, illustrated by Shephane Jorisch (picture book); *The Landing* by John Ibbitson (novel); *Scaredy Squirrel* by Melanie Watt, illustrated by Melanie Watt (picture book).

NONFICTION Picture books: activity books, animal, arts/crafts, biography, careers, concept, health, history, hobbies, how-to, multicultural, nature/environment, science, social issues, special needs, sports. Young readers: activity books, animal, arts/crafts, biography, careers, concept, history, hobbies, how-to, multicultural. Middle readers: cooking, music/dance. Average word length: picture books 500-1,250; young readers 750-2,000; middle readers 5,000-15,000. Recently published *The Kids Book of Canadian Geography*, by Jane Drake and Ann Love (informational activity); *Science, Nature, Environment*; *Moving Day*, by Pamela Hickman, illustrated by Geraldo Valerio (animal/nature); *Everywear*, by Ellen Warwick, illustrated by Bernice Lum (craft book).

HOW TO CONTACT Fiction/nonfiction: Submit outline/synopsis and 2-3 sample chapters. For picture books submit complete ms. Responds within 6 months only if interested. Publishes a book 18-24 months after acceptance.

ILLUSTRATION Works with 40 illustrators/year. Reviews ms/illustration packages from artists. Send color copies of illustration portfolio, cover letter outlining other experience. Contact: Art Director. Illustrations only: Send tearsheets, color photocopies. Responds only if interested.

KOALA BOOKS

P.O. Box 626, Mascot, NSW 1460, Australia. (61)02 9667-2997. Fax: (61)02 9667-2881. E-mail: admin@koalabooks.com.au. Website: www.koalabooks.com. au. **Manuscript Acquisitions:** Children's Editor. **Art Acquisitions:** Children's Designer, deb@koalabooks. com.au. "KOALA Books is an independent wholly Australian-owned children's book publishing house. Our strength is providing quality books for children at competitive prices."

HOW TO CONTACT Accepts material from residents of Australia only. Hard copy only. Picture books only: Submit complete ms, blurb, brief author biography, list of author's published works. Also SASE large enough for ms return. Responds to mss in 3 months.

ILLUSTRATION Accepts material from residents of Australia only. Illustrations only: Send cover letter, brief bio, list of published works and samples (color photographs or photocopies) in A4 folder suitable for filing." Contact: Children's Designer. Responds only if interested. Samples not returned; samples filed.

TERMS Pays authors royalty of 10% based on retail price or work purchased outright occasionally (may be split with illustrator).

TIPS "Take a look at our website to get an idea of the kinds of books we publish. A few hours research in a quality children's bookshop would be helpful when choosing a publisher."

FRANCES LINCOLN CHILDREN'S BOOKS

Frances Lincoln, 4 Torriano Mew, Torriano Ave., London NW5 2RZ. (020)7284-4009. E-mail: FLCB@franceslincoln.com. Website: www.franceslincoln.com. Estab. 1977. Specializes in trade books, nonfiction, fiction, multicultural material. Publishes 84 picture books/year; 2 young readers/year; 11 middle readers/year; 2 young adult titles/readers; 6% of books by first-time authors. "Our company was founded by Frances Lincoln in 1977. We published our first books two years later, and we have been creating illustrated books of the highest quality ever since, with special emphasis on gardening, walking and the outdoors, art, architecture, design and landscape. In 1983, we

started to publish illustrated books for children. Since then we have won many awards and prizes with both fiction and nonfiction children's books."

FICTION Picture books, young readers, middle readers, young adults: adventure, animal, anthology, fantasy, folktales, health, history, humor, multicultural, nature/environment, special needs, sports. Average word length: picture books—1,000; young readers—9,788; middle readers—20,653; young adults—35,407. Recently published *The Sniper*, by James Riordan (young adult/teen novel); *Amazons! Women Warriors of the World*, by Sally Pomme Clayton, illustrated by Sophie Herxheimer (picture book); *Young Inferno*, by John Agard, illustrated by Satoshi Kitamura (graphic novel/picture book).

NONFICTION Picture books, young readers, middle readers, young adult: activity books, animal, biography, careers, cooking, graphic novels, history, multicultural, nature/environment, religion, social issues, special needs. Average word length: picture books—1,000; middle readers—29,768. Recently published *Tail-End Charlie,* by Mick Manning and Brita Granstroöm (picture book); *Our World of Water,* by Beatrice Hollyer, with photographers by Oxfam (picture book); *Look! Drawing the Line in Art,* by Gillian Wolfe (picture book).

HOW TO CONTACT Fiction/nonfiction: Submit query (by e-mail—letter queries are rarely responded to). Responds as soon as possible; mss in minimum 6 weeks. Publishes a book 18 months after acceptance. Will consider e-mail submissions, simultaneous submissions, and previously published work.

ILLUSTRATION Works with approx 56 illustrators/year. Uses both color and b&w. Reviews ms/illustration packages from artist. Sample illustrations. Illustrations only: Query with samples. Responds only if interested. Samples are returned with SASE. Samples are kept on file only if interested.

PHOTOGRAPHY Buys stock images and assigns work. Uses children, multicultural photos. Submit cover letter, published samples, or portfolio.

TERMS Pays authors royalty. Offers advances. Originals returned to artist at job's completion. Catalog available on website.

LITTLE TIGER PRESS

1 The Coda Centre, 189 Munster Rd., London SW6 6AW, United Kingdom. Website: www.littletiger press.com.

FICTION Picture books: animal, concept, contemporary, humor. Average word length: picture books—750 words or less. Recently published *Gruff the Grump*, by Steve Smallman and Cee Biscoe (ages 3-7, picture book); *One Special Day*, by M. Christina Butler and Tina Macnaughton (ages 3-7, touch-and-feel, picture book).

ILLUSTRATION Digital submissions preferred; please send in digital samples as pdf or jpeg attachments to artsubmissions@littletiger.co.uk. Files should be flattened and no bigger than 1.0 MB per attachment. Include name and contact details on any attachments. Printed submissions please send in printed color samples as A4 printouts. Do not send in original artwork as we cannot be held responsible for unsolicited original artwork being lost or damaged in the post. We aim to acknowledge unsolicited material and to return material if so requested within three months. Please include SAE if return of material is requested.

TIPS "Every reasonable care is taken of the manuscripts and samples we receive, but we cannot accept responsibility for any loss or damage. Try to read or look at as many books on the Little Tiger Press list before sending in your material. Refer to our website www.littletigerpress.com for further details."

☺ LOBSTER PRESS

1620 Sherbrooke St. W.Suites C&D, Montreal QC H3H 1C9 Canada. (514)904-1100. Fax: (514)904-1101. E-mail: lobsterpresssubmissions@gmail.com. Website: www.lobsterpress.com. **Editorial Director**: Mahak Jain. Publishes picture books, fiction and nonfiction for all ages. We primarily publish manuscripts written by permanent residents or citizens of Canada, with some exceptions. Our goal is to publish original, lively, and engaging books that capture the reader's imagination and thrill minds.

FICTION: We are looking for fiction that emphasizes the emotional journey of its characters through strong, marketable plots. We especially favor genre stories that both inspire our fancy but also maintain a sense of realism—fantasy, mystery, horror, sci-fi, comedy, and more. Picture books should be no more than a 1,000 words. Chapter books for younger readers will ideally be around 10,000 words, though we are flexible. Middle readers should be 35-45,000 words. YA can be anywhere between 45,000 to 80,000 words (longer manuscripts are unlikely to be successful).

NONFICTION We are currently accepting proposals for nonfiction stories that are timely and relevant to the present concerns of children and teenagers. We favor books that address issues such as bullying, environmental concerns, volunteerism, etc., or that provide information in an original, fun manner on topics such as money, character building, developing good habits, etc. Successful writers will have an established platform either as an expert in their field or in journalism.

HOW TO CONTACT No mailed submissions will be accepted. All submissions must be e-mailed to lobsterpresssubmissions@gmail.com. We will only respond to those submissions that we are interested in pursuing. Please take a look at our submissions guidelines in detail before sending any manuscripts or proposals.

ILLUSTRATION Please e-mail lobsterpresssubmissions@gmail.com with a link to your online portfolio. Attachments will not be opened under any circumstances. Illustrators may mail samples of artwork, but this is not advised.

TERMS Authors and illustrators are paid through royalties (5-10%) and the amount varies with the project.

☺ MANOR HOUSE PUBLISHING, INC.

E-mail: mbdavie@manor-house.biz. Website: www.manor-house.biz. "We are a Canadian publisher, so manuscripts should be Canadian in content and aimed as much as possible at a wide, general audience. At this point in time, we are only publishing books by Canadian citizens residing in Canada." **Contact:** Mike Davie, president (novels, poetry and nonfiction). Publishes hardcover, trade paperback, and mass market paperback originals and reprints. 30 queries received/year. 20 mss received/year.

FICTION Stories should have Canadian settings and characters should be Canadian, but content should have universal appeal to wide audience. Query via e-mail. Submit proposal package, clips, bio, 3 sample chapters. Submit complete ms.

NONFICTION Query via e-mail. Submit proposal package, outline, bio, 3 sample chapters. Submit complete ms.

HOW TO CONTACT Query via e-mail. Submit proposal package, outline, bio, 3 sample chapters.

TIPS "Our audience includes everyone—the general public/mass audience. Self-edit your work first, make sure it is well written with strong Canadian content."

✎ MANTRA LINGUA

Global House, 303 Ballards Lane, London N12 8NP, United Kingdom. (44)(208)445-5123. Website: www.mantralingua.com. **Manuscript Acquisitions:** Series Editor.

○ Mantra Lingua publishes dual-language books in English and more that 42 languages. They also publish talking books and resources with their Talking Pen technology, which brings sound and interactivity to their products. They will consider good contemporary stories, myths and folklore for picture books only.

FICTION Picture books, young readers, middle readers: folktales, multicultural stories, myths. Average word length: picture books—1,000-1,500; young readers—1,000-1,500. Recently published *Keeping Up With Cheetah,* by Lindsay Camp, illustrated by Jill Newton (ages 3-7); *Lion Fables*, by Heriette Barkow, illustrated by Jago Ormerod (ages 6-10).

HOW TO CONTACT Fiction: Submit outline/synopsis (250 words); mail submissions. Include SASE if you'd like ms returned.

ILLUSTRATION Uses 2D animation for CD-ROMs. Query with samples. Responds only if interested. Samples not returned; samples filed.

◐ MOOSE ENTERPRISE BOOK & THEATRE PLAY PUBLISHING

Imprint of Moose Hide Books, 684 Walls Rd. Sault Ste. Marie ON P6A 5K6 Canada. E-mail: mooseenterprises@on.aibn.com. Website: www.moosehidebooks.com. **Manuscript Acquisitions:** Edmond Alcid. Publishes 2 middle readers/year; 2 young adult titles/year. 75% of books by first-time authors. Editorial philosophy: "To assist the new writers of moral standards."

○ This publisher does not offer payment for stories published in its anthologies and/or book collections. Be sure to send a SASE for guidelines.

FICTION Middle readers, young adults: adventure, fantasy, humor, suspense/mystery, story poetry. Recently published *Realm of the Golden Feather,* by C.R. Ginter (ages 12 and up, fantasy); *Tell Me a Story*, short story collection by various authors (ages 9-11, humor/adventure); *Spirits of Lost Lake*, by James Walters (ages 12 and up, adventure); *Rusty Butt-Treasure of the Ocean Mist*, by R.E. Forester.

NONFICTION Middle readers, young adults: biography, history, multicultural.

HOW TO CONTACT Fiction/nonfiction: Query. Responds to queries in 1 month; mss in 3 months. Publishes book 1 year after acceptance. Will consider simultaneous submissions.

ILLUSTRATION Uses primarily b&w artwork for interiors, cover artwork in color. Illustrations only: Query with samples. Responds in 1 month, if interested. Samples returned with SASE; samples filed.

TERMS Pays royalties. Originals returned to artist at job's completion. Manuscript and art guidelines available for SASE.

TIPS "Do not copy trends; be yourself—give me something new, something different."

◑ ORCA BOOK PUBLISHERS

P.O. Box 5626, Stn. B, Victoria BC V8R 6S4, Canada. Fax: (877)408-1551. E-mail: orca@orcabook.com. Website: www.orcabook.com. Publishes 7 picture books/year; 16 middle readers/year; 10 young adult titles/year. 25% of books by first-time authors. **Contact:** Christi Howes, editor (picture books); Sarah Harvey, editor (young readers); Andrew Wooldridge, editor (juvenile and teen fiction); Bob Tyrrell, publisher (YA, teen). Publishes hardcover and trade paperback originals, and mass market paperback originals and reprints. 2,500 queries received/year. 1,000 mss received/year.

○ Only publishes Canadian authors.

FICTION Picture books: animals, contemporary, history, nature/environment. Middle readers: contemporary, history, fantasy, nature/environment, problem novels, graphic novels. Young adults: adventure, contemporary, hi-lo (Orca Soundings), history, multicultural, nature/environment, problem novels, suspense/mystery, graphic novels. Average word length: picture books—500-1,500; middle readers—20,000-35,000; young adult—25,000-45,000; Orca Soundings—13,000-15,000; Orca Currents—13,000-15,000. Published *Tall in the Saddle,* by Anne Carter, illustrated by David McPhail (ages 4-8, picture book); *Me and Mr. Mah,* by Andrea Spalding, illustrated by Janet Wilson (ages 5 and up, picture book); *Alone at Ninety Foot*, by Katherine Holubitsky (young adult). Ask for guidelines, find out what we publish. Looking for children's fiction. No romance, science fiction. Query with SASE. Submit proposal package, outline, clips, 2-5 sample chapters, SASE.

NONFICTION Only publishes Canadian authors. Query with SASE.

HOW TO CONTACT Fiction: Submit complete ms if picture book; submit outline/synopsis and 3 sample chapters. "All queries or unsolicited submissions should be accompanied by a SASE." Responds to queries in 2 months; mss in 3 months. Publishes a book 18-36 months after acceptance. Submission guidelines available online.

ILLUSTRATION Works with 8-10 illustrators/year. Reviews ms/illustration packages from artists. Submit ms with 3-4 pieces of final art. "Reproductions only, no original art please." Illustrations only: Query with samples; provide résumé, slides. Responds in 2 months. Samples returned with SASE; samples filed.

TERMS Pays authors royalty of 5% for picture books, 10% for novels, based on retail price. Offers advances (average amount: $2,000). Pays illustrators royalty of 5% minimum based on retail price and advance on royalty. Sends galleys to authors. Original artwork returned at job's completion if picture books. Book catalog available for SASE with $2 first-class postage. Manuscript guidelines available for SASE. Art guidelines not available.

TIPS "Our audience is students in grades K-12. Know our books, and know the market."

PEMMICAN PUBLICATIONS, INC.

150 Henry Ave., Winnipeg MB R3B 0J7, Canada. (204)589-6346. Fax: (204)589-2063. E-mail: pemmican@pemmican.mb.ca. Website: www.pemmican.mb.ca. **Contact:** Randal McILroy, managing editor (Metis culture & heritage). "Pemmican Publications is a Metis publishing house, with a mandate to publish books by Metis authors and illustrators and with an emphasis on culturally relevant stories. We encourage writers to learn a little about Pemmican before sending samples. Pemmican publishes titles in the following genres: Adult Fiction, which includes novels, story collections and anthologies; Nonfiction, with an emphasis on social history and biography reflecting Metis experience; Children's and Young Adult titles; Aboriginal languages, including Michif and Cree." Publishes trade paperback originals and reprints. 120 queries received/year. 120 mss received/year.

FICTION All manuscripts must be Metis culture and heritage related. Submit proposal package including outline and 3 sample chapters.

NONFICTION All mss must be Metis culture and heritage related. Submit proposal package including outline and 3 sample chapters.

TIPS "Our mandate is to promote Metis authors, illustrators and stories. No agent is necessary."

PICCADILLY PRESS

5 Castle Rd.London NW1 8PR United Kingdom. (44)(207)267-4492. Fax: (44)(207)267-4493. E-mail: books@piccadillypress.co.uk Website: www.piccadillypress.co.uk.

FICTION Picture books: animal, contemporary, fantasy, nature/environment. Young adults: contemporary, humor, problem novels. Average word length: picture books—500-1,000; young adults—25,000-35,000. Recently published *Fifty Fifty*, by S.L. Powell (young adult); *Camden Town Tales: The Celeb Next Door*, by Hilary Freeman (young adult); *Letters From an Alien Schoolboy*, by Ros Asquit (Children Age 6+); *Grub in Love*, by Abi Burlingham and Sarah Warburton (picture book).

NONFICTION Young adults: self help (humorous). Average word length: young adults—25,000-35,000. *Everything You Wanted to Ask About Periods*, by Tricia Kreitman, Dr. Fiona Findlay & Dr. Rosemary Jones.

HOW TO CONTACT Fiction: Submit complete ms for picture books or submit outline/synopsis and 2 sample chapters for YA. Enclose a brief cover letter and SASE for reply. Nonfiction: Submit outline/synopsis and 2 sample chapters. Responds to mss in approximately 6 weeks.

ILLUSTRATION Illustrations only: Query with samples (do not send originals).

TIPS "Keep a copy of your manuscript on file."

PIPERS' ASH, LTD.

Pipers' Ash, Church Road, Christian Malford, Chippenham, Wiltshire SN15 4BW, United Kingdom. (44)(124)972-0563. Fax: (44)(870)056-8916. E-mail: pipersash@supamasu.com. Website: www.supamasu.com. Publishes 1 middle reader/year; 2 young adult titles/year. 90% of books by first-time authors. Editorial philosophy is "to discover new authors with talent and potential." **Contact:** Manuscript Evaluation Desk. Publishes hardcover and paperback editions. 1,000 queries received/year. 400 mss received/year.

FICTION Young readers, middle readers: adventure. Young adults: problem novels. Average word length: young readers—10,000; middle readers—20,000; young adults—30,000. Visit website. We publish 30,000-word novels and short story collections. Query with SASE. Submit sample chapters, 25-word synopsis (that sorts out the writers from the wafflers).

NONFICTION Young readers: history, multicultural, nature/environment. Middle readers: biography, history, multicultural, nature/environment, sports. Young adults: self help, social issues, special needs. Average word length: young readers—10,000; middle readers—20,000; young adults—30,000. Query with SASE.

HOW TO CONTACT Fiction/nonfiction: Query. Responds to queries in 1 week; mss in 3 months. Publishes book 2 months after acceptance. Will consider e-mail submissions, previously published work.

TERMS Pays authors royalty of 10% based on wholesale price. Sends galleys to authors. Offers ms guidelines for SASE. "Include adequate postage for return of manuscript plus publisher's guidelines."

TIPS "Study the market! Check your selected publisher's catalogue and website."

● MATHEW PRICE LTD.

Albany Court, Albury, Thame, Oxon OX9 2LP, United Kingdom. Website: www.mathewprice.com. U.S. address: 12300 Ford St., Suite 455, Dallas, TX. 75234. E-mail: info@mathewprice.com. **Manuscript Acquisitions:** Mathew Price, chairman. Publishes 2-3 picture books/year; 2 young readers/year; 1-2 gift book/year. We accept submissions by e-mail only. Looking especially for stories for 2- to 4-year-olds and fiction for young adults, especially fantasy. "Mathew Price Ltd. works to bring to market talented authors and artists profitably by publishing books for children that lift the hearts of people young and old all over the world."

FICTION Will consider any category.

HOW TO CONTACT Submit mss by e-mail only to submissions@mathewprice.com.

ILLUSTRATION Accepts material from artists in other countries. Uses color artwork only. Reviews ms/illustration packages from artists sent by e-mail only. Illustrations only: send PDFs or JPEGs by e-mail.

TERMS Originals returned to artist at job's completion. Book catalog available. All imprints included in a single catalog. Catalog available on website.

TIPS "Study the market; keep a copy of all your work."

●● QED PUBLISHING

The Quarto Group, 226 City Rd., London EC1V 2TT, United Kingdom. +44 (0)20 7812 8633. Fax: +44 (0)20 7253 4370. E-mail: zetad@quarto.com. Website: www.qed-publishing.co.uk. Estab. 2003. Specializes in trade books, educational material, multicultural material. **Associate Publisher:** Zeta Davies. Produces 8 picture books/year; 20 nonfiction readers/year, 40 general reference books/year. Strives for "editorial excellence with ground-breaking design."

FICTION Average word length: picture books—500; young readers—3,000; middle readers—3,500. Recently published *The Tickety Tale Teller*, by Maureen Haselhurst, illustrated by Barbara Vagnozzi (ages 4+); *The Thief of Bracken Farm*, by Emma Barnes, illustrated by Hannah Wood (ages 4+); *The Big Fuzzy*, by Caroline Castle, illustrated by Daniel Howarth (ages 4+).

NONFICTION Picture books: animal, arts/crafts, biography, geography, reference, science. Young readers: activity books, animal, arts/crafts, biography, geography, reference, science. Middle readers: activity books, animal, arts/crafts, biography, geography, science. Average word length: picture books—500; young readers—3,000; middle readers—3,500. Recently published *Exploring the Earth*, by Peter Grego (ages 7 and up); *The Ancient Egyptians*, by Fiona Macdonald (ages 7+, science); *The Great Big Book of Pirated*, by John Malam (ages 7+, history).

HOW TO CONTACT Fiction/nonfiction: Query.

ILLUSTRATION Accepts material from international illustrators. Works with 25 illustrators/year. For ms/illustration packages: Submit ms with 2 pieces of final art. Reviews work for future assignments. Submit samples to Amanda Askew, editor. Responds in 2 weeks. Samples filed.

PHOTOGRAPHY Buys stock images and assigns work. Submit photos to Zeta Davies, creative director. Uses step-by-step photos. For first contact, send CD of work or online URL.

TIPS "Be persistent."

◐ RAINCOAST BOOK DISTRIBUTION, LTD.

(604)448-7100. Fax: (604)270-7161. E-mail: info@raincoast.com. Website: www.raincoast.com. Publishes hardcover and trade paperback originals and reprints. 3,000 queries received/year.

FICTION *No unsolicited mss.*

NONFICTION *No unsolicited mss.* Query with SASE.

● RANDOM HOUSE CHILDREN'S BOOKS

61-63 Uxbridge Rd., London W5 5SA, England. (44)(208)579-2652. Fax: (44)(208)579-5479. E-mail: childrenseditorial@randomhouse.co.uk. Website: www.kidsatrandomhouse.co.uk. Book publisher. **Manuscript Acquisitions:** Philippa Dickinson, managing director. Imprints: Doubleday, Corgi, Johnathan Cape, Hutchinson, Bodley Head, Red Fox, David Fickling Books, Tamarind Books. Publishes 120 picture books/year; 120 fiction titles/year.

FICTION Picture books: adventure, animal, anthology, contemporary, fantasy, folktales, humor, multicultural, nature/environment, poetry, suspense/mystery. Young readers: adventure, animal, anthology, contemporary, fantasy, folktales, humor, multicultural, nature/environment, poetry, sports, suspense/mystery. Middle readers: adventure, animal, anthology, contemporary, fantasy, folktales, humor, multicultural, nature/environment, problem novels, romance, sports, suspense/mystery. Young adults: adventure, contemporary, fantasy, humor, multicultural, nature/environment, problem novels, romance, science fiction, suspense/mystery. Average word length: picture books—800; young readers—1,500-6,000; middle readers—10,000-15,000; young adults—20,000-45,000.

HOW TO CONTACT Only interested in agented material. No unsolicited mss or picture books.

ILLUSTRATION Works with 50 illustrators/year. Reviews ms/illustration packages from artists. Query with samples. Contact: Margaret Hope. Samples are returned with SASE (IRC).

PHOTOGRAPHY Buys photos from freelancers. Contact: Margaret Hope. Photo captions required. Uses color or b&w prints. Submit cover letter, published samples.

TERMS Pays authors royalty. Offers advances. Pays illustrators by the project or royalty. Pays photographers by the project or per photo.

TIPS "Although Random House is a big publisher, each imprint only publishes a small number of books each year. Our lists for the next few years are already full. Any book we take on from a previously unpublished author has to be truly exceptional. Manuscripts should be sent to us via literary agents."

◎ RONSDALE PRESS

3350 W. 21st Ave. Vancouver BC V6S 1G7 Canada. (604)738-4688. Fax: (604)731-4548. E-mail: ronsdale@shaw.ca. Website: ronsdalepress.com. Estab. 1988. Book publisher. **Manuscript/Art Acquisitions:** Veronica Hatch, children's editor. Publishes 3 children's books/year. 40% of titles by first-time authors. "Ronsdale Press is a Canadian literary publishing house that publishes 12 books each year, three of which are children's titles. Of particular interest are books involving children exploring and discovering new aspects of Canadian history." **Contact:** Ronald B. Hatch, director (fiction, poetry, social commentary); Veronica Hatch, managing director (children's literature). Canadian authors only. Ronsdale publishes fiction, poetry, regional history, biography and autobiography, books of ideas about Canada, as well as young adult historical fiction. Publishes trade paperback originals. 300 queries received/year. 800 mss received/year.

FICTION Young adults: Canadian novels. Average word length: middle readers and young adults—50,000. Recently published *Red Goodwin*, by John Wilson (ages 10-14); *Tragic Links*, by Cathy Beveridge (ages 10-14); *Dark Times*, edited by Ann Walsh (anthology of short stories, ages 10 and up); *Submarine Outlaw*, by Phillip Roy; *The Way Lies North*, by Jean Rae Baxter (ages 10-14). *Canadian authors only.* Query with at least the first 80 pages. Short stories must have some previous magazine publication.

NONFICTION Middle readers, young adults: animal, biography, history, multicultural, social issues. Average word length: young readers—90; middle readers—90. "We publish a number of books for children and young adults in the age 8 to 15 range. We are especially interested in YA historical novels. **We regret that we can no longer publish picture books.**"

HOW TO CONTACT Accepts material from residents of Canada only. Fiction/nonfiction: Submit complete ms. Responds to queries in 2 weeks; mss in 2 months. Publishes a book 1 year after acceptance. Will consider simultaneous submissions.

ILLUSTRATION Works with 2 illustrators/year. Reviews ms/illustration packages from artists. Requires only cover art. Responds in 2 weeks. Samples returned with SASE. Originals returned to artist at job's completion.

TERMS Pays authors royalty of 10% based on retail price. Pays illustrators by the project $400-800. Sends galleys to authors. Book catalog available for 8½×11 envelope and $1 postage; ms and art guidelines available for SASE.

TIPS "Ronsdale Press is a literary publishing house, based in Vancouver, and dedicated to publishing books from across Canada, books that give Canadians new insights into themselves and their country. We aim to publish the best Canadian writers."

☼ SECOND STORY PRESS

20 Maud St., Suite 401, Toronto ON M5V 2M5, Canada. (416)537-7850. Fax: (416)537-0588. E-mail: info@secondstorypress.ca. Website: www.secondstorypress.ca.

FICTION Considers non-sexist, non-racist and non-violent stories, as well as historical fiction, chapter books, picture books. Recently published *Lilly and the Paper Man*, by Rebecca Upjohn; *Mom and Mum Are Getting Married!*, by Ken Setterington.

NONFICTION Picture books: biography. Recently published *Hiding Edith: A True Story*, by Kathy Kacer (a new addition to our Holocaust remembrance series for young readers).

HOW TO CONTACT Accepts appropriate material from residents of Canada only. Fiction and nonfiction: Submit complete ms or submit outline and sample chapters by postal mail only. No electronic submissions or queries.

☻ TAFELBERG PUBLISHERS

Imprint of NB Publishers, 40 Heerengracht, Cape Town, Western Cape 8001 South Africa. (27)(21)406-3033. Fax: (27)(21)406-3812. E-mail: lsteyn@tafelberg.com. Website: www.tafelberg.com. **Manuscript Acquisitions:** Louise Steyn, publisher. Publishes 3 picture books/year; 2 young readers/year; 2 middle readers/year; 4 young adult titles/year. 40% of books by first-time authors. **Contact:** Danita van Romburgh, editorial secretary. General publisher best known for Afrikaans fiction, authoritative political works, children's/youth literature, and a variety of illustrated and nonillustrated nonfiction.

FICTION Picture books, young readers: animal, anthology, contemporary, fantasy, folktales, hi-lo, humor, multicultural, nature/environment, science fiction, special needs. Middle readers, young adults: animal (middle reader only), contemporary, fantasy, hi-lo, humor, multicultural, nature/environment, problem novels, science fiction, special needs, sports, suspense/mystery. Average word length: picture books—1,500-7,500; young readers—25,000; middle readers—15,000; young adults—40,000. Recently published *Because Pula Means Rain*, by Jenny Robson (ages 12-15, realism); *BreinBliksem*, by Fanie Viljoen (ages 13-18, realism); *SuperZero*, by Darrel Bristow-Bovey (ages 9-12, realism/humor). Submit complete ms.

NONFICTION Submit complete ms.

HOW TO CONTACT Fiction: Query or submit complete ms. Responds to queries in 2 weeks; mss in 2-6 months. Publishes book 1 year after acceptance.

ILLUSTRATION Works with 2-3 illustrators/year. Reviews ms/illustration packages from artists. Send ms with dummy or e-mail and jpegs. Contact: Louise Steyn, publisher. Illustrations only: Query with brochure, photocopies, résumé, URL, jpegs. Responds only if interested. Samples not returned.

TERMS Pays authors royalty of 15-18% based on wholesale price. Pays illustrators by the project or royalty based on wholesale price. Sends galleys to authors. Originals returned to artist at job's completion.

TIPS "Writers: Story needs to have a South African or African style. Illustrators: I'd like to look, but the chances of getting commissioned are slim. The market is small and difficult. Do not expect huge advances. Editorial staff attended or plans to attend the following conferences: IBBY, Frankfurt, SCBWI Bologna."

☼ THISTLEDOWN PRESS LTD.

Website: www.thistledownpress.com/. 118 20th Street West, Saskatoon, SK, S7M 0W6 Canada. (306)244-1722. Fax: (306)244-1762. E-mail: tdpress@thistledown.sk.com. **Acquisitions:** Allan Forrie, publisher. Publishes numerous middle reader and young adult titles/year. "Thistledown originates books by Canadian authors only, although we have co-published titles by authors outside Canada. We do not publish children's picture books."

○ Thistledown publishes books by Canadian authors only.

FICTION Middle readers, young adults: adventure, anthology, contemporary, fantasy, humor, poetry, romance, science fiction, suspense/mystery, short stories. Average word length: young adults—40,000. Recently published *Up All Night*, edited by R.P. MacIntyre (young adult, anthology); *Offside*, by Cathy Beveridge (young adult, novel); *Cheeseburger Subversive*, by Richard Scarsbrook; *The Alchemist's Daughter*, by Eileen Kernaghan.

HOW TO CONTACT Submit outline/synopsis and sample chapters. "We do not accept unsolicted full-length manuscripts. These will be returned." Responds to queries in 4 months. Publishes a book about 1 year after acceptance. No simultaneous submissions. No e-mailed submissions.

ILLUSTRATION Prefers agented illustrators but "not mandatory." Works with few illustrators. Illustrations only: Query with samples, promo sheet, slides, tearsheets. Responds only if interested. Samples returned with SASE; samples filed.

TERMS Pays authors royalty of 10-12% based on net dollar sales. Pays illustrators and photographers by the project (range: $250-750). Sends galleys to authors. Original artwork returned at job's completion. Book catalog free on request. Manuscript guidelines for #10 envelope and IRC.

TIPS "Send cover letter including publishing history and SASE."

○ TRADEWIND BOOKS

(604)662-4405. E-mail: tradewindbooks@mail.lycos.com. Website: www.tradewindbooks.com. **Manuscript Acquisitions**: Michael Katz, publisher. **Art Acquisitions:** Carol Frank, art director. Senior Editor: R. David Stephens. Publishes 2-3 picture books; 3 young adult titles/year; 1 book of poetry; 1 chapter book. 15% of books by first-time authors. **Contact:** Michael Katz, publisher; Carol Frank, art director. "Tradewind Books publishes juvenile picture books and young adult novels. Requires that submissions include evidence that author has read at least 3 titles published by Tradewind Books." Publishes hardcover and trade paperback originals.

FICTION Picture books: adventure, multicultural, folktales. Average word length: 900 words. Recently published *City Kids*, by X.J. Kennedy and illustrated by Phillpe Beha; *Roxy*, by PJ Reece; *Viva Zapata!* by Emilie Smith and illustrated by Stefan Czernecki. Send complete ms for picture books.

HOW TO CONTACT Picture books: Submit complete ms. YA novels by Canadian authors only. Chapter books by U.S. authors considered. Will consider simultaneous submissions. Do not send query letter. Responds to mss in 12 weeks. Unsolicited submissions accepted only if authors have read a selection of books published by Tradewind Books. Submissions must include a reference to these books.

ILLUSTRATION Works with 3-4 illustrators/year. Reviews ms/illustration packages from artists. Send illustrated ms as dummy. Illustrations only: Query with samples. Responds only if interested. Samples returned with SASE; samples filed.

TERMS Royalties negotiable. Offers advances against royalties. Originals returned to artist at job's completion. Catalog available on website.

○ USBORNE PUBLISHING

83-85 Saffron Hill, London EC1N 8RT, United Kingdom. (44)(020)7430-2800. Fax: (44)(020)7430-1562. Website: www.usborne.com. **Manuscript Acquisitions:** Fiction Editorial Assistant. **Art Acquisitions:** Usborne Art Department. "Usborne Publishing is a multiple-award-winning, world-wide children's publishing company specializing in superbly researched and produced information books with a unique appeal to young readers."

FICTION Young readers, middle readers: adventure, contemporary, fantasy, history, humor, multi-cultural, nature/environment, science fiction, suspense/mystery, strong concept-based or character-led series. Average word length: young readers—5,000-10,000; middle readers—25,000-50,000. Recently published *Secret Mermaid series* by Sue Mongredien (ages 7 and up); *School Friends* by Ann Bryant (ages 9 and up).

HOW TO CONTACT Refer to guidelines on website or request from above address. Fiction: No unsolicited submissions accepted. Does not accept submissions for nonfiction or picture books.

ILLUSTRATION Works with 100 illustrators per year. Illustrations only: Query with samples. Samples not returned; samples filed.

PHOTOGRAPHY Contact: Usborne Art Department. Submit samples.

TERMS Pays authors royalty.

TIPS "Do not send any original work and, sorry, but we cannot guarantee a reply."

○ WEIGL EDUCATIONAL PUBLISHERS LIMITED

6325 Tenth St. SE, Calgary AB T2H 2Z9, Canada. (403)233-7747. Fax: (403)233-7769. E-mail: linda@weigl.com. Website: www.weigl.ca. Publishes textbooks, library and multimedia resources. Subjects include social studies, biography, life skills, environment/science studies, multicultural, language arts, geography. Photos used for text illustrations, book covers. "Textbook publisher catering to juvenile and young adult audience (K-12)." Makes outright purchase. Responds ASAP to queries. Query with SASE. Publishes hardcover originals and reprints, school library softcover.

✪ WHITECAP BOOKS, LTD.

(640)980-9852. Fax: (604)980-8197. E-mail: white cap@whitecap.ca. Website: www.whitecap.ca. Publishes 0-1 young reader/year; 0-1 middle reader/year; 3-4 young adult/year. Whitecap Books is currently de-emphasizing the children's and YA adventure in series only. Manuscript guidelines available on website. **Contact:** Rights & Acquisitions. "Whitecap Books is a general trade publisher with a focus on food and wine titles. Although we are interested in reviewing unsolicited ms submissions, please note that we only accept submissions that meet the needs of our current publishing program. Please see some of most recent releases to get an idea of the kinds of titles we are interested in." Publishes hardcover and trade paperback originals. 500 queries received/year. 1,000 mss received/year.

FICTION No children's picture books or adult fiction. See guidelines.

NONFICTION Young children's and middle reader's nonfiction focusing mainly on nature, wildlife and animals. "Writers should take the time to research our list and read the submission guidelines on our website. This is especially important for children's writers and cookbook authors. We will only consider submissions that fall into these categories: cookbooks, wine and spirits, regional travel, home and garden, Canadian history, North American natural history, juvenile series-based fiction." "At this time, we are not accepting the following categories: self-help or inspirational books, political, social commentary, or issue books, general how-to books, biographies or memoirs, business and finance, art and architecture, religion and spirituality." Submit cover letter, synopsis, SASE via ground mail. See guidelines online at website.

HOW TO CONTACT Query to Rights and Acquisitions. Accepts unagented work and multiple submissions. Responds to queries/ms in 6 months. Publishes a book approximately 1 year after acceptance. Include SASE with sufficient return postage. Mark envelopes "submissions." Please send international postal vouchers with SASE if submission is from U.S.A. No e-mail submissions.

ILLUSTRATION Works with 1-2 illustrators/year. Uses color artwork only. Reviews ms/illustration packages from artists. Query. Contact: Rights and Acquisitions. Illustrations only: Send postcard sample with tearsheets. Contact: Michelle Mayne, art director. Responds only if interested.

PHOTOGRAPHY Only accepts digital photography. Submit stock photo list. Buys stock and assigns work. Model/property releases required; captions required.

TERMS Pays authors a negotiated royalty or purchases work outright. Offers advances. Pays illustrators and photographers negotiated amount. Originals returned to artist at job's completion.

TIPS "We want well-written, well-researched material that presents a fresh approach to a particular topic."

MAGAZINES

///

Children's magazines are a great place for unpublished writers and illustrators to break into the market. Writers, illustrators and photographers alike may find it easier to get book assignments if they have tearsheets from magazines. Having magazine work under your belt shows you're professional and have experience working with editors and art directors and meeting deadlines.

But magazines aren't merely a breaking-in point. Writing, illustration and photo assignments for magazines let you see your work in print quickly, and the magazine market can offer steady work and regular paychecks (a number of them pay on acceptance). Book authors and illustrators may have to wait a year or two before receiving royalties from a project. The magazine market is also a good place to use research material that didn't make it into a book project you're working on. You may even work on a magazine idea that blossoms into a book project.

TARGETING YOUR SUBMISSIONS

It's important to know the topics typically covered by different children's magazines. To help you match your work with the right publications, we've included an index in the back of this book.

If you're a writer, targeting the correct age group with your submission is an important consideration. Many rejection slips are sent because a writer has not targeted a manuscript to the correct age. Few magazines are aimed at children of all ages, so you must be certain your manuscript is written for the audience level of the particular magazine you're submitting to. Magazines for children (just as magazines for adults) may also target a specific gender.

Each magazine has a different editorial philosophy. Language usage also varies between periodicals, as does the length of feature articles and the use of artwork and photographs. Reading magazines *before* submitting is the best way to determine if your material is appropriate. Also, because magazines targeted to specific age groups have a natural turnover in readership every few years, old topics (with a new slant) can be recycled.

Since many kids' magazines sell subscriptions through direct mail or schools, you may not be able to find a particular publication at bookstores or newsstands. Check your local library, or send for copies of the magazines you're interested in. Most magazines in this section have sample copies available and will send them for a SASE or small fee.

Also, many magazines have submission guidelines and theme lists available for a SASE. Check magazines' websites, too. Many offer excerpts of articles, submission guidelines and theme lists and will give you a feel for the editorial focus of the publication.

Watch for the Canadian and International symbols. These publications' needs and requirements may differ from their U.S. counterparts.

ADVENTURES

WordAction Publications, 2923 Troost Ave., Kansas City, MO 64109. (816)931-1900. Fax: (816)412-8312. E-mail: dfillmore@nazarene.org. Website: www.nph.com. **Articles Editor:** Donna Filmore. Weekly magazine. "*Adventures* is a full-color story paper for first and second graders. It is designed to connect Sunday School learning with the daily living experiences of the early elementary child. The reading level should be beginning. The intent of *Adventures* is to provide a life-related paper enabling Christian values, encouraging good choices and providing reinforcement for biblical concepts taught in WordAction Sunday School curriculum." Entire publication aimed at juvenile market.

FICTION Picture-Oriented Material: contemporary, inspirational, religious. Young Readers: contemporary, inspirational, religious. Byline given.

HOW TO CONTACT Fiction: Send complete ms. Responds to queries in 6 weeks; to mss in 6 weeks.

TERMS Pays on acceptance. Buys all rights. Writer's guidelines free for SASE.

TIPS "Send SASE for themes and guidelines or e-mail acallison@nazarene.org. Stories should realistically portray the life experiences of first- and second-grade children from a variety of ethnic and social backgrounds. We also need simple puzzles, easy recipes and easy-to-do craft ideas."

ADVOCATE, PKA'S PUBLICATION

1881 Little Westkill Rd., Prattsville NY 12468. (518)299-3103. E-mail: advoad@localnet.com. Website: http://Advocatepka.weebly.com or www.facebook.com/pages/Advocate-PKAs-Publication/111826035499969. **Publisher:** Patricia Keller. Bimonthly tabloid. Estab. 1987. Circ. 12,000. "Advocates for good writers and quality writings. We publish art, fiction, photos and poetry. *Advocate*'s submitters are talented people of all ages who do not earn their livings as writers. We wish to promote the arts and to give those we publish the opportunity to be published." **Contact:** Patricia Keller, publisher.

⭕ Gaited Horse Association newsletter is included in this publication. Horse-oriented stories, poetry, art and photos are currently needed.

FICTION Middle readers, young adults/teens; adults: adventure, animal, contemporary, fantasy, folktales, health, humorous, nature/environment, problem-solving, romance, science fiction, sports, suspense/mystery. Looks for "well written, entertaining work, whether fiction or nonfiction." Buys approximately 42 mss/year. Prose pieces should not exceed 1,500 words. Byline given. Wants to see more humorous material, nature/environment and romantic comedy.

NONFICTION Middle readers, young adults/teens: animal, arts/crafts, biography, careers, concept, cooking, fashion, games/puzzles, geography, history, hobbies, how-to, humorous, interview/profile, nature/environment, problem-solving, science, social issues, sports, travel. Buys 10 mss/year. Prose pieces should not exceed 1,500 words. Byline given.

POETRY Reviews poetry any length. *Advocate, PKA's Publication*, published bimonthly, is an advertiser-supported tabloid using "original, previously unpublished works, such as feature stories, essays, 'think' pieces, letters to the editor, profiles, humor, fiction, poetry, puzzles, cartoons, or line drawings." Wants "nearly any kind of poetry, any length. Circulation is 10,000; all distributed free. Subscription: $16.50 (6 issues). Sample: $5 (includes guidelines). Occasionally comments on rejected poems. Responds in 2 months. Guidelines available with sample copy ($5). Pays 2 contributor's copies. Acquires first rights only. No religious or pornographic poetry.

HOW TO CONTACT Fiction/nonfiction: send complete ms. Responds to queries in 6 weeks; mss in 2 months. Publishes ms 2-18 months after acceptance.

ILLUSTRATION Uses b&w artwork only. Uses cartoons. Reviews ms/illustration packages from artists. Submit a photo print (b&w or color), an excellent copy of work (no larger than 8×10) or original. Prints in black and white but accepts color work that converts well to gray scale. Illustrations only: "Send previous unpublished art with SASE, please." Responds in 2 months. Samples returned with SASE; samples not filed. Credit line given.

PHOTOS Buys photos from freelancers. Model/property releases required. Uses color and b&w prints (no slides). Send unsolicited photos by mail with SASE. Responds in 2 months. Wants nature, artistic and humorous photos.

TERMS Pays on publication with contributor's copies. Acquires first rights for mss, artwork and photographs. Pays in copies. Sample copies for $5. For a yearly subscription, published 6 times per year-$16.50. Writer's/illustrator/photo guidelines with sample copy.

TIPS "Please, no simultaneous submissions, work that has appeared on the Internet, pornography, overt religiosity, anti-environmentalism or gratuitous violence. Artists and photographers should keep in mind that we are a b&w paper. Please do not send postcards. Use envelope with SASE."

AIM MAGAZINE

P.O. Box 390, Milton WA 98354-0390. E-mail: submissions@aimmagazine.org; information@aimmagazine.org. Website: www.aimmagazine.org. **Contact:** Ruth Apilado, associate editor. Quarterly magazine. Circ. 8,000. "Readers are high school and college students, teachers, adults interested in helping to purge racism from the human blood stream by the way of the written word—that is our goal!" 15% of material aimed at juvenile audience.

FICTION Young adults/teens: adventure, folktales, humorous, history, multicultural, "stories with social significance." Wants stories that teach children that people are more alike than they are different. Does not want to see religious fiction. Buys 20 mss/year. Average word length: 1,000-4,000. Byline given.

NONFICTION Young adults/teens: biography, interview/profile, multicultural, "stuff with social significance." Does not want to see religious nonfiction. Buys 20 mss/year. Average word length: 500-2,000. Byline given.

HOW TO CONTACT Fiction: Send complete ms. Nonfiction: Query with published clips. Responds to queries/mss in 1 month. Will consider simultaneous submissions.

ILLUSTRATION Buys 6 illustrations/issue. Preferred theme: Overcoming social injustices through nonviolent means. Reviews ms/illustration packages from artists. Query first. Illustrations only: Query with tearsheets. Responds to art samples in 1 month. Samples filed. Original artwork returned at job's completion "if desired." Credit line given.

PHOTOS Wants "photos of activists who are trying to contribute to social improvement."

TERMS Pays on acceptance. Buys first North American serial rights. Pays $15-25 for stories/articles. Pays in contributor copies if copies are requested. Pays $25 for b&w cover illustration. Photographers paid by the project. Sample copies for $5.

TIPS "Write about what you know."

AMERICAN CAREERS

(800)669-7795. E-mail: ccinfor@carcom.com. Website: www.carcom.com; www.americancareersonline.com. Published 1 time/year. Circ. 400,000. Publishes career and education information for students in grades 6-12. Buys 5 mss/year. Average word length: 300-800. Byline given. Jerry Kanabel, art director. **Contact:** Mary Pitchford. Student publication covering careers, career statistics, skills needed to get jobs. Sample copy for $4. Guidelines for #10 SASE.

NONFICTION Query by mail only with published clips. Length: 300-1,000 words. Pays $100-450.

HOW TO CONTACT Query in writing with résumé and published clips. Acknowledges queries within 30 days. Keeps queries on file up to 2 years. Accepts simultaneous submissions with notification.

PHOTOS State availability. Captions, identification of subjects, model releases required. Negotiates payment individually.

TERMS Pays on acceptance. Pays writers variable amount.

TIPS Letters of introduction or query letters with samples and resumes are ways we get to know writers. Samples should include how-to articles and career-related articles. Articles written for teenagers also would make good samples. Short feature articles on careers, career-related how-to articles, and self-assessment tools (10-20 point quizzes with scoring information) are primarily what we publish.

AMERICAN CHEERLEADER

American Cheerleader Media LLC,110 William St., 23rd fl., New York NY 10038. (646)459-4800. Fax: (646)459-4900. E-mail: acmail@americancheerleader.com. Website: www.americancheerleader.com. Bimonthly magazine. Estab. 1995. Circ. 150,000. Special interest teen magazine for kids who cheer. Bimonthly magazine covering high school, college, and competitive cheerleading. Editorial lead time 3 months. Sample copy for $2.95. Guidelines free.

NONFICTION Young adults: biography, interview/profile (sports personalities), careers, fashion, beauty, health, how-to (cheering techniques, routines, pep songs, etc.), problem-solving, sports, cheerleading specific material. "We're looking for authors who know cheerleading." Buys 20 mss/year. Average word length: 750-2,000. Byline given. Query with samples; provide résumé, business card, tearsheets to be kept on file. Sample copies for $4." Query with published clips. Length: 400-1,500 words. Pays $100-250 for assigned articles. Pays $100 maximum for unsolicited articles.

HOW TO CONTACT Query with published clips. Responds to queries/mss in 3 months. Publishes ms 3 months after acceptance. Will consider electronic submission via disk or e-mail. Buys 2 illustrations/issue; 12-20 illustrations/year. Works on assignment only.

ILLUSTRATION Reviews ms/illustration packages from artists. Illustrations only: Query with samples; arrange portfolio review. Responds only if interested. Samples filed. Originals not returned at job's completion. Credit line given.

PHOTOS State availability. Model releases required. Reviews transparencies, 5x7 prints. Offers $50/photo.

TERMS Pays on publication. Buys all rights for mss, artwork and photographs. Pays $100-300 for stories. Pays illustrators $50-200 for b&w inside, $100-300 for color inside.

TIPS We invite proposals from freelance writers who are involved in or have been involved in cheerleading—i.e., coaches, sponsors, or cheerleaders. Our writing style is upbeat and 'sporty' to catch and hold the attention of our teenaged readers. Articles should be broken down into lots of sidebars, bulleted lists, Q&As, etc.

APPLESEEDS

30 Grove Street, Suite C, Peterborough NH 03458. (800)821-0115. Fax: (603)924-7380. E-mail: susanbuckleynyc@gmail.com. Website: www.cobblestonepub.com. **Contact:** Susan Buckley, editor. Magazine published 9 times annually. *AppleSeeds* is a 36-page, multidisciplinary, nonfiction social studies magazine from Cobblestone Publishing for ages 8-10. Each issue focuses on one theme.

> Requests for sample issues should be mailed to Cobblestone directly. See website for current theme list (www.cobblestonepub.com/guidesAAP.html).

HOW TO CONTACT Nonfiction: Query only. Send all queries to Susan Buckley. See website for submission guidelines and theme list. E-mail queries only. See website for editorial guidelines.

ILLUSTRATION Contact Ann Dillon at Cobblestone. See website for illustration guidelines.

TIPS "Submit queries specifically focused on the theme of an upcoming issue. We generally work 6 months ahead on themes. We look for unusual perspectives, original ideas, and excellent scholarship. We accept **no unsolicited manuscripts**. Writers should check our website at cobblestonepub.com/pages/writersAPPguides/html for current guidelines, topics, and query deadlines. We use very little fiction. Illustrators should not submit unsolicited art."

AQUILA

New Leaf Publishing, P.O. Box 2518, Eastbourne BN22 8AP United Kingdom. (44)(132)343-1313. Fax: (44)(132)373-1136. E-mail: info@aquila.co.uk. Website: www.aquila.co.uk. **Submissions Editor:** Jackie Berry and Anji Ansty-Holroyd. Monthly magazine. Estab. 1993. "*Aquila* is an educational magazine for readers ages 8-13 including factual articles (no pop/celebrity material), arts/crafts and puzzles." Entire publication aimed at juvenile market.

FICTION Young Readers: animal, contemporary, fantasy, folktales, health, history, humorous, multicultural, nature/environment, problem solving, religious, science fiction, sports, suspense/mystery. Middle Readers: animal, contemporary, fantasy, folktales, health, history, humorous, multicultural, nature/environment, problem solving, religious, romance, science fiction, sports, suspense/mystery. Buys 6-8 mss/year. Byline given.

NONFICTION Considers Young Readers: animal, arts/crafts, concept, cooking, games/puzzles, health, history, how-to, interview/profile, math, nature/environment, science, sports. Middle Readers: animal, arts/crafts, concept, cooking, games/puzzles, health, history, interview/profile, math, nature/environment, science, sports. Buys 48 mss/year. Average word length: 350-750.

HOW TO CONTACT Fiction: Query with published clips. Nonfiction: Query with published clips. Responds to queries in 6-8 weeks. Publishes ms 1 year after acceptance. Considers electronic submissions via disk or e-mail, previously published work.

ILLUSTRATION Color artwork only. Works on assignment only. For first contact, query with samples. Submit samples to Jackie Berry, Editor. Responds only if interested. Samples not returned. Samples filed.

TERMS Buys exclusive magazine rights. Buys exclusive magazine rights for artwork. Pays $150-200 for stories; $50-100 for articles. Additional payment for ms/illustration packages. Additional payment for ms/photo packages. Pays illustrators $130-150 for color cover. Sample copies (€5 sterling) this must be bankers cheque in sterling, not US dollars. Writer's guidelines free for SASE. Publishes work by children.

TIPS "We only accept a high level of educational material for children ages 8-13 with a good standard of literacy and ability."

◑ ARC POETRY MAGAZINE

P.O. Box 81060, Ottawa ON K1P 1B1, Canada. E-mail: editor@arcpoetry.ca. Website: www.arcpoetry.ca. **Contact:** Pauline Conley, managing editor.

◐ ASK

70 E. Lake St., Chicago IL 60601. E-mail: ask@ask mag.com. Website: www.cricketmag.com. Magazine published 9 times/year. Estab. 2002. *Ask* is a magazine of arts and sciences for curious kids who like to find out how the world works. **Contact:** Liz Huyck, editor; Karen Kohn, art director.

NONFICTION Young readers, middle readers: science, engineering, invention, machines, archaeology, animals, nature/environment, history, history of science. Average word length: 150-1,600. Byline given.

HOW TO CONTACT *Ask* commissions most articles but welcomes queries from authors on all nonfiction subjects. Particularly looking for odd, unusual, and interesting stories likely to interest science-oriented kids. See www.cricketmag.com/19-Submission-Guidelines-for-ASK-magazine-for-children-ages-6-9 for current issue theme list and calendar. Writers interested in working for *Ask* should send a resume and writing sample (including at least one page un-edited) for consideration.

ILLUSTRATION Buys 10 illustrations/issue; 60 illustrations/year. Works on assignment only. For illustrations, send query with samples.

BABAGANEWZ

Jewish Family & Life, P.O. Box 9129, Newton, MA 02464. (888) 458-8535. Fax: (617) 965-7772. Website: www.babaganewz.com. **Articles Editor:** Mark Levine. **Managing Editor:** Jean Max. Monthly magazine. Estab. 2001. Circ. 40,000. "*BabagaNewzC* helps middle school students explore Jewish values that are at the core of Jewish beliefs and practices."

FICTION Middle readers: religious, Jewish themes. Buys 1 ms/year. Average word length: 1,000-1,500. Byline given.

NONFICTION Middle readers: arts/crafts, concept, games/puzzles, geography, history, humorous, interview/profile, nature/environment, religion, science, social issues. Most articles are written by assignment. Average word length: 350-1,000. Byline given.

HOW TO CONTACT Queries only for fiction; queries preferred for nonfiction. No unsolicited manuscripts.

ILLUSTRATION Uses color artwork only. Works on assignment only. Illustrations only: Send postcard sample with promo sheet, resume, URL. Responds only if interested. Credit line given.

PHOTOS Photos by assignment.

TERMS Pays on acceptance. Usually buys all rights for mss. Original artwork returned at job's completion only if requested. Sample copies free for SAE 9×12 and 4 first-class stamps.

TIPS "Most work is done on assignment. We are looking for freelance writers with experience writing nonfiction for 9- to 13-year-olds, especially on Jewish-related themes. No unsolicited manuscripts."

BABYBUG

Carus Publishing, 70 East Lake St., Chicago IL 60601. E-mail: babybug@caruspub.com. Website: www.cricketmag.com. Published 10 times/year (monthly except for combined May/June and July/August issues). "A listening and looking magazine for infants and toddlers ages 6 to 24 months, *Babybug* is 6×7, 24 pages long, printed in large type on high-quality cardboard stock with rounded corners and no staples." **Contact:** Marianne Carus, editor-in-chief. Guidelines available online.

FICTION Looking for very simple and concrete stories, 4-6 short sentences maximum. Length: 2-8 short sentences. $25 min.

NONFICTION Must use very basic words and concepts, 10 words maximum. Submit complete ms, SASE. Length: 10 words/max. Pays $25.

POETRY Maximum length 8 lines. Looking for rhythmic, rhyming poems. Pays $25 minimum on publication. Acquires North American publication rights for previously published poems; rights vary for unpublished poems.

HOW TO CONTACT "Please do not query first." Send complete ms with SASE. "Submissions without SASE will be discarded." Responds in 6 months.

ILLUSTRATION Uses color artwork only. Works on assignment only. Reviews ms/illustration packages from artists. "The manuscripts will be evaluated for quality of concept and text before the art is considered." Contact: Suzanne Beck. Illustrations only: Send tearsheets or photo prints/photocopies with SASE.

"Submissions without SASE will be discarded." Responds in 3 months. Samples filed.

PHOTOS Pays $500/spread; $250/page.

TERMS Rights purchased vary. Original artwork returned at job's completion. Rates vary ($25 minimum for mss; $250 minimum for art). Sample copy for $5. Guidelines free for SASE or available on website; FAQ at www.cricketmag.com.

TIPS "*Babybug* would like to reach as many children's authors and artists as possible for original contributions, but our standards are very high, and we will accept only top-quality material. Before attempting to write for *Babybug*, be sure to familiarize yourself with this age child. Imagine having to read your story or poem—out loud—50 times or more! That's what parents will have to do. Babies and toddlers demand, 'Read it again!' Your material must hold up under repetition. And humor is much appreciated by all."

BOYS' LIFE

(972)580-2366. Fax: (972)580-2079. Website: www.boyslife.org. J. D. Owen, editor-in-chief; Michael Goldman, managing editor; Aaron Derr, senior writer. Sample copies for $3.95 plus 9x12 SASE. Guidelines available with SASE and online.

NONFICTION Query with SASE. No phone queries. Averge word length for articles: 500-1,500 words, including sidebars and boxes. Average word length for columns: 300-750. Pay ranges from $300 and up.

ILLUSTRATION Buys 10-12 illustrations/issue; 100-125 illustrations/year. Works on assignment only. Reviews ms/illustration packages from artists. "Query first." Illustrations only: Send tearsheets. Responds to art samples only if interested. Samples returned with SASE. Original artwork returned at job's completion. Works on assignment only

PHOTOS Photo guidelines free with SASE. Boy Scouts of America Magazine Division also publishes *Scouting* magazine. "Most photographs are from specific assignments that freelance photojournalists shoot for *Boys' Life*. Interested in all photographers, but do not send unsolicited images." Pays $500 base editorial day rate against placement fees, plus expenses. **Pays on acceptance.** Buys one-time rights.

TERMS Pays on acceptance: $1,500-3,000 for color cover; $100-1,500 for color inside; $750 and up for fiction; $40-1,500 for major articles; $150-400 for columns; $250-300 for how-to features. Guidelines available with SASE.

TIPS "We strongly recommend reading at least 12 issues of the magazine before submitting queries. We are a good market for any writer willing to do the necessary homework. Write for a boy you know who is 12. Our readers demand punchy writing in relatively short, straightforward sentences. The editors demand well-reported articles that demonstrate high standards of journalism. We follow the *Associated Press* manual of style and usage. Learn and read our publications before submitting anything."

BOYS' QUEST

P.O. Box 227, Bluffton OH 45817-0227. (419)358-4610 ext.101. Fax: (419)358-8020. E-mail: hsbq@wcoil.com. E-mail: submissions@funforkidz.com. Website: boysquest.com. Bi-monthly magazine. "*Boys' Quest* is a magazine created for boys from 5 to 14 years, with youngsters 8, 9 and 10 the specific target age. Our point of view is that every young boy deserves the right to be a young boy for a number of years before he becomes a young adult. As a result, *Boys' Quest* looks for articles, fiction, nonfiction, and poetry that deal with timeless topics, such as pets, nature, hobbies, science, games, sports, careers, simple cooking, and anything else likely to interest a young boy." Contact: Marilyn Edwards, Bethany Sneed.

FICTION Picture-oriented material, young readers, middle readers: adventure, animal, history, humorous, multicultural, nature/environment, problem-solving, sports. Does not want to see violence, teenage themes. Buys 30 mss/year. Average word length: 200-500. Byline given. Length: 500 words.

NONFICTION Picture-oriented material, young readers, middle readers: animal, arts/crafts, cooking, games/puzzles, history, hobbies, how-to, humorous, math, problem-solving, sports. Prefer photo support with nonfiction. Buys 30 mss/year. Average word length: 200-500. Byline given. Length: 500 words.

POETRY Reviews poetry. Maximum length: 21 lines. Limit submissions to 6 poems.

HOW TO CONTACT All writers should consult the theme list before sending in articles. To receive current theme list, send a SASE. Fiction/nonfiction: Query or send complete ms (preferred). Send SASE with correct postage. No faxed or e-mailed material. Responds to queries in 2 weeks; mss in 2 weeks (if rejected); 5 weeks (if scheduled). Publishes ms 3 months-

3 years after acceptance. Will consider simultaneous submissions and previously published work.

ILLUSTRATION Buys 10 illustrations/issue; 60-70 illustrations/year. Uses b&w artwork only. Works on assignment only. Reviews ms/illustration packages from artists. Illustrations only: Query with samples, tearsheets. Responds in 1 month only if interested and a SASE. Samples returned with SASE; samples filed. Credit line given.

PHOTOS Photos used for support of nonfiction. "Excellent photographs included with a nonfiction story is considered very seriously." Model/property releases required. Uses b&w, 5×7 or 3×5 prints. Query with samples; send unsolicited photos by mail. Responds in 3 weeks. "We use a number of photos, printed in black and white, inside the magazine. These photos support the articles." $5/photo.

TERMS Pays on publication. Buys first North American serial rights for mss. Buys first rights for artwork. Pays $0.05/word for stories and articles. Additional payment for ms/illustration packages and for photos accompanying articles. Pays $150-200 for color cover; $25-35 for b&w inside. Pays photographers per photo (range: $5-10). Originals returned to artist at job's completion. Sample copies for $6 (there is a direct charge by the post office of $4.50 per issue for air mail to other countries), $8 for Canada, and $10.50 for all other countries. Writer's/illustrator's/photographer's guidelines and theme list are free for SASE.

TIPS "First be familiar with our magazines. We are looking for lively writing, most of it from a young boy's point of view—with the boy or boys directly involved in an activity that is both wholesome and unusual. We need nonfiction with photos and fiction stories—around 500 words—puzzles, poems, cooking, carpentry projects, jokes and riddles. Nonfiction pieces that are accompanied by black and white photos are far more likely to be accepted than those that need illustrations. We will entertain simultaneous submissions as long as that fact is noted on the manuscript."

BREAD FOR GOD'S CHILDREN

P.O. Box 1017, Arcadia FL 34265-1017. (863)494-6214. Fax: (863)993-0154. E-mail: bread@breadministries.org. Website: www.breadministries.org. **Contact:** Judith M. Gibbs, editor. Bimonthly magazine. "*Bread* is designed as a teaching tool for Christian families." 85% of publication aimed at juvenile market. Three

sample copies for 9x12 SAE and 5 first-class stamps. Guidelines for #10 SASE.

FICTION Young readers, middle readers, young adult/teen: adventure, religious, problem-solving, sports. Looks for "teaching stories that portray Christian lifestyles without preaching." Buys approximately 10-15 mss/year. Average word length: 900-1,500 (for teens); 600-900 (for young children). Byline given. "We are looking for writers who have a solid knowledge of Biblical principles and are concerned for the youth of today living by those principles. Our stories must be well written, with the story itself getting the message across—no preaching, moralizing, or tag endings." No fantasy, science fiction, or non-Christian themes. Send complete ms. Length: 600-800 words/young children; 900-1,500 words/older children. Pays $40-50.

NONFICTION All levels: how-to. "We do not want anything detrimental to solid family values. Most topics will fit if they are slanted to our basic needs." Buys 3-4 mss/year. Average word length: 500-800. Byline given.

HOW TO CONTACT Fiction/nonfiction: Send complete ms. Responds to mss in 6 months "if considered for use." Will consider simultaneous submissions and previously published work.

ILLUSTRATION "The only illustrations we purchase are those occasional good ones accompanying an accepted story."

TERMS Pays on publication. Pays $30-50 for stories; $30 for articles. Sample copies free for 9×12 SAE and 5 first-class stamps (for 2 copies).

TIPS "We want stories or articles that illustrate overcoming obstacles by faith and living solid, Christian lives. Know our publication and what we have used in the past. Know the readership and publisher's guidelines. Stories should teach the value of morality and honesty without preaching. Edit carefully for content and grammar."

🌐😊 BRILLIANT STAR

National Spiritual Assembly of the Bahá'ís of the U.S. 1233 Central St., Evanston IL 60201. Phone: (847)853-2354. Fax: (847)425-7951. E-mail: brilliant@usbnc.org. Website: www.brilliantstarmagazine.org. Publishes 6 issues/year. Estab. 1969. Magazine is designed for children ages 8-12. *Brilliant Star* presents Bahá'ís history and principles through fiction, nonfiction, activities, interviews, puzzles, cartoons, games, music, and art. Universal values of good character, such as kindness, courage, creativity, and helpfulness are incorporated into the magazine.

FICTION Middle readers: contemporary, fantasy, folktale, multicultural, nature/environment, problem-solving, religious. Average word length: 700-1,400. Byline given.

NONFICTION Middle readers: arts/crafts, games/puzzles, geography, how-to, humorous, multicultural, nature/environment, religion, social issues. Buys 6 mss/year. Average word length: 300-700. Byline given.

POETRY "We only publish poetry written by children at the moment."

HOW TO CONTACT Fiction: Send complete ms. Nonfiction: Query. Responds to queries/mss in 6 weeks. Publishes ms 6 months-1 year after acceptance. Prefers e-mail submissions.

ILLUSTRATION Works on assignment only. Reviews ms/illustration packages from artists. Illustrations only: Query with samples. Contact: Aaron Kreader, graphic designer. Responds only if interested. Samples kept on file. Credit line given.

PHOTOS Buys photos with accompanying ms only. Model/property release required; captions required. Responds only if interested.

TERMS Pays 2 copies of issue. Buys first rights and reprint rights for mss, artwork, and photos. Sample copies for $3 and SASE for 4 ounces. Writer's/illustrator's/photo guidelines for SASE.

TIPS "*Brilliant Star*'s content is developed with a focus on children in their 'tween' years, ages 8-12. This is a period of intense emotional, physical, and psychological development. Familiarize yourself with the interests and challenges of children in this age range. Protagonists in our fiction are usually in the upper part of our age range: 10-12 years old. They solve their problems without adult intervention. We appreciate seeing a sense of humor but not related to bodily functions or put-downs. Keep your language and concepts age-appropriate. Use short words, sentences, and paragraphs. Activities and games may be submitted in rough or final form. Send us a description of your activity along with short, simple instructions. We avoid long, complicated activities that require adult supervision. If you think they will be helpful, please try to provide step-by-step rough sketches of the instructions. You may also submit photographs to illustrate the activity."

☺ CADET QUEST MAGAZINE

Calvinist Cadet Corps, P.O. Box 7259, Grand Rapids MI 49510. (616)241-5616. Fax: (616)241-5558. E-mail: submissions@calvinistcadets.org. Website: www.calvinistcadets.org. **Editor:** G. Richard Broene. Magazine published 7 times/year. Circ. 7,500. "Our magazine is for members of the Calvinist Cadet Corps—boys aged 9-14. Our purpose is to show how God is at work in their lives and in the world around them. Our magazine offers nonfiction articles and fast-moving fiction—everything to appeal to the interests and concerns of boys and teach Christian values." **Contact:** G. Richard Broene, editor. Sample copy for 9x12 SASE. Guidelines for #10 SASE.

○ Accepts submissions by mail or by e-mail (must include ms in text of e-mail). Will not open attachments.

FICTION Middle readers, boys/early teens: adventure, humorous, multicultural, problem-solving, religious, sports. Buys 14 mss/year. Average word length: 900-1,500. Middle readers, boys/early teens: arts/crafts, games/puzzles, hobbies, how-to, humorous, interview/profile, problem-solving, science, sports. Buys 6-12 mss/year. Average word length: 400-900. Considerable fiction is used. Fast-moving stories that appeal to a boy's sense of adventure or sense of humor are welcome. Avoid preachiness. Avoid simplistic answers to complicated problems. Avoid long dialogue and little action. No fantasy, science fiction, fashion, horror or erotica. Send complete ms. Length: 900-1,500 words. Pays 4-5¢/word, and 1 contributor's copy.

NONFICTION Send complete ms. Length: 500-1,500 words. Pays 4-5¢/word.

HOW TO CONTACT Fiction/nonfiction: Send complete ms by mail with SASE or by e-mail. Please note: E-mail submissions must have material in the body of the e-mail. Will not open attachments. Responds to mss in 2 months. Will consider simultaneous submissions.

ILLUSTRATION Buys 2 illustrations/issue; buys 12 illustrations/year. Works on assignment only. Reviews ms/illustration packages from artists.

PHOTOS Pays $20-30 for photos purchased with ms.

TERMS Responds in 5 weeks. Samples returned with SASE. Originals returned to artist at job's completion. Credit line given.

TIPS "Best time to submit stories/articles is early in the year (February-April). Also remember readers are boys ages 9-14. Stories must reflect or add to the theme of the issue and be from a Christian perspective."

CALLIOPE

Cobblestone Publishing Co., 30 Grove St., Suite C, Peterborough NH 03458-1454. (603)924-7209. Fax: (603)924-7380. E-mail: cfbakeriii@meganet.net. Website: www.cobblestonepub.com. "*Calliope* covers world history (East/West), and lively, original approaches to the subject are the primary concerns of the editors in choosing material." Pays 20-25¢/word for stories/articles. Pays on an individual basis for poetry, activities, games/puzzles. Writer's/illustrator's/photo guidelines for SASE. Lou Waryncia, editorial director; Ann Dillon, art director. **Contact:** Rosalie Baker & Charles Baker, co-editors. Magazine published 9 times/year covering world history (East and West) through 1800 AD for 8 to 14-year-old kids. Sample copy for $5.95, $2 shipping and handling, and 10x13 SASE. Guidelines available online.

For themes and queries deadlines, visit the Calliope website at: www.cobblestonepub. com/magazine/CAL. 2010 themes included: Isabella of Spain-Queen of a New World; Michelangelo; Dutch East India Company; Exploring Africa with Stanley & Livingstone; Meaning of Numbers; Shades of Indigo; The Nile river; and the Zodiac.

FICTION Length: 1,000 words maximum. Pays 20-25¢/word.

NONFICTION Query with writing sample, 1-page outline, bibliography, SASE. 400-1000/feature articles; 300-600 words/supplemental nonfiction. Pays 20-25¢/word.

HOW TO CONTACT A query must consist of the following to be considered (please use nonerasable paper): a brief cover letter stating subject and word length of the proposed article; a detailed one-page outline explaining the information to be presented in the article; a bibliography of materials the author intends to use in preparing the article; a self-addressed stamped envelope. Writers new to *Calliope* should send a writing sample with query. In all correspondence, please include your complete address as well as a telephone number where you can be reached. A writer may send as many queries for one issue as he or she wishes, but each query must have a separate cover letter, outline and bibliography as well as a SASE. Telephone and e-mail queries are not accepted. Handwritten queries will not be considered. Queries may be submitted at any time, but queries sent well in advance of deadline *may not be answered for several months*. Go-aheads requesting material proposed in queries are usually sent 10 months prior to publication date. Unused queries will be returned approximately three to four months prior to publication date.

PHOTOS Illustrations only: Send tearsheets, photocopies. Original work returned upon job's completion (upon written request).Buys photos from freelancers. Wants photos pertaining to any upcoming themes. Uses b&w/color prints, 35mm transparencies and 300 DPI digital images. Send unsolicited photos by mail (on speculation). Buys all rights for mss and artwork. If you have photographs pertaining to any upcoming theme, please contact the editor by mail or fax, or send them with your query. You may also send images on speculation. Model/property release preferred. Reviews b&w prints, color slides. Reviews photos with or without accompanying manuscript. We buy one-time use. Our suggested fee range for professional quality photographs follows: ¼ page to full page b/w $15-100; color $25-100. Please note that fees for non-professional quality photographs are negotiated. Cover fees are set on an individual basis for one-time use, plus promotional use. All cover images are color. Prices set by museums, societies, stock photography houses, etc., are paid or negotiated. Photographs that are promotional in nature (e.g., from tourist agencies, organizations, special events, etc.) are usually submitted at no charge. Pays on publication. Credit line given. Buys one-time rights; negotiable.

TIPS "Authors are urged to use primary resources and up-to-date scholarly resources in their bibliography. In all correspondence, please include your complete address and a telephone number where you can be reached."

CAREERS AND COLLEGES

A division of Alloy Education, an Alloy Media + Marketing Company, 10 Abeel Rd., Cranbury NJ 08512. (609) 619- 8739. Website: www.careersandcolleges.com. **SVP/Managing Director:** Jayne Pennington. Editor: Don Rauf. Magazine published 3 times a year (2 issues direct-to-home in July and 1 to 10,000 high schools in December). Circulation: 760,000. Distributed to 760,000 homes of 15- to 17-year-olds and college-bound high school graduates, and 10,000 high schools. *Careers and Colleges* magazine provides juniors and seniors in high school with editorial, tips, trends, and websites to assist them in the transition to college, career, young adulthood, and independence.

NONFICTION Young adults/teens: careers, college, health, how-to, humorous, interview/profile, personal development, problem-solving, social issues, sports, travel. Buys 10-20 mss/year. Average word length: 1,000-1,500. Byline given.

HOW TO CONTACT Nonfiction: Query. Responds to queries in 6 weeks. Will consider electronic submissions.

ILLUSTRATION Buys 2 illustrations/issue; buys 8 illustrations/year. Works on assignment only. Reviews samples online. Query first. Credit line given.

TERMS Pays on acceptance plus 45 days. Buys all rights. Pays $100-600 for assigned/unsolicited articles. Additional payment for ms/illustration packages "must be negotiated." Pays $300-1,000 for color illustration; $200-700 for b&w/color inside illustration. Pays photographers by the project. Sample copy $5. Contributor's guidelines are available electronically.

TIPS "Articles with great quotes, good reporting, good writing. Rich with examples and anecdotes. Must tie in with the objective to help teenaged readers plan for their futures. Current trends, policy changes and information regarding college admissions, financial aid, and career opportunities."

CARUS PUBLISHING COMPANY

30 Grove St., Suite C, Peterborough NH 03458. Website: www.cricketmag.com.

○ See listings for *Babybug, Cicada, Click, Cricket, Ladybug, Muse, Spider* and *ASK*. Carus Publishing owns Cobblestone Publishing, publisher of *AppleSeeds, Calliope, Cobblestone, Dig, Faces* and *Odyssey*.

TERMS "Our 'bug magazines' accept unsolicited manuscripts."

CATHOLIC FORESTER

Fax: (630)983-3384. E-mail: magazine@catholicforester.org. Website: www.catholicforester.org. Quarterly magazine. Targets members of the Catholic Order of Foresters. In addition to the organization's news, it offers general interest pieces on health, finance, family life. Danielle Marsh, art director. **Contact:** Patricia Baron, assoc. editor. Quarterly magazine for members of the Catholic Order of Foresters, a fraternal insurance benefit society. Editorial lead time 6 months. Sample copy for 9x12 SAE and 4 first-class stamps. Guidelines available online.

FICTION Uses inspirational and humorous fiction. "A good children's story with a positive lesson or message would rate high on our list." Length: 500-1,500 words. Pays 50¢/word.

NONFICTION General interest pieces on health, finance, family life; inspirational. Will consider previously published work. Send complete ms by mail, fax, or e-mail. Rejected material will not be returned without accompanying SASE. Length: 500-1,500 words. Pays 50¢/word.

POETRY 15 lines maximum. Pays 30¢/word.

HOW TO CONTACT Submit complete ms. Responds in 4 months.

ILLUSTRATION Buys 2-4 illustrations/issue. Uses color artwork only.

PHOTOS State availability. Negotiates payment individually.

TERMS Buys 6-10 mss/year. Average word length: 500-1,500. Works on assignment only. Sample copies for 9×12 SASE with 3 first-class stamps. Writer's guidelines free for SASE.

TIPS "Our audience includes a broad age spectrum, ranging from youth to seniors."

CELEBRATE

Word Action Publishing Co. Church of the Nazarene, 2923 Troost Ave, Kansas City MO 64109. (816)931-1900, ext. 8228. Fax: (816)412-8306. E-mail: dxb@nph.com. Website: www.wordaction.com. **Editor:** Abigail L. Takala. **Assistant Editor:** Danielle J. Broadbooks. Weekly publication. Estab. 2001. Circ. 30,000. "This weekly take-home paper connects Sunday School learning to life for preschoolers (age 3 and 4), kindergartners (age 5 and 6) and their families." 75% of publication aimed at juvenile market; 25% parents.

NONFICTION Picture-oriented material: arts/crafts, cooking, poems, action rhymes, piggyback songs (theme based). 50% of mss nonfiction. Byline given.

POETRY Reviews poetry. Maximum length: 4-8 lines. Unlimited submissions.

HOW TO CONTACT Nonfiction: query. Responds to queries in 1 month. Responds to mss in 6 weeks. Publishes ms 1 year after acceptance. Will accept electronic submission via e-mail.

TERMS Pays on acceptance. Buys all rights, multiuse rights. Pays $15 for activities, crafts, recipes, songs, rhymes, and poems. Compensation includes 2 contributor copies. Sample copy for SASE.

🌑 CHALLENGE

Website: www.pearson.com.au/schools. Pearson Education Australia, 20 Thackray Rd., Port Melbourne VIC 3205 Australia. (61)03 9245 7111. Fax: (61)03 9245 7333. E-mail: magazines@pearson.com.au. Website: www.pearson.com.au/schools. **Articles Editor:** Petra Poupa. **Fiction Editor:** Meredith Costain. Quarterly Magazine. Circ. 20,000. "Magazines are educational and fun. We publish mainly nonfiction articles in a variety of genres and text types. They must be appropriate, factually correct, and of high interest. We publish interviews, recounts, informational and argumentative articles."

○ *Challenge* is a theme-based publication geared to ages 11-14. Check the website to see upcoming themes and deadlines. *Challenge* is a theme-based publication geared to ages 11-14. Check the website to see upcoming themes and deadlines.

FICTION Middle readers, young adults: adventure, animal, contemporary, fantasy, folktale, humorous, multicultural, problem-solving, science fiction, sports, suspense/mystery. Buys 12 mss/year. Average word length: 400-1,000. Byline given.

NONFICTION Middle readers, young adults: animal, arts/crafts, biography, careers, cooking, fashion, geography, health, history, hobbies, how-to, humorous, interview/profile, math, multicultural, nature/environment, problem-solving, science, social issues, sports, travel (depends on theme of issue). Buys 100 ms/year. Average word length: 200-600. Byline given.

POETRY Reviews poetry.

HOW TO CONTACT Fiction/nonfiction: Send complete ms. Responds to queries in 4-5 months; mss in 3 months. Publishes ms 3 months after acceptance. Will consider simultaneous submissions and electronic submissions via disk or e-mail.

PHOTOS Looking for photos to suit various themes; photos needed depend on stories. Model/property release required; captions required. Uses color, standard sized, prints, high resolution digital images and 35mm transparencies. Provide résumé, business card, promotional literature and tearsheets to be kept on file.

TERMS Pays on publication. Buys first Australian serial rights. Pays $80-200 (Australian) for stories; $100-220 (Australian) for articles.

TIPS "Check out our website for information about our publications." Also see listings for *Comet* and *Explore*.

◯ CHEMMATTERS

American Chemical Society, 1155 16th St., NW, Washington DC 20036. (202)872-6164. Fax: (202)833-7732. E-mail: chemmatters@acs.org. Website: www.acs.org/chemmatters. **Editor:** Pat Pages. **Art Director:** Cornithia Harris. Quarterly magazine. **Contact:** Pat Pages, editor. Covers content covered in a standard high school chemistry textbook.

NONFICTION Query with published clips. Pays $500-$1,000 for article. Additional payment for mss/illustration packages and for photos accompanying articles.

HOW TO CONTACT Query with published clips. E-mail or mail submissions will be considered. Responds to queries/mss in 2 weeks. Publishes ms 6 months after acceptance. Will consider simultaneous submissions, e-mail submissions.

ILLUSTRATION Buys 3 illustrations/issue; 12 illustrations/year. Uses color artwork only. Works on assignment only. Reviews manuscript/illustration packages from artists. Query. Contact: Cornithia Harris, art director *ChemMatters*. Illustrations only: Query with promo sheet, resume. Responds in 2 weeks. Samples returned with SASE; samples not filed. Credit line given.

PHOTOS Looking for photos of high school students engaged in science-related activities. Model/property release required; captions required. Uses color prints, but prefers high-resolution PDFs. Query with samples. Responds in 2 weeks.

TERMS Pays on acceptance. Minimally buys first North American serial rights, but prefers to buy all rights, reprint rights, electronic rights for manuscripts. Buys all rights for artwork; non-exclusive first rights for photos. Pays $500-$1,000 for article. Additional payment for manuscript/illustration packages and for photos accompanying articles. Sample copies free for 10x13 SASE and 3 first-class stamps. Writer's guidelines free for SASE (available as e-mail attachment upon request).

TIPS "Be aware of the content covered in a standard high school chemistry textbook. Choose themes and topics that are timely, interesting, fun, *and* that relate to the content and concepts of the first-year chemistry course. Articles should describe real people involved with real science. Best articles feature young people making a difference or solving a problem."

CHILDREN'S BETTER HEALTH INSTITUTE

P.O. Box 567, Indianapolis IN 46206. Website: www. cbhi.org. See listings for *Jack and Jill* and *Turtle*.

CICADA MAGAZINE

Carus Publishing Company, 70 East Lake St., Suite 300, Chicago IL 60601. (312)701-1720. Fax: (312)701-1728. E-mail: mail@cicadamag.com. Website: www. cicadamag.com. **Editor-in-Chief:** Marianne Carus. **Executive Editor:** Deborah Vetter. **Art Director:** John Sandford. Bimonthly magazine. Estab. 1998. *Cicada* publishes fiction and poetry with a genuine teen sensibility, aimed at the high school and college-age market. The editors are looking for stories and poems that are thought-provoking but entertaining. Byline given. **Contact:** Deborah Vetter, executive editor; John Sandford, art director. Guidelines available online.

FICTION Young adults: adventure, contemporary, fantasy, historical, humor/satire, multicultural, nature/environment, romance, science fiction, sports, suspense/mystery. Buys up to 42 mss/year. Average word length: about 5,000 words for short stories; up to 10,000 for novellas (one novella per issue). The main protagonist should be at least 14 and preferably older. Stories should have a genuine teen sensibility and be aimed at readers in high school or college. 5,000 words maximum (up to 15,000 words/novellas). Pays up to 25¢/word.

NONFICTION Young adults: first-person, coming-of-age experiences that are relevant to teens and young adults (example: life in the Peace Corps). Buys up to 6 mss/year. Average word length: about 5,000 words. Submit complete ms, SASE. 5,000 words maximum; 300-500 words/book reviews. Pays up to 25¢/word.

POETRY Reviews serious, humorous, free verse, rhyming (if done well) poetry. Maximum length: up to 25 lines. Limit submissions to 5 poems. Pays up to $3/line on publication.

HOW TO CONTACT Fiction/nonfiction: send complete ms. Responds to mss in 3 months. Publishes ms 1-2 years after acceptance. Will consider simultaneous submissions if author lets us know. Important: See www.cicadamag.com. For updated submissions guidelines as editorial needs fluctuate.

ILLUSTRATION Buys 20 illustrations/issue; 120 illustrations/year. Uses color artwork for cover; b&w

for interior. Works on assignment only. Reviews ms/illustration packages from artists. To submit samples, e-mail a link to your online portfolio to: dvetter@cicadamag.com. You may also e-mail a sample up to a maximum attachment size of 50 KB. We will keep your samples on file and contact you if we find an assignment that suits your style.

PHOTOS Wants documentary photos (clear shots that illustrate specific artifacts, persons, locations, phenomena, etc., cited in the text) and "art" shots of teens in photo montage/lighting effects etc. Send photocopies/tearsheets of artwork.

TERMS Credit line given. Pays on publication. Rates and contract rights vary.

TIPS "Quality writing, good literary style, genuine teen sensibility, depth, humor, good character development, avoidance of stereotypes. Read several issues to familarize yourself with our style."

CLICK

30 Grove St., Suite C, Peterborough, NH 03458. E-mail: click@caruspub.com. Website: www.cricket mag.com. **Editor:** Amy Tao. **Art Director:** Deb Porter. 9 issues/year. Estab. 1998. "*Click* is a science and exploration magazine for children ages 3 to 7. Designed and written with the idea that it's never too early to encourage achild's natural curiosity about the world, *Click*'s 40 full-color pages are filled with amazing photographs, beautiful illustrations, and stories and articles that are both entertaining and thought-provoking."

NONFICTION Young readers: animals, nature/environment, science. Average word length: 100-900. Byline given.

HOW TO CONTACT *Click* does not accept unsolicited manuscripts or queries. All articles are commissioned. To be considered for assignments, experienced science writers may send a resume and three published clips.

ILLUSTRATION Buys 10 illustrations/issue; 100 illustrations/year. Works on assignment only. Query with samples. Responds only if interested. Credit line given.

COBBLESTONE

Cobblestone Publishing, 30 Grove Street, Suite C, Peterborough NH 03458. (800)821-0115. Fax: (603)924-7380. E-mail: customerservice@caruspub.com. Website: www.cobblestonepub.com. Magazine published 9 times/year. Circ. 27,000. "*Cobblestone* is theme-related. Writers should request editorial guidelines which explain procedure and list upcoming themes. Queries must relate to an upcoming theme. It is recommended that writers become familiar with the magazine (sample copies available). All articles must relate to the issue's theme. Buys 120 mss/year. Average word length: 600-800. Byline given. Preferred theme or style: Material that is fun, clear and accurate but not too juvenile. Historically accurate sources are a must. Works on assignment only. Writers: "Submit detailed queries that show attention to historical accuracy and that offer interesting and entertaining information. Study past issues to know what we look for. All feature articles, recipes, activities, fiction and supplemental nonfiction are freelance contributions." Covers material for ages 9-14. Guidelines available on website or with SASE; sample copy for $6.95, $2 shipping/handling, 10x13 SASE.

○ "*Cobblestone* stands apart from other children's magazines by offering a solid look at one subject and stressing strong editorial content, color photographs throughout, and original illustrations." *Cobblestone* themes and deadline are available on website or with SASE.

FICTION Middle readers, young adults: folktales, history, multicultural. 800 words maximum. Pays 20-25¢/word.

NONFICTION Middle readers (school ages 9-14): arts/crafts, biography, geography, history (world and American), multicultural, social issues. Query with writing sample, 1-page outline, bibliography, SASE. 800 words/feature articles; 300-600 words/supplemental nonfiction; up to 700 words maximum/activities. Pays 20-25¢/word.

POETRY "Clear, objective imagery. Serious and light verse considered." Must have clear, objective imagery. 50 lines maximum. Pays on an individual basis. Acquires all rights.

HOW TO CONTACT Fiction/nonfiction: Query. Include: a brief cover letter, a detailed one-page outline, an extensive bibliography of materials, a SASE. Writers new to *Cobblestone* should send a writing sample with query. Include SASE. In all correspondence, please include your complete address as well as a telephone number where you can be reached. Each query must have a separate cover letter, outline, bibliography and SASE. Telephone queries are not accepted. Handwritten queries will not be considered. Queries may be submitted at any time, but queries sent well in advance of deadline *may not be answered for several months.* Go-aheads requesting material proposed in queries are usually sent 5 months prior to publication date. Unused queries will not be returned."

ILLUSTRATION Reviews ms/illustration packages from artists. Query. Illustrations only: Send photocopies, tearsheets, or other nonreturnable samples. "Illustrators should consult issues of *Cobblestone* to familiarize themselves with our needs." Responds to art samples in 1 month. Samples are not returned; samples filed. Original artwork returned at job's completion (upon written request). Credit line given. Illustrators: "Submit color samples, not too juvenile. Study past issues to know what we look for. The illustration we use is generally for stories, recipes and activities."

PHOTOS Captions, identification of subjects required, model release. Reviews contact sheets, transparencies, prints. $15-100/b&w. Pays on publication. Credit line given. Buys one-time rights. Our suggested fee range for professional quality photographs follows: ¼ page to full page b/w $15 to $100; color $25 to $100. Please note that fees for non-professional quality photographs are negotiated.

TERMS Pays on an individual basis. Must relate to theme. Buys 5 color illustrations/issue; 45 illustrations/year. Pays after publication. Buys all rights to articles and artwork. Pays 20-25¢/word for articles/stories. Pays on an individual basis for poetry, activities, games/puzzles. Pays photographers per photo ($50-100 for color). Sample copy $5.95 with 9×12 SAE and 4 first-class stamps; writer's/illustrator's/photo guidelines free with SAE and 1 first-class stamp.

TIPS "Review theme lists and past issues to see what we're looking for."

⊕ CRICKET

Carus Publishing Company, 70 East Lake, Suite 300, Chicago, IL 60601. (312)701-1270. Website: www.cricketmag.com. **Editor-in-Chief:** Marianne Carus. **Executive Editor:** Lonnie Plecha. **Senior Art Director:** Karen Kohn. Publishes 9 issues/year. Estab. 1973. Circ. 55,000. Children's literary magazine for ages 9-14. **Contact:** Submissions Editor. Monthly magazine for children ages 9-14. Guidelines available online.

FICTION Middle readers, young adults/teens: contemporary, fantasy, folk and fairy tales, history, humorous, science fiction, suspense/mystery. Buys 70 mss/year. Maximum word length: 2,000. Byline given. No didactic, sex, religious, or horror stories. Length:

200-2,000 words. Pays 25¢/word maximum, and 6 contributor's copies; $2.50 charge for extras.

NONFICTION Middle readers, young adults/teens: adventure, architecture, archaeology, biography, foreign culture, games/puzzles, geography, natural history, science and technology, social science, sports, travel. Multicultural needs include articles on customs and cultures. Requests bibliography with submissions. Buys 30 mss/year. Average word length: 200-1,500. Byline given. Submit complete ms, SASE. Length: 200-1,500 words. Pays 25¢/word maximum.

POETRY Reviews poems, 1-page maximum length. Limit submission to 5 poems or less. Serious, humorous, nonsense rhymes. 50 lines maximum. Pays $3/line maximum.

HOW TO CONTACT Send complete ms. Do not query first. Responds to mss in 4-6 months. Does not like but will consider simultaneous submissions. SASE required for response, IRC's for international submissions.

ILLUSTRATION Buys 22 illustrations (7 separate commissions)/issue; 198 illustrations/year. Preferred theme for style: "stylized realism; strong people, especially kids; good action illustration; whimsical and humorous. All media, generally full color." Reviews ms/illustration packages from artists, "but reserves option to re-illustrate." Send complete ms with sample and query. Illustrations only: Provide link to website or tearsheets and good quality photocopies to be kept on file. SASE required for response/return of samples.

PHOTOS Purchases photos with accompanying ms only. Model/property releases required. Uses 300 DPI digital files, color glossy prints. Commissions all art separately from the text. Tearsheets/photocopies of both color and b&w work are considered. Accepts artwork done in pencil, pen and ink, watercolor, acrylic, oil, pastels, scratchboard, and woodcut. Does not want work that is overly caricatured or cartoony. It is especially helpful to see pieces showing young people, animals, action scenes, and several scenes from a narrative showing a character in different situations and emotional states.

TERMS Pays 30 days after publication. Rights purchased vary. Do not send original artwork. Pays up to 25¢/word for unsolicited articles; up to $3/line for poetry. Pays $750 for color cover; $150-250 for color inside. Writer's/illustrator's guidelines for SASE. Sample issue for $5, check made out to Cricket Magazine Group.

TIPS Writers: "Read copies of back issues and current issues. Adhere to specified word limits. *Please* do not query." Would currently like to see more fantasy and science fiction. Illustrators: "Send only your best work and be able to reproduce that quality in assignments. Put name and address on *all* samples. Know a publication before you submit."

DAVEY AND GOLIATH'S DEVOTIONS

Augsburg Fortress Publishers, P.O. Box 1209, Minneapolis MN 55440-1209. E-mail: cllsub@augsburgfortress.org. Website: www.augsburgfortress.org. **Editor:** Becky Carlson. Quarterly magazine. Circ. approximately 40,000. This is a booklet of interactive conversations and activities related to weekly devotional material. Used primarily by Lutheran families with elementary school-aged children. "*Davey and Goliath*'s devotions is a magazine with concrete ideas that families can use to build biblical literacy and share faith and serve others. It includes Bible stories, family activities, crafts, games, and a section of puzzles, and mazes."

HOW TO CONTACT Visit www.augsburgfortress.org/media/company/downloads/FamilyDevotionalSampleBriefing.oc to view sample briefing. Follow instructions in briefing if interested in submitting a sample for the devotional. Published material is 100% assigned.

TERMS Pays on acceptance of final ms assignment. Buys all rights. Pays $40/printed page on assignment. Free sample and information for prospective writers. Include 6×9 SAE and postage.

TIPS "Pay attention to details in the sample devotional. Follow the process laid out in the information for prospective writers. Ability to interpret Bible texts appropriately for children is required. Content must be doable and fun for families on the go."

DIG

30 Grove St., Suite C, Peterborough NH 03450. (603)924-7209. Fax: (603)924-7380. E-mail: cfbakeriii@meganet.net. Website: www.cobblestonepub.com. Website: www.cobblestonepub.com. **Editor:** Rosalie Baker. **Editorial Director:** Lou Waryncia. **Art Director:** Ann Dillon. Magazine published 9 times/year. Estab. 1999. Circ. 18,000. An archaeology magazine for kids ages 8-14. Publishes entertaining and educational stories about discoveries, artifacts, archaeologists.

◯*Dig* was purchased by Cobblestone Publishing, a division of Carus Publishing.

NONFICTION Middle readers, young adults: biography, games/puzzles, history, science, archaeology. Buys 50 mss/year. Average word length: 400-800. Byline given.

HOW TO CONTACT Fiction/nonfiction: Query. "A query must consist of all of the following to be considered: a brief cover letter stating the subject and word length of the proposed article, a detailed one-page outline explaining the information to be presented in the article, a bibliography of materials the author intends to use in preparing the article, and a SASE. Writers new to *Dig* should send a writing sample with query." Multiple queries accepted, may not be answered for many months. Go-aheads requesting material proposed in queries are usually sent 10 months prior to publication date. Unused queries will be returned approximately 3-4 months prior to publication date.

ILLUSTRATION Buys 10-15 illustrations/issue; 60-75 illustrations/year. Prefers color artwork. Works on assignment only. Reviews ms/illustration packages from artists. Query. Illustrations only: Query with samples. Arrange portfolio review. Send tearsheets. Responds in 2 months only if interested. Samples not returned; samples filed. Credit line given.

PHOTOS Uses anything related to archaeology, history, artifacts, and current archaeological events that relate to kids. Uses color prints and 35mm transparencies and 300 DPI digital images. Provide resume, promotional literature or tearsheets to be kept on file. Responds only if interested.

TERMS Pays on publication. Buys all rights for mss. Buys first North American rights for photos. Original artwork returned at job's completion. Pays 20-25¢/word. Additional payment for ms/illustration packages and for photos accompanying articles. Pays per photo.

TIPS "We are looking for writers who can communicate archaeological concepts in a conversational, interesting, informative and *accurate* style for kids. Writers should have some idea where photography can be located to support their articles."

DRAMATICS MAGAZINE

Educational Theatre Association, 2343 Auburn Ave., Cincinnati OH 45219. (513)421-3900. E-mail: dcorathers@edta.org. Website: www.edta.org. **Articles Editor:** Don Corathers. **Graphic Design:** Kay Walters. Published monthly September-May. Estab. 1929. Circ. 35,000. "*Dramatics* is for students (mainly high school age) and teachers of theater. Mix includes how-to (tech theater, acting, directing, etc.), informational, interview, photo feature, humorous, profile, technical. We want our student readers to grow as theater artists and become a more discerning and appreciative audience. Material is directed to both theater students and their teachers, with strong student slant."

FICTION Young adults: drama (one-act and full-length plays). Does not want to see plays that show no understanding of the conventions of the theater. No plays for children, no Christmas or didactic "message" plays. "We prefer unpublished scripts that have been produced at least once." Buys 5-9 plays/year. Emerging playwrights have better chances with résumé of credits.

NONFICTION Young adults: arts/crafts, careers, how-to, interview/profile, multicultural (all theater-related). "We try to portray the theater community in all its diversity." Does not want to see academic treatises. Buys 50 mss/year. Average word length: 750-3,000. Byline given.

HOW TO CONTACT Send complete ms. Responds in 3 months (longer for plays). Publishes ms 3 months after acceptance. Will consider simultaneous submissions and previously published work occasionally.

ILLUSTRATION Buys 0-2 illustrations/year. Works on assignment only. Arrange portfolio review; send résumé, promo sheets and tearsheets. Responds only if interested. Samples returned with SASE; sample not filed. Credit line given.

PHOTOS Buys photos with accompanying ms only. Looking for "good-quality production or candid photography to accompany article. We very occasionally publish photo essays." Model/property release and captions required. Prefers hi-res jpg files. Will consider prints or transparencies. Query with reésumeé of credits. Responds only if interested.

TERMS Pays on acceptance. Buys one-time print and short-term Web rights. Buys one-time rights for artwork and photos. Original artwork returned at job's completion. Pays $100-500 for plays; $50-500 for articles; up to $100 for illustrations. Pays photographers by the project or per photo. Sometimes offers additional payment for ms/illustration packages and photos accompanying a ms. Sample copy available for 9×12 SAE with 4 ounces first-class postage.

Writer's and photo guidelines available for SASE or via website.

TIPS "Obtain our writer's guidelines and look at recent back issues. The best way to break in is to know our audience—drama students, teachers and others interested in theater—and write for them. Writers who have some practical experience in theater, especially in technical areas, have an advantage, but we'll work with anybody who has a good idea. Some freelancers have become regular contributors."

🌀 EXPLORE

Pearson Education Australia, 20 Thackray Rd., Port Melbourne VIC 3207 Australia. (61)03 3245 7111. Fax: (61)03 9245 7333. E-mail: magazines@pearson.com.au. Website: www.pearson.com.au/schools. Quarterly Magazine. Circ. 20,000. Pearson Education publishes "educational magazines that include a variety of nonfiction articles in a variety of genres and text types (interviews, diary, informational, recount, argumentative, etc.). They must be appropriate, factually correct and of high interest.

⭕ *Explore* is a theme based publication. Check the website to see upcoming themes and deadlines.

FICTION Young readers, middle readers: adventure, animal, contemporary, fantasy, folktale, humorous, multicultural, nature/environment, problem-solving, suspense/mystery. Middle readers: science fiction, sports. Average word length: 400-1,000. Byline given.

NONFICTION Young readers, middle readers: animal, arts/crafts, biography, careers, cooking, health, history, hobbies, how-to, interview/profile, math, multicultural, nature/environment, problem-solving, science, social issues, sports, travel. Young readers: games/puzzles. Middle readers: concept, fashion, geography. Average word length: 200-600. Byline given.

POETRY Reviews poetry.

HOW TO CONTACT Fiction/nonfiction: Send complete ms. Responds to queries in 1 month; mss in 3 months. Publishes ms 3 months after acceptance. Will consider simultaneous submissions and electronic submissions via disk or e-mail.

PHOTOS Looking for photos to suit various themes; photos needed depend on stories. Model/property release required; captions required. Uses color, standard sized, prints, high resolution digital images and 35mm transparencies. Provide résumé, business card, promotional literature and tearsheets to be kept on file.

TERMS Pays on publication. Buys first Australian rights. Pays $80-200 (Australian) for stories; $100-220 (Australian) for articles.

TIPS "Check out our website for information about our publications." Also see listings for *Challenge* and *Comet*.

FACES

Cobblestone Publishing,, 30 Grove St., Suite C, Peterborough NH 03458. (603)924-7209; (800)821-0115. Fax: (603)924-7380. E-mail: customerservice@caruspub.com. Website: www.cobblestonepub.com. Magazine published 9 times/year (September-May) with combined issues in May/June, July/August, and November/December. Circ. 15,000. *Faces* is a theme-related magazine; writers should send for theme list before submitting ideas/queries. Each month a different world culture is featured through the use of feature articles, activities and photographs and illustrations. Sample copy for $6.95, $2 shipping and handling, 10 x 13 SASE. Guidelines with SASE or online.

FICTION Middle readers, young adults/teens: adventure, folktales, history, multicultural, plays, religious, travel. Does not want to see material that does not relate to a specific upcoming theme. Buys 9 mss/year. Maximum word length: 800. Byline given. 800 words maximum. Pays 20-25¢/word.

NONFICTION Middle readers and young adults/teens: animal, anthropology, arts/crafts, biography, cooking, fashion, games/puzzles, geography, history, how-to, humorous, interview/profile, nature/environment, religious, social issues, sports, travel. Does not want to see material not related to a specific upcoming theme. Buys 63 mss/year. Average word length: 300-600. Byline given. Query with writing sample, 1-page outline, bibliography, SASE. 800 words/feature articles; 300-600/supplemental nonfiction; up to 700 words/activities. Pays 20-25¢/word.

POETRY Serious and light verse considered. Must have clear, objective imagery. 100 lines maximum. Pays on an individual basis.

HOW TO CONTACT Fiction/nonfiction: Query with published clips and 2-3 line biographical sketch. "Ideas should be submitted 6-9 months prior to the publication date. Responses to ideas are usually sent approximately 4 months before the publication date." Guidelines online.

ILLUSTRATION Buys 3 illustrations/issue; buys 27 illustrations/year. Preferred theme or style: Material that is meticulously researched (most articles are written by professional anthropologists); simple, direct style preferred, but not too juvenile. Works on assignment only. Roughs required. Reviews ms/illustration packages from artists. Illustrations only: Send samples of b&w work. "Illustrators should consult issues of *Faces* to familiarize themselves with our needs." Responds to art samples only if interested. Samples returned with SASE. Original artwork returned at job's completion (upon written request). Credit line given.

PHOTOS Wants photos relating to forthcoming themes. "Contact the editor by mail or fax, or send photos with your query. You may also send images on speculation." Captions, identification of subjects, model releases required. Reviews contact sheets, transparencies, prints. Pays $15-100/b&w; $25-100/color; cover fees are negotiated.

TERMS Pays on publication. Buys all rights for mss and artwork. Pays 20-25¢/word for articles/stories. Pays on an individual basis for poetry. Covers are assigned and paid on an individual basis. Pays illustrators $50-300 for color inside. Pays photographers per photo ($25-100 for color). Sample copy $6.95 with 7½×10½ SAE and 5 first-class stamps. Writer's/illustrator's/photo guidelines via website or free with SASE and 1 first-class stamp.

TIPS "Writers are encouraged to study past issues of the magazine to become familiar with our style and content. Writers with anthropological and/or travel experience are particularly encouraged; *Faces* is about world cultures. All feature articles, recipes and activities are freelance contributions. Illustrators: Submit b&w samples, not too juvenile. Study past issues to know what we look for. The illustration we use is generally for retold legends, recipes and activities."

THE FRIEND MAGAZINE

The Church of Jesus Christ of Latter-day Saints, 50 E. North Temple St., Room 2432, Salt Lake City, UT 84150-3226. (801)240-2210. E-mail: friend@ldschurch.org. Website: www.lds.org. **Art Director:** Mark Robison. Monthly magazine for 3-12 year olds. Estab. 1971. Circ. 275,000.

NONFICTION Publishes children's/true stories—adventure, ethnic, some historical, humor, mainstream,

religious/inspirational, nature. Length: 1,000 words maximum. Also publishes family- and gospel-oriented puzzles, games and cartoons. Simple recipes and handicraft projects welcome.

POETRY Reviews poetry. Maximum length: 20 lines. "We are looking for easy-to-illustrate peoms with catchy cadences. Poems should convey a sense of joy adn reflect gospel teachings. Also brief poems that will appeal to preschoolers."

HOW TO CONTACT Send complete ms. Responds to mss in 2 months.

ILLUSTRATION Illustrations only: Query with samples; arrange personal interview to show portfolio; provide résumé and tearsheets for files.

TERMS Pays on acceptance. Buys all rights for mss. Pays $100-150 (400 words and up) for stories; $30 for poems; $20 minimum for activities and games. Contributors are encouraged to send for sample copy for $1.50, 9×12 envelope and four 41-cent stamps. Free writer's guidelines.

TIPS "*The Friend* is published by The Church of Jesus Christ of Latter-day Saints for boys and girls up to 11 years of age. All submissions are carefully read by the *Friend* staff, and those not accepted are returned within 2 months for SASE. Submit seasonal material at least one year in advance. Query letters and simultaneous submissions are not encouraged. Authors may request rights to have their work reprinted after their manuscript is published."

FUN FOR KIDZ

Website: http://funforkidz.com. P.O. Box 227, Bluffton OH 45817-0227. (419)358-4610. Fax: (419)358-5027. E-mail: submissions@funforkidz.com. Website: www.funforkidz.com. **Articles Editor:** Marilyn Edwards. Bimonthly magazine. Estab. 2002. "*Fun for Kidz* is a magazine created for boys and girls ages 5-14, with youngsters 8, 9, and 10 the specific target age. The magazine is designed as an activity publication to be enjoyed by both boys and girls on the alternative months of *Hopscotch* and *Boys' Quest* magazines."

○*Fun for Kidz* is theme-oriented. Send SASE for theme list and writer's guidelines.

FICTION Picture-oriented material, young readers, middle readers: adventure, animal, history, humorous, problem-solving, multicultural, nature/environment, sports. Average word length: 300-700.

NONFICTION Picture-oriented material, young readers, middle readers: animal, arts/crafts, cooking, games/puzzles, history, hobbies, how-to, humorous, problem-solving, sports, carpentry projects. Average word length: 300-700. Byline given.

POETRY Reviews poetry.

HOW TO CONTACT Fiction/nonfiction: Send complete ms. Responds to queries in 2 weeks; mss in 5 weeks. Will consider simultaneous submissions.

ILLUSTRATION Works on assignment mostly. "We are anxious to find artists capable of illustrating stories and features. Our inside art is pen and ink." Query with samples. Samples kept on file.

PHOTOS "We use a number of b&w photos inside the magazine; most support the articles used."

TERMS Pays on publication. Buys first American serial rights. Buys first American serial rights and photos for artwork. Pays $0.05/word; $10/poem or puzzle; $35 for art (full page); $25 for art (partial page). Pays illustrators $5-10 for b&w photos. Sample copies available for $6 (there is a direct charge by the post office of $4.50 per issue for airmail to other countries); $8 for Canada, and $10.50 for all other countries.

TIPS "Our point of view is that every child deserves the right to be a child for a number of years before he or she becomes a young adult. As a result, *Fun for Kidz* looks for activities that deal with timeless topics, such as pets, nature, hobbies, science, games, sports, careers, simple cooking, and anything else likely to interest a child."

GIRLS' LIFE

Monarch Publishing, 4529 Harford Rd., Baltimore MD 21214. (410)426-9600. Fax: (410)254-0991. E-mail: katiea@girlslife.com. Website: www.girlslife. com. **Contact:** Katie Abbondanza, senior editor. Bi-monthly magazine for girls, ages 9-15. Estab.1994. Circ. 400,000. Editorial lead time 4 months. Sample copy for $5 or online. Guidelines available online.

FICTION "We accept short fiction. They should be stand-alone stories and are generally 2,500-3,500 words."

NONFICTION "Features and articles should speak to young women ages 10-15 looking for new ideas about relationships, family, friends, school, etc., with fresh, savvy advice. Front-of-the-book columns and quizzes are a good place to start." Buys 40 mss/year. Length: 700-2,000 words. Pays $350/regular column; $500/feature. Query by mail with published clips. Submit complete mss on spec only. Length: 700-2,000 words. Pays $350/regular column; $500/feature.

HOW TO CONTACT Accepts queries by mail or e-mail. Query with published clips. Submit complete mss on spec only. Responds in 3 month to queries.

PHOTOS State availability with submission if applicable. Reviews contact sheets, negatives, transparencies. Negotiates payment individually. Captions, identification of subjects, model releases required.

TERMS Pays on publication. Publishes ms an average of 3 months after acceptance. Byline given. Buys all rights. Editorial lead time 4 months. Submit seasonal material 5 months in advance. Sample copy for $5 or online. Writer's guidelines online.

TIPS "Send queries with published writing samples and detailed resume. Have new ideas, a voice that speaks to our audience—not *down* to our audience—and supply artwork source."

GREEN TEACHER

95 Robert St., Toronto ON M2S 2K5.(416)960-1244. Fax: (416)925-3474. E-mail: info@greenteacher.com. Website: www.greenteacher.com. **Article Editor/Photo Editor:** Gail Littlejohn and Tim Grant. Estab. 1991. Circ. 15,000. "*Green Teacher* is a magazine that helps youth educators enhance environmental and global education inside and outside of schools."

NONFICTION Considers all levels: multicultural, nature/environment. Average word length: 750-2,500.

HOW TO CONTACT Nonfiction: Query. Responds to queries in 1 weeks; Publishes ms 8 months after acceptance. Considers electronic submissions via disk or e-mail.

ILLUSTRATION Buys 3 illustrations/issue from freelancers; 10 illustrations/year from freelancers. Black & white artwork only. Works on assignment only. Reviews ms/illustration packages from artists. Query. **Contact:** Gail Littlejohn, editor. Illustrations only: Query with samples; tearsheets. Responds only if interested. Samples not returned. Samples filed. Credit line given.

PHOTOS Purchases photos both separately and with accompanying mss. "Activity photos, environmental photos." Uses b&w prints. Query with samples. Responds only of interested.

TERMS Pays on acceptance.

GUIDE MAGAZINE

Review and Herald Publishing Association, 55 W. Oak Ridge Dr., Hagerstown MD 21740. (301)393-4037. Fax: (301)393-4055. E-mail: guide@rhpa.org. Website: www.guidemagazine.org. **Editor:** Randy

Fishell. **Designer:** Brandon Reese. Weekly magazine. Estab. 1953. Circ. 27,000. "Ours is a weekly Christian journal written for middle readers and young teens (ages 10-14), presenting true stories relevant to the needs of today's young person, emphasizing positive aspects of Christian living." Guidelines available online at website.

> "*Guide* is a Christian story magazine for young people ages 10-14. The 32-page, 4-color publication is published weekly by the Review and Herald Publishing Association. Our mission is to show readers, through stories that illustrate Bible truth, how to walk with God now and forever."

NONFICTION Middle readers, young adults/teens: adventure, animal, character-building, contemporary, games/puzzles, humorous, multicultural, problem-solving, religious. "We need true happenings, not merely true-to-life. Our stories and puzzles must have a spiritual emphasis." No violence. No articles. "We always need humor and adventure stories." Buys 150 mss/year. Average word length: 500-600 minimum, 1,200-1,300 maximum. Byline given. Each issue includes 3-4 true stories. *Guide* does not publish fiction, poetry, or articles (devotionals, how-to, profiles, etc.). However, we sometimes accept quizzes and other unique nonstory formats. Each piece should include a clear spiritual element. Standard feature-length stories are 1,000-1,200 words, but we also accept shorter pieces of 450 words and up. Payment is 7-10 cents/word upon acceptance for first serial rights."

HOW TO CONTACT Nonfiction: Send complete ms. Responds in 6 weeks. Will consider simultaneous submissions. "We can pay half of the regular amount for reprints." Responds to queries/mss in 6 weeks. Credit line given. "We encourage e-mail submissions."

TERMS Pays on acceptance. Buys first world serial rights; first rights; one-time rights; second serial (reprint rights); simultaneous rights. Pays 6-12¢/word for stories and articles. "Writer receives 3 complimentary copies of issue in which work appears." Sample copy free with 6×9 SAE and 2 first-class stamps. Writer's guidelines for SASE.

TIPS "Children's magazines want mystery, action, discovery, suspense and humor—no matter what the topic. For us, truth is stronger than fiction."

HIGHLIGHTS FOR CHILDREN

803 Church St., Honesdale PA 18431. (570)253-1080. E-mail: eds@highlights-corp.com. Website: www.High lights.com. **Contacts:** Christine French Clark. editor-in-chief, and Cindy Smith, art director. Monthly magazine. Estab. 1946. Circ. approximately 2 million. "Our motto is 'Fun With a Purpose.' We are looking for quality fiction and nonfiction that appeals to children, encourages them to read, and reinforces positive values. All art is done on assignment." Monthly magazine for children up to age 12. Sample copy free. Guidelines on website in "About Us" area.

FICTION Picture-oriented material, young readers, middle readers: adventure, animal, contemporary, fantasy, folktales, history, humorous, multicultural, problem-solving, sports. Multicultural needs include first-person accounts of children from other cultures and first-person accounts of children from other countries. Does not want to see war, crime, violence. "We see too many stories with overt morals." Would like to see more contemporary, multicultural and world culture fiction, mystery stories, action/adventure stories, humorous stories, and fiction for younger readers. Buys 150 mss/year. Average word length: 500-800. Byline given. Meaningful stories appealing to both girls and boys, up to age 12. Vivid, full of action. Engaging plot, strong characterization, lively language. Prefers stories in which a child protagonist solves a dilemma through his or her own resources. Seeks stories that the child ages 8-12 will eagerly read, and the child ages 2-7 will like to hear when read aloud (500-800 words). Stories require interesting plots and a number of illustration possiblities. Also need rebuses (picture stories 120 words or under), stories with urban settings, stories for beginning readers (100-500 words), sports and humorous stories, adventures, holiday stories, and mysteries. We also would like to see more material of 1-page length (300 words), both fiction and factual. Send complete ms. Length: words. Pays $150 minimum.

NONFICTION Picture-oriented material, young readers, middle readers: animal, arts/crafts, biography, careers, games/puzzles, geography, health, history, hobbies, how-to, interview/profile, multicultural, nature/environment, problem-solving, science, sports. Multicultural needs include articles set in a country *about* the people of the country. Does not want to see trendy topics, fads, personalities who would not be good role models for children, guns, war, crime, violence. "We'd like to see more nonfiction for younger readers—maximum of 500 words. We still need older-reader material, too—500-800 words." Buys 200 mss/year. Maximum word length: 800. Byline given. "Generally we prefer to see a manuscript rather than a query. However, we will review queries regarding nonfiction." Pays $25 for craft ideas and puzzles; $25 for fingerplays; $150 and up for articles.

POETRY Lines/poem: 16 or less ("most poems are shorter"). Considers simultaneous submissions ("please indicate"); no previously published poetry. No e-mail submissions. "Submit typed manuscript with very brief cover letter." Occasionally comments on submissions "if manuscript has merit or author seems to have potential for our market." Guidelines available for SASE. Responds "generally within one month." Always sends prepublication galleys. Pays 2 contributor's copies; "money varies." Acquires all rights.

HOW TO CONTACT Send complete ms. Responds to queries in 1 month; mss in 6 weeks.

ILLUSTRATION Buys 25-30 illustrations/issue. Preferred theme or style: Realistic, some stylization. Works on assignment only. Reviews ms/illustration packages from artists. Illustrations only: photocopies, promo sheet, tearsheets, or slides. Résumé optional. Portfolio only if requested. Contact: Art Director. Responds to art samples in 2 months. Samples returned with SASE; samples filed. Credit line given.

PHOTOS Reviews color 35mm slides, photos, or electronic files.

TERMS Pays on acceptance. Buys all rights for mss. Pays $50 and up for unsolicited articles. Pays illustrators $700 for color front cover; $25-200 for b&w inside, $100-500 for color inside. Sample copies $3.95 and send SASE with 4 first-class stamps. Writer's/illustrator's guidelines free with SASE and on website.

TIPS "We are pleased that many authors of children's literature report that their first published work was in the pages of *Highlights*. It is not our policy to consider fiction on the strength of the reputation of the author. We judge each submission on its own merits. With factual material, however, we do prefer that writers be authorities in their field or people with first-hand experience. In this manner we can avoid the encyclopedic article that merely restates information readily available elsewhere. We don't make assignments. Query with simple letter to establish whether the nonfiction subject is likely to be of interest. A beginning writer should first become famil-

iar with the type of material that *Highlights* publishes. Include special qualifications, if any, of author. Write for the child, not the editor. Write in a voice that children understand and relate to. Speak to today's kids, avoiding didactic, overt messages. Even though our general principles haven't changed over the years, we are contemporary in our approach to issues. Avoid worn themes."

⊕ HIGHLIGHTS HIGH FIVE

807 Church St., Honesdale PA 18431. Fax: (570)251-7847. Website: www.highlights.com/highfive. **Contact:** Kathleen Hayes, editor. Guidelines available at website online.

🔾"Our newest magazine."

TIPS "Writers may find it helpful to read several issues of *High Five*."

HOPSCOTCH

The Magazine for Girls, P.O. Box 227, Bluffton OH 45817-0164. (419)358-4610. Fax: (419)358-5027. Website: http://hopscotchmagazine.com. E-mail: submissions@funforkidz.com. **Editor:** Marilyn Edwards. Bimonthly magazine. Estab. 1989. Circ. 14,000. For girls from ages 5- 14, featuring traditional subjects—pets, games, hobbies, nature, science, sports, etc.—with an emphasis on articles that show girls actively involved in unusual and/or worthwhile activities."

FICTION Picture-oriented material, young readers, middle readers: adventure, animal, history, humorous, nature/environment, sports, suspense/mystery. Does not want to see stories dealing with dating, sex, fashion, hard rock music. Buys 30 mss/year. Average word length: 300-700. Byline given.

NONFICTION Picture-oriented material, young readers, middle readers: animal, arts/crafts, biography, cooking, games/puzzles, geography, hobbies, how-to, humorous, math, nature/environment, science. Does not want to see pieces dealing with dating, sex, fashion, hard rock music. "Need more nonfiction with quality photos about a *Hopscotch*-age girl involved in a worthwhile activity." Buys 46 mss/year. Average word length: 400-700. Byline given.

POETRY Reviews traditional, wholesome, humorous poems. Maximum word length: 300; maximum line length: 20. Will accept 6 submissions/author.

HOW TO CONTACT All writers should consult the theme list before sending in articles. To receive a current theme list, send a SASE. Fiction: Send complete ms. Nonfiction: Query or send complete ms.

Responds to queries in 2 weeks; mss in 5 weeks. Will consider simultaneous submissions.

ILLUSTRATION Buys approximately 10 illustrations/issue; buys 60-70 articles/year. "Generally, the illustrations are assigned after we have purchased a piece (usually fiction). Occasionally, we will use a painting—in any given medium—for the cover, and these are usually seasonal." Uses b&w artwork only for inside; color for cover. Reviews ms/illustration packages from artists. Query first or send complete ms with final art. Illustrations only: Send résumé, portfolio, client list and tearsheets. Responds to art samples only if interested and SASE in 1 month. Samples returned with SASE. Credit line given.

PHOTOS Purchases photos separately (cover only) and with accompanying ms only. Looking for photos to accompany article. Model/property releases required. Uses 5×7, b&w prints; 35mm transparencies. Black & white photos should go with ms. Should show girl or girls ages 6-12.

TERMS For mss: pays on publication. For mss, artwork and photos, buys first North American serial rights; second serial (reprint rights). Original artwork returned at job's completion. Pays 5¢/word and $5-10/photo. "We always send a copy of the issue to the writer or illustrator." Text and art are treated separately. Pays $200 maximum for color cover; $25-35 for b&w inside. Sample copy for $6 (there is a direct charge by the post office of $4.50 per issue for airmail to other countries) and 8×12 SASE; $8 for Canada, and $10.50 for all other countries. Writer's/illustrator's/photo guidelines, theme list free for #10 SASE.

TIPS "Remember we publish only six issues a year, which means our editorial needs are extremely limited. Please look at our guidelines and our magazine.. and remember, we use far more nonfiction than fiction. Guidelines and current theme list can be downloaded from our website. If decent photos accompany the piece, it stands an even better chance of being accepted. We believe it is the responsibility of the contributor to come up with photos. Please remember, our readers are 6-12 years—most are 8-10—and your text should reflect that. Many magazines try to entertain first and educate second. We try to do the reverse. Our magazine is more simplistic, like a book to be read from cover to cover. We are looking for wholesome, non-dated material."

◎ HORSEPOWER

P.O. Box 670, Aurora ON L4G 4J9, Canada. (800)505-7428. Fax: (905)841-1530. E-mail: info@horse-canada.com. Website: www.horse-canada.com. **Managing Editor**: Susan Stafford. Estab. 1988. Circ. 17,000. Bimonthly 16-page magazine, bound into *Horse Canada*, a bimonthly family horse magazine. "*Horsepower* offers how-to articles and stories relating to horse care for kids ages 6-16, with a focus on safety."

◎*Horsepower* no longer accepts fiction.

NONFICTION Middle readers, young adults: arts/crafts, biography, careers, fashion, games/puzzles, health, history, hobbies, how-to, humorous, interview/profile, problem-solving, travel. Buys 6-10 mss/year. Average word length: 500-1,200. Byline given.

HOW TO CONTACT Fiction: query. Nonfiction: send complete ms. Responds to queries in 6 months; mss in 3 months. Publishes ms 6 months after acceptance. Will consider simultaneous submissions, electronic submission via disk or e-mail, previously published work.

ILLUSTRATION Buys 3 illustrations/year. Reviews ms/illustration packages from artists. Contact: Editor. Query with samples. Responds only if interested. Samples returned with SASE; samples kept on file. Credit line given.

PHOTOS Looks for photos of kids and horses, instructional/educational, relating to riding or horse care. Uses color matte or glossy prints. Query with samples. Responds only if interested. Accepts TIFF or JPEG 300 dpi, disk or e-mail. Children on horseback must be wearing riding helmets or photos cannot be published.

TERMS Pays on publication. Buys one-time rights for mss. Original artwork returned at job's completion if SASE provided. Pays $50-75 for stories. Additional payment for ms/illustration packages and for photos accompanying articles. Pays illustrators $25-50 for color inside. Pays photographers per photo (range: $15). Sample copies for $4.50. Writer's/illustrator's/photo guidelines for SASE.

TIPS "Articles must be easy to understand, yet detailed and accurate. How-to or other educational features must be written by, or in conjunction with, a riding/teaching professional. Fiction is not encouraged, unless it is outstanding and teaches a moral or practical lesson. Note: Preference will be given to Canadian writers and photographers due to Canadian content laws. Non-Canadian contributors accepted on a very limited basis."

IMAGINATION CAFÉ

P.O. Box 1536, Valparaiso IN 46384.(219)510-4467. E-mail: editor@imagination-cafe.com. Website: www.imagionation-cafe.com. **Articles Editor:** Rosanne Tolin. **Art Director:** Photo Editor. Estab. 2006. *"Imagination Café* is dedicated to empowering kids and tweens by encouraging curiosity in the world around them, as well as exploration of their talents and aspirations. *Imagination Café*'s mission is to offer children tools to discover their passions by providing them with reliable information, resources and safe opportunities for self-expression. *Imagination Café* publishes general interest articles with an emphasis on career exploration for kids. There is also material on school, science, history, and sports. Plus, celebrity briefs, recipes, animals, and other general interest pieces." Publication is aimed at juvenile market.

NONFICTION Buys 72 mss/year. Average word length: 150-500. Byline given.

HOW TO CONTACT *Agented submissions only.* Nonfiction: Query or query with published clips. Send complete ms. Responds to queries in 1 day to 2 weeks. Publishes ms 1 month after acceptance. Considers simultaneous submissions.

TERMS Pays on acceptance. Buys electronic and non-exclusive print rights. Originals not returned. Pays $15-75 for stories. Additional payment for ms/illustration packages.

TIPS *"Imagination Café* is not a beginner's market. Most of our contributors are published writers. Please study the website before submitting, and make sure your writing is clearly directed to a kid audience, no adults. That means informative, interesting text written in a clear, concise, even clever manner that suitable for the online reader. Have fun with it and be sure include web-friendly, relevant links and sidebars."

JACK AND JILL

Children's Better Health Institute, P.O. Box 567, Indianapolis IN 46206-0567. (317)636-8881. E-mail: j.goodman@cbhi.org. Website: www.jackandjillmag.org. "Write entertaining and imaginative stories for kids, not just about them. Writers should understand what is funny to kids, what's important to them, what excites them. Don't write from an adult 'kids are so cute' perspective. We're also looking for health and healthful lifestyle stories and articles, but don't be preachy." Bimonthly magazine published 6 times/year for children ages 8-12. Guidelines available online.

FICTION Young readers and middle readers: adventure, contemporary, folktales, health, history, humorous, nature, sports. Buys 30-35 mss/year. Average word length: 700. Byline given. Pays 30¢/word minimum.

NONFICTION Young readers, middle readers: animal, arts/crafts, cooking, games/puzzles, history, hobbies, how-to, humorous, interview/profile, nature, science, sports. Buys 8-10 mss/year. Average word length: 500. Byline given.

POETRY Reviews poetry.

HOW TO CONTACT Fiction/nonfiction: Send complete ms. Queries not accepted. Responds to mss in 3 months. Guidelines by request with a #10 SASE.

ILLUSTRATION Buys 15 illustrations/issue; 90 illustrations/year. Responds only if interested. Samples not returned; samples filed. Credit line given.

PHOTOS Publishes writing/art/photos by children.

TERMS Pays on publication; up to 25¢/word. Pays illustrators $275 for color cover; $35-90 for b&w, $70-155 for color inside. Pays photographers negotiated rate. Sample copies $1.25. Buys all rights to mss and one-time rights to photos.

TIPS "We are constantly looking for new writers who can tell good stories with interesting slants—stories that are not full of out-dated and time-worn expressions. We like to see stories about kids who are smart and capable, but not sarcastic or smug. Problem-solving skills, personal responsibility, and integrity are good topics for us. Obtain current issues of the magazine and study them to determine our present needs and editorial style."

JUNIOR BASEBALL

(203)210-5726. E-mail: jim@juniorbaseball.com. Website: www.juniorbaseball.com. Bimonthly magazine covering youth baseball. Focused on youth baseball players ages 7-17 (including high school) and their parents/coaches. Edited to various reading levels, depending upon age/skill level of feature. Buys all rights. Pays on publication. No kill fee. 25% freelance written. Byline given. Publishes ms an average of 4 months after acceptance. Submit seasonal material 4 months in advance. Responds in 2 weeks to queries. Responds in 1 month to mss. Editorial lead time 3 months. Sample copy for $5 and online. **Contact:** Jim Beecher, publisher.

NONFICTION Query. Length: 500-1,000 words. Pays $50-100.

HOW TO CONTACT Query.

PHOTOS Photos can be e-mailed in 300 dpi JPEGs. State availability. Captions, identification of subjects required. Reviews 35mm transparencies, 3 x 5 prints. Offers $10-100/photo; negotiates payment individually.

TERMS Accepts 8-12 mss/year. Length: 500-1,000 words. Pays $50-100.

TIPS "Must be well-versed in baseball! Have a child who is very involved in the sport, or have extensive hands-on experience in coaching baseball, at the youth, high school or higher level. We can always use accurate, authoritative skills information and good photos to accompany is a big advantage! This magazine is read by experts. No fiction, poems, games, puzzles, etc." Does not want first-person articles about your child.

THE KERF

E-mail: ken-letko@redwoods.edu. Website: http://redwoods.edu/Departments/english/poets&writers/clm.htm. *The Kerf*, published annually in fall, features "poetry that speaks to the environment and humanity." Wants "poetry that exhibits an environmental consciousness." Considers poetry by children and teens. Has published poetry by Ruth Daigon, Alice D'Alessio, James Grabill, George Keithley, and Paul Willis. *The Kerf* is 54 pages, digest-sized, printed via Docutech, saddle-stapled, with CS2 coverstock. Receives about 1,000 poems/year, accepts up to 3%. Press run is 400 (150 shelf sales); 100 distributed free to contributors and writing centers. Sample: $5. Make checks payable to College of the Redwoods. **Contact:** Ken Letko, editor.

KEYS FOR KIDS

CBH Ministries, Box 1001, Grand Rapids MI 49501-1001. (616)647-4971. Fax: (616)647-4950. E-mail: hazel@cbhministries.org. Website: www.cbhministries.org. **Fiction Editor:** Hazel Marett. Bimonthly devotional booklet. Estab. 1982. "This is a devotional booklet for children and is also widely used for family devotions." **Contact:** Hazel Marett, fiction editor.

FICTION Young readers, middle readers: religious. Buys 60 mss/year. Average word length: 400. Word Length: 600

HOW TO CONTACT Fiction: Send complete ms. Will consider simultaneous submissions.

TERMS Pays on acceptance. Buys reprint rights or first rights for mss. Pays $25 for stories. Sample copies free for SAE 6×9 and 3 first-class stamps. Writer's guidelines for SASE.

TIPS "Be sure to *follow* guidelines after studying sample copy of the publication."

KIDZ CHAT

Standard Publishing, 8805 Governor's Hill Dr., Suite 400, Cincinnati OH 45249. (513)931-4050. Fax: (877)867-5751. E-mail: mredford@standardpub.com. Website: www.standardpub.com. **Editor:** Marjorie Redford. Weekly magazine. Circ. 55,000.

> ◯ *Kidz Chat* has decided to reuse much of the material that was a part of the first publication cycle. They will not be sending out theme lists, sample copies or writers guidelines or accepting any unsolicited material because of this policy.

⊕ LADYBUG

(312)701-1720. Website: www.cricketmag.com. Monthly literary magazine for children 3-6, with stories, poems, activities, songs and picture stories. **Contact:** Marianne Carus, editor-in-chief; Suzanne Beck, managing art director. Guidelines available online.

FICTION Picture-oriented material: adventure, animal, fantasy, folktales, humorous, multicultural, nature/environment, problem-solving, science fiction, sports, suspense/mystery. "Open to any easy fiction stories." Buys 50 mss/year. Story length: limit 800 words. Byline given. Read-aloud stories, picture stories, original retellings of folk and fairy tales, multicultural stories. 800 words maximum. Pays 25¢/word ($25 minimum).

NONFICTION Picture-oriented material: activities, animal, arts/crafts, concept, cooking, humorous, math, nature/environment, problem-solving, science. Buys 35 mss/year. Story length: limit 800 words. Send complete ms, SASE. Length: 400-700 words. Pays 25¢/word ($25 minimum).

POETRY Reviews poems, 20-line maximum length; limit submissions to 5 poems. Uses lyrical, humorous, simple language, action rhymes. 20 lines maximum. Pays $3/line ($25 minimum).

HOW TO CONTACT Fiction/nonfiction: Send complete ms. Queries not accepted. Responds to mss in 6 months. Publishes ms up to 3 years after acceptance. Will consider simultaneous submissions if informed. Submissions without SASE will be discarded.

ILLUSTRATION Buys 12 illustrations/issue; 145 illustrations/year. Prefers "bright colors; all media, but uses watercolor and acrylics most often; same size as magazine is preferred but not required." To be considered for future assignments: Submit promo sheet, slides, tearsheets, color and b&w photocopies. Responds to art samples in 3 months. Submissions without SASE will be discarded.

PHOTOS Artists should submit tearsheets/photocopies of artwork to be kept in our illustrator files. Pays $500/spread; $250/page.

TERMS Pays on publication for mss; after delivery of completed assignment for illustrators. Rights purchased vary. Original artwork returned at job's completion. Pays 25¢/word for prose; $3/line for poetry. Pays $750 for color (cover) illustration, $50-100 for b&w (inside) illustration, $250/page for color (inside). Sample copy for $5. Writer's/illustrator's guidelines free for SASE or available on website; FAQ at www.cricketmag.com.

TIPS "Reread ms before sending. Keep within specified word limits. Study back issues before submitting to learn about the types of material we're looking for. Writing style is paramount. We look for rich, evocative language and a sense of joy or wonder. Remember that you're writing for preschoolers—be age-appropriate, but not condescending or preachy. A story must hold enjoyment for both parent and child through repeated read-aloud sessions. Remember that people come in all colors, sizes, physical conditions, and have special needs. Be inclusive!"

LEADING EDGE

E-mail: editor@leadingedgemagazine.com. Website: www.leadingedgemagazine.com. "We strive to encourage developing and established talent and provide high quality speculative fiction to our readers." Does not accept mss with sex, excessive violence, or profanity. Semiannual magazine covering science fiction and fantasy. Sample copy for $5.95. Guidelines available online at website.

○Accepts unsolicited submissions.

FICTION Young adults: fantasy, science fiction. Buys 16 mss/year. Average word length: up to 15,000. Byline given. Send complete ms by mail. Length: 12,500 words maximum. Pays 1¢/word; $10 minimum.

POETRY "Publishes 2-4 poems per issue. Poetry should reflect both literary value and popular appeal and should deal with science fiction- or fantasy-related themes." Pays $10 for first 4 pages; $1.50/each subsequent page.

HOW TO CONTACT Fiction: Send complete ms c/o Fiction Director. Responds to queries/mss in 4 months. Publishes ms 2-6 months after acceptance.

ILLUSTRATION Buys 24 illustrations/issue; 48 illustrations/year. Uses b&w artwork only. Works on assignment only. Contact: Art Director. Illustrations only: Send postcard sample with portfolio, samples, URL. Responds only if interested. Samples filed. Credit line given.

TERMS Pays on publication. Buys first North American serial rights for mss. Buys first North American serial rights for artwork. Original artwork returned at job's completion. Pays $0.01/word for stories. Pays illustrators $50 for color cover, $30 for b&w inside. Sample copies for $5.95. Writer's/illustrator's guidelines for SASE or visit the website.

TIPS "Buy a sample issue to know what is currently selling in our magazine. Also, make sure to follow the writer's guidelines when submitting."

LISTEN

55 West Oak Ridge Dr., Hagerstown MD 21740. (301)393-4019; (301)393-4082. Fax: (301) 393-3294. E-mail: editor@listenmagazine.org. **Editor:** Céleste Perrino-Walker. Monthly magazine, 9 issues. Estab. 1948. Circ. 12,000. "Listen offers positive alternatives to drug use for its teenage readers. Helps them have a happy and productive life by making the right choices."

NONFICTION How-to, health, humorous, life skills, problem-solving, social issues, drug facts, drug-free living. Wants to see more factual articles on drug abuse. Buys 50 mss/year. Average word length: 700. Byline given.

HOW TO CONTACT Nonfiction: Query. Considers manuscripts once a year, in October. Will consider simultaneous submissions, e-mail and previously published work.

ILLUSTRATION Buys 3-6 illustrations/issue; 50 illustrators/year. Reviews ms/illustration packages from artists. Manuscript/illustration packages and illustration only: Query. Contact: Doug Bendall at doug@dougbendall.com, designer. Responds only if interested. Originals returned at job's completion. Samples returned with SASE. Credit line given.

PHOTOS Purchases photos from freelancers. Photos purchased with accompanying ms only. Uses color and b&w photos; digital, 35mm, transparencies or prints. Query with samples. Looks for "youth oriented—action (sports, outdoors), personality photos."

TERMS Pays on acceptance. Buys exclusive magazine rights for mss. Buys one-time rights for artwork and photographs. Pays $80-250 for articles. Pays illustrators $500 for color cover; $75-225 for b&w inside; $135-450 for color inside. Pays photographers by the project (range: $125-500); pays per photo (range: $125-500). Additional payment forms/illustration packages and photos accompanying articles. Sample copy for $2 and 9×12 SASE and 2 first class stamps. Writer's guidelines free with SASE.

TIPS "*Listen* is a magazine for teenagers. It encourages development of good habits and high ideals of physical, social and mental health. It bases its editorial philosophy of primary drug prevention on total abstinence from tobacco, alcohol, and other drugs. Because it is used extensively in public high school classes, it does not accept articles and stories with overt religious emphasis. Four specific purposes guide the editors in selecting materials for *Listen*: (1) To portray a positive lifestyle and to foster skills and values that will help teenagers deal with contemporary problems, including smoking, drinking, and using drugs. This is *Listen*'s primary purpose. (2) To offer positive alternatives to a lifestyle of drug use of any kind. (3) To present scientifically accurate information about the nature and effects of tobacco, alcohol, and other drugs. (4) To report medical research, community programs, and educational efforts that are solving problems connected with smoking, alcohol, and other drugs. Articles should offer their readers activities that increase one's sense of self-worth through achievement and/or involvement in helping others. They are often categorized by three kinds of focus: (1) Hobbies, (2) Recreation, (3) Community Service."

LIVE WIRE

Standard Publishing. 8805 Governor's Hill Drive, Suite 400, Cincinnati OH 45249. (513)931-4050. Fax: (877)867-5751. E-mail: mredford@standardpub.com. Website: www.standardpub.com. **Editor:** Marjorie Redford. Published quarterly in weekly parts. Circ. 40,000.

○ *Live Wire* has decided to reuse much of the material that was a part of the first publication cycle. They will not be sending out theme lists, sample copies, or writers guidelines or accepting any unsolicited material because of this policy.

⊕ LYRICAL PASSION POETRY E-ZINE

P.O. Box 17331, Arlington TX 22216. Website: http://lyricalpassionpoetry.yolasite.com. **Contact:** Raquel D. Bailey, founding editor. Guidelines and upcoming themes available on website.

FICTION Cover letter preferred. Fiction should be typed, double-spaced.

POETRY Does not return manuscripts. Multiple submissions are permitted but no more than 3 submissions in a 6 month period. Does not want: dark, cliché, limerick, erotica, extremely explicit, violent or depressing literature. Free verse poetry length: between 1 and 40 lines.

MUSE

Website: www.cricketmag.com. "The goal of *Muse* is to give as many children as possible access to the most important ideas and concepts underlying the principal areas of human knowledge. Articles should meet the highest possible standards of clarity and transparency aided, wherever possible, by a tone of skepticism, humor, and irreverence."

NONFICTION Middle readers, young adult: animal, arts, history, math, nature/environment, problem-solving, science, social issues.

HOW TO CONTACT *Muse is not accepting unsolicited mss or queries.* All articles are commissioned. To be considered for assignments, experienced science writers may send a résumé and 3 published clips.

ILLUSTRATION Works on assignment only. Credit line given. Send prints or tearsheets, but please, no portfolios or original art, and above all, DO NOT SEND SAMPLES THAT NEED TO BE RETURNED.

PHOTOS Needs vary. Query with samples to photo editor.

NATIONAL GEOGRAPHIC KIDS

National Geographic Society, 1145 17th St. NW, Washington DC 20036. Website: www.kidsnationalgeographic.com. Magazine published 10 times/year. Editorial lead time 6+ months. Sample copy for #10 SAE. Guidelines free.

NONFICTION Query with published clips and resume. Length: 100-1,000 words. Pays $1/word for assigned articles.

PHOTOS State availability. Captions, identification of subjects, model releases required. Reviews contact sheets, negatives, transparencies, prints. Negotiates payment individually.

TIPS "Submit relevant clips. Writers must have demonstrated experience writing for kids. Read the magazine before submitting. Send query and clips via snail mail—materials will not be returned. No SASE required unless sample copy is requested."

NATURE FRIEND MAGAZINE

4253 Woodcock Lane, Dayton VA 22821. (540)867-0764. E-mail: photos@naturefriendmagazine.com. Website: www.dogwoodridgeoutdoors.com; www.naturefriendmagazine.com. Monthly magazine. Picture-oriented material, conversational, no talking animal stories. No evolutionary material. Buys 50 mss/year. Average word length: 500. Byline given. **Contact:** Kevin Shank, editor. Monthly magazine covering nature. Editorial lead time 4 months. Sample copy and writer's guidelines for $10 postage paid.

NONFICTION Animal, how-to, nature, photo-essays. Send complete ms. Length: 250-900 words. Pays 5¢/word.

HOW TO CONTACT Submit on CD with color printout.

PHOTOS Send photos. Captions, identification of subjects required. Reviews prints. Offers $20-75/photo.

TERMS Photo guidelines free with SASE. Pays $75 for front cover photo; $50 for back cover photo, $25 inside photo. Pays on publication. Buy one-time rights. Offers sample copy and writer's/photographer's guidelines for $10. Pays .05¢ per edited word.

TIPS "We want to bring joy and knowledge to children by opening the world of God's creation to them. We endeavor to create a sense of awe about nature's creator and a respect for His creation. I'd like to see more submissions on hands-on things to do with a nature theme (not collecting rocks or leaves—real stuff). Also looking for good stories that are accompanied by good photography."

NEW MOON

New Moon Publishing, Inc., P.O. Box 161287, Duluth MN 55816. (218)728-5507. Fax: (218)728-0314. E-mail: girl@newmoon.org. Website: www.newmoon.org. "*New Moon Girls* is for every girl who wants her voice heard and her dreams taken seriously. *New Moon Girls* portrays strong female role models of all ages, backgrounds and cultures now and in the past." Bimonthly magazine covering girls ages 8-14, edited by girls aged 8-14. Editorial lead time 6 months. Sample copy for $7 or online. Guidelines for SASE or online.

FICTION Middle readers, young adults: adventure, contemporary, fantasy, folktales, history, humorous, multicultural, nature/environment, problem-solving, religious, science fiction, sports, suspense/mystery, travel. Buys 6 mss/year. Average word length: 1,200-1,600. Byline given. Prefers girl-written material. All girl-centered. Send complete ms. Pays 6-12¢/word.

NONFICTION Middle readers, young adults: animal, arts/crafts, biography, careers, cooking, games/puzzles, health, history, hobbies, humorous, interview/profile, math, multicultural, nature/environment, problem-solving, science, social issues, sports, travel, stories about real girls. Does not want to see how-to stories. Wants more stories about real girls doing real things written *by girls*. Buys 6-12 adult-written mss/year; 30 girl-written mss/year. Average word length: 600. Byline given. Send complete ms. Length: 600 words. Pays 6-12¢/word.

POETRY No poetry by adults.

HOW TO CONTACT Fiction/Nonfiction: Does not return or acknowledge unsolicited mss. Send copies only. Responds only if interested. Will consider simultaneous and e-mail submissions.

ILLUSTRATION Buys 6-12 illustrations/year from freelancers. *New Moon Girls* seeks 4-color cover illustrations. Reviews ms/illustrations packages from artists. Query. Submit ms with rough sketches. Illustration only: Query; send portfolio and tearsheets. Samples not returned; samples filed. Responds in 6 months only if interested. Credit line given.

PHOTOS State availability. Captions, identification of subjects required. Negotiates payment individually.

TERMS Pays on publication. Buys all rights for mss. Buys one-time rights, reprint rights for artwork. Original artwork returned at job's completion. Pays 6-12¢/word for stories and articles plus contributor's copies. Pays illustrators $400 for color cover; $50-300 for color inside. Sample copies for $7. Writer's/cover art guidelines for SASE or available on website.

TIPS "We'd like to see more girl-written feature articles that relate to a theme. These can be about anything the girl has done personally, or she can write about something she's studied. Please read *New Moon* before submitting to get a sense of our style. Writers and artists who comprehend our goals have the best chance of publication. We love creative articles—both nonfiction and fiction—that are not condescending to our readers. Keep articles to suggested word lengths; avoid stereotypes. Refer to our guidelines and upcoming themes."

ON COURSE

A Magazine for Teens, 1445 Boonville Ave., Springfield, MO 65802-1894. (417)862-2781. Fax: (417)862-1693. E-mail: oncourse@ag.org. Website: www.oncourse.ag.org. **Editor:** Amber Weigand-Buckley. **Art Director:** Ryan Strong. Biannual magazine. Estab. 1991. Circ. 160,000. *On Course* is a magazine to empower students to grow in a real-life relationship with Christ.

⬤ *On Course* no longer uses illustrations, only photos.

FICTION Young adults: Christian discipleship, contemporary, humorous, multicultural, problem-solving, sports. Average word length: 800. Byline given.

NONFICTION Young adults: careers, interview/profile, multicultural, religion, social issues, college life, Christian discipleship.

HOW TO CONTACT Works on assignment basis only. Resumes and writing samples will be considered for inclusion in Writer's File to receive story assignments.

PHOTOS Buys photos from freelancers. "Teen life, church life, college life; unposed; often used for illustrative purposes." Model/property releases required. Uses color glossy prints and 35mm or $2\frac{1}{4}\times2\frac{1}{4}$ transparencies. Query with samples; send business card, promotional literature, tearsheets or catalog. Responds only if interested.

TERMS Pays on acceptance. Buys first or reprint rights for mss. Buys one-time rights for photographs. Pays $30 per assigned stories/articles. Pays illustrators and photographers "as negotiated." Sample copies free for 9×11 SASE. Writer's guidelines for SASE.

POCKETS

Upper Room, P.O. Box 340004, 1908 Grand Ave., Nashville TN 37203-0004. (800)972-0433. Fax: (615)340-7275. E-mail: pockets@upperroom.org. Website: http://pockets.upperroom.org/. Magazine published 11 times/year. "*Pockets* is a Christian devotional magazine for children ages 8-12. Stories should help children experience a Christian lifestyle that is not always a neatly wrapped moral package but is open to the continuing revelation of God's will." Monthly (except February) magazine covering children's and families' spiritual formation. Each issue reflects a specific theme. Sample copy available with a 9x12 SASE with 4 first-class stamps attached to envelope. Guidelines on website.

FICTION Picture-oriented, young readers, middle readers: adventure, contemporary, occasional folktales, multicultural, nature/environment, problem-solving, religious. Does not accept violence or talking animal stories. Buys 25-30 mss/year. Average word length: 600-1,000. Byline given. *Pockets* also accepts short-short stories (no more than 600 words) for children 5-7. Buys 11 mss/year. "Submissions should contain lots of action, use believable dialogue, be simply written, and be relevant to the problems faced by this age group in everyday life. Children need to be able to see themselves in the pages of the magazine. It is important that the tone not be 'preachy' or didactic. Use short sentences and paragraphs. When possible, use concrete words instead of abstractions." No violence, science fiction, romance, fantasy, or talking animal stories. Send complete ms. Length: 600-1,000 words. Pays 14¢/word.

NONFICTION Picture-oriented, young readers, middle readers: cooking, games/puzzles. "*Pockets* seeks biographical sketches of persons, famous or unknown, whose lives reflect their Christian commitment, written in a way that appeals to children." Does not accept how-to articles. "Nonfiction reads like a story." Multicultural needs include: stories that feature children of various racial/ethnic groups and do so in a way that is true to those depicted. Buys 10 mss/year. Average word length: 400-1,000. Byline given. Length: 400-1,000 words. Pays 14¢/word.

POETRY *Pockets*, published monthly (except February), is an interdenominational magazine for children ages 8-12. "Each issue is built around a specific theme, with material (including poetry) that can be used by children in a variety of ways. Submissions do not need to be overly religious; they should help children experience a Christian lifestyle that is not always a neatly wrapped moral package but is open to the continuing revelation of God's will." Considers poetry by children. Length: 4-20 lines. Pays $25 minimum.

HOW TO CONTACT Fiction/nonfiction: Send complete ms. "We do not accept queries." Responds to mss in 6 weeks. Will consider simultaneous submissions.

ILLUSTRATION Buys 25-35 illustrations/issue. Preferred theme or style: varied; both 4-color. Works on assignment only. Illustrations only: Send promo sheet, tearsheets.

PHOTOS Send 4-6 close-up photos of children actively involved in peacemakers at work activities. Send photos, contact sheets, prints, or digital images. Must be 300 dpi. Pays $25/photo.

TIPS "Theme stories, role models, and retold scripture stories are most open to freelancers. Poetry is also open. It is very helpful if writers read our writers' guidelines and themes on our website."

RAINBOW RUMPUS

The Magazine for Kids with LGBT Parents, P.O. Box 6881, Minneapolis MN 55406. (612)721-6442. E-mail: fictionandpoetry@rainbowrumpus.org. Website: www.rainbowrumpus.org. **Article Editors:** Deb Carver, Al Onkka, Aja McCullough. **Fiction Editor:** Beth Wallace. **Art/photo Acquisitions:** Beth Wallace. Monthly online magazine. Estab. 2005. Circ. 250 visits/day. "*Rainbow Rumpus* is an online magazine for 4- to 18-year-olds who have lesbian, gay, bisexual or transgender (LGBT) parents. The magazine has three sections: one for children, one for grownups. We are looking for children's fiction, young adult fiction, and poetry. *Rainbow Rumpus* publishes and reviews work that is written from the point of view of youth who have LGBT parents or connections with the LGBT community, celebrates the diversity of LGBT-headed families, and is of high quality." 75% of publication aimed at young readers. **Contact:** Beth Wallace, editor-in-chief.

FICTION All levels: adventure, animal, contemporary, fantasy, folktales, history, humorous, multicultural, nature/environment, problem solving, science fiction, sports, suspense/mystery. Buys 24 mss/year. Average word length: 800-5,000. Byline given.

NONFICTION All levels: Interview/profile, social issues. Average word length: 800-5,000. Byline given.

POETRY Maximum of 5 poems per submission.

HOW TO CONTACT Send complete ms via e-mail to fictionandpoetry@rainbowrumpus.org with the word "Submission" in the subject line. Responds to mss in 6 weeks. Considers electronic submissions and previously published work.

ILLUSTRATION Buys 1 illustration/issue. Uses both b&w and color artwork. Reviews ms/illustration packages from artists: Query. Illustrations only: Query with samples. Contact: Beth Wallace, editor-in-chief. Samples not returned; samples filed depending on the level of interest. Credit line given.

TERMS Pays on publication. Buys first rights for mss; may request print anthology and audio or recording rights. Buys first rights for artwork. Pays $75 per story. Pays illustrators $100 for color. Writer's guidelines available on website.

TIPS If you wish to submit nonfiction, please query by e-mail to editorinchief@rainbowrumpus.org. Emerging writers encouraged to submit. You do not need to be a member of the LGBT community to participate.

READ

Weekly Reader Publishing Group, 1 Reader's Digest Rd., Pleasantville NY 10570. Website: www.weeklyreader.com. *READ* no longer accepts unsolicited manuscripts. Those that are sent will not be read, responded to, or returned.

RED LIGHTS

2740 Andrea Drive, Allentown PA 18103-4602. (212)875-9342. E-mail: mhazelton@rcn.com; marilynhazelton@rcn.com. *red lights*, published semiannually in January and June, is devoted to English-language tanka and tanka sequences. *red lights* is 36-40 pages, $8\frac{1}{2} \times 3\frac{3}{4}$, offset-printed, saddle-stapled, with Japanese textured paper cover; copies are numbered. Receives about 1,200 poems/year, accepts about 20%. Press run is 320. Single copy: $8; subscription: $16 U.S., $18 USD Canada, $20 USD foreign. Make checks payable to "red lights" in the U.S. **Contact:** Marilyn Hazelton, editor.

POETRY Wants "print-only tanka, mainly 'free-form' but also strictly syllabic 5-7-5-7-7; will consider tanka sequences and tan-renga." Considers poetry by children and teens. Has published poetry by Sanford Goldstein, Michael McClintock, Laura Maffei, Linda Jeannette Ward, Jane Reichhold, and Michael Dylan Welch.

TIPS "Each issue features a 'red lights featured tanka' on the theme of 'red lights.' Poet whose poem is selected receives 1 contributor's copy."

SCIENCE WEEKLY

CAM Publishing Group, Inc., P.O. Box 70638, Chevy Chase, MD 20813. (301)680-8804. Fax: (301)680-9240. E-mail: scienceweekly@erols.com. Website: www.scienceweekly.com. **Publisher:** Dr. Claude Mayberry. Magazine published 14 times/year. Estab. 1984.

Circ. 200,000. *Science Weekly* uses freelance writers to develop and write an entire issue on a single science topic. Send résumé only, not submissions. Authors preferred within the greater D.C./Virginia/Maryland area. *Science Weekly* works on assignment only.

NONFICTION Young readers, middle readers (K-6th grade): Science/math education, education, problem-solving.

TERMS Pays on publication. Prefers people with education, science and children's writing background. *Send resume only.* Sample copies free with SAE and 3 first-class stamps. Free samples on website www.scienceweekly.com.

ⒶSEVENTEEN MAGAZINE

300 W. 57th St., 17th Floor, New York NY 10019. (917)934-6500. E-mail: mail@seventeen.com. Website: www.seventeen.com. Monthly magazine. "We reach 14.5 million girls each month. Over the past five decades, *Seventeen* has helped shape teenage life in America. We represent an important rite of passage, helping to define, socialize and empower young women. We create notions of beauty and style, proclaim what's hot in popular culture and identify social issues."

◖*Seventeen* no longer accepts fiction submissions.

NONFICTION Young adults: careers, cooking, hobbies, how-to, humorous, interview/profile, multicultural, social issues. Buys 7-12 mss/year. Word length: Varies from 200-2,000 words for articles. Byline sometimes given.

ILLUSTRATION *Only interested in agented material.* Buys 10 illustrations/issue; 120 illustrations/year. Works on assignment only. Reviews ms/illustration packages. Illustrations only: Query with samples. Responds only if interested. Samples not returned; samples filed. Credit line given.

PHOTOS Looking for photos to match current stories. Model/property releases required; captions required. Uses color, 8×10 prints; 35mm, $2^1_4 \times 2^1_4$, 4×5 or 8×10 transparencies. Query with samples or résumé of credits, or submit portfolio for review. Responds only if interested.

TERMS Pays on publication. Buys first North American serial rights, first rights or all rights for mss. Buys exclusive rights for 3 months; online rights for photos. Original artwork returned at job's completion. Pays $1/word for articles/stories (varies by ex-

perience). Additional payment for photos accompanying articles. Pays illustrators/photographers $150-500. Sample copies not available. Writer's guidelines for SASE.

TIPS Send for guidelines before submitting.

SHARING THE VICTORY

Fellowship of Christian Athletes, 8701 Leeds Rd., Kansas City MO 64129. (816)921-0909. Fax: (816)921-8755. E-mail: stv@fca.org. Website: www.fca.org. **Articles/Photo Editor:** Jill Ewert. **Art Director:** Mat Casner. Magazine published 9 times a year. Estab. 1982. Circ. 80,000. Purpose is to serve as a ministry tool of the Fellowship of Christian Athletes (FCA) by aligning with its mission to present to athletes and coaches and all whom they influence, the challenge and adventure of receiving Jesus Christ as Savior and Lord. **Contact:** Jill Ewert, managing editor. Sample copy for $1 and 9x12 SASE with 3 first-class stamps. Guidelines available online.

NONFICTION Young adults/teens: religion, sports. Average word length: 700-1,200. Byline given.

HOW TO CONTACT Nonfiction: Query with published clips. Publishes ms 3 months after acceptance. Will consider electronic submissions via e-mail. Query. Length: 500-1,000 words.

PHOTOS Purchases photos separately. Looking for photos of sports action. Uses color prints and high resolution electronic files of 300 dpi or higher. State availability. Reviews contact sheets. Payment based on size of photo.

TERMS Pays on publication. Buys first rights and second serial (reprint) rights. Pays $150-400 for assigned and unsolicited articles. Photographers paid per photo. Sample copies for 9×12 SASE and $1. Writer's/photo guidelines for SASE.

TIPS "Profiles and interviews of particular interest to coed athlete, primarily high school and college age. Our graphics and editorial content appeal to youth. The area most open to freelancers is profiles on or interviews with well-known athletes or coaches (male, female, minorities) who have been or are involved in some capacity with FCA."

SHINE BRIGHTLY

GEMS Girls' Clubs, P.O. Box 7259, Grand Rapids MI 49510. (616)241-5616. Fax: (616)241-5558. E-mail: shinebrightly@gemsgc.org. Website: www.gemsgc.org. **Contacts:** Jan Boone, editor; Kelli Ponstein, managing editor. Monthly (with combined June/July/Au-

gust summer issue) magazine. Circ. 17,000. "*SHINE brightly* is designed to help girls ages 9-14 see how God is at work in their lives and in the world around them."
Contact: Jan Boone, editor; Kelli Ponstein, managing editor. Sample copy with 9x12 SASE with 3 first class stamps and $1. Guidelines available online.

FICTION Middle readers: adventure, animal, contemporary, health, history, humorous, multicultural, nature/environment, problem-solving, religious, sports. Does not want to see unrealistic stories and those with trite, easy endings. We are interested in manuscripts that show how girls can change the world. Buys 30 mss/year. Average word length: 400-900. Byline given. Send complete ms. Pays up to $35.

NONFICTION Middle readers: animal, arts/crafts, careers, cooking, fashion, games/puzzles, health, hobbies, how-to, humorous, nature/environment, multicultural, problem-solving, religious, service projects, social issues, sports, travel, also movies, music and musicians, famous people, interacting with family and friends. We are currently looking for inspirational biographies; stories from Zambia, Africa; and articles about living a green lifestyle. Buys 9 mss/year. Average word length: 100-800. Byline given. Send complete ms to shinebrightly@gemsgc.org. Length: 100-900 words. Pays 3-5¢/word, plus 2 copies.

POETRY Pays $5-15.

HOW TO CONTACT Annual theme update available online. Fiction/nonfiction: E-mail complete manuscript. Place manuscript within body of e-mail. No attachments. Send complete ms. Responds to mss in 3 months. Will consider simultaneous submissions. Guidelines on website.

ILLUSTRATION Samples returned with SASE. Credit line given.

PHOTOS Purchased with or without ms. Appreciate multicultural subjects. Reviews 5x7 or 8x10 clear color glossy prints. Pays $25-50 on publication.

TERMS Pays on publication. Buys first North American serial rights, first rights, second serial (reprint rights) or simultaneous rights. Original artwork not returned at job's completion. Pays up to $35 for stories, assigned articles and unsolicited articles. Games and puzzles are $5-10. "We send complimentary copies in addition to pay." Pays $25-50 for color inside illustration.

TIPS Writers: "Please check our website before submitting. We have a specific style and theme that deals with how girls can impact the world. The stories should be current, deal with pre-adolescent problems and joys, and help girls see God at work in their lives through humor as well as problem-solving. We prefer not to see anything on the adult level, secular material, or violence. Writers frequently oversimplify the articles and often write with a Pollyanna attitude. An author should be able to see his/her writing style as exciting and appealing to girls ages 9-14. The style can be fun, but also teach a truth. Subjects should be current and important to *SHINE brightly* readers. Use our theme update as a guide. We would like to receive material with a multicultural slant."

SKIPPING STONES: A MULTICULTURAL LITERARY MAGAZINE

P.O. Box 3939, Eugene OR 97403-0939. (541)342-4956. Fax: Call for number. E-mail: Editor@Skippingstones.org. Website: www.Skippingstones.org. **Contact:** Arun N. Toke, articles/photo/fiction editor. Bi-monthly magazine. Estab. 1988. Circ. 2,200. "*Skipping Stones* is an award-winning multicultural, nonprofit magazine designed to promote cooperation, creativity and celebration of cultural and ecological richness. We encourage submissions by children of color, minorities and under-represented populations."
Contact: Arun Toke, editor. Editorial lead time 3-4 months. Sample copy for $6. Writer's guidelines online or for business-sized envelope.

FICTION Middle readers, young adult/teens: contemporary, meaningful, humorous. All levels: folktales, multicultural, nature/environment. Multicultural needs include: bilingual or multilingual pieces; use of words from other languages; settings in other countries, cultures or multi-ethnic communities. Send complete ms. Length: 300-800 words. Pays with contributor copies.

NONFICTION All levels: animal, biography, cooking, games/puzzles, history, humorous, interview/profile, multicultural, nature/environment, creative problem-solving, religion and cultural celebrations, sports, travel, social and international awareness. Does not want to see preaching, violence or abusive language; no poems by authors over 18 years old; no suspense or romance stories. Average word length: 1,000 max. Byline given. Send complete ms. Length: 400-800 words.

POETRY Only accepts poetry from youth under age 18. Length: 30 lines maximum.

HOW TO CONTACT Fiction: Query/complete ms. Nonfiction: Send query. Responds to queries in 1 month; mss in 4 months. Will consider simultaneous submissions; reviews artwork for future assignments. Please include your name and address on each page.

ILLUSTRATION Prefers illustrations by teenagers and young adults. Will consider all illustration packages. Manuscript/illustration packages: Query; submit complete ms with final art; submit tearsheets. Responds in 4 months. Credit line given.

PHOTOS B&w photos preferred, but color photos with good contrast are welcome. Needs: youth 7-17, international, nature, celebrations. Send photos. Captions required. Reviews 4x6 prints, low-res JPEG files. Offers no additional payment for photos.

TERMS Acquires first and non-exclusive reprint rights for mss and photographs. Pays in copies for authors, photographers and illustrators. Sample copy for $5 with SAE and 4 first-class stamps. Writer's/illustrator's guidelines for 4×9 SASE. "We want material meant for children and young adults/teenagers with multicultural or ecological awareness themes. Think, live and write as if you were a child, tween or teen." Wants "material that gives insight to cultural celebrations, lifestyle, customs and traditions, glimpse of daily life in other countries and cultures. Photos, songs, artwork are most welcome if they illustrate/highlight the points. Translations are invited if your submission is in a language other than English. Upcoming themes will include cultural celebrations, living abroad, challenging, hospitality customs of various cultures, cross-cultural understanding, African, Asian and Latin American cultures, humor, international understanding, turning points and magical moments in life, caring for the earth, spirituality, and multicutural awareness."

TIPS "Be original and innovative. Use multicultural, nature, or cross-cultural themes. Multilingual submissions are welcome."

SPARKLE

GEMS Girls' Clubs, 1333 Alger SE, P.O. Box 7295, Grand Rapids MI 49510. (616)241-5616. Fax: (616)241-5558. E-mail: sparkle@gemsgc.org. Website: www.gemsgc.org. **Senior Editor:** Sara Lynn Hilton. **Art Director/Photo Editor:** Sara DeRidder. Magazine published 6 times/year. Estab. 2002. Circ. 5,119. "Our mission is to prepare young girls to live out their faith and become world-changers. We strive to help girls make a difference in the world. We look at the application of scripture to everyday life. We strive to delight the reader and cause the reader to evalute her own life in light of the truth presented. Finally, we strive to teach practical life skills." Editorial lead time 3 months. Sample copy for 9x13 SAE, 3 first-class stamps, and $1 for coverage/publication cost. Writer's guidelines for #10 SASE or online.

FICTION Young readers: adventure, animal, contemporary, fantasy, folktale, health, history, humorous, multicultural, music and musicians, nature/environment, problem-solving, religious, recipes, service projects, sports, suspense/mystery, interacting with family and friends. "We are currently looking for inspirational biographies; stories form Zambia, Africa; and ideas on how to live a green lifestyle." Buys 10 mss/year. Average word length: 100-400. Byline given. Send complete ms. Pays $20/story.

NONFICTION Young readers: animal, arts/crafts, biography, careers, cooking, concept, games/puzzles, geography, health, history, hobbies, how-to, interview/profile, math, multicultural, nature/environment, problem-solving, quizzes, science, social issues, sports, travel, personal experience, inspirational, music/drama/art. Buys 15 mss/year. Average word length: 100-400. Byline given. Send complete ms. Pays $20/article.

POETRY Looks for simple poems about God's creation or traditional Bible truths. Maximum length: 15 lines. We do not wish to see anything that is too difficult for a first grader to read. We wish it to remain light. The style can be fun, but also teach a truth. No violence or secular material.

HOW TO CONTACT Fiction/nonfiction: E-mail complete manuscript. Place manuscript within body of e-mail. No attachments. Responds to ms in 6 weeks. Publishes ms 6 months after acceptance. Will consider simultaneous submissions and previously published work.

ILLUSTRATION Buys 1-2 illustrations/issue; 8-10 illustrations/year. Uses color artwork only. Works on assignment only. Reviews ms/illustration packages from artists. Send ms with dummy. Contact: Sara DeRidder, graphic and web designer. Illustrations only: send promo sheet. Contact: Sara DeRidder. Responds in 3 weeks only if interested. Samples returned with SASE; samples filed. Credit line given.

PHOTOS Send photos. Identification of subjects required. Reviews at least 5X7 clear color glossy prints, GIF/JPEG files on CD. Offers $25-50/photo.

TERMS Pays on publication. Buys first North American serial rights, second serial (reprint rights) or simultaneous rights for mss, artwork and photos. Pays $20 minimum for stories and articles. Pays illustrators $50 for color cover; $25 for color inside. Original artwork not returned at job's completion. Sample copies for $1. Writer's/illustrator/photo guidelines free for SASE or available on website.

TIPS "Keep it simple. We are writing to 1st-3rd graders. It must be simple yet interesting. Manuscripts should build girls up in Christian character but not be preachy. They are just learning about God and how He wants them to live. Manuscripts should be delightful as well as educational and inspirational. Writers should keep stories simple but not write with a 'Pollyanna' attitude. Authors should see their writing style as exciting and appealing to girls ages 6-9. Subjects should be current and important to *Sparkle* readers. Use our theme as a guide. We would like to receive material with a multicultural slant.

SPIDER

(312)701-1720. Fax: (312)701-1728. Website: www.cricketmag.com. Magazine published 9x/year, monthly except for combined May/June, July/August, and November/December issues. Circ. 50,000. Spider publishes high-quality literature for beginning readers, primarily ages 6-9. Guidelines available online.

FICTION Young readers: adventure, contemporary, fantasy, folktales, humor, science fiction. "Authentic stories from all cultures are welcome. No didactic, religious, or violent stories, or anything that talks down to children." Average word length: 300-1,000. Byline given. Stories should be easy to read. Pays up to 25¢/word

NONFICTION Young readers: animal, arts/crafts, cooking, games/puzzles, geography, history, human interest, math, multicultural, nature/environment, problem-solving, science. "Well-researched articles on topics are welcome. Would like to see more games, puzzles, and activities, especially ones adaptable to *Spider*'s takeout pages. No encyclopedic or overtly educational articles." Average word length: 300-800. Byline given. Submit complete ms, bibliography, SASE. Pays up to 25¢/word.

POETRY Serious, humorous. Maximum length: 20 lines. Pays $3/line maximum

HOW TO CONTACT Fiction/nonfiction: Send complete ms with SASE. Do not query. Responds to mss in 6 months. Publishes ms 2-3 years after acceptance. Will consider simultaneous submissions and previously published work.

ILLUSTRATION Buys 5-10 illustrations/issue; 45-90 illustrations/year. Uses color artwork only. "We prefer that you work on flexible or strippable stock, no larger than 20 × 22 (image area 19 × 21). This will allow us to put the art directly on the drum of our separator's laser scanner. Art on disk CMYK, 300 dpi. We use more realism than cartoon-style art." Works on assignment only. Reviews ms/illustration packages from artists. Illustrations only: Send promo sheet and tearsheets. Responds in 3 months. Samples returned with SASE; samples filed. Credit line given.

PHOTOS Buys photos from freelancers. Buys photos with accompanying ms only. Model/property releases and captions required. Uses 35mm, $2^1_4 \times 2^1_4$ transparencies or digital files. Send unsolicited photos by mail; provide résumé and tearsheets. Responds in 3 months. For art samples, it is especially helpful to see pieces showing children, animals, action scenes, and several scenes from a narrative showing a character in different situations. Send photocopies/tearsheets. Also considers photo essays (prefers color, but b&w is also accepted). Captions, identification of subjects, model releases required. Reviews contact sheets, transparencies, 8×10 prints.

TERMS Pays on publication. Rights purchased vary. Buys first and promotional rights for artwork; one-time rights for photographs. Original artwork returned at job's completion. Pays up to 25¢/word for previously unpublished stories/articles. Authors also receive 6 complimentary copies of the issue in which work appears. Additional payment for ms/illustration packages and for photos accompanying articles. Pays illustrators $750 for color cover; $200-300 for color inside. Pays photographers per photo (range: $25-75). Sample copies for $5. Writer's/illustrator's guidelines online at www.cricketmag.com or for SASE.

TIPS We'd like to see more of the following: engaging nonfiction, fillers, and 'takeout page' activities; folktales, fairy tales, science fiction, and humorous stories. Most importantly, do not write down to children.

STONE SOUP

(831)426-5557. Fax: (831)426-1161. E-mail: editor@
stonesoup.com. Website: www.stonesoup.com. *Stone
Soup*, published 6 times/year, showcases writing and
art by children ages 13 and under. "We have a preference for writing and art based on real-life experiences;
no formula stories or poems. We only publish writing
by children ages 8 to 13. We do not publish writing
by adults." Bimonthly. Circ. 15,000. "We do not like
assignments or formula stories of any kind." Receives
1,000 unsolicited mss/month. Accepts 10 mss/issue.
Publishes ms 4 months after acceptance. **Publishes
some new writers/year.** Also publishes literary essays,
poetry. Send complete ms. "We like to learn a little
about our young writers, why they like to write, and
how they came to write the story they are submitting."
Sample copy by phone. Writer's guidelines online. No
simultaneous submissions. No e-mail submissions.
Include name, age, home address, and phone number. Guidelines available on website. Responds in up
to 6 weeks. Acquires all rights. Returns rights upon
request. Open to reviews by children. **Contact:** Ms.
Gerry Mandel, editor.

> "Stories and poems from past issues are avail-
> able online."

FICTION Adventure, ethnic/multicultural, experimental, fantasy, historical, humor/satire, mystery/sus-
pense, science fiction, slice-of-life vignettes, suspense.
"We do not like assignments or formula stories of any
kind." Send complete ms. Length: 150-2,500 words.
Pays $40 for stories. Authors also receive 2 copies, a
certificate, and discounts on additional copies and
on subscriptions.

NONFICTION Historical, personal experience, book
reviews. Pays $40.

POETRY Wants free verse poetry. Does not want
rhyming poetry, haiku, or cinquain. No simultaneous submissions. No e-mail submissions. Guidelines
available on website. Responds in up to 6 weeks. Acquires all rights. Returns rights upon request. Open
to reviews by children. Pays $40/poem, a certificate,
and 2 contributor's copies plus discounts.

HOW TO CONTACT "Submissions can be any
number of pages, any format. Don't include SASE;
we respond only to those submissions under consideration and cannot return mss."

TIPS "All writing we publish is by young people
ages 13 and under. We do not publish any writing by
adults. We can't emphasize enough how important it

is to read a couple of issues of the magazine. You can
read stories and poems from past issues online. We
have a strong preference for writing on subjects that
mean a lot to the author. If you feel strongly about
something that happened to you or something you
observed, use that feeling as the basis for your story or poem. Stories should have good descriptions,
realistic dialogue, and a point to make. In a poem,
each word must be chosen carefully. Your poem
should present a view of your subject, and a way of
using words that are special and all your own."

TURTLE MAGAZINE

For Preschool Kids, 1100 Waterway Blvd., Indianapolis, IN 46202. (317)636-8881. Fax: (317)684-8094.
Website: www.turtlemag.org. **Editor:** Terry Harsh-
man. **Art Director:** Bart Rivers. Bimonthly magazine
published 6 times/year. Circ. 300,000. *Turtle* uses
read-aloud stories, especially suitable for bedtime
or naptime reading, for children ages 2-5. Also uses
poems, simple science experiments, easy recipes and
health-related articles.

FICTION Picture-oriented material: health-related,
medical, history, humorous, multicultural, nature/en-
vironment, problem-solving, sports, recipes, simple
science experiments. Avoid stories in which the characters indulge in unhealthy activities. Buys 20 mss/year.
Average word length: 150-300. Byline given. Currently
accepting submissions for Rebus stories only.

NONFICTION Picture-oriented material: cooking,
health, sports, simple science. "We use very simple
experiments illustrating basic science concepts. These
should be pretested. We also publish simple, healthful recipes." Buys 24 mss/year. Average word length:
100-300. Byline given.

POETRY "We're especially looking for short poems
(4-8 lines) and slightly longer action rhymes to foster
creative movement in preschoolers. We also use short
verse on our inside front cover and back cover."

HOW TO CONTACT Fiction/nonfiction: Send
complete mss. Queries are not accepted. Responds
to mss in 3 months.

TERMS Pays on publication. Buys all rights for mss.
Pays up to 22¢/word for stories and articles (depending upon length and quality) and 10 complimentary
copies. Pays $25 minimum for poems. Sample copy
$3.95. Writer's guidelines free with SASE and on
website.

TIPS "Our need for health-related material, especially features that encourage fitness, is ongoing. Health subjects must be age-appropriate. When writing about them, think creatively and lighten up! Always keep in mind that in order for a story or article to educate preschoolers, it first must be entertaining—warm and engaging, exciting, or genuinely funny. Here the trend is toward leaner, lighter writing. There will be a growing need for interactive activities. Writers might want to consider developing an activity to accompany their concise manuscripts."

U.S. KIDS

Children's Better Health Institute, 1100 Waterway Blvd., P.O. Box 567, Indianapolis IN 46202. (317)636-8881. Website: www.uskidsmag.com. **Editor:** Daniel Lee. **Art Director:** Greg Vanzo. Magazine for children ages 6-11. Estab. 1987. Circ. 230,000. Magazine featuring kids doing extraordinary things, especially activities related to health, sports, the arts, interesting hobbies, the environment, computers, etc. Editorial lead time 6 months. Sample copy for $2.95 or online. Guidelines for #10 SASE.

> *U.S. Kids* is being retargeted to a younger audience. Closed to submissions until further notice.

FICTION Young readers: adventure, animal, contemporary, health, history, humorous, multicultural, nature/environment, problem-solving, sports, suspense/mystery. Buys limited number of stories/year. Query first. Average word length: 500-800. Byline given. Buys very little fictional material. Send complete ms. Pays up to 25¢/word.

NONFICTION Young readers: animal, arts/crafts, cooking, games/puzzles, health, history, hobbies, how-to, humorous, interview/profile, multicultural, nature/environment, science, social issues, sports, travel. Wants to see interviews with kids ages 5-10, who have done something unusual or different. Buys 30-40 mss/year. Average word length: 400. Byline given. Send complete ms. Pays up to 25¢/word.

POETRY Maximum length: 8-24 lines. Pays $25-50.

HOW TO CONTACT Fiction: Send complete ms. Responds to queries and mss in 3 months.

ILLUSTRATION Buys 8 illustrations/issue; 70 illustrations/year. Color artwork only. Works on assignment only. Reviews ms/illustration packages from artists. Query. Illustrations only: Send resume and tearsheets. Responds only if interested. Samples re-turned with SASE; samples kept on file. Does not return originals. Credit line given.

PHOTOS Purchases photography from freelancers. Looking for photos that pertain to children ages 5-10. Model/property release required. Uses color and b&w prints; 35mm, $2^1/_4 \times 2^1/_4$, 4×5 and 8×10 transparencies. Photographers should provide resume, business card, promotional literature or tearsheets to be kept on file. Responds only if interested. State availability. Captions, identification of subjects, model releases required. Reviews contact sheets, negatives, transparencies, color photocopies, or prints. Negotiates payment individually.

TERMS Pays on publication. Buys all rights for mss. Purchases all rights for artwork. Purchases one-time rights for photographs. Pays 17¢/word minimum. Additional payment for ms/illustration packages. Pays illustrators $155/page for color inside. Photographers paid by the project or per photo (negotiable). Sample copies for $3.95. Writer's/illustrator/photo guidelines for #10 SASE.

TIPS We are retargeting the magazine for first-, second-, and third-graders, and looking for fun and informative articles on activities and hobbies of interest to younger kids. Special emphasis on fitness, sports, and health. Availability of good photos a plus. "Write clearly and concisely without preaching or being obvious."

WHAT IF?

Canada's Creative Magazine for Teens. 19 Lynwood Place, Guelph ON N1G 2V9 Canada. (519)823-2941. Fax: (519)823-8081. E-mail: editor@whatifmagazine.com. Website: www.whatifmagazine.com. **Art Director:** Jean Leslie. Quarterly magazine. Estab. 2003. Circ. 5,000. "The goal of *What If?* is to help Canadian young adults get published for the first time in a quality literary setting."

FICTION Young adults: adventure, contemporary, fantasy, folktale, health, humorous, multicultural, nature/environment, problem-solving, science fiction, sports, suspense/mystery. Buys 48 mss/year. Average word length: 500-3,000. Byline given.

NONFICTION Young adults: Personal essays and opinion pieces to a maximum of 1,500 words. Byline given.

POETRY Reviews poetry: all styles. Maximum length: 20 lines. Limit submissions to 4 poems.

HOW TO CONTACT Fiction/Nonfiction: Send complete ms. Responds to mss in 3 months. Publishes ms 4 months after acceptance. Will consider e-mail submissions, previously published work if the author owns all rights.

ILLUSTRATION Uses approximately 150 illustrations/year. Reviews ms/illustration packages from young adult artists. Send ms with dummy. Query with samples. Contact: Jean Leslie, production manager. Responds in 2 months. Samples returned with SASE. Credit line given.

TERMS Pays on publication. Acquires first rights for mss and artwork. Original artwork returned at job's completion. Pays 2 copies for stories; 2 copy for articles; 2 copies for illustration and 2 copies for poems. Sample copies for $10. Writer's/illustrator's guidelines for SASE or available by e-mail.

TIPS "Read our magazine. The majority of the material we publish (90%) is by Canadian young adults. Another 10% is staff written. We are currently accepting material from Canadian teens only."

☉ YES MAG

Canada's Science Magazine for Kids 501-3960 Quadra St., Victoria, BC, V8X 4A3 Canada. Fax: (250)477-5390. E-mail: editor@yesmag.ca; jude@yesmag.com. Website: www.yesmag.ca. Bimonthly magazine. Estab. 1996. Circ. 22,000. "YES Mag is designed to make science accessible, interesting, exciting, and fun. Written for children ages 10 to 15, YES Mag covers a range of topics including science and technology news, environmental updates, do-at-home projects and articles about Canadian science and scientists." **Contact:** Jude Isabella, managing editor; David Garrison, publisher; Shannon Hunt, editor. Sample copies available. Writer's guidelines available on the website under "Contact" information.

NONFICTION Middle readers: All the sciences-math, engineering, biology, physics, chemistry, etc. Buys 30 mss/year. Average word length: 250- 800. Byline given. Query with published clips.

HOW TO CONTACT Nonfiction: Query with published clips. "We prefer e-mail queries." Responds to queries/mss in 6 weeks. Generally publishes ms 3 months after acceptance. **Emphasis on Canadian writers.**

ILLUSTRATION Buys 2 illustrations/issue; 10 illustrations/year. Uses color artwork only. Works on assignment only. Reviews ms/illustration packages from artists. Query. Illustration only: Query with samples. Responds in 6 weeks. Samples filed. Credit line given.

PHOTOS "Looking for science, technology, nature/environment photos based on current editorial needs." Photo captions required. Uses color prints. Provide resume, business card, promotional literature, tearsheets if possible. Will buy if photo is appropriate. Usually uses stock agencies.

TERMS Pays on publication. Buys one-time rights for mss. Buys one-time rights for artwork/photos. Original artwork returned at job's completion. Pays $70-200 for stories and articles. Sample copies for $5. Writer's guidelines available on the website under "Contact" information.

TIPS "We do not publish fiction or science fiction or poetry. Visit our website for more information and sample articles. Articles relating to the physical sciences and mathematics are encouraged."

YOUNG RIDER

The Magazine for Horse and Pony Lovers, P.O. Box 8237, Lexington KY 40533. (859)260-9800. Fax: (859)260-9814. Website: www.youngrider.com. **Editor:** Lesley Ward. Bimonthly magazine. Estab. 1994. "*Young Rider* magazine teaches young people, in an easy-to-read and entertaining way, how to look after their horses properly, and how to improve their riding skills safely."

FICTION Young adults: adventure, animal, horses, horse celebrities, famous equestrians. Buys 10 mss/year. Average word length: 1,500 maximum. Byline given.

NONFICTION Young adults: animal, careers, health (horse), sports, riding. Buys 20-30 mss/year. Average word length: 1,000 maximum. Byline given.

HOW TO CONTACT Fiction/nonfiction: Query with published clips. Responds to queries in 2 weeks. Publishes ms 6-12 months after acceptance. Will consider simultaneous submissions, electronic submissions via disk or modem, previously published work.

ILLUSTRATION Buys 2 illustrations/issue; 10 illustrations/year. Works on assignment only. Reviews ms/illustration packages from artists. Query. Contact: Lesley Ward, editor. Illustrations only: Query with samples. Contact: Lesley Ward, editor. Responds in 2 weeks. Samples returned with SASE. Credit line given.

PHOTOS Buys photos with accompanying ms only. Uses high-res digital images only—in focus, good light. Model/property release required; captions required. Query with samples. Responds in 2 weeks.

TERMS Pays on publication. Buys first North American serial rights for mss, artwork, photos. Original artwork returned at job's completion. Pays $150 maximum for stories; $250 maximum for articles. Additional payment for ms/illustration packages and for photos accompanying articles. Pays $70-140 for color inside. Pays photographers per photo (range: $65-155). Sample copies for $3.50. Writer's/illustrator's/photo guidelines for SASE.

TIPS "Fiction must be in third person. Read magazine before sending in a query. No 'true story from when I was a youngster.' No moralistic stories. Fiction must be up-to-date and humorous, teen-oriented. Need horsy interest or celebrity rider features. No practical or how-to articles—all done in-house."

AGENTS & ART REPS

This section features listings of literary agents and art reps who either specialize in, or represent a good percentage of, children's writers and/or illustrators. While there are a number of children's publishers who are open to non-agented material, using the services of an agent or rep can be beneficial to a writer or artist. Agents and reps can get your work seen by editors and art directors more quickly. They are familiar with the market and have insights into which editors and art directors would be most interested in your work. Also, they negotiate contracts and will likely be able to get you a better deal than you could get on your own.

Agents and reps make their income by taking a percentage of what writers and illustrators receive from publishers. The standard percentage for agents is 10 to 15 percent; art reps generally take 25 to 30 percent. We have not included any agencies in this section that charge reading fees.

WHAT TO SEND

When putting together a package for an agent or rep, follow the guidelines given in their listings. Most agents open to submissions prefer initially to receive a query letter describing your work. For novels and longer works, some agents ask for an outline and a number of sample chapters, but you should send these only if you're asked to do so. Never fax or e-mail query letters or sample chapters to agents without their permission. Just as with publishers, agents receive a large volume of submissions. It may take them a long time to reply, so you may want to query several agents at one time. It's best, however, to have a complete manuscript considered by only one agent at a time. Always include a self-addressed, stamped envelope (SASE).

For initial contact with art reps, send a brief query letter and self-promo pieces, following the guidelines given in the listings. If you don't have a flier or brochure, send photocopies. Always include a SASE.

For those who both write and illustrate, some agents listed will consider the work of author/illustrators. Read through the listings for details.

As you consider approaching agents and reps with your work, keep in mind that they are very choosy about who they take on to represent. Your work must be high quality and presented professionally to make an impression on them. For more information on approaching agents and additional listings, see *Guide to Literary Agents* (Writer's Digest Books). For additional listings of art reps see *Artist's & Graphic Designer's Market* (Writer's Digest Books).

AN ORGANIZATION FOR AGENTS

In some listings of agents you'll see references to AAR (The Association of Authors' Representatives). This organization requires its members to meet an established list of professional standards and a code of ethics.

The objectives of AAR include keeping agents informed about conditions in publishing and related fields; encouraging cooperation among literary organizations; and assisting agents in representing their author-clients' interests. Officially, members are prohibited from directly or indirectly charging reading fees. The AAR offers writers a list of member agents on their website. They also offer a list of recommended questions an author should ask an agent and other FAQs, all found on their website. They can be contacted at AAR, 676A 9th Ave. #312, New York NY 10036. (212)840-5777. E-mail: aarinc@mindspring.com. Website: www.aar-online.org.

AGENTS

ADAMS LITERARY

7845 Colony Rd., C4 #215, Charlotte NC 28226. E-mail: info@adamsliterary.com. E-mail: submissions@adamsliterary.com. Website: www.adamsliterary.com. Fax: (704)542-1450. Member of AAR. Other memberships include SCBWI and WNBA. Adams Literary is a full-service literary agency exclusively representing children's book authors and artists. **Contact:** Tracey Adams, Josh Adams, Quinlan Lee.

REPRESENTS "The finest children's book authors and artists."

TERMS Agent receives 15% commission on domestic sales; 20% on foreign sales. Offers written contract.

HOW TO CONTACT Contact through online form on website only. Or send e-mail if that is not operating correctly. "All submissions and queries must be made through the online form on our website. We will not review—and will promptly recycle—any unsolicited submissions or queries we receive by post. Before submitting your work for consideration, please carefully review our complete guidelines." "While we have an established client list, we do seek new talent—and we accept submissions from both published and aspiring authors and artists."

TIPS "Guidelines are posted (and frequently updated) on our website."

BOOKSTOP LITERARY AGENCY

67 Meadow View Rd., Orinda, CA 94563. (925)254-2664. Fax: (925)254-2668. E-mail: info@bookstopliterary.com. Website: www.bookstopliterary.com. Seeking both new and established writers and illustrators. Estab. 1983. 100% of material handled is books for children and young adults.

REPRESENTS fiction, nonfiction, picture books, middle grade, young adult, and illustrations. "Special interest in Hispanic, Asian American, and African American writers; quirky picture books; clever adventure/mystery novels; and authentic and emotional young adult voices."

TERMS Agent receives 15% commission on domestic sales. Offers written contract, binding for 1 year.

HOW TO CONTACT Please send: cover letter, entire ms for picture books; first 30 pages of novels; proposal and sample chapters ok for nonfiction. E-mail submissions: Paste cover letter and first 10 pages of manuscript into body of e-mail, send to info@bookstopliterary.com. Send sample illustrations only if you are an illustrator.

ANDREA BROWN LITERARY AGENCY, INC.

Website: www.andreabrownlit.com. 1076 Eagle Dr. Salinas CA 93905. (831)422-5925. **President:** Andrea Brown. Estab. 1981. Member of SCBWI and WNBA. Mostly obtains new clients through recommendations, editors, clients and agents. **Contact:** Andrea Brown, president. There are eight different agents at this agency.

REPRESENTS 20% of clients are new/previously unpublished writers. Specializes in "all kinds of children's books—illustrators and authors." 98% juvenile books. Considers: Nonfiction (animals, anthropology/archaeology, art/architecture/design, biography/autobiography, current affairs, ethnic/cultural interests, history, how-to, nature/environment, photography, popular culture, science/technology, sociology, sports); fiction (historical, science fiction); picture books, young adult. This agency specializes in children's books, though each agent has differing tastes.

RECENT SALES *Chloe*, by Catherine Ryan Hyde (Knopf); Sasha Cohen autobiography (HarperCollins); *The Five Ancestors*, by Jeff Stone (Random House); *Thirteen Reasons Why*, by Jay Asher (Penguin); *Identical*, by Ellen Hopkins (S&S).

TERMS Agent receives 15% commission on domestic sales. Agent receives 20% commission on foreign sales. Offers written contract.

HOW TO CONTACT Query. Responds in 3 months to queries and mss. E-mail queries only. For picture books, submit complete ms, SASE. For fiction, submit short synopsis, SASE, first 3 chapters. For nonfiction, submit proposal, 1-2 sample chapters. For illustrations, submit 4-5 color samples (no originals). "We only accept queries via e-mail. No attachments, with the exception of jpeg illustrations from illustrators." Visit the agents' bios on our website and choose only one agent to whom you will submit your e-query. Send a short e-mail query letter to that agent with QUERY in the subject field. Obtains most new clients through referrals from editors, clients and agents. Check website for guidelines and information.

CURTIS BROWN, LTD.

(212)473-5400. E-mail: gknowlton@cbltd.com. Website: www.curtisbrown.com. Seeking both new and established writers. Members of AAR and SCBWI. Signatory of WGA. **Staff includes:** Ginger Clark, VP; Elizabeth Harding; Ginger Knowlton, Exec. VP; Mitchell Waters; and Anna J. Webman. Represents authors and illustrators of fiction, nonfiction, picture books, middle grade, young adult. **Contact:** Ginger Knowlton. Alternate address: Peter Ginsberg, president at CBSF, 1750 Montgomery St., San Francisco CA 94111. (415)954-8566.

RECENT SALES This agency prefers not to share information on specific sales.

TERMS Agent receives 15% commission on domestic sales; 20% on foreign sales. Offers written contract. 75 days notice must be given to terminate contract. Charges for some postage (overseas, etc.).

HOW TO CONTACT Query with SASE. If a picture book, send only one picture book ms. Considers simultaneous queries, "but please tell us." Returns material only with SASE. Prefers to read materials exclusively. *No unsolicited mss.* Obtains most new clients through recommendations from others, solicitations, conferences.

BROWNE & MILLER LITERARY ASSOCIATES, LLC

410 S. Michigan Ave., Suite 460, Chicago, IL 60605. (312)922-3063. Fax: (312)922-1905. E-mail: mail@browneandmiller.com. Website: www.browneandmiller.com. **Contact:** Danielle Egan-Miller, president. Prefers to work with established writers. Handles only certain types of work. Estab. 1971. Member of AAR, RWA, MWA. Represents 85+ clients. 5% of clients are new/previously unpublished writers. 15% of material handled is books for young readers.

○ Prior to opening the agency, Danielle Egan-Miller worked as an editor.

REPRESENTS Considers primarily YA fiction. "We love great writing and have a wonderful list of authors writing YA in particular." Not looking for picture books, middle grade.

RECENT SALES Sold 10 books for young readers in the last year.

TERMS Agent receives 15% commission on domestic sales; 20% on foreign sales. Offers written contract, binding for 2 years. 30 days notice must be given to terminate contract.

HOW TO CONTACT Query with SASE. Accepts queries by e-mail. Considers simultaneous queries. Responds in 2-4 weeks to queries; 4-6 months to mss. Returns material only with SASE. Obtains clients through recommendations from others.

TIPS "We are very hands-on and do much editorial work with our clients. We are passionate about the books we represent and work hard to help clients reach their publishing goals."

PEMA BROWNE LTD.

Website: www.pemabrowneltd.com. 11 Tena Place, Valley Cottage NY 10989. (845)268-0029. **Contact:** Pema Browne. Estab. 1966. Represents 2 illustrators. 10% of artwork handled is children's book illustration. Specializes in general commercial. Markets include: all publishing areas; children's picture books. Clients include HarperCollins, Holiday House, Bantam Doubleday Dell, Nelson/Word, Hyperion, Putnam. Client list available upon request.

REPRESENTS Fiction, nonfiction, picture books, middle grade, young adult, manuscript/illustration packages. Looking for "professional and unique" talent.

RECENT SALES *The Daring Ms. Quimby*, by Suzanne Whitaker (Holiday House).

TERMS Rep receives 30% illustration commission; 20% author commission. Exclusive area representation is required. For promotional purposes, talent must provide color mailers to distribute. Representative pays mailing costs on promotion mailings.

HOW TO CONTACT For first contact, send query letter, direct mail flier/brochure and SASE. If interested will ask to mail appropriate materials for review. Portfolios should include tearsheets and transparencies or good color photocopies, plus SASE. Accepts queries by mail only. Obtains new talent through recommendations and interviews (portfolio review).

TIPS "We are doing more publishing—all types—less advertising." Looks for "continuity of illustration and dedication to work."

LIZA DAWSON ASSOCIATES

(212)465-9071. Fax: (212)947-0460. E-mail: queryliza@lizadawsonassociates.com. Website: www.lizadawsonassociates.com. 350 7th Ave, Suite 2003, New York, NY 10001. E-mail: anna@olswanger.com. Website: www.olswanger.com. **Contact:** Anna Olswanger. Member of SCBWI, WNBA, Authors Guild. Represents 10 clients. 30% of clients are new/unpublished writers. 75% of material handled is books for young readers.

REPRESENTS Fiction, nonfiction; author-illustrator picture books. "This agency specializes in readable literary fiction, thrillers, mainstream historicals, women's fiction, academics, historians, business, journalists and psychology."

TERMS Agent receives 15% commission on domestic sales; 20% commission on foreign sales. Offers written contract. Charges clients for photocopying and overseas postage.

HOW TO CONTACT Query with first 5 pages. Query by e-mail only. No phone calls. Considers simultaneous queries. Responds in 4 weeks to queries; 8 weeks to mss. Individual query e-mails are query[agentfirstname]@lizadawsonassociates.com. We prefer to see only a query letter first. If we are intrigued, we'll ask to see a portion of the manuscript. Obtains most new clients through recommendations from others, conferences.

DUNHAM LITERARY, INC.

(212)929-0994. Website: www.dunhamlit.com. **Contact:** Jennie Dunham. Seeking both new and established writers but prefers to work with established writers. Estab. 2000. Member of AAR, signatory of SCBWI. Represents 50 clients. 15% of clients are new/previously unpublished writers. 50% of material handled is books of young readers. **Contact:** Jennie Dunham.

REPRESENTS Considers fiction, picture books, middle grade, young adult. Most agents represent children's books or adult books, and this agency represents both. Actively seeking mss with great story and voice. Not looking for activity books, workbooks, educational books, poetry.

RECENT SALES Sold 30 books for young readers in the last year. *Peter Pan*, by Robert Sabuda (Little Simon); *Flamingos On the Roof*, by Calef Brown (Houghton); *Adele and Simon In America*, by Barbara McClintock (Farrar, Straus & Giroux); *Caught Between the Pages*, by Marlene Carvell (Dutton); *Waiting For Normal*, by Leslie Connor (HarperCollins); *The Gollywhopper Games*, by Jody Feldman (Greenwillow); *America the Beautiful* by Robert Sabuda; *Dahlia*, by Barbara McClintock; *Living Dead Girl*, by Tod Goldberg; *In My Mother's House* by Margaret McMulla; *Black Hawk Down* by Mark Bowden; *Look Back All the Green Valley* by Fred Chappell; *Under a Wing* by Reeve Lindbergh; *I Am Madame X*, by Gioia Diliberto.

TERMS Agent receives 15% commission on domestic sales; 20-25% on foreign sales. Offers written contract. 60 days notice must be given to terminate contract.

HOW TO CONTACT Query with SASE. Considers simultaneous queries and submissions. Responds in 2 weeks to queries; 2 months to mss. Returns material only with SASE. Obtains clients through recommendations from others.

DWYER & O'GRADY, INC.

P.O. Box 790, Cedar Key FL 32625-0790. (352)543-9307. Fax: (603)375-5373. Website: www.dwyerogrady.com. Contact: Jeffrey P. Dwyer. Agents for authors and illustrators of children's books. Estab. 1990. Member of Society of Illustrators, Author's Guild, SCBWI, Graphic Artist's Guild. Represents 12 illustrators and 20 writers. Staff includes Elizabeth O'Grady and Jeffrey Dwyer. Specializes in children's books (picture books, middle grade and young adult). Markets include: publishing/books, audio/film. **Contact:** Elizabeth O'Grady.

REPRESENTS "We are not accepting new clients at this time. This agency represents only writers and illustrators of children's books."

TERMS Receives 15% commission domestic, 20% foreign. Additional fees are negotiable. Exclusive representation is required (world rights). Advertising costs are paid by representative. Offers written contract; 1-month notice must be given to terminate contract. This agency charges clients for photocopying of longer mss or mutually agreed upon marketing expenses.

HOW TO CONTACT For first contact, send query letter by postal mail only. Do not send unsolicited material. We are not adding new clients. Check website to see if policy changes. Obtains most new clients through recommendations from others, direct approach by agent to writer whose work they've read.

TIPS "This agency previously had an address in New Hampshire. Mail all materials to the new Florida address."

DYSTEL & GODERICH LITERARY MANAGEMENT

(212)627-9100. Fax: (212)627-9313. E-mail: mbourret@dystel.com. Website: www.dystel.com. **Contact:** Michael Bourret and Jim McCarthy.

REPRESENTS Fiction, picture books, middle grade, and young adult novels. "We are actively seeking fiction for all ages, in all genres. We're especially interested in quality young adult fiction, from realistic to paranormal, and all kinds of middle grade, from funny boy books to more sentimental fare. Though we are open to author/illustrators, we are not looking for picture book manuscripts. And, while we would like to see more YA memoir, nonfiction is not something we usually handle." "This agency specializes in cookbooks and commercial and literary fiction and nonfiction." No plays, screenplays or poetry.

TERMS Agent receives 15% commission on domestic sales, 20% commission on foreign sales. Offers written contract.

HOW TO CONTACT Query with SASE. Please include the first three chapters in the body of the e-mail. E-mail queries preferred; Michael Bourret only accepts e-mail queries. Accepts simultaneous submissions. Responds within 8 weeks. Returns mss only with SASE. Obtains new clients by recommendations from others, queries/solicitations, and conferences.

TIPS "DGLM prides itself on being a full-service agency. We're involved in every stage of the publishing process, from offering substantial editing on mss and proposals, to coming up with book ideas for authors looking for their next project, negotiating contracts and collecting monies for our clients. We follow a book from its inception through its sale to a publisher, its publication, and beyond. Our commitment to our writers does not, by any means, end when we have collected our commission. This is one of the many things that makes us unique in a very competitive business."

○ EDUCATIONAL DESIGN SERVICES LLC

5750 Bou Ave, Ste. 1508, N. Bethesda, MD 20852. E-mail: blinder@educationaldesignservices.com. Website: www.educationaldesignservices.com. **Contact:** B. Linder. Handles only certain types of work—educational materials aimed at teacher development or the K-12 Market. Estab. 1981. 80% of clients are new/previously unpublished writers.

REPRESENTS Considers text materials for K-12 market. "We specialize in educational materials to be used in classrooms (in class sets), for staff development or in teacher education classes." Actively seeking educational, text materials. Not looking for picture books, story books, fiction; no illustrators.

RECENT SALES *How to Solve Word Problems in Mathematics*, by Wayne (McGraw-Hill); *Prepar-*

ing for the 8th Grade Test in Social Studies, by Farran-Paci (Amsco); *Minority Report*, by Gunn-Singh (Scarecrow Education); *No Parent Left Behind,* by Petrosino & Spiegel (Rowman & Littlefield); *Teaching Test-taking Skills* (R&L Education); *10 Languages You'll Need Most in the Classroom,* by Sundem, Krieger, Pickiewicz (Corwin Press); *Kids, Classrooms & Capital Hill,* by Flynn (R&L Education).

TERMS Agent receives 15% commission on domestic sales; 25% on foreign sales. Offers written contract, binding until any party opts out. Terminate contract through certified letter.

HOW TO CONTACT Query by e-mail or with SASE or send outline and 1 sample chapter. Considers simultaneous queries and submissions if so indicated. Responds in 6-8 weeks to queries/mss. Returns material only with SASE. Obtains clients through recommendations from others, queries/solicitations or through conferences.

ETHAN ELLENBERG LITERARY AGENCY

E-mail: agent@ethanellenberg.com. Website: ethanellenberg.com. 548 Broadway, #5-E, New York NY 10012. (212)431-4554. Fax: (212)941-4652. **Contact:** Ethan Ellenberg. Estab. 1983. Represents 80 clients. 10% of clients are new/previously unpublished writers. "Children's books are an important area for us." **Contact:** Ethan Ellenberg.

REPRESENTS Considers: picture books, middle grade, YA and selected. "This agency specializes in commercial fiction—especially thrillers, romance/women's, and specialized nonfiction. We also do a lot of children's books." "Actively seeking commercial fiction as noted above—romance/fiction for women, science fiction and fantasy, thrillers, suspense and mysteries. Our other two main areas of interest are children's books and narrative nonfiction. We are actively seeking clients; follow the directions on our website." Does not want to receive poetry, short stories or screenplays.

TERMS Agent receives 15% on domestic sales; 20% on foreign sales. Offers written contract, "flexible." Charges for "direct expenses only: photocopying for manuscript submissions, postage for submission and foreign rights sales."

HOW TO CONTACT Picture books—send full ms with SASE. Illustrators: Send a representative portfolio with color copies and SASE. No original artwork. Young adults—send outline plus 3 sample chapters with SASE. Accepts queries by e-mail; does not accept attachments to e-mail queries or fax queries. Considers simultaneous queries and submissions. Responds in 6 weeks to snail mail queries; only responds to e-mail queries if interested. Returns materials only with SASE. "See website for detailed instructions; please follow them carefully." No phone calls. For fiction, send introductory letter, outline, first 3 chapters, SASE. For nonfiction, send query letter, proposal, 1 sample chapter, SASE. For children's books, send introductory letter, up to 3 picture book mss, outline, first 3 chapters, SASE.

TIPS We do consider new material from unsolicited authors. Write a good, clear letter with a succinct description of your book. We prefer the first 3 chapters when we consider fiction. For all submissions, you must include a SASE or the material will be discarded. It's always hard to break in, but talent will find a home. Check our website for complete submission guidelines. We continue to see natural storytellers and nonfiction writers with important books.

THE ELAINE P. ENGLISH LITERARY AGENCY

4710 41st St. NW, Suite D, Washington DC 20016. (202)362-5190. Fax: (202)362-5192. E-mail: queries@elaineenglish.com. elaine@elaineenglish.com. Website: www.elaineenglish.com/literary.php. **Contact:** Elaine English.

REPRESENTS Actively seeking women's fiction, including single-title romances, and young adult fiction. Does not want to receive any science fiction, time travel, or picture books.

RECENT SALES Have been to Sourcebooks, Tor, Harlequin.

TERMS Agent receives 15% commission on domestic sales. Agent receives 20% commission on foreign sales. Offers written contract; 30-day notice must be given to terminate contract. Charges only for shipping expenses; generally taken from proceeds.

HOW TO CONTACT Generally prefers e-queries sent to queries@elaineenglish.com or YA sent to naomi@elaineenglish.com. If requested, submit synopsis, first 3 chapters, SASE. Please check website for further details. Obtains most new clients through recommendations from others, conferences, submissions. Responds in 4-8 weeks to queries; 3 months to requested submissions.

FLANNERY LITERARY

1140 Wickfield Ct., Naperville IL 60563. (630)428-2682. Fax: (630)428-2683. E-mail: FlanLit@aol.com. **Contact:** Jennifer Flannery. Estab. 1992. Represents 40 clients. 95% of clients are new/previously unpublished writers. Specializes in children's and young adult, juvenile fiction and nonfiction. **Contact:** Jennifer Flannery.

REPRESENTS 100% juvenile books. Considers: nonfiction, fiction, picture books, middle grade, young adult. Obtains new clients through referrals and queries. This agency specializes in children's and young adult fiction and nonfiction. It also accepts picture books.

TERMS Agent receives 15% commission on domestic sales; 20% on foreign sales. Offers written contract, binding for life of book in print, with 30-day cancellation clause. 100% of business is derived from commissions on sales.

HOW TO CONTACT "No e-mail or fax queries, please." Responds in 2 weeks to queries; 5 weeks to mss. Query with SASE. Obtains most new clients through recommendations from others, submissions.

TIPS "Write an engrossing, succinct query describing your work. We are always looking for a fresh new voice."

BARRY GOLDBLATT LITERARY LLC

320 Seventh Ave.#266, Brooklyn NY 11215. (718)832-8787. Fax: (718)832-5558. Website: www.bgliterary.com. Estab. 2000. Member of AAR, SCBWI. **Staff includes:** Barry Goldblatt, Beth Fleisher and Joe Monti. Represents 95% juvenile and young adult books. Considers graphic novels, fiction, nonfiction, middle grade, young adult.

RECENT SALES The Infernal Devices trilogy, by Cassandra Clare; *Clappy as a Ham*, by Michael Ian Black; *Pearl*, by Jo Knowles; *The Book of Blood and Shadows* by Robin Wasserman; *Summerton* by Karen Healey; *The Deviners* by Libba Bray.

TERMS Agent receives 15% commission on domestic sales; 20% on foreign and dramatic sales. Offers written contract. 60 days notice must be given to terminate contract.

HOW TO CONTACT "Please see our website for specific submission guidelines and information on agents' particular tastes." Obtains clients through referrals, queries, conferences.

TIPS "We're a group of hands-on agents, with wide

ranging interests. Get us hooked with a great query letter, then convince us with an unforgettable manuscript."

➕ DOUG GRAD LITERARY AGENCY, INC.

156 Prospect Park West, Brooklyn NY 11215. (718)788-6067. E-mail: doug.grad@dgliterary.com. query@dgliterary.com. Website: www.dgliterary.com. **Contact:** Doug Grad.

RECENT SALES *Drink the Tea*, by Thomas Kaufman (St. Martin's); *15 Minutes: The Impossible Math of Nuclear War*, by L. Douglas Keeney (St. Martin's)

HOW TO CONTACT Query by e-mail first at query@dgliterary.com. No sample material unless requested.

ASHLEY GRAYSON LITERARY AGENCY

E-mail: graysonagent@earthlink.net. Website: www.graysonagency.com/blog. 1342 18th St. San Pedro CA 90732. (310) 514-0267. Fax: (310) 831-0036. Seeking established writers; willing to consider some new writers. Estab. 1976. Agents are members of AAR, SCBWI, SFWA, RWA. **Represents** 75 clients. 2% new writers. 35% books for young readers. Staff includes Ashley Grayson, young adult and middle grade; Carolyn Grayson, young adult, middle grade, very few picture books; Denise Dumars, young adult. Handles fiction, middle grade, young adult. "We represent top authors in the field and we market their books to publishers worldwide." Actively seeking fiction of high commercial potential from established authors and new authors who clearly demonstrate on the first page they can write a break-in/break-out novel. Unpublished authors should provide recommendations from published authors who have actually read the work in question and recommend it. For tips on writing and publishing, follow our blog at http://graysonagency.com/blog.

HOW TO CONTACT Ashley Grayson and Carolyn Grayson prefer queries by e-mail. Please paste the first 3 pages of manuscript into the body of the e-mail. If querying about a picture book, paste entire text. Denise Dumars prefers queries by post; include first three pages of manuscript and SASE. Do not query more than one person in the agency. Response: 1 month after query, 2-3 months after ms. Returns mss only with SASE. Obtains new clients through recommendations from others, queries/solicitations, conferences.

RECENT SALES Sold 25+ books last year. *Juliet Dove, Queen of Love*, by Bruce Coville (Harcourt); *Alosha*,

by Christopher Pike (TOR); *Sleeping Freshmen Never Lie*, by David Lubar (Dutton); *Ball Don't Lie*, by Matt de la Peña (Delacorte); *Wiley & Grampa's Creature Features*, by Kirk Scroggs (10-book series, Little Brown); *Snitch*, by Allison van Diepen (Simon Pulse). Also represents: J.B. Cheaney (Knopf), Bruce Wetter (Atheneum).

TERMS Agent receives 15% on domestic sales, 20% on foreign sales. Offers written contract. Contract binding for 1 year. 30 days notice must be given for termination of contract.

TIPS "We do request revisions as they are required. We are long-time agents, professional and known in the business. We perform professionally for our clients and we ask the same of them."

REPRESENTS "We prefer to work with published (traditional print), established authors. We will give first consideration to authors who come recommended to us by our clients or other publishing professionals. We accept a very small number of new, previously unpublished authors." "The agency is temporarily closed to queries from writers who are not published at book length (self-published or print-on-demand do not count). There are only three exceptions to this policy: (1) Unpublished authors who have received an offer from a reputable publisher, who need an agent before beginning contract negotiations; (2) Authors who are recommended by a published author, editor or agent who has read the work in question; (3) Authors whom we have met at conferences and from whom we have requested submissions. Unpublished authors—nonfiction: Authors who are recognized within their field or area may still query with proposals." "We are seeking more mysteries and thrillers."

THE GREENHOUSE LITERARY AGENCY

11308 Lapham Dr., Oakton VA 22124. E-mail: submissions@greenhouseliterary.com. Website: www.greenhouseliterary.com. Contact: Sarah Davies. Young agency actively seeking clients. Seeking both new and established writers. Member of SCBWI. Represents 20 authors. 100% fiction for young readers. Staff includes Sarah Davies in USA and Julia Churchill in UK. **Contact:** Sarah Davies.

◑ Sarah Davies has had an editorial and management career in children's publishing spanning 25 years; for 5 years prior to launching the Greenhouse she was publishing director of Macmillan Children's Books in London, and publishing leading authors from both sides of the Atlantic.

REPRESENTS Handles fiction, middle grade, 'tween, young adult. "Sarah Davies (who is British) represents authors personally to both the USA and UK, and the Greenhouse has offices in both countries. Commission structure reflects this as the agency takes the same commission for both the USA and UK, treating both as the 'domestic' market. Foreign rights are sold by Rights People (a separate business but also part of the Greenhouse's parent company), a dedicated team of rights-selling experts with a fast-growing international track record. This means sub-agents are rarely used, giving the agency an exceptionally cohesive presence around the world and a truly global reach. Davies has a strong editorial background and is able, as necessary, to work creatively with authors in a very hands-on way to help them reach submission point." Actively seeking children's and YA fiction of all genres, from high-concept, character-led chapter-book series through teen and crossover. Does not seek short stories, poetry or nonfiction, or work aimed at adults. Only represents picture-book texts by existing clients initially taken on for older fiction. "We exclusively represent authors writing fiction for children and teens. The agency has offices in both the USA and UK, and Sarah Davies (who is British) personally represents authors to both markets. The agency's commission structure reflects this—taking 15% for sales to both US and UK, thus treating both as 'domestic' market.'" All genres of children's and YA fiction ages 5+. Does not want to receive nonfiction, poetry, picture books (text or illustration) or work aimed at adults; short stories, educational or religious/inspirational work, pre-school/novelty material, or screenplays.

RECENT SALES *Princess for Hire*, by Lindsey Leavitt (Hyperion); *What Happened on Fox Street*, by Tricia Springstubb (Harpercollins); *The Replacement*, by Brenna Yovanoff (Razorbill); *Just Add Magic*, by Cindy Callaghan (Aladdin).

TERMS Receives 15% commission on sales to both US and UK; 25% on foreign sales. Offers written contract. Sarah Davies attends Bologna Children's Bookfair in Bologna, Italy; SCBWI conferences; BookExpo America; and other conferences—see website for information.

TIPS "It's very important to me to have a strong, long-term relationship with clients. Having been 25 years in the publishing industry, I know the business from the inside and have excellent contacts in both the US and UK. I work hard to find every client the very best publisher and deal for their writing. My editorial background means I can work creatively with authors where necessary; I aim to submit high-quality manuscripts to publishers while respecting the role of the editor who will have their own publishing vision. Before submitting, prospective authors should read up-to-date submissions guidelines on website and also look at the Greenhouse's 'Top 10 tips for authors of children's fiction', which can be found on www.greenhouseliterary.com". This agency charges very occasionally for copies for submission to film agents or foreign publishers.

HOW TO CONTACT E-queries only as per guidelines given on website. Query should contain one-paragraph synopsis, one-paragraph bio, up to 5 sample pages pasted into e-mail. Replies to all submissions mostly within 2 weeks, but leave 6 weeks before chasing for response. Responds in 6-8 weeks to requested full manuscripts. Our current policy on picture books is that we do not solicit either texts or illustrators, but *do* represent picture books by authors whom we have already taken on for their older, longer work. Obtains most new clients through recommendations from others, solicitations, conferences.

TIPS "Before submitting material, authors should read the Greenhouse's 'Top 10 Tips for Authors of Children's Fiction,' which can be found on our website."

🌑 JANKLOW & NESBIT ASSOCIATES

445 Park Ave., New York NY 10022. Phone: (212)-421-1700; Fax: (212)980-3671. E-mail: info@janklow.com. Website: janklowandnesbit.com. Accepts simultaneous submissions. **Contact:** Julie Just, Literary Agent.

REPRESENTS Juvenile fiction and nonfiction, all genres; picture books, young readers, middle readers, young adult/teen mass market books, trade books. Does not want to receive unsolicited submissions or queries.

HOW TO CONTACT Query with samples. Considers electronic submissions. Obtains most new clients through recommendations from others.

TIPS "Please send a short query with sample chapters or artwork."

BARBARA S. KOUTS, LITERARY AGENT

(631)286-1278. Fax: (631) 286-1538. Member of AAR. Represent 50 clients. 10% of clients are new/previously unpublished writers. Specializes in children's books. **Contact:** Barbara S. Kouts.

REPRESENTS 100% juvenile books. Considers: nonfiction, fiction, picture books, ms/illustration packages, middle grade, young adult. Obtains new clients through recommendations from others, solicitation, at conferences, etc. This agency specializes in children's books.

RECENT SALES *Code Talker*, by Joseph Bruchac (Dial); *The Penderwicks*, by Jeanne Birdsall (Knopf); *Froggy's Baby Sister*, by Jonathan London (Viking).

TERMS Agent receives 10% commission on domestic sales; 20% on foreign sales. Charges for photocopying.

HOW TO CONTACT Responds in 1 week to queries; 6 weeks to mss. Query with SASE. Obtains most new clients through recommendations from others, solicitations, conferences.

TIPS "Write, do not call. Be professional in your writing."

GINA MACCOBY LITERARY AGENCY

P.O. Box 60, Chappaqua NY 10514. (914)238-5630. **Contact:** Gina Maccoby. Estab. 1986. Represents writers and illustrators of children's books. **Contact:** Gina Maccoby.

REPRESENTS 33% juvenile books. Considers: nonfiction, fiction, young adult. Usually obtains new clients through recommendations from own clients and/or editors.

TERMS Agent receives 15% commission on domestic sales; 25% on foreign sales. Charges for photocopying. May recover certain costs such as airmail postage to Europe or Japan or legal fees. Agent receives 15% commission on domestic sales.

HOW TO CONTACT Query with SASE. "Please, no unsolicited manuscripts." Considers simultaneous queries and submissions. Responds to queries in 3 months. Returns materials only with SASE. If querying by e-mail, put "query" in subject line. Obtains

most new clients through recommendations from clients and publishers.

TIPS This agency sold 21 titles last year.

MCINTOSH & OTIS, INC.

353 Lexington Ave., New York, NY 10016. (212)687-7400. Fax: (212)687-6894. E-mail: info@mcintoshandotis.com. Website: www.mcintoshandotis.net. **Contact:** Edward Necarsulmer IV. Seeking both new and established writers. Estab. 1927. Member of AAR and SCBWI. 30% of clients are new/previously unpublished writers. 90% of material handled is books for young readers.

REPRESENTS Considers fiction, middle grade, young adult. "McIntosh & Otis has a long history of representing authors of adult and children's books. The children's department is a separate division." Actively seeking "books with memorable characters, distinctive voice and a great plot." Not looking for educational, activity books, coloring books.

TERMS Agent receives 15% commission on domestic sales; 20% on foreign sales.

HOW TO CONTACT Query with SASE. Exclusive submission only. Responds in 6–8 weeks. Returns material only with SASE. Obtains clients through recommendations from others, editors, conferences and queries.

TIPS "No e-mail or phone calls!"

✪ THE MCVEIGH AGENCY

345 West 21st St., New York NY 10011-3035. E-mail: queries@themcveighagency.com. Website: www.themcveighagency.com. **Contact:** Linda Epstein.

REPRESENTS Considers nonfiction, fiction, picture books, middle grade, young adult, other. "I'm an experienced editor who knows virtually everyone in the field, having worked at almost every major publishing house. My knowledge of how to line edit a manuscript combined with my contacts allows me to help both new and established talent publish their works." Actively seeking everything form picture books to YA. Actively seeking genre mashups, a book that combines two common but disparate themes and combines them to comic or dramatic effect. As far as MG and YA, this agency seeks everything, but especially scary books, historical steampunk, and books that would appeal to children of color.

TERMS Agent receives 15% on domestic sales, 15% on foreign sales. Offers written contract. 30 days notice must be given for termination of contract.

HOW TO CONTACT E-mail query. Considers simultaneous queries, submissions. Responds 2 weeks after query; 4 weeks after ms. Returns mss only with SASE. Obtains new clients through recommendations from others, queries/solicitations, conferences. For e-queries: In the subject line of your e-mail, please write: "Query," then the type of manuscript (e.g. YA, MG, PB, adult, nonfiction), and then the title of your book. The body of your e-mail should consist of your query letter, followed by the first 20 pages of your manuscript (for fiction) or your full proposal (for nonfiction). Please do not add your manuscript as an attachment. If the agency is interested in reading more, they'll request that you e-mail the full manuscript.

TIPS "I am a very hands-on, old-school agent who likes to edit manuscripts as much as I like to negotiate deals. My favorite agents were always what I called 'honest sharks,' out to get the best deal for their client, always looking ahead, but always conduct business in such a way that everyone came away as happy as possible. In short—they had integrity and determination to represent their clients to the best of their abilities, and that's what I aspire to."

ERIN MURPHY LITERARY AGENCY

2700 Woodlands Village, #300-458, Flagstaff AZ 86001-7172. (928)525-2056. Fax: (928)525-2480. Website: emliterary.com. Closed to unsolicited queries and submissions. Considers both new and established writers, by referral from industry professionals she knows or personal contact (such as conferences) only. Estab. 1999. Member of SCBWI. Represents 70 active clients. 25% of clients are new/previously unpublished writers. 100% of material handled is books of young readers. **Contact:** Erin Murphy, president; Ammi-Joan Paquette, associate agent.

REPRESENTS Picture books, middle grade, young adult. "This agency only represents children's books. We do not accept unsolicited manuscripts or queries. We consider new clients by referral or personal contact only."

TERMS Agent receives 15% commission on domestic sales; 25% on foreign sales. Offers written contract. 30 days notice must be given to terminate contract.

MUSE LITERARY MANAGEMENT

189 Waverly Place, #4, New York NY 10014-3135. (212)925-3721. E-mail: museliterarymgmt@aol.com. Website: www.museliterary.com. Agency is member of Children's Literature Network. Represents 10 clients. 90% new writers. 60% books for young readers. **Contact:** Deborah Carter.

REPRESENTS Handles nonfiction, fiction, picture books, middle grade, young adult. As an independent literary agent, Deborah Carter focuses on manuscript development; the sale and administration of print, performance and foreign rights to literary works; and post-publication publicity and appearances. Works in both children's and adult books. Actively seeking fiction and nonfiction for young children to young adult by writers with original outlook who follow their segment of the industry. Not interested in category sci-fi, fantasy or horror. No gross or copycat books. Special interest in African-American and multicultural titles. Looking for picture books and novels that bring something new to their bookselling category. Prefers writers who interact with the age groups they're writing for. Originality and imagination are treasured. See "Bookshelf"page at www.museliterary.com for links to favorite books. Actively pursuing new writers with formal training and published authors who want to try something new. Those who submit should be receptive to editorial feedback and willing to revise to be competitive. Writers are encouraged to read *Publishers Weekly* to develop an awareness of the marketplace and bookselling categories for their book. Does not want vulgar subject matter or books that copy others. "I'm only interested in intelligent books." Does not want "manuscripts that have been worked over by book doctors (collaborative projects ok, but writers must have chops); category romance, chick lit, sci-fi, fantasy, horror, stories about cats and dogs, vampires or serial killers, fiction or nonfiction with religious or spiritual subject matter."

TERMS Agent receives 15% commission on domestic sales; 20% on foreign sales. Offers written contract. Contract binding for 1 year. One day's notice must be given for termination of contract. One-year contract offered when writer and agent agree that the manuscript is ready for submission; manuscripts in development are not bound by contract. Sometimes charges for postage and photocopying. All expenses are preapproved by the client.

HOW TO CONTACT Seeking both new and established writers. Accepts queries by e-mail, mail. Considers simultaneous queries, submissions. Responds in 1-2 weeks to queries; 2-3 weeks to ms. Query with

SASE. Query via e-mail (no attachments). Discards unwanted queries. Obtains most new clients through recommendations from others, conferences.

TIPS "I give editorial feedback and work on revisions on spec. Agency agreement is offered when the writer and I feel the manuscript is ready for submission to publishers. Writers should also be open to doing revisions with editors who express serious interest in their work, prior to any offer of a publishing contract. All aspects of career strategy are discussed with writers, and all decisions are ultimately theirs. I make multiple and simultaneous submissions when looking for rights opportunities, and share all correspondence. All agreements are signed by the writers. Reimbursement for expenses is subject to client's approval, limited to photocopying (usually press clips) and postage. I always submit fresh manuscripts to publishers printed in my office with no charge to the writer."

JEAN V. NAGGAR LITERARY AGENCY, INC.

(212)794-1082. E-mail: jweltz@jvnla.com; jvnla@jvnla.com; jregel@jvnla.com; atasman@jvnla.com. Website: www.jvnla.com. Seeking both new and established writers. Estab. 1978. Member of AAR, SCBWI. Represents over 450 clients. Large percentage of clients are new/previously unpublished writers. Accepts queries by e-mail. Prefers to read materials exclusively. **Contact:** Jean Naggar.

REPRESENTS Handles nonfiction, fiction, picture books, middle grade, young adult. 25% material handled is books for young readers. Jennifer Weltz (subrights, children's, adults); Jessica Regel (young adult, adult, subrights); Jean Naggar (taking no new clients); see website for client list; Alice Tasman (adult, children's); Elizabeth Evans (adult nonfiction, some fiction and YA). This agency specializes in mainstream fiction and nonfiction and literary fiction with commercial potential.

RECENT SALES *Night Navigation* by Ginnah Howard; *After Hours At the Almost Home,* by Tara Yelen; *An Entirely Synthetic Fish: A Biography of Rainbow Trout* by Anders Halverson; *The Patron Saint of Butterflies* by Cecilia Galante; *Wondrous Strange* by Lesley Livingston; *6 Sick Hipsters* by Rayo Casablanca; *The Last Bridge* by Teri Coyne; *Gypsy Goodbye* by Nancy Springer; *Commuters* by Emily Tedrowe; *The Language of Secrets* by Dianne Dixon; *Smiling to Freedom* by Martin Benoit Stiles; *The Tale of Halcyon Crane* by Wendy Webb; *Fugitive* by Phillip Margolin; *BlackBerry Girl* by Aidan Donnelley Rowley; *Wild Girls* by Pat Murphy.

TERMS Agent receives 15% commission on domestic sales. Agent receives 20% commission on foreign sales. Offers written contract. Charges for overseas mailing, messenger services, book purchases, long-distance telephone, photocopying—all deductible from royalties received.

HOW TO CONTACT Responds in 2 weeks to query if interested. Will not respond if not interested. Response time for ms depends on the agent queried. Obtains new clients through recommendations from others, queries/solicitations, conferences. Query via e-mail. Prefers to read materials exclusively. No fax queries. Obtains most new clients through recommendations from others.

TIPS "Use a professional presentation. Because of the avalanche of unsolicited queries that flood the agency every week, we have had to modify our policy. We will now only guarantee to read and respond to queries from writers who come recommended by someone we know. Our areas are general fiction and nonfiction—no children's books by unpublished writers, no multimedia, no screenplays, no formula fiction, and no mysteries by unpublished writers. We recommend patience and fortitude: the courage to be true to your own vision, the fortitude to finish a novel and polish it again and again before sending it out, and the patience to accept rejection gracefully and wait for the stars to align themselves appropriately for success."

ALISON PICARD, LITERARY AGENT

P.O. Box 2000, Cotuit MA 02635. **Contact:** Alison Picard. Seeking both new and established writers. Estab. 1985. Represents 50 clients. 40% of clients are new/previously unpublished writers. 20% of material handled is books for young readers.

○ Prior to opening her agency, Alison Picard was an assistant at a large New York agency before co-founding Kidde, Hoyt & Picard in 1982. She became an independent agent in 1985.

REPRESENTS Considers nonfiction, fiction, a very few picture books, middle grade, young adult. "I represent juvenile and YA books. I do not handle short stories, articles, poetry or plays. I am especially interested in commercial nonfiction, romances and mysteries/suspense/thrillers. I work with agencies in Europe and Los Angeles to sell foreign and TV/film rights. "Actively seeking middle grade fiction. Not looking for poetry or plays."

RECENT SALES *Funerals and Fly Fishing*, by Mary Bartek (Henry Holt & Co.); *Playing Dad's Song*, by Dina Friedman (Farrar Straus & Giroux); *Escaping into the Night*, by Dina Friedman (Simon & Schuster); *Celebritrees* and *The Peace Bell*, by Margi Preus (Henry Holt & Co.).

TERMS Receives 15% commission on domestic sales; 20-25% on foreign sales. Offers written contract, binding for 1 year. 1-week notice must be given to terminate contract.

HOW TO CONTACT Query with SASE. Accepts queries by e-mail with no attachments. Considers simultaneous queries and submissions. Responds in 2 weeks to queries; 4 months to mss. Returns material only with SASE. Obtains clients through queries/solicitations.

TIPS "We currently have a backlog of submissions."

PROSPECT AGENCY

551 Valley Road, PMB 377, Upper Montclair, NJ 02043. (718)788-3217. Fax: (718)360-9582. E-mail: esk@prospectagency.com. Website: www.prospectagency.com. **Contact:** Emily Sylvan Kim, Becca Stumpf, Rachel Orr, Teresa Keitlinski. Seeking both new and established writers. Estab. 2005. Agent is member of AAR. Represents 80 clients and growing. 70% of clients are new/previously unpublished writers. 60% of material handled is books for young readers. Staff includes Emily Sylvan, Becca Stumpf, and Rachel Orr. Emily handles young adult, tween and middle grade literary and commercial fiction, with a special interest in edgy books and books for boys. Becca Stumpf handals young adult and middle grade literary and commercial fiction, with a special interest in fantasy and science fiction with cross-genre appeal. Rachel Orr handles picture books, beginning readers, chapter books, middle grade/YA novels, children's nonfiction, and children's illustrators. Teresa Kietlinski hadles picture books authors and illustrators. She also seeks children's picture book illustrators and graphic novels.

○ For some of us, it's all we've ever known. Others have worked in various facets of publishing and law.

REPRESENTS Handles nonfiction, fiction, picture books, middle grade, young adult. "Prospect Agency focuses on adult and children's literature, and is currently looking for the next generation of writers and illustrators to shape the literary landscape. We are a small, personal agency that focuses on helping each client reach success through hands-on editorial assistance and professional contract negotiations. We also strive to be on the cutting edge technologically. The agents here spend a lot of time forming personal relationships with authors and their work. Every agent here has incredibly strong editorial skills, and works directly with clients to balance the goals of selling individual books and managing a career." We're looking for strong, unique voices and unforgettable stories and characters.

RECENT SALES Sold 15 books for young readers in the last year. (Also represents adult fiction.) Recent sales include: *Ollie and Claire* (Philomel); *Vicious*, (Bloomsbury); *Temptest Rising* (Walker Books); *Where Do Diggers Sleep at Night* (Random House Children's); *A DJ Called Tomorrow* (Little, Brown); *Princesses of Iowa* (Candlewick); and others. .

TERMS Agent receives 15% on domestic sales, 20% on foreign sales sold directly and 25% on sales using a subagent. Offers written contract.

HOW TO CONTACT Send outline and 3 sample chapters. Accepts queries through website ONLY. Considers simultaneous queries and submissions. However, we do not accept submissions to multiple Prospect agents (please submit to only one agent at Prospect Agency). Responds in 1 week to 3 months following an initial query. 1 week to 2 months after a mss has been requested. All submissions are elcetronic; manuscripts and queries that are not a good fit for our agency are rejected via e-mail. We obtain new clients through conferences, recommendations, queries and some scouting.

WENDY SCHMALZ AGENCY

P.O. Box 831, Hudson NY 12534. (518)672-7697. E-mail: wendy@schmalzagency.com. Website:www.schmalzagency.com. Seeking both new and established writers. Estab. 2002. Member of AAR. Represents 35 clients. 10% of clients are new/previously unpublished writers. 70% of material handled is books for young readers. **Contact:** Wendy Schmalz.

○ Prior to opening her agency, Wendy Schmalz was an agent for 23 years at Harold Ober Associates.

REPRESENTS Considers nonfiction, fiction, middle grade, young adult. Actively seeking young adult novels, middle grade novels. Not looking for picture books, science fiction or fantasy.

TERMS Agent receives 15% commission on domestic sales; 20% on foreign sales; 25% for Asian sales. Fees for photocopying and FedEx. Agent receives 15% commission on domestic sales; 20% on foreign sales; 25% for Asian sales.

HOW TO CONTACT Query with SASE. Accepts queries by e-mail. Responds in 4 weeks to queries; 4-6 weeks to mss. Returns material only with SASE. Obtains clients through recommendations from others.

SUSAN SCHULMAN LITERARY AGENCY

454 W. 44th, New York NY 10036. (212)713-1633. Fax: (212)581-8830. E-mail: schulman@aol.com. Website: www.Schulmanagency.com. **Contact:** Susan Schulman. Seeking both new and established writers. Estab. 1980. Member of AAR, WGA, SCBWI, Dramatists Guild, New York Women in Film, League of New York Theater Professional Women, Women's Media Group. 15% of material handled is books for young readers. Staff includes Emily Uhry, YA; Linda Kiss, picture books. **Contact:** Susan Schulman.

REPRESENTS Handles nonfiction, fiction, picture books, middle grade, young adult. Actively seeking well-written, original stories for any age group. "We specialize in books for, by and about women and women's issues including nonfiction self-help books, fiction and theater projects. We also handle the film, television and allied rights for several agencies as well as foreign rights for several publishing houses." Actively seeking new nonfiction. Considers plays. Does not want to receive poetry, television scripts or concepts for television.

RECENT SALES Sold 50 titles in the last year; hundred of subsidiary rights deals.

TERMS Agent receives 15% on domestic sales, 20% on foreign sales. Schulman describes her agency as "professional boutique, long-standing, eclectic." Offers written contract; 30-day notice must be given to terminate contract.

HOW TO CONTACT Query with SASE. Accepts queries by e-mail but responds only to e-mail queries which interest agency. Considers simultaneous queries and submissions. Returns mss only with SASE. Obtains new clients through recommendations from others, queries/solicitations, conferences. Query with SASE. Submit outline, synopsis, author

bio, 3 sample chapters. Obtains most new clients through recommendations from others, solicitations, conferences.

TIPS "Keep writing!"

SERENDIPITY LITERARY AGENCY, LLC

305 Gates Ave., Brooklyn NY 11216. (718)230-7689. Fax: (718)230-7829. E-mail: rbrooks@serendipitylit. com. Website: www.serendipitylit.com. **Contact:** Regina Brooks. Estab. 2000. Represents 50 clients. 65% of clients are new/unpublished writers. 50% of material handled is books for young readers. Handles all children's books areas from picture books to young adult, both fiction and nonfiction. Actively seeking young adult novels with an urban flair and juvenile books. Accepts e-mail queries. **Contact:** Regina Brooks.

REPRESENTS "I adore working with first-time authors whose books challenge the readers emotionally; tears and laughter. I also represent award-winning illustrators." Regina Brooks: African-American nonfiction, commercial fiction, young adult novels with an urban flair and juvenile books. No stage plays, screenplays or poetry.

RECENT SALES *A Wreath for Emmitt Till*, by Marilyn Nelson (Houghton Mifflin); *A Song for Present Existence*, by Marilyn Nelson and Tonya Hegamin (Scholastic); *Ruby and the Booker Boys*, by Derrick Barnes (Scholastic); *Brenda Buckley's Universe and Everything In It*, by Sundee Frazier (Delacorte Books for Young Readers); *Wait Until the Black Girl Sings*, by Bil Wright (Scholastic); *First Semester*, by Cecil R. Cross II (KimaniTru/ Harlequin).

TERMS Agent receives 15% commission on domestic sales. Agent receives 20% commission on foreign sales. Offers written contract; 2-month notice must be given to terminate contract. Charges clients for office fees, which are taken from any advance.

HOW TO CONTACT Prefers to read materials exclusively. For nonfiction, submit proposal, outline, 1 sample chapter (electronically), SASE. Write the field on the back of the envelope. For adult fiction, please send a query letter that includes basic information that describes your project. Your query letter should include the title, premise, and length of the manuscript. See our guidelines onine. Write the genre of your book on the back of your envelope. Based on your initial query letter and synopsis, our office may request sample chapters, or your ms in its entirety. Obtains most new clients through conferences, referrals.

TIPS "See *Writing Great Books For Young Adults.* Looking for high concept ideas with big hooks."

THE SPIELER AGENCY

E-mail: thespieleragency@gmail.com. **Contact:** Katya Balter, acquisitions.

TERMS Agent receives 15% commission on domestic sales. Charges clients for messenger bills, photocopying, postage.

HOW TO CONTACT Accepts electronic submissions, or send query letter and sample chapters. Returns materials only with SASE; otherwise materials are discarded when rejected. Obtains most new clients through recommendations, listing in *Guide to Literary Agents*.

TIPS "Check www.publishersmarketplace.com/ members/spielerlit/."

STIMOLA LITERARY STUDIO, INC.

Fax: /Phone: (201)945-9353. E-mail: info@stimolaliterarystudio.com. Website: www.stimolaliterarystudio.com. **Contact:** Rosemary B. Stimola. Seeking both new and established writers. Estab. 1997. Member of AAR, SCBWI, ALA, NCTE. Represents 45+ clients. 25% of clients are new/previously unpublished writers. 85% of material handled is books for young readers.

REPRESENTS Preschool through young adult, fiction and nonfiction. Agency is owned and operated by a former educator and children's bookseller with a Ph.D in Linguistics. Actively seeking remarkable young adult fiction and debut picture book author/illustrators. No institutional books.

HOW TO CONTACT Query via e-mail. No attachments, please! Considers simultaneous queries. Responds in 3 weeks to queries of interest; 6-8 weeks to requested mss. Returns snail mail material with SASE. While unsolicited queries are welcome, most clients come through editor, agent, client referrals.

⭕ Prior to opening her agency, Rosemary Stimola was an independent children's bookseller.

RECENT SALES Sold 40 books for young readers in the last year. Among these, *A Touch Mortal*, by Leah Clifford (Greenwillow/Harper Collins); *Black Hole Sun*, by David Gill (Greenwillow/Harper Collins); *Dot*, by Patricia Intriago (FSG/Macmillan); *Inside Out and Back Again*, by Thanhha Lai (Harper Collins); *The Fox Inheritance*, by Mary Pearson (Henry Holt/Macmillan); *Henry Aaron's Dream*, by Matt Tavares (Candlewick Press); *Throat*, by R.A. Nelson (Knopf/RH).

TERMS Agent receives 15% commission on domestic sales; 20% on foreign sales (if subagents used). Offers written contract, binding for all children's projects. 60 days notice must be given to terminate contract. Charges $85 one-time fee per project to cover expenses. Client provides all hard copy and e-files required for submission."

TIPS Query via e-mail (no unsolicited attachments). Obtains most new clients through referrals. Unsolicited submissions are still accepted. Agent is hands-on, no-nonsense. May request revisions. Does not edit but may offer suggestions for improvement. Well-respected by clients and editors. "A firm but reasonable deal negotiator."

➕ THE STRINGER LITERARY AGENCY, LLC

E-mail: stringerlit@comcast.net. Website: www. stringerlit.com. **Contact:** Marlene Stringer.

REPRESENTS This agency specializes in fiction. Does not want to receive picture books, plays, short stories or poetry.

RECENT SALES *Out for Blood* and *Stolen*, by Alyxandra Harvey (Walker Books); *Change of Heart*, by Shari Maurer, (WestSide Books); *I Stole Johnny Depp's Alien Girlfriend*, by Gary Ghislain (Chronicle Books); *The Land of Hope & Glory Trilogy*, by Geoffrey Wilson to Hodder; *..And On The Piano, Nicky Hopkins!* by Julian Dawson to Plus One Press; *Poison Kissed*, by Erica Hayes (St. Martin's); *Possum Summer*, by Jen K. Blom (Holiday House); *An Echo Through the Snow* (Forge).

HOW TO CONTACT Electronic submissions only.

TIPS "If your manuscript falls between categories, or you are not sure of the category, query and we'll let you know if we'd like to take a look. We strive to respond as quickly as possible. If you have not received a response in the time period indicated, please re-query."

ANN TOBIAS: A LITERARY AGENCY FOR CHILDREN'S BOOKS

E-mail: AnnTobias84@hotmail.com. **Contact:** Ann Tobias.

REPRESENTS This agency specializes in books for children.

TERMS Agent receives 15% commission on domestic sales; 20% on foreign sales.

HOW TO CONTACT Send a one-page letter of inquiry accompanied by a one-page writing sample, double-spaced. No e-mail, fax or phone queries. Cannot sign for receipt of ms. Accepts simultaneous submissions for queries only. Must have 1 month exclusive basis for considering an entire ms after inviting author to submit. Responds to all queries accompanied by SASE; 2 months to mss. Returns material only with SASE. For all age groups and genres: Send a one-page letter of inquiry accompanied by a one-page writing sample, double-spaced. No attachments will be opened. Obtains most new clients through recommendations from editors.

TIPS "Read at least 200 children's books in the age group and genre in which you hope to be published. Follow this by reading another 100 children's books in other age groups and genres so you will have a feel for the field as a whole."

S©OTT TREIMEL NY

S©OTT TREIMEL NY; 0434 Lafayette St., New York, NY 10003. (212)505-8353. E-mail: general@scotttreimelny.com. Website: scotttreimelny.com. **Contact:** John M. Cusick.

REPRESENTS 100% juvenile books. Actively seeking career clients, especially middle grade and teen authors. Not seeking picture book authors, but author/illustrators may submit. This agency specializes in tightly focused segments of the trade and institutional markets. Seeks career clients.

RECENT SALES *The Hunchback Assignments*, by Arthur Slade (Random House, HarperCollins Canada; HarperCollins Australia); *Shotgun Serenade*, by Gail Giles (Little, Brown); *Laundry Day*, by Maurie Manning (Clarion); *The P.S. Brothers*, by Maribeth Boelts (Harcourt); *The First Five Fourths*, by Pat Hughes (Viking); *Old Robert and the Troubadour Cats*, by Barbara Joosse (Philomel); *Ends*, by David Ward (Abrams); *Dear Canada*, by Barbara Haworth-Attard (Scholastic); *Soccer Dreams*, by Maribeth Boelts (Candlewick); *Lucky Me*, by Richard Scrimger (Tundra); *Play, Louie, Play*, by Muriel Harris Weinstein (Bloomsbury).

TERMS Agent receives 15-20% commission on domestic sales; 25% on foreign sales. Offers verbal or written contract, binding on a "contract-by-contract basis." Offers extensive editorial guidance "to ensure submissions are of the high quality for which we are known." Charges clients for photocopying, express postage, messengers and books needed to sell foreign, film and other rights.

HOW TO CONTACT Submissions accepted via website submission form.

TIPS "We look for dedicated authors and illustrators able to sustain longtime careers in our increasingly competitive field. I want fresh, not derivative story concepts with overly familiar characters. We look for gripping stories, characters, pacing and themes. We remain mindful of an authentic (to the age) point-of-view, and look for original voices. We spend significant time hunting for the best new work, and do launch debut talent each year. It is best *not* to send manuscripts with lengthy submission histories already."

WRITERS HOUSE

E-mail: mmejias@writershouse.com; smalk@writershouse.com. 21 W. 26th St.New York NY 10010. (212)685-2400. Fax: (212)685-1781. Website: www.writershouse.com. Estab. 1974. Member of AAR. Writers House represents all types of fiction and nonfiction, specializing in children's and young adult literature, form picture books to YA, authors and illustrators. Client include winners of the Caldecott, Newbery, and Printz Medals and Honors in addition to recipients of the National Book Award in young people's literature and numerous other prizes. Clients' books have appeared on the *New York Times* Children's picture book, chapter book, paperback, and series lists including the phenomenon, *Twilight*. Information on submissions policies and specific agent guidelines can be found on our website. New clients are found through unsolicited submissions as well as other means. **Contact:** Michael Mejias.

REPRESENTS This agency specializes in all types of popular fiction and nonfiction. Does not want to receive scholarly, professional, poetry, plays or screenplays.

TERMS Agent receives 15% commission on domestic sales; 20% on foreign sales. Offers written contract, binding for 1 year. Agency charges fees for copying mss/proposals and overseas airmail of books.

HOW TO CONTACT Query with SASE. Please send us a query letter of no more than 2 pages, which includes your credentials, an explanation of what makes your book unique and special, and a synopsis. (If submitting to Steven Malk: Writers House, 7660 Fay Ave., #338H, La Jolla, CA 92037.) Obtains most new clients through recommendations from authors and editors.

TIPS "Do not send manuscripts. Write a compelling letter. If you do, we'll ask to see your work. Follow submission guidelines and please do not simultaneously submit your work to more than one Writer's House agent."

ART REPS

ART FACTORY

925 Elm Grove Rd., Elm Grove, WI 53122. (262)785-1940. Fax: (262)785-1611. E-mail: tstocki@artfactoryltd.com. Website: www.artfactoryillustrators.com. **Contact:** Tom Stocki. Commercial illustration representative. Estab. 1978. Represents 9 illustrators including: Tom Buchs, Tom Nachreiner, Todd Dakins, Linda Godfrey, Larry Mikec, Bill Scott, Gary Shea, Terry Herman, Troy Allen. 10% of artwork handled is children's book illustration. Currently open to illustrators seeking representation. Open to both new and established illustrators.

REPRESENTS Illustration.

TERMS Receives 25-30% commission. Offers written contract. Advertising costs are split: 75% paid by illustrators; 25% paid by rep. "We try to mail samples of all our illustrators at one time and we try to update our website; so we ask the illustrators to keep up with new samples." Advertises in *Picturebook, Workbook*.

HOW TO CONTACT For first contact, send query letter, tearsheets. Responds only if interested. Call to schedule an appointment. Portfolio should include tearsheets. Finds illustrators through queries/solicitations.

TIPS "Have a unique style."

ASCIUTTO ART REPS. INC.

1712 E. Butler Circle, Chandler AZ 85225. (480)814-8010 Website: www.Aartreps.com E-mail: Aartreps@cox.net. **Contact:** Mary Anne Asciutto, art agent. Children's book illustration representative since 1980. Specializing in children's illustrations for children's educational text books, grades K-8, children's trade books, children's magazines, posters, packaging, etc.

RECENT SALES *Bats, Sharks, Whales, Snakes, Penguins, Alligators and Crocodiles*, illustrated by Meryl Henderson for Boyds Mills Press.

TERMS Agency receives 25% commission. Advertising and promotion costs are split: 75% paid by talent; 25% paid by representative. U.S. citizens only.

HOW TO CONTACT Send samples via e-mail with a cover letter, résumé. Submit sample portfolio for review with SASE. Responds in 2 to 4 weeks. Portfolio should include at least 12 samples of original art, printed tearsheets, photocopies or color prints of most recent work.

TIPS In obtaining representation, "be sure to connect with an agent who handles the kind of work, you (the artist) *want*."

CAROL BANCROFT & FRIENDS

P.O. Box 2030, Danbury CT 06813. (203)730-8270 or (800)720-7020. Fax: (203)730-8275. E-mail: cb_friends8270@sbcglobal.net or cbfriends@sbcglobal.net; artists@carolbancroft.com. Website: www.carolbancroft.com. Illustration representative for all aspects of children's publishing and design. Member of, Society of Illustrators, Graphic Artists Guild, National Art Education Association, SCBWI. Represents 30+ illustrators. Specializes in illustration for children's publishing—text and trade; any children's-related material. Clients include, but not limited to, Scholastic, Houghton Mifflin, HarperCollins, Dutton, Harcourt, Marshall Cavendish, McGraw Hill, Hay House. **Contact:** Joy Tricarico, owner.

REPRESENTS Illustration for children of all ages including young adults. Advertises in Picture Book, Directory of Illustration.

TERMS Rep receives 25% commission. Advertising costs are split: 75% paid by talent; 25% paid by representative. For promotional purposes, artists must provide "laser copies (not slides), tearsheets, promo pieces, good color photocopies, etc.; 6 pieces or more is best; narrative scenes and children interacting."

HOW TO CONTACT Send either 2-3 samples with your address to the e-mail address above or mail 6-10 samples, along with a SASE to the above P.O. box.

TIPS "We look for artists who can draw animals and people with imagination and energy, depicting engaging characters with action in situational settings."

PEMA BROWNE LTD.

11 Tena Place, Valley Cottage NY 10989. (845)268-0029. **Contact:** Pema Browne. Estab. 1966. Represents 2 illustrators. 10% of artwork handled is children's book illustration. Specializes in general commercial. Markets include: all publishing areas; children's pic-

ture books. Clients include HarperCollins, Holiday House, Bantam Doubleday Dell, Nelson/Word, Hyperion, Putnam. Client list available upon request.

REPRESENTS Fiction, nonfiction, picture books, middle grade, young adult, manuscript/illustration packages. Looking for "professional and unique" talent.

RECENT SALES *The Daring Ms. Quimby*, by Suzanne Whitaker (Holiday House).

TERMS Rep receives 30% illustration commission; 20% author commission. Exclusive area representation is required. For promotional purposes, talent must provide color mailers to distribute. Representative pays mailing costs on promotion mailings.

HOW TO CONTACT For first contact, send query letter, direct mail flier/brochure and SASE. If interested will ask to mail appropriate materials for review. Portfolios should include tearsheets and transparencies or good color photocopies, plus SASE. Accepts queries by mail only. Obtains new talent through recommendations and interviews (portfolio review).

TIPS "We are doing more publishing—all types— less advertising." Looks for "continuity of illustration and dedication to work."

CATUGEAU: ARTIST AGENT, LLC

3009 Margaret Jones Lane, Williamsburg, VA 23185. (757)221-0666. Fax: (757)221-6669. E-mail: chris@catugeau.com. Website: www.CATugeau.com. **Owner/ Agent:** Christina Tugeau. Children's publishing trade book, mass market, educational. Estab. 1994. Member of SPAR, SCBWI, Graphic Artists Guild. Represents about 38 illustrators. 95% of artwork handled is children's book illustration.

◯Accepting limited new artists from North America only.

REPRESENTS Illustration ONLY (and book ideas from agency artists).

TERMS Receives 25% commission. "Artists responsible for providing samples for portfolios, promotional books and mailings." Exclusive representation required in educational. Trade "house accounts" acceptable. Offers written contract. Advertises in *Picturebook* and *Directory of Illustration*.

HOW TO CONTACT For first contact, e-mail samples and live website link, with note. No CDs. Responds ASAP. Finds illustrators through recommendations from others, conferences, personal search.

TIPS "Do research, read articles on CAT website,

study picture books at bookstores, promote yourself a bit to learn the industry. Be professional. Know what you do best, and be prepared to give rep what they need to present you! Do have e-mail and scanning capabilities, too."

◯ CORNELL & McCARTHY, LLC

(203)454-4210. Fax: (203)454-4258. E-mail: contact@ cmartreps.com. Children's book illustration representatives. Member of SCBWI and Graphic Artists Guild. Represents 30 illustrators. Specializes in children's books: trade, mass market, educational. Obtains new talent through recommendations, solicitation, conferences.

TERMS Agent receives 25% commission. Advertising costs are split: 75% paid by talent; 25% paid by representative. For promotional purposes, talent must provide 10-12 strong portfolio pieces relating to children's publishing.

HOW TO CONTACT For first contact, send query letter, direct mail flier/brochure, tearsheets, photocopies and SASE or e-mail. Responds in 1 month.

TIPS "Work hard on your portfolio."

CREATIVE FREELANCERS, INC.

P.O. Box 366, Tallevast FL 34270 (800)398-9544. Website: www.illustratorsonline.com. **Contact:** Marilyn Howard. Commercial illustration representative. Estab. 1988. Represents over 30 illustrators. "Our staff members have art direction, art buying or illustration backgrounds." Specializes in children's books, advertising, architectural, conceptual. Markets include: advertising agencies; corporations/client direct; design firms; editorial/magazines; paper products/greeting cards; publishing/books; sales/ promotion firms.

REPRESENTS Illustration. Artists must have published work.

TERMS Rep receives 30% commission. Exclusive area representation is preferred. Advertising costs are split: 75% paid by talent; 25% paid by representative. For promotional purposes, talent must provide scans of artwork. Advertises in *American Showcase*, *Workbook*.

HOW TO CONTACT For first contact, send tearsheets, low res jpegs or "whatever best shows work." Responds back only if interested.

TIPS Looks for experience, professionalism and consistency of style. Obtains new talent through "word of mouth and website."

DIMENSION

13420 Morgan Ave. S.Burnsville MN 55337. (952)201-3981. E-mail: jkoltes@dimensioncreative.com. Website: www.dimensioncreative.com. **Contact:** Joanne Koltes. Commercial illustration representative. Estab. 1982. Member of MN Book Builder. Represents 12 illustrators. 65% of artwork handled is children's book illustration. Staff includes Joanne Koltes.

TERMS Advertises in *Picturebook* and *Minnesota Creative.*

HOW TO CONTACT Contact with samples via e-mail. Responds only if interested.

PAT HACKETT/ARTIST REP

7014 N. Mercer Way, Mercer Island WA 98040-2130. (206)447-1600. Website: www.pathackett.com. **Contact:** Pat Hackett. Commercial illustration representative. Estab. 1979. Member of Graphic Artists Guild. Represents 10 illustrators. 10% of artwork handled is children's book illustration. Currently open to illustrators seeking representation. Open to both new and established illustrators.

REPRESENTS Illustration. Looking for illustrators with unique, strong, salable style. Bryan Ballinger, Kooch Campbell, Jonathan Combs, Eldon Doty, Ed Fotheringham, John Fretz, Lilly Lee, Bruce Morser, Dennis Ochsner, Mark Zingarelli.

TERMS Receives 25-33% commission. Advertising costs are split: 75% paid by illustrators; 25% paid by rep. Illustrator must provide portfolios (2-3) and promotional pieces. Advertises in *Picturebook*, *Workbook.*

HOW TO CONTACT For first contact, send query letter, tearsheets, SASE, direct mail flyer/brochure, or e-mail. Responds only if interested. Wait for response.

TIPS "Send query plus 1-2 samples, either by regular mail or e-mail."

LEVY CREATIVE MANAGEMENT

245 E. 63rd St., Suite 1622, New York NY 10065. (212)687-6465. Fax: (212)661-4839. E-mail: info@levycreative.com. Website: www.levycreative.com. Member of Society of Illustrators. Represents 13 illustrators including: Kako, Orit Berman, Michael Byers, Robin Eley, Brian Hubble, Rory Kurtz, Jorge Mascarenhas, Christopher Nelsen, Laura Osorno, Trip Park, Kyung Soon Park, Koren Shadmi, Jason Tharp, Andrea Wicklund. 30% of artwork handled

is children's book illustration. Currently open to illustrators seeking representation. Open to both new and established illustrators. Submission guidelines available on website.

REPRESENTS Illustration, manuscript/illustration packages.

TERMS Exclusive representation required. Offers written contract. Advertising costs are split: 75% paid by illustrators; 25% paid by rep. Portfolio should include professionally presented materials. Finds illustrators through recommendations from others, word of mouth, competitions.

HOW TO CONTACT For first contact, send tearsheets, photocopies, SASE. See website for submission guidelines. Responds only if interested.

MARLENA AGENCY, INC.

322 Ewing St., Princeton, NJ 08540. (609)252-9405. Fax: (609)252-1949. E-mail: marlena@marlenaagency.com. Website: www.marlenaagency.com. Commercial illustration representative. Estab. 1990. Member of Society of Illustrators. Represents over 30 international illustrators including: Gerard Dubois, Linda Helton, Paul Zwolak, Martin Jarrie, Serge Bloch, Hadley Hooper, Jean-François Martin Perre Mornet, Pep Montserrat, Tomasz Walenta, Istvan Orosz, Lorenzo Petrantoni, Scott Mckowen and Carmen Segovia. Staff includes Marlena Torzecka, Marie Joanne Wimmer, Anna Pluskota, Sophie Mialhe. Currently open to illustrators seeking representation. Open to both new and established illustrators. Submission guidelines available for #10 SASE.

REPRESENTS Illustration.

RECENT SALES *Sees Behind Trees*, by Linda Helton (Harcourt); *Ms. Rubinstein's Beauty*, by Pep Montserrat (Sterling); *ABC USA*, by Martin Jarrie (Sterling); *My Cat*, by Linda Helton (Scholastic); *The McElderry Book of Greek Myths*, by Pep Monserrat (McElderly Books).

TERMS Exclusive representation required. Offers written contract. Requires printed portfolios, digital files, direct mail piece (such as postcards) printed samples. Advertises in *Workbook.*

HOW TO CONTACT For first contact, send tearsheets, photocopies, or e-mail low resolution samples only. Responds only if interested. Drop off or mail portfolio, photocopies. Portfolio should include tearsheets, photocopies. Finds illustrators through queries/solicitations, magazines and graphic design.

TIPS "Be creative and persistent."

MB ARTISTS

(formerly HK Portfolio), 775 Sixth Avenue, #6, New York NY 10001. (212)689-7830. E-mail: mela@mbartists.com. Website: www.mbartists.com. **Contact:** Mela Bolinao. Illustration representative. Estab. 1986. Member of SPAR, Society of Illustrators and Graphic Artists Guild. Represents over 60 illustrators. Specializes in illustration for juvenile markets. Markets include: advertising agencies; editorial/magazines; publishing/books.

REPRESENTS Illustration.

RECENT SALES *Peanut Butter and Homework Sandwiches*, illustrated by Jack E. Davis (Putnam); *Pirate Goes to School*, illustrated by John Manders (Scholastic); *The Adventures of Granny Clearwater*, illustrated by by Laura Huliska Beith (Henry Holt); *Grandma Calls Me Gigglepie*, illustrated by Hiroe Nakata (Robin Corey Books); *Twelve Haunted Rooms of Halloween*, illustrated by Macky Pamintuan (Sterling).

TERMS Rep receives 25% commission. No geographic restrictions. Advertising costs are split: 75% paid by talent; 25% paid by representative. Advertises in *Picturebook*, *Directory of Illustration*, *Play* and *Workbook*.

HOW TO CONTACT No geographic restrictions. For first contact, send query letter, direct mail flier/brochure, website address, tearsheets, slides, photographs or color copies and SASE or send website link to mela@mbartists.com. Responds in 1 week. Portfolio should include at least 12 images appropriate for the juvenile market.

THE NEIS GROUP

14600 Sawyer Ranch Rd., Dripping Springs TX 78620. (616)450-1533. Website: www.neisgroup.com. E-mail: jneis@neisgroup.com. **Contact:** Judy Neis. Commercial illustration representative. Estab. 1982. Represents 45 illustrators including: Lyn Boyer, Pam Thomson, Dan Sharp, Terry Workman, Garry Colby, Clint Hansen, Julie Borden, Diana Magnuson, Jacqueline Rogers, Johnna Hogenkamp, Jack Pennington, Gary Ferster, Mark and Lee Fullerton, James Palmer, Brandon Reese, Joel Spector, John White, Neverne Covington, Ruth Pettis, Laura Nikiel, Brandon Fall, Carol Newsom, Joel Aaron Carlson, Gary Freeman. 60% of artwork handled is children's book illustration.

Currently open to illustrators seeking representation. Looking for established illustrators only.

REPRESENTS Illustration, photography and calligraphy/manuscript packages.

TERMS Receives 25% commission. "I prefer portfolios on disc, color printouts and e-mail capabilities whenever possible." Advertises in *Picturebook* and *Creative Black Book*.

HOW TO CONTACT For first contact, send bio, tearsheets, direct mail flier/brochure. Responds only if interested. After initial contact, drop off portfolio of nonreturnables. Portfolio should include tearsheets, photocopies. Obtains new talent through recommendations from others and queries/solicitations.

WANDA NOWAK/CREATIVE ILLUSTRATORS AGENCY

231 E. 76th St.5D, New York NY 10021. (212)535-0438. E-mail: wanda@wandanow.com. Website: www.wandanow.com. **Contact:** Wanda Nowak. Commercial illustration representative. Estab. 1996. Represents 20 illustrators including: Emilie Chollat, Thea Kliros, Frederique Bertrand, Ilja Bereznickas, Boris Kulikov, Yayo, Laurence Cleyet-Merle, E. Kerner, Ellen Usdin, Stephane Jorisch, Oliver Latyk, Benoit Laverdiere, Anne-Sophie Lanquetin, Andre Letria. 50% of artwork handled is children's book illustration. Staff includes Wanda Nowak. Open to both new and established illustrators.

REPRESENTS Illustration. Looking for "unique, individual style."

TERMS Receives 30% commission. Exclusive representation required. Offers written contract. Advertising costs are split: 70% paid by illustrators; 30% paid by rep. Advertises *Workbook*, *American Illustrators*.

HOW TO CONTACT For first contact, send e-mail with PDF. Finds illustrators through recommendations from others, sourcebooks, exhibitions.

TIPS "Develop your own style. Send a little illustrated story, which will prove you can carry a character in different situations with facial expressions, etc."

LIZ SANDERS AGENCY

2415 E. Hangman Creek Lane, Spokane WA USA 99224-8514. E-mail: liz@lizsanders.com. Website: ww.lizsanders.com. **Contact:** Liz Sanders. Commercial illustration representative. Estab. 1985. Represents Kyle Poling, Jared Beckstand, Craig Orback, Amy Ning, Tom Pansini, Chris Lensch, Lynn Gesue,

Poozie, Susan Synarski, Sudi McCollum, Suzanne Beaky and more. Currently open to illustrators seeking representation. Open to both new and established illustrators. Handles illustration. Markets include publishing, licensed properties, entertainment and advertising.

TERMS Receives 30% commission against pro bono mailing program. Offers written contract. Advertises in *Picturebook* and picture-book.com, *Directory of Illustration*, childrensillustrators.com, theispot. com, folioplanet.com. No geographic restrictions.

HOW TO CONTACT For first contact, send tearsheets, direct mail flier/brochure, color copies, non-returnable or e-mail to submissions@lizsanders. com. Responds only if interested. Obtains new talent through recommendations from industry contacts, conferences and queries/solicitations, Literary Market Place.

S.I. INTERNATIONAL

43 E. 19th St., 2nd Floor, New York, NY 10003. (212)254-4996. Fax: (212)995-0911. E-mail: information@si-i.com. Website: www.si-i.com. Commercial illustration representative. Estab. 1983. Member of SPAR, Graphic Artists Guild. Represents 50 illustrators. Specializes in license characters, educational publishing and children's illustration, digital art and design, mass market paperbacks. Markets include design firms; publishing/books; sales/promotion firms; licensing firms; digital art and design firms.

REPRESENTS Illustration. Looking for artists "who have the ability to do children's illustration and to do licensed characters either digitally or reflectively."

TERMS Rep receives 25-30% commission. Advertising costs are split: 70% paid by talent; 30% paid by representative. "Contact agency for details. Must have mailer." Advertises in *Picturebook*.

HOW TO CONTACT For first contact, send query letter, tearsheets. Responds in 3 weeks. After initial contact, write for appointment to show portfolio of tearsheets, slides.

🔴 THOROGOOD KIDS

11-15 Betterton St., Covent Garden, London WC2H 9BP United Kingdom . (347)627-0243. E-mail: draw@goodillustration.com. Website: www.goodillustration.

com. Represents 30 illustrators including: Bill Dare, Kanako and Yuzuru, Shaunna Peterson, Nicola Slater, Dan Hambe, David Bromley, Robin Heighway-Bury, Anja Boretzki, Olivier Latyk, Al Sacui, John Woodcock, Carol Morley, Leo Timmers, Christiane Engel, Anne Yvonne Gilbert, Philip Nicholson, Adria Fruitos, Ester Garcia Cortes, Lisa Zibamanzar, Alessandra Cimatoribus, Marta and Leonor, Iryna Bodnaruk. Open to illustrators seeking representation. Accepting both new and established illustrators. Guidelines not available.

REPRESENTS Accepts illustration, illustration/manuscript packages.

HOW TO CONTACT "For first contact, send tearsheets, photocopies, SASE, direct mail flyer/brochure. After initial contact, we will contact the illustrator if we want to see the portfolio. Portfolio should include tearsheets, photocopies. Finds illustrators through queries/solicitations, conferences."

TIPS "Be unique and research your market. Talent will win out!"

GWEN WALTERS ARTIST REPRESENTATIVE

1801 S. Flagler Dr.,#1202, W. Palm Beach FL 33401. (561)805-7739. E-mail: artincgw@aol.com. Website: www.gwenwaltersartrep.com. **Contact:** Gwen Walters. Commercial illustration representative. Estab. 1976. Represents 18 illustrators. 90% of artwork handled is children's book illustration. Currently open to illustrators seeking representation. Looking for established illustrators only.

REPRESENTS Illustration.

RECENT SALES Sells to "all major book publishers."

TERMS Receives 30% commission. Artist needs to supply all promo material. Offers written contract. Advertising costs are split: 70% paid by illustrator; 30% paid by rep. Advertises in *Picturebook*, *RSVP*, *Directory of Illustration*.

HOW TO CONTACT For first contact, send tearsheets. Responds only if interested. Finds illustrators through recommendations from others.

TIPS "You need to pound the pavement for a couple of years to get some experience under your belt. Don't forget to sign all artwork. So many artists forget to stamp their samples."

CLUBS & ORGANIZATIONS

Contacts made through organizations such as the ones listed in this section can be quite beneficial for children's writers and illustrators. Professional organizations provide numerous educational, business and legal services in the form of newsletters, workshops or seminars. Organizations can provide tips about how to be a more successful writer or artist, as well as what types of business cards to keep, health and life insurance coverage to carry, and competitions to consider.

An added benefit of belonging to an organization is the opportunity to network with those who have similar interests, creating a support system. As in any business, knowing the right people can often help your career, and important contacts can be made through your peers. Membership in a writer's or artist's organization also shows publishers you're serious about your craft. This provides no guarantee your work will be published, but it gives you an added dimension of credibility and professionalism.

Some of the organizations listed here welcome anyone with an interest, while others are only open to published writers and professional artists. Organizations such as the Society of Children's Book Writers and Illustrators (SCBWI, www.scbwi.org) have varying levels of membership. SCBWI offers associate membership to those with no publishing credits, and full membership to those who have had work for children published. International organizations such as SCBWI also have regional chapters throughout the U.S. and the world. Write or call for more information regarding any group that interests you, or check the websites of the many organizations that list them. Be sure to get information about local chapters, membership qualifications and services offered.

AMERICAN ALLIANCE FOR THEATRE & EDUCATION

7979 Old Georgetown Rd., 10th Floor, Bethesda, MD 20814. (301)951-7977. E-mail: info@aate.com. Website: www.aate.com. Purpose of organization: to promote standards of excellence in theatre and drama education. "We achieve this by assimilating quality practices in theatre and theatre education, connecting artists, educators, researchers and scholars with each other, and by providing opportunities for our members to learn, exchange and diversify their work, their audiences and their perspectives." Membership cost: $115 annually for individual in U.S. and Canada, $220 annually for organization, $60 annually for students, and $70 annually for retired people, $310 annually for University Departmental memberships; add $30 outside Canada and U.S. Holds annual conference (July or August). Contests held for unpublished play reading project and annual awards in various categories. Awards plaque and stickers for published playbooks. Publishes list of unpublished plays deemed worthy of performance and stages readings at conference. Contact national office at number above or see website for contact information for Playwriting Network Chairpersons.

AMERICAN SOCIETY OF JOURNALISTS AND AUTHORS

1501 Broadway, Suite 302, New York, NY 10036. Website: www.asja.org. **Executive Director:** Alexandra Owens. Qualifications for membership: "Need to be a professional freelance nonfiction writer. Refer to website for further qualifications." Membership cost: Application fee—$50; annual dues—$195. Group sponsors national conferences. Professional seminars online and in person around the country. Workshops/conferences open to nonmembers. Publishes a newsletter for members that provides confidential information for nonfiction writers.

ARIZONA AUTHORS ASSOCIATION

6145 W. Echo Lane, Glendale AZ 85302. (623)847-9343. E-mail: info@azauthors.com. Website: www.azauthors.com. **President:** Toby Heathcotte. Estab. 1978. Purpose of organization: to offer professional, educational and social opportunities to writers and authors, and serve as a network. Members must be authors, writers working toward publication, agents, publishers, publicists, printers, illustrators, etc. Membership cost: $45/year writers; $30/year students; $60/year other professionals in publishing industry. Holds regular workshops and meetings. Publishes bimonthly newsletter and *Arizona Literary Magazine*. Sponsors Annual Literary Contest in poetry, essays, short stories, novels and published books with cash prizes and awards bestowed at a public banquet. Winning entries are also published or advertised in the *Arizona Literary Magazine*. First and second place winners in poetry, essay and short story categories are entered in the Pushcart Prize. Winners in published categories receive free listings by www.fivestarpublications.com. Send SASE or view website for guidelines.

THE AUTHORS GUILD, INC.

31 East 32nd Street 7th floor; New York, NY 10016. (212)563-5904. Fax: (212)564-5363. E-mail: staff@authorsguild.org. Website: www.authorsguild.org. **Executive Director:** Paul Aiken. Purpose of organization: to offer services and materials intended to help authors with the business and legal aspects of their work, including contract problems, copyright matters, freedom of expression and taxation. Guild has 8,000 members. Qualifications for membership: Must be book author published by an established American publisher within 7 years or any author who has had 3 works (fiction or nonfiction) published by a magazine or magazines of general circulation in the last 18 months. Associate membership also available. Annual dues: $90. Different levels of membership include: associate membership with all rights except voting available to an author who has a firm contract offer or is currently negotiating a royalty contract from an established American publisher. "The Guild offers free contract reviews to its members. The Guild conducts several symposia each year at which experts provide information, offer advice and answer questions on subjects of interest and concern to authors. Typical subjects have been the rights of privacy and publicity, libel, wills and estates, taxation, copyright, editors and editing, the art of interviewing, standards of criticism and book reviewing. Transcripts of these symposia are published and circulated to members. The *Authors Guild Bulletin*, a quarterly journal, contains articles on matters of interest to writers, reports of Guild activities, contract surveys, advice on problem clauses in contracts, transcripts of Guild and League symposia and information on a variety of professional topics. Subscription included in the cost of the annual dues." **Contact:** Paul Aiken, Exec. Director.

⟳ CANADIAN SOCIETY OF CHILDREN'S AUTHORS, ILLUSTRATORS AND PERFORMERS

104-40 Orchard View Blvd., Toronto, ON M4R 1B9 Canada. (416)515-1559. E-mail: office@canscaip.org. Website: www.canscaip.org. **Administrative Director:** Lena Coakley. Purpose of organization: development of Canadian children's culture and support for authors, illustrators and performers working in this field. Qualifications for membership: Members—professionals who have been published (not self-published) or have paid public performances/records/tapes to their credit. Friends—share interest in field of children's culture. Membership cost: $85 (Members dues), $45 (Friends dues). Sponsors workshops/conferences. Manuscript evaluation services; publishes newsletter: includes profiles of members; news round-up of members' activities countrywide; market news; news on awards, grants, etc; columns related to professional concerns.

LEWIS CARROLL SOCIETY OF NORTH AMERICA

11935 Beltsville Dr.Beltsville MD 20705. E-mail: secretary@lewiscarroll.org. Website: www.lewiscarroll.org. **Secretary:** Clare Imholtz. "We are an organization of Carroll admirers of all ages and interests and a center for Carroll studies." Qualifications for membership: "An interest in Lewis Carroll and a simple love for Alice (or the Snark for that matter)." Membership cost: $35 (regular membership), $50 (foreign membership), $100 (sustaining membership). The Society meets twice a year—in spring and in fall; locations vary. Publishes a semi-annual journal, *Knight Letter*, and maintains an active publishing program.

THE CHILDREN'S BOOK COUNCIL, INC.

54 W. 39th St., 14th Floor, New York, NY 10018. (212)966-1990. Fax: (212)966-2073. E-mail: cbc.info@cbcbooks.org. Website: www.cbcbooks.org. **Executive Director:** Robin Adelson. Purpose of organization: A nonprofit trade association of children's and young adult publishers and packagers, CBC promotes the enjoyment of books for children and young adults and works with national and international organizations to that end. The CBC has sponsored Children's Book Week since 1945 and Young People's Poetry Week since 1999. Qualifications for membership: trade publishers and packagers of children's and young adult books and related literary materials are eligible for membership. Publishers wishing to join should contact the CBC for dues information. Sponsors workshops and seminars for publishing company personnel. Children's Book Week poster and downloadable bookmark available, information at www.bookweekonline.com.

FLORIDA FREELANCE WRITERS ASSOCIATION

Writers-Editors Network, P.O. Box A, North Stratford NH 03590. (603)922-8338. E-mail: FFWA@Writers-Editors.com. Websites: www.ffwamembers.com and www.writers-editors.com. **Executive Director:** Dana K. Cassell. Purpose of organization: To provide a link between Florida writers and buyers of the written word; to help writers run more effective editorial businesses. Qualifications for membership: "None. We provide a variety of services and information, some for beginners and some for established pros." Membership cost: $90/year. Publishes a newsletter focusing on market news, business news, how-to tips for the serious writer. Annual Directory of Florida Markets included in FFWA newsletter section and electronic download. Publishes annual *Guide to CNW/Florida Writers*, which is distributed to editors around the country. Sponsors contest: annual deadline March 15. Guidelines on website. Categories: juvenile, adult nonfiction, adult fiction and poetry. Awards include cash for top prizes, certificate for others. Contest open to nonmembers.

GRAPHIC ARTISTS GUILD

32 Broadway, Suite 1114, New York NY 10004. E-mail: admin@gag.org; Patricia@gag.org. Website: www.graphicartistsguild.org. Purpose of organization: "To promote and protect the economic interests of member artists. It is committed to improving conditions for all creators of graphic arts and raising standards for the entire industry." Qualification for full membership: 50% of income derived from the creation of graphic artwork. Associate members include those in allied fields and students. Initiation fee: $30. Full memberships: $200; student membership: $75/year. Associate membership: $170/year. Publishes *Graphic Artists Guild Handbook*, *Pricing and Ethical Guidelines* (members receive a copy as part of their membership). **Contact:** Patricia McKiernan.

HORROR WRITERS ASSOCIATION

244 5th Avenue, Suite 2767, New York NY 10001. E-mail: hwa@horror.org. Website: www.horror.org. **Office Manager:** John Little. Purpose of organization: To encourage public interest in horror and dark fantasy and to provide networking and career tools for members. Qualifications for membership: Complete membership rules online at www.horror.org/memrule.htm. At least one low-level sale is required to join as an affiliate. Non-writing professionals who can show income from a horror-related field may join as an associate (booksellers, editors, agents, librarians, etc.). To qualify for full active membership, you must be a published, professional writer of horror. Membership cost: $65 annually. Holds annual Stoker Awards Weekend and HWA Business Meeting. Publishes monthly newsletter focusing on market news, industry news, HWA business for members. Sponsors awards. We give the Bram Stoker Awards for superior achievement in horror annually. Awards include a handmade Stoker trophy designed by sculptor Stephen Kirk. Awards open to nonmembers.

INTERNATIONAL READING ASSOCIATION

800 Barksdale Rd., P.O. Box 8139, Newark, DE 19714-8139. (302)731-1600, ext. 293. Fax: (302)731-1057. E-mail: pubinfo@reading.org. Website: www.reading.org. Purpose of organization: "Formed in 1956, the International Reading Association seeks to promote high levels of literacy for all by improving the quality of reading instruction through studying the reading process and teaching techniques; serving as a clearinghouse for the dissemination of reading research through conferences, journals, and other publications; and actively encouraging the lifetime reading habit. Its goals include professional development, advocacy, partnerships, research, and global literacy development." **Open to students.** Sponsors annual convention. Publishes a newsletter called "Reading Today." Sponsors a number of awards and fellowships. Visit the IRA website for more information on membership, conventions and awards.

INTERNATIONAL WOMEN'S WRITING GUILD

P.O. Box 810, Gracie Station, New York NY 10028. (212)737-7536. Fax: (212)737-9469. E-mail: iwwg@iwwg.org; dirhahn@iwwg.org. Website: www.iwwg.org. IWWG is "a network for the personal and professional empowerment of women through writing." Qualifications: Open to any woman connected to the written word regardless of professional portfolio. Membership cost: $55/65 annually. "IWWG sponsors several annual conferences a year in all areas of the U.S. The major conference is held in June of each year at Yale University in New Haven, Connecticut. It is a week-long conference attracting 350 women internationally." Also publishes a 32-page newsletter, *Network*, 4 times/year; offers dental and vision insurance at group rates, referrals to literary agents. **Contact:** Hannelore Hahn, exec. editor.

⬡ LEAGUE OF CANADIAN POETS

920 Yonge St. Suite 608, Toronto ON M4W 3C7 Canada. (416)504-1657. Fax: (416)504-0096. Website: www.poets.ca. **Executive Director:** Joanna Poblocka. President: Joe Blades. Inquiries to Joanna Poblocka. The L.C.P. is a national organization of published Canadian poets. Our constitutional objectives are to advance poetry in Canada and to promote the professional interests of the members. Qualifications for membership: full—publication of at least 1 book of poetry by a professional publisher; associate membership—an active interest in poetry, demonstrated by several magazine/periodical publication credits; student—an active interest in poetry, 12 sample poems required; supporting—any friend of poetry. Membership fees: full—$175/year, associate—$60, student—$20, supporting—$100. Holds an Annual General Meeting every spring; some events open to nonmembers. "We also organize reading programs in schools and public venues. We publish a newsletter which includes information on poetry/poetics in Canada and beyond. Also publish the books *Poetry Markets for Canadians; Who's Who in the League of Canadian Poets; Poets in the Classroom* (teaching guide), and online publications. The Gerald Lampert Memorial Award for the best first book of poetry published in Canada in the preceding year and The Pat Lowther Memorial Award for the best book of poetry by a Canadian woman published in the preceding year. Deadline for awards: November 1. Visit www.poets.ca for more details. Sponsors youth poetry competition. Visit www.youngpoets.ca for details.

LITERARY MANAGERS AND DRAMATURGS OF THE AMERICAS

P.O. Box 36. 20985, P.A.C.C. New York NY 10129. E-mail: lmda@lmda.org or lmdanyc@hotmail.com.

Website: www.lmda.org. LMDA is a not-for-profit service organization for the professions of literary management and dramaturgy. Student Membership: $25/year. Open to students in dramaturgy, performing arts and literature programs, or related disciplines. Proof of student status required. Includes national conference, New Dramaturg activities, local symposia, job phone and select membership meetings. Active Membership: $60/year. Open to full-time and part-time professionals working in the fields of literary management and dramaturgy. All privileges and services including voting rights and eligibility for office. Institutional Membership: $200/year. Open to theaters, universities and other organizations. Includes all privileges and services except voting rights and eligibility for office. Publishes a newsletter featuring articles on literary management, dramaturgy, LMDA program updates and other articles of interest. Spotlight sponsor membership $500/year; open to theatres,universities and other organizations; includes all priviledges for up to six individual members, plus additional promotional benefits.

THE NATIONAL LEAGUE OF AMERICAN PEN WOMEN

Pen Arts Building, 1300 17th St. N.W., Washington, DC 20036-1973. (202)785-1997. Fax: (202)452-8868. E-mail: nlapw1@verizon.net. Website: www.americanpenwomen.org. **President:** Jean Elizabeth Holmes. Purpose of organization: to promote professional work in art, letters and music since 1897. Qualifications for membership: An applicant must show "proof of sale" in each chosen category—art, letters and music. Levels of membership include: Active, Associate, International Affiliate, Members-at-Large, Honorary Members (in one or more of the following classifications: Art, Letters and Music). Holds workshops/conferences. Publishes magazine 4 times/year titled *The Pen Woman*. Sponsors various contests in areas of Art, Letters, and Music. Awards made at Biennial Convention. Biannual scholarships awarded to non-Pen Women for mature women. Awards include cash prizes—up to $1,000. Specialized contests open to nonmembers.

NATIONAL WRITERS ASSOCIATION

10904 S. Parker Rd., #508, Parker CO 80138. (303)841-0246. Fax: (303)841-2607. E-mail: natlwritersassn@hotmail.com. Website: www.nationalwriters.com. Estab. 1937. Purpose of organization: association for freelance writers. Qualifications for membership: as-

sociate membership—must be serious about writing; professional membership—must be published and paid writer (cite credentials). Membership cost: $65 associate; $85 professional; $35 student. Sponsors workshops/conferences: TV/screenwriting workshops, NWAF Annual Conferences, Literary Clearinghouse, editing and critiquing services, local chapters, National Writer's School. Open to non-members. Publishes industry news of interest to freelance writers; how-to articles; market information; member news and networking opportunities. Nonmember subscription: $20. Sponsors poetry contest; short story contest; article contest; novel contest. Awards cash for top 3 winners; books and/or certificates for other winners; honorable mention certificate places 5-10. Contests open to nonmembers.

NATIONAL WRITERS UNION

256 W. 38th St., Suite 703, New York NY 10018. (212)254-0279. Fax: (212)-254-0673. E-mail: nwu@nwu.org. Website: www.nwu.org. Students welcome. Purpose of organization: Advocacy for freelance writers. Qualifications for membership: "Membership in the NWU is open to all qualified writers, and no one shall be barred or in any manner prejudiced within the Union on account of race, age, sex, sexual orientation, disability, national origin, religion or ideology. You are eligible for membership if you have published a book, a play, three articles, five poems, one short story or an equivalent amount of newsletter, publicity, technical, commercial, government or institutional copy. You are also eligible for membership if you have written an equal amount of unpublished material and you are actively writing and attempting to publish your work" Membership cost: annual writing income less than $5,000-$120/year; $5,001-15,000-$195; $15,001-30,000-$265/year; $30,001-$45,000-$315 a year; $45,001- and up -$340/year. Holds workshops throughout the country. Members only section on website offers rich resources for freelance writers. Skilled contract advice and grievance help for members.

PEN AMERICAN CENTER

588 Broadway Suit 303, New York NY 10012. (212)334-1660. Fax: (212)334-2181. E-mail: pen@pen.org. Website: www.pen.org. Purpose of organization: "An association of writers working to advance literature, to defend free expression, and to foster international literary fellowship." Qualifications for membership: "The standard qualification for a writer to become a member

of PEN is publication of two or more books of a literary character, or one book generally acclaimed to be of exceptional distinction. Also eligible for membership: editors who have demonstrated commitment to excellence in their profession (usually construed as five years' service in book editing); translators who have published at least two book-length literary translations; playwrights whose works have been produced professionally; and literary essayists whose publications are extensive even if they have not yet been issued as a book. Candidates for membership may be nominated by a PEN member or they may nominate themselves with the support of two references from the literary community or from a current PEN member. Membership dues are $100 per year and many PEN members contribute their time by serving on committees, conducting campaigns and writing letters in connection with freedom-of-expression cases, contributing to the PEN journal, participating in PEN public events, helping to bring literature into underserved communities, and judging PEN literary awards. PEN members receive a subscription to the PEN journal, the PEN Annual Report, and have access to medical insurance at group rates. Members living in the New York metropolitan and tri-state area, or near the Branches, are invited to PEN events throughout the year. Membership in PEN American Center includes reciprocal privileges in PEN American Center branches and in foreign PEN Centers for those traveling abroad. Application forms are available on the Web at www.pen.org. Associate Membership is open to everyone who supports PEN's mission, and your annual dues ($40; $20 for students) provides crucial support to PEN's programs. When you join as an Associate Member, not only will you receive a subscription to the PEN Journal http://pen.org/page.php/prmID/150 and notices of all PEN events but you are also invited to participate in the work of PEN. PEN American Center is the largest of the 141 centers of PEN International, the world's oldest human rights organization and the oldest international literary organization. PEN International was founded in 1921 to dispel national, ethnic, and racial hatreds and to promote understanding among all countries. PEN American Center, founded a year later, works to advance literature, to defend free expression, and to foster international literary fellowship. The Center has a membership of 3,400 distinguished writers, editors, and translators. In addition to defending writers in prison or in danger of imprisonment for their work, PEN American Center sponsors public literary programs and forums on current issues, sends prominent authors to inner-city schools to encourage reading and writing, administers literary prizes, promotes international literature that might otherwise go unread in the United States, and offers grants and loans to writers facing financial or medical emergencies. In carrying out this work, PEN American Center builds upon the achievements of such dedicated past members as W.H. Auden, James Baldwin, Willa Cather, Robert Frost, Langston Hughes, Thomas Mann, Arthur Miller, Marianne Moore, Susan Sontag, and John Steinbeck. The Children's Book Authors' Committee sponsors annual public events focusing on the art of writing for children and young adults and on the diversity of literature for juvenile readers. The PEN/Phyllis Naylor Working Writer Fellowship was established in 2001 to assist a North American author of fiction for children or young adults (E-mail: awards@pen.org). Visit www.pen.org for complete information. Sponsors several competitions per year. Monetary awards range from $2,000-35,000.

PUPPETEERS OF AMERICA, INC.

Membership Office: 26 Howard Ave, New Haven, CT 06519-2809. (888)568-6235. E-mail: membership@puppeteers.org. Website: www.puppeteers.org. **Membership Officer:** Fred Thompson. Purpose of organization: to promote the art and appreciation of puppetry as a means of communications and as a performing art. The Puppeteers of America boasts an international membership. Qualifications for membership: interest in the art form. Membership cost: single adult, $55; seniors (65+) and youth members, (6-17 years of age), $35; full-time college student, $35; family, $75; couple, $65; senior couple, $55; company, $90. Membership discounts to festivals and puppetry store purchases, access to the Audio Visual Library & Consultants in many areas of Puppetry. *The Puppetry Journal*, a quarterly periodical, provides a color photo gallery, news about puppeteers, puppet theaters, exhibitions, touring companies, technical tips, new products, new books, films, television, and events sponsored by the Chartered Guilds in each of the 8 P of A regions. Includes *Playboard*, The P of A newsletter; subscription to the *Puppetry Journal* only, $40 (libraries/ institutions only).

SCIENCE-FICTION AND FANTASY WRITERS OF AMERICA, INC.

Website: www.sfwa.org. P.O. Box 877, Chestertown, MD 21620. E-mail: execdir@sfwa.org. Website: www.

sfwa.org. **Executive Director:** Jane Jewell. Purpose of organization: to encourage public interest in science fiction literature and provide organization format for writers/editors/artists within the genre. Qualifications for membership: at least 1 professional sale or other professional involvement within the field. Membership cost: annual active dues—$70; affiliate—$55; one-time installation fee of $10; dues year begins July 1. Different levels of membership include: active—requires 3 professional short stories or 1 novel published; associate—requires 1 professional sale; or affiliate—which requires some other professional involvement such as artist, editor, librarian, bookseller, teacher, etc. Workshops/conferences: annual awards banquet, usually in April or May. Open to nonmembers. Publishes quarterly journal, the *SFWA Bulletin*. Nonmember subscription: $18/year in U.S. Sponsors Nebula Awards for best published science fiction or fantasy in the categories of novel, novella, novelette and short story. Awards trophy. Also presents the Damon Knight Memorial Grand Master Award for Lifetime Achievement, and, beginning in 2006, the Andre Norton Award for Outstanding Young Adult Science Fiction or Fantasy Book of the Year.

SOCIETY OF CHILDREN'S BOOK WRITERS AND ILLUSTRATORS

8271 Beverly Blvd., Los Angeles, CA 90048. (323)782-1010. Fax:(323)782-1892. E-mail: scbwi@scbwi.org. Website: www.scbwi.org. **President:** Stephen Mooser. **Executive Director:** Lin Oliver. Chairperson, Board of Advisors: Frank Sloan. Purpose of organization: to assist writers and illustrators working or interested in the field. Qualifications for membership: an interest in children's literature and illustration. Membership cost: $70/year. Plus one time $85 initiation fee. Different levels of membership include: P.A.L. membership—published by publisher listed in SCBWI Market Surveys; full membership—published authors/illustrators (includes self-published); associate membership—unpublished writers/illustrators. Holds 100 events (workshops/conferences) worldwide each year. National Conference open to nonmembers. Publishes bi-monthly magazine on writing and illustrating children's books. Sponsors annual awards and grants for writers and illustrators who are members.

SOCIETY OF ILLUSTRATORS

128 E. 63rd St., New York NY 10065. (212)838-2560. Fax: (212)838-2561. E-mail: info@societyillustrators.

org. Website: www.societyillustrators.org. **Contact:** Anelle Miller, director. "Our mission is to promote the art and appreciation of illustration, its history and evolving nature through exhibitions, lectures and education." Annual dues for nonresident Illustrator members (those living more than 125 air miles from SI's headquarters): $300. Dues for resident illustrator members: $500 per year; resident associate members: $500. Artist members shall include those who make illustration their profession and earn at least 60% of their income from their illustration. Associate members are those who earn their living in the arts or who have made a substantial contribution to the art of illustration. This includes art directors, art buyers, creative supervisors, instructors, publishers and like categories. The candidate must complete and sign the application form, which requires a brief biography, a listing of schools attended, other training and a résumé of his or her professional career. Candidates for illustrators membership, in addition to the above requirements, must submit examples of their work."

SOCIETY OF MIDLAND AUTHORS

P.O. 10419, Chicago, IL 60610-0419. Website: www.midlandauthors.com. **President:** Robert Loerzel. Purpose of organization: create closer association among writers of the Middle West; stimulate creative literary effort; maintain collection of members' works; encourage interest in reading and literature by cooperating with other educational and cultural agencies. Qualifications for membership: membership by invitation only. Must be author or co-author of a book demonstrating literary style and published by a recognized publisher and be identified through residence with Illinois, Indiana, Iowa, Kansas, Michigan, Minnesota, Missouri, Nebraska, North Dakota, Ohio, South Dakota or Wisconsin. **Open to students** (if authors). Membership cost: $35/year dues. Different levels of membership include: regular—published book authors; associate, nonvoting—not published as above but having some connection with literature, such as librarians, teachers, publishers and editors. Program meetings held 5 times a year, featuring authors, publishers, editors or the like individually or on panels. Usually second Tuesday of October, November, February, March and April. Also holds annual awards dinner in May. Publishes a newsletter focusing on news of members and general items of interest to writers. Sponsors contests. "Annual awards in six categories, given at annual dinner in

May. Monetary awards for books published that premiered professionally in previous calendar year. Send SASE to contact person for details." Categories include adult fiction, adult nonfiction, juvenile fiction, juvenile nonfiction, poetry, biography. No picture books. Contest open to nonmembers. Deadline for contest: February 1.

SOCIETY OF SOUTHWESTERN AUTHORS

Fax: (520)751-7877. E-mail: Information: Penny Porter wporter202@aol.com. Website: www.ssa-az.org. Purpose of organization: to promote fellowship among professional and associate members of the writing profession, to recognize members' achievements, to stimulate further achievement, and to assist persons seeking to become professional writers. Qualifications for membership: Professional Membership: proof of publication of a book, articles, TV screenplay, etc. Associate Membership: proof of desire to write, and/or become a professional. Self-published authors may receive status of Professional Membership at the discretion of the board of directors. Membership cost: $30 initiation plus $30/year dues. The Society of Southwestern Authors sponsors an annual 2-day writers' conference (all genres) held in September; watch website ssa-az.org. SSA publishes a bimonthly newsletter, *The Write Word*, promoting members' published works, advice to fellow writers, and up-to-the-minute trends in publishing and marketing. Yearly writing contest open to all writers; short story, memoir, poetry, children's stories. Applications available in February—e-mail Mike Rom at Mike_Rom@hotmail.com; Subject Line: "SSA Writer's Contest."

○ TEXT & ACADEMIC AUTHORS ASSOCIATION

9313 42nd St., Pinellas Park FL 33782. (727)563-0020. E-mail: richard.hull@taaonline.net; kim.pawlak@taaonline.net. Website: www.taaonline.net. TAA's overall mission is to enhance the quality of textbooks and other academic materials, such as journal articles, monographs and scholarly books, in all fields and disciplines. Qualifications for membership: all authors and prospective authors are welcome. Membership cost: $30 first year; graduated levels for following years. Workshops/conferences: June each year. Newsletter focuses on all areas of interest to textbook and academic authors. **Contact:** Richard T. Hall, exec. director.

THEATRE FOR YOUNG AUDIENCES/USA

2936 N. Southport Ave 3rd floor Chicago, IL 60657. E-mail: info@tyausa.org. Website: www.tyausa.org. Purpose of organization: to promote theater for children and young people by linking professional theaters and artists together; sponsoring national, international and regional conferences and providing publications and information. Also serves as U.S. Center for International Association of the Theatre for Children and Young People. Different levels of memberships include: organizations, individuals, students, retirees, libraries. TYA Today includes original articles, reviews and works of criticism and theory, all of interest to theater practitioners (included with membership). Publishes *Marquee*, a directory that focuses on information on members in U.S.

VOLUNTEER LAWYERS FOR THE ARTS

1 E. 53rd St.6th Floor, New York NY 10022-4201. (212)319-ARTS, ext. 1 (the Art Law Line). Fax: (212)752-6575. E-mail: epaul@vlany.org. Website: www.vlany.org. **Executive Director:** Elena M. Paul. Purpose of organization: Volunteer Lawyers for the Arts is dedicated to providing free arts-related legal assistance to low-income artists and not-for-profit arts organizations in all creative fields. Over 1,000 attorneys in the New York area donate their time through VLA to artists and arts organizations unable to afford legal counsel. Everyone is welcome to use VLA's Art Law Line, a legal hotline for any artist or arts organization needing quick answers to arts-related questions. VLA also provides clinics, seminars and publications designed to educate artists on legal issues that affect their careers. Members receive discounts on publications and seminars as well as other benefits. Some of the many publications we carry are *All You Need to Know About the Music Business; Business and Legal Forms for Fine Artists, Photographers & Authors & Self-Publishers; Contracts for the Film & TV Industry*, plus many more.

WESTERN WRITERS OF AMERICA, INC.

1012 Mesa Vista Hall, MSCO6 3770, 1 University of New Mexico, Albuquerque NM 87131-0001. (505)277-5234. E-mail: wwa@unm.edu; rod@holmesco.com. Website: www.westernwriters.org. **Executive Director:** Paul Andrew Hutton. Open to students. Purpose of organization: to further all types of literature that pertains to the American West. Membership requirements: must be a published author of Western material. Membership cost: $75/year ($90 foreign). Different levels of membership include: active and associate—the two vary upon number of books or articles published. Holds annual conference. The 2008 conference held in Scottsdale, AZ; 2009 held in Midwest City, Oklahoma. Publishes bimonthly magazine focusing on Western literature, market trends, bookreviews, news of members, etc. Nonmembers may subscribe for $30 ($50 foreign). Sponsors youth writing contests. Spur awards given annually for a variety of types of writing. Awards include plaque, certificate, publicity. Contest and Spur Awards open to nonmembers.

☾ WRITERS' FEDERATION OF NEW BRUNSWICK

P.O. Box 306, Moncton, NB E1C 8L4. Canada. (506)459-7228. E-mail: wfnb@nb.aibn.com. Website: www.umce.ca/wfnb. **Executive Director:** Lee Thompson. Purpose of organization: "to promote New Brunswick writing and to help writers at all stages of their development." Qualifications for membership: interest in writing. Membership cost: $40, basic annual membership; $20, high school students; $45, family membership; $50, institutional membership; $100, sustaining member; $250, patron; and $1,000, lifetime member. Holds workshops/conferences. Publishes a newsletter with articles concerning the craft of writing, member news, contests, markets, workshops and conference listings. Sponsors annual literary competition, $15 entry fee for members, $20 for nonmembers. Categories: fiction, nonfiction, poetry, children's literature—3 prizes per category of $150, $75, $50; Alfred Bailey Prize of $400 for poetry ms; The Richards Prize of $400 for short novel, collection of short stories or section of long novel; The Sheree Fitch Prize for writing by young people (14-18 years of age). Contest open to nonmembers (residents of Canada only).

☾ WRITERS' FEDERATION OF NOVA SCOTIA

1113 Marginal Rd., Halifax NS B3H 4P7 Canada. (902)423-8116. Fax: (902)422-0881. E-mail: talk@writers.ns.ca. Website: www.writers.ns.ca.

☾ WRITERS GUILD OF ALBERTA

11759 Groat Rd. Edmonton AB T5M 3K6 Canada. (780)422-8174. Fax: (780)422-2663. E-mail: mail@writersguild.ab.ca. Website: www.writersguild.ab.ca. Purpose of organization: to support, encourage and promote writers and writing, to safeguard the freedom to write and to read, and to advocate for the well-being of writers in Alberta. Membership cost: $60/year; $30 for seniors/students. Holds workshops/conferences. Publishes a newsletter focusing on markets, competitions, contemporary issues related to the literary arts (writing, publishing, censorship, royalties etc.). Sponsors annual Literary Awards in five categories (novel, nonfiction, children's literature, poetry, drama). Awards include $1,500, leather-bound book, promotion and publicity. Open to nonmembers.

WRITERS OF KERN

P.O. Box 22335, Bakersfield CA 93390. (661)399-0423. E-mail: WritersOfKern@gmail.com. Website: www.writersofkern.com. **Membership:** Sandy Moffett. Open to published writers and any person interested in writing. Dues: $45/year, $20 for students; $20 initiation fee. Types of memberships: Active Writers with published work; Associate Writers working toward publication; Affiliate—beginners and students. Monthly meetings held on the third Saturday of every month. Annual writers' workshops, with speakers who are authors, agents, etc. on topics pertaining to writing; critique groups for several fiction genres, poetry, children's, nonfiction, journalism and screenwriting which meet bimonthly. Members receive a monthly newsletter from WOK and CWC with marketing tips, conferences and contests.

CONFERENCES & WORKSHOPS

Writers and illustrators eager to expand their knowledge of the children's publishing industry should consider attending one of the many conferences and workshops held each year. Whether you're a novice or seasoned professional, conferences and workshops are great places to pick up information on a variety of topics and network with experts in the publishing industry, as well as with your peers.

Listings in this section provide details about what conference and workshop courses are offered, where and when they are held, and the costs. Some of the national writing and art organizations also offer regional workshops throughout the year. Write, call or visit websites for information.

Writers can find listings of more than 1,000 conferences on the WritersMarket.com Paid Services site—writersmarket.com/paidservices.

Members of the Society of Children's Book Writers and Illustrators can find information on conferences in national and local SCBWI newsletters. Nonmembers may attend SCBWI events as well. SCBWI conferences are listed in the beginning of this section under a separate subheading. For information on SCBWI's annual national conferences, contact them at (323)782-1010 or check their website for a complete calendar of national and regional events (scbwi.org).

SCBWI CONFERENCES

BOISE REGIONAL CONFERENCE FOR UTAH/SOUTHERN IDAHO SCBWI

E-mail: neysajensen@msn.com. One day workshop focuses on the craft of writing, as well as getting to know an editor. One-on-one critiques available for an additional fee. Event held in Boise, Idaho every spring. **Contact:** Sydney Husseman, Regional Advisor; Neysa Jensen, Assis. Regional Advisor.

SCBWI; ANNUAL CONFERENCES ON WRITING AND ILLUSTRATING FOR CHILDREN

Website: www.scbwi.org. **Conference Director:** Lin Oliver. Writer and illustrator workshops geared toward all levels. **Open to students.** Covers all aspects of children's book and magazine publishing—the novel, illustration techniques, marketing, etc. Annual conferences held in August in Los Angeles and in New York in February. Cost of conference (LA): approximately $390; includes all 4 days and one banquet meal. Write for more information or visit website.

SCBWI—ARIZONA; EVENTS

P.O. Box 26384, Scottsdale, AZ 85255-0123. E-mail: RegionalAdvisor@scbwi-az.org. Website: www. scbwi-az.org. **Regional Advisor:** Michelle Parker-Rock. SCBWI Arizona will offer a variety of workshops, retreats, intensives, conferences, meetings and other craft and industry-related events throughout 2011-2012. Open to members and nonmembers, published and nonpublished. Registration to major events is usually limited. Pre-registration always required. Visit website, write or e-mail for more information.

☻ SCBWI BOLOGNA BIENNIAL CONFERENCE

Website: www.scbwibologna.org. The SCBWI Showcase Booth at the Bologna Book Fair: The next SCBWI Showcase Booth will take place during the 2012 Bologna Book Fair. It will feature authors and illustrators from SCBWI regions, SCBWI PAL members, and special author and illustrator events. For more information e-mail: Angela@SCBWIBologna.org or Kathleen@SCBWIBologna.org

☻ SCBWI—CANADA EAST

Website: www.scbwicanada.org/east. E-mail: araeast@scbwicanada.org; raeast@scbwicanada.org.

Website: www.scbwicanada.org/east. **Regional Advisor:** Lizann Flatt. Writer and illustrator events geared toward all levels. Usually offers one event in spring and another in the fall. Check website Events pages for updated information. **Contact:** Lizann Flatt, Regional Advisor.

SCBWI—DAKOTAS; SPRING CONFERENCE

2521 S 40th St., Grand Forks, ND 58201. E-mail: cdrylander@yahoo.com. Website: www.dakotas-scbwi. org. **Regional Advisor:** Chris Rylander. This is a conference for writers and illustrators of all levels. Previous conferences have included speakers Tim Gilner, S.T. Underdahl, Roxane Salonen, and Marilyn Kratz. Annual event held every spring. Check website for details.

SCBWI—DAKOTAS; WRITERS CONFERENCE IN CHILDREN'S LITERATURE

Grand Forks, ND 58201. (701)720-0464. E-mail: cdrylander@yahoo.com. Website: www.dakotas-scbwi. org. **Regional Advisor:** Chris Rylander. Conference sessions geared toward all levels. "Although the conference attendees are mostly writers, we encourage and welcome illustrators of every level." Open to students. "Our conference offers 3-4 children's authors, editors, publishers, illustrators, or agents. Past conferences have included Kent Brown (publisher, Boyds Mills Press); Alexandra Penfold (editor, Simon & Schuster); Jane Kurtz (author); Anastasia Suen (author); and Karen Ritz (illustrator). Conference held each fall. "Please call or e-mail to confirm dates. Writers and illustrators come from throughout the northern plains, including North Dakota, South Dakota, Montana, Minnesota, Iowa, and Canada." Writing facilities available: campus of University of North Dakota. Local art exhibits and/or concerts may coincide with conference. Cost of conference includes Friday evening reception and sessions, Saturday's sessions, and lunch. A manuscript may be submitted 1 month in advance for critique (extra charge). E-mail for more information.

SCBWI—DAKOTAS/UND WRITERS CONFERENCE IN CHILDREN'S LITERATURE

Department of English, Merrifield Hall, Room 110, 276 Centennial Drive, Stop 7209, Univeristy of North Dakota, Grand Forks, ND 58202. (701)777-3321 or

(701)777-3984. E-mail: cdrylander@yahoo.com. Website: www.und.edu or www.dakotas-scbwi.org. **Regional Advisor**: Chris Rylander. Conference for all levels. "Our conference offers 3-4 chlidren's authors, editors, publishers, illustrators or agents. Past conferences have included Elaine Marie Alphin (author), Jane Kurtz (author), Alexandra Penfold (editor), Kent Brown (publisher), and Karen Ritz (illustrator)." Annual conference held every fall. "Please call or e-mail to confirm dates." Cost of conference to be determined. Cost included Friday evening sessions, Saturday sessions, and Saturday lunch. "We welcome writers, illustrators, and others who are interested in children's literature."

⊕ SCBWI–EASTERN PENNSYLVANIA

Two events this fall! Critique Fest, September 10, 2011, at the Mulberry Art Studio, Lancaster, PA. One day event for 60 participants that offers three critiques, one with an editor, one with an agent, one with an author. Critiquers also participate in group critiques. Visit website for registration, which will open in early July. Second event this fall: Tri region event, November 11-13, 2011, held at the Wyndham in Gettysburg, PA. This event is hosted by three regions, Eastern PA, Western PA and MD/DE/VA region. This is a first time event that has the large conference opportunities with small retreat appeal. Watch website for more details, www.scbwiepa.org.

SCBWI–FLORIDA;
MID-YEAR WRITING WORKSHOP

12973 SW 112 Court, Miami, FL 33186. (305)382-2677. E-mail: LindaBernfeld@gmail.com. Website: www. scbwiflorida.com. **Regional Advisor**: Linda Rodriguez Bernfeld. Annual workshop held in June in Orlando. Workshop is geared toward helping everyone hone their writing skills. Attendees choose one track and spend the day with industry leaders who share valuable information about that area of children's book writing. There are a minimum of 3 tracks, picture book, middle grade and young adult. The 4th and 5th tracks are variable, covering subjects such as poetry, nonfiction, humor or writing for magazines. E-mail for more information.

SCBWI–FLORIDA;
REGIONAL CONFERENCE

12973 SW 112 Court, Miami, FL 33186. (305)382-2677. E-mail: lindabernfeld@gmail.com. Website: www.

scbwiflorida.com. **Regional Advisor**: Linda Rodriguez Bernfeld. Annual conference held in January in Miami. Past keynote speakers have included Linda Sue Park, Richard Peck, Bruce Coville, Bruce Hale, Arthur A. Levine, Judy Blume, Kate Dicamillo. Cost of conference: approximately $225. The 3-day conference will have workshops Friday afternoon and a field trip to Books and Books Friday evening. For more information, contact e-mail Linda Rodriguez Bernfeld at lindabernfeld@gmail.com.

⊕ SCBWI–ILLINOIS;
PRAIRIE WRITERS DAY

Website: www.scbwi-illinois.org. Chicago, IL E-mail: biermanlisa@hotmail.com. Website: www.scbwi-illinois.org/events. **Regional Advisors**: Lisa Bierman and Alice McGinty. All-day conference November 12, 2011, at the Wojcik Conference Center, Harper College, 1200 W. Algonquin Rd., Palatine, IL 60067. Full day of guest speakers, editors/agents TBD. Ms. critiques available as well as break-out sessions on career and craft. See website for complete description.

SCBWI–IOWA CONFERENCES

P.O. Box 1436, Bettendorf IA 52722-0024. E-mail: hecklit@aol.com. Website: www.scbwi-iowa.org/. Writer and illustrator workshops in all genres of children writing. The Iowa Region offers conferences of high-quality events usually over a three-day period with registration options. Recent speakers included Allyn Johnston, Marla Frazee, Julie Romeis, Samantha McFerrin, Scott Treimel. Holds spring and fall events on a regional level, and network events across that state. Individual critiques and portfolio review offerings vary with the program and presenters. For more information e-mail or visit website. **Contact:** Connie Heckert, regional advisor.

SCBWI–LOS ANGELES; EVENTS

P.O. Box 1728, Pacific Palisades, CA 90272. (310)573-7318. Website: www.scbwisocal.org. **Co-regional Advisors:** Sarah Laurenson (sarah.laurenson@gmail.com) and Edie Pagliasotti (ediescbwi@sbcglobal.net). SCBWI—Los Angeles hosts 6 major events each year: **Writer's Workshop** (winter)—half-day workshop featuring speaker demonstrating nuts and bolts techniques on the craft of writing for childrens; **Writer's Day** (spring)—a one-day conference featuring speakers, a professional forum, writing contests and awards; **Critiquenic** (summer)—a free informal critiquing session for writers and illustrators facilitated by published authors/illustrators, held after a picnic lunch; **Writers & Illustrator's Sunday Field Trip** (fall)—hands-on creative field trip for writers and illustrators; **Working Writer's Retreat** (fall)—a 3-day, 2-night retreat featuring an editor/agent, speakers, and intensive critiquing. **Illustrator's Day** (winter)— A one-day conference featuring speakers, juried art competition, contests, portfolio review/display. See calendar of events on website for more details and dates.

SCBWI—METRO NEW YORK; PROFESSIONAL SERIES

P.O. Box 1475, Cooper Station, New York, NY 10276-1475. (212)545-3719. E-mail: scbwi_metrony@yahoo.com. Website: http://metro.nyscbwi.org. **Regional Advisor:** Seta Toroyan. Writer and illustrator workshops geared toward all levels. The Metro New York Professional Series generally meets the second Tuesday of each month, from September to June, 7:30-9:30 p.m. Check website to confirm location, dates, times and speakers. Cost of workshop: $15 for SCBWI members; $20 for nonmembers. "We feature an informal evening with coffee, cookies and top editors, art directors, agents, publicity and marketing people, librarians, reviewers and more."

SCBWI—MICHIGAN; CONFERENCES

Website: www.Kidsbooklink.org. **Co-Regional Advisors:** Monica Harris and Leslie Helakoski. One-day conference held in April/May and 3-day fall conference held in September. Workshops periodically. Speakers TBA. See website for details on all upcoming events.

SCBWI—MIDATLANTIC; ANNUAL FALL CONFERENCE

Mid-Atlantic SCBWI, P.O. Box 3215, Reston, VA 20195-1215. E-mail: scbwimidatlantic@gmail.com. Website: www.scbwi-midatlantic.org. Conference takes place Saturday, October 22, 2011 in Arlington, VA from 8 to 5. Keynote speaker TBA. For updates and details visit website. Registration limited to 200. Conference fills quickly. Cost: $115 for SCBWI members; $145 for nonmembers. Includes continental breakfast. Lunch is on your own. (The food court at the Ballston Common Mall is two blocks away.) **Contact:** Sydney Dunlap and Erin Teagan, conference co-chairs. Ellen Braaf, regional advisor.

SCBWI—MIDSOUTH FALL CONFERENCE

P.O. Box 396, Cordova, TN 38088. E-mail: expressdog@bellsouth.net or cameron_s_e@yahoo.com. Website: www.scbwi-midsouth.org. **Conference Coordinators:** Genetta Adair and Sharon Cameron. Conference for writers and illustrators of all experience. 2011 conference will be held September 17-18 in Nashville. In the past, workshops were offered on Plotting Your Novel, Understanding the Language of Editors, Landing an Agent, How to Prepare a Portfolio, Negotiating a Contract, The Basics for Beginners, and many others. Attendees are invited to bring a manuscript and/or art portfolio to share in the optional, no-charge critique group session. Illustrators are invited to bring color copies of their art (not originals) to be displayed in the illustrators' showcase. For an additional fee, attendees may schedule a 15-minute manuscript critique or portfolio critique by the editor, art director or other expert consultant. Annual conference held in September. Registration limited to 130 attendees. Cost to be determined. The 2010 Midsouth Fall Conference included Balzer & Bray editor Ruta Rimas; nonfiction book pakager and editor Lionel Bender from London, England; Andrea Brown agent Kelly Sonnack; ICM agent Tina Wexler; award-winning author Linda Sue Park and more.

SCBWI—MISSOURI; CHILDREN'S WRITER'S CONFERENCE

St. Charles County Community College, P.O. Box 76975, 103 CEAC, St. Peters MO 63376-0975. (636)922-8233, ext. 4108. Website: www.moscbwi.org. **Regional Advisor:** Stephanie Bearce. Writer and illustrator conference geared toward all levels. **Open to students.** Speakers include editors, writers, agents, and other professionals. Topics vary from year to year, but each conference offers sessions for both writers and illustrators as well as for newcomers and published writers. Previous topics included: "What Happens When Your Manuscript is Accepted" by Dawn Weinstock, editor; "Writing—Hobby or Vocation?" by Chris Kelleher; "Mother Time Gives Advice: Perspectives from a 25 Year Veteran" by Judith Mathews, editor; "Don't Be a Starving Writer" by Vicki Berger Erwin, author; and "Words & Pictures: History in the Making," by author-illustrator Cheryl Harness. Annual conference held in early November. For exact date, see SCBWI Website: www.scbwi.org or the events page of the Missouri SCBWI website. Registration limited to 75-90. Cost of conference includes one-day workshop (8 a.m. to 5 p.m.) plus lunch. Write for more information.

SCBWI—NEW ENGLAND; ANNUAL CONFERENCE

Nashua, NH 03063. E-mail: northernnera@scbwi.org. Website: www.nescbwi.org. **Regional Advisor:** Anna Boll. Conference is for all levels of writers and illustrators. **Open to students.** "We offer many workshops at each conference, and often there is a multi-day format. Examples of subjects addressed: manuscript development, revision, marketing your work, productive school visits, picture book dummy formatting, adding texture to your illustrations, etc." Annual conference held in mid-May. Registration limited to 450. Cost: TBD; includes pre-conference social, great keynote speaker, many workshop options, lunch, snacks, etc. Keynote speaker for 2008 conference was Laurie Halse Anderson. "Details (additional speakers, theme, number of workshop choices, etc.) will be posted to our website as they become available. Registration will not start until March. Opportunities for one-on-one manuscript critiques and portfolio reviews will be available at the conference."

SCBWI—NEW JERSEY; ANNUAL SPRING CONFERENCE

E-mail: njscbwi@newjerseyscbwi.com. Website: www.newjerseyscbwi.com. **Regional Advisor:** Kathy Temean. This two-day conference is always held the first weekend in June in Princeton, NJ. "How to" workshops, first page sessions, agent pitches, one-on-one critiques, consultations, portolio reviews, mix and mingle, group critiques, contests, interaction with the faculty of editors, agents, art director and authors are some of the highlights of the weekend. Published authors and illustrators attending the conference are invited to do a book signing and sell their books on Saturday afternoon. Illustrators have the opportunity to exhibit their artwork and display their portolio throughout the conference. Meals are included with the cost of admission. Illustrator and writing craft workshops held before conference for additional cost. Conference is known for its high ratio of faculty to attendees.

➕ SCBWI—NEW JERSEY; ANNUAL SUMMER CONFERENCE

SCBWI-New Jersey: Society of Children's Book Writers & Illustrators, Website: www.newjerseyscbwi.com.

This weekend conference is held in the beginning of June in Princeton, NJ. Multiple one-on-one critiques; "how-to" workshops for every level, first page sessions, agent pitches and interaction with the faculty of editors, agents, art director and authors are some of the highlights of the weekend. On Friday attendees can sign up for writing intensives or register for illustrators' day with the art directors. Published authors attending the conference can sign up to participate in the bookfair to sell and autograph their books; illustrators have the opportunity to display their artwork. Attendees have the option to participate in group critiques after dinner on Saturday evening and attend a mix and mingle with the faculty on Friday night. Meals are included with the cost of admission. Conference is known for its high ratio of faculty to attendees and interaction opportunities. **Contact:** Kathy Termean, Regional Advisor.

SCBWI—NEW JERSEY; FIRST PAGE SESSIONS

E-mail: njscbwi@newjerseyscbwi.com; kathy@newjerseyscbwi.com; laurie@newjerseyscbwi.com. Website: www.newjerseyscbwi.com. Held 4 times a year in Princeton, NJ. Two editors/agents give their first impression of a first page and let participants know if they would read more. These sessions are held late afternoon during the week and are limited to 30 people. Attendees can choose to have dinner with the editors after the session. Please visit www.newjerseyscbwi.com for more information.

SCBWI—NEW JERSEY; MENTORING WORKSHOPS

E-mail: njscbwi@newjerseyscbwi.com. Website: www.newjerseyscbwi.com. **Regional Advisor:** Kathy Temean. These workshops have become very popular and fill quickly. Workshops provide an inspiring environment for writers to work on their manuscript and have personal contact with their mentor/editor. Each workshop consists of 14 writers and two editors or 28 people and 4 editors. Weekend workshops allow writers to spend 45 minutes, one-on-one, with their mentor to discuss their manuscript and career direction, first page critiques, pitch sessions and other fun writing activities. One day workshops consist of 20 minute one-on-one critiques and Q&A session, plus first-page critiques. These workshops are held in the winter, spring, and fall each year Princeton, New Jersey. Please visit www.newjerseyscbwi.com for more information.

SCBWI—NEW MEXICO; HANDSPRINGS: A CONFERENCE FOR CHILDREN'S WRITERS AND ILLUSTRATORS

P.O. Box 1084, Socorro NM. E-mail: handsprings@ scbwi-nm.org. Website: www.scbwi-nm.org. **Registrar:** Lois Bradley. **Regional Advisor:** Chris Eboch. Conference for beginner and intermediate writers and illustrators. "The 2011 conference features four keynote speakers—editors, agents, art directors and/or illustrators and authors. 2011 speakers will lead 2½ hour intensive, craft-based workshops. Annual conference held in October 8, 2011. Registration limited to 100. "Offers intensive craft-based workshops and large-group presentations." Cost: $110-150 for basic Saturday registration dependent on registration; $40-50 for private critiques (lowest prices are for SCBWI members). "The Friday evening party included social time and mini book launches. Saturday features a full day of keynote speeches by visiting editors, agents and/or art directors; breakout workshops on the craft and business of writing; and optional written critiques with the editors or written portfolio review by the art director."

SCBWI—NORCA (SAN FRANCISCO/ SOUTH); GOLDEN GATE CONFERENCE AT ASILOMAR

Website: www.scbwisf.org. **Co-Regional Advisors:** Amy Laughlin and Kristin Howell. "We welcome published and 'not-yet-published' writers and illustrators. Lectures and workshops are geared toward professionals and those striving to become professional. Program topics cover aspects of writing or illustrating, and marketing, from picture books to young adult novels. Past speakers include editors, agents, art directors, Newbery Award-winning authors, and Caldecott Award-winning illustrators. Annual conference, generally held third or fourth weekend in February; Friday evening through Sunday lunch. Registration limited to approximately 140. Manuscript or portfolio review available. Most rooms shared with one other person. Additional charge for single when available. Desks available in most rooms. All rooms have private baths. Conference center is set in wooded campus on Asilomar Beach in Pacific Grove, California. Approximate cost: $465 for SCBWI members, $610 for nonmembers; includes shared room, 6 meals and all conference activities. Vegetarian meals available. Coming together for shared meals and activities builds a strong feeling of community among the speakers and conferees. Scholarships

available to SCBWI members. Registration opens end of October/November. For more information, including exact costs and dates, visit our website."

SCBWI—NORTHERN OHIO; ANNUAL CONFERENCE

E-mail: vselvaggio@windstream.net. Website: www. nohscbwi.org. **Regional Advisor:** Victoria A. Selvaggio. Northern Ohio's conference is crafted for all levels of writers and illustrators of children's literature. The dates for the 2011 conference are September 23 and 24. "Our annual event will be held at the Sheraton Cleveland Airport Hotel. Conference costs will be posted on our website with registration information. SCBWI members receive a discount. Additional fees apply for late registration, critiques, or portfolio reviews. Cost includes an optional Friday evening Opening Banquet from 6-10 p.m. with a keynote speaker; Saturday event from 8:30 a.m. to 5 p.m. which includes breakfast snack, full-day conference with headliner presentations, general sessions, breakout workshops, lunch, panel discussion, bookstore, and autograph session. The Illustrator Showcase is open to all attendees at no additional cost. Grand door prize drawn at the end of the day Saturday, is free admission to the following year's conference. Further information, including headliner speakers will be posted on our website. All questions can be directed to vselvaggio@windstream.net."

SCBWI—OREGON CONFERENCES

E-mail: robink@scbwior.com. Website: www.scbwior. com. Writer and illustrator workshops and presentations geared toward all levels. "We invite editors, art directors, agents, attorneys, authors, illustrators and others in the business of writing and illustrating for children. Faculty members offer craft presentations, workshops, first-page sessions and individual critiques as well as informal networking opportunities. Critique group network opportunities for local group meetings and regional retreats; see website for details. Two main events per year: Writers and Illustrators Retreat: held near Portland Thurs-Sun the 2nd weekend in October. Cost of retreat: $355 plus $35 critique fee includes double occupancy and all meals; Spring Conference: Held in the Portland area (2 day event the third Fri-Sat in May (one-day attendance is permitted); cost for presentations and workshops: about $150 includes continental breakfast and lunch on Saturday, critique fee $35.00-attendees only; Friday: intensive sessions cost about $100 for the day with professional tracks in writing and illustrating. Registration limited to 300 for the conference and 55 for the retreat. SCBWI Oregon is a regional chapter of the Society of Children's Book Writers and Illustrators. SCBWI Members receive a discount for all events. Oregon and S. Washington members get preference.

SCBWI–POCONO MOUNTAINS RETREAT

Website: www.scbwiepa.org. Held in the spring at Shawnee Inn, Shawnee on the Delaware, PA. Faculty addresses craft, web design, school visits, writing, illustration and publishing. Registration limited to 150. Cost of retreat: tuition $140, meals, room and board averages $250 for the weekend. For information, online registration and brochure, visit website.

SCBWI–SAN DIEGO; CHAPTER MEETINGS & WORKSHOPS

San Diego—SCBWI, San Diego, CA. E-mail: ra-sd@ sandiego-scbwi.org. Website: www.sandiego-scbwi. org. **Regional Advisor:** Janice M. Yuwiler. Writer and illustrator meetings and workshops geared toward all levels. Topics vary but emphasize writing and illustrating for children. Check website, e-mail or call (619)713-5462 for more information. "The San Diego chapter holds meetings the second Saturday of each month from September-May at the University of San Diego from 2-4 p.m.; cost $7 (members), $9 (nonmembers). Check website for room, speaker and directions." Check website for 2012 meeting schedule. Published members share lessons learned and holiday book sale. 2012 conference to be held in February, Writer's Retreat in May. Check website for details. Season tickets include all regular chapter meetings during the season and newsletter issues for one calendar year as well as discounts on conferences/retreats. See the website for conference/workshop dates, times and prices. Chapter also helps members find critique groups for on-going enhancement of skills.

SCBWI–SOUTHERN BREEZE; SPRINGMINGLE

Website: www.southern-breeze.net. **Regional Advisors:** Jo Kittinger and Claudia Pearson. Writer and illustrator conference geared toward intermediate, advanced and professional levels. Speakers typically include agents, editors, authors, art directors, illustrators. **Open to SCBWI members, non-members and college students.** Annual conference held in Atlanta, Georgia. Usually held in late February. Registration limited. Cost of conference: approximately $225; Typically includes Friday dinner, Saturday lunch and Saturday banquet. Manuscript critiques and portfolio reviews available for additional fee. Pre-registration is necessary. Send a SASE to Southern Breeze, P.O. Box 26282, Birmingham AL 35260 for more information or visit website: www.southern-breeze.net.

SCBWI–SOUTHERN BREEZE; WRITING AND ILLUSTRATING FOR KIDS

P.O. Box 26282, Birmingham AL 35260. E-mail: sjkit tinger@gmail.com. Website: www.southern-breeze. org. Writer and illustrator workshops geared toward all levels. Open to SCBWI members, non-members and college students. All sessions pertain specifically to the production and support of quality children's literature. This one-day conference offers about 30 workshops on craft and the business of writing. Picture books, chapter books, novels covered. Entry and professional level topics addressed by published writers and illustrators, editors and agents. Annual conference. Fall conference is held the third weekend in October in the Birmingham, AL, metropolitan area. (Museums, shopping, zoo, gardens, universities and colleges are within a short driving distance.) All workshops are limited to 30 or fewer people. Pre-registration is necessary. Some workshops fill quickly. Cost of conference: approximately $110 for members, $135 for nonmembers, $120 for students; program includes keynote speaker, 4 workshops (selected from 30), lunch, and Friday night dessert party. Mss critiques and portfolio reviews are available for an additional fee; mss must be sent early. Registration is by mail ahead of time. Manuscript and portfolio reviews must be pre-paid and scheduled. Send a SASE to: Southern Breeze, P.O. Box 26282, Birmingham AL 35260 or visit website. Fall conference is always held in Birmingham, Alabama. Room block at a hotel near conference site (usually a school) is by individual reservation and offers a conference rate. Keynote for WIK10 was Darcy Pattison. Additional speakers include editors, agents, art directors, authors, and/or illustrators. WIK12 speakers to be announced. **Contact:** Jo Kittinger.

SCBWI–VENTURA/SANTA BARBARA; FALL CONFERENCE

E-mail: alexisinca@aol.com. Website: www.scbwisocal. org/calendar. Writers' conference geared toward all levels. Speakers include editors, authors, illustrators and agents. Fiction and nonfiction picture books, middle grade and YA novels, and magazine submissions addressed. Annual writing contest in all genres plus illustration display. Conference held November 5, 2011 at California Lutheran University in Thousand Oaks, California in cooperation with the CLU School of Education. For fees and other information, e-mail or go to website. **Contact:** Alexis O'Neill, Regional Advisor.

SCBWI—VENTURA/SANTA BARBARA; RETREAT FOR CHILDREN'S AUTHORS AND ILLUSTRATORS

E-mail: alexisinca@aol.com. Website: www.scbwiso cal.org. The Winter Retreat, held in Santa Barbara in January, focuses on craft or business issues. Go to website or e-mail for upcoming date, theme and fee.

SCBWI—WESTERN WASHINGTON STATE; CONFERENCE & RETREAT

SCBWI Western Washington; Conference & Retreat P.O. Box 156, Enumclaw WA 98022. E-mail: info@ scbwi-washington.org. Website: www.scbwi-washington.org. **Co-Regional Advisors:** Joni Sensel and Laurie Thompson. "The Western Washington region of SCBWI hosts an annual conference in April, a retreat in November, and monthly meetings and events throughout the year. Please visit the website for complete details."

SCBWI—WISCONSIN; FALL RETREAT FOR WORKING WRITERS

Regional Advisor: Pam Beres. Writer and illustrator conference geared toward all levels. All our sessions pertain to children's writing/illustration. Faculty addresses writing/illustrating/publishing. Annual conference held October. Go to our website for more information:www.scbwi-wi.com.

OTHER CONFERENCES

AEC CONFERENCE ON SOUTHERN LITERATURE

Arts & Education Council (AEC), 3069 S. Broad St., Suite 2, Chattanooga TN 37408-3056. (423)267-1218 or (800)267-4232. Fax: (423)267-1018. E-mail: srobinson@ artsedcouncil.org. Website: http://artsedcouncil.org; http://southernlitconference.org. Executive Director: Susan Robinson. Open to students and adults. Recently described as "the leading literary event in the South," by literary critic Louis D. Rubin, Jr., the AEC Confer-

ence attracts over 1,000 readers and writers from all over the United States. See website for cost and location. Features panel discussions, readings and commentaries for adults and students by today's foremost Southern writers. **Contact:** Susan Robinson.

○ "Get ready for the 2012 Conference: Download the Suggested Reading List online."

ANNUAL SPRING POETRY FESTIVAL

City College, 160 Convent Ave., New York NY 10031. (212)650-6356. E-mail: bigapplepoetpam@aol.com. Website:www1.ccny.cuny.edu/prospective/humanities/poetry. **Director, Poetry Outreach Center:** Pam Laskin. Writer workshops geared to all levels. **Open to students.** Annual poetry festival. Festival held May 17, 2011. Registration limited to 325. Cost of workshops and festival: free. Write for more information. Site: Theater B of Aaron Davis Hall.

BIG SUR WRITING WORKSHOP

Henry Miller Library, Highway One, Big Sur CA 93920. (831)667-2574. E-mail: box601@gmail.com; magnus@ henrymiller.org. Website: www.henrymiller.org/ CWW.html. **Contact:** Magnus Toren, executive director. Annual workshops are held in December and March focusing on children's and young adult writing. Workshop held in Big Sur Lodge in Pfeiffer State Park. Cost of workshop: $720; included meals, lodging, workshop, Saturday evening reception; $600 if lodging not needed.

○ BOOMING GROUND ONLINE WRITERS STUDIO

Buch E-462, 1866 Main Mall, UBC, Vancouver BC V6T 1Z1Canada . Fax: (604)648-8848. E-mail: contact@boomingground.com. Website: www.boomingground.com. **Director:** Jordan Hall. Writer mentorships geared toward beginner, intermediate, and advanced levels in novel, short fiction, poetry, nonfiction, and children's writing and more. **Open to students.** Online mentorship program—students work for 6 months with a mentor by e-mail, allowing up to 120-240 pages of material to be created. Program cost: $500 (Canadian). Site: online and by e-mail. **Contact:** Jordan Hall, director.

CAT WRITERS' ASSOCIATION ANNUAL WRITERS CONFERENCE

66 Adams Street, Jamestown NY 14701. (716)484-6155. E-mail: dogwriter@windstream.net. Website:

www.catwriters.org. The Cat Writers' Association holds an annual conference at varying locations around the US. The agenda for the conference is filled with seminars, editor appointments, an autograph party, networking breakfast, reception and annual awards banquet, as well as the annual meeting of the association. See website for details. **Contact:** Susan M. Ewing, president.

CHILDREN'S AUTHORS' BOOTCAMP

P.O. Box 231, Allenspark CO 80510. (303)747-1014. E-mail: CABootcamp@msn.com. Website: www. WeMakeWriters.com. Writer workshops geared toward beginner and intermediate levels. "Children's Authors' Bootcamp provides two full, information-packed days on the fundamentals of writing fiction for children. The workshop covers developing strong, unique characters; well-constructed plots; believable dialogue; seamless description and pacing; point of view; editing your own work; marketing your manuscripts to publishers, and more. Each day also includes in-class writing exercises and small group activities." Workshop held several times per year at various locations throughout the United States. Please check our website for upcoming dates and locations. Maximum size is 55; average workshop has 30 participants. Cost of workshop varies; see website for details. Cost includes tuition for both Saturday and Sunday (9:00 a.m. to 4:30 p.m.); morning and afternoon snacks; lunch; handout packet. "Check website for details."

CONFERENCE FOR WRITERS & ILLUSTRATORS OF CHILDREN'S BOOKS

Website: www.bookpassage.com. Book Passage, 51 Tamal Vista Blvd.Corte Madera CA 94925. (415)927-0960, ext. 239. Fax: (415)927-3069. E-mail: bpconferences@bookpassage.com. Website: www.bookpassage.com. **Conference Coordinator:** Kathryn Petrocelli. Writer and illustrator conference geared toward beginner and intermediate levels. Sessions cover such topics as the nuts and bolts of writing and illustrating, publisher's spotlight, market trends, developing characters/finding voice in your writing, and the author/agent relationship. Four-day conference held each summer. Includes opening night dinner, 3 lunches and a closing reception.

THE DIY BOOK FESTIVAL

7095 Hollywood Blvd.Suite 864, Los Angeles CA 90028-0893. (323)665-8080. Fax: (323)372-3883. E-mail: diyconvention@aol.com. Website: www.diyconvention.com. **Managing Director:** Bruce Haring. Writer and illustrator workshops geared toward beginner and intermediate levels. **Open to students.** Festival focus on getting your book into print, book marketing and promotion. Annual workshop. Workshop held February-October, various cities. Cost of workshop: $50; includes admission to event, entry to prize competition, lunch for some events. Check out our website for current dates and locations: www.diyconvention.com.

DUKE UNIVERSITY YOUTH PROGRAMS: CREATIVE WRITERS' WORKSHOP

Campus Box 90700, Room 201, The Bishop's House, Durham NC 27708. Website: www.learnmore.uke.edu/youth. **Contact:** Duke Youth Programs. **Open to students.** The Creative Writers' Workshop provides an intensive creative writing experience for advanced high school age writers who want to improve their skills in a community of writers. "The interactive format gives participants the opportunity to share their work in small groups, one-on-one with instructors, and receive feedback in a supportive environment. The review and critique process helps writers sharpen critical thinking skills and learn how to revise their work." Annual workshop. Every summer there is one 2-week residential session. Costs for 2011—$1,775 for residential campers; $1,145 for extended day campers. Visit website for more information. www.learnmore.duke.edu/youth

DUKE UNIVERSITY YOUTH PROGRAMS: YOUNG WRITERS' CAMP

P.O. Box 90702, Durham NC 27708. (919)684-2827. Fax: (919)681-8235. E-mail: youth@duke.edu. Website: www.learnmore.uke.edu/youth. **Contact:** Duke Youth Programs (919)684-6259. Beginner and intermediate levels writing workshops for middle and high school students. **Open to students** (grades 6-11). Summer Camp. The Young Writers' Camp offers courses to enhance participants skills in creative and expository writing. "Through a core curriculum of short fiction, poetry, journalism and playwriting students choose two courses for study to develop creative and analytical processes of writing. Students work on assignments and projects in and out of class, such as newspaper features, short stories, character studies, and journals." Annual workshop. Every summer there are three 2-week sessions with residential and day options. Costs for 2011—$1,175 for residential campers; $1,145 for extended day campers; $865 for day campers. Visit website or call for more information.

FISHTRAP, INC.

400 Grant Street, P.O. Box 38, Enterprise OR 97828-0038. (541)426-3623. E-mail: director@fishtrap.org. Website: www.fishtrap.org. Writer workshops geared toward beginner, intermediate, advanced and professional levels. Open to students, scholarships available. A series of writing workshops and a writers' gathering is held each July. During the school year Fishtrap brings writers into local schools and offers workshops for teachers and writers of children's and young adult books. Other programs include writing and K-12 teaching residencies, writers' retreats, and lectures. College credit available for many workshops. See website for full program descriptions and to get on the e-mail and mail lists. **Contact:** Barbara Dills, Interim Director.

INDIANAPOLIS YOUTH LITERATURE CONFERENCE

Chaired by Dr. Marilyn Irwin, School of Library and Information Science, Indiana University, Purdue University, Indianapolis. (317)278-2375 or (317)275-4100. Annual conference held the last Saturday of January each year featuring top writers in the field of children's literature. Registration limited to 300. Cost of conference: $75. Three plenary addresses, 2 workshops, book signing, reception and conference bookstore. The conference is geared toward three groups: teachers, librarians and writers/illustrators. Co-sponsors include the Indianapolis Marion County Public Library, Indiana State Library, and Kids Ink Children's Bookstore.

INTERNATIONAL CREATIVE WRITING CAMP

(701)838-8472. Fax: (701)838-1351. E-mail: info@international musiccamp.com. Website: www.internationalmusiccamp.com. **Camp Director:** Dr. Timothy Wollenzien. Writer and illustrator workshops geared toward beginner, intermediate and advanced levels. **Open to students.** Sessions offered include those covering poems, plays, mystery stories, essays. Workshop held June 26-July 2, 2011. Registration limited to 40. The summer camp location at the International Peace Garden on the Border between Manitoba and North Dakota is an ideal site for creative thinking. Excellent food, housing and recreation facilities are available.

Cost of workshop: Before May 1st -$355.00; after May 1st - $370.00. Write for more information. **Contact:** Dr. Timothy Wollenzien. Airline and depot shuttles are available upon request. Housing is included in the fee. Conference information is available in September. For brochure visit website, e-mail, call or fax. Accepts inquiries by e-mail, phone and fax.

IWWG ANNUAL SUMMER CONFERENCE

International Women's Writing Guild, P.O. Box 810, Gracie Station, New York NY 10028. (212)737-7536. Fax: (212)737-9469. E-mail: iwwg@iwwg.org. Website: www.iwwg.org. Writer and illustrator workshops geared toward all levels. Held June 24-July 1, 2011. Offers over 50 different workshops—some are for children's book writers and illustrators. Also sponsors other events throughout the U.S. Annual workshops. "Remember the Magic" workshops held every summer for a week. Length of each session: 90 minutes; sessions take place for an entire week. Registration limited to 500. Cost of workshop: $1,399 (includes complete program, room and board). Write for more information. "This workshop takes place at Yale University, New Haven, CT." **Contact:** Hannelore Hahn, executive director.

KINDLING WORDS EAST

Annual retreat held in late January near Burlington, Vermont. A retreat with three strands: writer, illustrator and editor; professional level. Intensive workshops for each strand, and an open schedule for conversations and networking. Registration limited to approximately 70. Hosted by the 4-star Inn at Essex (room and board extra). Participants must be published by a CCBC listed publisher, or if in publishing, occupy a professional position. Registration opens August 1 or as posted on the website, and fills quickly. Check website to see if spaces are available, to sign up to be notified when registration opens each year, or for more information.

KINDLING WORDS WEST

Website: www.KindlingWords.org. Annual retreat held in late May at a stunning and sacred location: Mable Dodge Luhan House, in Taos New Mexico. KWW is an artist's colony- style week with workshops by gifted teachers followed by a working retreat. Participants gather just before dinner to have white-space discussions; evenings include fireside readings, star gazing and songs. $400 tuition; room/board extra.

Participants must be published by CBC-recognized publisher. Go to www.kindlingwords.org to view speakers and register.

LA JOLLA WRITERS CONFERENCE

P.O. Box 178122, San Diego CA 92177. (858)467-1978. Website: www.lajollawritersconference.com. Antoinette Kuritz, Founder. Established 2001. Annual. 2011 Conference held November 4-6 at the Paradise Point Resort & Spa (San Diego). Conference duration: 3 days. Maximum attendance limited to 200. The La Jolla Writers Conference welcomes writers of all levels of experience. This three-day event, now in its 11th year, always boasts exciting, interactive workshops, lectures, and presentations by an outstanding and freely accessible faculty comprised of best-selling authors, editors from major publishing houses, and literary agents, all of whom value meeting and working with a diverse group of creative people passionate about writing. The LJWC uniquely covers the art, craft and business of writing for both fiction and nonfiction with a 5 to 1 student to faculty ratio. Costs $295 Early, $385 Regular, $435 after August 1. Conference registration includes access to more than 75 classes, three keynote addresses, two meals, appetizer reception, and faculty author signing. Additional Information: Private Read & Critiques available for an additional fee of $50 each. **Contact:** Jared Kuritz, director. Conference held November 4-6, 2011 at the Paradise Point Resort & Spa (San Diego). A discounted rate with the hotel that hosts the conference is arranged. Please refer to the website.

LEAGUE OF UTAH WRITERS' ANNUAL ROUNDUP

P.O. Box 18430, Kearns UT 84118. (435) 313-4459. E-mail: natpace@yahoo.com. Website: www.luwrite.com. **President:** Natalie Pace. **President Elect:** Mike Eldredge. **Membership Chairman:** Dorothy Crofts. Writer workshops geared toward beginner, intermediate or advanced. Annual conference. Roundup will be held at the Homestead in Midway Utah, September 18-19, 2009. Registration limited to 300. Cost is $99 for members/$129 for nonmembers registering before August 15; $120 for members; $150 non-members after August 19. Cost includes 3 meals, all workshops, general sessions, a syllabus, handouts and conference packet. Contact Natalie Pace (natpace@yahoo.com) with questions or (435)674-9792 or above e-mail address. Send registration to Dorothy Crofts, Member-ship Chairman, P.O. Box 18430, Kearns, UT 84118. Check website for updates, price changes and specifics. **Contact:** Edwin Smith, President; Tim Keller, President Elect. Roundup will be held at The Riverwoods Conference Center with lodging available at the Marriott Springhill Suites, (adjacent to the Conference Center) phone 435-750-5180 in Logan, Utah, September 16 & 17, 2011.

MANHATTANVILLE SUMMER WRITERS' WEEK

2900 Purchase St., Purchase NY 10577-2103. (914)323-5239. Fax: (914)323-3122. E-mail: sirabiank@mville.edu. Website: www.manhattanville.edu. **Program Director:** Karen Sirabian. Writer workshops geared toward writers and aspiring writers. **Open to students.** Writers' week offers a special workshop for writers interested in children's/young adult writing. We have featured such workshop leaders as: Patricia Gauch, Richard Peck, Elizabeth Winthrop and Janet Lisle. In 2009, James Howe conducted a workshop entitled "Writing for Children & Young Adults." Annual workshop held in June. Cost of workshop: $725 (noncredit); includes a full week of writing activities, 5-day workshop on children's literature; lectures; readings; sessions with editors and agents; major speaker, Rick Moody; etc. Workshop may be taken for 2 graduate credits. Write or e-mail for more information.

THE MANUSCRIPT WORKSHOP IN VERMONT

P.O. Box 529, Londonderry VT 05148. E-mail: aplbrk2@earthlink.net. Website: www.barbaraseul ing.com. **Director:** Barbara Seuling. Writer workshop for all levels. Annual workshop estab. 1992. Generally held mid to late July and August and sometimes early September. The time is divided among instructive hands-on sessions in the mornings, writing time in the afternoons, and critiquing in the evenings. A guest speaker from the world of children's books may be a guest at the workshops. Cost of workshop: $750 per person; applicants are responsible for their accommodations and meals at the inn.

☼ MARITIME WRITERS' WORKSHOP

UNB College of Extended Learning, P.O. Box 4400, Fredericton NB E3B 5A3 Canada. (506)458-7106 or (506)453-4646. E-mail: bpaynter@unb.ca. Website: www.unb.ca/cel/programs/creative/maritime-writ ers/index.html. **Coordinator:** Beth Paynter. Day-long workshops during the week of July 4-8, 2011. Workshops run from 9 a.m.- 4 p.m. daily, on topics such as life writing, fiction and how to get published. Group workshop plus individual conferences, public readings, etc. Registration limited. Cost: $125; students: $75.

MIDWEST WRITERS WORKSHOP

Department of Journalism, Ball State University, Muncie IN 47306. (765)282-1055. E-mail: midwestwriters@yahoo.com. Website: www.midwestwriters.org. **Director:** Jama Kehoe Bigger. Writer workshops geared toward intermediate level. Topics include most genres. Our faculty/speakers have included Joyce Carol Oates, George Plimpton, Clive Cussler, Haven Kimmel, James Alexander Thom, Wiliam Zinsser, Phillip Gulley and children's writers Rebecca Kai Dotlich, April Pulley Sayre, Peter Welling, Claire Ewert and Michelle Medlock Adams. Workshop also includes agent pitch sessions ms evaluation and a writing contest. Annual workshop held in late July. Registration tentatively limited to 125. Cost: $115-325. Most meals included. Offers scholarships. See website for more information.

MISSOURI WRITERS' GUILD ANNUAL STATE CONFERENCE

E-mail: mwgvpchair@gmail.com. Website: www.missouriwritersguild.org. **Contact:** Tricia Sanders, vice president and conference chairman. Writer and illustrator workshops geared to all levels. **Open to students.** Annual conference held early April or early May each year. Annual conference "gives writers the opportunity to hear outstanding speakers and to receive information on marketing, research, and writing techniques."

MOONDANCE INTERNATIONAL FILM FESTIVAL

970 Ninth St.Boulder CO 80302. (303)545-0202. E-mail: director@moondancefilmfestival.com. Website: www.moondancefilmfestival.com. **Executive Director:** Elizabeth English. Moondance Film Festival Workshop Sessions include screenwriting, playwriting, short stories, filmmaking (feature, documentary, short, animation), TV and video filmmaking, writing for TV (MOW, sitcoms, drama), writing for animation, adaptation to screenplays (novels and short stories), how to get an agent, what agents want to see and pitch panels. Check website for more information and registration forms. "The Moondance competition includes special categories for writers and filmmak-

ers who create work for the children's market!" Entry forms and guidelines are on the website.

NANCY SONDEL'S PACIFIC COAST CHILDREN'S WRITERS WORKSHOP

P.O. Box 244, Aptos CA 95001. Website: www.childrenswritersworkshop.com. Established in 2003, our seminar serves semi-advanced through professional-level adult writers. A concurrent, intergenerational workshop is open to students age 14 and up, who give adults target-reader feedback. Intensive focus on craft as a marketing tool. Team-taught master classes (open clinics for manuscript critiques) explore such topics as "Envision and Edit Your Whole Novel" and "Story Architecture and Arcs." Continuous close contact with faculty, who have included literary agent Andrea Brown and Dial Books senior editor Kate Harrison. **Next seminars:** October 7-9, 2011 and October 5-7, 2012. Registration limited to 12 adults and 6 teens. **Cost of workshop:** Approx $450 (teens) to $600; includes lodging, most meals, and up to two in-person faculty critiques of partials. Optional: whole-novel critiques, plus two consults with editor or agent, for additional $400-$600. Limited work scholarships. For the most critique options, submit sample chapters and synopsis with e-application by mid May; open until filled. **Content:** Character-driven novels with protagonists ages 11 and older. Collegial format; 90 percent hands-on, with dialogues between seasoned faculty and savvy, congenial peers. Our faculty critiques early as well as optional later chapters, plus synopses. Our pre-workshop anthology of peer manuscripts maximizes learning and networking. Several enrollees have landed contracts as a direct result of our seminar. **Details:** visit our website and e-mail us via the contact form." Our venue, Pajaro Dunes Conference Center and Resort, offers free use of business center with DSL Internet access in enrollees' beachfront townhomes.

OHIO KENTUCKY INDIANA CHILDREN'S LITERATURE CONFERENCE

<c/o> Jennifer Smith, Northern Kentucky University, 405 Steely Library, Highland Heights, KY 41099. (859)572-6620. Fax: (859)572-5390. E-mail: smithjen@nku.edu. Website:http://oki.nku.edu. **Staff Development Coordinator:** Jennifer Smith. Writer and illustrator conference geared toward all levels. **Open to University.** Annual conference. Emphasizes multicultural literature for children and young adults. Con-

ference held annually in November. Contact Jennifer Smith for more information. Cost of conference: $75; includes registration/attendance at all workshop sessions, *Tri-state Authors and Illustrators of Childrens Books Directory*, continental breakfast, lunch, author/illustrator signings. Manuscript critiques are available for an additional cost. E-mail or call for more information.

OKLAHOMA WRITERS' FEDERATION, INC. ANNUAL CONFERENCE

Website: www.owfi.org. **President:** Linda Apple (please see website for most current info): www.owfi.org. Writer workshops geared toward all levels. **Open to students.** "Forty seminars, with 30 speakers consisting of editors, literary agents and many best-selling authors. Topics range widely to include craft, marketing, and all genres of writing." Annual conference. Held first weekend in May each year. Writing facilities available: book room, autograph party, two lunch workshops. Cost of conference: $150 before March 15; $175 after March 15; $70 for single days; $25 for lunch workshops. Full tuition includes 2-day conference (all events except lunch workshops) and 2 dinners plus one 10-minute appointment with an attending editor or agent of your choice (must be reserved in advance). "If writers would like to participate in the annual writing contest, they must become members of OWFI. You don't have to be a member to attend the conference." See website for more information.

OUTDOOR WRITERS ASSOCIATION OF AMERICA ANNUAL CONFERENCE

615 Oak St., Suite 201, Missoula MT 59801. (406)728-7434. E-mail: info@owaa.org; rginer@owaa.org. Website: http://owaa.org. **Meeting Planner:** Robin Giner. Writer workshops geared toward all levels. Annual four-day conference. Craft improvement seminars; newsmaker sessions. 2011 conference held in Salt Lake City, UT. Cost of workshop: $390-450; includes attendance at all workshops and most meals. Attendees must have prior approval from executive director before attendance is permitted. Write for more information.

OZARK CREATIVE WRITERS, INC. CONFERENCE

P.O. Box 424, Eureka Springs AR 72632. E-mail: ozarkcreativewriters@gmail.com. Website: www.ozarkcreativewriters.org. Open to professional and amateur writers, workshops are geared to all levels and all forms of the creative process and literary arts. Sessions sometimes include songwriting, with presentations by best-selling authors, editors and agents. The OCW Conference promotes writing by offering competition in all genres. The annual event is held on the second full weekend in October (October 6-11, 2011) at the Inn of the Ozarks, in the resort town of Eureka Springs, Arkansas. Approximately 200 attend each year; many also enter the creative writing competitions.

PACIFIC NORTHWEST CHILDREN'S BOOK CONFERENCE

Portland State University, Continuing Education, Graduate School of Education, P.O. Box 751, Portland, OR 97207. (503)725-9786 or (800)547-8887, ext. 9786. Fax: (503)725-5595. E-mail: snydere@pdx.edu. Website: www.ceed.pdx.edu/children/. **Contact:** Elizabeth Snyder. Focus on the craft of writing and illustrating for children while working with an outstanding faculty of acclaimed editors, authors, and illustrators. Daily afternoon faculty-led writing and illustration workshops. Acquire specific information on how to become a professional in the field of children's literature. Annual workshop for all levels. Cost depends on options selected, including: noncredit or 3 graduate credits or graduate credits; individual ms/portfolio reviews and room and board at Reed campus.

PACIFIC NORTHWEST WRITER ASSN. SUMMER WRITER'S CONFERENCE

PMB 2717, 1420 NW Gilman Blvd, Suite 2, Issaquah, WA 98027. (425) 673-BOOK (2665). E-mail: staff@pnwa.org. Website: www.pnwa.org. Writer conference geared toward beginner, intermediate, advanced and professional levels. Meet agents and editors. Learn craft from renowned authors. Uncover new marketing secrets. PNWA's 56th Annual Conference was held August 4-7, 2011, at the Hyatt Regency, Bellevue, WA 98004.

PIMA WRITERS' WORKSHOP

Pima College, 2202 W. Anklam Rd., Tucson AZ 85709-0170. (520)206-6084. Fax: (520)206-6020. E-mail: mfiles@pima.edu. Writer conference geared toward beginner, intermediate and advanced levels. **Open to students.** The conference features presentations and writing exercises on writing and publishing stories for children and young adults, among other genres. Annual conference. Workshop held in May. 2011 dates: May 27-29. Cost: $100 (can include ms critique). Participants may attend for college credit. Meals and accommodations not included. Features a dozen authors, editors and agents talking about writing and publishing fiction, nonfiction, poetry and stories for children. Write for more information.

PUBLISHINGGAME.COM WORKSHOP

Newton MA 02459. (617)630-0945. E-mail: Alyza@publishinggame.com. Website: www.publishinggame.com. **Coordinator:** Alyza Harris. Fern Reiss, author of the popular "Publishing Game" book series and CEO of Expertizing.com, will teach this one-day workshop. Writer workshops geared toward beginner, intermediate and advanced levels. Sessions will include: Find a Literary Agent, Self-Publish Your Children's Book, Book Promotion for Children's Books. September—New York; October—Boston; November—New York; December—Philadelphia; January—Washington, DC; February—New York; March—New York; April—New York; May—Boston; June—Los Angeles, CA; July—San Francisco; August—Boston. Please see http://www.publishinggame.com for current schedule. Registration limited to 18. Fills quickly! Cost of workshop: $195; included information-packed course binder and light refreshments. E-mail for more information. Workshop now available as a 5-CD audio workshop. For information on getting more media attention for your novel, nonfiction or children's book, see Fern Reiss' complementary Expertizing workshop at www.expertizing.com.

ROBERT QUACKENBUSH'S CHILDREN'S BOOK WRITING AND ILLUSTRATING WORKSHOP

460 E. 79th St., New York NY 10075. Phone/fax: (212)861-2761. E-mail: rqstudios@aol.com. Website: www.rquackenbush.com. Studio address: 223 East 79th St. New York, NY 10075. **Contact:** Robert Quackenbush. A 4-day extensive workshop on writing and illustrating books for young readers held annually the second week in July at author/artist Robert Quackenbush's Manhattan studio for beginning and advance writers and illustrators. The focus of this workshop is on creating manuscripts and/or illustrated book dummies from start to finish for picture books and beginning reader chapter books ready to submit to publishers. Also covered

is writing fiction and nonfiction for middle grades and young adults, if that is the attendee's interest. In addition, attention is given to review of illustrator's portfolios, and new trends in illustration, including animation for films, are explored. During the 4 days, the workshop meets from 9 a.m–4 p.m. including one hour for lunch. Registration is limited to 10. Some writing and/or art supplies are available at the studio and there is an art store nearby, if needed. There are also electrical outlets for attendees' laptop computers. Cost of workshop is $750. A $100 non-refundable deposit is required to enroll; balance is due three weeks prior the workshop. Attendees are responsible for arranging for their own hotel and meals. On request, suggestions are given for economical places to stay and eat. Recommended by Foder's Great American Learning Vacations, which says, "This unique workshop, held annually since 1982, provides the opportunity to work with Robert Quackenbush, a prolific author and illustrator of children's books with more than 200 fiction and nonfiction books for young readers to his credit, including mysteries, biographies and songbooks. The workshop attracts both professional and beginning writers and artists of different ages from all over the world." Brochure available. Also inquire about fall, winter and spring workshops that meet once a week for ten weeks each that are offered to artists and writers in the New York area. A list of recommended hotels and restaurants is sent upon receipt of deposit to applicants living out of the area of New York City.

♲ SASKATCHEWAN FESTIVAL OF WORDS AND WORKSHOPS

217 Main St. N., Moose Jaw SK S6H 0W1 Canada . E-mail: word.festival@sasktel.net. Website: www.festivalofwords.com. Writer workshops geared toward beginner and intermediate levels. **Open to students.** Readings that include a wide spectrum of genres—fiction, creative nonfiction, poetry, songwriting, screenwriting, playwriting, dramatic reading with actors, graphic novels, Great Big Book Club Discussion with author, children's writing, panels, independent film screening, panels, slam poetry, interviews and performances. Annual festival. Workshop held third weekend in July. Cost of workshop varies from $10 for a single reading to $200 for a full pass (as of 2011). Trivia Night Fun ticket is ex-

tra. Visit website for more information. **Contact:** Donna Lee Howes.

SOUTHEASTERN WRITERS ASSOCIATION—ANNUAL WRITERS WORKSHOP

161 Woodstone, Athens GA 30605. E-mail: purple@southeasternwriters.com. Website: www.southeasternwriters.com. **Open to all writers**. Contests with cash prizes. Instruction offered for novel and short fiction, nonfiction, writing for children, humor, inspirational writing and poetry. Manuscript deadline April 1st, includes free evaluation conference(s) with instructor(s). Agent in residence. Annual 4-day workshop held in June. Cost of workshop: $395 for 4 days or $150-350 daily tuition. Accommodations: Offers overnight accommodations on workshop site. Visit website for more information and cost of overnight accommodations. E-mail or send SASE for brochure. **Contact:** Amy Munnell & Sheila Hudson, presidents.

SPLIT ROCK ARTS PROGRAM

Split Rock Arts Program, University of Minnesota, 360 Coffey Hall, 1420 Eckles Ave.St. Paul MN 55108-6084. (612)625-8100. Fax: (612)624-5359. E-mail: splitrockarts@umn.edu. Website: www.cce.umn.edu/Split-Rock-Arts-Program. Summer workshops and seasonal retreats, including autobiography, poetry, fiction, creative nonfiction, memoir, writing for children; book arts, comic illustration, calligraphy, picture books illustration, graphic novel and a variety of special topics and forms, are taught by renowned writers and illustrators. Held on the Twin Cities campus and at the University's Cloquet Forestry Center in northern Minnesota. Writing instructors for 2010-11 includes: Jessica Abel, Brenda Caȷrdenas, Nancy Carlson, Jack El-Hai, Heid Erdrich, John Hildebrand, Jim Moore, Gregory Orfalea, Shannon Olson, Sun Yung Shin, Joyce Sutphen, Richard Terrill, Catherine Watson, and more. Three-day seasonal retreats are offered in February, April, and October; weeklong and three-day summer workshops and retreats are offered in June and July. Registration limited to 17 per workshop/retreat. Graduate/undergraduate credit, scholarships and on-campus accommodations available. Cost of workshop: $370-555. Registration is ongoing.

SURREY INTERNATIONAL WRITERS CONFERENCE

SIWC c/o SD 36, Unit 400, 9260-140 Street, Surrey BC V3V 5Z4 Canada . E-mail: kcdyer@telus.net. Website: www.siwc.ca. Coordinator: Kathy Chung. Writing workshops geared toward beginner, intermediate and advanced levels. More than 70 workshops and panels, on all topics and genres. Blue Pencil and Agent/Editor Pitch sessions included. Annual Conference held every October. Different conference price packages available. Check our website for more information, or e-mail conference coordinator Kathy Chung at kathychung@siwc.ca.

SYDNEY CHILDREN'S WRITERS AND ILLUSTRATORS NETWORK

The Hughenden Boutique Hotel, 14 Queen St., Woollahra NS 2025 Australia . (61) 2 9363 4863. Fax: (61) 2 9362 0398. Website: www.sgervay.com.au. Writer and illustrator network geared toward professionals. Topics emphasized include networking, information and expertise about Australian children's publishing industry. Network held the first Wednesday of every month, except for January, commencing at 10:30 a.m. Registration limited to 30. Writing facilities available: Internet and conference facilities. Payment of personal beverages and lunch. As a prerequisite must be published in a commercial or have a book contract. E-mail for more information. "This is a professional meeting which aims at an interchange of ideas and information between professional children's authors and illustrators. Editors and other invited guests speak from time to time." **Contact:** Susanne Gervay.

UMKC WRITERS WORKSHOPS

5300 Rockhill Rd.Kansas City MO 64110-2450. (816)235-2736. Fax: (816)235-5279. E-mail:whittfeldk@umkc.edu. Website: www.newletters.org/writingConferences.asp. **Contact:** Kathi Wittfeld. Mark Twain Workshop was held Monday, June 6-24, 2011 at 104 Cockefair Hall and New Letters Weekend Writing Conference held on Friday, Saturday and Sunday, June 24-26, 2011 at Diastole. New Letters Writer's Conference and Mark Twain Writer's Workshop are geared toward intermediate, advanced and professional levels. Workshops open to students and community. Annual workshops. Workshops held in Summer. Cost of workshop varies. Write for more information. **Contact:** Kathi Wittfeld.

WHIDBEY ISLAND WRITERS' CONFERENCE (10TH ANNUAL)

P.O. Box 1289, Langley, WA 98260. (360)331-6714. E-mail: writers@whidbey.com. Website: www.writeon whidbey.org. **Writers Contact:** Conference Director. Three days focused on the tools you need to become a great writer. Learn from a variety of award-winning children's book authors and very experienced literary agents. Variety of preconference workshops and conference topics. Conference held in early spring. Registration limited to 290. Cost: $395; early bird and member discounts available. Registration includes workshops, fireside chats, book-signing reception, various activities, and daily luncheons. The conference offers consultation appointments with editors and agents. Registrants may reduce the cost of their conference by volunteering. See the website for more information. "The uniquely personal and friendly weekend is designed to be highly interactive."

WILLAMETTE WRITERS ANNUAL WRITERS CONFERENCE

2108 Buck St., West Linn OR 97068. (503)305-6729. Fax: (503)344-6174. E-mail: wilwrite@williamette writers.com. Website: www.willamettewriters.com. **Office Manager:** Bill Johnson. Writer workshops geared toward all levels. Emphasizes all areas of writing, including children's and young adult. Opportunities to meet one-on-one with leading literary agents and editors. Workshops held in August. Cost of conference: $230-$430; includes membership.

WRITE-BY-THE-LAKE WRITER'S WORKSHOP & RETREAT

21 N. Park St., 7th Floor, Madison WI 53715. (608)262-3447. E-mail: cdesmet@dcs.wisc.edu. Website: www. dcs.wisc.edu/lsa/writing. **Coordinator:** Christine DeSmet. Writer workshops geared toward beginner, intermediate, and advanced levels. **Open to students** (1-3 graduate credits available in English). "One week-long session is devoted to writing for children." Annual workshop held in mid-June. Registration limited to 15. Writing facilities available: computer labs. Cost of workshop: $345 before May 16; $395 after May 17. Cost includes instruction, welcome luncheon, and pastry/coffee each day. E-mail for more information. "Brochure goes online every January for the following June."

WRITERS' LEAGUE OF TEXAS WORKSHOPS AND SUMMER WRITING RETREAT

611 S. Congress Ave., Suite 130, Austin TX 78704. (512)499-8914. Fax: (512)499-0441. E-mail: wlt@ writersleague.org. Website: www.writersleague.org. "Classes and workshops provide practical advice and guidance on the craft of writing for writers at all stages of their career." Retreat: Annual Summer Writing Academy in Alpine, TX, is a week-long writing intensive with five tracks. Special presentations: "The Secrets of the Agents" series of workshops with visiting literary agents. Classes and Workshops: Topics: e-publishing; creative nonfiction; screenwriting; novel writing; short fiction; journaling; manuscript revision; memoir writing; poetry; essays; freelance writing; publicity; author/book websites; and blogging. **Contact:** Sara Kocek, program coordinator.

☉ THE WRITERS RETREATS' NETWORK

Website: www.writersretreat.com. E-mail: info@writ ersretreat.com. Contact: Micheline Cote. A worldwide selection of residential retreats opened year-round to writers—most of them offering on-site coaching and mentoring. The retreats cater to writers of all genres and offer on-site support such as mentoring, workshops, editing and lodging; some of them offer scholarships. To start and operate a retreat in your area, visit our website and find out about the new handbook *A Writers' Retreat: Starting from Scratch to Success!*

WRITERS RETREAT WORKSHOP

E-mail: wrw04@netscape.net (brochure and other information). Website: www.writersretreatworkshop. com. **Director:** Jason Sitzes. Intensive workshops geared toward beginner, intermediate and advanced levels. Annual workshop, held in Marydale Retreat Center, Erlanger KY in late May, early June. Registration limited to 32: beginners and advanced. Writing facilities available: private rooms with desks. Cost includes tuition, food and lodging for 9 nights, daily classes, writing space, time and assignments, consultation and instruction. One annual scholarship available: February deadline. Requirements: short synopsis required to determine appropriateness of novel for our nuts-and-bolts approach to getting the work in shape for publication. Write for more information. For complete updated details, visit www.writersretreatworkshop.com.

CONTESTS, AWARDS & GRANTS

Publication is not the only way to get your work recognized. Contests and awards can also be great ways to gain recognition in the industry. Grants, offered by organizations like SCBWI, offer monetary recognition to writers, giving them more financial freedom as they work on projects.

When considering contests or applying for grants, be sure to study guidelines and requirements. Regard entry deadlines as gospel and follow the rules to the letter.

Note that some contests require nominations. For published authors and illustrators, competitions provide an excellent way to promote your work. Your publisher may not be aware of local competitions such as state-sponsored awards—if your book is eligible, have the appropriate person at your publishing company nominate or enter your work for consideration.

To select potential contests and grants, read through the listings that interest you, then send for more information about the types of written or illustrated material considered and other important details. A number of contests offer information through websites given in their listings.

If you are interested in knowing who has received certain awards in the past, check your local library or bookstores or consult *Children's Books: Awards & Honors*, compiled and edited by the Children's Book Council (www.cbcbooks.org). Many bookstores have special sections for books that are Caldecott and Newbery Medal winners. Visit the American Library Association website, www.ala.org, for information on the Caldecott, Newbery, Coretta Scott King and Printz Awards. Visit www.hbook.com for information on The Boston Globe-Horn Book Award. Visit www.scbwi.org for information on The Golden Kite Award.

⊙ ALCUIN CITATION AWARD

The Alcuin Society, P.O. Box 3216, Vancouver BC V6B 3X8 Canada. (604)732-5403. E-mail: awards@ alcuinsociety.com. Website: www.alcuinsociety.com/ awards. Annual award. Estab. 1981. Purpose of contest: Alcuin Citations are awarded annually for excellence in Canadian book design. Previously published submissions from the year prior to the Award's Call for Entries (i.e. 2010 awards went to books published in 2009). Submissions made by the publisher, author or designer. Deadline for entries: mid-March. Entry fee is $30/book for Society members; $35/book for non-members; include cheque and entry form with book; downloadable entry form available at website. Awards certificate. Winning books are exhibited nationally and internationally at the Tokyo, Frankfurt and Leipzig Book Fairs, and are Canada's entries in the international competition in Leipzig, "Book Design from all over the World" in the following Spring. Judging by professionals and those experienced in the field of book design. Requirements for entrants: Winners are selected from books designed and published in Canada. Awards are presented annually at appropriate ceremonies held in each year.

AMERICA & ME ESSAY CONTEST

P.O. Box 30400, 7373 W. Saginaw, Lansing MI 48909-7900. E-mail: lfedewa@fbinsmi.com. Website: http://www.farmbureauinsurance-mi.com/pages/events/essay.htm. Annual contest. **Open to students only.** Estab. 1968. Purpose of the contest: to give Michigan 8th graders the opportunity to write about their American heroes, especially the people who have made a big difference in the students' personal lives. Unpublished submissions only. Deadline for entries: mid-November. SASE for contest rules and entry forms. "We have a school mailing list. Any school located in Michigan is eligible to participate." Entries not returned. No entry fee. Cash awards, savings bonds and plaques for state top ten ($1,000), certificates and plaques for top 3 winners from each school. Each school may submit up to 10 essays for judging. Judging by home office employee volunteers. Requirements for entrants: participants must work through their schools or our agents' sponsoring schools. No individual submissions will be accepted. Top ten essays and excerpts from other essays are published in booklet form following the contest. State capitol/schools receive copies."

AMERICAN ASSOCIATION OF UNIVERSITY WOMEN AWARD IN JUVENILE LITERATURE

4610 Mail Service Center, Raleigh NC 27699-4610. (919)733-9375. E-mail: michael.hill@ncdcr.gov. Annual award. Purpose of award: to recognize the year's best work of juvenile literature by a North Carolina resident. Book must be published during the year ending June 30. Submissions made by author, author's agent or publisher. Deadline for entries: July 15. SASE for contest rules. Awards a cup to the winner and winner's name inscribed on a plaque displayed within the North Carolina Office of Archives and History. Judging by Board of Award selected by sponsoring organization. Requirements for entrants: Author must have maintained either legal residence or actual physical residence, or a combination of both, in the state of North Carolina for three years immediately preceding the close of the contest period. Only published work (books) eligible. **Contact:** Michael Hill, awards coordinator. Judged by three-judge panel.

○ Competition receives 10-15 submissions per category.

AMERICAS AWARD

Website: http://www4.uwm.edu/clacs/aa/index.cfm. Annual award. Estab. 1993. Purpose of contest: Up to two awards are given each spring in recognition of U.S. published works (from the previous year) of fiction, poetry, folklore or selected nonfiction (from picture books to works for young adults) in English or Spanish which authentically and engagingly relate to Latin America, the Caribbean, or to Latinos in the United States. By combining both and linking the "Americas," the intent is to reach beyond geographic borders, as well as multicultural-international boundaries, focusing instead upon cultural heritages within the hemisphere. Previously published submissions only. Submissions open to anyone with an interest in the theme of the award. Deadline for entries: January 15. Visit website or send SASE for contest rules and any committee changes. Awards $500 cash prize, plaque and a formal presentation at the Library of Congress, Washington DC. Judging by a review committee consisting of individuals in teaching, library work, outreach and children's literature specialists.

HANS CHRISTIAN ANDERSEN AWARD

IBBY International Board on Books for Young People, Nonnenweg 12, Postfach CH-4003 Basel Switzerland. (004161)272 29 17. Fax: (004161)272 27 57. E-mail: ibby@ibby.org. Website: www.ibby.org. **Director:** Liz Page. Award offered every two years. Purpose of award: A Hans Christian Andersen Medal shall be awarded every two years by the International Board on Books for Young People (IBBY) to an author and to an illustrator, living at the time of the nomination, who by the outstanding value of their work are judged to have made a lasting contribution to literature for children and young people. The complete works of the author and of the illustrator will be taken into consideration in awarding the medal, which will be accompanied by a diploma. Candidates are nominated by National Sections of IBBY in good standing. The Hans Christian Andersen Award is the highest international recognition given to an author and an illustrator of children's books. The Author's Award has been given since 1956, the Illustrator's Award since 1966. Her Majesty Queen Margrethe II of Denmark is the patron of the Hans Christian Andersen Awards. The Hans Christian Andersen Jury judges the books submitted for medals according to literary and artistic criteria. The awards are presented at the biennial congresses of IBBY.

ATLANTIC WRITING COMPETITION FOR UNPUBLISHED MANUSCRIPTS

Writer's Federation of Nova Scotia, 1113 Marginal Rd. Halifax NS B3H 4P7 Canada. (902)423-8116. Fax: (902)422-0881. E-mail: talk@writers.ns.ca. Website: www.writers.ns.ca/awc.html. Annual contest. Purpose is to encourage emerging writers in Atlantic Canada to explore their talents by sending unpublished work to any of five categories: novel, short story, poetry, writing for younger children, writing for juvenile/young adult. Unpublished submissions only. Only open to residents of Atlantic Canada who are unpublished in category they enter. Visit website for more information. **Contact:** Nate Crawford, program coordinator. Deadline: First Friday in December. Prize: **Novel**—1st Place: $200; 2nd Place: $150; 3rd Place: $75. **Writing for Younger Children and Juvenile/Young Adult**—1st Place: $150; 2nd Place: $75; 3rd Place: $50. **Poetry and Short Story**—1st Place: $150; 2nd Place: $75; 3rd Place: $50. Judged by a team of 2-3 professional writers, editors, booksellers, librarians or teachers.

AUSTIN PUBLIC LIBRARY FRIENDS FOUNDATION AWARDS FOR BEST CHILDREN'S BOOK ($500) AND BEST YOUNG ADULT BOOK ($500)

P.O. Box 609, Round Rock TX 78680. Website: http://texasinstituteofletters.org/. Website: www.smu.edu/english/creativewriting/The_Texas_Institute_of_Letters.htm. Offered annually for works published January 1-December 31 of previous year to recognize the best book for children and young people. Writer must have been born in Texas or have lived in the state for at least 2 consecutive years at one time, or the subject matter must be associated with the state. See website for information on eligibility, deadlines and the judges names and addresses to whom the books should be sent. Prize: $500 for each award winner. **Contact:** W.K. (Kip) Stratton, acquisitions.

MARILYN BAILLIE PICTURE BOOK AWARD

40 Orchard View Blvd., Suite 101, Toronto ON M4R 1B9 Canada. (416)975-0010. Fax: (416)975-8970. E-mail: meghan@bookcentre.ca. Website: www.bookcentre.ca. "Honours excellence in the illustrated picture book format." Prize: $20,000.

BAKER'S PLAYS HIGH SCHOOL PLAYWRITING CONTEST

Baker's Plays, 45 W. 25th St. New York NY 10010. E-mail: publications@bakersplays.com Website: www.bakersplays.com. **Contest Director:** Roxanne Heinze-Bradshaw. **Open to any high school students.** Annual contest. Estab. 1990. Purpose of the contest: to encourage playwrights at the high school level and to ensure the future of American theater. Unpublished submissions only. Postmark deadline: January 30. Notification: May. SASE for contest rules and entry forms. No entry fee. Awards $500 to the first place playwright with publication by Baker's Plays; $250 to the second place playwright with an honorable mention; and $100 to the third place playwright with an honorable mention in the series. Judged anonymously. Plays must be accompanied by the signature of a sponsoring high school drama or English teacher, and it is recommended that the play receive a production or a public reading prior to the submission. To ensure return of manuscripts, please include SASE. Teachers must not submit student's work. The winning work will be listed in the *Baker's Plays Catalogue*, which is distributed to 50,000 prospective producing organizations.

JOHN AND PATRICIA BEATTY AWARD

California Library Association, 950 Glenn Drive, Suite 150, Folsom, CA 95630. (916)233-3298. Fax: (916)932-2209. E-mail: hollym@cla-net.org. Website: www.cla-net.org. **Executive Director:** Holly Macriss. Annual award. Estab. 1987. Purpose of award: "The purpose of the John and Patricia Beatty Award is to encourage the writing of quality children's books highlighting California, its culture, heritage and/or future." Previously published submissions only. Submissions made by the author, author's agent or review copies sent by publisher. The award is given to the author of a children's book published the preceding year. Deadline for entries: Submissions may be made January-December. Contact CLA Executive Director who will liaison with Beatty Award Committee. Awards cash prize of $500 and an engraved plaque. Judging by a 5-member selection committee appointed by the president of the California Library Association. Requirements for entrants: "Any children's or young adult book set in California and published in the U.S. during the calendar year preceding the presentation of the award is eligible for consideration. This includes works of fiction as well as nonfiction for children and young people of all ages. Reprints and compilations are not eligible. The California setting must be depicted authentically and must serve as an integral focus for the book." Winning selection is announced through press release during National Library Week in April. Author is presented with award at annual California Library Association Conference in November.

☺ THE GEOFFREY BILSON AWARD FOR HISTORICAL FICTION FOR YOUNG PEOPLE

The Canadian Children's Book Centre, 40 Orchard View Blvd., Suite 217, Toronto, ON M4R 1B9, Canada. (416)975-0010. Fax: (416)975-8970. E-mail: meghan@bookcentre.ca. Website: www.bookcentre.ca. **Contact:** Meghan Howe. Created in Geoffrey Bilson's memory in 1988. Awarded annually to reward excellence in the writing of an outstanding work of historical fiction for young readers, by a Canadian author, published in the previous calendar year. Open to Ca-

nadian citizens and residents of Canada for at least 2 years. Deadline: Mid-December. Prize: $5,000. Please visit website for submissions guidelines and eligibility criteria, as well as specific submission deadline.

THE IRMA S. AND JAMES H. BLACK BOOK AWARD

Bank Street College of Education, 610 W. 112th St., New York NY 10025-1898. (212)875-4458. Fax: (212)875-4558. E-mail: kfreda@bankstreet.edu; apryce@bankstreet.edu. Website: www.bankstreet.edu/childrenslibrary/irmasimontonblackhome.html. **Contact:** Kristin Freda. Annual award. Estab. 1972. Purpose of award: "The award is given each spring for a book for young children, published in the previous year, for excellence of both text and illustrations." Entries must have been published during the previous calendar year (between January '11 and December '11 for 2012 award). Deadline for entries: mid-December. "Publishers submit books to us by sending them here to me at the Bank Street Library. Authors may ask their publishers to submit their books. Out of these, three to five books are chosen by a committee of older children and children's literature professionals. These books are then presented to children in selected first-, second-, and third-grade classes here and at a number of other cooperating schools. These children are the final judges who pick the actual award winner. A scroll (one each for the author and illustrator, if they're different) with the recipient's name and a gold seal designed by Maurice Sendak are awarded in May."

WALDO M. AND GRACE C. BONDERMAN BIENNIAL NATIONAL YOUTH THEATRE PLAYWRITING COMPETITION AND DEVELOPMENT WORKSHOP AND SYMPOSIUM

Bonderman Youth Theatre Playwriting Workshop, Indiana Repertory Theatre, 140 W. Washington St. Indianapolis, IN 46204. E-mail: bonderma@iupui.edu. Website: www.Irtlive.com. **Artistic Director**: Janet Allen. Open to professional and non-professional American playwrights. See website for deadline. Estab. 1985. Entries not returned. No entry fee. Judging by professional theatre directors, teachers and artists. Requirements for entrants: Contest opens only to American playwrights with plays not previously produced professionally and not currently in development with a theatre.

BOSTON GLOBE-HORN BOOK AWARDS

The Boston Globe & The Horn Book, Inc. The Horn Book, 56 Roland St., Suite 200, Boston MA 02129. (617)628-0225. Fax: (617)628-0882. E-mail: info@hbook.com. Website: www.hbook.com/bghb/submissions_bghb.asp. Annual award. Estab. 1967. Purpose of award: To reward literary excellence in children's and young adult books. Awards are for picture books, nonfiction, fiction and poetry. Up to two honor books may be chosen for each category. Books must be published between June 1, 2010 and May 31, 2011. Deadline for entries: May 31, 2011. Textboks, e-books, and audiobooks will not be considered, nor will manuscripts. Books should be submitted by publishers, although the judges reserve the right to honor any eligible book. Award winners receive $500 and silver engraved bowl, honor book winners receive a silver engraved plate. Judging by 3 judges involved in children's book field. The book must have been published in the U.S. *The Horn Book Magazine* publishes speeches given at awards ceremonies. **Contact:** Katrina Hedeen.

☻ ANN CONNOR BRIMER AWARD

Website: www.nsla.ns.ca/index.php/about/awards/ann-connor-brimer-award/ann-connor-brimer/. **Award Director:** Heather MacKenzie. Annual award. Estab. 1991. Purpose of the contest: to recognize excellence in writing. Given to an author of a children's book who resides in Atlantic Canada. Previously published submissions only. Submissions made by the author's agent or nominated by a person or group of people. Must be published in previous year. Deadline for entries: October 15. SASE for contest rules and entry forms. Please go to website for contest rules and entry forms: http://www.nsla.ns.ca/index.php/about/awards/ann-connor-brimer-award/ann-connor-brimer/. No entry fee but four copies of the title must accompany the submission. Awards $2,000 and framed certificate. Judging by a selection committee. Requirements for entrants: Book must be intended for use up to age 15; in print and readily available; fiction or nonfiction except textbooks.

BUCKEYE CHILDREN'S BOOK AWARD

Website: www.bcbookaward.info. **President:** Christine Watters. Correspondence should be sent to Christine Watters via the website. **Open to Ohio students.** Award offered every year. Estab. 1981. Purpose of the award: The Buckeye Children's Book Award Program was designed to encourage children to read literature critically, to promote teacher and librarian involvement in children's literature programs, and to commend authors of such literature, as well as to promote the use of libraries. Nominees are submitted by students between January 1 and March 15. Votes are cast between September 1 and November 10. Winning titles are posted on the website on December 1.

RANDOLPH CALDECOTT MEDAL

Association for Library Service to Children, Division of the American Library Association, 50 E. Huron, Chicago IL 60611. (312)280-2163. E-mail: alscawards@ala.org. Website: www.ala.org/alsc/caldecott.cfm. Annual award. Estab. 1938. Purpose of the award: to honor the artist of the most outstanding picture book for children published in the U.S. (Illustrator must be U.S. citizen or resident.) Must be published year preceding award. Deadline for entries: December 31. SASE for award rules. Entries not returned. No entry fee. "Medal given at ALA Annual Conference during the Newbery/Caldecott Banquet."

CALIFORNIA YOUNG PLAYWRIGHTS CONTEST

Playwrights Project, 2590 Truxton Rd.,Ste. 202, San Diego CA, 92106-6145. (619)239-8222. Fax: (619)239-8225. E-mail: write@playwrightsproject.org. Website: www.playwrightsproject.org. **Open to Californians under age 19.** Annual contest. Estab. 1985. "Our organization and the contest is designed to nurture promising young writers. We hope to develop playwrights and audiences for live theater. We also teach playwriting." Submissions required to be unpublished and not produced professionally. Submissions made by the author. Deadline for entries: June 1. SASE for contest rules and entry form. No entry fee. Judging by professionals in the theater community, a committee of 5-7; changes somewhat each year. Works performed in San Diego at a professional theatre. Writers submitting scripts of 10 or more pages receive a detailed script evaluation letter upon request. **Contact:** Cecelia Kouma, executive director. Deadline: June 1. Prize: Professional production of 2-4 winning plays at a professional theatre in San Diego, plus royalty.

CALLIOPE FICTION CONTEST

Writers' Specialized Interest Group (SIG) of American Mensa, Ltd., 5975 W. Western Way, PMB 116Y,

Tucson, AZ 85713. E-mail: sreditor@clearwire.net; cynthia@theriver.com. Website: www.calliopewriters.org. **Fiction Editor:** Sandy Raschke. **Open to students.** Annual contest. Estab. 1991. Purpose of contest: "To promote good writing and opportunities for getting published. To give our member/subscribers and others an entertaining and fun exercise in writing." Unpublished submissions only (all genres, no violence, profanity or extreme horror). Submissions made by author. Deadline for entries: Changes annually. Entry fee is $5 for nonsubscribers; subscribers get first entry fee. Awards small amount of cash (up to $75 for 1st place, to $10 for 3rd), certificates, full or mini-subscriptions to *Calliope* and various premiums and books, depending on donations. All winners are published in subsequent issues of *Calliope*. Judging by fiction editor, with concurrence of other editors, if needed. Requirements for entrants: winners must retain sufficient rights to have their stories published in the January/February issue, or their entries will be disqualified; one-time rights. Open to all writers. No special considerations—other than following the guidelines. Contest theme, due dates and sometimes entry fees change annually. Always send SASE for complete rules; available after March 15 each year. Sample copies with prior winners are available for $3.

CANADA COUNCIL GOVERNOR GENERAL'S LITERARY AWARDS

350 Albert St.Ottawa ON K1P 5V8 Canada. (613)566-4410, ext. 5573. Fax: (613)566-4410. www.canadacouncil.ca/prizes/ggla. Annual award. Purpose of award: given to the best English-language and the best French-language work in each of the 7 categories of Fiction, Literary Nonfiction, Poetry, Drama, Children's Literature (text), Children's Literature (illustration) and Translation. Books must be first-edition trade books that have been written, translated or illustrated by Canadian citizens or permanent residents of Canada. In the case of translation, the original work written in English or French, must also be a Canadian-authored title. English titles must be published between September 1, 2010 and September 30, 2011. Books must be submitted by publishers. Deadline depends on the book's publication date. For books published in English: March 15, June 1 and August 7. For books published in French: March 15 and July 15. The awards ceremony is scheduled mid-November.

Amount of award: $25,000 to winning authors; $1,000 to non-winning finalists.

CAROL OTIS HURST CHILDREN'S BOOK PRIZE

Westfield Athenaeum, 6 Elm St., Westfield MA 01085. (413)568-7833. Website: www.westath.org. The Carol Otis Hurst Children's Book Prize honors outstanding works of fiction and nonfiction written for children and young adults through the age of 18. Books must have been copyrighted in their original format during the calendar year, January 1 to December 31, of the prize year. Neither anthologies nor updated or revised editions of previously published works are eligible. The prize may be awarded to a single author or co-authors, as named on the title page of the book. Nominees for the prize must be living at the time that their books are submitted. Any individual, publisher, or organization may nominate a book. Books may be self-published. All questions of eligibility will be resolved and final decisions rendered by the Hurst Prize judges. Complete an entry rorm for each title submitted. The form may be found on the Westfield Athenaeum website. The book's cover, brief excerpts from the text, and its illustrations may be used to publicize the prize and its recipient. **Deadline:** Dec. 31. For a work to be considered, the writer must either be a native or a current resident of New England. While the prize (together with a monetary award of $500) is presented annually to an author whose work best exemplifies the highest standards of writing for this age group regardless of genre or topic or geographical setting, the prize committee is especially interested in those books that treat life in the region. Further, entries will be judged on how well they succeed in portraying one or more of the following elements: childhood, adolescence, family life, schooling, social and political developments, fine and performing artistic expression, domestic arts, environmental issues, transportation and communication, changing technology, military experience at home and abroad, business and manufacturing, workers and the labor movement, agriculture and its transformation, racial and ethnic diversity, religious life and institutions, immigration and adjustment, sports at all levels, and the evolution of popular entertainment. **Contact:** Ralph Melnick, assistant director, Westfield Athenaeum. Established to celebrate the life and work of noted children's author Carol Otis Hurst.

CHILDREN'S AFRICANA BOOK AWARD

E-mail: harrietmcguire@earthlink.net. Outreach Council of the African Studies Association, c/o Rutgers University, 132 George St. New Brunswick NJ 08901. (732)932-8173. Fax: (732)932-3394. Website: www.africanstudies.org. Administered by Africa Access, P.O. Box 8028, Silver Spring MD 20910. (301)585-9136. E-mail: africaaccess@aol.com. Website: www.africaaccessreview.org. **Chairperson**: Brenda Randolph. Annually. Estab. 1991. Purpose of contest: "The Children's Africana Book Awards are presented annually to the authors and illustrators of the best books on Africa for children and young people published or republished in the U.S. The awards were created by the Outreach Council of the African Studies Association (ASA) to dispel stereotypes and encourage the publication and use of accurate, balanced children's materials about Africa. The awards are presented in 2 categories: Young Children and Older Readers. Since 1991, 63 books have been recognized." Entries must have been published in the calendar year previous to the award. No entry fee. Awards plaque, ceremony in Washington D.C., announcement each spring, reviews published at Africa Access Review website and in *Sankofa: Journal of African Children's & Young Adult Literature*. Judging by Outreach Council of ASA and children's literature scholars. "Work submitted for awards must be suitable for children ages 4-18; a significant portion of books' content must be about Africa; must by copyrighted in the calendar year prior to award year; must be published or republished in the US. New in 2010, the jury has added designation of 'Noteworthy Books,' flagged for special attention by teachers and librarians. Award winners, Honor Books and Noteworthy books will all be featured in our publicity materials." **Contact:** Harriet McGuire.

CHILDREN'S BOOK GUILD AWARD FOR NONFICTION

E-mail: theguild@childrensbookguild.org. Website: www.childrensbookguild.org. Estab. 1977. Annual award. Purpose of award: "to honor an author or illustrator whose total work has contributed significantly to the quality of nonfiction for children." Award includes a cash prize and an engraved crystal paperweight. Judging by a jury of Children's Book Guild specialists, authors, and illustrators. "One doesn't enter. One is selected. Our jury annually selects one author for the award." **Contact:** President; changes yearly.

CHILDREN'S WRITER WRITING CONTESTS

93 Long Ridge Rd., West Redding, CT 06896-1124. (203)792-8600. Fax: (203)792-8406. Website: www.childrenswriter.com. Contest offered twice per year by *Children's Writer*, the monthly newsletter of writing and publishing trends. Purpose of the award: To promote higher quality children's literature. "Each contest has its own theme. Any original unpublished piece, not accepted by any publisher at the time of submission, is eligible." Submissions made by the author. Deadline for entries: Last weekday in February and October. "We charge a $10 entry fee for nonsubscribers only, which is applicable against a subscription to *Children's Writer*. Awards: 1st place—$250 or $500, a certificate and publication in *Children's Writer*; 2nd place—$100 or $250, and certificate; 3rd-5th places—$50 or $100 and certificates. To obtain the rules and theme for the current contest go to the website and click on "Writing Contests," or send a SASE to *Children's Writer* at the above address. Put "Contest Request" in the lower left of your envelope. Judging by a panel of 4 selected from the staff of the Institute of Children's Literature. "We acquire First North American Serial Rights (to print the winner in *Children's Writer*), after which all rights revert to author." Open to any writer. Entries are judged on age targeting, originality, quality of writing and, for nonfiction, how well the information is conveyed and accuracy. "Submit clear photocopies only, not originals; submission will not be returned. Manuscripts should be typed double-spaced. No pieces containing violence or derogatory, racist or sexist language or situations will be accepted, at the sole discretion of the judges."

CHRISTIAN BOOK AWARDS

Evangelical Christian Publishers Assocation, 9633 South 48th St., Suite 140, Phoenix, AZ 85044. (480)966-3998. Fax: (480)966-1944. E-mail: info@ecpa.org. Website: www.ecpa.org. **President:** Mark W. Kuyper. Annual award. Established 1978. Categories include Children & Youth. "All entries must be evangelical in nature and cannot be contrary to ECPA's Statement of Faith (stated in official rules)." Deadline for entry: January (see website for specific date). Guidelines available on website in October. "The work must be submitted by an ECPA member publisher." Awards a Christian Book Award plaque.

COLORADO BOOK AWARDS

(303)894-7951, ext. 21. Fax: (303)864-9361. E-mail: long@coloradohumanities.org. Website: www.colo radocenterforthebook.org. Offered annually for work published by December of previous year. "The purpose is to champion all Colorado authors, editors, illustrators and photographers, and in particular, to honor the award winners raising the profiles of both their work and Colorado as a state whose people promote and support reading, writing and literacy through books. The categories are generally: children's literature, young adult and juvenile literature, fiction, genre fiction (romance, mystery/thriller, science fiction/fantasy, historical), biography, history, anthology, poetry, pictorial, graphic novel/comic, creative nonfiction, and general nonfiction, as well as other categories as determined each year. Open to authors who reside or have resided in Colorado." Cost: $53 fee. Needs fiction, nonfiction, poetry, juvenile, novels. Deadline: January 16, 2012. **Contact:** Margaret Coval, exec. director, or Jennifer Long, prog. adjudicator. Deadline: January 16, 2012.

CRICKET LEAGUE

Cricket League, P.O. Box 300, Peru IL 61354. mail@ cricketmagkids.com. Website: www.cricketmagkids. com/contests. Address entries to: Cricket League, P.O. Box 300, Peru IL 61354. Open to children of all ages. Nine contests per year. Estab. 1973. "The purpose of Cricket League contests is to encourage creativity and give young people an opportunity to express themselves in writing, drawing, painting or photography. There is a contest in each issue. Possible categories include story, poetry, art, or photography. Each contest relates to a specific theme described on each *Cricket* issue's Cricket League page and on the website. Signature verifying originality, age and address of entrant and permission to publish required. Entries that do not relate to the current month's theme cannot be considered." Unpublished submissions only. Deadline for entries: the 25th of the month. Cricket League rules, contest theme, and submission deadline information can be found in the current issue of *Cricket* and via website. "We prefer that children who enter the contests subscribe to the magazine or that *Cricket* read Cricket in their school or library." No entry fee. Awards certificate suitable for framing and children's

books or art/writing supplies. Judging by Cricket editors. Obtains right to print prizewinning entries in magazine and/or on the website. Refer to contest rules in current Cricket issue. Winning entries are published on the Cricket League pages in a subsequent Cricket magazine. Current theme, rules, and prizewinning entries also posted on the website.

DOROTHY CANFIELD FISHER CHILDREN'S BOOK AWARD

578 Paine Tpke. N., Berlin VT 05602. Website: www. dcfaward.org. (802)828-6954. E-mail: grace.greene@ state.vt.us. Website: www.dcfaward.org. **Chair:** Mary Linney. Annual award. Purpose of the award: to encourage Vermont children to become enthusiastic and discriminating readers by providing them with books of good quality by living American or Canadian authors published in the current year. Deadline for entries: December of year book was published. E-mail for entry rules. No entry fee. Awards a scroll presented to the winning author at an award ceremony. Judging is by the children grades 4-8. They vote for their favorite book. Requirements for entrants: "Titles must be original work, published in the U.S., and be appropriate to children in grades 4-8. The book must be copyrighted in the current year. It must be written by an American author living in the U.S. or Canada, or a Canadian author living in Canada or the U.S."

MARGARET A. EDWARDS AWARD

50 East Huron St. Chicago IL 60611-2795. (312)280-4390 or (800)545-2433. Fax: (312)280-5276. E-mail: yalsa@ala.org. Website: www.ala.org/yalsa/edwards. Annual award administered by the Young Adult Library Services Association (YALSA) of the American Library Association (ALA) and sponsored by *School Library Journal* magazine. Purpose of award: ALA's Young Adult Library Services Association (YALSA), recognizes an author and a specific work or works for significant and lasting contribution to young adult literature. Submissions must be previously published no less than five years prior to the first meeting of the current Margaret A. Edwards Award Committee at Midwinter Meeting. Nomination form is available on the YALSA website. No entry fee. Judging by members of the Young Adult Library Services Association. Deadline for entry: December 1. "The award will be given annually to an author whose book or books, over a period of time, have been accepted by young adults as an authentic voice that continues to

illuminate their experiences and emotions, giving insight into their lives. The book or books should enable them to understand themselves, the world in which they live, and their relationship with others and with society. The book or books must be in print at the time of the nomination."

SHUBERT FENDRICH MEMORIAL PLAYWRITING CONTEST

Pioneer Drama Service, Inc., P.O. Box 4267, Englewood CO 80155-4267. Fax: (303)779-4315. E-mail: submissions@pioneerdrama.com. Website: www.pioneerdrama.com. **Director:** Lori Conary, submissions editor. Annual contest. Estab. 1990. Purpose of the contest: "To encourage the development of quality theatrical material for educational and family theater." Previously unpublished submissions only. Open to all writers not currently published by Pioneer Drama Service. SASE for contest rules and guidelines or view online. No entry fee. Cover letter, SASE for return of ms, and proof of production or staged reading must accompany all submissions. Awards $1,000 royalty advance and publication. Upon receipt of signed contracts, plays will be published and made available in our next catalog. Judging by editors. All rights acquired with acceptance of contract for publication. Restrictions for entrants: Any writers currently published by Pioneer Drama Service are not eligible. **Contact:** Lori Conary, Submissions Editor. **Deadline**: December 31 (postmarked).

○ THE NORMA FLECK AWARD FOR CANADIAN CHILDREN'S NONFICTION

Website: www.bookcentre.ca. The Canadian Children's Book Centre, 40 Orchard View Blvd., Suite 217, Toronto, ON M4R 1B9 Canada. (416)975-0010. Fax: (416)975-8970. E-mail: info@bookcentre.ca. Website: www.bookcentre.ca. **Contact:** Meghan Howe, library coordinator. The Norma Fleck Award was established by the Fleck Family Foundation in May 1999 to honour the life of Norma Marie Fleck, and to recognize exceptional Canadian nonfiction books for young people. Publishers are welcome to nominate books using the online form. Offered annually for books published between January 1 and December 31 of the previous calendar year. Open to Canadian citizens or landed immigrants. The jury will always include at least 3 of the following: a teacher, a librarian, a bookseller, and a reviewer. A juror will have a deep understanding of, and some involvement with, Canadian

children's books. The Canadian Children's Book Centre will select the jury members. Deadline: Mid-December (annually). Prize: $10,000 goes to the author (unless 40% or more of the text area is composed of original illustrations, in which case the award will be divided equally between the author and the artist).

FLICKER TALE CHILDREN'S BOOK AWARD

Flicker Tale Award Committee, North Dakota Library Association, Morton Mandan Public Library, 609 W. Main St., Mandan, ND 58554. E-mail: laustin@cdln.info. Website: www.ndla.info/ftaward.htm. **Contact:** Linda Austin. Estab. 1979. Purpose of award: to give children across the state of North Dakota a chance to vote for their book of choice from a nominated list of 20: 4 in the picture book category; 4 in the intermediate category; 4 in the juvenile category (for more advanced readers); 4 in the upper garage level nonfiction category. Also, to promote awareness of quality literature for children. Previously published submissions only. Submissions nominated by librarians and teachers across the state of North Dakota. Awards a plaque from North Dakota Library Association and banquet dinner. Judging by children in North Dakota. Entry deadline in April.

DON FREEMAN MEMORIAL GRANT-IN-AID

Society of Children's Book Writers and Illustrators, 8271 Beverly Blvd.Los Angeles CA 90048.(323)782-1010. Fax: (323) 782-1892. E-mail: scbwi@scbwi.org. Website: www.scbwi.org. Estab. 1974. Purpose of award: to "enable picture book artists to further their understanding, training and work in the picture book genre." Applications and prepared materials are available in October and must be postmarked between February 1 and March 1. Grant awarded and announced in August. SASE for award rules and entry forms. SASE for return of entries. No entry fee. Annually awards one grant of $1,500 and one runner-up grant of $500. "The grant-in-aid is available to both full and associate members of the SCBWI who, as artists, seriously intend to make picture books their chief contribution to the field of children's literature."

⊕ THEODOR SEUSS GEISEL AWARD

Association for Library Service to Children, Division of the American Library Association, 50 E. Huron, Chicago. IL 60611. (800)-545-2433. E-mail: ala@ala.org. Website: www.ala.org. The Theodor Seuss Geisel Award, established in 2004, is given annually beginning in 2006 to the author(s) and illustrator(s) of the most distinguished American book for beginning readers published in English in the United States during the preceding year. The award is to recognize the author(s) and illustrator(s) who demonstrate great creativity and imagination in his/her/their literary and artistic achievements to engage children in reading. Deadline for entries: December 31. Entries not returned. Not entry fee. Medal given at awards ceremony during ALA Annual Conference.

☯ AMELIA FRANCES HOWARD GIBBON AWARD FOR ILLUSTRATION

1150 Morrison Drive, Suite 400, Ottawa ON K 2H859 Canada. (613)232-9625. Fax: (613)563-9895. E-mail: carol.mcdougall@iwk.nshealth.ca. Website: www.cla. ca. **Contact:** Committee Chair. Annual award. Estab. 1971. Purpose of the award: "to honor excellence in the illustration of children's book(s) in Canada. To merit consideration the book must have been published in Canada and its illustrator must be a Canadian citizen or a permanent resident of Canada." Previously published submissions only; must be published between January 1 and December 31 of the previous year. Deadline for entries: December 31. See website for award rules. Entries not returned. No entry fee. Judging by selection committee of members of Canadian Association of Children's Librarians. Requirements for entrants: illustrator must be Canadian or Canadian resident.

GOLDEN KITE AWARDS

Society of Children's Book Writers and Illustrators, 8271 Beverly Blvd.Los Angeles CA 90048. (323)782-1010. E-mail: scbwi@scbwi.org. Website: www.scbwi. org. **Contact:** SCBWI Golden Kite Coordinator. Annual award. Estab. 1973. "The works chosen will be those that the judges feel exhibit excellence in writing and in the case of the picture—illustrated books—in illustration, and genuinely appeal to the interests and concerns of children. For the fiction and nonfiction awards, original works and single-author collections of stories or poems of which at least half are new and never before published in book form are eligible—anthologies and translations are not. For the picture-illustration awards, the art or photographs must be original works (the texts—which may be fiction or nonfiction—may be original, public domain or previously published). Deadline for entries: December 15. SASE for award rules. No entry fee. Awards: In addi-

tion to statuettes and plaques, the four winners receive $2,500 cash award plus trip to LA SCBWI Conference. The panel of judges will consist of professional authors, illustrators, editors or agents." Requirements for entrants: "must be a member of SCBWI and books must be published in that year." Winning books will be displayed at national conference in August. Books to be entered, as well as further inquiries, should be submitted to: The Society of Children's Book Writers and Illustrators, above address.

✚☯ GOVERNOR GENERAL'S LITERARY AWARDS

Canada Council for the Arts, 350 Albert St., P.O. Box 1047, Ottawa ON K1P 5V8 Canada. (613)566-4414, ext. 5573. Fax: (613)566-4410. Website: www.canad acouncil.ca/prizes/ggla. Publishers submit titles for consideration. Deadlines depend on the book's publication date. For books published in English: March 15, June 1 and August 7. For books published in french: March 15 and July 15. Prize: Each laureate receives $25,000; non-winning finalists receive $1,000.

✚ THE MARILYN HALL AWARDS FOR YOUTH THEATRE

Beverly Hills Theatre Guild, P.O. Box 148, Beverly Hills, CA 90213. Website: www.beverlyhillsthe atreguild.com. **Contact:** Candace Coster, competition coordinator. **Open to students.** Annual contest. Estab. 1998/99. Purpose of contest: "To encourage the creation and development of new plays for youth theatre." Unpublished submissions only. Authors must be U.S. citizens or legal residents and must sign entry form personally. Deadline for entries: between January 15 and last day of February each year (postmark accepted). Playwrights may submit up to two scripts. One nonprofessional production acceptable for eligibility. SASE for contest rules and entry forms. No entry fee. Awards: $700, 1st prize; $300, 2nd prize. Judging by theatre professionals cognizant of youth theatre and writing/producing.

HIGHLIGHTS FOR CHILDREN FICTION CONTEST

803 Church St., Honesdale PA 18431-1824. (570)253-1080. Fax: (570)251-7847. E-mail: eds@highlights-corp.com. Website: www.Highlights.com. **Fiction Contest Editor:** Christine French Cully. Annual contest. Estab. 1980. Purpose of the contest: to stimulate interest in writing for children and reward and

recognize excellence. Unpublished submissions only. Deadline for entries: January 31; entries accepted after January 1 only. SASE for contest rules and return of entries. No entry fee. Awards 3 prizes of $1,000 each in cash and a pewter bowl (or, at the winner's election, attendance at the Highlights Foundation Writers Workshop at Chautauqua) and a pewter bowl. Judging by a panel of *Highlights* editors and outside judges. Winning pieces are purchased for the cash prize of $1,000 and published in Highlights; other entries are considered for purchase at regular rates. Requirements for entrants: open to any writer 16 years of age or older. Winners announced in May. Length up to 800 words. Stories for beginning readers should not exceed 500 words. Stories should be consistent with *Highlights* editorial requirements. No violence, crime or derogatory humor. Send SASE or visit website for guidelines and current theme. **Contact:** Joëlle Dujardin, senior editor.

MARILYN HOLINSHEAD VISITING SCHOLARS FELLOWSHIP

Kerlan Grant-in-Aid, University of Minnesota, 113 Anderson Library, 222 21st Ave. South, Minneapolis MN 55455. E-mail: circ@umn.edu. Website: http://special.lib.umn.edu/clrc/kerlan/index.php. This fellowship provides grants-in-aid for travel to the Kerlan Collection. These grants will be available for research study in 2011. The Kerlan Collection is one of the world's finest research collections in children's literature and contains over 100,000 books and original art and manuscript material for approximately 16,000 titles. For more information about our holdings, please visit the Kerlan Collection's website. Applicants may request up to $1,500. Send a letter with the proposed purpose, a plan to use specific research materials (manuscripts and art), dates and budget (including airfare and per diem) to above address. The deadline for receipt of all materials is January 30, 2011. Travel and a written report on the project must be completed and submitted in 2011. Deadline: Jan. 30, 2011.

THE JULIA WARD HOWE/BOSTON AUTHORS AWARD

(617)783-1357. E-mail: bostonauthors@aol.com; lawson@bc.edu. Website: www.bostonauthorsclub.org. **Contact:** Alan Lawson. Deadline: January 15, 2012. Prize: $1,000 in each category.

HRC SHOWCASE THEATRE PLAYWRITING CONTEST

P.O. Box 940, Hudson NY 12534. (518)851-7244. Website: www.hrc-showcasetheatre.com. Annual contest. HRC Showcase Theatre is a not-for-profit professional theater company dedicated to the advancement of performing in the Hudson River Valley area through reading of plays and providing opportunities for new and established playwrights. Unpublished submissions only. Submissions made by author and by the author's agent. Deadlines for entries: May 1. SASE for contest rules and entry forms. Entry fee is $5. Awards $500 cash plus concert reading by professional actors for winning play and $100 for each of the four other plays that will be given a staged reading. Judging by panel selected by Board of Directors. Requirements for entrants: Entrants must live in the northeastern U.S.

INSIGHT WRITING CONTEST

Insight Magazine, 55 W. Oak Ridge Dr., Hagerstown, MD 21740-7390. (301) 393-4038. E-mail: insight@rhpa.org. Website: www.insightmagazine.org. **Open to students.** Annual contest. Unpublished submissions only. Submissions made by author. Deadline for entries: June. SASE for contest rules and entry forms. Awards first prizes, $100-250; second prizes, $75-200; third prizes, $50-150. Winning entries will be published in *Insight*. Contest includes three categories: Student Short Story, General Short Story and Student Poetry. You must be age 22 or under to enter the student categories. Entries must include cover sheet form available with SASE or on website.

IRA CHILDREN'S AND YOUNG ADULT'S BOOK AWARD

(302)731-1600. Fax: (302)731-1057. E-mail: kbaughman@reading.org; exec@reading.org. Website: www.reading.org. Annual award. Awards are given for an author's first or second published book for fiction and nonfiction in 3 categories: primary (ages preschool-8), intermediate (ages 9-13) and young adult (ages 14-17). This award is intended for newly published authors who show unusual promise in the children's book field. Deadline for entries: See website. Awards $1,000. For guidelines, write or e-mail exec@reading.org. **Contact:** Kathy Baughman.

EZRA JACK KEATS/KERLAN MEMORIAL FELLOWSHIP

Ezra Jack Keats/Kerlan Collection, Memorial Fellowship Committee, 113 Andersen Library, 222 21st Ave. S., University of Minnesota, Minneapolis, MN 55455. Website: http://special.lib.umn.edu/clrc/kerlan/awards.php. This fellowship from the Ezra Jack Keats Foundation will provide $1,500 to a "talented writer and/or illustrator of children's books who wishes to use the Kerlan Collection for the furtherance of his or her artistic development." Special consideration will be given to someone who would find it difficult to finance a visit to the Kerlan Collection. The Ezra Jack Keats Fellowship recipient will receive transportation costs and a per diem allotment. See website for application deadline and for digital application materials. For paper copies of the application send a large (6×9 or 9×12) SAE with 97¢ postage to above address.

THE EZRA JACK KEATS NEW WRITER AND NEW ILLUSTRATOR AWARDS

Ezra Jack Keats Foundation/Administered by The Office of Children's Services, The New York Public Library, 450 14th St., Brooklyn NY 11215. E-mail: jchang@nypl.org. Website: www.ezra-jack-keats.org. **Program Coordinator:** Julia Chang. Annual awards. Purpose of the awards: "The awards will be given to a promising new writer of picture books for children and a promising new illustrator of picture books for children. Selection criteria include books for children (ages 9 and under) that reflect the tradition of Ezra Jack Keats. These books portray: the universal qualities of childhood, strong and supportive family and adult relationships, the multicultural nature of our world." Submissions made by the publisher. Must be published in the preceding year. Deadline for entries: mid-December. SASE for contest rules and entry forms or e-mail Julia Chang at jchang@nypl.org. No entry fee. Awards $1,000 coupled with Ezra Jack Keats Bronze Medal. Judging by a panel of experts. "The author or illustrator should have published no more than 3 children's books. Entries are judged on the outstanding features of the text, complemented by illustrations. Candidates need not be both author and illustrator. Entries should carry a 2011 copyright (for the 2012 award)." Winning books and authors to be presented at reception at The New York Public Library.

KENTUCKY BLUEGRASS AWARD

Lincoln County High School Media Center, 60 Education Way, Stanford KY 40484. (606)365-9111. Fax: (606)365-1750. E-mail: kay.hensley@lincoln.kyschools.us. Website: www.kyreading.org. **Award Director:** Kay Renee Hensley. Submit entries to: Kay Renee Hensley. Annual award. Estab. 1983. Purpose of award: to promote readership among young children and young adolescents. Also to recognize exceptional creative efforts of authors and illustrators. Previously published submissions only. Submissions made by author, made by author's agent, nominated by teachers or librarians. Must be published no more than 3 years prior to the award year. Deadline for entries: March 15. Contest rules and entry forms are available from the website. No entry fee. Awards a framed certificate and invitation to be recognized at the annual luncheon of the Kentucky Bluegrass Award. Judging by children who participate through their schools or libraries. "Books are reviewed by a panel of teachers and librarians before they are placed on a master list for the year. These books must have been published within a three-year period prior to the review. Winners are chosen from this list of preselected books. Books are divided into four divisions, K-2, 3-5, 6-8, 9-12 grades. Winners are chosen by children who either read the books or have the books read to them. Children from the entire state of Kentucky are involved in the selection of the annual winners for each of the divisions."

CORETTA SCOTT KING BOOK AWARDS

Coretta Scott King Book Awards Committee, Ethnic and Multicultural Information Exchange Round Table, American Library Association, 50 E. Huron St.Chicago IL 60611. (800)545-2433 ext: 4297. Fax: (312)280-3256. E-mail: olos@ala.org. Website: www.ala.org/csk. "The Coretta Scott King Book Awards is an annual award celebrating African American experience. A new talent award may also be selected. An awards jury of Children's Librarians judge the books form the previous year, and select the winners in January at the ALA Midwinter meeting. A copy of an entry must be sent to each juror by December 1 of the juried year. A copy of the jury list and directions for submitting titles can be found on website. Call or e-mail ALA Office for Literacy and Outreach Services for jury list. Awards breakfast held on Tuesday morning during ALA. Annual Conference in June. See schedule at website.

LOUISE LOUIS/EMILY F. BOURNE STUDENT POETRY AWARD

Poetry Society of America, 15 Gramercy Park, New York, NY 10003. (212)254-9628. Fax: (212)673-2352. Website: www.poetrysociety.org. **Contact:** Program Director. *Open to students.* Annual award. Purpose of the award: award is for the best unpublished poem by a high or preparatory school student (grades 9-12) from the U.S. and its territories. Unpublished submissions only. Deadline for entries: October 1-December 22. SASE for award rules and entry forms. Entries not returned. "High schools can send an unlimited number of submissions with one entry per individual student for a flat fee of $20. (High school students may send a single entry for $5.)" Award: $250. Judging by a professional poet. Requirements for entrants: Award open to all high school and preparatory students from the U.S. and its territories. School attended, as well as name and address, should be noted. PSA submission guidelines must be followed. These are printed in our fall calendar on our website and are readily available if those interested send us a SASE. Line limit: none. "The award-winning poem will be included in a sheaf of poems that will be part of the program at the award ceremony and sent to all PSA members."

MCLAREN MEMORIAL COMEDY PLAY WRITING COMPETITION

Midland Community Theatre, 2000 W. Wadley, Midland, TX 79705. (432)682-2544. Fax: (432)682-6136. E-mail: mclaren1@mctmidland.org. Website: www. mctmidland.org. Estab. 1989. *Open to students.* Annual contest. Purpose of conference: "The McLaren Memorial Comedy Play Writing Competition was established in 1989 to honor long-time MCT volunteer Mike McLaren who loved a good comedy, whether he was on stage or in the front row." Unpublished submissions only. Submissions made by author. Deadline for entries: February 28th (scripts are accepted January 1 through the end of February each year). SASE for contest rules and entry forms. Entry fee is $10 per script. Awards $400 for full-length winner and $200 for one-act winner as well as staged readings for 3 finalists in each category. Judging by the audience present at the McLaren festival when the staged readings are performed. Rights to winning material acquired or purchased. 1st right of production or refusal is ac-

quired by MCT. Requirements for entrants: "Yes, the contest is open to any playwright, but the play submitted must be unpublished and never produced in a for-profit setting. One previous production in a non-profit theatre is acceptable. 'Readings' do not count as productions."

☺ THE VICKY METCALF AWARD FOR CHILDREN'S LITERATURE

(416)504-8222. Fax: (416)504-9090. E-mail: info@ writerstrust.com. Website: www.writerstrust.com. **Administrator:** Amanda Hopkins, program coordinator. The Vicky Metcalf Award is presented each fall to a Canadian writer for a body of work in children's literature at The Writers' Trust Awards event in Toronto. Prize: $20,000. Open to Canadian residents only.

MIDLAND AUTHORS AWARD

E-mail: writercc@aol.com. Website: www.midland authors.com. **Contact:** Carol Jean Carlson. Deadline: February 15. Prize: Monetary award given to winner in each category.

MILKWEED NATIONAL FICTION PRIZE

1011 Washington Ave. S., Suite 300, Minneapolis MN 55415. (612)332-3192. Fax: (612)215-2550. E-mail: editor@milkweed.org. Website: www.milkweed.org. **Award Director:** Daniel Slager, Publisher. Annual award. Estab. 1993. Purpose of the award: to recognize an outstanding literary novel for readers ages 8-13 and encourage writers to turn their attention to readers in this age group. Unpublished submissions only "in book form." Please send SASE or visit website for award guidelines. The prize is awarded to the best work for children ages 8-13 that Milkweed agrees to publish in a calendar year. The prize consists of a $5,000 advance against royalties agreed to at the time of acceptance. Submissions must follow our usual children's guidelines. **Contact:** The Editors. Deadline: Open. Prize: Publication by Milkweed Editions and a cash advance of $5,000 against royalties agreed upon in the contractual arrangement negotiated at the time of acceptance.

MINNESOTA BOOK AWARDS

325 Cedar Street, Suite 555, St. Paul MN 55101. E-mail: ann@thefriends.org; mnbookawards@thefriends.org; friends@thefriends.org. Website: www.thefriends. org. The Friends of the Saint Paul Public Library. An-

nual award. Purpose of contest: To recognize and honor achievement by members of Minnesota's book community.

☺ MUNICIPAL CHAPTER OF TORONTO IODE JEAN THROOP BOOK AWARD

Toronto Municipal IODE, 40 St. Clair Ave. E., Suite 205, Toronto, ON M4T 1M9, Canada. (416)925-5078. Fax: (416)925-5127. E-mail: iodetoronto@bellnet.ca. Website: www.bookcentre.ca/awards/iode_book_award_municipal_chapter_toronto. **Contest Director:** Jennifer Werry. Submit entries to: Theo Heras, Lillian Smith Library, 239 College St., Toronto. Annual contest. Estab. 1974. Previously published submissions only. Submissions made by author. Deadline for entries: November 1. No entry fee. Awards: $1,000. If the illustrator is different from the author, the prize money is divided. Judging by book award committee comprised of members of Toronto Municipal Chapter IODE. Requirements for entrants: Authors and illustrators must be Canadian and live within the GTA.

NATIONAL CHILDREN'S THEATRE FESTIVAL

(305)444-9293, ext. 615. Fax: (305)444-4181. E-mail: maulding@actorsplayhouse.org. Website: www.actorsplayhouse.org. Purpose of contest: to bring together the excitement of the theater arts and the magic of young audiences through the creation of new musical works and to create a venue for playwrights/composers to showcase their artistic products. Submissions must be unpublished. Submissions are made by author or author's agent. Deadline for entries: April 1 annually. Visit website or send SASE for contest rules and entry forms. Entry fee is $10. Awards: first prize of $500, full production, and transportation to festival weekend based on availability. Past judges include Joseph Robinette, Moses Goldberg and Luis Santeiro.

NATIONAL FOUNDATION FOR ADVANCEMENT IN THE ARTS

youngARTS, 777 Brickell Ave., Suite 370, Miami, FL 33131. (305)377-1140. Fax: (305)377-1149. E-mail: info@nfaa.org. Website: www.youngARTS.org. **Contact:** Carla Hill. *Open to students/high school seniors or other 17- and 18-year-olds.* Created to recognize and reward outstanding accomplishment in cinematic arts, dance, jazz, music, photography, theater, voice, visual arts and/or writing. youngARTS is an innovative national program of the National Foundation for Advancement in the Arts (NFAA). Established in 1981, youngARTS touches the lives of gifted young people across the country, providing financial support, scholarships and goal-oriented artistic, educational and career opportunities. Each year, from a pool of more than 8,000 applicants, an average of 800 youngARTS winners are chosen for NFAA support by panels of distinguished artists and educators. Deadline for registration: June 1 (early) and October 1. Deadline for submission of work: Nov. 3. Entry fee is $35 (online)/$40(paper). Fee waivers available based on need. Awards $100-10,000—unrestricted cash grants. Judging by a panel of artists and educators recognized in the field. Rights to submitted/winning material: NFAA/youngARTS retains the right to duplicate work in an anthology or in Foundation literature unless otherwise specified by the artist. Requirements for entrants: Artists must be high school seniors or, if not enrolled in high school, must be 17 or 18 years old. Applicants must be U.S. citizens or residents, unless applying in jazz. Literary and visual works will be published in an anthology distributed during youngARTS Week in Miami when the final adjudication takes place. NFAA invites up to 150 finalists to participate in youngARTS Week in January in Miami-Dade County, Florida. youngARTS Week is a once-in-a-lifetime experience consisting of performances, master classes, workshops, readings, exhibits, and enrichment activities with renowned artists and arts educators. All expenses are paid by NFAA, including airfare, hotel, meals and ground transportation.

NATIONAL PEACE ESSAY CONTEST

1200 17th St. NW, Washington DC 20036. (202)457-1700. Fax: (202)429.6063. E-mail: essaycontest@usip.org. Website: www.usip.org/NPEC. **Open to high school students.** Annual contest. Estab. 1987. "The contest gives students the opportunity to do valuable research, writing and thinking on a topic of importance to international peace and conflict resolution. Teaching guides are available for teachers who allow the contest to be used as a classroom assignment." Deadline for entries is February 1, 2012. "Interested students, teachers and others may visit the website to download or request contest materials. Please do not include SASE." Guidelines and rules on website. No entry fee. State-level awards are $1,000 college scholarships. National winners are selected from among the 1st place state winners. National winners receive scholarships in the following amounts: first place $10,000; second $5,000; third $2,500. National amount includes state award. First-place state winners invited to an expenses-paid awards program in Washington, DC in June. Judging is conducted by education professionals from across the country and by the board of directors of the United States Institute of Peace. "All submissions become property of the U.S. Institute of Peace to use at its discretion and without royalty or any limitation. Students grades 9-12 in the U.S., its territories and overseas schools may submit essays for review by completing the application process. U.S. citizenship required for students attending overseas schools. National winning essays will be published by the U.S. Institute of Peace."

NATIONAL WRITERS ASSOCIATION NONFICTION CONTEST

(303)841-0246. Fax: (303)841-2607. E-mail: natlwrit ersassn@hotmail.com. Website: www.nationalwrit ers.com. 10940 S. Parker Rd.#508, Parker CO 80134. (303)841-0246. **Executive Director:** Sandy Whelchel. Annual contest. Estab. 1971. Purpose of contest: "to encourage and recognize those who excel in nonfiction writing." Submissions made by author. Deadline for entries: December 31. SASE for contest rules and entry forms. Entry fee is $18. Awards 3 cash prizes; choice of books; Honorable Mention Certificate. "Two people read each entry; third party picks three top winners from top five." Judging sheets sent if entry accompanied by SASE. Condensed version of 1st place may be published in *Authorship*. **Contact:** Sandy Whelchel, director. Deadline: December 31. Prize: 1st Place: $200; 2nd Place: $100; 3rd Place: $50.

JOHN NEWBERY MEDAL

Association for Library Service to Children, Division of the American Library Association, 50 E. Huron, Chicago, IL 60611. (800)545-2433, ext. 2153. Fax: (312)280-5271 E-mail:library@ala.org. Website: www. ala.org. Annual award. Estab. 1922. Purpose of award: to recognize the most distinguished contribution to American children's literature published in the U.S. Previously published submissions only; must be published prior to year award is given. Deadline for entries: December 31. SASE for award rules. Entries not returned. No entry fee. Medal awarded at Caldecott/ Newbery banquet during ALA annual conference. Judging by Newbery Award Selection Committee.

NEW ENGLAND BOOK AWARDS

New England Independent Booksellers Association, 297 Broadway, #212, Arlington MA 02474. (781)316-8894. Fax: (781)316-2605. E-mail: nan@ neba.org. Website: www.newenglandbooks.org/De fault.aspx?pageId=234046. Annual award. Previously published submissions only. Submissions made by New England booksellers; publishers. "Award is given to a specific title, fiction, nonfiction, children's. The titles must be either about New England, set in New England or by an author residing in New England. The titles must be hardcover, paperback orginal or reissue that was published between September 1 and August 31. Entries must be still in print and available. No entry fee. Judging by NEIBA membership. Requirements for entrants: Author/illustrator must live in New England. Submit written nominations only; actual books should not be sent. Member bookstores receive materials to display winners' books. Submission deadline: July 2. **Contact:** Nan Sorenson, assistant exec. director.

NEW VOICES AWARD

Website: www.leeandlow.com. **Open to students.** Annual award. Estab. 2000. Purpose of contest: To encourage writers of color to enter the world of children's books. Lee & Low Books is one of the few minority-owned publishing companies in the country. We have published more than 90 first-time writers and illustrators. Winning titles include *The Blue Roses*, winner of a Patterson Prize for Books for Young People, *Janna and the Kings*, an IRA Children's Book Award Notable, and *Sixteen Years in Sixteen Seconds*, selected for the Texas Bluebonnet Award Masterlist. Submissions made by author. Deadline for entries: September 30. SASE for contest rules or visit website. No entry fee. Awards New Voices Award—$1,000 prize and standard publication contract (regardless of whether or not writer has an agent) along with an advance against royalties; New Voices Honor Award—$500 prize. Judging by Lee & Low editors. Restrictions of media for illustrators: The author must be a writer of color who is a resident of the U.S. and who has not previously published a children's picture book. For additional information, send SASE or visit Lee & Low's website (www.leeandlow.com/p/new_voic es_award.mhtml).

NORTH AMERICAN INTERNATIONAL AUTO SHOW HIGH SCHOOL POSTER CONTEST

Detroit Auto Dealers Association, 1900 W. Big Beaver Rd., Troy MI 48084-3531. (248)643-0250. Fax: (248)283-5148. E-mail: sherp@dada.org. Website: www.naias.com. **Open to students.** Annual contest. Submissions made by the author and illustrator. Contact: Detroit Auto Dealers Association (DADA) for contest rules and entry forms or retrieve rules from website. No entry fee. Awards in the High School Poster Contest are as follows: Chairman's Award— $1,000; State Farm Insurance Award—$1,000; Designer's Best of Show (Digital and Traditional)—$500; Best Theme—$250; Best Use of Color—$250; Most Creative—$250. A winner will be chosen in each category from grades 10, 11 and 12. Prizes: 1st place in 10, 11, 12—$500; 2nd place—$250; 3rd place—$100. The winners of the Designer's Best of Show Digital and Traditional will each receive $500. The winner of the Chairman's Award will receive $1,000. Entries will be judged by an independent panel of recognized representatives of the art community. Entrants must be Michigan high school students enrolled in grades 10-12. Winning posters may be displayed at the NAIAS 2012 and reproduced in the official NAIAS program, which is available to the public, international media, corporate executives and automotive suppliers. Winning posters may also be displayed on the official NAIAS website at the sole discretion of the NAIAS. Deadline: November 2011.

NORTHERN CALIFORNIA BOOK AWARDS

c/o Poetry Flash, 1450 Fourth St. #4, Berkeley CA 94710. (510)525-5476. E-mail: editor@poetryflash. org. Website: www.poetryflash.org. **Contact:** Joyce Jenkins. Annual Northern California Book Award for outstanding book in literature, open to books published in the current calendar year by Northern California authors. Annual award. NCBR presents annual awards to Bay Area (northern California) authors annually in fiction, nonfiction, poetry and children's literature. Purpose is to encourage writers and stimulate interest in books and reading." Previously published books only. Must be published the calendar year prior to spring awards ceremony. Submissions nominated by publishers; author or agent could also nominate published work. No entry forms. Send 3 copies of the book to attention: NCBR. No entry fee. Awards $100 honorarium and award certificate. Judging by voting members of the Northern California Book Reviewers. Books that reach the "finals" (usually 3-5 per category) displayed at annual award ceremonies (spring). Nominated books are displayed and sold at the Northern California Book Awards in the spring of each year; the winner is asked to read at the San Francisco Public Library's Main Branch. **Contact:** Joyce Jenkins, exec. director. (Specialized: Northern California). Purpose is to recognize "the best of Northern California (from Fresno north) fiction, poetry, nonfiction, and children's literature, as chosen by the Northern California Book Reviewers Association." Deadline: Dec. 1.

OHIOANA BOOK AWARDS

Ohioana Library Association, 274 E. 1st Ave., Suite 300, Columbus OH 43201-3673. (614)466-3831. Fax: (614)728-6974. E-mail: ohioana@ohioana.org. Website: www.ohioana.org. Offered annually to bring national attention to Ohio authors and their books, published in the last 2 years. (Books can only be considered once.) Categories: Fiction, nonfiction, juvenile, poetry, and books about Ohio or an Ohioan. Writers must have been born in Ohio or lived in Ohio for at least 5 years, but books about Ohio or an Ohioan need not be written by an Ohioan. Prize: certificate and glass sculpture. Judged by a jury selected by librarians, book reviewers, writers and other knowledgeable people. Each winter the jury considers all books received since the previous jury. No entry fee. **Deadline: December 31.** A copy of the book must be received by the Ohioana Library by December 31 prior to the year the award is given; literary quality of the book must be outstanding. No entry forms are needed, but they are available July 1 of each year. Specific questions should be sent to Ohioana. Results announced in August or September. Winners notified by mail in May. **Contact:** Linda Hengst, executive director.

OKLAHOMA BOOK AWARDS

Oklahoma Center for the Book, 200 NE 18th, Oklahoma City OK 73105. (405)521-2502. Fax: (405)525-7804. E-mail: carmstrong@oltn.odl.state.ok.us. Website: www.odl.state.ok.us/ocb. **Executive Director:** Connie Armstrong. Annual award. Estab. 1989. Purpose of award: "to honor Oklahoma writers and books about our state." Previously published submissions only. Submissions made by the author, author's agent, or entered by a person or group of people, including the publisher. Must be published during the calendar year preceding the award. Awards are presented to best books in fiction, nonfiction, children's, design and illustration, and poetry books about Oklahoma or books written by an author who was born, is living or has lived in Oklahoma. Deadline for entries: early January. SASE for award rules and entry forms. Entry fee $25. Awards a medal—no cash prize. Judging by a panel of 5 people for each category—a librarian, a working writer in the genre, booksellers, editors, etc. Requirements for entrants: author must be an Oklahoma native, resident, former resident or have written a book with Oklahoma theme. Winner will be announced at banquet in Oklahoma City. The Arrell Gibson Lifetime Achievement Award is also presented each year for a body of work.

ONCE UPON A WORLD CHILDREN'S BOOK AWARD

Simon Wiesenthal Center and Museum of Tolerance Library and Archives, 1399 S. Roxbury Dr., Los Angeles, CA 90035-4709. (310)772-7605. Fax: (310)772-7628. E-mail: bookaward@wiesenthal.net. Website: www.wiesenthal.com/library. **Award Director**: Adaire J. Klein. Submit 4 copies of each entry to: Adaire J. Klein, director of library and archival services. Annual award. Estab. 1996. Submissions made by publishers, author or author's agent. Suggestions from educators, libraries, and others accepted. Must be published January-December of previous year. Deadline for entries: March 31. SASE for contest rules and entry forms. Awards $1,000 each to two authors honoring a book for children age 6-10 and one for age 11 and up. Recognition of Honor Books if deemed appropriate. Judging is by 6 independent judges familiar with children's literature. Award open to any writer with work in English language on subjects of tolerance, diversity, human understanding, and social justice. Book Seals available from the library.

ORBIS PICTUS AWARD FOR OUTSTANDING NONFICTION FOR CHILDREN

The National Council of Teachers of English, 1111 W. Kenyon Rd., Urbana IL 61801-1096. (217)328-3870. Fax: (217)328-0977. E-mail: dzagorski@ncte.org. Website: www.ncte.org/awards/orbispictus. **Chair, NCTE Committee on the Orbis Pictus Award for Outstanding Nonfiction for Children:** Fran Wilson, Cincinnati, OH. Annual award. Estab. 1989. Purpose of award: To promote and recognize excellence in the writing of nonfiction for children. Previously published submissions only. Submissions made by author, author's agent, by a person or group of people. Must be published January 1-December 31 of contest year. Deadline for entries: December 31. Call for award information. No entry fee. Awards a plaque given at the NCTE Elementary Section Luncheon at the NCTE Annual Convention in November. Judging by a committee. "The name Orbis Pictus commemorates the work of Johannes Amos Comenius, 'Orbis Pictus—The World in Pictures' (1657), considered to be the first book actually planned for children."

OREGON BOOK AWARDS

Literary Arts, 224 NW 13th Ave., Ste. 306, Portland OR 97209. (503)227-2583. E-mail: susan@literary-arts.org. Website: www.literary-arts.org. The annual Oregon Book Awards celebrate Oregon authors in the areas of poetry, fiction, nonfiction, drama and young readers' literature published between August 1, 2010 and July 31, 2011. Prize: Finalists are invited on a statewide reading tour and are promoted in bookstores and libraries across the state. Judged by writers who are selected from outside Oregon for their expertise in a genre. Past judges include Mark Doty, Colson Whitehead and Kim Barnes. Entry fee determined by initial print run; see website for details. Deadline: last Friday in August. Entries must be previously published. Oregon residents only. Accepts inquiries by phone and e-mail. Finalists announced in January. Winners announced at an awards ceremony in November. List of winners available in April. **Contact:** Susan Denning.

THE ORIGINAL ART

128 E. 63rd St., New York NY 10065. (212)838-2560. Fax: (212)838-2561. E-mail: kim@societyillustrators.org; info@societyillustrators.org. Website: www.societyillustrators.org. **Contact**: Kate Feirtag, exhibition director. Annual contest. Estab. 1981. Purpose of contest: to celebrate the fine art of children's book illustration. Previously published submissions only. Deadline for entries: July 18. Request "call for entries" to receive contest rules and entry forms. Entry fee is $30/book. Judging by seven professional artists and editors. Works will be displayed at the Society of Illustrators Museum of American Illustration in New York City October-November annually. Medals awarded; catalog published.

HELEN KEATING OTT AWARD FOR OUTSTANDING CONTRIBUTION TO CHILDREN'S LITERATURE

Church and Synagogue Library Association, 2920 SW Dolph Ct Ste 3A, Portland OR 97219. (503)244-6919. Fax: (503)977-3734. E-mail: csla@worldaccessnet.com. Website: www.cslainfo.org. **Chair of Committee:** Jeri Baker. Annual award. Estab. 1980. "This award is given to a person or organization that has made a significant contribution to promoting high moral and ethical values through children's literature." Deadline for entries: April 1. "Recipient is honored in July during the conference." Awards certificate of recognition, the awards banquet, and one night's stay in the hotel. "A nomination for an award may be made by anyone. An application form is available by contacting Judy Janzen, administrator of CSLA, via e-mail at csla@worldaccessnet.com or by calling 1-800-LIB-CSLA. Elements of creativity and innovation will be given high priority by the judges." **Contact:** Jeri Baker, Chair of Committee.

PATERSON PRIZE FOR BOOKS FOR YOUNG PEOPLE

One College Blvd., Paterson NJ 07505-1179. (973)523-6085. Fax: (973)523-6085. E-mail: mgillan@pccc.edu. Website: www.pccc.edu/poetry. Part of the Poetry Center's mission is "to recognize excellence in books for young people." Published submissions only. Submissions made by author, author's agent or publisher. Must be published between January 1-December 31 of year previous to award year. Deadline for entries: March 15. SASE for contest rules and entry forms or visit website. Awards $500 for the author in either of 3 categories: PreK-Grade 3; Grades 4-6, Grades 7-12. Judging by a professional writer selected by the Poetry Center. Contest is open to any writer/illustrator. **Contact:** Maria Mazziotti Gillan, exec. director. Deadline: March 15. Prize: $500 in each category.

PENNSYLVANIA YOUNG READERS' CHOICE AWARDS PROGRAM

148 S. Bethelehem Pike, Ambler PA 19002-5822. (215)643-5048. E-mail: bellavance@verizon.net. Website: http://www.psla.org. **Coordinator:** Jean B. Bellavance. Annual award. Estab. 1991. Submissions nominated by a person or group. Must be published within 5 years of the award—for example, books published in 2007 to present are eligible for the 2011-2012

award. Deadline for entries: September 1. SASE for contest rules and entry forms. No entry fee. Framed certificate to winning authors. Judging by children of Pennsylvania (they vote). Requirements for entrants: currently living in North America. Reader's Choice Award is to promote reading of quality books by young people in the Commonwealth of Pennsylvania, to promote teacher and librarian involvement in children's literature, and to honor authors whose work has been recognized by the children of Pennsylvania. Four awards are given, one for each of the following grade level divisions: K-3, 3-6, 6-8, YA. View information at the Pennsylvania School Librarians website.

PEN/PHYLLIS NAYLOR WORKING WRITER FELLOWSHIP

PEN, 588 Broadway, New York NY 10012. (212)334-1660, ext. 108. Fax: (212)334-2181. E-mail: awards@pen.org. Website: www.pen.org. Submit entries to: awards coordinator. Must have published 2 books for children or young adults to be eligible. Annual contest. Estab. 2001. To support writers with a financial need and recognize work of high literary caliber. Unpublished submissions only. Submissions nominated. Deadline for entries: Feb. 3, 2011. Awards $5,000. Upon nomination by an editor or fellow writer, a panel of judges will select the winning book. Open to a writer of children's or young adult fiction in financial need, who has published at least two books. Please visit our website for full guidelines. **Contact:** Nick Burd, awards program director.

PLEASE TOUCH MUSEUM BOOK AWARD

Please Touch Museum, Memorial Hall in Fairmont Park, 4231 Avenue of the Republic, Philadelphia, PA 19131. (215)578-3153. Fax: (215)578-5171. E-mail: brafter@pleasetouchmuseum.org. Website: www.pleasetouchmuseum.org/events/special_events_awards/ptm_book_awards. **Contact:** Brian Rafter. Annual award. Estab. 1985. Purpose of the award: "to recognize and encourage the publication of high-quality books for young children. The award is given to books that are imaginative, exceptionally illustrated, and help to foster a child's life-long love of reading. Each year, the museum selects one winner in two age categories— ages 3 and under and ages 4 to 7. These age categories reflect the age of the children Please Touch Museum serves. To be eligible for consideration, a book must: (1) Be distinguished in text, illustration, and ability to explore and clarify an idea for young children (ages 7 and under). (2) Be published within the last year by an American publisher. (3) Be by an American author and/or illustrator." SASE for award rules and entry forms. No entry fee. Publishing date deadlines apply. Judging by jury of select museum staff, children's literature experts, librarians, and early childhood educators. Please Touch Museum's Kid's Store purchases books for selling at Annual Book Award Ceremony and throughout the year. Winning author autographing sessions may be held at Please Touch Museum, and at the Delaware Valley Association for the Education of Young Children' Annual Conference in Philadelphia.

PNWA LITERARY CONTEST

PMB 2717-1420 NW Gilman Blvd, Ste 2, Issaquah WA 98027. (425)673-2665. Fax: (206)824-4559. E-mail: staff@pnwa.org. Website: www.pnwa.org. **Open to students.** Annual contest. Purpose of contest: "Valuable tool for writers as contest submissions are critiqued (2 critiques)." Unpublished submissions only. Submissions made by author. Deadline for entries: February 18, 2011. Entry fee is $35/entry for members, $50/entry for nonmembers. Awards $700-1st; $300-2nd. Awards in all 12 categories. **Contact:** Kelli Liddane.

POCKETS FICTION-WRITING CONTEST

P.O. Box 340004, Nashville TN 37203-0004. E-mail: pockets@upperroom.org;theupperroommagazine@ upperroom.org. Website: www.pockets.upperroom. org. Upper Room Publications, P.O. Box 340004, Nashville TN 37203-0004. (615) 340-7333. Fax: (615) 340-7267. **Contact:** Lynn W. Gilliam, senior editor. *Pockets* is a devotional magazine for children between the ages of 6 and 11. Contest offered annually for unpublished work to discover new children's writers. Prize: $1,000 and publication in *Pockets*. Categories: short stories. Judged by *Pockets* staff and staff of other Upper Room Publications. No entry fee. Guidelines available on website or send #10 SASE. **Deadline: Must be postmarked between March 1-August 15.** Entries must be unpublished. Because the purpose of the contest is to discover new writers, previous winners are not eligible. No violence, science fiction, romance, fantasy or talking animal stories. Word length 1,000-1,600 words. Open to any writer. Winner announced November 1 and notified by U.S. mail. Contest submissions accompanied by SASE will be returned Nov. 1. "Send SASE with 4 first-class stamps to request guidelines and a past issue, or go to: http:// pockets.upperroom.org." We do not accept manuscripts sent by fax or e-mail. Purpose of contest is to discover new children's fiction writers.

EDGAR ALLAN POE AWARD

1140 Broadway, Suite 1507, New York NY 10001. E-mail: mwa@mysterywriters.org. Website: www.mysterywriters.org. Mystery Writers of America, Inc. Work must be published/produced the year of the contest. Purpose of the award: to honor authors of distinguished works in the mystery field. Previously published submissions only. Submissions made by the author, author's agent; "normally by the publisher." Submission information can be found at: www.mysterywriters.org. No entry fee. Judging by professional members of Mystery Writers of America (writers). Nominee press release sent in mid-January. Winner announced at the Edgar® Awards Banquet, held in late April/early May. **Deadline:** Must be received by Nov. 30. Prize: Awards ceramic bust of "Edgar" for winner; scrolls for all nominees.

MICHAEL L. PRINTZ AWARD

Young Adult Library Services Association, Division of the American Library Association, 50 E. Huron, Chicago IL 60611. Fax: (312)280-5276. E-mail: yalsa@ ala.org. Website: www.ala.org/yalsa/printz. Annual award. The Michael L. Printz Award is an award for a book that exemplifies literary excellence in young adult literature. It is named for a Topeka, Kansas school librarian who was a long-time active member of the Young Adult Library Services Association. It will be selected annually by an award committee that can also name as many as 4 honor books. The award-winning book can be fiction, nonfiction, poetry or an anthology, and can be a work of joint authorship or editorship. The books must be published between January 1 and December 31 of the preceding year and be designated by its publisher as being either a young adult book or one published for the age range that YALSA defines as young adult, e.g. ages 12 through 18. The deadline for both committee and field nominations will be December 1.

PURPLE DRAGONFLY BOOK AWARDS

4696 W. Tyson St., Chandler AZ 85226-2903. (480)940-8182. Fax: (480)940-8787. E-mail: info@fivestarpublications.com. Website: www.fivestarpublications.com; www.fivestarbookawards.com. **Contact:** Lynda Exley, contest coordinator. The awards are open to books published in any calendar year and in any country that are available for purchase. Books entered must be printed in English. Traditionally published, partnership published and self-published books are permitted, as long as they fit the above criteria. E-books are not permitted; although, Five Star does have plans for an e-book contest in the future, so please check www.FiveStar BookAwards.com periodically for notification of contest launch. Final deadline for submissions is May 1, 2012; to be eligible, submissions must be postmarked May 1, 2012 or earlier. The deadline is the same each year. Submissions postmarked March 1, 2012 or earlier that meet all submission requirements are eligible for the Early Bird reward: a free copy of "The Economical Guide to Self-Publishing" or "Promote Like a Pro: Small Budget, Big Show." Prize: The grand prize winner will receive a $300 cash prize, 100 foil award seals (more can be ordered for an extra charge), one hour of marketing consultation from Five Star Publications and $100 worth of Five Star Publications' titles, as well as publicity on Five Star Publications' websites and inclusion in a winners' news release sent to a comprehensive list of media outlets. The grand prize winner will also be placed in the Five Star Dragonfly Book Awards virtual bookstore with a thumbnail of the book's cover, price, one-sentence description and link to Amazon.com for purchasing purposes, if applicable. First place: All first place winners of categories will be put into a drawing for a $100 prize. In addition, each first place winner in each category receives a certificate commemorating their accomplishment, 25 foil award seals (more can be ordered for an extra charge) and mention on Five Star Publications' websites. Our judges are industry experts with specific knowledge about the categories over which they preside. Being honored with a Purple Dragonfly Award confers credibility upon the winner, as well as provides positive publicity to further their success. The goal of these awards is to give published authors the recognition they deserve and provide a helping hand to further their careers.

QUILL AND SCROLL INTERNATIONAL WRITING/PHOTO CONTEST

Quill and Scroll, School of Journalism and Mass Communication, University of Iowa, Iowa City IA 52242-2004. (319)335-3457. Fax: (319)335-3989. E-mail: quill-scroll@uiowa.edu. Website: www.uiowa.

edu/~quill-sc. **Open to students.** Annual contest. Previously published submissions only. Submissions made by the author or school newspaper adviser. Must be published within the last year. Deadline for entries: February 5. Visit website for more information and entry forms. Entry fee is $2/entry. Engraved plaque awarded to sweepstakes winners. Judging by various judges. *Quill and Scroll* acquires the right to publish submitted material in its magazine or website if it is chosen as a winning entry. Requirements for entrants: must be students in grades 9-12 for high school division. Entry form available on website. **Contact:** Vanessa Shelton. Prize: Winners will receive *Quill and Scroll*'s National Award Gold Key and, if seniors, are eligible to apply for one of the scholarships offered by *Quill and Scroll*. All winning entries are automatically eligible for the International Writing and Photo Sweepstakes Awards. Engraved plaque awarded to sweepstakes winners. Judged by various judges.

🕒 RED HOUSE CHILDREN'S BOOK AWARD

Federation of Children's Book Groups, 2 Bridge Wood View, Horsforth, Leeds, West Yorkshire LS18 5PE, England. (44)(113)258-8910. E-mail: marianne adey@aol.com. Website: www.redhousechildrensboo kaward.co.uk. Purpose of the award: "The R.H.C.B.A. is an annual prize for the best children's book of the year judged by the children themselves." Categories: (I) books for younger children, (II) books for younger readers, (III) books for older readers. Estab. 1980. Works must be published in the United Kingdom. **Deadline for entries**: December 31. SASE or e-mail for rules. Entries not returned. Awards "a magnificent silver and oak trophy worth over €6,000." Silver dishes to each category winner. Portfolios of children's work to all Top Ten authors and illustrators. Judging by children. Requirements for entrants: Work must be fiction and published in the UK during the current year (poetry is ineligible). Top 50 Books of the year will be published in current "Pick of the Year" publication.

TOMÁS RIVERA MEXICAN AMERICAN CHILDREN'S BOOK AWARD

Texas State University-San Marcos, EDU, 601 University Dr., San Marcos TX 78666-4613. (512)245-3839. Fax: (512)245-7911. E-mail: JesseGainer@txstate. edu. Website: www.education.txstate.edu/depart ments/Tomas-Rivera-Book-Award-Project-Link.

html. **Award Director:** Dr. Jesse Gainer. Competition open to adults. Annual contest. Estab. 1995. Purpose of award: "To encourage authors, illustrators and publishers to produce books that authentically reflect the lives of Mexican Americans appropriate for children and young adults in the United States." Unpublished mss not accepted. Submissions made by "any interested individual or publishing company." Must be published during the two years prior to the year of consideration for the appropriate category "Works for Younger Children" or " Works for Older Children." **Deadline for entries:** November 1 of publication year. Contact Dr. Jesse Gainer for information and send copy of book. No entry fee. Awards $2,000 per book. Judging of nominations by a regional committee, national committee judges finalists. Annual ceremony honoring the book and author/illustrator is held during the fall at Texas State University-San Marcos in collaboration with the Texas Book Festival. **Contact:** Dr. Jesse Gainer, Director. Judging of nominations by a regional committee, national committee judges finalists.

ROCKY MOUNTAIN BOOK AWARD: ALBERTA CHILDREN'S CHOICE BOOK AWARD

Rocky Mountain Book Award Committee, Box 42, Lethbridge AB T1J 3Y3 Canada. (403)381-0855. E-mail: rockymountainbookaward@shaw.ca. Website: http://rmba.lethsd.ab.ca. **Contest Director:** Michelle Dimnik. Submit entries to: Richard Chase, board member. *Open to students.* Annual contest. Estab. 2001. Purpose of contest: "Reading motivation for students, promotion of Canadian authors, illustrators and publishers." Previously unpublished submissions only. Submissions made by author's agent or nominated by a person or group. SASE for contest rules and entry forms. No entry fee. Awards: Gold medal and author tour of selected Alberta schools. Judging by students. Requirements for entrants: Canadian authors and illustrators only.

ROYAL DRAGONFLY BOOK AWARDS

4696 W. Tyson St., Chandler AZ 85226-2903. (480)940-8182. Fax: (480)940-8787. E-mail: info@fivestarpublications.com. Website: www.fivestarpublications.com; www.fivestarbookawards.com; www.royaldragonfly bookawards.com. **Contact:** Lynda Exley. No publication date limit for entries as long as the book is still in print. Deadline: February 1. Prize: Grand Prize: $300, plus other recognition. First Place: $100, plus other prizes. Second Place: Certificate. Judged by industry experts with specific knowledge about the categories over which they preside. No rights to submitted material are acquired when writers enter work for this contest.

SASKATCHEWAN CHILDREN'S LITERATURE AWARD

Saskatchewan Book Awards, 205B-2314 11th Avenue, Regina SK S4P 0K1 Canada. (306)569-1585. Fax: (306)569-4187. E-mail: director@bookawards.sk.ca. Website: www.bookawards.sk.ca. **Book Submissions:** Jacki Lay, exec. director. Open to Saskatchewan authors only. Annual award. Estab. 1995. Purpose of contest: to celebrate Saskatchewan books and authors and to promote their work. Previously published submissions only. Submissions made by author, author's agent or publisher by September 15, 2010-October 31, 2011. SASE for contest rules and entry forms. Entry fee is $25 (Canadian). Awards $2,000 (Canadian). Judging by three children's literature authors outside of Saskatchewan. Requirements for entrants: Must be Saskatchewan resident; book must have ISBN number; book must have been published within the last year. Award-winning book will appear on TV talk shows and be pictured on bookmarks distributed to libraries, schools and bookstores in Saskatchewan. **Contact:** Jackie Lay, executive director, book submissions. Deadline: November 1, 2011.

SCBWI MAGAZINE MERIT AWARDS

Website: www.scbwi.org. **Award Coordinator:** Stephanie Gordon. Annual award. Estab. 1988. Purpose of the award: "to recognize outstanding original magazine work for young people published during that year and having been written or illustrated by members of SCBWI." Previously published submissions only. Entries must be submitted between January 1 and December 15 of the year of publication. For rules and procedures see website. No entry fee. Must be a SCBWI member. Awards plaques and honor certificates for each of 4 categories (fiction, nonfiction, illustration, poetry). Judging by a magazine editor and two "full" SCBWI members. "All magazine work for young people by an SCBWI member—writer, artist or photographer—is eligible during the year of original publication. In the case of co-authored work, both authors must be SCBWI members. Members must submit their own work." Requirements for entrants: 4 copies each of the published work and proof of publication (may be contents page) showing the name of the magazine and the date of issue. The SCBWI is a professional organization of writers and illustrators and others interested in children's literature. Membership is open to the general public at large.

SCBWI WORK-IN-PROGRESS GRANTS

Society of Children's Book Writers and Illustrators, 8271 Beverly Blvd., Los Angeles CA 90048. (323)782-1010. Fax: (323)782-1892. E-mail: scbwi@scbwi.org. Website: www.scbwi.org. Annual award. "The SCBWI Work-in-Progress Grants have been established to assist children's book writers in the completion of a specific project." Four categories: (1) General Work-in-Progress Grant. (2) Grant for a Contemporary Novel for Young People. (3) Nonfiction Research Grant. (4) Grant for a Work Whose Author Has Never Had a Book Published. Requests for applications may be made beginning October 1. Completed applications accepted February 1-April 1 of each year. SASE for applications for grants. In any year, an applicant may apply for any of the grants except the one awarded for a work whose author has never had a book published. (The recipient of this grant will be chosen from entries in all categories.) Five grants of $1,500 will be awarded annually. Runner-up grants of $500 (one in each category) will also be awarded. "The grants are available to both full and associate members of the SCBWI. They are not available for projects on which there are already contracts." Previous recipients not eligible to apply.

SKIPPING STONES BOOK AWARDS

Skipping Stones, P.O. Box 3939, Eugene OR 97403-0939. (541)342-4956. E-mail: editor@skippingstones.org. Website: www.skippingstones.org. Open to published books, publications/magazines, educational videos, and DVDs. Annual awards since 1994. Purpose of contest: To recognize exceptional, literary and artistic contributions to juvenile/children's literature, as well as teaching resources and educational audio/video resources in the areas of multicultural awareness, nature and ecology, social issues, peace and nonviolence. Submissions made by the author or publishers and/or producers. **Deadline for entries**: February 1. Send request for contest rules and entry forms or visit website. Entry fee is $50; 50% discount for small nonprofit publishers. Each year, an honor roll of about 20 to 25 books and A/V with teaching resources are selected by a multicultural selection committee of editors, students, parents,

teachers and librarians. Winners receive gold honor award seals, attractive honor certificates and publicity via multiple outlets. Many educational publications announce the winners of our book awards. The reviews of winning books and educational videos/DVDs are published in the May-August issue of *Skipping Stones* (and/or on our website), now in its 23rd year.

SKIPPING STONES YOUTH HONOR AWARDS

P.O. Box 3939, Eugene OR 97403-0939. (541)342-4956. E-mail: editor@SkippingStones.org. Website: www.SkippingStones.org. **Open to students.** Annual awards. Purpose of contest: "to recognize youth, 7 to 17, for their contributions to multicultural awareness, nature and ecology, social issues, peace and nonviolence. Also to promote creativity, self-esteem and writing skills and to recognize important work being done by youth organizations." Submissions made by the author. **Deadline for entries**: June 25. SASE for contest rules or download from www.skippingstones.org/youthhonor-02.htm. Entries must include certificate of originality by a parent and/or teacher and a cover letter that included cultural background information on the author. Submissions can either be mailed or e-mailed. Entry fee is $3 fee is waived for low-income students. Everyone who enters the contest receives the September-October issue featuring Youth Awards. Judging by *Skipping Stones* staff. "Up to ten awards are given in three categories: (1) Compositions—(essays, poems, short stories, songs, travelogues, etc.) should be typed (double-spaced) or neatly handwritten. Fiction or nonfiction should be limited to 1,000 words; poems to 30 lines. Non-English writings are also welcome. (2) Artwork—(drawings, cartoons, paintings or photo essays with captions) should have the artist's name, age and address on the back of each page. Send the originals with SASE. Black & white photos are especially welcome. Limit: 8 pieces. (3) Youth Organizations—Tell us how your club or group works to: (a) preserve the nature and ecology in your area, (b) enhance the quality of life for low-income, minority or disabled or (c) improve racial or cultural harmony in your school or community. Use the same format as for compositions." The winners are published in the September-October issue of *Skipping Stones*. Now in its 23rd year, *Skipping Stones* is a winner of N.A.M.E.EDPRESS, Newsstand Resources and Parent's Choice Awards.

KAY SNOW WRITERS' CONTEST

9045 SW Barbur Blvd. #5A, Portland OR 97219-4027. (503)452-1592. Fax: (503)452-0372. E-mail: wilwrite@teleport.com. Website: www.willamettewriters.com. Annual contest. **Open to students.** Purpose of contest: "to encourage beginning and established writers to continue the craft." Unpublished, original submissions only. Submissions made by the author. **Deadline for entries**: April 23rd. SASE for contest rules and entry forms. Entry fee is $10, Williamette Writers' members; $15, nonmembers; free for student writers grades 1-12. Awards cash prize of $300 per category (fiction, nonfiction, juvenile, poetry, script writing), $50 for students in three divisions: 1-5, 6-8, 9-12. Judges are anonymous. **Contact:** Lizzy Shannon, contest director. Purpose of contest is "to encourage beginning and established writers to continue the craft."

SOUTHWEST WRITERS

3721 Morris NE, Suite A, Albuquerque NM 87111. (505)265-9485. Fax: (505)265-9483. E-mail: swwriters@juno.com. Website: www.southwestwriters.org. Non-profit organization dedicated to helping members of all levels in their writing. Members enjoy perks such as networking with professional and aspiring writers; substantial discounts on mini-conferences, workshops, writing classes, and annual and quarterly SWW writing contest; monthly newsletter; two writing programs per month; critique groups, critique service (also for nonmembers); discounts at bookstores and other businesses; and website linking. Cost of membership: Individual, $60/year, $100/2 years; Two People, $50 each/year; Student, $40/year; Student under 18, $25/year; Outside U.S.$65/year; Lifetime, $750. See website for information. Submit first 20 pages and 1 page synopsis (using industry-standard formatting, Courier font, brad-bound). **Deadline**: May 1-May 16. Prize: Up to $1,000 grand prize. All mss will be screened by a panel and the top 10 in each category will be sent to appropriate editors or literary agents to determine the final top 3 places. The top 3 winners will also receive a critique from the judging editor or literary agent. Contacting any judge about an entry is an automatic disqualification. 12. Entrants retain all rights to their entries. By entering this contest, you agree to abide by the rules, agree that decisions by the judges are final, and agree that no refunds will be awarded.

SOUTHWEST WRITERS ANNUAL CONTEST

SouthWest Writers, 3721 Morris NE, Suite A, Albuquerque NM 87111. (505)265-9485. Website: www.southwestwriters.com. Submit entries to: Contest Chair. **Open to adults and students.** Annual contest. Estab. 1982. Purpose of contest: to encourage writers of all genres. Also offers mini-conferences, critique service, (for $60/year, offers 2 monthly programs, monthly newsletter, annual writing and bi-monthly writing contests, other workshops, various discount perks, website linking, e-mail addresses, classes and critique service (open to nonmembers). See website for more information or call or write.

➕ SYDNEY TAYLOR BOOK AWARD

Association of Jewish Libraries, P.O. Box 1118, Teaneck, NJ 07666. (212)725-5359. E-mail: chair@sydney taylorbookaward.org. Website: www.sydneytaylor bookaward.org. **Contact:** Barbara Bietz, chair. Offered annually for work published during the current year. "Given to distinguished contributions to Jewish literature for children. One award for younder readers, one for older readers, and one for teens." Publishers submit books. **Deadline**: December 31, but we cannot guarantee that books received after December 1 will be considered. Guidelines on website. Awards certificate, cash award, and gold or silver seals for cover of winning book.

SYDNEY TAYLOR MANUSCRIPT COMPETITION

Association of Jewish Libraries, 204 Park St., Montclair, NJ 07042. E-mail: stmacajl@aol.com. Website: www.jewishlibrarics.org. **Coordinator:** Aileen Grossberg. **Open to students** and to any unpublished writer of fiction. Annual contest. Estab. 1985. Purpose of the contest: "This competition is for unpublished writers of fiction. Material should be for readers ages 8-11, with universal appeal that will serve to deepen the understanding of Judaism for all children, revealing positive aspects of Jewish life." Unpublished submissions only. **Deadline for entries**: December 15. Download rules and forms from website. No entry fee. Awards $1,000. Award winner will be notified in April, and the award will be presented at the convention in June. Judging by qualified judges from within the Association of Jewish Libraries. Requirements for entrants: must be an unpublished fiction writer; also, books must range from 64-200 pages in length. "AJL assumes no responsibility for publication, but hopes this cash incentive will serve to encourage new writers of children's stories with Jewish themes for all children." **Contact:** Aileen Grossberg.

☺ THE TORONTO BOOK AWARDS

Website: http://www.toronto.ca/book_awards/index. htm. City of Toronto, 100 Queen St. W, 2nd Floor, West Tower, Toronto ON M5H 2N2 Canada. (416)392-4674. E-mail: bkurmey@toronto.ca. **Submit entries to:** Bev Kurmey, Protocol Officer. Annual award. Estab. 1974. Recognizes books of literary or artistic merit that are evocative of Toronto. Submissions made by author, author's agent or nominated by a person or group. Must be published the calendar year prior to the award year. **Deadline for entries:** last week day of March annually. Awards $15,000 in prize money. Judging by committee.

VEGETARIAN ESSAY CONTEST

The Vegetarian Resource Group, P.O. Box 1463, Baltimore MD 21203. (410)366-VEGE. Fax: (410)366-8804. E-mail: vrg@vrg.org. Website: www.vrg.org. Annual contest. **Open to students.** Estab. 1985. Purpose of contest: to promote vegetarianism in young people. Unpublished submissions only. **Deadline for entries**: May 1 of each year. SASE for contest rules and entry forms. No entry fee. Awards $50 savings bond. Judging by awards committee. Acquires right for The Vegetarian Resource Group to reprint essays. Requirements for entrants: age 18 and under. Winning works may be published in *Vegetarian Journal*, instructional materials for students. Submit 2-3 page essay on any aspect of vegetarianism, which is the abstinence of meat, fish and fowl. Entrants can base paper on interviewing, research or personal opinion. Need not be vegetarian to enter. To promote vegetarianism in young people.

VFW VOICE OF DEMOCRACY

Veterans of Foreign Wars of the U.S., 406 W. 34th St., Kansas City, MO 64111. (816)756-3390. E-mail: kharmer@vfw.org. Website: www.vfw.org. **Open to high school students.** Annual contest. Estab. 1960. Purpose of contest: to give high school students the opportunity to voice their opinions about their responsibility to our country and to convey those opinions via the broadcast media to all of America. **Deadline for entries**: November 1. No entry fee. Winners

receive awards ranging from $1,000-30,000. Requirements for entrants: "9th-12th grade students in public, parochial, private and home schools are eligible to compete. Former first place state winners are not eligible to compete again. Contact your participating high school teacher, counselor, our website www.vfw. org or your local VFW Post to enter."

VIRGINIA LIBRARY ASSOCIATION/ JEFFERSON CUP

Virginia Library Association, P.O. Box 56312, Virginia Beach, VA 23456. (757)507-1097. Fax: (757)447-3478. E-mail: hhinkle@bcps.k12.va.us. Website: www.vla. org. Award director changes year to year. Estab. 1983. Purpose of award "The Jefferson Cup honors a distinguished biography, historical fiction or American history book for young people. Presented since 1983, the Jefferson Cup Committee's goal is to promote reading about America's past; to encourage the quality writing of United States history, biography and historical fiction for young people and to recognize authors in these disciplines." Entries must be published in the year prior to selection. **Deadline for entries**: January 31. Additional information on the Jefferson Cup and criteria on making submissions is available on the VLA website. Judging by committee. The book must be about U.S. history or an American person, 1492 to present, or fiction that highlights the U.S. past; author must reside in the U.S. The book must be published especially for young people.

WESTERN HERITAGE AWARDS

National Cowboy & Western Heritage Museum, 1700 NE 63rd St., Oklahoma City, OK 73111-7997. (405)478-2250. Fax: (405)478-4714. E-mail: ssimpson@nationalcowboymuseum.org. Website: www.nationalcowboymuseum.org. **Contact:** Shayla Simpson. Annual award. Estab. 1961. Purpose of award: The WHA are presented annually to encourage the accurate and artistic telling of great stories of the West through 16 categories of western literature, television, film and music; including fiction, nonfiction, children's books and poetry. Previously published submissions only; must be published the calendar year before the awards are presented. **Deadline for literary entries**: November 30. **Deadline for film, music and television entries**: December 31. Entries not returned. Entry fee is $50/entry. Awards a Wrangler bronze sculpture designed by famed western artist, John Free. Judging by a panel of judges selected each year with distinction in various fields of western art and heritage. Requirements for entrants: The material must pertain to the development or preservation of the West, either from a historical or contemporary viewpoint. Literary entries must have been published between December 1 and November 30 of calendar year. Film, music or television entries must have been released or aired between January 1 and December 31 of calendar year of entry. Works recognized during special awards ceremonies held annually at the museum. There is an autograph party preceding the awards. Awards ceremonies are sometimes broadcast. **Contact:** Shayla Simpson, PR director.

JACKIE WHITE MEMORIAL NATIONAL CHILDREN'S PLAY WRITING CONTEST

1800 Nelwood, Columbia MO 65202-1447. (573)874-5628. E-mail: bybetsy@yahoo.com. Website: www.cectheatre.org. Send scripts to 309 Parkade Blvd., Columbia MO 65202. Annual contest. Estab. 1988. Purpose of contest: "To encourage writing of family-friendly scripts." Previously unpublished submissions only. Submissions made by author. **Deadline for entries**: June 1, 2011. SASE for contest rules and entry forms. Entry fee is $25. Awards $500 with production possible. Judging by current and past board members of CEC and by non-board members who direct plays at CEC. Play may be performed during the following season. We reserve the right to award 1st place and prize monies without a production. All submissions will be read by at least three readers. Author will receive a written evaluation of the script. **Contact:** Betsy Phillips, contest director.

WILLA LITERARY AWARD

(801)573-5309. E-mail: alicetrego@mac.com. Website: www.womenwritingthewest.org. **Contact:** Alice D. Trego, contest director. **Deadline:** February 1. Prize: Each winner receives $100 and a trophy. Each finalist receives a plaque. Award announcement is in early August, and awards are presented to the winners and finalists at the annual WWW Fall Conference. professional librarians not affiliated with WWW.

RITA WILLIAMS YOUNG ADULT PROSE PRIZE

National League of American Pen Women, Nob Hill, San Francisco Branch, 1544 Sweetwood Dr., Broadmoor Vlg. CA 94015-2029. E-mail: pennobhill@aol.com. Website: www.soulmakingcontest.us. **Contact:** Eileen Malone. **Open to students.** Up to 3,000 words in story, essay, journal entry, creative nonfiction or memoir by writers in grades 9-12. See judges online at website. Annual prize. **Deadline**: November 30. Guidelines for SASE or at www.soulmaking contest.us. Charges $5/entry (make checks payable to NLAPW, Nob Hill Branch). International entrants please send Travelers Check drawn on a USA bank. Prize: 1st Place: $100; 2nd Place: $50; 3rd Place: $25. Open to any writer in grade 9-12 or equivalent. No e-mail entries or those mailed special delivery, certified or registered will be accepted. Do enclose SASE in your entry package if you wish to receive contest results. **Contact:** Eileen Malone.

PAUL A. WITTY OUTSTANDING LITERATURE AWARD

International Reading Association, Special Interest Group, Reading for Gifted and Creative Learning, School of Education, Lamar University, P.O. Box 10034, Beaumont, TX 77710. (409)880-8046. Fax: (409)880-8384. E-mail: dorothy.sisk@lamar.edu. Website: www.reading.org. **Award Director:** Dorothy Sisk. **Open to students.** Annual award. Estab. 1979. Categories of entries: poetry/prose at elementary, junior high and senior high levels. Unpublished submissions only. **Deadline for entries**: February 1. SASE for award rules and entry forms. SASE for return of entries. No entry fee. Awards $25 and plaque, also certificates of merit. Judging by 2 committees for screening and awarding. "The elementary students' entries must be legible and may not exceed 1,000 words. Secondary students' prose entries should be typed and may exceed 1,000 words if necessary. At both elementary and secondary levels, if poetry is entered, a set of five poems must be submitted. All entries and requests for applications must include a self-addressed, stamped envelope."

PAUL A. WITTY SHORT STORY AWARD

(302)731-1600, ext. 229. Fax: (302)731-1057. E-mail: committees@reading.org. Website: www.reading.org. "The entry must be an original short story appearing in a young children's periodical for the first time. The short story should serve as a literary standard that encourages young readers to read periodicals." **Deadline for entries**: The entry must have been published for the first time in the eligibility year; the short story must be submitted during the calendar year of publication. Anyone wishing to nominate a short story should send it to the designated Paul A. Witty Short Award Committee by November 1. Award is $1,000 and recognition at the annual IRA Convention. **Deadline**: December 1.

ALICE WOOD MEMORIAL OHIOANA AWARD FOR CHILDREN'S LITERATURE

274 E. First Ave., Suite 300, Columbus OH 43201. (614)466-3831. Fax: (614)728-6974. E-mail: ohioana@ohioana.org. Website: www.ohioana.org. Offered to an author whose body of work has made, and continues to make, a significant contribution to literature for children or young adults and through their work as a writer, teacher, administrator, and community member, interest in children's literature has been encouraged and children have become involved with reading. Nomination forms for SASE. Recipient must have been born in Ohio or lived in Ohio at least 5 years. **Deadline**: December 31. Awards $1,000 cash prize. **Contact**: Linda R. Hengst.

WRITE IT NOW!

SmartWriters.com, 10823 Worthing Ave. San Diego CA 92126-2665. (858)689-2665. E-mail: editor@smartwriters.com. Website: www.SmartWriters.com. Estab. 1994. Annual contest. "Our purpose is to encourage new writers and help get their manuscripts into the hands of people who can help further their careers." Unpublished submissions only. Submissions made by author. **Deadline for entries**: May 1. SASE for contest rules and entry forms; also see website. Entry fee is $15 for initial entry, $10 for additional entries. Awards a cash prize, books about writing, and an editorial review of the winning manuscripts. Judging by published writers and editors. Requirement for entrants: "This contest is open to all writers age 18 and older. There are 5 categories: young adult, middle grade, picture book, nonfiction and illustration." See website for more details, FAQ and rules updates. **Contact**: Roxyanne Young, editorial director.

WRITERS-EDITORS NETWORK ANNUAL INTERNATIONAL WRITING COMPETITION

(formerly Florida State Writing Competition), CNW/FFWA, P.O. Box A, North Stratford NH 03590. (603)922-8338. Fax: (603)922-8339. E-mail: contest@writers-editors.com. Website: www.writers-editors.com. Annual contest. Estab. 1984. Categories include children's literature (length appropriate to age cat-

egory). Entry form online at website. Entry fee is $5 (members), $10 (nonmembers) or $10-20 for entries longer than 3,000 words. Awards $100 first prize, $75 second prize, $50 third prize, certificates for honorable mentions. Judging by librarians, editors and published authors. Judging criteria: interest and readability within age group, writing style and mechanics, originality, salability. **Deadline**: March 15. For copy of official entry form, send #10 SASE or visit website. List of winners on website. **Contact**: Dana K. Cassell, executive director.

WRITERS' LEAGUE OF TEXAS BOOK AWARDS

Writers' League of Texas, 611 S. Congress Ave. Suite 130, Austin TX 78704. (512)499-8914. Fax: (512)499-0441. E-mail: wlt@writersleague.org. Website: www.writersleague.org. Offered annually for books published in the previous year. Honors outstanding children's books in short-works categories. Awards at the Texas Book Festival in Austin, Texas. **Deadline**: See website.

WRITING CONFERENCE WRITING CONTESTS

The Writing Conference, Inc., P.O. Box 664, Ottawa KS 66067. Phone/fax: (785)242-1995. E-mail: jbushman@writingconference.com. Website: www.writingconference.com. **Contest Director**: John H. Bushman. **Open to students.** Annual contest. Estab. 1988. Purpose of contest: to further writing by students with awards for narration, exposition and poetry at the elementary, middle school and high school levels. Unpublished submissions only. Submissions made by the author or teacher. **Deadline for entries**: January 8. Consult website for guidelines and entry form. No entry fee. Awards plaque and publication of winning entry in The Writers' Slate online, April issue. Judging by a panel of teachers. Requirements for entrants: must be enrolled in school—K-12th grade—or home schooled.

YEARBOOK EXCELLENCE CONTEST

Quill and Scroll Society, School of Journalism and Mass Communication, 100 Adler Building, Room E346, Iowa City IA 52242-2004. (319)335-3457. Fax: (319)335-3989. E-mail: quill-scroll@uiowa.edu. Website: www.uiowa.edu/~quill-sc. **Executive Director**: Vanessa Shelton. **Open to students whose schools have Quill and Scroll charters.** Annual contest. Estab. 1987. Purpose of contest: to recognize and reward student journalists for their work in yearbooks and to provide student winners an opportunity to apply for a scholarship to be used freshman year in college for students planning to major in journalism. Previously published submissions only. Submissions made by the author or school yearbook adviser. Must be published between in the 12-month span prior to contest deadline. **Deadline for entries**: November 1. Visit our website for list of current and previous winners.

☺ YOUNG ADULT CANADIAN BOOK AWARD

Canadian Library Association/ Association canndienne des bibliothèques, 1150 Morrison Drive, Suite 400, Ottawa ON K2H 8S9 Canada. (613)232-9625. Fax: (613)563-9895. Website: www.cla.ca. **Contact:** Committee Chair. Annual award. Estab. 1981. This award recognizes an author of an outstanding English language Canadian book which appeals to young adults between the ages of 13 and 18. To be eligible for consideration, the following must apply: It must be a work of fiction (novel, collection of short stories, or graphic novel), the title must be a Canadian publication in either hardcover or paperback, and the author must be a Canadian citizen or landed immigrant. The award is given annually, when merited, at the Canadian Library Association's annual conference. Established in 1980 by the Young Adult Caucus of the Saskatchewan Library Association. Nominations should be sent by December 31, annually.

THE YOUTH HONOR AWARD PROGRAM

Skipping Stones, P.O. Box 3939, Eugene OR 97403. (514)342-4956. E-mail: editor@skippingstones.org. Website: www.skippingstones.org. **Director of Publicty, Editor:** Arun N. Toke. **Open to students.** Annual contest. Estab. 1994. Purpose of contest: "To recognize creative and artistic works by young people that promote multicultural awareness and nature appreciation." Unpublished submissions only. Submissions made by author. **Deadline for entries**: June 25. SASE for contest rules and entry forms also available

on our website. Entry fee is $3; low-income entrants, free. "Ten winners and some noteworthy entries will be published in our fall issue. Winners will also receive an Honor Award Certificate, a subscription to *Skipping Stones* and five nature and/or multicultural books." Requirements for entrants: Original writing (essays, interviews, poems, plays, short stories, etc.) and art (photos, paintings, cartoons, etc.) are accepted from youth ages 7 to 17. Non-English and bilingual writings are welcome. Also, you must include a certificate of originality signed by a parent or teacher. "Include a cover letter telling about yourself and your submissions, your age, and contact information. Every student who enters will receive a copy of *Skipping Stones* fall issue featuring the 10 winning entries."

ANNA ZORNIO MEMORIAL CHILDREN'S THEATRE PLAYWRITING COMPETITION

(University of New Hampshire, Department of Theatre and Dance, Paul Creative Arts Center, 30 Academic Way. Durham NH 03824-3538. (603)862-3038. Fax: (603)862-0298. E-mail: mike.wood@unh.edu. Website: www.unh.edu/theatre-dance/zornio. **Contact:** Michael Wood. Contest every 4 years; next contest is November 2012 for 2013-2014 season. Estab. 1979. Purpose of the award: "to honor the late Anna Zornio, an alumna of The University of New Hampshire, for dedication to and inspiration of playwriting for young people, K-12th grade. Open to playwrights who are residents of the U.S. and Canada. Plays or musicals should run about 45 minutes." Unpublished submissions only. Submissions made by the author. **Deadline for entries**: March 2, 2012. No entry fee. Awards $500 plus guaranteed production. Judging by faculty committee. Acquires rights to campus production. For entry form and more information visit www.unh.edu/theatre-dance/zornio. Prize: Up to $500. The play is also produced and underwritten as part of the 2013-2014 season by the UNH Department of Theatre and Dance. Winner will be notified on or after Dec. 15, 2012.

GLOSSARY

AAR. Association of Authors' Representatives.

ABA. American Booksellers Association.

ABC. Association of Booksellers for Children.

ADVANCE. A sum of money a publisher pays a writer or illustrator prior to the publication of a book. It is usually paid in installments, such as one half on signing the contract, one half on delivery of a complete and satisfactory manuscript. The advance is paid against the royalty money that will be earned by the book.

ALA. American Library Association.

ALL RIGHTS. The rights contracted to a publisher permitting the use of material anywhere and in any form, including movie and book club sales, without additional payment to the creator.

ANTHOLOGY. A collection of selected writings by various authors or gatherings of works by one author.

ANTHROPOMORPHIZATION. The act of attributing human form and personality to things not human (such as animals).

ASAP. As soon as possible.

ASSIGNMENT. An editor or art director asks a writer, illustrator or photographer to produce a specific piece for an agreed-upon fee.

B&W. Black and white.

BACKLIST. A publisher's list of books not published during the current season but still in print.

BEA. BookExpo America.

BIENNIALLY. Occurring once every 2 years.

BIMONTHLY. Occurring once every 2 months.

BIWEEKLY. Occurring once every 2 weeks.

BOOK PACKAGER. A company that draws all elements of a book together, from the initial concept to writing and marketing strategies, then sells the book package to a book publisher and/or movie producer. Also known as book producer or book developer.

BOOK PROPOSAL. Package submitted to a publisher for consideration usually consisting of a synopsis and outline as well as sample chapters.

BUSINESS-SIZE ENVELOPE. Also known as a #10 envelope. The standard size used in sending business correspondence.

CAMERA-READY. Refers to art that is completely prepared for copy camera platemaking.

CAPTION. A description of the subject matter of an illustration or photograph; photo captions include persons' names where appropriate. Also called cutline.

CBC. Children's Book Council.

CLEAN-COPY. A manuscript free of errors and needing no editing; it is ready for typesetting.

CLIPS. Samples, usually from newspapers or magazines, of a writer's published work.

CONCEPT BOOKS. Books that deal with ideas, concepts and large-scale problems, promoting an understanding of what's happening in a child's world. Most prevalent are alphabet and counting books, but also includes books dealing with specific concerns facing young people (such as divorce, birth of a sibling, friendship or moving).

CONTRACT. A written agreement stating the rights to be purchased by an editor, art director or producer and the amount of payment the writer, illustrator or photographer will receive for that sale. (See the article "Running Your Business.")

CONTRIBUTOR'S COPIES. The magazine issues sent to an author, illustrator or photographer in which her work appears.

CO-OP PUBLISHER. A publisher that shares production costs with an author but, unlike subsidy publishers, handles all marketing and distribution. An author receives a high percentage of royalties until her initial investment is recouped, then standard royalties. (*Children's Writer's & Illustrator's Market* does not include co-op publishers.)

COPY. The actual written material of a manuscript.

COPYEDITING. Editing a manuscript for grammar usage, spelling, punctuation and general style.

COPYRIGHT. A means to legally protect an author's/illustrator's/photographer's work. This can be shown by writing the creator's name and the year of work's creation.

COVER LETTER. A brief letter, accompanying a complete manuscript, especially useful if responding to an editor's request for a manuscript. May also accompany a book proposal.

CUTLINE. See caption.

DIVISION. An unincorporated branch of a company.

DUMMY. A loose mock-up of a book showing placement of text and artwork.

ELECTRONIC SUBMISSION. A submission of material by e-mail or web form.

FINAL DRAFT. The last version of a polished manuscript ready for submission to an editor.

FIRST NORTH AMERICAN SERIAL RIGHTS. The right to publish material in a periodical for the first time, in the U.S. or Canada. (See the article "Running Your Business.")

F&GS. Folded and gathered sheets. An early, not-yet-bound copy of a picture book.

FLAT FEE. A one-time payment.

GALLEYS. The first typeset version of a manuscript that has not yet been divided into pages.

GENRE. A formulaic type of fiction, such as horror, mystery, romance, science fiction or western.

GLOSSY. A photograph with a shiny surface as opposed to one with a non-shiny matte finish.

GOUACHE. Opaque watercolor with an appreciable film thickness and an actual paint layer.

HALFTONE. Reproduction of a continuous tone illustration with the image formed by dots produced by a camera lens screen.

HARD COPY. The printed copy of a computer's output.

HARDWARE. All the mechanically-integrated components of a computer that are not software—circuit boards, transistors and the machines that are the actual computer.

HI-LO. High interest, low reading level.

HOME PAGE. The first page of a website.

IBBY. International Board on Books for Young People.

IMPRINT. Name applied to a publisher's specific line of books.

INTERNET. A worldwide network of computers that offers access to a wide variety of electronic resources.

IRA. International Reading Association.

IRC. International Reply Coupon. Sold at the post office to enclose with text or artwork sent to a recipient outside your own country to cover postage costs when replying or returning work.

KEYLINE. Identification of the positions of illustrations and copy for the printer.

LAYOUT. Arrangement of illustrations, photographs, text and headlines for printed material.

LINE DRAWING. Illustration done with pencil or ink using no wash or other shading.

MASS MARKET BOOKS. Paperback books directed toward an extremely large audience sold in supermarkets, drugstores, airports, newsstands, online retailers and bookstores.

MECHANICALS. Paste-up or preparation of work for printing.

MIDDLE GRADE OR MID-GRADE. See middle reader.

MIDDLE READER. The general classifiwcation of books written for readers approximately ages 9–11. Often called middle grade or mid-grade.

MS (MSS). Manuscript(s).

MULTIPLE SUBMISSIONS. See simultaneous submissions.

NCTE. National Council of Teachers of English.

ONE-TIME RIGHTS. Permission to publish a story in periodical or book form one time only. (See the article "Running Your Business.")

OUTLINE. A summary of a book's contents; often in the form of chapter headings with a descriptive sentence or two under each heading to show the scope of the book.

PACKAGE SALE. The sale of a manuscript and illustrations/photos as a "package" paid for with one check.

PAYMENT ON ACCEPTANCE. The writer, artist or photographer is paid for her work at the time the editor or art director decides to buy it.

PAYMENT ON PUBLICATION. The writer, artist or photographer is paid for her work when it is published.

PICTURE BOOK. A type of book aimed at preschoolers to 8-year-olds that tells a story using a combination of text and artwork, or artwork only.

PRINT. An impression pulled from an original plate, stone, block, screen or negative; also a positive made from a photographic negative.

PROOFREADING. Reading text to correct typographical errors.

QUERY. A letter to an editor or agent designed to capture interest in an article or book you have written or propose to write. (See the article "Before Your First Sale.")

READING FEE. Money charged by some agents and publishers to read a submitted manuscript. (*Children's Writer's & Illustrator's Market* does not include agencies that charge reading fees.)

REPRINT RIGHTS. Permission to print an already published work whose first rights have been sold to another magazine or book publisher. (See the article "Running Your Business.")

RESPONSE TIME. The average length of time it takes an editor or art director to accept or reject a query or submission and inform the creator of the decision.

RIGHTS. The bundle of permissions offered to an editor or art director in exchange for printing a manuscript, artwork or photographs. (See the article "Running Your Business.")

ROUGH DRAFT. A manuscript that has not been checked for errors in grammar, punctuation, spelling or content.

ROUGHS. Preliminary sketches or drawings.

ROYALTY. An agreed percentage paid by a publisher to a writer, illustrator or photographer for each copy of her work sold.

SAE. Self-addressed envelope.

SASE. Self-addressed, stamped envelope.

SCBWI. The Society of Children's Book Writers and Illustrators. (See listing in Clubs & Organizations section.)

SECOND SERIAL RIGHTS. Permission for the reprinting of a work in another periodical after its first publication in book or magazine form. (See the article "Running Your Business.")

SEMIANNUAL. Occurring every 6 months or twice a year.

SEMIMONTHLY. Occurring twice a month.

SEMIWEEKLY. Occurring twice a week.

SERIAL RIGHTS. The rights given by an author to a publisher to print a piece in one or more periodicals. (See the article "Running Your Business.")

SIMULTANEOUS SUBMISSIONS. Queries or proposals sent to several publishers at the same time. Also called multiple submissions. (See the article "Before Your First Sale.")

SLANT. The approach to a story or piece of artwork that will appeal to readers of a particular publication.

SLUSH PILE. Editors' term for their collections of unsolicited manuscripts.

SOFTWARE. Programs and related documentation for use with a computer.

SOLICITED MANUSCRIPT. Material that an editor has asked for or agreed to consider before being sent by a writer.

SPAR. Society of Photographers and Artists Representatives.

SPECULATION (SPEC). Creating a piece with no assurance from an editor or art director that it will be purchased or any reimbursements for material or labor paid.

SUBSIDIARY RIGHTS. All rights other than book publishing rights included in a book contract, such as paperback, book club and movie rights. (See the article "Running Your Business.")

SUBSIDY PUBLISHER. A book publisher that charges the author for the cost of typesetting, printing and promoting a book. Also called a vanity publisher. (*Children's Writer's & Illustrator's Market* does not include subsidy publishers.)

SYNOPSIS. A brief summary of a story or novel. Usually a page to a page and a half, singlespaced, if part of a book proposal.

TABLOID. Publication printed on an ordinary newspaper page turned sideways and folded in half.

TEARSHEET. Page from a magazine or newspaper containing your printed art, story, article, poem or photo.

THUMBNAIL. A rough layout in miniature.

TRADE BOOKS. Books sold in bookstores and through online retailers, aimed at a smaller audience than mass market books, and printed in smaller quantities by publishers.

TRANSPARENCIES. Positive color slides; not color prints.

UNSOLICITED MANUSCRIPT. Material sent without an editor's, art director's or agent's request.

VANITY PUBLISHER. See subsidy publisher.

WORK-FOR-HIRE. An arrangement between a writer, illustrator or photographer and a company under which the company retains complete control of the work's copyright. (See the article "Running Your Business.")

YA. See young adult.

YOUNG ADULT. The general classification of books written for readers approximately ages 12–18. Often referred to as YA.

YOUNG READER. The general classification of books written for readers approximately ages 5–8.

SUBJECT INDEX

//

This index lists book and magazine publishers by the fiction and nonfiction subject areas in which they publish. Use it to locate appropriate markets for your work, then carefully read the listings and follow the guidelines of each publisher.

ANIMAL

CONTEMPORARY

FANTASY

FOLKTALES

HEALTH

HI-LO

HUMOR

MULTICULTURAL

NATURE/ENVIRONMENT

POETRY

SPORTS

SUSPENSE/MYSTERY

BOOK PUBLISHERS - NONFICTION

ACTIVITY BOOKS

ANIMAL

ARTS/CRAFTS

BIOGRAPHY

HOBBIES

HOW-TO

MULTICULTURAL

SCIENCE

SPECIAL NEEDS

SPORTS

TEXTBOOKS

MAGAZINES—FICTION

FICTIONADVENTURE

EDITOR NAMES INDEX

May, Steven Allen (Plan B Press) 482

Mayorga, Patricia (poetsespresso) 346

McBride, Greg (Innisfree Poetry Journal) 275

McCarthy, M.L. (Candelabrum Poetry
    Magazine) 217

McCourt, Theresa (Tule Review, The) 421

McCrary Sullivan, Anne (English Journal) 246

McDowell, Michael (Windfall: A Journal of
    Poetry of Place) 435

McGuire, Devin (Aurorean, The) 407

McIsaac, Bonnie (Antigonish Review, The) 191

McKinsey, Dillon (Ardent!) 194

McMahon, Jeff (Contrary) 232

McNutt, Donald (Blueline) 210

Meischen, David (Texas Poetry Calendar) 406

Mellichamp-Milliken, Jean (Lyric, The) 411

Menendez, Didi (Poets and Artists) 345

Metz, Scott (Roadrunner Haiku Journal) 367

Milam, Andrew Wright
    (Seaweed Sideshow Circus) 486

Miller, E. Ethelbert (Poet Lore) 341

Miller, Philip (Same, The) 369

Miller, Sandi (devozine) 239

Minter, Sheryl (Willow, The) 434

Moffitt, Julie (Earthshine) 243

Molini, Sally (Cerise Press) 220

Monaghan, Tim (Ledge Magazine, The) 287

Moon, Susan (Nocturnal Lyric, The) 414

Moore, Aaron (Floyd County Moonshine) 253

Moorhead, Andrea (Osiris) 323

Moramarco, Fred (Poetry International) 343

Morgan, Amanda (Splizz) 390

Morris, Kelly (Poet's Ink) 347

Morrisey, Brian (POESY Magazine) 339

Morrison, Charles (Pirene's Fountain) 335

Moss, Jo-Ann (Raving Dove) 361

Mowery, Betty (Shepherd, The) 375

Musto, Ronald G. (Italica Press) 474

N

Narvaez, R. (asinine poetry) 197

Nash, Sydney
    (View From Here Magazine, The) 415

Neeley, Stacia Dunn (Aries: A Journal of
    Creative Expression) 194

Nelson, Cami (Quarterly West) 357

Newbern, Laura (Arts & Letters Journal of
    Contemporary Culture) 196

Newman, Karen L. (Illumen) 272

Nguyen, Phong (Pleiades: A Journal of New
    Writing) 336

Nicholl, Greg
    (Johns Hopkins University Press, The) 489

Nielsen, Ayaz Daryl (bear creek haiku) 205

Nunn, Graham (SpeedPoets Zine) 387

O

Ochester, Ed (5 am) 180

Ogroske, Leon (Writers' Journal) 438

Orgera, Alexis (New CollAge) 310

Osborne, JoAn (Tiger's Eye) 418

Ostrander, Fred (Blue Unicorn, A Tri-Quarterly
    of Poetry) 210

Owens, Scott (Wild Goose Poetry Review) 432

Oxley, Patricia (Acumen Magazine) 184

P

Page, Jeremy (Frogmore Papers, The) 257

Paine, Patty (Diode Poetry Journal) 240

Palley, Julian (California Quarterly) 215

Pargitter, M. (Hippopotamus Press) 473

Parham, Robert (Southern Poetry Review) 383

Partridge, Dixie (Sunstone) 399

Pawlak, Mark (Hanging Loose) 265

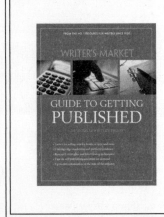